Evangelical Lutheran

Hymn-Book

With Tunes

Concordia Publishing House

St. Louis

Contents

The Order of Morning Service,

or the Communion

A Hymn of Invocation of the Holy Ghost may be sung.

The Congregation shall rise, and the Minister, standing at the Altar, shall say:

In the Name of the Father, and of the Son, and of the Holy Ghost.

The Congregation shall sing or say:

A - - - - - men.

Then shall be said the Confession of Sins, *as here followeth:*

The Confession of Sins.

Beloved in the Lord! Let us draw near with a true heart, and confess our sins unto God our Father, beseeching Him, in the Name of our Lord Jesus Christ, to grant us forgiveness.

Then, all kneeling or standing, shall be sung or said:

Minister. Our help is in the Name of the Lord.

Congregation:

Minister. I said, I will confess my transgressions unto the Lord.

Congregation:

Who made heav'n and earth.
And Thou forgavest the iniquity of my sin.

Then shall the Minister say:

Almighty God, our Maker and Redeemer, we poor sinners confess unto Thee, that we are by nature sinful and unclean, and that we have sinned against Thee, by thought, word, and deed. Wherefore we flee for refuge to Thine infinite mercy, seeking and imploring Thy grace, for the sake of our Lord Jesus Christ.

The Congregation shall say with the Minister:

O most merciful God, who hast given Thine Only-begotten Son to die for us, have mercy upon us, and for His sake grant us remission of all our sins: and by Thy Holy Spirit increase in us true knowledge of Thee, and of Thy will, and true obedience to Thy Word, to the end that by Thy grace we may come to everlasting life, through Jesus Christ our Lord. Amen.

Morning Service

Then the Minister, standing, shall say:

Almighty God, our heavenly Father, hath had mercy upon us, and hath given His Only Son to die for us, and for His sake forgiveth us all our sins. To them that believe on His Name, He giveth power to become the sons of God, and hath promised them His Holy Spirit. He that believeth, and is baptized, shall be saved. Grant this, Lord, unto us all.

Then shall the Congregation sing or say:

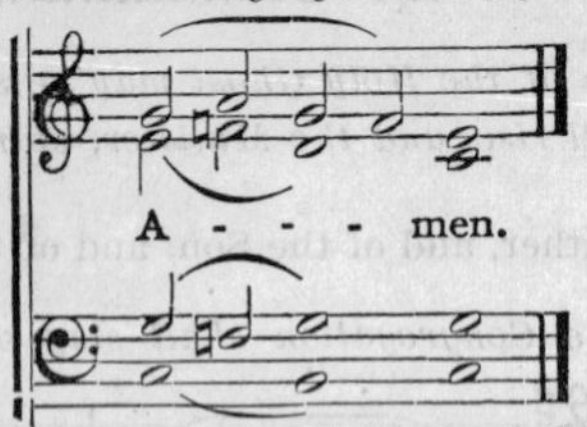
A - - - men.

Then, all standing to the close of the Collect, *shall be sung or said the* Introit *for the day.*

The Introit.

The Introit *with the* Gloria Patri *may be sung by the Choir; or the* Introit *may be said by the Minister, and the* Gloria Patri *sung or said by the Congregation. Instead of the* Introit *a Psalm or a Hymn may be used.*

Gloria Patri.

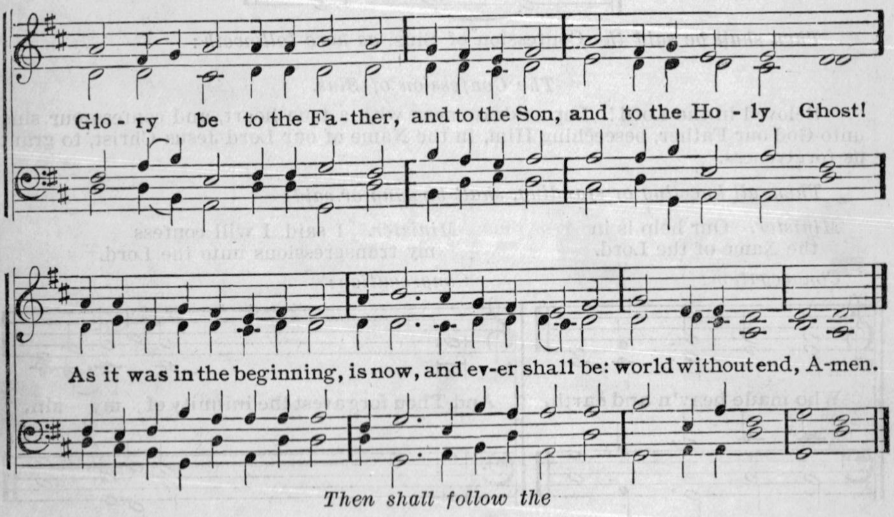
Glo - ry be to the Fa-ther, and to the Son, and to the Ho - ly Ghost!
As it was in the beginning, is now, and ev-er shall be: world without end, A-men.

Then shall follow the

Kyrie.

The Kyrie *may be sung or said by the Minister and Congregation, or each petition may be said by the Minister and sung or said by the Congregation in response.*

Congregation:

Lord, have mer - cy up - on us. Christ, have mer - cy up-

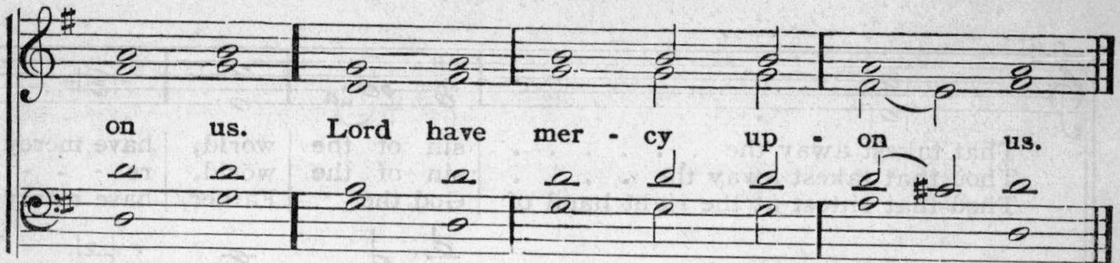
on us. Lord have mer - cy up - on us.

Then shall be sung the Gloria in Excelsis *as here followeth. Instead of the* Gloria in Excelsis, *another Canticle or Hymn of Praise may be sung, except on Festival days, and when there is a Communion.*

Gloria in Excelsis.

The Minister shall say:

Glory be to God on high!

Congregation:

Glory be to . . . . | God on | high:
We praise Thee, we bless Thee, we | wor - ship | Thee,

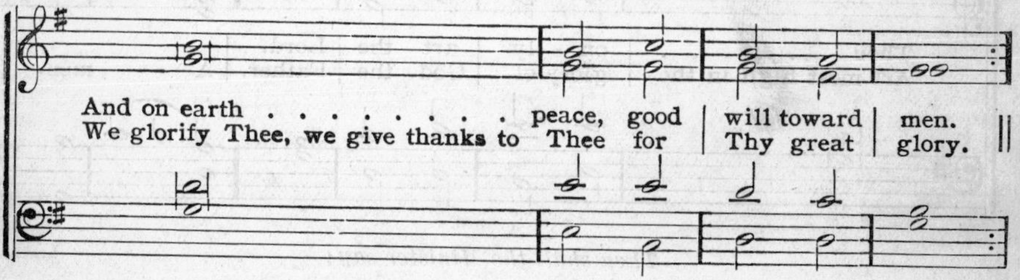

And on earth . . . . peace, good | will toward | men.
We glorify Thee, we give thanks to Thee for | Thy great | glory.

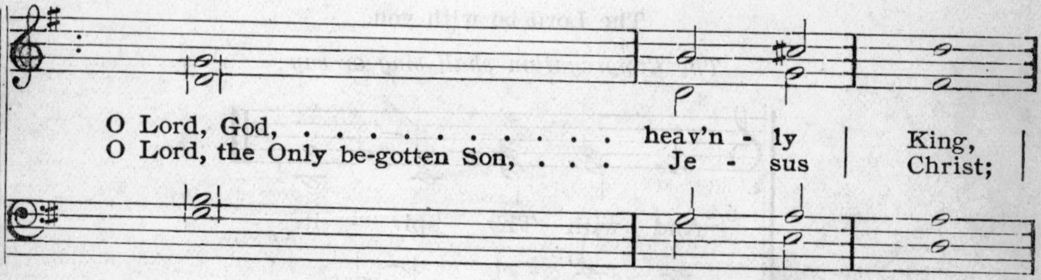

O Lord, God, ... heav'n - ly | King,
O Lord, the Only be-gotten Son, . . . Je - sus | Christ;

God the . . . . | Fa - ther | Al - - | mighty.
O Lord God, Lamb of God . . | Son . . | of the | Father.

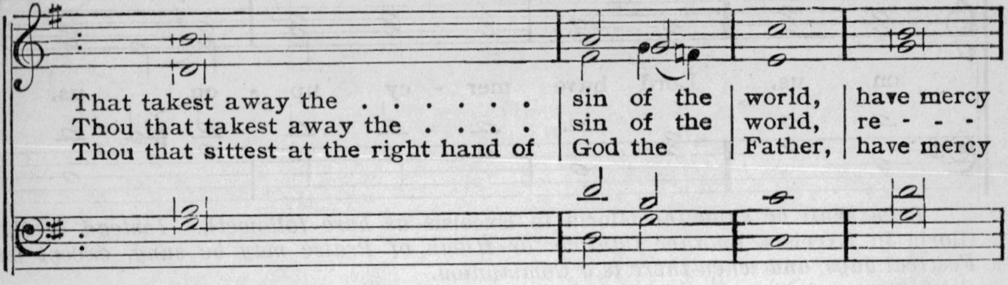

That takest away the . . . . | sin of the | world, | have mercy | up - on | us.
Thou that takest away the . . . . | sin of the | world, | re - - - | ceive our | prayer.
Thou that sittest at the right hand of | God the | Father, | have mercy | up - on | us.

For Thou . . . . only art | holy; | Thou . . . . | on - ly | art the | Lord.
Thou only, O Christ, with the Holy | Ghost, | Art most high in the | glory of | God the | Father. | A - - men.

Then shall the Minister say:

The Lord be with you.

The Congregation shall sing or say:

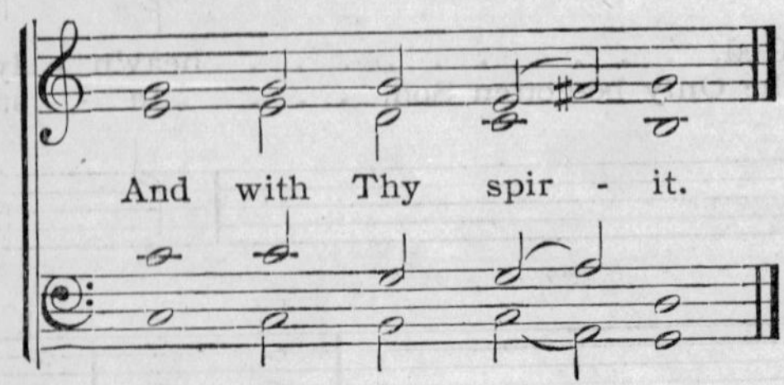
And with Thy spir - it.

The Minister shall say:

Let us pray.

Then shall the Minister say the Collect for the Day.

The Collect.

The Collect *ended, the Congregation shall sing or say:*

A - - - - - - - men.

Then shall the Minister read the Epistle for the Day. *Other* Scripture Lessons *may be read before the* Epistle, *but the* Epistle *and* Gospel for the Day *shall always be read. The Minister shall announce the* Epistle, *saying:*

The Epistle for (*here he shall name the Day*) is written in the——Chapter of——, beginning at the——Verse.

The Epistle for the Day.

The Epistle *ended, the Minister shall say:* Here endeth the Epistle.

Then shall the Hallelujah *be sung or said, except in the Passion season.*

The Hallelujah.

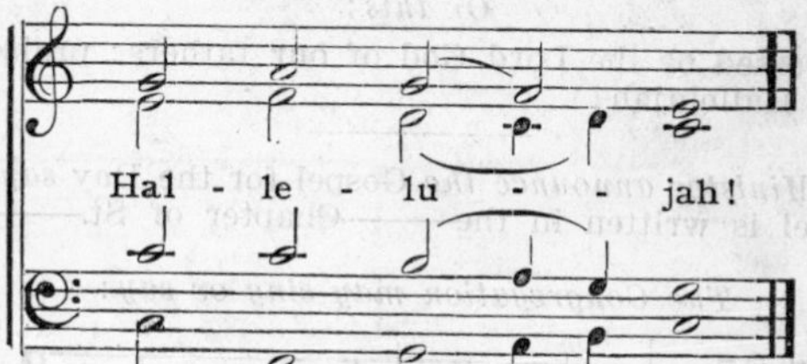

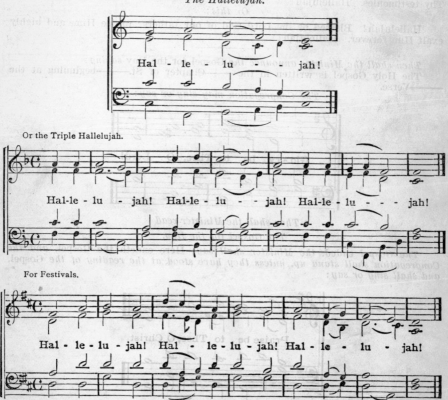

Hal - le - lu - - jah!

Or the Triple Hallelujah.

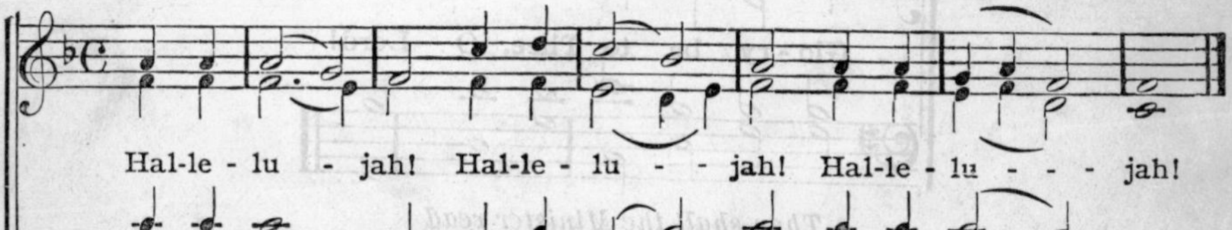

Hal-le - lu - jah! Hal-le - lu - - jah! Hal-le - lu - - - jah!

For Festivals.

Hal - le - lu - jah! Hal - le - lu - jah! Hal - le - lu - jah!

Instead of the simple Hallelujah, *a sentence for the Season of the Church-year may be sung with it; or a Psalm or Hymn may be sung after the* Hallelujah.

The Hallelujah and Sentence

Morning Service

For Advent.

Hallelujah! Remember, O Lord, Thy tender mercies: for they have been ever of old. Hallelujah!

For the Epiphany Season.

Hallelujah! O praise the Lord, all ye nations; and laud Him, all ye people. For His merciful kindness is great toward us: and the truth of the Lord endureth forever. Hallelujah!

For the Passion Season.

Christ hath humbled Himself, and become obedient unto death: even the death of the Cross.

For the Easter Season.

Hallelujah! Christ our Passover is sacrificed for us. Hallelujah!

For Whitsuntide.

Hallelujah! Thou sendest forth Thy Spirit, they are created: and Thou renewest the face of the earth. Hallelujah!

From Trinity to Advent.

Hallelujah! O Lord, deal with Thy servant according unto Thy mercy; and teach me Thy statutes. I am Thy servant, give me understanding: that I may know Thy testimonies. Hallelujah!

Or this:

Hallelujah! Blessed be the Lord God of our fathers: praise Him, and highly exalt Him forever. Hallelujah!

Then shall the Minister announce the Gospel for the Day *saying:*
The Holy Gospel is written in the——Chapter of St.——beginning at the ——Verse.

The Congregation may sing or say:

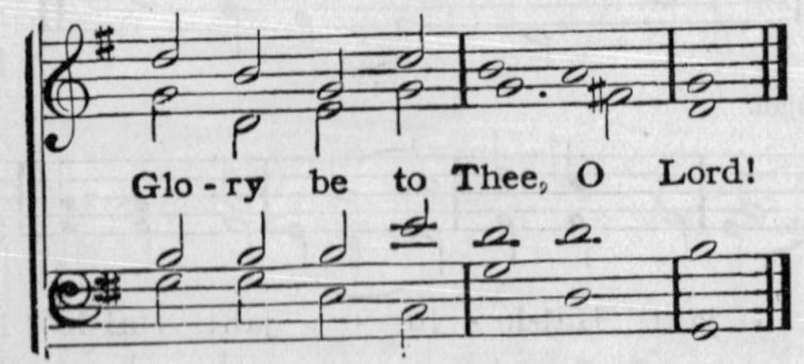
Glo - ry be to Thee, O Lord!

Then shall the Minister read
The Gospel for the Day.

The Gospel ended, the Minister shall say: Here endeth the Gospel, *and the Congregation shall stand up, unless they have stood at the reading of the* Gospel, *and shall sing or say:*

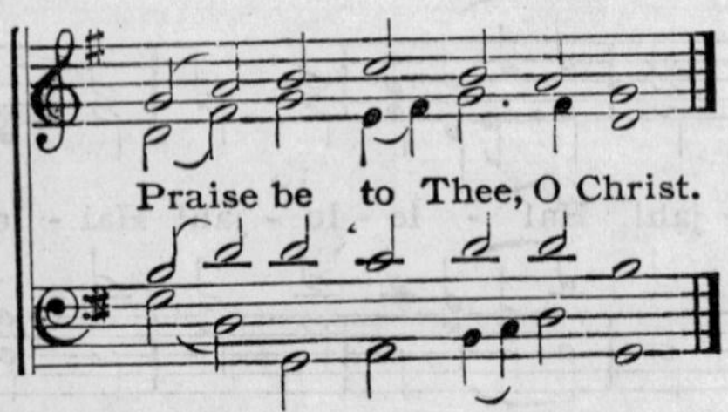
Praise be to Thee, O Christ.

Then shall be said or sung the Nicene Creed, *or the* Apostles' Creed; *but if there be a Communion, the* Nicene Creed *shall be used.*

The Nicene Creed.

I believe in one God, the Father Almighty, Maker of Heaven and earth, and of all things visible and invisible.

And in one Lord Jesus Christ, the Only-begotten Son of God, begotten of His Father before all worlds, God of God, Light of Light, Very God of Very God, Begotten, not made, Being of one substance with the Father, By whom all things were made; Who, for us men, and for our salvation, came down from heaven, And was incarnate by the Holy Ghost of the Virgin Mary, And was made man; And was crucified also for us under Pontius Pilate. He suffered and was buried: and the third day He rose again, according to the Scriptures; and ascended into heaven, And sitteth on the right hand of the Father; and He shall come again with glory to judge both the quick and the dead; Whose kingdom shall have no end.

And I believe in the Holy Ghost, The Lord and Giver of Life, Who proceedeth from the Father and the Son, Who with the Father and the Son together is worshipped and glorified, who spake by the Prophets. And I believe one holy Christian and Apostolic Church. I acknowledge one Baptism for the remission of sins; And I look for the Resurrection of the dead; And the life of the world to come. Amen.

The Apostles' Creed.

I believe in God the Father Almighty, Maker of Heaven and earth.

And in Jesus Christ His only Son, our Lord; Who was conceived by the Holy Ghost, Born of the Virgin Mary; Suffered under Pontius Pilate, Was crucified, dead, and buried; He descended into hell; The third day He rose again from the dead; He ascended into Heaven and sitteth on the right hand of God the Father Almighty; from thence He shall come to judge the quick and the dead.

I believe in the Holy Ghost; The holy Christian Church, the Communion of Saints; The Forgiveness of sins; the Resurrection of the body; And the Life everlasting. Amen.

Then may a Hymn be sung and the Minister shall go into the pulpit. After the Hymn shall follow

The Sermon.

The Sermon ended, the Congregation standing up, the Minister shall say:

The peace of God, which passeth all understanding, keep your hearts and minds through Christ Jesus.

The Offertory *shall then be sung, at the close of which the Congregation shall be seated.*

One of the Offertories *here following, or any other suitable Offertory, may be used.*

The Offertory.

I.

G. Winer, 1655

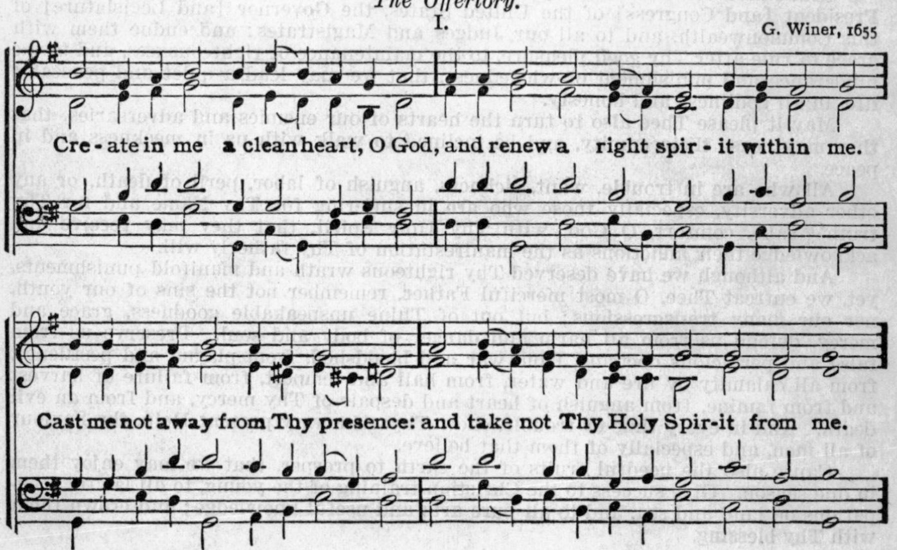
Cre-ate in me a clean heart, O God, and renew a right spir-it within me.
Cast me not away from Thy presence: and take not Thy Holy Spir-it from me.

Restore unto me the joy of Thy salvation, and uphold me with Thy free Spir-it.

II.

The sacrifices of God are a broken spirit: a broken and a contrite heart, O God, Thou wilt not despise.

Do good in Thy good pleasure unto Zion: Build Thou the walls of Jerusalem.

Then shalt Thou be pleased with the sacrifices of righteousness: with burnt-offering and whole burnt-offering.

The Offerings shall be gathered and brought to the Minister, who shall place them on the Altar.

Then shall the Minister make mention of any special petition, intercessions or thanksgivings which may have been requested. He may also make mention of the death of any member of the Congregation.

Then shall follow the General Prayer. *The Prayer here following may be used; or, if there be no Communion, the* Litany, *or a selection from the* Collects and Prayers, *or any other suitable prayer.*

The General Prayer.

Almighty and most merciful God, the Father of our Lord Jesus Christ: We give Thee thanks for all Thy goodness and tender mercies, especially for the gift of Thy dear Son, and for the revelation of Thy will and grace: and we beseech Thee so to implant Thy Word in us, that in good and honest hearts, we may keep it, and bring forth fruit by patient continuance in well doing.

Most heartily we beseech Thee so to rule and govern Thy Church universal, with all its pastors and ministers, that it may be preserved in the pure doctrine of Thy saving Word, whereby faith toward Thee may be strengthened, and charity increased in us toward all mankind.

Grant also health and prosperity to all that are in authority, especially to the President [and Congress] of the United States, the Governor [and Legislature] of this Commonwealth, and to all our Judges and Magistrates; and endue them with grace to rule after Thy good pleasure, to the maintenance of righteousness, and to the hinderance and punishment of wickedness, that we may lead a quiet and peaceable life, in all godliness and honesty.

May it please Thee also to turn the hearts of our enemies and adversaries, that they may cease their enmity, and be inclined to walk with us in meekness and in peace.

All who are in trouble, want, sickness, anguish of labor, peril of death, or any other adversity, especially those who are in suffering for Thy Name and for Thy truth's sake, comfort, O God, with Thy Holy Spirit, that they may receive and acknowledge their afflictions as the manifestation of Thy fatherly will.

And although we have deserved Thy righteous wrath and manifold punishments, yet, we entreat Thee, O most merciful Father, remember not the sins of our youth, nor our many transgressions; but out of Thine unspeakable goodness, grace and mercy, defend us from all harm and danger of body and soul. Preserve us from false and pernicious doctrine, from war and bloodshed, from plague and pestilence, from all calamity by fire and water, from hail and tempest, from failure of harvest and from famine, from anguish of heart and despair of Thy mercy, and from an evil death. And in every time of trouble, show Thyself a very present Help, the Saviour of all men, and especially of them that believe.

Cause also the needful fruits of the earth to prosper, that we may enjoy them in due season. Give success to the Christian training of the young, to all lawful occupations on land and sea, and to all pure arts and useful knowledge; and crown them with Thy blessing.

Here special Supplications, Intercessions and Prayers may be made.

These, and whatsoever other things Thou wouldest have us ask of Thee, O God, vouchsafe unto us for the sake of the bitter sufferings and death of Jesus Christ, Thine only Son, our Lord and Saviour, who liveth and reigneth with Thee and the Holy Ghost, ever one God, world without end.

Then shall the Minister, and the Congregation with him, say the Lord's Prayer.

The Lord's Prayer.

Our Father, who art in heaven; Hallowed by Thy Name; Thy kingdom come; Thy will be done on earth, as it is in heaven; Give us this day our daily bread; And forgive us our trespasses, as we forgive those who trespass against us; And lead us not into temptation; But deliver us from evil: For Thine is the kingdom, and the power, and the glory, for ever and ever. Amen.

Then shall be sung a Hymn.

If there be no Communion, a Doxology may be sung, and the Minister, standing at the Altar, shall pronounce the Benediction, *after which the Congregation shall offer silent prayer.*

The Benediction.

The Lord bless thee, and keep thee.

The Lord make His face shine upon thee, and be gracious unto thee.

The Lord lift up His countenance upon thee, and give thee peace.

The Congregation shall sing or say:

A - men, A - men, A - men.

Whilst the Hymn is sung, the Minister shall go to the Altar, make ready the Communion vessels and prepare for the administration of the Holy Communion.

The Hymn ended, the Congregation shall rise, and stand to the end of the Agnus Dei.

The Preface.

The Minister shall say:

The Lord be with you.

The Congregation shall sing or say:

And with thy Spir - it.

Minister. Lift up your hearts.

Congregation:

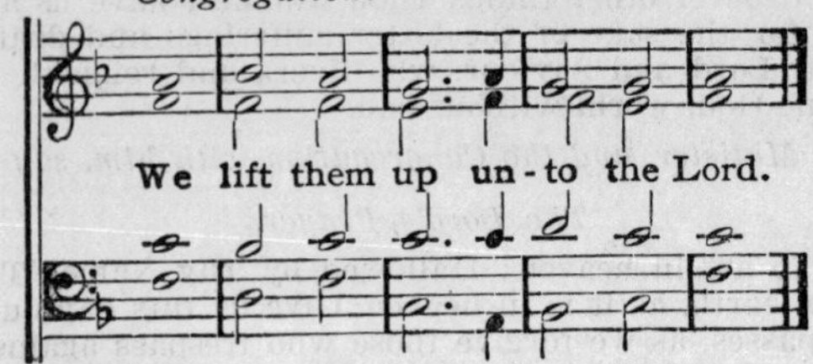
We lift them up un-to the Lord.

Minister. Let us give thanks unto the Lord our God.

Congregation:

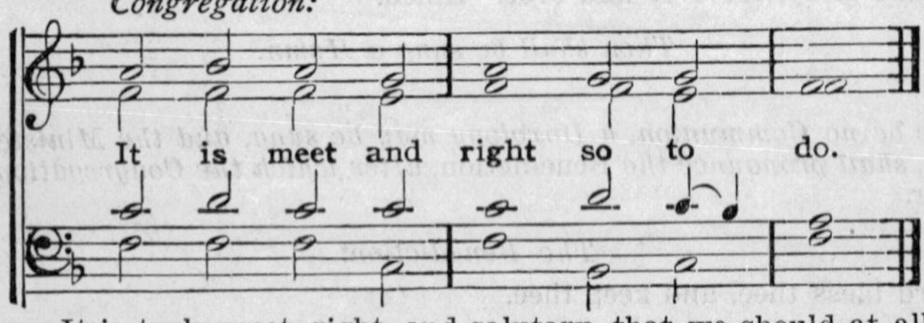
It is meet and right so to do.

Minister. It is truly meet, right and salutary, that we should at all times, and in all places, give thanks unto Thee, O Lord, Holy Father, Almighty Everlasting God.

Here shall follow the Proper Preface, *according to the time, if there be any specially appointed, or else immediately shall follow,* Therefore with angels, etc.

Proper Prefaces.

For Christmas.

For in the mystery of the Word made flesh, Thou hast given us a new revelation of Thy glory: that seeing Thee in the person of Thy Son, we may be drawn to the love of those things which are not seen. Therefore with Angels, etc.

For the Passion Season.

Who on the tree of the Cross didst give salvation unto mankind; that whence death arose, thence Life also might rise again: and that he who by a tree once overcame, might likewise by a tree be overcome, through Christ our Lord; through whom with Angels, etc.

For the Easter Season.

But chiefly are we bound to praise Thee for the glorious Resurrection of Thy Son Jesus Christ our Lord: for He is the very Paschal Lamb, which was offered for us, and hath taken away the sin of the world; Who by His death hath destroyed death, and by His rising to life again, hath restored to us everlasting life. Therefore with Angels, etc.

For Ascension Day.

Through Jesus Christ our Lord, Who after His Resurrection appeared openly to all His disciples, and in their sight was taken up into Heaven, that He might make us partakers of His Divine Nature. Therefore with Angels, etc.

For Whitsunday.

Through Jesus Christ, Thy dear Son, our Lord and Savior; Who ascended above the heavens, and sitting at Thy right hand, poured out on this day the Holy Spirit, as He had promised, upon the chosen disciples; whereat the whole earth rejoices with exceeding joy. Therefore with Angels, etc.

For the Festival of the Trinity.

Who with Thine Only-begotten Son, and the Holy Ghost, art one God, one Lord. And in the confession of the only true God, we worship the Trinity in Person, and the Unity in Substance, of Majesty co-equal. Therefore with Angels, etc.

After the Preface shall follow immediately:

Therefore with Angels and Archangels, and with all the company of heaven, we laud and magnify Thy glorious name; evermore praising Thee, and saying.

Then shall be said or sung the Sanctus.

Traditional
Ho - ly, ho - ly, ho - ly, Lord, God of Sa - ba - oth;
Heav'n and earth are full of Thy glo - ry; Ho - san - na, Ho-
Soli.
1st and 2nd Sop.
Alto.
san - na Ho - san - na in the high - est. Bless - ed is He
Tutti.
Congregation:
Bless-ed is He, Bless - ed is He, that com - eth in the name of the Lord.
Ho - san - na, Ho - san - na, Ho - san - na, in the high - est.

Then may the Minister give this Exhortation.

The Exhortation.

Dearly Beloved! Forasmuch as we purpose to come to the Holy Supper of our Lord Jesus Christ, it becometh us diligently to examine ourselves, as St. Paul exhorteth us. For this Holy Sacrament hath been instituted for the special comfort and strengthening of those who humbly confess their sins, and who hunger and thirst after righteousness.

But if we thus examine ourselves, we shall find nothing in us but only sin and death, from which we can in no wise set ourselves free. Therefore our Lord Jesus Christ hath had mercy upon us and hath taken upon Himself our nature, that so He might fulfill for us the whole will and law of God, and for us and for our deliverance suffer death and all that we by our sins have deserved. And to the end that we should the more confidently believe this, and be strengthened by our faith in a cheerful obedience to His holy will, He hath instituted the Holy Sacrament of His Supper, in which He feedeth us with His Body, and giveth us to drink of His Blood.

Therefore whoso eateth of this bread, and drinketh of this cup, firmly believing the words of Christ, dwelleth in Christ, and Christ in him, and hath eternal life.

We should also do this in remembrance of Him, showing His death, that He was delivered for our offences, and raised again for our justification, and rendering unto Him most hearty thanks for the same, take up our cross and follow Him, and according to His commandment, love one another even as He hath loved us. For we are all one bread and one body, even as we are all partakers of this one bread, and drink of this one cup.

Then the Minister, turning to the Altar, shall say:

Let us pray.

Our Father, who art in heaven; Hallowed be Thy Name; Thy kingdom come; Thy will be done on earth as it is in heaven; Give us this day our daily bread; And forgive us our trespasses, as we forgive those who trespass against us; And lead us not into temptation; But deliver us from evil.

Then shall the Congregation sing or say:

For Thine is the king-dom, and the power, and the
glo - ry, for - ev - er and ev - er. A - - men.

Then shall the Minister say:

Our Lord Jesus Christ, in the night in which He was betrayed, took bread; (*a*) and when He had given thanks He brake it and gave it to His disciples, saying: Take, eat; this is my Body, which is given for you; this do in remembrance of Me.

(*a*) *Here he shall take the Plate with the Bread in his hand.*

After the same manner, also, He took the cup, when He had supped, and when He had given thanks, He gave it to them, saying: Drink ye all of it; this cup is the New Testament in My Blood, which is shed for you, and for many, for the remission of sins; this do, as oft as ye drink it, in remembrance of Me."

(*b*) *Here he shall take the Cup in his hand.*

Then shall the Minister say:

The peace of the Lord be with you alway.

Then shall be sung or said the Agnus Dei, *and the distribution shall begin.*

Agnus Dei. Braunschweig, 1528

O Christ, Thou Lamb of God, that tak-est a-way the sin of the
world, have mer-cy up-on us! O Christ, Thou Lamb of God, that
tak-est a-way the sin of the world, have mer-cy up-on us!
O Christ, Thou Lamb of God, that tak-est a-way the sin of the
world, grant us Thy peace. A - - - - - men.

When the Minister giveth the Bread he shall say:

Take and eat, this is the true Body of Christ given for thee.

When he giveth the Cup he shall say:

Take and drink, this is the true Blood of the New Testament, shed for thy sins.

In dismissing the Communicants, the Minister may say:

The Body of our Lord Jesus Christ and His precious Blood strengthen and preserve you in the true faith unto everlasting life.

If the consecrated Bread or Wine be spent before all have communed, the Minister shall consecrate more, saying aloud so much of the words of institution as pertaineth to the element to be consecrated.

When all have communed, the Minister shall reverently cover what remaineth of the Bread and Wine.

Then all standing, may be sung or said the

Nunc Dimittis.

Pomeranian, 1535

1. Lord, now lettest Thou Thy servant de - - - - - - - part in peace: ac - cord - ing to Thy Word.
2. For mine eyes have seen Thy salvation: which Thou hast prepared be - fore the face of all peo - ple.
3. A light to light - en the Gen - tiles, and the glo - ry of Thy peo - ple Is - - - - ra - el.

4. Glo - ry | be to the Father, and . . . .
5. As it | was in the beginning, is now, and . . . . . .
to the Son: and to the Ho - ly Ghost.
ev - er shall be: world with - out end, A-men.

Then shall be said:

The Thanksgiving.

Minister.

O give thanks unto the Lord, for He is good.

The Congregation shall sing or say:

And His mercy en-dureth for - ev - - - er.

Minister.

We give thanks to Thee, Almighty God, that Thou hast refreshed us through this salutary gift; and we beseech Thee, that of Thy mercy Thou wouldst strengthen us through the same in faith towards Thee and in fervent love toward one another, through Jesus Christ, Thy dear Son, our Lord, who liveth and reigneth with Thee, and the Holy Ghost, ever one God, world without end.

The Congregation shall sing or say:

A - - men.

Then may be sung or said the

Benedicamus.

Minister. The Lord be with you.

Congregation:

And with Thy Spir - it.

Minister. Bless we the Lord.

Congregation:

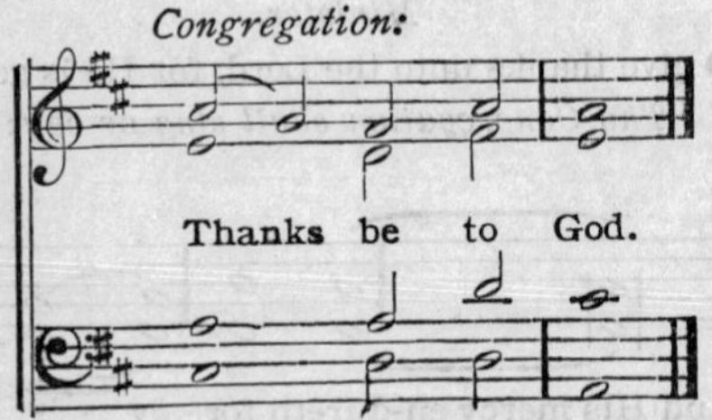
Thanks be to God.

Then shall the Minister say the Benediction *as here followeth, or he may say the words* 2 Cor. xiii. 14.

After the Benediction the Congregation should offer silent prayer.

The Benediction.

The Lord bless thee, and keep thee.
The Lord make His face shine upon thee, and be gracious unto thee.
The Lord lift up His countenance upon thee, and give thee peace.

The Congregation shall sing or say:

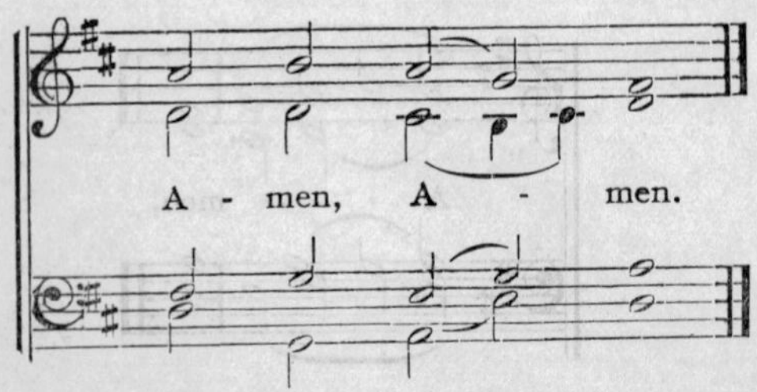
A - men, A - men.

Order of Evening Service, or Vespers

A Hymn of Invocation of the Holy Ghost, or another Hymn may be sung.

Then shall be sung or said responsively the Versicle *with the* Gloria Patri *as here followeth, all standing to the end of the* Psalm.

Versicle. O Lord, open Thou my lips.

Congregation:

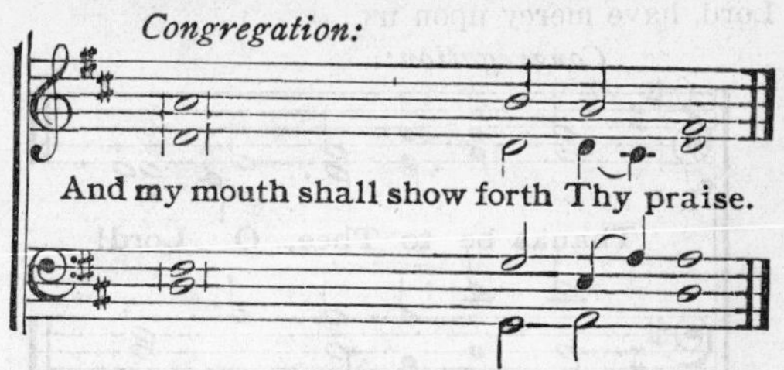
And my mouth shall show forth Thy praise.

Versicle. Make haste, O God, to deliver me.

Congregation.

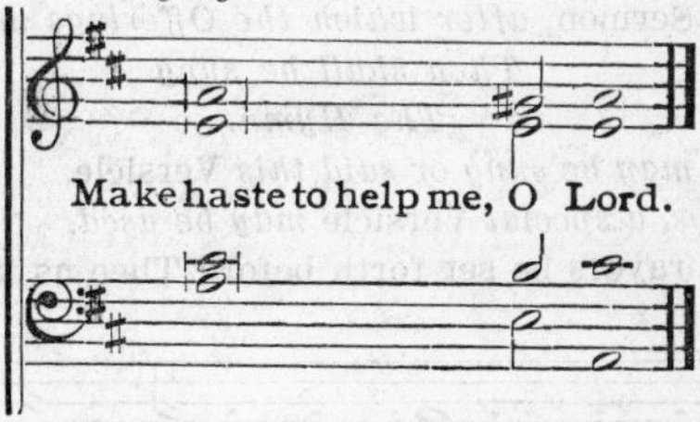

Make haste to help me, O Lord.

Glo - ry be to the Father and . . . . to the Son,

And to the Ho - ly Ghost: As it was in the be-gin-ning, is now,

and ever shall be, world with-out end. A - men. Hal - le - lu - jah.

Evening Service, or Vespers

During the Passion Season the Hallelujah *shall be omitted.*

The Psalm.

Then shall be sung or said one or more Psalms. *At the end of the* Psalm *the* Gloria Patri *shall be sung. An* Antiphon *may be used with each* Psalm.

The Lesson.

The Scripture Lessons *shall then be read, and after each* Lesson *may be sung or said*:

But Thou, O Lord, have mercy upon us.

Congregation:

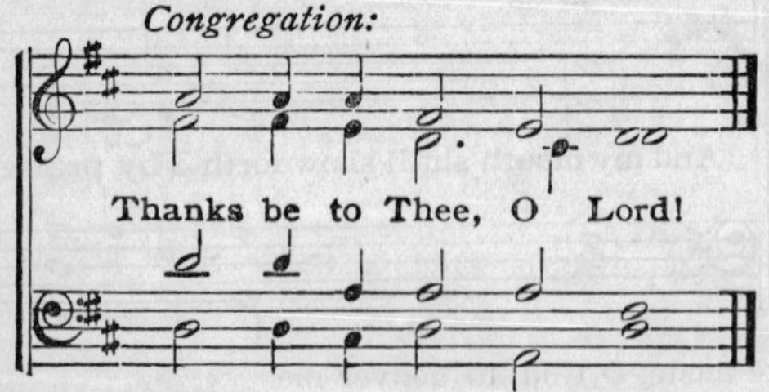
Thanks be to Thee, O Lord!

After the Lessons *a* Responsory *may be sung, or a* hymn.

Then may follow a Sermon, *after which the Offerings may be gathered.*

Then shall be sung

The Hymn.

Then, all standing, may be sung or said this Versicle.

But on Festival days, a special Versicle *may be used.*

Versicle. Let my prayers be set forth before Thee as incense:

Congregation:

And the lifting up of my hands as the eve - ning sac - ri - fice.

Then shall be sung the

The Canticle.

Magnificat. St. Luke i.

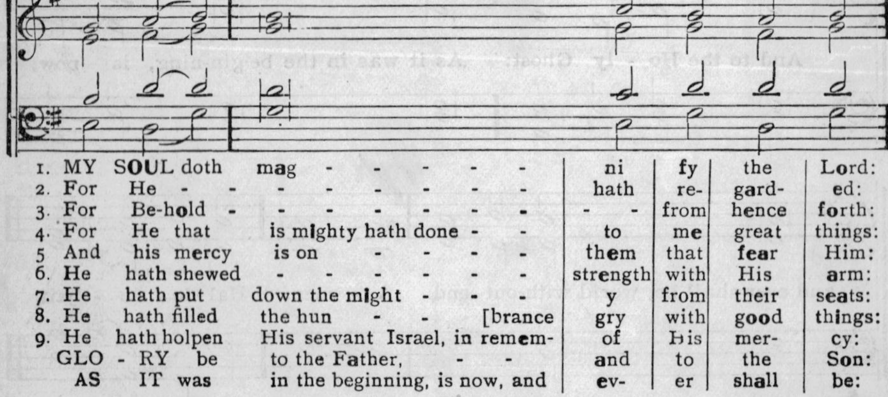

1.	MY SOUL doth mag - - - - - -	ni	fy	the	Lord:
2.	For He - - - - - - - - - -	hath	re-	gard-	ed:
3.	For Be-hold - - - - - - - - - -	- -	from	hence	forth:
4.	For He that is mighty hath done - -	to	me	great	things:
5	And his mercy is on - - - - -	them	that	fear	Him:
6.	He hath shewed - - - - - - -	strength	with	His	arm:
7.	He hath put down the might - - -	y	from	their	seats:
8.	He hath filled the hun - - [brance	gry	with	good	things:
9.	He hath holpen His servant Israel, in remem-	of	His	mer-	cy:
	GLO - RY be to the Father, - -	and	to	the	Son:
	AS IT was in the beginning, is now, and	ev-	er	shall	be:

Evening Service, or Vespers

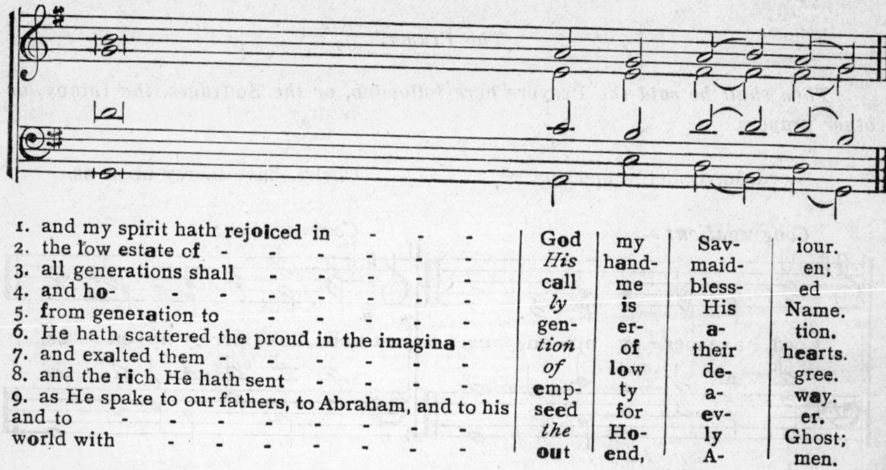
1. and my spirit hath rejoiced in - - - - | God | my | Sav- | iour.
2. the low estate of - - - - - | His | hand- | maid- | en;
3. all generations shall - - - - - | call | me | bless- | ed
4. and ho- - - - - - - - | ly | is | His | Name.
5. from generation to - - - - | gen- | er- | a- | tion.
6. He hath scattered the proud in the imagina - | tion | of | their | hearts.
7. and exalted them - - - - - - | of | low | de- | gree.
8. and the rich He hath sent - - - - | emp- | ty | a- | way.
9. as He spake to our fathers, to Abraham, and to his | seed | for | ev- | er.
and to - - - - - - - - | the | Ho- | ly | Ghost;
world with - - - - - - - | out | end, | A- | men.

Or the

Nunc Dimittis. St. Luke ii.

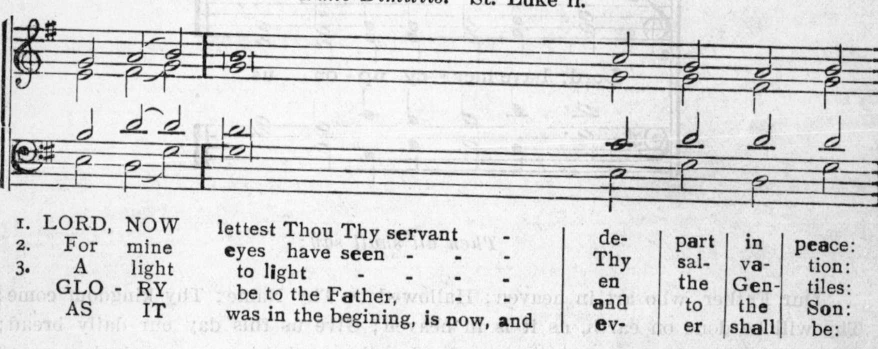
1. LORD, NOW lettest Thou Thy servant - | de- | part | in | peace:
2. For mine eyes have seen - - - | Thy | sal- | va- | tion:
3. A light to light - - - - | en | the | Gen- | tiles:
GLO - RY be to the Father, - - - | and | to | the | Son:
AS IT was in the begining, is now, and | ev- | er | shall | be:

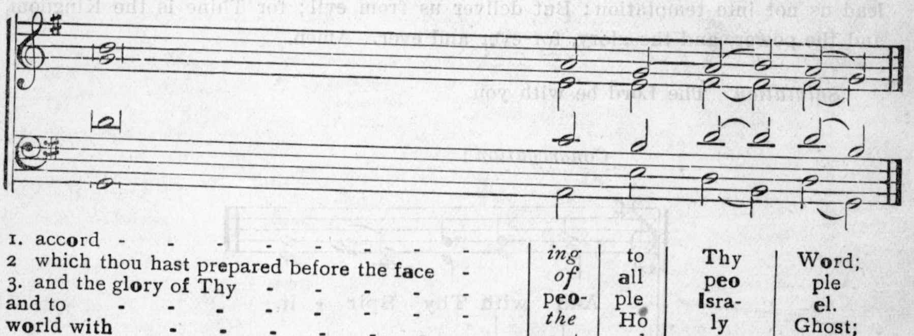
1. accord - - - - - - - - - | ing | to | Thy | Word;
2 which thou hast prepared before the face - | of | all | peo | ple
3. and the glory of Thy - - - - - - | peo- | ple | Isra- | el.
and to - - - - - - - - | the | Ho | ly | Ghost;
world with - - - - - - - | out | end. | A- | men.

An Antiphon may be sung with the Canticle.

The Prayer.

Then shall be said the Prayers *here following, or the* Suffrages, *the* Litany, *or other prayers.*

Lord, have mercy upon us. Christ, have mercy upon us.

Congregation: *Congregation:*

Lord, have mer - cy up - on us.
Christ, have mer-cy up - on us.

Lord, have mercy upon us.

Congregation:

Lord, have mer - cy up - on us.

Then all shall say:

Our Father, who art in heaven; Hallowed be Thy Name; Thy kingdom come; Thy will be done on earth, as it is in heaven; Give us this day our daily bread; And forgive us our trespasses, as we forgive those who trespass against us; and lead us not into temptation; But deliver us from evil; for Thine is the Kingdom, and the power, and the glory, for ever and ever. Amen.

Salutation. The Lord be with you.

Congregation:

And with Thy Spir - it.

Let us pray.

Then shall be said the Collect *for the day*: *the* Collect *for the Sunday is said throughout the week following until Friday, but on Saturday the* Collect *for the following Sunday is said. Then may be said any other* Collects *and after that this* Collect *for Peace. A* Versicle *may be used with the* Collect.

O God, from whom all holy desires, all good counsels, and all just works do proceed; Give unto Thy seravnts that peace which the world cannot give; that our hearts may be set to obey Thy commandments, and also that by Thee, we being defended from the fear of our enemies, may pass our time in rest and quietness; through the merits of Jesus Christ our Saviour.

Congregation:

A men.

Then may be sung or said the Benedicamus.

Bless we the Lord,

Congregation:

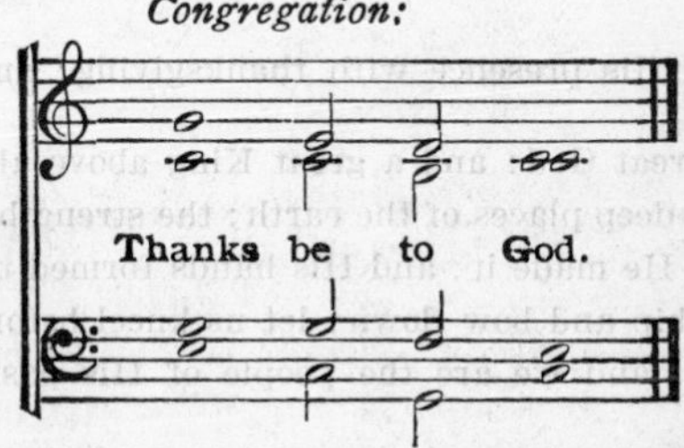
Thanks be to God.

The service may end with the Benedicamus; *or a Closing Hymn may be sung, after which may be said*

The grace of the Lord Jesus Christ, and the love of God, and the communion of the Holy Ghost, be with you all.

Congregation:

A - men, A - men, A - men.

At the close of the Service silent prayer should be offered.

The Order of Early Service, or Matins

A Hymn of Invocation of the Holy Ghost, or another Hymn may be sung.

Then shall be sung or said the Versicles *here following, all standing to the end of the Venite.*

Versicle. O Lord, open Thou my lips.

Answer. And my mouth shall show forth Thy praise.

Versicle. Make haste, O God, to deliver me.

Answer. Make haste to help me, O Lord.

Glory be to the Father, and to the Son: and to the Holy Ghost;

As it was in the beginning, is now, and ever shall be, world without end. Amen.

Hallelujah.

During the Passion season the Hallelujah *shall be omitted.*

Then shall follow the Invitatory *with the* Venite. *On Festival Days a special* Invitatory *may be used.*

The Invitatory.

O Come, let us worship the Lord:
For He is our Maker.

Venite Exultemus. Ps. xcv.

O come, let us sing unto the Lord: let us make a joyful noise to the Rock of our salvation.

Let us come before His presence with thanksgiving: and make a joyful noise unto Him with psalms.

For the Lord is a great God: and a great King above all gods.

In His hand are the deep places of the earth: the strength of the hills is His also.

The Sea is His, and He made it: and His hands formed the dry land.

O come, let us worship and bow down: let us kneel before the Lord our Maker.

For He is our God: and we are the people of His pasture, and the sheep of His hand.

Glory be to the Father, and to the Son, and to the Holy Ghost;

As it was in the beginning, is now, and ever shall be: world without end. Amen.

The Hymn.

The Hymn shall then be sung.

The Psalm.

Then, all standing to the end of the Psalm *shall be sung or said one or more* Psalms. *At the end of the* Psalm *the* Gloria Patri *shall be sung. An* Antiphon *may be used with each* Psalm.

The Lesson.

The Scripture Lessons *shall then be read. After each* Lesson *may be sung or said:*

But Thou, O Lord, have mercy upon us.

Answer. Thanks be to God.

After the Lessons *a* Responsory *may be sung.*

A brief Exhortation, *or* Sermon, *may then follow.*

The Canticle.

The Congregation shall stand and sing the Te Deum Laudamus, *or the* Benedictus. *An* Antiphon *may be sung with the* Benedictus.

Te Deum Laudamus.

We praise Thee, O God: we acknowledge Thee to be the Lord.

All the earth doth worship Thee: the Father everlasting.

To Thee all angels cry aloud: the heavens and all the powers therein.

To Thee Cherubim and Seraphim: continually do cry, Holy, Holy, Holy: Lord God of Sabaoth;

Heaven and earth are full of the majesty: of Thy Glory.

The glorious company of the Apostles: praise Thee.

The goodly fellowship of the Prophets: praise Thee.

The noble army of Martyrs: praise Thee.

The holy Church throughout all the world: doth acknowledge Thee;

The Father: of an infinite Majesty;

Thine adorable, true: and only Son;

Also the Holy Ghost: the Comforter.

Thou art the King of Glory: O Christ.

Thou art the everlasting Son: of the Father.

When Thou tookest upon Thee to deliver man: Thou didst humble Thyself to be born of a Virgin.

When Thou hadst overcome the sharpness of death: Thou didst open the kingdom of heaven to all believers.

Thou sittest at the right hand of God: in the glory of the Father.

We believe that Thou shalt come: to be our Judge.

We therefore pray Thee, help Thy servants: whom Thou hast redeemed with Thy precious blood.

Make them to be numbered with Thy saints: in glory everlasting.

O Lord, save Thy people: and bless Thine heritage.

Govern them: and lift them up forever.

Day by day: we magnify Thee.

And we worship Thy name: ever, world without end.

Vouchsafe, O Lord: to keep us this day without sin.

O Lord, have mercy upon us: have mercy upon us.

O Lord, let Thy mercy be upon us: as our trust is in Thee.

O Lord, in Thee have I trusted: let me never be confounded. Amen.

Or the

Benedictus. St. Luke i.

Blessed be the Lord God of Israel: for He hath visited and redeemed His people;

And hath raised up a horn of salvation for us: in the house of His servant David;

As He spake by the mouth of His holy prophets: which have been since the world began;

That we should be saved from our enemies: and from the hand of all that hate us;

To perform the mercy promised to our fathers: and to remember His holy covenant.

The oath which He sware to our father Abraham: that He would grant unto us;

That we, being delivered out of the hand of our enemies: might serve Him without fear,

In holiness and righteousness before Him: all the days of our life.

And thou, child, shalt be called the Prophet of the Highest: for thou shalt go before the face of the Lord to prepare His ways;

To give knowledge of salvation unto His people: by the remission of their sins,

Through the tender mercy of our God: whereby the dayspring from on high hath visited us;

To give light to them that sit in darkness and in the shadow of death: to guide our feet in the way of peace.

Glory be to the Father, and to the Son: and to the Holy Ghost;

As it was in the beginning, is now, and ever shall be: world without end. Amen.

The Prayer.

Then shall be said the Prayers *here following, or the* Suffrages, *the* Litany, *or other prayers.*

Lord, have mercy upon us.

Lord, have mercy upon us.

Christ, have mercy upon us.

Christ, have mercy upon us.

Lord, have mercy upon us.

Lord, have mercy upon us.

Then all shall say:

Our Father, who art in heaven; Hallowed be Thy Name; Thy kingdom come; Thy will be done on earth as it is in heaven; Give us this day our daily bread; And forgive us our trespasses, as we forgive those who trespass against us; and lead us not into temptation; But deliver us from evil; for Thine is the kingdom, and the power, and the glory, for ever and ever. Amen.

One or more Collects *may be used, with the* Salutation, *which may be preceded by a* Versicle. *After each* Collect *the Congregation shall sing or say*:

Amen.

Then may be sung or said the Benedicamus *with the* Salutation.

The Lord be with you.

Answer. And with thy spirit.

Benedicamus.

Bless we the Lord.

Answer. Thanks be to God,

The service may end with the Benedicamus *or a closing* Hymn *may be sung; after which may be said*

The grace of the Lord Jesus Christ, and the love of God, and the communion of the Holy Ghost, be with you all.

Amen.

At the close of the service silent prayer should be offered.

Introits and Collects for the Church Year

The Introits *have their proper music, but they may be sung to the Psalm tunes. The* Introit, *as far as the Psalm may be repeated after the* Gloria Patri.

FIRST SUNDAY IN ADVENT.

Introit.

Unto Thee, O Lord, do I lift up my soul: O my God, I trust in Thee;
Let me not be ashamed: Let not mine enemies triumph over me;
Yea, let none that wait on Thee: be ashamed.
Psalm. Shew me Thy ways, O Lord: teach me Thy paths.
Glory be to the Father, &c.

Collect.

Stir up, we beseech Thee, Thy power, O Lord, and come; that by Thy protection we may be rescued from the threatening perils of our sins, and saved by Thy mighty deliverance; Who livest and reignest with the Father and the Holy Ghost, ever one God, world without end. *Amen.*

Epistle, Rom. xiii: 11-14. *Gospel,* Matt. xxi: 1-9.

SECOND SUNDAY IN ADVENT.

Introit.

Daughter of Zion: behold thy salvation cometh. The Lord shall cause His glorious voice to be heard: and ye shall have gladness of heart.

Ps. Give ear, O shepherd of Israel: Thou that leadest Joseph like a flock.

Glory be to the Father, &c.

Collect.

Stir up our hearts, O Lord, to make ready the way of Thine Only-Begotten Son, so that by His coming we may be enabled to serve Thee with pure minds; Who liveth and reigneth with Thee and the Holy Ghost, ever one God, world without end. *Amen.*

Epistle, Romans xv: 4-13. *Gospel,* Luke xxi: 25-36.

THIRD SUNDAY IN ADVENT.

Introit.

Rejoice in the Lord alway: and again I say, Rejoice.
Let your moderation be known unto all men: the Lord is at hand.
Be careful for nothing: but in everything by prayer and supplication with thanksgiving let your requests be made known unto God.

Ps. Lord, Thou hast been favorable unto Thy land: Thou hast brought back the captivity of Jacob.

Glory be to the Father, &c.

Collect.

Lord, we beseech Thee, give ear to our prayers, and lighten the darkness of our hearts, by Thy gracious visitation: Who livest and reignest with the Father and the Holy Ghost, ever one God, world without end. *Amen.*
Epistle, 1 Cor. iv: 1-5. *Gospel,* Matt. xi: 2-10.

FOURTH SUNDAY IN ADVENT.

Introit.

Drop down, ye heavens, from above: and let the skies pour down righteousness:
Let the earth open: and bring forth salvation.
Ps. The heavens declare the glory of God: and the firmament sheweth His handiwork.

Glory be to the Father, &c.

Collect.

Stir up, O Lord, we beseech Thee, Thy power, and come, and with great might succor us, that by the help of Thy grace whatsoever is hindered by our sins may be speedily accomplished, through Thy mercy and satisfaction; Who livest and reignest with the Father and the Holy Ghost, ever one God, world without end. *Amen.*

Epistle, Philippians iv: 4-7. *Gospel,* John i: 19-28.

Other Collects for the Season of Advent.

Mercifully hear, O Lord, the prayers of Thy people; that as they rejoice in the Advent of Thine Only-Begotten Son according to the flesh, so when He cometh a second time in His Majesty, they may receive the reward of eternal life; through the same Jesus Christ our Lord; Who liveth, &c.

O God, Who dost gladden us with the early anticipation of our Redemption; Grant that we who now joyfully receive Thine Only-Begotten Son as our Redeemer, may also behold Him without fear when He cometh as our Judge; Who liveth, &c.

Most merciful God, Who hast given Thine eternal Word to be made incarnate of the pure Virgin; Grant unto Thy people grace to put away fleshly lusts, that so they may be ready for Thy visitation; through the same, Thy Son, Jesus Christ, our Lord, who liveth and reigneth, &c.

CHRISTMAS.

Introit.

Unto us a Child is born, unto us a Son is given: and the government shall be upon His shoulder.

And His Name shall be called Wonderful, Counsellor, the Mighty God: the Everlasting Father, the Prince of Peace.

Ps. O sing unto the Lord a new song: for He hath done marvelous things.

Glory be to the Father, &c.

Collect for Christmas Night.

O God, Who hast made this most holy night to shine with the brightness of the true Light; Grant, we beseech Thee, that as we have known on earth the mysteries of that Light, we may also come to the fullness of its joys in heaven; through the same our Lord Jesus Christ, who liveth and reigneth with Thee and the Holy Ghost, ever one God, world without end. *Amen.*

Collect for Christmas Day.

Grant, we beseech Thee, Almighty God, that the new birth of Thine Only-Begotten Son in the flesh may set us free who are held in the old bondage under the yoke of sin; through the same, Thy Son, Jesus Christ, our Lord, who liveth and reigneth with Thee and the Holy Ghost, ever one God, world without end. *Amen.*

Epistle, Tit. ii: 11-14; Isa. ix: 2-7. *Gospel,* Luke ii: 1-14.

SECOND CHRISTMAS DAY.

[*The* Introit *and* Collect *are the same as for Christmas Day.*]

Epistle, Titus iii: 4-7. *Gospel,* Luke ii: 15-20.

SUNDAY AFTER CHRISTMAS.

Introit.

Thy testimonies are very sure: holiness becometh Thine house, O Lord, forever. Thy throne is established of old: Thou art from everlasting.

Ps. The Lord reigneth, He is clothed with majesty: the Lord is clothed with strength, wherewith He hath girded Himself.

Glory be to the Father, &c.

Collect.

Almighty and Everlasting God, direct our actions according to Thy good pleasure, that in the Name of Thy beloved Son, we may be made to abound in good works; through the same Jesus Christ, our Lord, who liveth and reigneth with Thee and the Holy Ghost, ever one God, world without end. *Amen.*

Epistle, Galatians iv: 1-7. *Gospel,* Luke ii: 33-40.

THE CIRCUMCISION OF CHRIST—NEW YEAR.

Introit.

O Lord, our Lord, how excellent is Thy Name in all the earth: Who hast set Thy glory above the heavens. What is man that Thou art mindful of him: and the Son of man that Thou visitest him?

Ps. Thou, O Lord, art our Father and our Redeemer: from everlasting is Thy Name.

Glory be to the Father, &c.

Collect.

O Lord God, Who, for our sakes, hast made Thy Blessed Son, our Saviour, subject to the Law, and caused Him to endure the circumcision of the flesh; Grant us the true circumcision of the Spirit, that our hearts may be pure from all sinful desires and lusts, through the same, Thy Son, our Lord Jesus Christ, who liveth and reigneth with Thee and the Holy Ghost, ever one God, world without end. *Amen.*

Almighty and Everlasting God, from whom cometh down every good and perfect gift; we give Thee thanks for all Thy benefits, temporal and spiritual, bestowed upon us in the year past, and we beseech Thee of Thy goodness, grant us a favorable and joyful year, defend us from all dangers and adversities, and send upon us the fulness of Thy blessing; through Jesus Christ, Thy Son, our Lord, &c.

Epistle, Galatians iii: 23-29. *Gospel,* Luke ii: 21.

SUNDAY AFTER NEW YEAR.

[*The* Introit *and* Collect *are the same as for the Sunday after Christmas.*]

Epistle, 1 Peter iv: 12-19. *Gospel,* Matt. ii: 13-23.

EPIPHANY.

Introit.

Behold the Lord, the Ruler hath come: and the Kingdom, and the power, and the glory are in His hand.

Ps. Give the King Thy judgments, O God: and Thy righteousness unto the King's Son.

Glory be to the Father, &c.

Collect.

O God, Who by the leading of a star didst manifest Thy Only-Begotten Son to the Gentiles; Mercifully grant, that we, who know Thee now by faith, may after this life have the fruition of Thy glorious Godhead; through the same, Thy Son, Jesus Christ our Lord, who liveth and reigneth with Thee and the Holy Ghost, ever one God, world without end. *Amen.*

Epistle, Isaiah lx: 1-6. *Gospel,* Matt. ii: 1-12.

FIRST SUNDAY AFTER EPIPHANY.

Introit.

I saw also the Lord sitting upon a throne: high and lifted up.

And I heard the voice of a great multitude, saying, Alleluia: for the Lord God Omnipotent reigneth.

Ps. Make a joyful noise unto the Lord, all ye lands: serve the Lord with gladness.

Glory be to the Father, &c.

Collect.

O Lord, we beseech Thee mercifully to receive the prayers of Thy people who call upon Thee; and grant that they may both perceive and know what things they ought to do, and also may have grace and power faithfully to fulfil the same; through Jesus Christ, Thy Son, our Lord, who liveth and reigneth with Thee and the Holy Ghost, ever one God, world without end. *Amen.*

Epistle, Rom. xii: 1-5. *Gospel,* Luke ii: 41-52.

SECOND SUNDAY AFTER EPIPHANY.

Introit.

All the earth shall worship Thee: and shall sing unto Thee, O God.

They shall sing to Thy Name: O Thou Most Highest.

Ps. Make a joyful noise unto God, all ye lands: sing forth the honor of His Name, make His praise glorious.

Glory be to the Father, &c.

Collect.

Almighty and Everlasting God, Who dost govern all things in heaven and earth; Mercifully hear the supplications of Thy people, and grant us Thy peace all the days of our life; through Thy Son, Jesus Christ, our Lord, who liveth and reigneth with Thee and the Holy Ghost, ever one God, world without end. *Amen.*

Epistle, Romans xii: 6-16. *Gospel,* John ii: 1-11.

THIRD SUNDAY AFTER EPIPHANY.

Introit.

Worship Him, all ye His angels: Zion heard and was glad.

The daughters of Judah rejoiced: because of Thy judgments, O Lord.

Ps. The Lord reigneth, let the earth rejoice: let the multitude of isles be glad thereof.

Glory be to the Father, &c.

Collect.

Almighty and Everlasting God, mercifully look upon our infirmities, and in all our dangers and necessities stretch forth the right hand of Thy Majesty, to help and defend us; through Jesus Christ, our Lord, who liveth and reigneth with Thee and the Holy Ghost, ever one God, world without end. *Amen.*

Epistle, Rom. xii: 16-21. *Gospel,* Matt. viii: 1-13.

FOURTH SUNDAY AFTER EPIPHANY.

[*The* Introit *is the same as for the Third Sunday after* Epiphany.]

Collect.

Almighty God, Who knowest us to be set in the midst of so many and great dangers, that by reason of the frailty of our nature we cannot always stand upright; Grant to us such strength and protection as may support us in all dangers, and carry us through all temptations; through Jesus Christ, our Lord, who liveth and reigneth with Thee and the Holy Ghost, ever one God, world without end. *Amen.*

Epistle, Rom. xiii: 8-10. *Gospel,* Matt. viii: 23-27.

FIFTH SUNDAY AFTER EPIPHANY.

[*The* Introit *is the same as for the Third Sunday after* Epiphany.]

Collect.

O Lord, we beseech Thee to keep Thy Church and Household continually in Thy true religion; that they who do lean upon the hope of Thy heavenly grace may evermore be defended by Thy mighty power; through Jesus Christ, Thy Son, our Lord, who liveth and reigneth with Thee and the Holy Ghost, ever one God, world without end. *Amen.*

Epistle, Col. iii: 12-17. *Gospel,* Matt. xiii: 24-30.

SIXTH SUNDAY AFTER EPIPHANY.

Introit.

The lightnings lightened the world: the earth trembled and shook.

Ps. How amiable are Thy tabernacles, O Lord of Hosts: My soul longeth, yea, even fainteth for the courts of the Lord.

Glory be to the Father, &c.

Collect.

O God, Who in the glorious Transfiguration of Thy Only-Begotten Son, hast confirmed the mysteries of the faith by the testimony of the fathers, and who, in the voice that came from the bright cloud, didst in a wonderful manner foreshow the adoption of sons: Mercifully vouchsafe to make us co-heirs with the King of his glory, and bring us to the enjoyment of the same; through the same, our Lord Jesus Christ, who liveth and reigneth with Thee and the Holy Ghost, ever one God, world without end. *Amen.*

Epistle, 2 Peter i: 16-21. *Gospel*, Matt. xvii: 1-9.

SEPTUAGESIMA SUNDAY.

Introit.

The sorrows of death compassed me: the sorrows of hell compassed me about.
In my distress, I called upon the Lord: and He heard my voice out of His temple.
Ps. I will love Thee, O Lord my Strength: the Lord is my Rock and my Fortress!
Glory be to the Father, &c.

Collect.

O Lord, we beseech Thee favorably to hear the prayers of Thy people: that we, who are justly punished for our offences, may be mercifully delivered by Thy goodness, for the glory of Thy Name; through Jesus Christ, Thy Son, our Saviour, who liveth and reigneth with Thee and the Holy Ghost, ever one God, world without end. *Amen.*

Epistle, 1 Cor. ix: 24—x: 5. *Gospel*, Matt. xx: 1-16.

SEXAGESIMA SUNDAY.

Introit.

Awake, why sleepest Thou, O Lord?: Arise, cast us not off forever.
Wherefore hidest Thou Thy face: and forgettest our affliction?
Our soul is bowed down to the dust: arise for our help and redeem us.
Ps. We have heard with our ears, O God: our fathers have told us what work Thou didst in their days.
Glory be to the Father, &c.

Collect.

O God, Who seest that we put not our trust in anything that we do: Mercifully grant, that by Thy power we may be defended against all adversity; through Jesus Christ, our Lord, who liveth and reigneth with Thee and the Holy Ghost, ever one God, world without end. *Amen.*

Epistle, 2 Cor. xi: 19—xii: 9. *Gospel*, Luke viii: 4-15.

QUINQUAGESIMA SUNDAY.

Introit.

Be Thou my strong Rock: for an house of defence to save me.
Thou art my Rock and my Fortress: therefore for Thy Name's sake lead me and guide me.
Ps. In Thee, O Lord, do I put my trust; let me never be ashamed: deliver me in my righteousness.
Glory be to the Father, &c.

Collect.

O Lord, we beseech Thee mercifully hear our prayers, and, having set us free from the bonds of sin, defend us from all evil; through Jesus Christ, Thy Son, our Lord, who liveth and reigneth with Thee and the Holy Ghost, ever one God, world without end. *Amen.*

Epistle, 1 Cor. xiii: 1-13. *Gospel*, Luke xviii: 31-43.

ASH WEDNESDAY, OR FIRST DAY OF LENT.

Introit.

I will cry unto God Most High: unto God that performeth all things for me.

Yea, in the shadow of Thy wings will I make my refuge: until these calamities be overpast.

Ps. Be merciful unto me, O God, be merciful unto me: for my soul trusteth in Thee.

Glory be to the Father, &c.

Collect.

Almighty and Everlasting God, Who hatest nothing that Thou hast made, and dost forgive the sins of all those who are penitent; Create and make in us new and contrite hearts, that we, worthily lamenting our sins, and acknowledging our wretchedness, may obtain of Thee, the God of all mercy, perfect remission and forgiveness; through Jesus Christ, our Lord, who liveth and reigneth with Thee and the Holy Ghost, ever one God, world without end. *Amen.*

Epistle, Joel ii: 12-19. *Gospel,* Matt. vi: 16-21.

FIRST SUNDAY IN LENT (INVOCAVIT).

Introit.

He shall call upon Me, and I will answer him: I will deliver him and honor him.

With long life will I satisfy him: and show him my salvation.

Ps. He that dwelleth in the secret place of the Most High: shall abide under the shadow of the Almighty.

Glory be to the Father, &c.

Collect.

O Lord, mercifully hear our prayer, and stretch forth the right hand of Thy Majesty to defend us from them that rise up against us; through Jesus Christ, Thy Son, our Lord, who liveth and reigneth with Thee and the Holy Ghost, ever one God, world without end. *Amen.*

Epistle, 2 Cor. vi: 1-10. *Gospel,* Matt. iv: 1-11.

SECOND SUNDAY IN LENT (REMINISCERE).

Introit.

Remember, O Lord, Thy tender mercies and Thy loving kindnesses: for they have been ever of old.

Let not mine enemies triumph over me: God of Israel, deliver us out of all our troubles.

Ps. Unto Thee, O Lord, do I lift up my soul: O my God, I trust in Thee; let me not be ashamed.

Glory be to the Father, &c.

Collect.

O God, Who seest that of ourselves we have no strength, keep us both outwardly and inwardly; that we may be defended from all adversities which may happen to the body, and from all evil thoughts which may assault and hurt the soul; through Jesus Christ, Thy Son, our Lord, who liveth and reigneth with Thee and the Holy Ghost, ever one God, world without end. *Amen.*

Epistle, 1 Thess. iv: 1-7. *Gospel,* Matt. xv: 21-28.

THIRD SUNDAY IN LENT (OCULI).

Introit.

Mine eyes are ever toward the Lord: for He shall pluck my feet out of the net.
Turn Thee unto me, and have mercy upon me: for I am desolate and afflicted.
Ps. Unto Thee, O Lord, do I lift up my soul: O my God, I trust in Thee; let me not be ashamed.
Glory be to the Father, &c.

Collect.

We beseech Thee, Almighty God, look upon the hearty desires of Thy humble servants, and stretch forth the right hand of Thy Majesty to be our defence against all our enemies; through Jesus Christ, Thy Son, our Lord, who liveth and reigneth with Thee and the Holy Ghost, ever one God, world without end. *Amen.*

Epistle, Ephesians v: 1-9. *Gospel,* Luke xi: 14-28.

FOURTH SUNDAY IN LENT (LAETARE).

Introit.

Rejoice ye with Jerusalem, and be glad with her: all ye that love her.
Rejoice for joy with her: all ye that mourn for her.
Ps. I was glad when they said unto me: Let us go into the house of the Lord.
Glory be to the Father, &c.

Collect.

Grant, we beseech Thee, Almighty God, that we, who for our evil deeds do worthily deserve to be punished, by the comfort of Thy grace may mercifully be relieved; through our Lord and Saviour Jesus Christ, who liveth and reigneth with Thee and the Holy Ghost, ever one God, world without end. *Amen.*

Epistle, Galatians iv: 21-31. *Gospel,* John vi: 1-15.

FIFTH SUNDAY IN LENT (JUDICA).

Introit.

Judge me, O God: and plead my cause against an ungodly nation.
O deliver me from the deceitful and unjust man: for Thou art the God of my strength.
Ps. O send out Thy light and Thy truth: let them lead me; let them bring me unto Thy holy hill.
Glory be to the Father, &c.

Collect.

We beseech Thee, Almighty God, mercifully to look upon Thy people, that by Thy great goodness they may be governed and preserved evermore, both in body and soul; through Jesus Christ, Thy Son, our Lord, who liveth and reigneth with Thee and the Holy Ghost, ever one God, world without end. *Amen.*

Epistle, Hebrews ix: 11-15. *Gospel,* John viii: 46-59.

SIXTH SUNDAY IN LENT (PALMARUM).

Introit.

Be not Thou far from me, O Lord: O my strength, haste Thee to help me.
Save me from the lion's mouth: and deliver me from the horns of the unicorns.
Ps. My God, my God, why hast Thou forsaken me?: Why art Thou so far from helping me?
Glory be to the Father, &c.

Collect.

Almighty and Everlasting God, Who hast sent Thy Son, our Saviour Jesus Christ, to take upon Him our flesh, and to suffer death upon the cross, that all mankind should follow the example of His great humility: Mercifully grant that we may both follow the example of His patience, and also be made partakers of His resurrection; through the same Jesus Christ our Lord, who liveth and reigneth with Thee and the Holy Ghost, ever one God, world without end. *Amen.*

Epistle, Philippians ii: 5-11. *Gospel,* Matt. xxi: 1-9.

MONDAY IN HOLY WEEK.

Introit.

Plead my cause, O Lord, with them that strive with me: fight against them that fight against me.

Take hold of shield and buckler: and stand up for mine help.

Ps. Draw out also the spear, and stop the way against them that persecute me: say unto my soul, I am Thy salvation.

Glory be to the Father, &c.

Collect.

Grant, we beseech Thee, Almighty God, that we, who amid so many adversities do fail through our own infirmities, may be restored through the passion and intercession of Thine Only-Begotten Son, who liveth and reigneth with Thee and the Holy Ghost ever one God, world without end. *Amen.*

Epistle, Is. l: 5-10. *Gospel,* John xii: 1-23, or The Passion History.

TUESDAY IN HOLY WEEK.

Introit.

God forbid that I should glory: save in the Cross of our Lord Jesus Christ.

In Him is salvation, life, and resurrection from the dead: by Him we are redeemed and set at liberty.

Ps. God be merciful unto us, and bless us: and cause his face to shine upon us.

Glory be to the Father, &c.

Collect.

Almighty and Everlasting God, Grant us grace so to pass through this holy time of our Lord's Passion, that we may obtain the pardon of our sins; through the same, Thy Son, who liveth and reigneth with Thee and the Holy Ghost, ever one God, world without end. *Amen.*

Epistle, Jer. xi: 18-20. *Gospel,* John xii: 24-43, or The Passion History.

WEDNESDAY IN HOLY WEEK.

Introit.

At the Name of Jesus every knee shall bow: of things in heaven, and things in earth, and things under the earth.

For He became obedient unto death, even the death of the Cross: wherefore He is Lord, to the glory of God the Father.

Ps. Hear my prayer, O Lord: and let my cry come unto Thee.

Glory be to the Father, &c.

Collect.

Grant, we beseech Thee, Almighty God, that we, who for our evil deeds are continually afflicted, may mercifully be relieved by the Passion of Thine Only-Begotten Son, who liveth and reigneth with Thee and the Holy Ghost, ever one God, world without end. *Amen.*

Epistle, Is. lxii: 11; lxiii: 1-7. *Gospel,* Luke xxii: 1-xxiii: 42, or The Passion History.

THURSDAY IN HOLY WEEK.

The Introit *is the same as for Tuesday.*

O Lord God, Who hast left unto us in a wonderful Sacrament a memorial of Thy Passion; Grant, we beseech Thee, that we may so use this Sacrament of Thy Body and Blood, that the fruits of Thy redemption may continually be manifest in us; Thou, who livest and reignest with the Father and the Holy Ghost, ever one God, world without end. *Amen.*

Epistle, 1 Cor. xi: 23-32. *Gospel,* John xiii: 1-15, or The Passion History.

GOOD FRIDAY.

The same Introit *as for Tuesday, or this*:

Surely He hath borne our griefs and carried our sorrows: He was wounded for our transgressions, He was bruised for our iniquities.

All we like sheep have gone astray: and the Lord hath laid on Him the iniquity of us all.

Ps. Hear my prayer, O Lord: and let my cry come unto Thee.

Glory be to the Father, &c.

Collects.

Almighty God, we beseech Thee graciously to behold this Thy family, for which our Lord Jesus Christ was contented to be betrayed, and given up into the hands of wicked men, and to suffer death upon the Cross; who now liveth and reigneth with Thee and the Holy Ghost, ever one God, world without end. *Amen.*

Merciful and Everlasting God, Who hast not spared Thine only Son, but delivered Him up for us all, that He might bear our sins upon the Cross; Grant that our hearts may be so fixed with steadfast faith in Him that we may not fear the power of any adversaries; through the same, Thy Son, Jesus Christ our Lord. *Amen.*

Almighty and Everlasting God, Who hast willed that Thy Son should bear for us the pains of the Cross, that Thou mightest remove from us the power of the adversary; Help us so to remember and give thanks for our Lord's Passion that we may obtain remission of sin and redemption from everlasting death; through the same, our Lord Jesus Christ. *Amen.*

Epistle, Isa. lii: 13-liii: 12. *Gospel.* John xviii: 1-xix: 42, or The Passion History.

EASTER.

Introit.

When I awake I am still with Thee. Hallelujah!: Thou hast laid Thine hand upon me. Hallelujah!

Such knowledge is too wonderful for me: it is high, I cannot attain unto it. Hallelujah! Hallelujah!

Ps. O Lord, Thou hast searched me, and known me: Thou knowest my downsitting and mine uprising.

Glory be to the Father, &c.

or

He is risen, Hallelujah!: Why seek ye the Living among the dead? Hallelujah!

Remember how He spake unto you, Hallelujah: the Son of man must be crucified, and the third day rise again. Hallelujah! Hallelujah!

Ps. Thou crownedst Him with glory and honor: Thou madest Him to have dominion over the works of Thy hands.

Glory be to the Father, &c.

The Collect *for Easter Eve.*

O God, Who didst enlighten this most holy night with the glory of the Lord's Resurrection; Preserve in all Thy people the spirit of adoption which Thou hast given, so that renewed in body and soul they may perform unto Thee a pure service; through the same, our Lord Jesus Christ, who liveth and reigneth with Thee and the Holy Ghost, ever one God, world without end. *Amen.*

The Collect *for Easter Day.*

Almighty God, Who, through Thine Only-Begotten Son, Jesus Christ, hast overcome death, and opened unto us the gate of everlasting life; We humbly beseech Thee, that, as Thou dost put into our minds good desires, so by Thy continual help we may bring the same to good effect; through Jesus Christ, our Lord, who liveth and reigneth with Thee and the Holy Ghost, ever one God, world without end. *Amen.*

Other Easter Collects.

Grant, we beseech Thee, Almighty God, that we who celebrate Thy Paschal Feast, kindled with heavenly desires, may ever thirst for the Fountain of Life, Jesus Christ, Thy Son, our Lord. *Amen.*

Grant, we beseech Thee, Almighty God, that we who celebrate the solemnities of the Lord's Resurrection, may by the renewal of Thy Holy Spirit rise again from the death of the soul; through the same Jesus Christ our Lord. *Amen.*

Epistle, 1 Cor. v: 6-8. *Gospel,* Mark xvi: 1-8.

EASTER MONDAY.

The Introit *and the* Collect *are the same as for Easter Day.*

Epistle, Acts x: 34-41. *Gospel,* Luke xxiv: 13-35.

FIRST SUNDAY AFTER EASTER (QUASIMODOGENITI).

Introit.

As newborn babes: desire the sincere milk of the Word.

Hear, O my people, and I will testify unto Thee: O Israel, if thou wilt hearken unto me.

Ps. Sing aloud unto God our strength: make a joyful noise unto the God of Jacob.

Glory be to the Father, &c.

Collect.

Grant, we beseech Thee, Almighty God, that we who have celebrated the solemnities of the Lord's Resurrection, may, by the help of Thy grace, bring forth the fruits thereof in our life and conversation; through the same Jesus Christ, Thy Son, our Lord, who liveth and reigneth with Thee and the Holy Ghost, ever one God, world without end. *Amen.*

Epistle, 1 John v: 4-12. *Gospel,* John xx: 19-31.

SECOND SUNDAY AFTER EASTER (MISERICORDIAS).

Introit.

The earth is full of the goodness of the Lord:

By the Word of the Lord were the heavens made.

Ps. Rejoice in the Lord, O ye righteous: for praise is comely for the upright.

Glory be to the Father, &c.

Collect.

God, Who, by the humiliation of Thy Son, didst raise up the fallen world; Grant unto Thy faithful ones perpetual gladness, and those whom Thou hast delivered from the danger of everlasting death, do Thou make partakers of eternal joys; through the same Jesus Christ our Lord, who liveth and reigneth with Thee and the Holy Ghost, ever one God, world without end. *Amen.*

Epistle, 1 Peter ii: 21-25. *Gospel,* John x: 11-16.

THIRD SUNDAY AFTER EASTER (JUBILATE).

Introit.

Make a joyful noise unto God, all ye lands:

Sing forth the honor of His Name; make His praise glorious.

Ps. Say unto God, how terrible art Thou in Thy works: through the greatness of Thy power shall Thine enemies submit themselves unto Thee.

Glory be to the Father, &c.

Collect.

Almighty God, Who showest to them that be in error the light of Thy truth, to the intent that they may return into the way of righteousness; Grant unto all them that are admitted into the fellowship of Christ's Religion that they may eschew those things that are contrary to their profession, and follow all such things as are agreeable to the same; through our Lord Jesus Christ, who liveth and reigneth with Thee and the Holy Ghost, ever one God, world without end. *Amen.*

Epistle, 1 Peter ii: 11-20. *Gospel,* John xvi: 16-23.

FOURTH SUNDAY AFTER EASTER (CANTATE).

Introit.

O sing unto the Lord a new song: for He hath done marvellous things.

The Lord hath made known His salvation: His righteousness hath He openly showed in the sight of the heathen.

Ps. His right hand, and His holy arm: hath gotten Him the victory.

Glory be to the Father, &c.

Collect.

O God, Who makest the minds of the faithful to be of one will; Grant unto Thy people that they may love what Thou commandest, and desire what Thou dost promise; that among the manifold changes of this world, our hearts may there be fixed where true joys are to be found; through Jesus Christ, Thy Son, our Lord, who liveth and reigneth with Thee and the Holy Ghost, ever one God, world without end. *Amen.*

Epistle, James i: 16-21. *Gospel,* John xvi: 5-15.

FIFTH SUNDAY AFTER EASTER (ROGATE).

Introit.

With the voice of singing declare ye, and tell this: utter it even to the end of the earth. Hallelujah!

The Lord hath redeemed His servant Jacob: Hallelujah, Hallelujah!

Ps. Make a joyful noise unto God, all ye lands: sing forth the honor of His Name; make His praise glorious.

Glory be to the Father, &c.

Collect.

O God, from Whom all good things do come; Grant to us Thy humble servants, that by Thy holy inspiration we may think those things that be right, and by Thy merciful guiding may perform the same; through Jesus Christ, Thy Son, our Lord, who liveth and reigneth with Thee and the Holy Ghost, ever one God, world without end. *Amen.*

Epistle, James i: 22-27. *Gospel,* John xvi: 23-30.

ASCENSION DAY.

Introit.

Ye men of Gallilee, why stand ye gazing up into heaven? : Hallelujah!

This same Jesus which is taken up from you into heaven, shall so come in like manner as ye have seen Him go into heaven: Hallelujah! Hallelujah!

Ps. O clap your hands, all ye people: shout unto God with the voice of triumph.

Glory be to the Father, &c.

Collect.

Grant, we beseech Thee, Almighty God, that like as we do believe Thy Only-Begotten Son, our Lord Jesus Christ, to have ascended into the heavens; so may we also in heart and mind thither ascend, and with Him continually dwell, who liveth and reigneth with Thee and the Holy Ghost, ever one God, world without end. *Amen.*

O King of Glory, Lord of Hosts, Who didst this Day ascend in triumph far above all heavens; We beseech Thee leave us not comfortless, but send to us the Spirit of Truth, promised of the Father; O Thou, who, with the Father and the Holy Ghost, livest and reignest ever one God, world without end. *Amen.*

Epistle, Acts i: 1-11. *Gospel*, Mark xvi: 14-20.

SUNDAY AFTER ASCENSION (EXAUDI).

Introit.

Hear, O Lord, when I cry with my voice: Hallelujah!

When Thou saidst, seek ye My face; my heart said unto Thee, Thy face, Lord, will I seek: Hide not Thy face from me. Hallelujah, Hallelujah!

Ps. The Lord is my Light, and my Salvation: whom shall I fear?

Glory be to the Father, &c.

Collect.

Almighty, Everlasting God; Make us to have always a devout will towards Thee, and to serve Thy Majesty with a pure heart; through Thy Son, Jesus Christ our Lord, who liveth and reigneth with Thee and the Holy Ghost, ever one God, world without end. *Amen.*

Epistle, 1 Peter iv: 7-11. *Gospel*, John xv: 26—xvi: 4.

WHITSUNDAY.

Introit.

The Spirit of the Lord filleth the world: Hallelujah!

Let the righteous be glad; let them rejoice before God: yea, let them exceedingly rejoice. Hallelujah! Hallelujah!

Ps. Let God arise; let His enemies be scattered: let them also that hate Him flee before Him.

Glory be to the Father, &c.

Collect.

O God, Who didst teach the hearts of Thy faithful people, by sending to them the light of Thy Holy Spirit; Grant us by the same Spirit to have a right judgment in all things, and evermore to rejoice in His holy comfort; through our Lord Jesus Christ, Thy Son, who with Thee and the Holy Ghost liveth and reigneth, ever one God, world without end. *Amen.*

Epistle, Acts ii: 1-13. *Gospel*, John xiv: 23-31.

MONDAY IN WHITSUN-WEEK.

The Introit *is the same as for Whitsunday.*

Collect.

O God, Who didst give Thy Holy Spirit to Thine Apostles; Grant unto Thy people the performance of their petitions, so that on us to whom Thou hast given faith, Thou mayest also bestow peace; through our Lord Jesus Christ, Thy Son, who with Thee and the Holy Ghost liveth and reigneth, ever one God, world without end. *Amen.*

Epistle, Acts x: 42-48. *Gospel*, John iii: 16-21.

THE FESTIVAL OF THE TRINITY.

Introit.

Blessed be the Holy Trinity, and the undivided Unity: Let us give glory to Him because He hath shown His mercy to us.

Ps. O Lord, our Lord: how excellent is Thy Name in all the earth!

Glory be to the Father, &c.

Or,

Holy, Holy, Holy, is the Lord of Hosts: of Him, and through Him, and to Him, are all things.

Ps. O Lord, our Lord: how excellent is Thy Name in all the earth.

Glory be to the Father, &c.

Collect.

Almighty and Everlasting God, Who hast given unto us, Thy servants, grace, by the confession of a true faith, to acknowledge the glory of the Eternal Trinity, and in the power of the Divine Majesty to worship the Unity; We beseech Thee, that Thou wouldst keep us steadfast in this faith, and evermore defend us from all adversities, who livest and reignest, one God, world without end. *Amen.*

Epistle, Romans xi: 33-36. *Gospel,* John iii: 1-15.

FIRST SUNDAY AFTER TRINITY.

Introit.

O Lord, I have trusted in Thy mercy: my heart shall rejoice in Thy salvation.
I will sing unto the Lord: because He hath dealt bountifully with me.

Ps. How long wilt Thou forget me, O Lord?: How long wilt Thou hide Thy face from me?

Glory be to the Father, &c.

Collect.

O God, the strength of all them that put their trust in Thee; Mercifully accept our prayers; and because through the weakness of our mortal nature we can do no good thing without Thee, grant us the help of Thy grace, that in keeping Thy commandments we may please Thee, both in will and deed; through Jesus Christ our Lord, who liveth and reigneth with Thee and the Holy Ghost, ever one God, world without end. *Amen.*

Epistle, 1 John iv: 16-21. *Gospel,* Luke xvi: 19-31.

SECOND SUNDAY AFTER TRINITY.

Introit.

The Lord was my stay; He brought me forth also into a large place:
He delivered me, because He delighted in me.

Ps. I will love Thee, O Lord, my strength: The Lord is my Rock, and my Fortress.

Glory be to the Father, &c.

Collect.

O Lord, Who never failest to help and govern those whom Thou dost bring up in Thy steadfast fear and love; Make us to have a perpetual fear and love of Thy Holy Name; through Jesus Christ, Thy Son, our Lord, who liveth and reigneth with Thee and the Holy Ghost, ever one God, world without end. *Amen.*

Epistle, 1 John iii: 13-18. *Gospel,* Luke xiv: 16-24.

THIRD SUNDAY AFTER TRINITY.

Introit.

Turn Thee unto me, and have mercy upon me: for I am desolate and afflicted.
Look upon mine affliction and my pain: and forgive all my sins.

Ps. Unto Thee, O Lord, do I lift up my soul: O my God, I trust in Thee, let me not be ashamed.

Glory be to the Father, &c.

Collect.

O God, the Protector of all that trust in Thee, without whom nothing is strong, nothing is holy; increase and multiply upon us Thy mercy; that Thou being our Ruler and Guide, we may so pass through things temporal that we finally lose not the things eternal; through Jesus Christ our Lord, who liveth and reigneth with Thee and the Holy Ghost, ever one God, world without end. *Amen.*

Epistle, 1 Peter v: 6-11. *Gospel,* Luke xv: 1-10.

FOURTH SUNDAY AFTER TRINITY.

Introit.

The Lord is my Light and my Salvation; whom shall I fear?: The Lord is the strength of my life; of whom shall I be afraid?

When the wicked, even mine enemies and my foes came upon me: they stumbled and fell.

Ps. Though an host should encamp against me: my heart shall not fear.

Glory be to the Father, &c.

Collect.

Grant, O Lord, we beseech Thee, that the course of this world may be so peaceably ordered by Thy governance, that Thy Church may joyfully serve Thee in all godly quietness; through Jesus Christ, Thy Son, our Lord, who liveth and reigneth with Thee and the Holy Ghost, ever one God, world without end. *Amen.*

Epistle, Rom. viii: 18-23. *Gospel,* Luke vi: 36-42.

FIFTH SUNDAY AFTER TRINITY.

Introit.

Hear, O Lord, when I cry with my voice: Thou hast been my help.

Leave me not, neither forsake me: O God of my salvation.

Ps. The Lord is my Light and my Salvation: whom shall I fear?

Glory be to the Father, &c.

Collect.

O God, Who hast prepared for them that love Thee such good things as pass man's understanding; Pour into our hearts such love toward Thee, that we, loving Thee above all things, may obtain Thy promises, which exceed all that we can desire; through Jesus Christ, Thy Son, our Lord, who liveth and reigneth with Thee and the Holy Ghost, ever one God, world without end. *Amen.*

Epistle, 1 Peter iii: 8-15. *Gospel,* Luke v: 1-11.

SIXTH SUNDAY AFTER TRINITY.

Introit.

The Lord is the strength of His people: He is the saving strength of His anointed.

Save Thy people, and bless Thine inheritance: feed them also, and lift them up forever.

Ps. Unto Thee will I cry, O Lord, my Rock; be not silent unto me: lest if Thou be silent to me, I become like them that go down into the pit.

Glory be to the Father, &c.

Collect.

Lord of all power and might, Who art the Author and Giver of all good things; Graft in our hearts the love of Thy Name, increase in us true religion, nourish us with all goodness, and of Thy great mercy keep us in the same; through Jesus Christ, Thy Son, our Lord, who liveth and reigneth with Thee and the Holy Ghost, ever one God, world without end. *Amen.*

Epistle, Rom. vi: 3-11. *Gospel,* Matt. v: 20-26.

SEVENTH SUNDAY AFTER TRINITY.

Introit.

O clap your hands, all ye people: Shout unto God with the voice of triumph.

Ps. He shall subdue the people under us: and the nations under our feet.

Glory be to the Father, &c.

Collect.

O God, Whose never-failing Providence ordereth all things both in heaven and earth; We humbly beseech Thee to put away from us all hurtful things, and to give us those things which be profitable for us; through Jesus Christ, Thy Son, our Lord, who liveth and reigneth with Thee and the Holy Ghost, ever one God, world without end. *Amen.*

Epistle, Romans vi: 19-23. *Gospel,* Mark viii: 1-9.

EIGHTH SUNDAY AFTER TRINITY.

Introit.

We have thought of Thy loving kindness, O God: in the midst of Thy Temple.

According to Thy Name, O God, so is Thy praise unto the ends of the earth: Thy right hand is full of righteousness.

Ps. Great is the Lord, and greatly to be praised: in the city of our God, in the mountain of His holiness.

Glory be to the Father, &c.

Collect.

Grant to us, Lord, we beseech Thee, the Spirit to think and do always such things as are right; that we, who cannot do anything that is good without Thee, may by Thee be enabled to live according to Thy will; through Jesus Christ, Thy Son, our Lord, who liveth and reigneth with Thee and the Holy Ghost, ever one God, world without end. *Amen.*

Epistle, Romans viii: 12-17. *Gospel,* Matt. vii: 15-23.

NINTH SUNDAY AFTER TRINITY.

Introit.

Behold God is mine Helper: the Lord is with them that uphold my soul.

He shall reward evil unto mine enemies: cut them off in Thy truth, O Lord.

Ps. Save me, O God, by Thy Name: and judge me by Thy strength.

Glory be to the Father, &c.

Collect.

Let Thy merciful ears, O Lord, be open to the prayers of Thy humble servants; and that they may obtain their petitions make them to ask such things as shall please Thee; through Jesus Christ, Thy Son, our Lord, who liveth and reigneth with Thee and the Holy Ghost, ever one God, world without end. *Amen.*

Epistle, 1 Cor. x: 6-13. *Gospel,* Luke xvi: 1-9.

TENTH SUNDAY AFTER TRINITY.

Introit.

As for me, I will call upon God; and He shall hear my voice: He hath delivered my soul in peace from the battle that was against me.

God shall hear and afflict them; even He that abideth of old: Cast thy burden upon the Lord, and He shall sustain thee.

Ps. Give ear to my prayer, O God: and hide not Thyself from my supplication.

Glory be to the Father, &c.

Collect.

O God, Who declarest Thine Almighty power chiefly in showing mercy and pity; mercifully grant unto us such a measure of Thy grace, that we, running the way of Thy commandments, may obtain Thy gracious promises, and be made partakers of Thy heavenly treasure; through Jesus Christ, Thy Son, our Lord, who liveth and reigneth with Thee and the Holy Ghost, ever one God, world without end. *Amen.*

Epistle, 1 Cor. xii: 1-11. *Gospel,* Luke xix: 41-48.

ELEVENTH SUNDAY AFTER TRINITY.

Introit.

God is in His holy habitation, He is God who setteth the solitary in families:
The God of Israel is He that giveth strength and power unto his people.

Ps. Let God arise, let his enemies be scattered: let them also that hate Him flee before Him.

Glory be to the Father, &c.

Collect.

Almighty and Everlasting God, Who art always more ready to hear than we to pray, and art wont to give more than either we desire or deserve; Pour down upon us the abundance of Thy mercy, forgiving us those things whereof our conscience is afraid, and giving us those good things which we are not worthy to ask, but through the merits and mediation of Jesus Christ, Thy Son, our Lord, who liveth and reigneth with Thee and the Holy Ghost, ever one God, world without end. *Amen.*

Epistle, 1 Cor. xv: 1-10. *Gospel,* Luke xviii: 9-14.

TWELFTH SUNDAY AFTER TRINITY.

Introit.

Make haste, O God, to deliver me: make haste to help me, O Lord.
Let them be ashamed and confounded: that seek after my soul.

Ps. Let them be turned backward, and put to confusion: that desire my hurt.

Glory be to the Father, &c.

Collect.

Almighty and merciful God, of Whose only gift it cometh that Thy faithful people do unto Thee true and laudable service; Grant, we beseech Thee, that we may so faithfully serve Thee in this life, that we fail not finally to attain Thy Heavenly promises; through Jesus Christ, Thy Son, our Lord, who liveth and reigneth with Thee and the Holy Ghost, true God, world without end. *Amen.*

Epistle, 2 Cor. iii: 4-11. *Gospel,* Mark vii: 31-37.

THIRTEENTH SUNDAY AFTER TRINITY.

Introit.

Have respect, O Lord, unto Thy covenant: O let not the oppressed return ashamed.

Arise, O God, plead Thine own cause: and forget not the voice of Thine enemies.

Ps. O God, why hast Thou cast us off forever: Why doth Thine anger smoke against the sheep of Thy pasture?

Glory be to the Father, &c.

Collect.

Almighty and Everlasting God, give unto us the increase of faith, hope, and charity; and that we may obtain that which Thou dost promise, make us to love that which Thou dost command; through Jesus Christ, Thy Son, our Lord, who liveth and reigneth with Thee and the Holy Ghost, ever one God, world without end. *Amen.*

Epistle, Gal. iii: 15-22. *Gospel,* Luke x: 23-37.

FOURTEENTH SUNDAY AFTER TRINITY.

Introit.

Behold, O God our shield, and look upon the face of Thine Anointed:

For a day in Thy courts is better than a thousand.

Ps. How amiable are Thy tabernacles, O Lord of Hosts: My soul longeth, yea, even fainteth for the courts of the Lord.

Glory be to the Father, &c.

Collect.

Keep, we beseech Thee, O Lord, Thy Church with Thy perpetual mercy; and because the frailty of man without Thee cannot but fall, keep us ever by Thy help from all things hurtful, and lead us to all things profitable to our salvation; through Jesus Christ, Thy Son, our Lord, who liveth and reigneth with Thee and the Holy Ghost, ever one God, world without end. *Amen.*

Epistle, Gal. v: 16-24. *Gospel,* Luke xvii: 11-19.

FIFTEENTH SUNDAY AFTER TRINITY.

Introit.

Bow down Thine ear, O Lord, hear me: O Thou, my God, save Thy servant that trusteth in Thee.

Be merciful to me, O Lord: for I cry unto Thee daily.

Ps. Rejoice the soul of Thy servant: for unto Thee, O Lord, do I lift up my soul.

Glory be to the Father, &c.

Collect.

O Lord, we beseech Thee, Let continual pity cleanse and defend Thy Church; and because it cannot continue in safety without Thy succor, preserve it evermore by Thy help and goodness; through Jesus Christ, Thy Son, our Lord, who liveth and reigneth with Thee and the Holy Ghost, ever one God, world without end. *Amen.*

Epistle, Gal. v: 25—vi: 10. *Gospel,* Matt. vi: 24-34.

SIXTEENTH SUNDAY AFTER TRINITY.

Introit.

Be merciful unto me, O Lord: for I cry unto Thee daily.

For Thou, Lord, art good, and ready to forgive: and plenteous in mercy unto all them that call upon Thee.

Ps. Bow down Thine ear, O Lord, hear me: for I am poor and needy.

Glory be to the Father, &c.

Collect.

Lord, we pray Thee, that Thy grace may always go before and follow after us, and make us continually to be given to all good works; through Jesus Christ, Thy Son, our Lord, who liveth and reigneth with Thee and the Holy Ghost, ever one God, world without end. *Amen.*

Epistle, Eph. iii: 13-21. *Gospel,* Luke vii: 11-17.

SEVENTEENTH SUNDAY AFTER TRINITY.

Introit.

Righteous art Thou, O Lord, and upright art Thy judgments:

Deal with Thy servant according to Thy mercy.

Ps. Blessed are the undefiled in the way: who walk in the law of the Lord.

Glory be to the Father, &c.

Collect.

Lord, we beseech Thee, Grant Thy people grace, to withstand the temptations of the devil, and with pure hearts and minds to follow Thee, the only God; through Jesus Christ, Thy Son, our Lord, who liveth and reigneth with Thee and the Holy Ghost, ever one God, world without end. *Amen.*

Epistle, Eph. iv: 1-6. *Gospel,* Luke xiv: 1-11.

EIGHTEENTH SUNDAY AFTER TRINITY.

Introit.

Reward them that wait for Thee, O Lord: and let Thy prophets be found faithful.

Hear the prayer of Thy servants: and of Thy people Israel.

Ps. I was glad when they said unto me: Let us go into the house of the Lord.

Glory be to the Father, &c.

Collect.

O God, forasmuch as without Thee we are not able to please Thee; Mercifully grant, that Thy Holy Spirit may in all things direct and rule our hearts; through Jesus Christ, Thy Son, our Lord, who liveth and reigneth with Thee and the Holy Ghost, ever one God, world without end. *Amen.*

Epistle, 1 Cor. i: 4-9. *Gospel,* Matt. xxii: 34-46.

NINETEENTH SUNDAY AFTER TRINITY.

Introit.

Say unto my soul, I am Thy salvation:
The righteous cry, and the Lord heareth;
He delivereth them out of their troubles: He is their God for ever and ever.

Ps. Give ear, O my people, to my law: incline your ears to the words of my mouth.

Glory be to the Father, &c.

Collect.

O Almighty and most merciful God, of Thy bountiful goodness keep us, we beseech Thee, from all things that may hurt us; that we, being ready, both in body and soul, may cheerfully accomplish those things that Thou wouldst have done; through Jesus Christ, Thy Son, our Lord, who liveth and reigneth with Thee and the Holy Ghost, ever one God, world without end. *Amen.*

Epistle, Eph. iv: 22-28. *Gospel,* Matt. ix: 1-8.

TWENTIETH SUNDAY AFTER TRINITY.

Introit.

The Lord our God is righteous in all his works which He doeth: for we obeyed not His voice.

Give glory to Thy Name, O Lord: and deal with us according to the multitude of Thy mercies.

Ps. Great is the Lord, and greatly to be praised: in the city of our God, in the mountain of His holiness.

Glory be to the Father, &c.

Collect.

Grant, we beseech Thee, merciful Lord, to Thy faithful people pardon and peace, that they may be cleansed from all their sins, and serve Thee with a quiet mind; through Jesus Christ, Thy Son, our Lord, who liveth and reigneth with Thee and the Holy Ghost, ever one God, world without end. *Amen.*

Epistle, Eph. v: 15-21. *Gospel,* Matt. xxii: 1-14.

TWENTY-FIRST SUNDAY AFTER TRINITY.

Introit.

The whole world is in Thy power, O Lord, King Almighty: there is no man that can gainsay Thee.

For Thou hast made heaven and earth, and all the wondrous things under the heaven: Thou art Lord of all.

Ps. Blessed are the undefiled in the way: who walk in the law of the Lord.

Glory be to the Father, &c.

Collect.

Lord, we beseech Thee to keep Thy household, the Church, in continual godliness; that through Thy protection it may be free from all adversities, and devoutly given to serve Thee in good works, to the glory of Thy Name; through Jesus Christ, Thy Son, our Lord, who liveth and reigneth with Thee and the Holy Ghost, ever one God, world without end. *Amen.*

Epistle, Eph. vi: 10-17. *Gospel,* John iv: 46-54.

TWENTY-SECOND SUNDAY AFTER TRINITY.

Introit.

If Thou, Lord, shouldest mark iniquities: O Lord, who shall stand?

But there is forgiveness with Thee: that Thou mayest be feared, O God of Israel.

Ps. Out of the depths have I cried unto Thee, O Lord: Lord, hear my voice.

Glory be to the Father, &c.

Collect.

O God, our refuge and strength, Who art the Author of all godliness; Be ready, we beseech Thee, to hear the devout prayers of Thy Church: and grant that those things which we ask faithfully, we may obtain effectually; through Jesus Christ, Thy Son, our Lord, who liveth and reigneth with Thee and the Holy Ghost, ever one God, world without end. *Amen.*

Epistle, Phil. i: 3-11. *Gospel,* Matt. xviii: 23-35.

TWENTY-THIRD SUNDAY AFTER TRINITY.

Introit.

I know the thoughts that I think toward you, saith the Lord: thoughts of peace, and not of evil.

Then shall ye call upon Me, and pray unto Me, and I will hearken unto you: and I will turn your captivity, and gather you from all nations and from all places.

Ps. Lord, Thou hast been favorable unto Thy land: Thou hast brought back the captivity of Jacob.

Glory be to the Father, &c.

Collect.

Absolve, we beseech Thee, O Lord, Thy people from their offences; that from the bonds of our sins which, by reason of our frailty, we have brought upon us, we may be delivered by Thy bountiful goodness; through Jesus Christ, Thy Son, our Lord, who liveth and reigneth with Thee and the Holy Ghost, ever one God, world without end. *Amen.*

Epistle, Phil. iii: 17-21. *Gospel,* Matt. xxii: 15-22.

TWENTY-FOURTH SUNDAY AFTER TRINITY.

Introit.

O come, let us worship and bow down: let us kneel before the Lord our Maker.

For He is our God: and we are the people of His pasture, and the sheep of His hand.

Ps. O come, let us sing unto the Lord: let us make a joyful noise to the Rock of our salvation.

Glory be to the Father, &c.

Collect.

Stir up, we beseech Thee, O Lord, the wills of Thy faithful people; that they, plenteously bringing forth the fruit of good works, may of Thee be plenteously rewarded; through Jesus Christ, Thy Son, our Lord, who liveth and reigneth with Thee and the Holy Ghost, ever one God, world without end. *Amen.*

Epistle, Col. i: 9-14. *Gospel,* Matt. ix: 18-26.

TWENTY-FIFTH SUNDAY AFTER TRINITY.

Introit.

Have mercy upon me, O Lord, for I am in trouble: deliver me from the hand of mine enemies, and from them that persecute me.

Let me not be ashamed, O Lord: for I have called upon Thee.

Ps. In Thee, O Lord, do I put my trust: let me never be ashamed.

Glory be to the Father, &c.

Almighty God, we beseech Thee, Show Thy mercy unto thy humble servants, that we who put no trust in our merits may not be dealt with after the severity of Thy judgment, but according to Thy mercy; through Jesus Christ, Thy Son, our Lord, who liveth and reigneth with Thee and the Holy Ghost, ever one God, world without end. *Amen.*

Epistle, 1 Thess. iv: 13-18. *Gospel,* Matt. xxiv: 15-28.

TWENTY-SIXTH SUNDAY AFTER TRINITY.

Introit.

Save me, O God, by Thy Name, and judge me by Thy strength:

Hear my prayer, O God; give ear to the words of my mouth.

Ps. He shall reward evil to mine enemies: cut them off in Thy truth.

Glory be to the Father, &c.

Collect.

O God, so rule and govern our hearts and minds by Thy Holy Spirit, that being ever-mindful of the end of all things, and the day of Thy just judgment, we may be stirred up to holiness of living here, and dwell with Thee forever hereafter; through Jesus Christ, Thy Son, our Lord, who liveth and reigneth with Thee and the Holy Ghost, ever one God, world without end. *Amen.*

Epistle, 2 Peter iii: 3-14, or 2 Thess. i: 3-10. *Gospel,* Matt. xxv: 31-46.

TWENTY-SEVENTH SUNDAY AFTER TRINITY.

The Introit *and* Collect *for the Twenty-third Sunday after Trinity shall be used on the last Sunday after Trinity in each year.*

Epistle, 1 Thess. v: 1-11. *Gospel,* Matt. xxv: 1-13.

THE FESTIVAL OF HARVEST.

Introit.

O Lord, Thou crownest the year with Thy goodness: and Thy paths drop fatness.

Thou visitest the earth and waterest it: Thou blessest the springing thereof.

Ps. Praise waiteth for Thee, O God, in Zion: and unto Thee shall the vow be performed.

Glory be to the Father, &c.

Collect.

Almighty God, most merciful Father, Who openest Thy hand, and satisfiest the desire of every living thing; we give Thee most humble and hearty thanks that Thou hast crowned the fields with Thy blessing, and hast permitted us once more to gather in the fruits of the earth; and we beseech Thee to bless and protect the living seed of Thy Word sown in our hearts, that in the plenteous fruits of righteousness we may always present to Thee an acceptable thank-offering; through Jesus Christ, Thy Son, our Lord, who liveth and reigneth with Thee and the Holy Ghost, ever one God, world without end. *Amen.*

THE FESTIVAL OF THE REFORMATION.

Introit.

The Lord of Hosts is with us: the God of Jacob is our refuge.

Therefore will not we fear, though the earth be removed: and though the mountains be carried into the midst of the sea.

Ps. God is our refuge and strength: a very present help in trouble.

Glory be to the Father, &c.

Collect.

O Lord God, Heavenly Father; Pour out, we beseech Thee, Thy Holy Spirit upon Thy faithful people, keep them steadfast in Thy grace and truth, protect and comfort them in all temptation, defend them against all enemies of Thy Word, and bestow upon Christ's Church militant Thy saving peace; through the same Thy Son, our Lord, who liveth and reigneth with Thee and the Holy Ghost, ever one God, world without end. *Amen.*

A DAY OF HUMILIATION AND PRAYER.

Introit.

Hear, O heavens, and give ear, for the Lord hath spoken: I have nourished and brought up children, and they have rebelled against me.

They have forsaken the Lord, they have provoked the Holy One of Israel unto anger: they are gone away backward.

Ps. If Thou, Lord, should mark iniquities: O Lord, who shall stand?

[*On this day the* Gloria Patri *is omitted.*]

Collect.

Almighty and most merciful God, our heavenly Father, of whose compassion there is no end, Who art long-suffering, gracious, and plenteous in goodness and truth; forgiving iniquity, transgression and sin; we have sinned and done perversely, we have forsaken and grievously offended Thee; against Thee, Thee only, have we sinned and done evil in Thy sight; But we beseech Thee, O Lord, remember not against us former iniquities; let Thy tender mercies speedily prevent us, for we are brought very low; help us, O God of our salvation, and purge away our sins, for the glory of Thy holy Name, and for the sake of Thy dear Son, our Saviour, Jesus Christ, who liveth and reigneth with Thee and the Holy Ghost, ever one God, world without end. *Amen.*

A DAY OF GENERAL OR SPECIAL THANKSGIVING.

Introit.

Let every thing that hath breath praise the Lord: praise ye the Lord.

Praise Him for His mighty acts: praise Him according to His excellent greatness.

Ps. Praise ye the Lord; praise God in His sanctuary; praise Him in the firmament of His power.

Glory be to the Father, &c.

Collect.

Almighty God, our Heavenly Father, Whose mercies are new unto us every morning, and who, though we have in no wise deserved Thy goodness, dost abundantly provide for all our wants of body and soul; Give us, we pray Thee, Thy Holy Spirit, that we may heartily acknowledge Thy merciful goodness toward us, give thanks for all Thy benefits, and serve Thee in willing obedience: through Jesus Christ, Thy Son, our Lord, who liveth and reigneth with Thee and the Holy Ghost, ever one God, world without end. *Amen.*

Introits and Collects

THE PRESENTATION OF CHRIST.

The Introit *is the same as for the Eighth Sunday after Trinity.*

Collect.

Almighty and Everliving God, we humbly beseech Thy Majesty, that as Thine Only-Begotten Son was this day presented in the temple in substance of our flesh, so we may be presented unto Thee with pure and clean hearts, by the same Thy Son, Jesus Christ, our Lord, who liveth and reigneth with Thee and the Holy Ghost, ever one God, world without end. *Amen.*

Epistle, Malachi iii: 1-4. *Gospel,* Luke ii: 22-32.

THE ANNUNCIATION.

Introit.

All the rich among the people shall entreat Thy favor.
She shall be brought unto the King in raiment of needle-work.
Her companions shall be brought unto Thee: with gladness and rejoicing.

Ps. My heart is inditing a good matter: I speak of the things which I have made touching the King.

Glory be to the Father, &c.

Collect.

We beseech Thee, O Lord, Pour Thy grace into our hearts; that as we have known the Incarnation of Thy Son Jesus Christ by the message of an angel, so by His Cross and Passion we may be brought unto the glory of His Resurrection; through the same Jesus Christ, our Lord, who liveth and reigneth with Thee and the Holy Ghost, ever one God, world without end.

Epistle, Isaiah vii: 10-16. *Gospel,* Luke i: 26-38.

THE VISITATION.

The Introit *is the same as for the Annunciation.*

Collect.

Almighty God, Who hast dealt wonderfully with Thy handmaiden the Virgin Mary, and hast chosen her to be the mother of Thy Son, and hast graciously made known that Thou regardest the poor and lowly and the despised; Grant us grace in all humility and meekness to receive Thy Word with hearty faith, and so be made one with Thy dear Son; who liveth and reigneth with Thee and the Holy Ghost, ever one God, world without end. *Amen.*

Epistle, Isaiah xi: 1-5. *Gospel,* Luke i: 39-56.

EVANGELISTS', APOSTLES', AND MARTYRS' DAYS.

Introit.

I know whom I have believed: and am persuaded that He is able to keep that which I have committed unto Him against that day.

There is laid up for me a crown of righteousness: which the Lord, the righteous Judge, shall give me.

Ps. O Lord, Thou hast searched me and know me: Thou knowest my down-sitting and mine uprising.

Glory be to the Father, &c.

Collect.

O Almighty God, Who hast built Thy Church upon the foundation of the Apostles and Prophets, Jesus Christ Himself being the Head Corner-Stone; Grant us to be joined together in unity of spirit by their doctrine, that we may be made a holy temple acceptable unto Thee; through Jesus Christ, Thy Son, our Lord, who liveth and reigneth with Thee and the Holy Ghost, ever one God, world without end. *Amen.*

O Almighty God, Who hast instructed Thy holy Church with the heavenly doctrine of Thy Evangelists and Apostles; Give us grace, that being not like children carried away with every blast of vain doctrine, we may be established in the truth of Thy holy Gospel; through Jesus Christ, Thy Son, our Lord, who liveth and reigneth with Thee and the Holy Ghost, ever one God, world without end. *Amen.*

O Almighty God, Who hast knit together Thine elect in one communion and fellowship in the mystical body of Thy Son Christ our Lord; Grant us grace so to follow Thy blessed Saints in all virtuous and godly living, that we may come to those unspeakable joys which Thou hast prepared for those who unfeignedly love Thee; through Jesus Christ our Lord, who liveth and reigneth with Thee and the Holy Ghost, ever one God, world without end. *Amen.*

[*The* Epistles *and* Gospels *for Apostles' Days and other Minor Festivals are to be found in the Tables.*]

ST. MICHAEL'S DAY.

Introit.

Bless the Lord, ye His Angels, that excel in strength: that do his commandments, hearkening unto the voice of His word.

Bless ye the Lord, all ye His hosts: ye ministers of His that do His pleasure.

Ps. Bless the Lord, O my soul: and all that is within me bless His holy Name.

Glory be to the Father, &c.

Collect.

O Everlasting God, Who hast ordained and constituted the services of Angels and men in a wonderful order; Mercifully grant, that as Thy holy Angels always do Thee service in heaven, so by Thy appointment they may succor and defend us on earth; through Jesus Christ our Lord. *Amen.*

Epistle, Revelation xii: 7-12. *Gospel,* Matt. xviii:1-11.

Invitatories, Antiphons, Responsories and Versicles for the Church Year

The Invitatory *varies with the Season, and is always used with* Psalm xcv. *at Matins. It is divided into two parts separately by a colon. The first part, or the whole, of the* Invitatory *may be sung or said by the Minister, or sung by a single voice, or by the choir, before the Psalm; and after the Psalm and* Gloria Patri *the whole* Invitatory *shall be sung.*

An Antiphon *is used at Matins and Vespers to the Psalms, the* Magnificat, *the* Nunc Dimittis, *and the* Benedictus. *It is used in the same manner as the* Invitatory.

The Responsory *varies with the Season, and may be sung after the last* Lesson *at Vespers and Matins. At the end of the* Responsory *is sung* Glory be to the Father, and to the Son, and to the Holy Ghost (*but not "As it was in the beginning, &c."*), *followed by the repetition of the last sentence of the* Responsory.

A Versicle *may be used at Vespers after the* Hymn, *and at Vespers and Matins before the closing* Collect. *A* Versicle *is used before the* Litany Collects. *The first part of the* Versicle *is said by the Minister, and the second part sung or said* by the people.

ADVENT.

Invitatory.

Behold, the King cometh: O come, let us worship Him.

Antiphons.

1. Behold, the Name of the Lord cometh from far: and let the whole earth be filled with His glory.
2. Come, O Lord, and make no tarrying: loosen the bonds of Thy people Israel.
3. Rejoice greatly, O Jerusalem: behold, Thy King cometh.
4. Behold, the Lord shall come, and all His saints with Him: and in that day the light shall be great. Hallelujah.

Responsory.

Behold, the days come, saith the Lord, that I will raise unto David a righteous Branch, and a King shall reign and prosper, and shall execute judgment and justice in the earth. And this is His Name whereby He shall be called, The Lord our Righteousness.

Verse. In His days shall Judah be saved, and Israel shall dwell safely.
And this is His Name whereby He shall be called, the Lord our Righteousness.
Glory be to the Father, and to the Son, and to the Holy Ghost.
And this is His Name whereby he shall be called, the Lord our Righteousness.

Versicles.

1. Out of Zion, the perfection of beauty, God hath shined:
Answer. Our God shall come. Hallelujah.
2. Prepare ye the way of the Lord. Hallelujah.
Make his paths straight. Hallelujah.
3. Drop down, ye heavens, from above, and let the skies pour down righteousness:
Let the earth open and bring forth salvation.

Responsories, Versicles

CHRISTMAS.

Invitatory.

Unto us the Christ is born: O come, let us worship Him.

Antiphons.

1. The Lord hath said unto me: Thou art my Son, this day have I begotten Thee.
2. The Lord hath sent redemption unto His people: He hath commanded His covenant forever.
3. Of the fruit of thy body: will I set upon thy throne.
4. Christ the Lord, our Saviour, Everlasting God and Mary's Son: we praise Thee evermore.

Responsory.

The Word was made flesh and dwelt among us. And we beheld His glory. the glory as of the Only-Begotten of the Father, full of grace and truth.

Verse. In the beginning was the Word, and the Word was with God, and the Word was God.

Full of grace and truth.

Glory be to the Father, and to the Son, and to the Holy Ghost.

Full of grace and truth.

Versicles.

1. At even ye shall know that the Lord will come: And in the morning, then shall ye see the glory of the Lord.
2. As the bridegroom from His chamber:
Cometh forth the Lord to run his race.
3. The Word was made flesh. Hallelujah.
And dwelt among us. Hallelujah.
4. Blessed is He that cometh in the Name of the Lord: God is the Lord, which hath showed us light.
5. Unto us a child is born. Hallelujah.
Unto us a Son is given. Hallelujah.
6. Unto you is born this day a Saviour: Hallelujah.
Which is Christ the Lord. Hallelujah.

THE EPIPHANY.

Invitatory.

Christ hath appeared unto us: O come, let us worship Him.

Antiphons.

1. Give unto the Lord glory and strength: worship the Lord in the beauty of holiness.
2. The Lord hath made known His Word. Hallelujah: the Word of His salvation. Hallelujah. Hallelujah.
3. A light to lighten the Gentiles: and the glory of Thy people Israel.
4. We have seen His star in the east: and are come to worship Him.

Responsory.

Arise, shine, for thy light is come, and the glory of the Lord is risen upon thee.

Verse. And the Gentiles shall come to Thy light, and kings to the brightness of thy rising.

And the glory of the Lord is risen upon thee.

Glory be to the Father, and to the Son, and to the Holy Ghost.

And the glory of the Lord is risen upon thee.

Versicles.

1. The kings of Tarshish and of the isles shall bring presents. Hallelujah.
The kings of Sheba and Seba shall offer gifts. Hallelujah.
2. All they from Sheba shall come. Hallelujah.
They shall bring gold and incense. Hallelujah.
3. O praise the Lord, all ye nations. Hallelujah.
Praise Him, all ye people. Hallelujah.

THE PASSION SEASON.

Antiphons.

1. Man shall not live by bread alone: but by every word that proceedeth out of the mouth of God.
2. Behold, now is the accepted time: behold, now is the day of salvation.
3. The kings of the earth set themselves, and the rulers take counsel together: against the Lord and against His anointed.
4. He was oppressed, and He was afflicted, yet he opened not His mouth: and the Lord hath laid on Him the iniquity of us all.

Responsory.

He was brought as a lamb to the slaughter, He was oppressed and He was afflicted, yet He opened not His mouth: He was delivered up to death, that He might quicken His people.
Verse. In Salem also is His tabernacle, and his dwelling place in Zion.
He was delivered up to death, that He might quicken His people.

Versicles.

1. Save me from the lion's mouth, O Lord.
And deliver me from the horns of the unicorns.
2. Christ became obedient unto death:
Even the death of the cross.
3. Christ was wounded for our transgressions:
He was bruised for our iniquities.

EASTER.

Invitatory.

The Lord is risen indeed: Hallelujah.

Antiphons.

1. Hallelujah!: Hallelujah! Hallelujah!
2. I laid me down and slept; I awaked: for the Lord sustained me. Hallelujah! Hallelujah!
3. Hallelujah! The Lord is risen. Hallelujah: As He said unto you. Hallelujah! Hallelujah!
4. Hallelujah! Abide with us, for it is toward evening: and the day is far spent. Hallelujah! Hallelujah!

Responsory.

Christ being raised from the dead dieth no more; death hath no more dominion over Him.
In that He liveth, He liveth unto God. Hallelujah! Hallelujah!
Verse. Christ was delivered for our offences and raised again for our justification.
In that He liveth, He liveth unto God. Hallelujah!
Glory be to the Father, and to the Son, and to the Holy Ghost.
In that He liveth, He liveth unto God. Hallelujah!

Versicles.

1. The Lord is risen from the grave. Hallelujah.
Who hung for us upon the tree. Hallelujah.
2. Then were the disciples glad. Hallelujah.
When they saw the Lord. Hallelujah.
3. This is the day which the Lord hath made. Hallelujah.
We will rejoice and be glad in it. Hallelujah.
4. The Lord is risen indeed. Hallelujah.
And hath appeared unto Simon. Hallelujah.

ASCENSION DAY.

Invitatory.

Hallelujah! The King ascendeth into Heaven: O come, let us worship Him. Hallelujah.

Antiphons.

1. If I go not away, the Comforter will not come unto you: but if I depart, I will send Him unto you. Hallelujah.

2. Hallelujah! Christ hath ascended up on high. Hallelujah!: And hath led captivity captive. Hallelujah! Hallelujah!

3. I ascend unto My Father and your Father: and to My God and your God. Hallelujah.

Responsory.

Go ye into all the world, and preach the Gospel. Hallelujah!
He that believeth and is baptized shall be saved. Hallelujah! Hallelujah!
Verse. In the Name of the Father, and of the Son, and of the Holy Ghost.
He that believeth and is baptized, shall be saved.
Glory be to the Father, and to the Son, and to the Holy Ghost.
He that believeth and is baptized, shall be saved.

Versicles.

1. I will not leave you comfortless: Hallelujah!
I go away and come again unto you. Hallelujah.
2. God is gone up with a shout. Hallelujah!
The Lord with the sound of a trumpet, Hallelujah.

WHITSUNTIDE.

Invitatory.

Hallelujah! The Spirit of the Lord filleth the world: O come, let us worship Him. Hallelujah!

Antiphons.

1. Come, Holy Ghost, and fill the hearts of Thy faithful people, and kindle in them the fire of Thy love: Thou, who through divers tongues gatherest together the nations in the unity of the faith. Hallelujah! Hallelujah!

2. Thou sendest forth Thy Spirit, they are created: and Thou renewest the face of the earth. Hallelujah! Hallelujah!

3. I will not leave you comfortless. Hallelujah!: I will come to you, and your heart shall rejoice. Hallelujah!

Responsory.

And there appeared unto the Apostles cloven tongues, like as of fire. Hallelujah!
And the Holy Ghost sat upon each of them. Hallelujah! Hallelujah!
Verse. And they began to speak with other tongues the wonderful works of God.
And the Holy Ghost sat upon each of them.
Glory be to the Father, and to the Son, and to the Holy Ghost.
And the Holy Ghost sat upon each of them.

Versicles.

1. The Comforter, which is the Holy Ghost. Hallelujah!
He shall teach you all things. Hallelujah!
2. And they were all filled with the Holy Ghost. Hallelujah!
And they began to speak. Hallelujah!
3. Create in me a clean heart, O God. Hallelujah!
And renew a right spirit within me. Hallelujah!

THE FESTIVAL OF TRINITY.

Invitatory.

The true God, One in Three, and Three in One: O come, let us worship Him.

Antiphons.

1. Unto Thee do we call, Thee do we praise, Thee do we worship: O blessed Trinity.
2. Glory be to Thee, Co-equal Trinity: one God before all worlds began, and now and forevermore.
3. Holy, Holy, Holy, Lord God Almighty: Which was, and is, and is to come.

Responsory.

We bless the Father, and the Son, and the Holy Ghost. Praise Him and magnify Him forever.

Verse. Blessed art Thou, O Lord, in the firmament of heaven, and above all to be praised and glorified forever.

Praise Him and magnify Him forever.
Glory be to the Father, and to the Son, and to the Holy Ghost.
Praise Him and magnify Him forever.

Versicle.

We bless the Father, and the Son, and the Holy Ghost; Praise Him and magnify Him forever.

THE FESTIVAL OF THE REFORMATION.

Antiphon.

I will speak of Thy testimonies also before kings: and will not be ashamed.

Versicles.

1. Thy Word is a lamp unto my feet. Hallelujah!
And a light unto my path. Hallelujah!
2. The Lord our God be with us. Hallelujah!
As he was with our fathers. Hallelujah!
3. Do good in Thy good pleasure unto Zion. Hallelujah.
Build Thou the walls of Jerusalem. Hallelujah.
4. Stand fast therefore in the liberty. Hallelujah!
Wherewith Christ hath made you free. Hallelujah!

A DAY OF HUMILIATION AND PRAYER.

Antiphons.

Be merciful unto me, O Lord, for I cry unto Thee daily: Bow down Thine ear, O Lord, hear me, for I am poor and needy.

Versicles.

1. Have mercy upon me, O God, according to Thy loving kindness:
According unto the multitude of Thy tender mercies blot out my transgressions.
2. Enter not into judgment with Thy servant, O Lord:
For in Thy sight shall no man living be justified.
3. Lord, deal not with us after our sins:
Nor reward us according to our iniquities.
4. Create in us a clean heart, O God.
And take not Thy Holy Spirit from us.
5. We have sinned with our fathers:
We have committed iniquity, we have done wickedly.

THE FESTIVAL OF CHURCH DEDICATION.

Antiphon.

The Lord is in His holy temple: the Lord's throne is in heaven.

Versicle.

Thy testimonies are very sure. Hallelujah!
Holiness becometh Thine house, O Lord, forever. Hallelujah!

THE COMMEMORATION OF THE DEAD.

Antiphons.

1. God shall wipe away all tears from their eyes: and there shall be no more death, neither sorrow, nor crying, neither shall there be any more pain; for the former things are passed away.

2. O how glorious is that kingdom: wherein all the saints do rejoice with Christ; they are clothed with white robes and follow the Lamb whithersoever He goeth.

Versicles.

1. We have here no continuing city. Hallelujah!
But we seek one to come. Hallelujah!
2. Blessed are the dead which die in the Lord. Hallelujah!
They rest from their labors and their works do follow them. Hallelujah!

FOR OTHER TIMES.

Antiphons.

1. Out of the depths: have I cried unto Thee, O Lord.
2. Out of Zion, the perfection of beauty: God hath shined.
3. Commit Thy way unto the Lord: trust also in Him.
4. Preserve my life: from the fear of the enemy.
5. It is good to sing praises: unto our God.
6. Forsake not the works: of Thine own hands.
7. The Lord: is the strength of my life.
8. The Lord said unto my Lord: sit Thou at my right hand.
9. Blessed be the Lord God: the God of Israel.
10. Blessed be the Lord out of Zion: Which dwelleth at Jerusalem.
11. Blessed: be His glorious Name forever.
12. I was glad when they said unto me: Let us go into the house of the Lord.
13. In the day of my trouble I will call upon Thee: for Thou wilt answer me.
14. I will praise Thy Name: forever and ever.
15. Thou wilt show me: the path of life.
16. We praise the Lord: now, henceforth and forever.
17. Blessed: is the man that feareth the Lord.

Responsory.

Forever, O Lord, Thy Word is settled in Heaven.
Thy Word is a lamp unto my feet, and a light unto my path.
Lord, I have loved the habitation of Thy house, and the place where Thine honor dwelleth.
Verse. **Blessed are they that hear the Word of God and keep it.**
Lord, I have loved the habitation of Thy house, and the place where Thine honor dwelleth.
Glory be to the Father, and to the Son, and to the Holy Ghost.
Lord, I have loved the habitation of Thy house, and the place where Thine honor dwelleth.

Versicles.

1. The eyes of all wait upon Thee:
And Thou givest them their meat in due season.

2. The Lord is merciful and gracious. Hallelujah!
Slow to anger, and plenteous in mercy. Hallelujah.

3. Pray ye therefore the Lord of the harvest:
That He would send forth laborers into His harvest.

4. Ask, and ye shall receive:
That your joy may be full.

5. O give thanks unto the Lord, for He is good. Hallelujah!
For his mercy endureth forever.

6. It is a good thing to give thanks unto the Lord:
And to sing praises unto Thy Name, O Most High.

7. Lord, Thou hast heard the desire of the humble:
Thou wilt preserve their heart, Thou wilt cause Thine ear to hear.

8. The Lord will give strength unto His people. Hallelujah!
The Lord will bless His people with peace. Hallelujah!

9. They that be wise, shall shine as the brightness of the firmament. Hallelujah!
And they that turn many to righteousness, as the stars forever and ever. Hallelujah!

10. By Me kings reign, and princes decree justice:
By Me princes rule, and nobles, even all the judges of the earth.

11. He shall give His angels charge over thee:
To keep Thee in all Thy ways.

12. The Lord God is a sun and shield; the Lord will give grace and glory. Hallelujah!
No good thing will He withhold from them that walk uprightly. Hallelujah!

13. Sanctify us through Thy truth. Hallelujah!
Thy Word is truth. Hallelujah!

14. Lord, teach me to do Thy will. Hallelujah!
Let Thy good Spirit lead me in the right way. Hallelujah!

15. Show me Thy ways, O Lord, Hallelujah!
Teach me Thy paths. Hallelujah!

16. Save Thy people, and bless Thine inheritance;
Feed them also, and lift them up forever.

17. Help us, O God of our salvation, for the glory of Thy Name:
Deliver us, and purge away our sins, for Thy Name's sake.

18. I have trusted in Thy mercy:
My heart shall rejoice in Thy salvation.

19. Suffer the little children to come unto Me, and forbid them not:
For of such is the kingdom of Heaven.

20. Bless the Lord, O my soul: and all that is within me, bless His holy Name:
Bless the Lord, O my soul, and forget not all His benefits. Hallelujah!

21. Call upon Me in the day of trouble:
I will deliver Thee, and Thou shalt glorify Me.

22. Make me to understand the way of Thy precepts:
Strengthen Thou me according to Thy Word.

Collects and Prayers

1.

Grant us, we beseech Thee, Almighty God, a steadfast faith in Jesus Christ, a cheerful hope in Thy mercy, and a sincere love to Thee and to all our fellow men; through Jesus Christ our Lord. *Amen.*

2.

O Lord God, heavenly Father, we give Thee thanks, that of Thy great goodness and mercy, Thou didst suffer Thine Only-Begotten Son to become incarnate, and to redeem us from sin and everlasting death; and we beseech Thee, enlighten our hearts, by Thy Holy Spirit, that we may evermore yield Thee unfeigned thanks for this Thy grace, and may comfort ourselves with the same in all time of tribulation and temptation; through the same Thy dear Son, Jesus Christ, our Lord. *Amen.*

3.

Almighty God, Who hast given us commandment to pray for the gift of the Holy Ghost; Most heartily we beseech Thee, through Jesus Christ our Advocate, to grant us Thy Holy Spirit, that He may quicken our hearts by Thy saving Word, and lead us into all truth, that He may guide, instruct, enlighten, govern, comfort and sanctify us into everlasting life; through the same, Jesus Christ our Lord. *Amen.*

4.

Send, we beseech Thee, Almighty God, Thy Holy Spirit into our hearts, that He may rule and direct us according to Thy will, comfort us in all our temptations and afflictions, defend us from all error, and lead us into all truth; that we, being steadfast in the faith, may increase in love and in all good works, and in the end obtain everlasting life; through Jesus Christ, Thy Son, our Lord. *Amen.*

5.

Almighty God, our heavenly Father, Who, of Thy tender love towards us sinners, hast given us Thy Son, that believing on Him we might have everlasting life; Grant us, we beseech Thee, Thy Holy Spirit, that we may continue steadfast in this faith to the end, and may come to everlasting life; through Jesus Christ our Lord. *Amen.*

6.

Almighty and Everlasting God, Who, by Thy Son, hast promised us forgiveness of sins and everlasting life; We beseech Thee so to rule and govern our hearts by Thy Holy Spirit, that in our daily need, and especially in all time of temptation, we may seek help from Him, and by a true and lively faith in Thy Word obtain the same; through Jesus Christ our Lord. *Amen.*

7.

O Lord God, heavenly Father, We beseech Thee, let Thy Holy Spirit dwell in us, that He may enlighten and lead us into all truth, and evermore defend us from all adversities; through Jesus Christ our Lord. *Amen.*

8.

O Lord God, heavenly Father, Who hast given Thine only Son to die for our sins, and to rise again for our justification; Quicken us; we beseech Thee, by Thy Holy Spirit, unto newness of life, that through the power of His resurrection, we may dwell with Christ forever; through the same, our Lord Jesus Christ. *Amen.*

9.

Almighty and Everliving God, Who makest us both to will and to do those things which are good, and acceptable unto Thy Divine Majesty; Let Thy Fatherly hand, we beseech Thee, ever be over us; let Thy Holy Spirit ever be with us; and so lead us in the knowledge and obedience of Thy Word, that in the end we may obtain everlasting life; through our Lord Jesus Christ. *Amen.*

FOR THE CHURCH.

10.

Grant, we beseech Thee, Almighty God, unto Thy Church, Thy Holy Spirit, and the wisdom which cometh down from above, that Thy word, as becometh it, may not be bound, but have free course and be preached to the joy and edifying of Christ's holy people, that in steadfast faith we may serve Thee, and in the confession of Thy Name abide unto the end; through Jesus Christ our Lord. *Amen.*

11.

Merciful Lord, we beseech Thee to cast the bright beams of Thy light upon Thy Church, that it being instructed by the doctrine of the blessed Apostles, may so walk in the light of Thy truth, that it may at length attain to the light of everlasting life; through Jesus Christ our Lord. *Amen.*

12.

O God, our Protector; Behold, and look upon the face of Thine Anointed, who hath given Himself for the redemption of all, and grant that from the rising of the sun to the going down thereof, Thy Name may be great among the Gentiles, and that in every place sacrifice and a pure offering may be made unto Thy Name; through Jesus Christ our Lord. *Amen.*

13.

O Lord, favorably receive the prayers of Thy Church, that being delivered from all adversity and error, it may serve Thee in safety and freedom; and grant us Thy peace in our time; through Jesus Christ our Lord. *Amen.*

14.

For the Children of the Church.

Almighty and Everlasting God, Who dost will that not one of these little ones should perish, and hast sent Thine only Son to seek and to save that which was lost, and through Him hast said, Suffer the little children to come unto Me, and forbid them not; for of such is the kingdom of God; Most heartily we beseech Thee so to bless and govern the children of Thy Church, by Thy Holy Spirit, that they may grow in grace and in the knowledge of Thy Word; protect and defend them against all danger and harm, giving Thy holy Angels charge over them; through Jesus Christ our Lord. *Amen.*

15.

For the Ministers of the Word.

Almighty and Everlasting God, Who alone doest great wonders; Send down upon Thy Ministers, and upon the congregations committed to their charge, the healthful Spirit of Thy grace; and, that they may truly please Thee, pour upon them the continual dew of Thy blessing; through Jesus Christ our Lord. *Amen.*

16.

Almighty and gracious God, the Father of our Lord Jesus Christ, Who hast commanded us to pray that Thou wouldest send forth laborers into Thy harvest; Of Thine infinite mercy give us true teachers and ministers of Thy Word, and put Thy saving Gospel in their hearts and on their lips, that they may truly fulfill Thy command, and preach nothing contrary to Thy holy Word; that we, being warned, instructed, nurtured, comforted and strengthened by Thy heavenly Word, may do those things which are well-pleasing to Thee, and profitable to us; through Jesus Christ our Lord. *Amen.*

17.

O Almighty God, Who by Thy Son Jesus Christ, didst give to Thy holy Apostles many excellent gifts, and commandedst them earnestly to feed Thy flock; Make, we beseech Thee, all Pastors diligently to preach Thy holy Word, and the people obediently to follow the same, that they may receive the crown of everlasting glory; through Jesus Christ our Lord. *Amen.*

18.

For the Church in its Conflicts.

Almighty and Everlasting God, Who wilt have all men to be saved, and to come to the knowledge of the truth; We beseech Thy glorious Majesty, through Jesus Christ our Lord and Saviour, impart the grace and help of Thy Holy Spirit to all ministers of Thy Word, that they may purely teach it to the saving of men; bring to nought by Thine Almighty power and unsearchable wisdom, all the counsels of those who hate Thy Word, and who, by corrupt teaching or with violent hands, would destroy it, and enlighten them with the knowledge of Thy glory; that we, leading a quiet and peaceable life, may, by a pure faith, learn the riches of Thy heavenly grace, and in holiness and righteousness serve Thee, the only true God; through Jesus Christ our Lord. ***Amen.***

19.

For those who have Erred.

Almighty God, our heavenly Father, Whose property it is always to have mercy; We most earnestly beseech Thee to visit with Thy Fatherly correction all such as have erred and gone astray from the truth of Thy holy Word, and to bring them to a due sense of their error, that they may again with hearty faith receive and hold fast Thine unchangeable truth; through Jesus Christ our Lord. ***Amen.***

20.

Almighty, Merciful, and Gracious God and Father, with our whole heart we beseech Thee for all who have forsaken the Christian faith, all who have wandered from any portion thereof, or are in doubt or temptation through the corruptors of Thy Word, that Thou wouldest visit them as a Father, reveal unto them their error, and bring them back from their wanderings, that they, in singleness of heart, taking pleasure alone in the pure truth of Thy Word, may be made wise thereby unto everlasting life; through faith in Jesus Christ, Thy Son, our Lord. ***Amen.***

21.

For Unity.

O God, Who restorest to the right way them that err, who gatherest them that are scattered, and preservest them that are gathered; Of Thy tender mercy, we beseech Thee, pour upon Thy Christian people the grace of Unity, that all schisms being healed, Thy flock, united to the true Shepherd of Thy Church, may worthily serve Thee; through Jesus Christ our Lord. ***Amen.***

22.

For the Removal of Schism.

Bring to nought, O Christ, the schisms of heresy, which seek to subvert Thy Truth; That as Thou art acknowledged in heaven and in earth as one and the same Lord, so Thy people, gathered from all nations, may serve Thee in unity of faith. ***Amen.***

23.

For the Jews.

Almighty and Everlasting God, Who lovest to show mercy; Hear the prayers which we offer unto Thee for Thine ancient people, that, acknowledging Jesus Christ, Who is the Light of truth, they may be delivered from their darkness; through the same, Thy Son, our Lord. ***Amen.***

24.

For the Heathen.

Almighty and Everlasting God, Who desirest not the death of a sinner, but wouldest have all men to repent and live; Hear our prayers for the Heathen; take away iniquity from their hearts, and turn them from their idols unto the living and true God, and to Thine only Son; and gather them into Thy holy Church, to the glory of Thy Name; through Jesus Christ our Lord. ***Amen.***

FOR THE CIVIL AUTHORITIES.

25.

O Merciful Father in heaven, Who holdest in Thy hand all the might of man, and who hast ordained the powers that be for the punishment of evil-doers, and for the praise of them that do well, and of whom is all rule and authority in the kingdoms of the world; We humbly beseech Thee, graciously regard Thy servants, the President of the United States, the Governor of this Commonwealth, our Judges and Magistrates, and all the rulers of the earth. May all that receive the sword, as Thy ministers, bear it according to Thy commandment. Enlighten and defend them by Thy Name, O God. Grant them wisdom and understanding, that under their peaceable governance, Thy people may be guarded and directed in righteousness, quietness, and unity. Protect and prolong their lives, O God of our salvation, that we, with them, may show forth the praise of Thy Name; through Jesus Christ our Lord. *Amen.*

26.

For our Enemies.

Forgive, we beseech Thee, O Lord, our enemies, and them that despitefully use us, and so change their hearts that they may walk with us in meekness and peace; through Jesus Christ our Lord. *Amen.*

27.

O Almighty, Everlasting God, Who through Thine Only Son, our blessed Lord, hast commanded us to love our enemies, to do good to them that hate us, and to pray for them that persecute us; We earnestly beseech Thee that by Thy gracious visitation they may be led to true repentance, and may have the same love, and be of one accord, and of one mind and heart with us, and with Thy whole Church; through the same, Thy dear Son, our Lord Jesus Christ. *Amen.*

28.

In time of National Calamity.

O Lord God, heavenly Father, we humbly confess unto Thee that by our evil doing and continual disobedience, we have deserved these Thy chastisements; But we earnestly beseech Thee, for Thy Name's sake, to spare us; restrain the harmful power of the enemy, and succor Thy suffering people, that Thy Word may be declared faithfully and without hinderance, and that we, amending our sinful lives, may walk obediently to Thy holy commandments; through Jesus Christ our Lord. *Amen.*

29.

Look mercifully, O Lord, we beseech Thee, on the affliction of Thy people; and let not our sin destroy us, but let Thine Almighty mercy save us; through Jesus Christ, Thy Son, our Lord. *Amen.*

30.

Most loving and gracious Lord God, Who for our many grievous sins art pleased sorely to chasten us, we flee to Thy tender and fatherly compassion alone, beseeching Thee that as a father pitieth his children, Thou wouldest pity us miserable sinners. Turn away Thy righteous wrath, and give us not over to deserved death, but deliver us, that we may now and evermore praise Thee, O gracious God and Father, who desirest not the death of a sinner, but rather that he may turn from his wickedness and live; through Jesus Christ, Thy Son, our Lord. *Amen.*

31.

For Prisoners.

Almighty God, Who didst bring the Apostle Peter forth out of prison; Have mercy upon all who are suffering imprisonment, and set them free from their bonds, that we may rejoice in their deliverance, and continually give praise to Thee; through Jesus Christ our Lord. *Amen.*

32.

For Peace and Quietness.

O Lord, we beseech Thee, mercifully to hear the prayers of Thy Church, that we, being delivered from all adversities, and serving Thee with a quiet mind, may enjoy Thy peace all the days of our life; through Jesus Christ our Lord. *Amen.*

IN TIME OF AFFLICTION AND DISTRESS.

33.

Almighty and Everlasting God, the Consolation of the sorrowful, and the Strength of the weak; May the prayers of them that in any tribulation or distress cry unto Thee, graciously come before Thee, so that in all their necessities they may mark and receive Thy manifold help and comfort; through Jesus Christ our Lord. *Amen.*

34.

Almighty and most merciful God, Who hast appointed us to endure sufferings and death with our Lord Jesus Christ, before we enter with Him into eternal Glory; Grant us grace at all times to subject ourselves to Thy Holy will, and to continue steadfast in the true faith unto the end of our lives, and at all times to find peace and joy in the blessed hope of the resurrection of the dead, and of the glory of the world to come; through Jesus Christ our Lord. *Amen.*

35.

Almighty God, Cast not away Thy people who cry unto Thee in their tribulation; but for the glory of Thy Name, be pleased to succor the afflicted; through Jesus Christ our Lord. *Amen.*

36.

For the Sick.

Almighty, Everlasting God, the eternal Salvation of them that believe; Hear our prayers in behalf of Thy servants who are sick, for whom we implore the aid of Thy mercy, that being restored to health, they may render thanks to Thee in Thy Church; through Jesus Christ our Lord. *Amen.*

37.

O Lord, look down from heaven, behold, visit and relieve Thy servants, for whom we offer our supplications; look upon *them* with the eyes of Thy mercy; give *them* comfort and sure confidence in Thee defend *them* from the danger of the enemy, and keep *them* in perpetual peace and safety; through Jesus Christ our Lord. *Amen.*

38.

For Mothers.

O Almighty, Everlasting God and Father, Creator of all things, Who by Thy grace, through Thy Son, our Lord, who hath redeemed us from the flesh and sin, makest the anguish of our human birth a holy and salutary cross; We pray Thee, O gracious Father, Lord and God, that Thou wouldest preserve and guard the work of Thine own hand. Forsake not them who cry to Thee in sore travail, but deliver them out of all their pains, to their joy, and to the glory of Thy goodness; through Jesus Christ our Lord. *Amen.*

39.

In time of Great Sickness.

Almighty and most merciful God, our heavenly Father, we Thine erring children humbly confess unto Thee, that we have justly deserved the chastening, which for our sins Thou hast sent upon us; But we entreat Thee, of Thy boundless goodness to grant us true repentance, graciously to forgive our sins, to remove from us or to lighten our merited punishment, and so to strengthen us by Thy grace that as obedient children we may be subject to Thy will, and bear our afflictions in patience; through Jesus Christ our Lord. *Amen.*

40.

In time of Drought.

O God, most merciful Father, we beseech Thee to open the windows of heaven, and to send a fruitful rain upon us, to revive the earth, and to refresh the fruits thereof, for all things droop and wither; graciously hear our prayer in this our necessity, that we may praise and glorify Thy Name forever and ever; through Jesus Christ our Lord. *Amen.*

41.

In time of Unseasonable Weather.

O Lord God, heavenly Father, Who art gracious and merciful, and hast promised that Thou wilt hear us when we call upon Thee in our troubles: We beseech Thee, look not upon our sins and evil doings, but upon our necessities, and according to Thy mercy send us such seasonable weather, that the earth may in due time yield her increase; that by Thy goodness we may receive our daily bread, and learn to know Thee as a merciful God, and evermore give thanks to Thee for Thy goodness; through Jesus Christ, Thy dear Son, our Lord. *Amen.*

THANKSGIVING.

42.

O Lord God, heavenly Father, from whom without ceasing we receive exceeding abundantly all good gifts, and who daily of Thy pure grace guardest us against all evil: Grant us we beseech Thee, Thy Holy Spirit, that acknowledging with our whole heart all this Thy goodness, we may now and evermore thank and praise Thy loving kindness and tender mercy; through Jesus Christ, Thy Son, our Lord. *Amen.*

43.

Almighty God, our heavenly Father, Whose mercies are new unto us every morning, and who, though we have in no wise deserved Thy goodness, dost abundantly provide for all our wants of body and soul; Give us, we pray Thee, Thy Holy Spirit, that we may heartily acknowledge Thy merciful goodness toward us, give thanks for all Thy benefits and serve Thee in willing obedience; through Jesus Christ, Thy Son, our Lord. *Amen.*

44.

Almighty and most merciful God, Who in Thy fatherly wisdom has chastened us on account of our sins, that we might not continue in impenitence and vain confidence, and thus perish with the ungodly; in the midst of wrath Thou hast remembered mercy, and hast graciously delivered us out of our affliction. We give Thee therefore most hearty thanks and praise, that Thou hast turned away from us Thy just anger, and shown Thyself favorable toward us Thine unworthy servants. Bless the Lord, O my soul: and all that is within me, bless His holy Name. Bless the Lord, O my soul, and forget not all His benefits. Thou Lord, art merciful and gracious, slow to anger, and plenteous in mercy. Glory be to Thee, O God, forever; through Jesus Christ our Lord. *Amen.*

45.

Glory be to Thee, O God Most Holy. Glory be to Thee, O God Most High. Glory be to Thee, O King of heaven and earth, Who, as a father pitieth his children, pitiest us. Fill us with joy and gladness in the Holy Ghost, that when Thou shalt render to every man according to his works, we may be found acceptable before Thee, through Him who hath redeemed us from the shame and curse of sin, even Jesus Christ, Thy dear Son, our Lord. *Amen.*

FOR SPECIAL GIFTS AND GRACES.

46.

For Protection During the Day.

O Lord, our heavenly Father, Almighty and Everlasting God, Who hast safely brought us to the beginning of this day; Defend us in the same with Thy mighty power: and grant that this day we fall into no sin, neither run into any kind of danger; but that all our doings, being ordered by Thy governance, may be righteous in Thy sight; through Jesus Christ our Lord. *Amen.*

47.

For Protection during the Night.

Lighten our darkness, we beseech Thee, O Lord; and by Thy great mercy defend us from all perils and dangers of this night; for the love of Thy Only Son, our Saviour, Jesus Christ. *Amen.*

48.

For Grace to use our Gifts.

O Lord God Almighty, Who dost endue Thy servants with divers and singular gifts of the Holy Ghost; Leave us not, we beseech Thee, destitute of Thy manifold gifts, nor yet of grace to use them alway to Thy honor and glory; through Jesus Christ our Lord. *Amen.*

49.

For Grace to receive the Word.

Blessed Lord, Who hast caused all Holy Scriptures to be written for our learning; Grant that we may in such wise hear them, read, mark, learn, and inwardly digest them, that by patience and comfort of Thy holy Word, we may embrace, and ever hold fast the blessed hope of everlasting life, which Thou hast given us in our Saviour Jesus Christ. *Amen.*

50.

For Grace to be led into all Truth.

Enlighten our minds, we beseech Thee, O God, by the Spirit which proceedeth from Thee; that as Thy Son hath promised, we may be led into all truth; through the same our Lord Jesus Christ. *Amen.*

51.

For Spiritual Renewal.

Almighty God, who hast given us Thy Only-Begotten Son to take our nature upon Him; Grant that we being regenerate, and made Thy children by adoption, and grace, may daily be renewed by Thy Holy Spirit; through the same our Lord Jesus Christ. *Amen.*

52.

For Penitence.

Merciful Father, Give us grace that we may never presume to sin; but if at any time we offend Thy Divine Majesty, may we truly repent and lament our offence, and by a lively faith obtain remission of all our sins, solely through the merits of Thy Son, our Saviour Jesus Christ. *Amen.*

53.

For Pardon.

Hear, we beseeech Thee, O Lord, the prayer of Thy suppliants, and spare those who confess their sins unto Thee, that Thou mayest bestow upon us both pardon and peace; through Jesus Christ our Lord. *Amen.*

54.

For Deliverance from Sin.

We beseech Thee, O Lord, in Thy clemency to show us Thine unspeakable mercy; that Thou mayest both set us free from our sins, and rescue us from the punishments which for our sins, we deserve; through Jesus Christ our Lord. *Amen.*

55.

For Grace to do God's Will.

Almighty God, give us grace that we may cast away the works of darkness, and put upon us the armor of light, now in the time of this mortal life, in which Thy Son Jesus Christ came to visit us in great humility; that in the last day, when He shall come again in His glorious Majesty to judge both the quick and the dead, we may rise to the life immortal; through Jesus Christ our Lord. *Amen.*

56.

For Grace to love and serve God.

O God, Who, through the grace of Thy Holy Spirit, dost pour the gifts of charity into the hearts of Thy faithful people; Grant unto Thy servants health both of mind and body, that they may love Thee with their whole strength, and with their whole heart perform those things which are pleasing unto Thee; through Jesus Christ our Lord. *Amen.*

57.

For Aid against Temptation.

O God, Who justifiest the ungōdly, and who desirest not the death of the sinner; We humbly implore Thy Majesty, that Thou wouldest graciously assist, by Thy heavenly aid, and evermore shield with Thy protection, Thy servants who trust in Thy mercy, that they may be separated by no temptations from Thee, and, without ceasing, may serve Thee, through Jesus Christ, Thy Son our Lord. *Amen.*

58.

For Faith.

Almighty and Everliving God, Who hast given to them that believe exceeding great and precious promises; Grant us so perfectly, and without all doubt, to believe in Thy Son Jesus Christ, that our faith in Thy sight may never be reproved. Hear us, O Lord, through the same our Saviour Jesus Christ. *Amen.*

59.

For Divine Guidance and Help.

Direct us, O Lord, in all our doings, with Thy most gracious favor, and further us with Thy continual help; that in all our works begun, continued, and ended in Thee, we may glorify Thy holy Name; and finally, by Thy mercy, obtain everlasting life; through Jesus Christ our Lord. *Amen.*

60.

O Almighty and Everlasting God, vouchsafe, we beseech Thee, to direct, sanctify and govern both our hearts and bodies in the ways of Thy laws, and in the works of Thy commandments; that through Thy most mighty protection, both here and ever, we may be preserved in body and in soul; through our Lord and Saviour Jesus Christ. *Amen.*

61.

For Spiritual Illumination.

Grant, we beseech Thee, Almighty God, that the brightness of Thy glory may shine forth upon us, and that the light of Thy light by the illumination of the Holy Spirit may stablish the hearts of all that have been born anew by Thy grace; through our Lord Jesus Christ. *Amen.*

62.

For Likeness to Christ.

Almighty God, Who hast given Thine Only Son to be unto us both a sacrifice for sin and also an ensample of godly life; Give us grace that we may always most thankfully receive that His inestimable benefit, and also daily endeavor ourselves to follow the blessed steps of His most holy life; through the same Jesus Christ our Lord. *Amen.*

63.

For a Right Knowledge of Christ.

O Almighty God, Whom to know is everlasting life; Grant us perfectly to know Thy Son Jesus Christ to be the way, the truth, and the life; that following His steps we may steadfastly walk in the way that leadeth to eternal life; through the same, Thy Son, Jesus Christ our Lord. *Amen.*

64.

For the Holy Spirit.

O Lord God, heavenly Father, Who by the blessed light of Thy divine Word hast led us to the knowledge of Thy Son; We most heartily beseech Thee so to replenish us with the grace of Thy Holy Spirit, that we may ever walk in the light of Thy truth and rejoicing with sure confidence in Christ our Saviour, may in the end be brought unto everlasting salvation; through the same, Thy Son, our Lord. *Amen.*

65.

Almighty and Everlasting God, Who of Thy great mercy in Jesus Christ Thy Son, dost grant us forgiveness of sin, and all things pertaining to life and godliness; Grant us, we beseech Thee, Thy Holy Spirit, that He may so rule our hearts, that we, being ever mindful of Thy fatherly mercy, may strive to mortify the flesh, and to overcome the world; and serving Thee in holiness and pureness of living, may give Thee continual thanks for all Thy goodness; through Jesus Christ, Thy Son, our Lord. *Amen.*

66.

For Purity.

Almighty God, unto Whom all hearts are open, all desires known, and from whom no secrets are hid; Cleanse the thoughts of our hearts by the inspiration of Thy Holy Spirit, that we may perfectly love Thee, and worthily magnify Thy holy Name; through Jesus Christ our Lord. *Amen.*

67.

For Innocency of Life.

O God, Whose strength is made perfect in weakness, Mortify and kill all vices in us, and so strengthen us by Thy grace, that by the innocency of our lives, and the constancy of our faith even unto death, we may glorify Thy holy Name; through Jesus Christ our Lord. *Amen.*

68.

For Love to God.

O God, Who makest all things to work together for good to them that love Thee; Pour into our hearts such steadfast love toward Thee, that the pure desires which by Thy Spirit have been stirred up in us, may not be turned aside by any temptation; through Jesus Christ our Lord. *Amen.*

69.

For Charity.

O Lord, Who hast taught us that all our doings without charity are nothing worth; Send Thy Holy Spirit and pour into our hearts that most excellent gift of Charity, the very bond of peace and all virtues, without which whosoever liveth is counted dead before Thee; grant this for Thine Only Son Jesus Christ's sake. *Amen.*

70.

For Humility.

O God, Who resistest the proud, and givest grace to the humble; Grant unto us true humility, after the likeness in which Thine Only Son hath revealed it in Himself, that we may never be lifted up and provoke Thy wrath, but in all lowliness be made partakers of the gifts of Thy grace; through Christ our Lord. *Amen.*

71.

For Patience.

O God, Who by the meek endurance of Thine Only-Begotten Son didst beat down the pride of the old enemy: Help us, we beseech Thee, rightly to treasure in our hearts what our Lord hath of His goodness borne for our sakes; that after His example we may bear with patience whatsoever things are adverse to us; through Christ our Lord. *Amen.*

72.

For a Happy Death.

Confirm, we beseech Thee, Almighty God, Thine unworthy servants in Thy grace; that in the hour of our death the adversary may not prevail against us, but that we may be found worthy of everlasting life; through Jesus Christ our Lord. *Amen.*

73.

For the Blessedness of Heaven.

Almighty, Everlasting God, Who didst give Thine Only Son to be a High Priest of good things to come; Hereafter grant unto us, Thine unworthy servants, to have our share in the company of the Blessed; through Jesus Christ our Lord. *Amen.*

74.

For Peace.

O God, Who art the Author of peace and Lover of concord, in knowledge of whom standeth our eternal life, whose service is perfect freedom; Defend us, Thy humble servants, in all assaults of our enemies; that we, surely trusting in Thy defence, may not fear the power of any adversaries, through the might of Jesus Christ our Lord. *Amen.*

FOR AN ANSWER TO PRAYER.

75.

Almighty God, Who hast given us grace at this time with one accord to make our common supplications unto Thee; and dost promise that when two or three are gathered together in Thy Name, Thou wilt grant their requests; Fulfill now, O Lord, the desires and petitions of Thy servants, as may be most expedient for them; granting us in this world knowledge of Thy truth, and in the world to come life everlasting. *Amen.*

76.

Almighty God, the fountain of all wisdom, Who knowest our necessities before we ask, and our ignorance in asking; We beseech Thee to have compassion upon our infirmities; and those things which for our unworthiness we dare not, and for our blindness we cannot ask, vouchsafe to give us, for the worthiness of Thy Son, Jesus Christ our Lord. *Amen.*

77.

Almighty God, Who hast promised to hear the petitions of those who ask in Thy Son's Name; We beseech Thee mercifully to incline Thine ears to us who have now made our prayers and supplications unto Thee; and grant that those things which we have faithfully asked according to Thy will, may effectually be obtained, to the relief of our necessity, and to the setting forth of Thy glory; through Jesus Christ our Lord. *Amen.*

General Prayers

I.

THE LITANY.

The Litany *may be used at* Evening Service *on Sundays, Wednesdays, and Fridays on Days of Humiliation and Prayer, and at* Morning Service *on Sundays when there is no Communion. The Responses in italics should be sung or said by the Congregation. The Responses may be repeated after each phrase, or only at the end of each group, as here followeth:*

Lord, have mercy upon us.
Lord, have mercy upon us.
Christ, have mercy upon us.
Christ, have mercy upon us.
Lord, have mercy upon us.
Lord, have mercy upon us.
O Christ, hear us.
O Christ, hear us.
O God, the Father in heaven;
Have mercy upon us.
O God the Son, Redeemer of the world;
Have mercy upon us.
O God, the Holy Ghost;
Have mercy upon us.
Be gracious unto us.
Spare us, good Lord.
Be gracious unto us.
Help us, good Lord.
From all sin;
From all error;
From all evil:
Good Lord, deliver us.
From the crafts and assaults of the devil;
From sudden and evil death;
From pestilence and famine;
From war and bloodshed;
From sedition and rebellion;
From lightning and tempest;
From all calamity by fire and water;
And from everlasting death:
Good Lord, deliver us.
By the mystery of Thy holy Incarnation;
By Thy holy Nativity;
By Thy Baptism, Fasting, and Temptation;
By Thine Agony and Bloody Sweat;
By Thy Cross and Passion;
By Thy precious Death and Burial;
By Thy glorious Resurrection and Ascension;
And by the coming of the Holy Ghost, the Comforter:
Help us, good Lord.
In all time of our tribulation;
In all time of our prosperity;
In the hour of death;
And in the day of judgment;
Help us, good Lord.
We poor sinners do beseech Thee;

To hear us, O Lord God.
And to rule and govern Thy holy Christian Church;
To preserve all pastors and ministers of Thy Church, in the true knowledge and understanding of Thy Word, and in holiness of life;
To put an end to all schisms and causes of offence;
To bring into the way of truth all such as have erred and are deceived;
To beat down Satan under feet;
To send faithful laborers into Thy harvest;
To accompany Thy Word with Thy Spirit and grace;
To raise up them that fall, and to strengthen such as do stand;
And to comfort and help the weak-hearted and the distressed:
We beseech Thee to hear us, good Lord.
To give to all nations peace and concord;
To preserve our country from discord and contention;
To give to our nation perpetual victory over all its enemies;
To direct and defend our President, and all in authority;
And to bless and keep our magistrates, and all our people:
We beseech Thee to hear us, good Lord.
To behold and succor all who are in danger, necessity and tribulation;
To protect all who travel by land or water;
To preserve all women in the perils of childbirth;
To strengthen and keep all sick persons and young children;
To set free all who are innocently imprisoned;
To defend and provide for all fatherless children and widows;
And to have mercy upon all men:
We beseech Thee to hear us, good Lord.
To forgive our enemies, persecutors, and slanderers, and to turn their hearts;
To give and preserve to our use the fruits of the earth;
And graciously to hear our prayers:
We beseech Thee to hear us, good Lord.
O Lord Jesus Christ, Son of God;
We beseech Thee to hear us, good Lord.
O Lamb of God, that takest away the sin of the world;
Have mercy upon us.
O Lamb of God, that takest away the sin of the world;
Have mercy upon us.
O Lamb of God, that takest away the sin of the world;
Grant us Thy peace.
O Christ, hear us.
O Christ, hear us.
Lord, have mercy upon us.
Lord, have mercy upon us.
Christ, have mercy upon us.
Christ, have mercy upon us.
Lord, have mercy upon us.
Lord, have mercy upon us, Amen.

Then shall the Minister, and the Congregation with him, say the Lord's Prayer, *after which may be said one or more of the* Litany Collects *here following.*

Our Father, who art in heaven; Hallowed be Thy Name; Thy kingdom come; Thy will be done on earth, as it is in heaven; Give us this day our daily bread; And forgive us our trespasses, as we forgive those who trespass against us; And lead us not into temptation; But deliver us from evil; For thine is the kingdom, and the power, and the glory, for ever and ever. *Amen.*

LITANY COLLECTS.

1.

M. O Lord, deal not with us after our sins.
C. Neither reward us according to our iniquities.

Almighty God, our heavenly Father, who desirest not the death of a sinner, but rather that he should turn from his evil way and live; We beseech Thee graciously to turn from us those punishments which we by our sins have deserved, and to grant us grace ever hereafter to serve Thee in holiness and pureness of living; through Jesus Christ our Lord. *Amen.*

2.

M. Help us, O God of our salvation, for the glory of Thy name.

C. Deliver us, and purge away our sins for Thy name's sake.

Almighty and Everlasting God, Who by Thy Holy Spirit dost govern and sanctify the whole Christian Church; Hear our prayers for all members of the same and mercifully grant, that by Thy grace they may serve Thee in true faith; through Jesus Christ Thy Son our Lord. *Amen.*

3.

M. O Lord, deal not with us after our sins.

C. Neither reward us according to our iniquities.

O God, merciful Father, Who despiseth not the sighing of a contrite heart, nor the desire of such as are sorrowful; Mercifully assist our prayers which we make before Thee in all our troubles and adversities, whensoever they oppress us; and graciously hear us, that those evils which the craft and subtilty of the devil or man worketh against us, may, by Thy good providence, be brought to naught; that we Thy servants, being hurt by no persecutions, may evermore give thanks unto Thee in Thy holy Church; through Jesus Christ Thy Son our Lord. *Amen.*

4.

M. O Lord, enter not into judgment with Thy servant.

C. For in Thy sight shall no man living be justified.

Almighty God, Who knowest us to be set in the midst of so many and great dangers, that by reason of the frailty of our nature we cannot always stand upright; Grant us such strength and protection, as may support us in all dangers, and carry us through all temptations; through Jesus Christ our Lord. *Amen.*

5.

M. Call upon Me in the day of trouble.

C. I will deliver thee, and thou shalt glorify Me.

Spare us, O Lord, and mercifully forgive us our sins, and though by our continual transgressions we have merited Thy punishments, be gracious unto us, and grant that all those evils which we have deserved, may be turned from us, and overruled to our everlasting good; through Jesus Christ Thy Son our Lord. *Amen.*

6.

For Peace.

M. The Lord will give strength unto His people.

C. The Lord will bless His people with peace.

O God, from Whom all holy desires, all good counsels, and all just works do proceed; Give unto Thy servants that peace, which the world cannot give; that our hearts may be set to obey Thy commandments, and also that by Thee, we, being defended from the fear of our enemies, may pass our time in rest and quietness; through the merits of Jesus Christ our Saviour. *Amen.*

II.

THE SUFFRAGES.

The Suffrages *may be used at* Early *or* Evening Service *in the same manner as the* Litany.

Lord, have mercy upon us.

Lord, have mercy upon us.

Christ, have mercy upon us.

Christ, have mercy upon us.

Lord, have mercy upon us.
Lord, have mercy upon us.

Our Father, who art in heaven; Hallowed be Thy Name; Thy kingdom come; Thy will be done on earth, as it is in heaven; Give us this day our daily bread; And forgive us our trespasses, as we forgive those who trespass against us; And lead us not into temptation;
But deliver us from evil.

I said; O Lord, be merciful unto me;
Heal my soul; for I have sinned against Thee.

Return, O Lord, how long?
And let it repent Thee concerning Thy servants.

Let Thy mercy, O Lord, be upon us;
According as we hope in Thee.

Let Thy priests be clothed with righteousness;
And let Thy saints shout for joy.

O Lord, save our rulers;
Let the King hear us when we call.

Save Thy people, and bless Thine inheritance.
Feed them also, and lift them up forever.

Remember thy congregation;
Which Thou hast purchased of old.

Peace be within thy walls;
And prosperity within thy palaces.

Let us pray for our absent brethren.
O Thou, our God, save Thy servants that trust in Thee.

Let us pray for the broken-hearted and the captives;
Redeem Israel, O God, out of all his troubles.

Send them help from the Sanctuary;
And strengthen them out of Zion.

Hear my prayer, O Lord;
And let my cry come unto Thee.

Then may be said responsively, by the Minister and Congregation the Psalm De Profundis *at* Early Morning Service, *and at* Evening Service *the Psalm* Miserere Mei.

Ps. cxxx. *De Profundis.*

Out of the depths have I cried:
Unto thee O Lord.

Lord, hear my voice:
Let thine ears be attentive to the voice of my supplications.

If Thou, Lord, shouldest mark iniquities:
O Lord, who shall stand?

But there is forgiveness with Thee:
That Thou mayest be feared.

I wait for the Lord, my soul doth wait:
And in His word do I hope.

My soul waiteth for the Lord more than they that watch for the morning:
I say, more than they that watch for the morning.

Let Israel hope in the Lord:
For with the Lord there is mercy, and with Him is plenteous redemption.

And He shall redeem Israel:
From all his iniquities.

Glory be to the Father, and to the Son, and to the Holy Ghost:
As it was in the beginning, is now, and ever shall be, world without end. Amen.

Or at Evening Service.

Ps. ii. *Miserere Mei.*

Have mercy upon me, O God, according to Thy loving kindness:
According unto the multitude of Thy tender mercies, blot out my transgressions.

Wash me thoroughly from mine iniquity:
And cleanse me from my sin.

For I acknowledge my transgressions:
And my sin is ever before me.
Against Thee, Thee only, have I sinned and done this evil in Thy sight:
That Thou mightest be justified when Thou speakest, and be clear when Thou judgest.
Behold, I was shapen in iniquity:
And in sin did my mother conceive me.
Behold, Thou desirest truth in the inward parts:
And in the hidden part shalt Thou make me to know wisdom.
Purge me with hyssop, and I shall be clean:
Wash me, and I shall be whiter than snow.
Make me to hear joy and gladness:
That the bones which Thou hast broken may rejoice.
Hide Thy face from my sins:
And blot out all mine iniquities.
Create in me a clean heart, O God:
And renew a right spirit within me.
Cast me not away from Thy presence:
And take not Thy Holy Spirit from me.
Restore unto me the joy of Thy salvation:
And uphold me with Thy free Spirit.
Then will I teach transgressors Thy ways:
And sinners shall be converted unto Thee.
Deliver me from blood-guiltiness, O God, Thou God of my salvation:
And my tongue shall sing aloud of Thy righteousness.
O Lord, open Thou my lips:
And my mouth shall show forth Thy praise.
For Thou desirest not sacrifice, else would I give it:
Thou delightest not in burnt offering.
The sacrifices of God are a broken spirit:
A broken and a contrite heart, O God, Thou wilt not despise.
Do good in Thy good pleasure unto Zion:
Build Thou the walls of Jerusalem.
Then shalt Thou be pleased with the sacrifices of righteousness, with burnt-offering and whole burnt-offering:
Then shall they offer bullocks upon Thine altar.
Glory be to the Father, and to the Son, and to the Holy Ghost:
As it was in the beginning, is now, and ever shall be, world without end. Amen.

Then shall be said:

Turn us again, O God of hosts,
Cause Thy face to shine and we shall be saved.
Arise, O Christ, for our help;
And redeem us for Thy mercy's sake.
Hear my prayer, O Lord;
And let my cry come unto Thee.
The Lord be with you.
And with thy spirit.
Let us pray.
Then may the Minister say a Collect *for the Season and any other suitable* Collects, *and after that he may say this* Collect *for peace.*
Give peace in our days, O Lord:
Because there is none other that fighteth for us, except Thou, our God.
O Lord, let there be peace in Thy strength:
And abundance in Thy towers.
Let us pray.
O God, from Whom all holy desires, all good counsels, and all just works do proceed; Give unto Thy servants that peace, which the world cannot give; that our

hearts may be set to obey Thy commandments, and also that by Thee, we, being defended from the fear of our enemies, may pass our time in rest and quietness; through the merits of Jesus Christ our Saviour. *Amen.*

Then may be sung or said the

Benedicamus.

Bless we the Lord:
Thanks be to God.

III.

THE MORNING SUFFRAGES.

To be said at Early Morning Service, *or in the* Morning Prayer of the Household.

Lord, have mercy upon us.
Lord, have mercy upon us.
Christ, have mercy upon us.
Christ, have mercy upon us.
Lord, have mercy upon us.
Lord, have mercy upon us.

Then shall all say the Lord's Prayer *and the* Apostles' Creed:

Our Father, Who art in heaven; Hallowed be Thy Name; Thy kingdom come; Thy will be done on earth, as it is in heaven; Give us this day our daily bread; And forgive us our trespasses, as we forgive those who trespass against us; And lead us not into temptation; But deliver us from evil. Amen.

I believe in God the Father Almighty, Maker of Heaven and earth; And in Jesus Christ His only Son, our Lord; Who was conceived by the Holy Ghost, Born of the Virgin Mary; Suffered under Pontius Pilate, Was crucified, dead, and buried; He descended into hell; The third day He rose again from the dead; He ascended into heaven, And sitteth on the right hand of God the Father Almighty; From thence He shall come to judge the quick and the dead.

I believe in the Holy Ghost; The Holy Christian Church, the Communion of Saints; The Forgiveness of sins; The Resurrection of the body; And the life everlasting. Amen.

Unto Thee have I cried, O Lord:
And in the morning shall my prayer prevent Thee.
Let my mouth be filled with thy praise:
And with Thy honor all the day.
O Lord, hide Thy face from my sins:
And blot out all mine iniquities.
Create in me, O God, a clean heart:
And renew a right spirit within me.
Cast me not away from Thy presence:
And take not Thy Holy Spirit from me.
Restore unto me the joy of Thy salvation:
And uphold me with Thy free Spirit.
Vouchsafe, O Lord, this day:
To keep us without sin.
Have mercy upon us, O Lord:
Have mercy upon us.
O Lord, let Thy mercy be upon us:
As our trust is in Thee.
Hear my prayer, O Lord:
And let my cry come unto Thee.
The Lord be with you:
And with thy spirit.

Let us pray.

Then shall be said the prayer here following, or No. 46, *or* No. 60 *of the* Collects *and* Prayers, *or any other suitable prayer.*

We give thanks unto Thee, Heavenly Father, through Jesus Christ Thy dear Son, that Thou hast protected us through the night from all danger and harm; and we beseech Thee to preserve and keep us, this day also, from all sin and evil; that in all our thoughts, words and deeds, we may serve and please Thee. Into Thy hands we commend our bodies and souls, and all that is ours. Let Thy holy angel have charge concerning us, that the wicked one have no power over us. ***Amen.***

Benedicamus.

Bless we the Lord.
Thanks be to God.

IV.

THE EVENING SUFFRAGES.

To be used at **Evening Service,** ***or at the*** **Evening Prayer of the Household.**

Lord, have mercy upon us.
Lord, have mercy upon us.

Christ, have mercy upon us.
Christ, have mercy upon us.

Lord, have mercy upon us.
Lord, have mercy upon us.

Then shall all say:

Our Father, Who art in heaven; Hallowed be Thy Name; Thy kingdom come; Thy will be done on earth, as it is in heaven; Give us this day our daily bread; And forgive us our trespasses, as we forgive those who trespass against us; And lead us not into temptation; But deliver us from evil. Amen.

I Believe in God the Father Almighty, Maker of Heaven and earth; And in Jesus Christ His Only Son, our Lord; Who was conceived by the Holy Ghost, Born of the Virgin Mary; Suffered under Pontius Pilate; Was crucified, dead, and buried; He descended into hell; The third day He rose again from the dead; He ascended into heaven; And sitteth on the right hand of God the Father Almighty; From thence He shall come to judge the quick and the dead.

I believe in the Holy Ghost; Thy holy Christian Church, the Communion of Saints; The Forgiveness of sins; The Resurrection of the body; And the Life everlasting. Amen.

Blessed art Thou, O Lord God of our fathers:
And greatly to be praised and glorified forever.

Bless we the Father, and the Son, and the Holy Ghost:
We praise and magnify Him forever.

Blessed art Thou, O Lord, in the firmament of heaven:
And greatly to be praised, and glorified, and highly exalted forever.

The Almighty and Merciful Lord, bless and preserve us.
Amen.

Vouchsafe, O Lord, this night:
To keep us without sin.

O Lord, have mercy upon us.
Have mercy upon us.

O Lord. let Thy mercy be upon us:
As our trust is in Thee.

Hear my prayer, O Lord:
And let my cry come unto Thee.

The Lord be with you.
And with thy spirit.

Let us pray.

Then shall be said the prayer here following, or **No. 47** ***of the*** **Collects** ***and*** **Prayers,** ***or any other suitable prayer.***

We give thanks unto Thee, heavenly Father, through Jesus Christ, Thy dear Son, that thou hast this day so graciously protected us, and we beseech Thee to forgive us all our sins, and the wrong which we have done, and by Thy great mercy defend us from all the perils and dangers of this night. Into Thy hands we commend our bodies and souls, and all that is ours. Let Thy holy angel have charge concerning us, that the wicked one have no power over us. *Amen.*

Benedicamus.

Bless we the Lord.
Thanks be to God.

V.

THE BIDDING PRAYER.

By ancient usage this prayer was specially appointed for Good Friday.

BRETHREN, let us pray for the whole *Christian Church*, that our Lord God would vouchsafe to defend it against all the assaults and temptations of the adversary, and to keep it perpetually upon the true foundation, Jesus Christ.

ALMIGHTY and everlasting God, Who hast revealed Thy glory to all nations in Jesus Christ and the word of His truth; Keep, we beseech Thee, in safety the works of Thy mercy, that so Thy Church, spread throughout all nations, may serve Thee in true faith, and persevere in the confession of Thy Name; through Jesus Christ our Lord. *Amen.*

Let us pray for the *Ministers* of the Word for all *estates* of men in the Church, and for all the *people of God.*

ALMIGHTY and everlasting God, by whose Spirit the whole body of the Church is governed and sanctified; Receive our supplications and prayers which we offer before Thee for all estates of men in Thy holy Church, that every member of the same, in his vocation and ministry, may truly and godly serve Thee; through Christ our Lord. *Amen.*

Let us pray for our *Catechumens*, that our Lord God would open their hearts and the door of His mercy, that having received the remission of all their sins by the washing of regeneration, they may be mindful of their baptismal covenant, and evermore be found in Christ Jesus our Lord.

ALMIGHTY and everlasting God, Who dost always multiply Thy Church, and with Thy light and grace dost strengthen the hearts of those whom Thou hast regenerated, confirming unto them Thy covenant and faithfulness; Grant unto our Catechumens increase both of faith and knowledge, that they may rejoice in their Baptism and really and heartily renew their covenant with Thee. *Amen.*

Let us pray *for all in authority*, and especially for the government of the United States, that we may lead a quiet and peaceable life in all godliness and honesty.

O MERCIFUL Father in heaven, Who holdest in Thy hand all the might of man, and who hast ordained the powers that be for the punishment of evil-doers, and for the praise of them that do well, and of whom is all rule and authority in the kingdoms of the world; We humbly beseech Thee, graciously regard Thy servants, the President of the United States, the Governor of this Commonwealth, our Judges and magistrates, and all the Rulers of the earth; that all who receive the sword, as Thy ministers, may bear it according to Thy commandment; through Christ our Lord. *Amen.*

Let us pray our Lord God Almighty that He would deliver the world from all *error*, take away *disease*, ward off *famine*, open the *prisons*, set free *those in bondage*, grant a safe return to the *wayfarers*, health to the *sick* and to our mariners a harbor of security.

ALMIGHTY and everlasting God, the Consolation of the sorrowful, and the Strength of the weak; May the prayers of them that in any tribulation or distress cry unto Thee graciously come before Thee, so that in all their necessities they may mark and receive Thy manifold help and comfort; through Christ our Lord. *Amen.*

Here may be offered prayers for Schismatics, Jews, and Heathen. See Collects and Prayers 19-24.

Let us pray for *peace*, that we may come to the knowledge of God's holy Word, and walk before Him as becometh Christians.

ALMIGHTY and everlasting God, King of glory, and Lord of heaven and earth, by whose Spirit all things are governed, by whose providence all things are ordered, who art the God of peace, and the author of all concord; Grant us, we beseech Thee, Thy heavenly peace and concord, that we may serve Thee in true fear, to the praise and glory of Thy Name; through Christ our Lord. *Amen.*

Let us pray for our *enemies*, that God would remember them in mercy, and graciously vouchsafe unto them such things as are both needful for them and profitable unto their salvation.

O ALMIGHTY, everlasting God, Who through Thine Only Son, our blessed Lord, hast commanded us to love our enemies, to do good to them that hate us, and to pray for them that persecute us; We earnestly beseech Thee, that by Thy gracious visitation all our enemies may be led to true repentance, and may have the same love, and be of one accord and of one mind and heart, with us and with Thy whole Christian Church; through Christ our Lord. *Amen.*

Let us pray for the *fruits of the earth*, that God would send down His blessing upon them, and graciously dispose our hearts to enjoy them in submission to His holy will.

O LORD, Father Almighty, Who by Thy Word hast created and dost bless and uphold all things; We pray Thee so to reveal unto us Thy Word our Lord Jesus Christ, that He dwelling in our hearts, we may by Thy grace be made meet to receive Thy blessing on all the fruits of the earth, and whatsoever pertains to our bodily need; through Christ our Lord. *Amen.*

Finally, let us pray for all those things for which our Lord would have us ask, saying:

OUR Father, Who art in heaven; Hallowed be Thy Name; Thy kingdom come; Thy will be done on earth, as it is in heaven; Give us this day our daily bread; And forgive us our trespasses, as we forgive those who trespass against us; And lead us not into temptation; But deliver us from evil; For Thine is the kingdom, and the power, and the glory, for ever and ever. *Amen.*

VI.

Almighty and Everlasting God, who art worthy to be had in reverence by all the children of men, we give Thee most humble and hearty thanks for the innumerable blessings, both temporal and spiritual, which, without any merit or worthiness on our part, Thou hast bestowed upon us.

We praise Thee, especially, that Thou [illegible]st preserved unto us, in their purity, Thy saving Word, and the sacred ordinances of [illegible] house. And we beseech Thee, O Lord, to grant and preserve unto Thy holy Church, throughout the world, purity of doctrine, and faithful pastors who shall preach Thy Word with power; and help all who hear, rightly to understand, and truly to believe the same. Be Thou the Protector and Defender of Thy people in all time of tribulation and danger; and may we, in communion with Thy Church, and in brotherly unity with all our fellow-Christians, fight the good fight of faith, and in the end receive the salvation of our souls.

Bestow Thy grace upon all the nations of the earth. Especially do we entreat Thee to bless our land, and all its inhabitants, and all who are in authority. Cause Thy glory to dwell among us, and let mercy and truth, righteousness and peace, everywhere prevail. To this end, we commend to Thy care all our schools, and pray Thee to make them nurseries of useful knowledge and christian virtues, that they may bring forth the wholesome fruits of life.

Graciously defend us from all calamities by fire and water, from war, and pestilence, from scarcity and famine. Protect and prosper every one in his appropriate calling, and cause all useful arts to flourish among us. Be Thou the God and Father of the widow and the fatherless children, the Helper of the sick and the needy, and the Comforter of the forsaken and distressed.

Here special Supplications, Intercessions and Prayers may be made.

And as we are strangers and pilgrims on earth, help us by true faith and a godly life to prepare for the world to come; doing the work which Thou hast given us to do while it is day; before the night cometh when no man can work. And when our last hour shall come, support us by Thy power, and receive us into Thine everlasting kingdom; through Jesus Christ Thy Son our Lord, Who liveth and reigneth with Thee and the Holy Ghost, for ever and ever *Amen.*

VII.

ALMIGHTY God, our heavenly Father, we Thine unworthy servants, do give Thee most humble and hearty thanks for all Thy goodness and loving kindness to us, and to all men. We bless Thee for our creation, preservation, and all the blessings of this life; but above all, for Thine inestimable love in the redemption of the world by our Lord and Saviour Jesus Christ, for the means of grace, and for the hope of glory. And, we beseech Thee, give us that due sense of all Thy mercies, that our hearts may be unfeignedly thankful, and that we may show forth Thy praise, not only with our lips, but in our lives: that walking before Thee in holiness and righteousness all our days, we may enjoy the testimony of a good conscience and the hope of Thy favor, be sustained and comforted under the troubles of this life, and finally be received into Thine everlasting kingdom, through Thine infinite mercy in Jesus Christ our Lord.

We offer unto Thee our common supplications for the good estate of Thy Church throughout the world; that it may be so guided and governed by Thy good Spirit, that all who profess themselves Christians may be led into the way of truth, and hold the faith in unity of spirit, in the bond of peace, and in righteousness of life. Send down upon all ministers of the gospel, and upon all congregations committed to their charge, the healthful spirit of Thy grace, and that they may truly please Thee, pour upon them the continual dew of Thy blessing.

Most heartily we beseech Thee, with Thy favor to behold the President [and Congress] of the United States, and all others in authority; and so replenish them with Thy grace, that they may always incline to Thy will, and walk in Thy way. Prosper all good counsels and all just works that peace and happiness, truth and righteousness, religion and piety, may be established among us throughout all generations.

We humbly entreat Thee also for all sorts and conditions of men; that Thou wouldest be pleased to make Thy ways known unto them, Thy saving health unto all nations.

May it please Thee to preserve all that travel by land or water; to succor all that are in peril or need; and to satisfy the wants of all Thy creatures.

We also commend to Thy fatherly goodness all those who are in any way afflicted or distressed, in mind, body, or estate; that it may please Thee to comfort and relieve them according to their several necessities, giving them patience under their sufferings, and a happy issue out of all their afflictions.

Here special Supplications, Intercessions and Prayers may be made.

Hear us, most merciful God, in these our humble requests, which we offer up unto Thee in the Name of Jesus Christ Thy Son, our Lord, to whom, with Thee and the Holy Ghost, be all honor and glory, world without end. *Amen.*

Psalms

Psalm i. *Beatus vir.*

Blessed is the man that walketh not in the counsel of the ungodly: nor standeth in the way of sinners, nor sitteth in the seat of the scornful.

But his delight is in the law of the LORD: and in his law doth he meditate day and night.

And he shall be like a tree planted by the rivers of water: that bringeth forth his fruit in his season.

His leaf also not wither: and whatsoever he doeth shall prosper.

The ungodly are not so: but are like the chaff which the wind driveth away.

Therefore the ungodly shall not stand in the judgment: nor sinners in the congregation of the righteous.

For the Lord knoweth the way of the righteous: but the way of the ungodly shall perish.

Psalm ii. *Quare fremuerunt gentes.*

Why do the heathen rage: and the people imagine a vain thing?

The kings of the earth set themselves, and the rulers take counsel together: against the LORD, and against his Anointed, saying,

Let us break their bands asunder: and cast away their cords from us.

He that sitteth in the heavens shall laugh: the Lord shall have them in derision.

Then shall He speak unto them in his wrath: and vex them in his sore displeasure.

Yet have I set my king: upon my holy hill of Zion.

I will declare the decree: the Lord hath said unto me, Thou art my Son; this day have I begotten Thee.

Ask of me, and I shall give thee the heathen for thine inheritance: and the uttermost parts of the earth for thy possession.

Thou shalt break them with a rod of iron: thou shalt dash them in pieces like a potter's vessel.

Be wise now therefore, O ye kings: be instructed, ye judges of the earth.

Serve the LORD with fear: and rejoice with trembling.

Kiss the Son, lest he be angry, and ye perish from the way, when his wrath is kindled but a little: blessed are they that put their trust in him.

Psalm vi. *Domine ne in furore.*

O LORD, rebuke me not in thine anger: neither chasten me in thy hot displeasure.

Have mercy upon me, O LORD; for I am weak: O Lord, heal me; for my bones are vexed.

My soul is also sore vexed: but Thou, O Lord, how long?

Return, O LORD, deliver my soul: oh save me for thy mercy's sake.

For in death there is no remembrance of thee: in the grave who shall give thee thanks?

I am weary with my groaning; all the night make I my bed to swim: I water my couch with my tears.

Mine eye is consumed because of grief: it waxeth old because of all mine enemies.

Depart from me all ye workers of iniquity: for the LORD hath heard the voice of my weeping.

The LORD hath heard my supplication: the LORD will receive my prayer.

Let all mine enemies be ashamed and sore vexed: let them return and be ashamed suddenly.

Psalm viii. *Domine, Dominus noster.*

O Lord, our Lord, how excellent is thy name in all the earth: Who hast set thy glory above the heavens.

Out of the mouth of babes and sucklings hast thou ordained strength because of thine enemies: that thou mightest still the enemy and the avenger.

When I consider thy heavens, the work of thy fingers: the moon and the stars, which thou hast ordained;

What is man, that thou art mindful of him: and the son of man, that thou visitest him?

For thou hast made him a little lower than the angels: and hast crowned him with glory and honor.

Thou madest him to have dominion over the works of thy hands: thou hast put all things under his feet;

All sheep and oxen: yea, and the beasts of the field;

The fowl of the air, and the fish of the sea: and whatsoever passeth through the paths of the seas.

O Lord our Lord: how excellent is thy name in all the earth!

Psalm xvi. *Conserva me, Domine.*

Preserve me, O God: for in thee do I put my trust.

O my soul, thou hast said unto the Lord, Thou art my Lord: my goodness extendeth not to thee;

But to the saints that are in the earth, and to the excellent: in whom is all my delight.

Their sorrows shall be multiplied: that hasten after another god;

Their drink offerings of blood will I not offer: nor take up their names into my lips.

The Lord is the portion of mine inheritance and of my cup: thou maintainest my lot.

The lines are fallen unto me in pleasant places: yea, I have a goodly heritage.

I will bless the Lord, who hath given me counsel: my reins also instruct me in the night-seasons.

I have set the Lord always before me: because he is at my right hand, I shall not be moved.

Therefore my heart is glad, and my glory rejoiceth: my flesh also shall rest in hope.

For thou wilt not leave my soul in hell: neither wilt thou suffer thine Holy One to see corruption.

Thou wilt shew me the path of life: in thy presence is fullness of joy; at thy right hand there are pleasures for evermore.

Psalm xviii. *Diligam te, Domine.*

I will love thee: O Lord, my strength.

The Lord is my rock, and my fortress, and my deliverer: my God, my strength, in whom I will trust; my buckler, and the horn of my salvation, and my high tower.

I will call upon the Lord, who is worthy to be praised, so shall I be saved from mine enemies.

The sorrows of death compassed me: and the floods of ungodly men made me afraid.

The sorrows of hell compassed me about: the snares of death prevented me.

In my distress I called upon the Lord: and cried unto my God.

He heard my voice out of his temple: and my cry came before him, even into his ears.

Then the earth shook and trembled: the foundations also of the hills moved and were shaken, because he was wroth.

There went up a smoke out of his nostrils, and fire out of his mouth devoured: coals were kindled by it.

He bowed the heavens also, and came down: and darkness was under his feet.

And he rode upon a cherub, and did fly: yea, he did fly upon the wings of the wind.

He made darkness his secret place: his pavilion round about him were dark waters and thick clouds of the skies.

At the brightness that was before him his thick clouds passed: hailstones and coals of fire.

The LORD also thundered in the heavens, and the Highest gave his voice: hailstones and coals of fire.

Yea, he sent out his arrows, and scattered them: and he shot out lightnings, and discomfited them.

Then the channels of waters were seen, and the foundations of the world were discovered: at thy rebuke, O LORD, at the blast of the breath of thy nostrils.

He sent from above, he took me: he drew me out of many waters.

He delivered me from my strong enemy, and from them which hated me: for they were too strong for me.

They prevented me in the day of my calamity: but the LORD was my stay.

He brought me forth also into a large place: he delivered me, because he delighted in me.

The LORD rewarded me according to my righteousness: according to the cleanness of my hands hath he recompensed me.

For I have kept the ways of the LORD: and have not wickedly departed from my God.

For all his judgments were before me: and I did not put away his statutes from me.

I was also upright before him: and I kept myself from mine iniquity.

Therefore hath the LORD recompensed me according to my righteousness: according to the cleanness of my hands in his eyesight.

With the merciful thou wilt shew thyself merciful: with an upright man thou wilt shew thyself upright;

With the pure thou wilt shew thyself pure: and with the froward thou wilt shew thyself froward.

For thou wilt save the afflicted people: but wilt bring down high looks.

For thou wilt light my candle: the LORD my God will enlighten my darkness.

For by thee I have run through a troop: and by my God have I leaped over a wall.

As for God, his way is perfect: the word of the LORD is tried; he is a buckler to all those that trust in him.

For who is God save the LORD: or who is a rock save our God?

It is God that girdeth me with strength: and maketh my way perfect.

He maketh my feet like hinds' feet: and setteth me upon my high places.

He teacheth my hands to war: so that a bow of steel is broken by mine arms.

Thou hast also given me the shield of thy salvation: and thy right hand hath holden me up, and thy gentleness hath made me great.

Thou hast enlarged my steps under me: that my feet did not slip.

I have pursued mine enemies and overtaken them: neither did I turn again till they were consumed.

I have wounded them that they were not able to rise: they are fallen under my feet.

For thou hast girded me with strength unto the battle: thou hast subdued under me those that rose up against me.

Thou hast also given me the necks of mine enemies: that I might destroy them that hate me.

They cried, but there was none to save them : even unto the LORD, but he answered them not.

Then did I beat them small as the dust before the wind : I did cast them out as the dirt in the streets.

Thou hast delivered me from the strivings of the people : and thou hast made me the head of the heathen.

A people whom I have not known : shall serve me.

As soon as they hear of me, they shall obey me : the strangers shall submit themselves unto me.

The strangers shall fade away : and be afraid out of their close places.

The LORD liveth, and blessed be my Rock : and let the God of my salvation be exalted.

It is God that avengeth me : and subdueth the people under me.

He delivered me from mine enemies ; yea, thou liftest me up above those that rise up against me ; thou hast delivered me from the violent man.

Therefore will I give thanks unto thee, O LORD, among the heathen : and sing praises unto thy name.

Great deliverance giveth he to his king: and sheweth mercy to his anointed, to David, and to his seed forevermore.

Psalm xix. *Coeli enarrant.*

The heavens declare the glory of God : and the firmament sheweth his handiwork.

Day unto day uttereth speech : and night unto night sheweth knowledge.

There is no speech nor language : where their voice is not heard.

Their line is gone out through all the earth : and their words to the end of the world.

In them hath he set a tabernacle for the sun : which is a bridegroom coming out of his chamber, and rejoiceth as a strong man to run a race.

His going forth is from the end of the heaven, and his circuit unto the ends of it : and there is nothing hid from the heat thereof.

The law of the LORD is perfect, converting the soul : the testimony of the LORD is sure, making wise the simple.

The statutes of the LORD are right, rejoicing the heart : the commandment of the LORD is pure, enlightening the eyes.

The fear of the LORD is clean, enduring forever : the judgments of the LORD are true and righteous altogether.

More to be desired are they than gold, yea, than much fine gold : sweeter also than honey and the honeycomb.

Moreover by them is thy servant warned : and in keeping of them there is great reward.

Who can understand his errors : cleanse thou me from secret faults.

Keep back thy servant also from presumptuous sins ; let them not have dominion over me : then shall I be upright and I shall be innocent from the great transgression.

Let the words of my mouth, and the meditation of my heart, be acceptable in thy sight ; O LORD, my strength, and my redeemer.

Psalm xxi. *Domine, in virtute tua.*

The king shall joy in thy strength, O LORD : and in thy salvation how greatly shall he rejoice !

Thou hast given him his heart's desire : and hast not withholden the request of his lips.

For thou preventest him with the blessings of goodness : thou settest a crown of pure gold on his head.

He asked life of thee and thou gavest it him : even length of days for ever and ever.

His glory is great in thy salvation: honor and majesty hast thou laid upon him.

For thou hast made him most blessed for ever: thou hast made him exceeding glad with thy countenance.

For the king trusteth in the LORD: and through the mercy of the Most High he shall not be moved.

Thine hand shall find out all thine enemies: thy right hand shall find out those that hate thee.

Thou shalt make them as a fiery oven in the time of thine anger: the LORD shall swallow them up in his wrath, and the fire shall devour them.

Their fruit shalt thou destroy from the earth: and their seed from among the children of men.

For they intended evil against thee: they imagined a mischievous device, which they are not able to perform.

Therefore shalt thou make them turn their back: when thou shalt make ready thine arrows upon thy strings against the face of them.

Be thou exalted, LORD, in thine own strength: so will we sing and praise thy power.

Psalm xxii. *Deus, Deus, meus.*

My God, my God, why hast thou forsaken me: why art thou so far from helping me, and from the words of my roaring?

O my God, I cry in the day time, but thou hearest not: and in the night season, and am not silent.

But thou art holy: O thou that inhabitest the praises of Israel.

Our fathers trusted in thee: they trusted, and thou didst deliver them.

They cried unto thee, and were delivered: they trusted in thee, and were not confounded.

But I am a worm, and no man: a reproach of men, and despised of the people.

All they that see me laugh me to scorn: they shoot out the lip, they shake the head saying

He trusted on the LORD that he would deliver him: let him deliver him, seeing he delighted in him.

But thou art he that took me out of the womb: thou didst make me hope when I was upon my mother's breasts.

I was cast upon thee from the womb: thou art my God from my mother's belly.

Be not far from me; for trouble is near: for there is none to help.

Many bulls have compassed me: strong bulls of Bashan have beset me round.

They gaped upon me with their mouths: as a ravening and a roaring lion.

I am poured out like water, and all my bones are out of joint: my heart is like wax; it is melted in the midst of my bowels.

My strength is dried up like a potsherd; and my tongue cleaveth to my jaws: and thou hast brought me into the dust of death.

For dogs have compassed me; the assembly of the wicked have inclosed me: they pierced my hands and my feet.

I may tell all my bones: they look and stare upon me.

They part my garments among them: and cast lots upon my vesture.

But be not thou far from me, O LORD: O my strength, haste thee to help me.

Deliver my soul from the sword: my darling from the power of the dog.

Save me from the lion's mouth: for thou hast heard me from the horns of the unicorns.

I will declare thy name unto my brethren: in the midst of the congregation will I praise thee.

Ye that fear the LORD, praise him; all ye the seed of Jacob, glorify him: and fear him all ye the seed of Israel.

For he hath not despised nor abhorred the affliction of the afflicted: neither hath he hid his face from him; but when he cried unto him, he heard.

My praise shall be of thee in the great congregation: I will pay my vows before them that fear him.

The meek shall eat and be satisfied: they shall praise the LORD that seek him; your heart shall live forever.

And the ends of the world shall remember and turn unto the LORD: and all the kindreds of the nations shall worship before thee.

For the kingdom is the LORD's: and he is the governor among the nations.

All they that be fat upon the earth: shall eat and worship.

All they that go down to the dust shall bow before him: and none can keep alive his own soul.

A seed shall serve him: it shall be accounted to the LORD for a generation.

They shall come, and shall declare his righteousness unto a people that shall be born: that he hath done this.

Psalm xxiii. *Dominus regit me.*

The LORD is my shepherd: I shall not want.

He maketh me to lie down in green pastures: he leadeth me beside the still waters.

He restoreth my soul: he leadeth me in the paths of righteousness for his name's sake.

Yea, though I walk through the valley of the shadow of death, I will fear no evil: for thou art with me; thy rod and thy staff they comfort me.

Thou preparest a table before me in the presence of mine enemies: thou anointest my head with oil; my cup runneth over.

Surely goodness and mercy shall follow me all the days of my life: and I will dwell in the house of the LORD for ever.

Psalm xxiv. *Domini est terra.*

The earth is the LORD's, and the fullness thereof: the world, and they that dwell therein.

For he hath founded it upon the seas: and established it upon the floods.

Who shall ascend into the hill of the LORD: or who shall stand in his holy place?

He that hath clean hands, and a pure heart: who hath not lifted up his soul unto vanity, nor sworn deceitfully.

He shall receive the blessing from the LORD: and righteousness from the God of his salvation.

This is the generation of them that seek him: that seek thy face, O Jacob.

Lift up your heads, O ye gates; and be ye lifted up, ye everlasting doors: and the King of glory shall come in.

Who is this King of glory: The LORD strong and mighty, the LORD mighty in battle.

Lift up your heads, O ye gates; even lift them up, ye everlasting doors: and the King of glory shall come in.

Who is this King of glory: The LORD of hosts, he is the King of glory.

Psalm xxv. *Ad te, Domine, levavi.*

Unto thee, O LORD: do I lift up my soul.

O my God, I trust in thee: let me not be ashamed, let not mine enemies triumph over me.

Yea, let none that wait upon thee be ashamed: let them be ashamed which transgress without cause.

Shew me thy ways, O LORD: teach me thy paths.

Lead me in thy truth, and teach me: for thou art the God of my salvation; on thee do I wait all the day.

Remember, O LORD, thy tender mercies and thy lovingkindnesses; for they have been ever of old.

Remember not the sins of my youth, nor my transgressions: according to thy mercy remember thou me for thy goodness sake, O LORD.

Good and upright is the LORD: therefore will he teach sinners in the way.

The meek will he guide in judgment: and the meek will he teach his way.

All the paths of the LORD are mercy and truth: unto such as keep his covenant and his testimonies.

For thy name's sake, O LORD, pardon mine iniquity: for it is great.

What man is he that feareth the LORD: him shall he teach in the way that he shall chose.

His soul shall dwell at ease: and his seed shall inherit the earth.

The secret of the LORD is with them that fear him: and he will shew them his covenant.

Mine eyes are ever toward the LORD: for he shall pluck my feet out of the net.

Turn thee unto me, and have mercy upon me: for I am desolate and afflicted.

The troubles of my heart are enlarged: O bring thou me out of my distresses.

Look upon mine affliction and my pain: and forgive all my sins.

Consider mine enemies, for they are many: and they hate me with cruel hatred.

O keep my soul, and deliver me: let me not be ashamed; for I put my trust in thee.

Let integrity and uprightness preserve me: for I wait on thee.

Redeem Israel, O God: out of all his troubles.

Psalm xxvii. *Dominus illuminatio.*

The LORD is my light and my salvation; whom shall I fear? the LORD is the strength of my life; of whom shall I be afraid?

When the wicked, even mine enemies and my foes, came upon me to eat my flesh: they stumbled and fell.

Though a host should encamp against me, my heart shall not fear: though war should rise against me, in this will I be confident.

One thing have I desired of the LORD, that will I seek after: that I may dwell in the house of the LORD all the days of my life, to behold the beauty of the LORD, and to inquire in his temple.

For in the time of trouble he shall hide me in his pavilion: in the secret of his tabernacle shall he hide me; he shall set me up upon a rock.

And now shall mine head be lifted up: above mine enemies round about me.

Therefore will I offer in his tabernacle sacrifices of joy: I will sing, yea, I will sing praises unto the LORD.

Hear, O LORD, when I cry with my voice: have mercy also upon me, and answer me.

When thou saidst, Seek ye my face: my heart said unto thee, Thy face, LORD, will I seek.

Hide not thy face far from me: put not thy servant away in anger.

Thou hast been my help: leave me not, neither forsake me, O God of my salvation.

When my father and my mother forsake me: then the LORD will take me up.

Teach me thy way, O LORD: and lead me in a plain path, because of mine enemies.

Deliver me not over unto the will of mine enemies: for false witnesses are risen up against me, and such as breathe out cruelty.

I had fainted: unless I had believed to see the goodness of the LORD in the land of the living.

Wait on the LORD; be of good courage, and he shall strengthen thine heart: wait, I say, on the LORD.

Psalm xxviii. *Ad te, Domine.*

Unto thee will I cry, O LORD my rock; be not silent to me: lest, if thou be silent to me, I become like them that go down into the pit.

Hear the voice of my supplications, when I cry unto thee: when I lift up my hands toward thy holy oracle.

Draw me not away with the wicked, and with the workers of iniquity: which speak peace to their neighbors, but mischief is in their hearts.

Give them according to their deeds: and according to the wickedness of their endeavors.

Give them after the work of their hands: render to them their desert.

Because they regard not the works of the LORD, nor the operation of his hand: he shall destroy them and not build them up.

Blessed be the LORD: because he hath heard the voice of my supplications.

The LORD is my strength and my shield; my heart trusteth in him, and I am helped: therefore my heart greatly rejoiceth; and with my song will I praise him.

The LORD is their strength: and he is the saving strength of his anointed.

Save thy people, and bless thine inheritance: feed them also, and lift them up for ever.

Psalm xxx. *Exaltabo te, Domine.*

I will extol thee, O LORD; for thou hast lifted me up: and hast not made my foes to rejoice over me.

O LORD my God, I cried unto thee: and thou hast healed me.

O LORD, thou hast brought up my soul from the grave: thou hast kept me alive, that I should not go down to the pit.

Sing unto the LORD, O ye saints of his: and give thanks at the remembrance of his holiness.

For his anger endureth but a moment; in his favor is life: weeping may endure for a night, but joy cometh in the morning.

And in my prosperity I said: I shall never be moved.

LORD, by thy favor thou hast made my mountain to stand strong: thou didst hide thy face, and I was troubled.

I cried to thee, O LORD: and unto the LORD I made supplication.

What profit is there in my blood, when I go down to the pit: Shall the dust praise thee? shall it declare thy truth?

Hear, O LORD, and have mercy upon me: LORD, be thou my helper.

Thou hast turned me from my mourning into dancing: thou hast put off my sackcloth, and girded me with gladness.

To the end that my glory may sing praise to thee, and not be silent: O LORD my God, I will give thanks unto thee forever.

Psalm xxxii. *Beati, quorum.*

Blessed is he whose transgression is forgiven: whose sin is covered.

Blessed is the man unto whom the LORD imputeth not iniquity: and in whose spirit there is no guile.

When I kept silence: my bones waxed old through my roaring all the day long.

For day and night thy hand was heavy upon me: my moisture is turned into the drought of summer.

I acknowledged my sin unto thee: and mine iniquity have I not hid.

I said, I will confess my transgressions unto the LORD: and thou forgavest the iniquity of my sin.

For this shall every one that is godly pray unto thee in a time when thou mayest be found: surely in the floods of great waters they shall not come nigh unto him.

Thou art my hiding place; thou shalt preserve me from trouble: thou shalt compass me about with songs of deliverance.

I will instruct thee and teach thee in the way which thou shalt go: I will guide thee with mine eye.

Be ye not as the horse, or as the mule, which have no understanding: whose mouth must be held in with bit and bridle, lest they come near unto thee.

Many sorrows shall be to the wicked: but he that trusteth in the LORD, mercy shall compass him about.

Be glad in the LORD, and rejoice, ye righteous: and shout for joy, all ye that are upright in heart.

Psalm xxxiii. *Exultate, justi.*

Rejoice in the LORD, O ye righteous: for praise is comely for the upright.

Praise the LORD with harp: sing unto him with the psaltery and an instrument of ten strings.

Sing unto him a new song: play skillfully with a [illegible] noise.

For the word of the LORD is right: and all his works are done in truth.

He loveth righteousness and judgment: the earth is full of the goodness of the LORD.

By the word of the LORD were the heavens made: and all the host of them by the breath of his mouth.

He gathereth the waters of the sea together as a heap: he layeth up the depth in storehouses.

Let all the earth fear the LORD: let all the inhabitants of the world stand in awe of him.

For he spake, and it was done: he commanded and it stood fast.

The LORD bringeth the counsel of the heathen to nought: he maketh the devices of the people of none effect.

The counsel of the LORD standeth for ever: the thoughts of his heart to all generations.

Blessed is the nation whose God is the LORD: and the people whom he hath chosen for his own inheritance.

The LORD looketh from heaven: he beholdeth all the sons of men.

From the place of his habitation he looketh: upon all the inhabitants of the earth.

He fashioneth their hearts alike: he considereth all their works.

There is no king saved by the multitude of a host: a mighty man is not delivered by much strength.

A horse is a vain thing for safety: neither shall he deliver any by his great strength.

Behold, the eye of the LORD is upon them that fear him: upon them that hope in his mercy.

To deliver their soul from death: and to keep them alive in famine.

Our soul waiteth for the LORD: he is our help and our shield.

For our heart shall rejoice in him: because we have trusted in his holy name.

Let thy mercy, O LORD, be upon us: according as we hope in thee.

Psalm xxxiv. *Benedicam Dominum.*

I will bless the LORD at all times: his praise shall continually be in my mouth.

My soul shall make her boast in the LORD; the humble shall hear thereof, and be glad.

O magnify the LORD with me: and let us exalt his name together.

I sought the LORD, and he heard me: and delivered me from all my fears.

They looked unto him, and were lightened: and their faces were not ashamed.

This poor man cried, and the LORD heard him: and saved him out of all his troubles.

The angel of the LORD encampeth round about them that fear him: and delivereth them.

O taste and see that the LORD is good: blessed is the man that trusteth in him.

O fear the LORD, ye his saints: for there is no want to them that fear him.

The young lions do lack, and suffer hunger: but they that seek the LORD shall not want any good thing.

Come, ye children, hearken unto me: I will teach you the fear of the LORD.

What man is he that desireth life: and loveth many days, that he may see good?

Keep thy tongue from evil: and thy lips from speaking guile.

Depart from evil, and do good: seek peace, and pursue it.

The eyes of the LORD are upon the righteous: and his ears are open unto their cry.

The face of the LORD is against them that do evil: to cut off the remembrance of them from the earth.

The righteous cry, and the LORD heareth: and delivereth them out of all their troubles.

The LORD is nigh unto them that are of broken heart: and saveth such as be of a contrite spirit.

Many are the afflictions of the righteous: but the LORD delivereth him out of them all.

He keepeth all his bones: not one of them is broken.

Evil shall slay the wicked: and they that hate the righteous shall be desolate.

The LORD redeemeth the soul of his servants: and none of them that trust in him shall be desolate.

Psalm xxxvi. *Dixit injustus.*

The transgression of the wicked saith within my heart: that there is no fear of God before his eyes.

For he flattereth himself in his own eyes: until his iniquity be found to be hateful.

The words of his mouth are iniquity and deceit: he hath left off to be wise, and to do good.

He deviseth mischief upon his bed: he setteth himself in a way that is not good; he abhorreth not evil.

Thy mercy, O LORD, is in the heavens: and thy faithfulness reacheth unto the clouds.

Thy righteousness is like the great mountains; thy judgments are a great deep: O LORD, thou preservest man and beast.

How excellent is thy lovingkindness, O God: therefore the children of men put their trust under the shadow of thy wings.

They shall be abundantly satisfied with the fatness of thy house: and thou shalt make them drink of the river of thy pleasures.

For with thee is the fountain of life: in thy light shall we see light.

O continue thy lovingkindness unto them that know thee: and thy righteousness to the upright in heart.

Let not the foot of pride come against me: and let not the hand of the wicked remove me.

There are the workers of iniquity fallen: they are cast down, and shall not be able to rise.

Psalm xl. *Expectans expectavi.*

I waited patiently for the LORD: and he inclined unto me and heard my voice.

He brought me up also out of a horrible pit, out of the miry clay: and set my feet upon a rock; and established my goings.

And he hath put a new song in my mouth, even praise unto our God: many shall see it, and fear, and shall trust in the LORD.

Blessed is the man that maketh the LORD his trust: and respecteth not the proud, nor such as turn aside to lies.

Many, O LORD my God, are thy wonderful works which thou hast done, and thy thoughts which are to us-ward: they cannot be reckoned up in order unto thee.

If I would declare and speak of them: they are more than can be numbered.

Sacrifice and offering thou didst not desire; mine ears hast thou opened: burnt offering and sin offering hast thou not required.

Then said I, Lo, I come: in the volume of the book it is written of me.

I delight to do thy will, O my God; yea, thy law is within my heart.

I have preached righteousness in the great congregation: lo I have not refrained my lips, O LORD, thou knowest.

I have not hid thy righteousness within my heart: I have declared thy faithfulness and thy salvation.

I have not concealed thy lovingkindness and thy truth: from the great congregation.

Withhold not thou thy tender mercies from me, O LORD: let thy lovingkindness and thy truth continually preserve me.

For innumerable evils have compassed me about; mine iniquities have taken hold upon me, so that I am not able to look up: they are more than the hairs of mine head; therefore my heart faileth me.

Be pleased, O LORD, to deliver me: O LORD, make haste to help me.

Let them be ashamed and confounded together that seek after my soul to destroy it: let them be driven backward and put to shame that wish me evil.

Let them be desolate for a reward of their shame: that say unto me, Aha, aha.

Let all those that seek thee rejoice and be glad in thee: let such as love thy salvation say continually, The LORD be magnified.

But I am poor and needy: yet the LORD thinketh upon me.

Thou art my helper and my deliverer: make no tarrying, O my God.

Psalm xliii. *Judica me, Deus.*

Judge me, O God, and plead my cause against an ungodly nation: O deliver me from the deceitful and unjust man.

For thou art the God of my strength, why dost thou cast me off: why go mourning because of the oppression of the enemy?

O send out thy light and thy truth, let them lead me: let them bring me unto thy holy hill, and to thy tabernacles.

Then will I go unto the altar of God, unto God my exceeding joy: yea, upon the harp will I praise thee, O God my God.

Why art thou cast down, O my soul? and why art thou disquieted within me? hope in God: for I shall yet praise him, who is the health of my countenance, and my God.

Psalm xlv. *Eructavit cor meum.*

My heart is inditing a good matter: I speak of the things which I have made touching the King.

My tongue is the pen: of a ready writer.

Thou art fairer than the children of men: grace is poured into thy lips; therefore God hath blessed thee forever.

Gird thy sword upon thy thigh, O most Mighty: with thy glory and thy majesty.

And in thy majesty ride prosperously, because of truth and meekness and righteousness: and thy right hand shall teach thee terrible things.

Thine arrows are sharp in the heart of the King's enemies: whereby the people fall under thee.

Thy throne, O God, is for ever and ever: the sceptre of thy kingdom is a right sceptre.

Thou lovest righteousness, and hatest wickedness: therefore God, thy God, hath anointed thee with the oil of gladness above thy fellows.

All thy garments smell of myrrh, and aloes, and cassia: out of the ivory palaces, whereby they have made thee glad.

King's daughters were among thy honourable women: upon thy right hand did stand the queen in gold of Ophir.

Hearken, O daughter, and consider, and incline thine ear: forget also thine own people, and thy father's house.

So shall the King greatly desire thy beauty: for he is thy Lord, and worship thou him.

And the daughter of Tyre shall be there with a gift: even the rich among the people shall entreat thy favor.

The King's daughter is all glorious within: her clothing is of wrought gold.

She shall be brought unto the king in raiment of needlework: the virgins her companions that follow her shall be brought unto thee.

With gladness and rejoicing shall they be brought: they shall enter into the King's palace.

Instead of thy fathers shall be thy children: whom thou mayest make princes in all the earth.

I will make thy name to be remembered in all generations: therefore shall the people praise thee for ever and ever.

Psalm xlvi. *Deus noster refugium.*

God is our refuge and strength: a very present help in trouble.

Therefore will not we fear, though the earth be removed: and though the mountains be carried into the midst of the sea;

Though the waters thereof roar and be troubled: though the mountains shake with the swelling thereof.

There is a river, the streams whereof shall make glad the city of God: the holy place of the tabernacles of the Most High.

God is in the midst of her; she shall not be moved: God shall help her, and that right early.

The heathen raged, the kingdoms were moved: he uttered his voice, the earth melted.

The LORD of hosts is with us: the God of Jacob is our refuge.

Come, behold the works of the LORD: what desolations he hath made in the earth.

He maketh wars to cease unto the end of the earth: he breaketh the bow, and cutteth the spear in sunder; he burneth the chariot in the fire.

Be still, and know that I am God: I will be exalted among the heathen, I will be exalted in the earth.

The LORD of hosts is with us: the God of Jacob is our refuge.

Psalm xlvii. *Omnes gentes, plaudite.*

O clap your hands all ye people: shout unto God with the voice of triumph.

For the LORD most high is terrible: he is a great King over all the earth.

He shall subdue the people under us: and the nations under our feet.

He shall choose our inheritance for us: the excellency of Jacob whom he loved.

God is gone up with a shout: the LORD with the sound of a trumpet.

Sing praises to God, sing praises: sing praises unto our King, sing praises.

For God is the King of all the earth: sing ye praises with understanding.

God reigneth over the heathen: God sitteth upon the throne of his holiness.

The princes of the people are gathered together, even the people of the God of Abraham: for the shields of the earth belong unto God; he is greatly exalted.

Psalm xlviii. *Magnus Dominus.*

Great is the Lord, and greatly to be praised: in the city of our God, in the mountain of his holiness.

Beautiful for situation, the joy of the whole earth, is mount Zion: on the sides of the north, the city of the great King.

God is known in her palaces: for a refuge.

For, lo, the kings were assembled: they passed by together.

They saw it, and so they marvelled: they were troubled, and hastened away.

Fear took hold upon them there, and pain: as of a woman in travail.

Thou breakest the ships of Tarshish: with an east wind.

As we have heard, so have we seen in the city of the Lord of hosts, in the city of our God: God will establish it forever.

We have thought of thy lovingkindness, O God: in the midst of thy temple.

According to thy name, O God, so is thy praise unto the ends of the earth: thy right hand is full of righteousness.

Let mount Zion rejoice, let the daughters of Judah be glad: because of thy judgments.

Walk about Zion, and go round about her: tell the towers thereof.

Mark ye well her bulwarks, consider her palaces: that ye may tell it to the generation following.

For this God is our God for ever and eve[illegible] will be our guide even unto death.

Psalm lvi. *Miserere mei, Deus.*

Be merciful unto me, O God; for man would swallow me up: he fighting daily oppresseth me.

Mine enemies would daily swallow me up: for they be many that fight against me, O thou Most High.

What time I am afraid: I will trust in thee.

In God I will praise his word: in God I have put my trust; I will not fear what flesh can do unto me.

Every day they wrest my words: all their thoughts are against me for evil.

They gather themselves together, they hide themselves: they mark my steps, when they wait for my soul.

Shall they escape by iniquity: in thine anger cast down the people, O God.

Thou tellest my wanderings; put thou my tears into thy bottle: are they not in thy book?

When I cry unto thee, then shall mine enemies turn back: this I know; for God is for me.

In God will I praise his word: in the Lord will I praise his word.

In God have I put my trust: I will not be afraid what man can do unto me.

Thy vows are upon me, O God: I will render praises unto thee.

For thou hast delivered my soul from death, wilt thou not deliver my feet from falling: that I may walk before God in the light of the living?

Psalm lxv. *Te decet hymnus.*

Praise waiteth for thee, O God, in Zion: and unto thee shall the vow be performed.

O thou that hearest prayer: unto thee shall all flesh come.

Iniquities prevail against me: as for our transgressions, thou shalt purge them away.

Blessed is the man whom thou choosest, and causest to approach unto thee, that he may dwell in thy courts: we shall be satisfied with the goodness of thy house, even of thy holy temple.

By terrible things in righteousness wilt thou answer us, O God of our salvation: who art the confidence of all the ends of the earth, and of them that are afar off upon the sea.

Which by his strength setteth fast the mountains: being girded with power.

Which stilleth the noise of the seas: the noise of their waves, and the tumult of the people.

They also that dwell in the uttermost parts are afraid at thy tokens: thou makest the outgoings of the morning and evening to rejoice.

Thou visitest the earth, and waterest it: thou greatly enrichest it with the river of God, which is full of water.

Thou preparest them corn: when thou hast so provided for it.

Thou waterest the ridges thereof abundantly; thou settlest the furrows thereof: thou makest it soft with showers; thou blessest the springing thereof.

Thou crownest the year with thy goodness: and thy paths drop fatness.

They drop upon the pastures of the wilderness: and the little hills rejoice on every side.

The pastures are clothed with flocks; the valleys also are covered over with corn: they shout for joy, they also sing.

Psalm lxvi. *Jubilate Deo.*

Make a joyful noise unto God, all ye lands: sing forth the honor of his name; make his praise glorious.

Say unto God, how terrible art thou in thy works: through the greatness of thy power shall thine enemies submit themselves unto thee.

All the earth shall worship thee, and shall sing unto thee: they shall sing to thy name.

Come and see the works of God: he is terrible in his doing toward the children of men.

He turned the sea into dry land: they went through the flood on foot; there did we rejoice in him.

He ruleth by his power for ever; his eyes behold the nations: let not the rebellious exalt themselves.

O bless our God, ye people: and make the voice of his praise to be heard.

Which holdeth our soul in life: and suffereth not our feet to be moved.

For thou, O God, hast proved us: thou hast tried us, as silver is tried.

Thou broughtest us into the net: thou laidst afflictions upon our loins.

Thou hast caused men to ride over our heads: we went through fire and through water; but thou broughtest us out into a wealthy place.

I will go into thy house with burnt offerings: I will pay thee my vows, which my lips have uttered, and my mouth hath spoken, when I was in trouble.

I will offer unto thee burnt sacrifices of fatlings, with the incense of rams: I will offer bullocks with goats.

Come and hear, all ye that fear God: and I will declare what he hath done for my soul.

I cried unto him with my mouth: and he was extolled with my tongue.

If I regard iniquity in my heart: the LORD will not hear me.

But verily God hath heard me: he hath attended to the voice of my prayer.

Blessed be God which hath not turned away my prayer: nor his mercy from me.

Psalm lxvii. *Deus misereatur.*

God be merciful unto us, and bless us: and cause his face to shine upon us.

That thy way may be known upon earth: thy saving health among all nations.

Let the people praise thee, O God: let all the people praise thee.

O let the nations be glad and sing for joy: for thou shalt judge the people righteously, and govern the nations upon earth.

Let the people praise thee, O God: let all the people praise thee.

Then shall the earth yield her increase: and God, even our own God, shall bless us.

God shall bless us: and all the ends of the earth shall fear him.

Psalm lxviii. *Exurgat Deus.*

Let God arise, let his enemies be scattered: let them also that hate him flee before him.

As smoke is driven away, so drive them away: as wax melteth before the fire, so let the wicked perish at the presence of God.

But let the righteous be glad; let them rejoice before God: yea, let them exceedingly rejoice.

Sing unto God, sing praises unto his name: extol him that rideth upon the heavens by his name JAH, and rejoice before him.

A father of the fatherless, and a judge of the widows: is God in his holy habitation.

God setteth the solitary in families; he bringeth out those which are bound with chains: but the rebellious dwell in a dry land.

O God, when thou wentest forth before thy people: when thou didst march through the wilderness.

The earth shook, the heavens also dropped at the presence of God: even Sinai itself was moved at the presence of God, the God of Israel.

Thou, O God, didst send a plentiful rain: whereby thou didst confirm thine inheritance, when it was weary.

Thy congregation has dwelt therein: thou, O God, hast prepared of thy goodness for the poor.

The LORD gave the word: great was the company of those that published it.

Kings of armies did flee apace: and she that tarried at home divided the spoil.

Though ye have lain among the pots, yet shall ye be as the wings of a dove: covered with silver, and her feathers with yellow gold.

When the Almighty scattered kings in it: it was white as snow in Salmon.

The hill of God is as the hill of Bashan: a high hill as the hill of Bashan.

Why leap ye, ye high hills? this is the hill which God desireth to dwell in: yea, the LORD will dwell in it forever.

The chariots of God are twenty thousand, even thousands of angels: the LORD is among them, as in Sinai, in the holy place.

Thou hast ascended on high, thou hast led captivity captive, thou hast received gifts for men: yea, for the rebellious also, that the LORD God might dwell among them.

Blessed be the LORD, who daily loadeth us with benefits: even the God of our salvation.

He that is our God is the God of salvation: and unto God the LORD belong the issues from death.

But God shall wound the head of his enemies: and the hairy scalp of such a one as goeth on still in his trespasses.

The LORD said, I will bring again from Bashan: I will bring my people again from the depths of the sea.

That thy foot may be dipped in the blood of thine enemies: and the tongue of thy dogs in the same.

They have seen thy goings, O God: even the goings of my God, my King, in the sanctuary.

The singers went before, the players on instruments followed after: among them were the damsels playing with timbrels.

Bless ye God in the congregations: even the LORD, from the fountain of Israel.

There is little Benjamin with their ruler, the princes of Judah and their council: the princes of Zebulun, and the princes of Naphtali.

Thy God hath commanded thy strength: strengthen, O God, that which thou hast wrought for us.

Because of thy temple at Jerusalem: shall kings bring presents unto thee.

Rebuke the company of spearmen, the multitude of the bulls, with the calves of the people, till every one submit himself with pieces of silver: scatter thou the people that delight in war.

Princes shall come out of Egypt: Ethiopia shall soon stretch out her hands unto God.

Sing unto God, ye kingdoms of the earth: O sing praises unto the Lord;

To him that rideth upon the heavens of heavens, which were of old: lo, he doth send out his voice, and that a mighty voice.

Ascribe ye strength unto God, his excellency is over Israel: and his strength is in the clouds.

O God, thou art terrible out of the holy places: the God of Israel is he that giveth strength and power unto his people. Blessed be God.

Psalm lxxii. *Deus, judicium.*

Give the king thy judgments, O God: and thy righteousness unto the king's son.

He shall judge thy people with righteousness: and the poor with judgment.

The mountains shall bring peace to the people: and the little hills, by righteousness.

He shall judge the poor of the people, he shall save the children of the needy: and shall break in pieces the oppressor.

They shall fear thee as long as the sun and moon endure: throughout all generations.

He shall come down like rain upon the mown grass: as showers that water the earth.

In his days shall the righteous flourish: and abundance of peace so long as the moon endureth.

He shall have dominion also from sea to sea: and from the rivers unto the ends of the earth.

They that dwell in the wilderness shall bow before him: and his enemies shall lick the dust.

The kings of Tarshish and of the isles shall bring presents: the kings of Sheba and Seba shall offer gifts.

Yea, all kings shall fall down before him: all nations shall serve him.

For he shall deliver the needy when he crieth: the poor also, and him that hath no helper.

He shall spare the poor and needy; and shall save the souls of the needy.

He shall redeem their souls from deceit and violence: and precious shall their blood be in his sight.

And he shall live, and to him shall be given of the gold of Sheba: prayer also shall be made for him continually, and daily shall he be praised.

There shall be a handful of corn in the earth upon the top of the mountains: the fruit thereof shall shake like Lebanon; and they of the city shall flourish like grass of the earth.

His name shall endure forever; his name shall be continued as long as the sun: and men shall be blessed in him; all nations shall call him blessed.

Blessed be the LORD God, the God of Israel: who only doeth wondrous things.

And blessed be his glorious name forever: and let the whole earth be filled with his glory. Amen, and Amen.

Psalm lxxvii. *Voce mea ad Dominum.*

I cried unto God with my voice: even unto God with my voice, and he gave ear unto me.

In the day of my trouble I sought the Lord: my sore ran in the night, and ceased not; my soul refused to be comforted.

I remembered God, and was troubled: I complained, and my spirit was overwhelmed.

Thou holdest mine eyes waking: I am so troubled that I cannot speak.

I have considered the days of old: the years of ancient times.

I call to remembrance my song in the night: I commune with mine own heart, and my spirit made diligent search.

Will the Lord cast off forever: and will he be favorable no more?

Is his mercy clean gone for ever: doth his promise fail forevermore?

Hath God forgotten to be gracious: hath he in anger shut up his tender mercies?

And I said, This is my infirmity: but I will remember the years of the right hand of the most high.

I will remember the works of the Lord: surely I will remember thy wonders of old.

I will meditate also of all thy work: and talk of thy doings.

Thy way, O God, is in the sanctuary: who is so great a God as our God?

Thou art the God that dost wonders: thou hast declared thy strength among the people.

Thou hast with thine arm redeemed thy people: the sons of Jacob and Joseph.

The waters saw thee, O God, the waters saw thee; they were afraid: the depths were also troubled.

The clouds poured out water; the skies sent out a sound: thine arrows also went abroad.

The voice of thy thunder was in the heaven: the lightnings lightened the world; the earth trembled and shook.

Thy way is in the sea, and thy path in the great waters: and thy footsteps are not known.

Thou leddest thy people like a flock: by the hand of Moses and Aaron.

Psalm lxxxv. *Benedixisti, Domine.*

Lord, thou hast been favorable unto thy land: thou hast brought back the captivity of Jacob.

Thou hast forgiven the iniquity of thy people: thou hast covered all their sin.

Thou hast taken away all thy wrath: thou hast turned thyself from the fierceness of thine anger.

Turn us, O God of our salvation: and cause thine anger towards us to cease.

Wilt thou be angry with us forever: wilt thou draw out thine anger to all generations?

Wilt thou not revive us again: that thy people may rejoice in thee?

Shew us thy mercy, O Lord: and grant us thy salvation.

I will hear what God the Lord will speak: for he will speak peace unto his people, and to his saints; but let them not again turn to folly.

Surely his salvation is nigh them that fear him: that glory may dwell in our land.

Mercy and truth are met together: righteousness and peace have kissed each other.

Truth shall spring out of the earth: and righteousness shall look down from heaven.

Yea, the Lord shall give that which is good: and our land shall yield her increase.

Righteousness shall go before him: and shall set us in the way of his steps.

Psalm lxxxvi. *Inclina, Domine.*

Bow down thine ear, O LORD, hear me : for I am poor and needy.

Preserve my soul ; for I am holy : O thou my God, save thy servant that trusteth in thee.

Be merciful unto me, O Lord : for I cry unto thee daily.

Rejoice the soul of thy servant : for unto thee, O Lord, do I lift up my soul.

For thou, Lord, art good, and ready to forgive : and plenteous in mercy unto all them that call upon thee.

Give ear, O LORD, unto my prayer : and attend to the voice of my supplications.

In the day of my trouble will I call upon thee : for thou wilt answer me.

Among the gods there is none like unto thee, O Lord : neither are there any works like unto thy works.

All nations whom thou hast made shall come and worship before thee, O Lord : and shall glorify thy name.

For thou art great, and doest wondrous things : thou art God alone.

Teach me thy way, O LORD ; I will walk in thy truth : unite my heart to fear thy name.

I will praise thee, O Lord my God, with all my heart : and I will glorify thy name for evermore.

For great is thy mercy toward me : and thou hast delivered my soul from the lowest hell.

O God, the proud are risen against me : and the assemblies of violent men have sought after my soul, and have not set thee before them.

But thou, O Lord, art a God full of compassion, and gracious : long suffering and plenteous in mercy and truth.

O turn unto me and have mercy upon me : give thy strength unto thy servant, and save the son of thine handmaid.

Shew me a token for good ; that they which hate me may see it, and be ashamed : because thou, LORD, hast holpen me, and comforted me.

Psalm lxxxvii. *Fundamenta ejus.*

His foundation : is in the holy mountains.

The LORD loveth the gates of Zion : more than all the dwellings of Jacob.

Glorious things are spoken of thee : O city of God.

I will make mention of Rahab and Babylon : to them that know me.

Behold Philistia, and Tyre, with Ethiopia : this man was born there.

And of Zion it shall be said, this and that man was born in her : and the highest himself shall establish her.

The LORD shall count when he writeth up the people : that this man was born there.

As well the singers as the players on instruments shall be there : all my springs are in thee.

Psalm lxxxix. *Misericordias Domini.*

I will sing of the mercies of the LORD, for ever : with my mouth will I make known thy faithfulness to all generations.

For I have said, Mercy shall be built up forever : thy faithfulness shalt thou establish in the very heavens.

I have made a covenant with my chosen : I have sworn unto David my servant.

Thy seed will I establish forever : and build up thy throne to all generations.

And the heaven shall praise thy wonders, O LORD : thy faithfulness also in the congregation of the saints.

For who in the heaven can be compared unto the Lord: who among the sons of the mighty can be likened unto the Lord?

God is greatly to be feared in the assembly of the saints: and to be had in reverence of all them that are about him.

O Lord God of hosts, who is a strong Lord like unto thee: or to thy faithfulness round about thee?

Thou rulest the raging of the sea: when the waves thereof arise, thou stillest them.

Thou hast broken Rahab in pieces, as one that is slain: thou hast scattered thine enemies with thy strong arms.

The heavens are thine, the earth also is thine: as for the world and the fulness thereof, thou hast founded them.

The north and the south, thou hast created them: Tabor and Hermon shall rejoice in thy name.

Thou hast a mighty arm: strong is thy hand, and high is thy right hand.

Justice and judgment are the habitation of thy throne: mercy and truth shall go before thy face.

Blessed is the people that know the joyful sound: they shall walk, O Lord, i the light of thy countenance.

In thy name shall they rejoice all the day: and in thy righteousness shall the be exalted.

For thou art the glory of their strength: and in thy favor our horn shal be exalted.

For the Lord is our defence: and the Holy one of Israel is our King.

Then thou spakest in vision to thy Holy One, and saidst: I have laid help u one that is mighty; I have exalted one chosen out of the people.

I have found David my servant: with my holy oil have I anointed him.

With whom my hand shall be established: mine arm also shall strengthen h

The enemy shall not exact upon him: nor the son of wickedness afflict him.

And I will beat down his foes before his face: and plague them that hate him.

But my faithfulness and my mercy shall be with him: and in my name shall horn be exalted.

I will set his hand also in the sea: and his right hand in the rivers.

He shall cry unto me, Thou art my Father: my God, and the Rock of my salv tion.

Also I will make him my firstborn: higher than the kings of the earth.

My mercy will I keep for him evermore: and my covenant shall stand fast wi him.

His seed also will I make to endure forever: and his throne as the days heaven.

If his children forsake my law: and walk not in my judgments;

If they break my statutes, and keep not my commandments: then will I visit their transgression with the rod; and their iniquity with stripes.

Nevertheless my lovingkindness will I not utterly take from him: nor suffer my faithfulness to fail.

My covenant will I not break, nor alter the thing that is gone out of my lips: once have I sworn by my holiness, that I will not lie unto David.

His seed shall endure forever: and his throne as the sun before me.

It shall be established forever as the moon: and as a faithful witness in heaven.

But thou hast cast off and abhorred: thou hast been wroth with thine anointed.

Thou hast made void the covenant of thy servant: thou hast profaned his crown by casting it to the ground.

Thou hast broken down all his hedges: thou hast brought his strongholds to ruin.

All that pass by the way spoil him: he is a reproach to his neighbors.

Thou hast set up the right hand of his adversaries: thou hast made all his enemies to rejoice.

Thou hast also turned the edge of his sword: and hast not made him to stand in the battle.

Thou hast made his glory to cease: and cast his throne down to the ground.

The days of his youth hast thou shortened: thou hast covered him with shame.

How long, LORD? wilt thou hide thyself for ever: shall thy wrath burn like fire?

Remember how short my time is: wherefore hast thou made all men in vain?

What man is he that liveth, and shall not see death: shall he deliver his soul from the hand of the grave?

Lord, where are thy former lovingkindnesses: which thou swearest unto David in thy truth?

Remember, Lord, the reproach of thy servants: how I do bear in my bosom the reproach of all the mighty people;

Wherewith thine enemies have reproached, O LORD; wherewith they have reproached the footsteps of thine anointed: blessed be the LORD for evermore. Amen, and Amen.

Psalm xc. *Domine refugium.*

LORD, thou hast been our dwellingplace: in all generations.

Before the mountains were brought forth, or ever thou hast formed the earth and the world: even from everlasting to everlasting, thou art God.

Thou turnest man to destruction: and sayest, Return, ye children of men.

For a thousand years in thy sight are but as yesterday when it is past: and as a watch in the night.

Thou carriest them away as with a flood; they are as a sleep: in the morning they are like grass which groweth up.

In the morning it flourisheth, and groweth up: in the evening it is cut down, and withereth.

For we are consumed by thine anger: and by thy wrath are we troubled.

Thou hast set our iniquities before thee: our secret sins in the light of thy countenance.

For all our days are passed away in thy wrath: we spend our years as a tale that is told.

The days of our years are threescore years and ten; and if by reason of strength they be fourscore years: yet is their strength labor and sorrow; for it is soon cut off, and we fly away.

Who knoweth the power of thine anger: even according to thy fear, so is thy wrath.

So teach us to number our days: that we may apply our hearts unto wisdom.

Return, O LORD, how long: and let it repent thee concerning thy servants.

O satisfy us early with thy mercy: that we may rejoice and be glad in our days.

Make us glad according to the days wherein thou hast afflicted us: and the years wherein we have seen evil.

Let thy work appear unto thy servants: and thy glory unto their children.

And let the beauty of the LORD our God be upon us: and establish thou the work of our hands upon us; yea, the work of our hands establish thou it.

Psalm xci. *Qui habitat.*

He that dwelleth in the secret place of the Most High: shall abide under the shadow of the Almighty.

I will say of the LORD, He is my refuge and my fortress: my God; in him will I trust.

Surely he shall deliver thee from the snare of the fowler: and from the noisome pestilence.

He shall cover thee with his feathers, and under his wings shalt thou trust: his truth shall be thy shield and buckler.

Thou shalt not be afraid for the terror by night: nor for the arrow that flieth by day;

Nor for the pestilence that walketh in darkness: nor for the destruction that wasteth at noonday.

A thousand shall fall at thy side, and ten thousand at thy right hand: but it shall not come nigh thee.

Only with thine eyes shalt thou behold: and see the reward of the wicked.

Because thou hast made the LORD which is my refuge: even the Most High, thy habitation;

There shall no evil befall thee: neither shall any plague come nigh thy dwelling.

For he shall give his angels charge over thee: to keep thee in all thy ways.

They shall bear thee up in their hands: lest thou dash thy foot against a stone.

Thou shalt tread upon the lion and adder: the young lion and the dragon shalt thou trample under feet.

Because he hath set his love upon me, therefore will I deliver him: I will set him on high, because he hath known my name.

He shall call upon me, and I will answer him: I will be with him in trouble; I will deliver him, and honor him.

With long life will I satisfy him: and show him my salvation.

Psalm xcii. *Bonum est confiteri.*

It is a good thing to give thanks unto the LORD: and to sing praises unto thy name, O Most High;

To show forth thy lovingkindness in the morning: and thy faithfulness every night.

Upon an instrument of ten strings, and upon the psaltery: upon the harp with a solemn sound.

For thou, LORD, hast made me glad through thy work: I will triumph in the works of thy hands.

O LORD, how great are thy works: and thy thoughts are very deep.

A brutish man knoweth not: neither doth a fool understand this.

When the wicked spring as the grass, and when all the workers of iniquity do flourish: it is that they shall be destroyed for ever; but thou, LORD, art most high for evermore.

For lo, thine enemies, O LORD, for, lo, thine enemies shall perish: all the workers of iniquity shall be scattered.

But my horn shalt thou exalt like the horn of a unicorn: I shall be anointed with fresh oil.

Mine eye also shall see my desire on mine enemies: and mine ears shall hear my desire of the wicked that rise up against me.

The righteous shall flourish like the palm tree: he shall grow like a cedar in Lebanon.

Those that be planted in the house of the LORD: shall flourish in the courts of our God.

They shall still bring forth fruit in old age: they shall be fat and flourishing;

To show that the LORD is upright; he is my rock: and there is no unrighteousness in him.

Psalm xciii. *Dominus regnavit.*

The LORD reigneth, he is clothed with majesty: the LORD is clothed with strength, wherewith he hath girded himself.

The world also is established: that it cannot be moved.

Thy throne is established of old: thou art from everlasting.

The floods have lifted up, O LORD, the floods have lifted up their voice: the floods lift up their waves.

The LORD on high is mightier than the noise of many waters: yea, than the mighty waves of the sea.

Thy testimonies are very sure: holiness becometh thine house, O LORD, forever.

Psalm xcv. *Venite exultemus.*

O come, let us sing unto the LORD: let us make a joyful noise unto the Rock of our salvation.

Let us come before his presence with thanksgiving: and make a joyful noise unto him with Psalms.

For the LORD is a great God: and a great King above all gods.

In his hand are the deep places of the earth: the strength of the hills is his also.

The sea is his, and he made it: and his hands formed the dry land.

O come, let us worship and bow down: let us kneel before the LORD our maker.

For he is our God: and we are the people of his pasture, and the sheep of his hand.

To-day if ye will hear his voice, harden not your heart: as in the provocation, and as in the day of temptation in the wilderness:

When your fathers tempted me: proved me, and saw my work.

Forty years long was I grieved with this generation, and said: it is a people [illegible]hat do err in their heart, and they have not known my ways;

Unto whom I sware in my wrath: that they should not enter into my re[illegible].

Psalm xcvii. *Dominus regnavit.*

The Lord reigneth, let the earth rejoice: let multitude of [illegible] glad thereof.

Clouds and darkness are round about him: righteousnes[illegible] judgment are the habitation of his throne.

A fire goeth before him: and burneth up his enemie[illegible]nd about.

His lightnings enlightened the world: the earth [illegible]nd trembled.

The hills melted like wax at the presence [illegible] LORD: at the presence of the Lord of the whole earth.

The heavens declare his righteousness: and [illegible] the people see his glory.

Confounded be all they that serve grave[illegible]mages, that boast themselves of idols: worship him all ye gods.

Zion heard, and was glad: and the daughters of Judah rejoiced because of thy judgments, O LORD.

For thou, LORD, art high above all the earth: thou are exalted far above all gods.

Ye that love the LORD hate evil: he preserveth the souls of his saints; he delivereth them out of the hand of the wicked.

Light is sown for the righteous: and gladness for the upright in heart.

Rejoice in the LORD, ye righteous: and give thanks at the remembrance of his holiness.

Psalm xcviii. *Cantate Domino.*

O sing unto the LORD a new song: for he hath done marvellous things.

His right hand, and his holy arm: hath gotten him the victory.

The LORD hath made known his salvation: his righteousness hath he openly shewed in the sight of the heathen.

He hath remembered his mercy and his truth toward the house of Israel: all the ends of the earth have seen the salvation of our God.

Make a joyful noise unto the LORD, all the earth: make a loud noise, and rejoice, and sing praise.

Sing unto the LORD with the harp: with the harp, and the voice of a Psalm.

With trumpets and sound of cornet: make a joyful noise before the LORD, the King.

Let the sea roar, and the fulness thereof: the world, and they that dwell therein.

Let the floods clap their hands, let the hills be joyful together before the LORD: for he cometh to judge the earth.

With righteousness shall he judge the world: and the people with equity.

Psalm c. *Jubilate Deo.*

Make a joyful noise unto the LORD, all ye lands: serve the LORD with gladness, come before his presence with singing.

Know ye that the LORD he is God: it is he that hath made us, and not we ourselves; we are his people, and the sheep of his pasture.

Enter into his gate with thanksgiving, and into his courts with praise: be thankful unto him, and bless his name.

For the LORD is good; his mercy is everlasting: and his truth endureth to all generations.

Psalm ciii. *Benedic, anima mea.*

Bless the LORD, O my soul: and all that is within me, bless his holy name.

Bless the LORD O my soul: and forget not all his benefits;

Who forgiveth all thine iniquities: who healeth all thy diseases;

Who redeemeth thy life from destruction: who crowneth thee with lovingkindness and tender mercies;

Who satisfieth thy mouth with good things: so that thy youth is renewed like the eagle's.

The LORD executeth righteousness and judgment: for all that are oppressed.

He made known his ways unto Moses: his acts unto the children of Israel.

The LORD is merciful and gracious: slow to anger, and plenteous in mercy.

He will not always chide: neither will he keep his anger forever.

He hath not dealt with us after our sins: nor rewarded us according to our iniquities.

For as the heaven is high above the earth: so great is his mercy toward them that fear him.

As far as the east is from the west: so far hath he removed our transgressions from us.

Like as a father pitieth his children: so the Lord pitieth them that fear him.

For he knoweth our frame: he remembereth that we are dust.

As for man, his days are as grass: as a flower of the field, so he flourisheth.

For the wind passeth over it, and it is gone: and the place thereof shall know it no more.

But the mercy of the Lord is from everlasting to everlasting upon them that fear him: and his righteousness unto children's children.

To such as keep his covenant: and to those that remember his commandments to do them.

The LORD hath prepared his throne in the heavens: and his kingdom ruleth over all.

Bless the LORD, ye his angels, that excel in strength: that do his commandments, hearkening unto the voice of his word.

Bless ye the LORD, all ye his hosts: ye ministers of his, that do his pleasure.

Bless the LORD, all his works, in all places of his dominion: bless the LORD, O my soul.

Psalm civ. *Benedic anima mea.*

Bless the Lord, O my soul: O Lord my God, thou art very great; thou art clothed with honour and majesty;

Who coverest thyself with light as with a garment: who stretchest out the heavens like a curtain;

Who layeth the beams of his chambers in the waters: who maketh the clouds his chariot; who walketh upon the wings of the wind:

Who maketh his angels spirits: his ministers a flaming fire;

Who laid the foundation of the earth: that it should not be removed forever.

Thou coveredst it with the deep as with a garment: the waters stood above the mountains.

At thy rebuke they fled: at the voice of thy thunder they hastened away.

They go up by the mountains; they go down by the valleys; unto the place which thou hast founded for them.

Thou hast set a bound that they may not pass over: that they turn not again to cover the earth.

He sendeth the springs into the valleys: which run among the hills.

They give drink to every beast of the field: the wild asses quench their thirst.

By them shall the fowls of the heaven have their habitation: which sing among the branches.

He watereth the hills from his chambers: the earth is satisfied with the fruit of thy works.

He causeth the grass to grow for the cattle: and herb for the service of man;

That he may bring forth food out of the earth, and wine that maketh glad the heart of man: and oil to make his face to shine, and bread which strengtheneth man's heart.

The trees of the Lord are full of sap: the cedars of Lebanon, which he hath planted;

Where the birds make their nests: as for the stork, the fir trees are her house.

The high hills are a refuge for the wild goats: and the rocks for the conies.

He appointed the moon for seasons: the sun knoweth his going down.

Thou makest darkness, and it is night: wherein all the beasts of the forests do creep forth.

The young lions roar after their prey: and seek their meat from God.

The sun ariseth, they gather themselves together: and lay them down in their dens.

Man goeth forth unto his work and to his labour: until the evening.

O Lord, how manifold are thy works: in wisdom hast thou made them all; the earth is full of thy riches.

So is this great and wide sea: wherein are things creeping innumerable, both small and great beasts.

There go the ships; there is that leviathan: whom thou hast made to play therein.

These wait all upon thee: that thou mayest give them their meat in due season.

That thou givest them they gather: thou openest thine hand, they are filled with good.

Thou hidest thy face, they are troubled: thou takest away their breath, they die, and return to their dust.

Thou sendest forth thy spirit, they are created: and thou renewest the face of the earth.

The glory of the Lord shall endure forever: the Lord shall rejoice in his works.

He looketh on the earth, and it trembleth: he toucheth the hills, and they smoke.

I will sing unto the LORD as long as I live: I will sing praise to my God while I have my being.

My meditation of him shall be sweet: I will be glad in the LORD.

Let the sinners be consumed out of the earth, and let the wicked be no more: Bless thou the LORD, O my soul. Praise ye the LORD.

Psalm cx. *Dixit Dominus.*

The LORD said unto my Lord: Sit thou at my right hand, until I make thine enemies thy footstool.

The LORD shall send the rod of thy strength out of Zion: rule thou in the midst of thine enemies.

Thy people shall be willing in the day of thy power, in the beauties of holiness from the womb of the morning: thou hast the dew of thy youth.

The LORD hath sworn, and will not repent: Thou art a priest for ever after the order of Melchizedek.

The Lord at thy right hand: shall strike through kings in the day of his wrath.

He shall judge among the heathen, he shall fill the places with the dead bodies: he shall wound the heads over many countries.

He shall drink of the brook in the way: therefore shall he lift up the head.

Psalm cxi. *Confitebor tibi.*

Praise ye the LORD. I will praise the LORD with my whole heart: in the assembly of the upright, and in the congregation.

The works of the LORD are great: sought out of all them that have pleasure therein.

His work is honourable and glorious: and his righteousness endureth forever.

He hath made his wonderful works to be remembered: the LORD is gracious and full of compassion.

He hath given meat unto them that fear him: he will ever be mindful of his covenant.

He hath shewed his people the power of his works: that he may give them the heritage of the heathen.

The works of his hands are verity and judgment: all his commandments are sure.

They stand fast for ever and ever: and are done in truth and uprightness.

He sent redemption unto his people: he hath commanded his covenant for ever; holy and reverend is his name.

The fear of the LORD is the beginning of wisdom: a good understanding have all they that do his commandments; his praise endureth forever.

Psalm cxiii. *Laudate, pueri.*

Praise ye the LORD. Praise, O ye servants of the LORD: praise the name of the LORD.

Blessed be the name of the LORD: from this time forth and for evermore.

From the rising of the sun unto the going down of the same: the LORD's name is to be praised.

The LORD is high above all nations: and his glory above the heavens.

Who is like unto the LORD our God, who dwelleth on high: who humbleth himself to behold the things that are in heaven, and in the earth!

He raiseth up the poor out of the dust: and lifteth the needy out of the dunghill;

That he may set him with princes: even with the princes of his people.

He maketh the barren woman to keep house: and to be a joyful mother of children. Praise ye the LORD.

Psalm cxv. *Non nobis Domine.*

Not unto us, O LORD, not unto us, but unto thy name give glory: for thy mercy, and for thy truth's sake.

Wherefore should the heathen say: Where is now their God?

But our God is in the heavens: he hath done whatsoever he hath pleased.

Their idols are silver and gold: the work of men's hands.

They have mouths but they speak not: eyes have they but they see not;

They have ears, but they hear not: noses have they, but they smell not;

They have hands, but they handle not; feet have they, but they walk not: neither speak they through their throat.

They that make them are like unto them: so is every one that trusteth in them.

O Israel, trust thou in the LORD: he is their help and their shield.

O house of Aaron, trust in the LORD: he is their help and their shield.

Ye that fear the LORD, trust in the LORD: he is their help and their shield.

The LORD hath been mindful of us; he will bless us: he will bless the house of Israel; he will bless the house of Aaron.

He will bless them that fear the LORD: both small and great.

The LORD shall increase you more and more: you and your children.

Ye are blessed of the LORD: which made heaven and earth.

The heaven, even the heavens, are the LORD'S: but the earth hath he given to the children of men.

The dead praise not the LORD: neither any that go down into silence.

But we will bless the LORD: from this time forth and forevermore. Praise the LORD.

Psalm cxvi. *Dilexi quoniam.*

I love the LORD: because he hath heard my voice and my supplications.

Because he hath inclined his ear unto me: therefore will I call upon him as long as I live.

The sorrows of death compassed me, and the pains of hell gat hold upon me: I found trouble and sorrow.

Then called I upon the name of the LORD: O LORD, I beseech thee, deliver my soul.

Gracious is the LORD, and righteous: yea, our God is merciful.

The LORD preserveth the simple: I was brought low, and he helped me.

Return unto thy rest, O my soul: for the LORD hath dealt bountifully with thee.

For thou hast delivered my soul from death: mine eyes from tears, and my feet from falling.

I will walk before the LORD: in the land of the living.

I believed, therefore have I spoken; I was greatly afflicted: I said in my haste, All men are liars.

What shall I render unto the LORD: for all his benefits toward me?

I will take the cup of salvation: and call upon the name of the LORD.

I will pay my vows unto the LORD now: in the presence of all his people.

Precious in the sight of the LORD: is the death of his saints.

O LORD, truly I am thy servant: I am thy servant, and the son of thine handmaid; thou hast loosed my bonds.

I will offer to thee the sacrifice of thanksgiving: and will call upon the name of the LORD.

I will pay my vows unto the LORD now, in the presence of all his people: in the courts of the LORD'S house, in the midst of thee, O Jerusalem. Praise ye the LORD.

So shall I have wherewith to answer him that reproacheth me: for I trust in thy word.

And take not the word of truth utterly out of my mouth: for I have hoped in thy judgments.

So shall I keep thy law continually: for ever and ever.

And I will walk at liberty: for I seek thy precepts.

I will speak of thy testimonies also before kings: and will not be ashamed.

And I will delight myself in thy commandments: which I have loved.

My hands also will I lift up unto thy commandments, which I have loved: and I will meditate in thy statutes.

VII. *Memor esto verbi tui.*

Remember the word unto thy servant: upon which thou hast caused me to hope.

This is my comfort in my affliction: for thy word hath quickened me.

The proud have had me greatly in derision: yet have I not declined from thy law.

I remembered thy judments of old, O LORD: and have comforted myself.

Horror hath taken hold upon me: because of the wicked that forsake thy law.

Thy statutes have been my songs: in the house of my pilgrimage.

I have remembered thy name, O LORD, in the night: and have kept thy law.

This I had: because I kept thy precepts.

VIII. *Portio mea Domine.*

Thou art my portion, O LORD: I have said that I would keep thy words.

I entreated thy favor with my whole heart: be merciful unto me according to thy word.

I thought on my ways: and turned my feet unto thy testimonies.

I made haste and delayed not: to keep thy commandments.

The bands of the wicked have robbed me: but I have not forgotten thy law.

At midnight I will rise to give thanks unto thee: because of thy righteous judgments.

I am a companion of all them that fear thee: and of them that keep thy precepts.

The earth, O LORD, is full of thy mercy: teach me thy statutes.

IX. *Bonitatem fecisti.*

Thou hast dealt well with thy servant: O LORD, according unto thy word.

Teach me good judgment and knowledge: for I have believed thy commandments.

Before I was afflicted I went astray: but now have I kept thy word.

Thou art good, and doest good: teach me thy statutes.

The proud have forged a lie against me: but I will keep thy precepts with my whole heart.

Their heart is as fat as grease: but I delight in thy law.

It is good for me that I have been afflicted: that I might learn thy statutes.

The law of thy mouth is better unto me: than thousands of gold and silver.

X. *Manus tuae fecerunt me.*

Thy hands have made me and fashioned me: give me understanding, that I may learn thy commandments.

They that fear thee will be glad when they see me: because I have hoped in the word.

I know, O LORD, that thy judgments are right: and that thou in faithfulness hast afflicted me.

Let, I pray thee, thy merciful kindness be for my comfort: according to thy word unto thy servant.

Let thy tender mercies come unto me, that I may live: for thy law is my delight.

Let the proud be ashamed; for they dealt perversely with me without a cause: but I will meditate in thy precepts.

Let those that fear thee turn unto me: and those that have known thy testimonies.

Let my heart be sound in thy statutes: that I be not ashamed.

XI. *Deficit anima mea.*

My soul fainteth for thy salvation: but I hope in thy word.

Mine eyes fail for thy word: saying, When wilt thou comfort me?

For I am become like a bottle in the smoke: yet do I not forget thy statutes.

How many are the days of thy servant: when wilt thou execute judgment on them that persecute me?

The proud have digged pits for me: which are not after thy law.

All thy commandments are faithful: they persecute me wrongfully; help thou me.

They had almost consumed me upon earth: but I forsook not thy precepts.

Quicken me after thy l[illegible]gkindness: so shall I keep the testimony of thy mouth.

XII. *In aeternum Domine.*

For ever, O [illegible] thy word is settled in heaven.

Thy fai[illegible]ss is unto all generations: thou hast established the earth, and it abideth.

T[illegible]tinue this day according to thine ordinances: for all are thy servants.

Un[illegible]s thy law had been my delight: I should then have perished in mine afflic[illegible].

[illegible] will never forget thy precepts: for with them thou hast quickened me.

I am thine, save me: for I have sought thy precepts.

The wicked have waited for me to destroy me: but I will consider thy testimonies.

I have seen an end of all perfection: but thy commandment is exceeding broad.

XIII. *Quomodo dilexi.*

O how love I thy law: it is my meditation all the day.

Thou through thy commandments hast made me wiser than mine enemies: for they are ever with me.

I have more understanding than all my teachers: for thy testimonies are my meditation.

I understand more than the ancients: because I keep thy precepts.

I have refrained my feet from every evil way: that I might keep thy word.

I have not departed from thy judgments: for thou hast taught me.

How sweet are thy words unto my taste: yea, sweeter than honey to my mouth.

Through thy precepts I get understanding: therefore I hate every false way.

XIV. *Lucerna pedibus meis.*

Thy word is a lamp unto my feet: and a light unto my path.

I have sworn and I will perform it: that I will keep thy righteous judgments.

I am afflicted very much: quicken me, O Lord, according unto thy word.

Accept, I beseech thee, the freewill offerings of my mouth, O Lord: and teach me thy judgments.

My soul is continually in my hand: yet do I not forget thy law.

The wicked have laid a snare for me: yet I erred not from thy precepts.

Thy testimonies have I taken as a heritage for ever: for they are the rejoicing of my heart.

I have inclined my heart to perform thy statutes always: even unto the end.

XV. *Iniquos odio habui.*

I hate vain thoughts: but thy law do I love.

Thou art my hiding place and my shield: I hope in thy word.

Depart from me, ye evil doers: for I will keep the commandments of my God.

Uphold me according unto thy word; that I may live: and let me not be ashamed of my hope.

Hold thou me up, and I shall be safe: and I will have respect unto thy statutes continually.

Thou hast trodden down all them that err from thy statutes: for their deceit is falsehood.

Thou puttest away all the wicked of the earth like dross: therefore I love thy testimonies.

My flesh trembleth for fear of thee: and I am afraid of thy judgments.

XVI. *Feci judicium.*

I have done judgment and justice: leave me not to mine oppressors.

Be surety for thy servant for good: let not the proud oppress me.

Mine eyes fail for thy salvation: and for the word of thy righteousness.

Deal with thy servant according unto thy mercy: and teach me thy statutes.

I am thy servant; give me understanding: that I may know thy testimonies.

It is time for thee, Lord, to work: for they have made void thy law.

Therefore I love thy commandments above gold: yea, above fine gold.

Therefore I esteem all thy precepts concerning all things to be right: and I hate every false way.

XVII. *Mirabilia.*

Thy testimonies are wonderful: therefore doth my soul keep them.

The entrance of thy words giveth light: it giveth understanding unto the simple.

I opened my mouth, and panted: for I longed for thy commandments.

Look thou upon me, and be merciful unto me: as thou usest to do unto those that love thy name.

Order my steps in thy word: and let not any iniquity have dominion over me.

Deliver me from the oppression of man: so will I keep thy precepts.

Make thy face to shine upon thy servant: and teach me thy statutes.

Rivers of waters run down mine eyes: because they keep not thy law.

XVIII. *Justus es, Domine.*

Righteous art thou, O Lord: and upright are thy judgments.

Thy testimonies that thou hast commanded: are righteous and very faithful.

My zeal hath consumed me: because mine enemies have forgotten thy words.

Thy word is very pure: therefore thy servant loveth it.

I am small and despised: yet do I not forget thy precepts.

Thy righteousness is an everlasting righteousness: and thy law is the truth.

Trouble and anguish have taken hold on me: yet thy commandments are my delights.

The righteousness of thy testimonies is everlasting: give me understanding, and I shall live.

XIX. *Clamavi in toto corde meo.*

I cried with my whole heart: hear me, O Lord; I will keep thy statutes.

I cried unto thee: save me, and I shall keep thy testimonies.

I prevented the dawning of the morning, and cried: I hoped in thy word.

Mine eyes prevent the night watches: that I might meditate in thy word.

Hear my voice according unto thy lovingkindness: O Lord, quicken me according to thy judgment.

They draw nigh that follow after mischief: they are far from thy law.

Thou art near, O Lord: and all thy commandments are truth.

Concerning thy testimonies, I have known of old: that thou hast founded them forever.

XX. *Vide humilitatem.*

Consider mine affliction, and deliver me: for I do not forget thy law.

Plead my cause and deliver me: quicken me according to thy word.

Salvation is far from the wicked: for they see not thy statutes.

Great are thy tender mercies, O Lord: quicken me according to thy judgments.

Many are my persecutors and mine enemies: yet do I not decline from thy testimonies.

I beheld the transgressors, and was grieved: because they kept not thy word.

Consider how I love thy precepts: quicken me O Lord, according to thy lovingkindness.

Thy word is true from the beginning: and every one of thy righteous judgments endureth forever.

XXI. *Principes persecuti sunt.*

Princes have persecuted me without a cause: but my heart standeth in awe of thy word.

I rejoice in thy word: as one that findeth great spoil.

I hate and abhor lying: but thy law do I love.

Seven times a day do I praise thee: because of thy righteous judgments.

Great peace have they which love thy law: and nothing shall offend them.

Lord, I have hoped for thy salvation: and done thy commandments.

My soul hath kept thy testimonies: and I love them exceedingly.

I have kept thy precepts and thy testimonies: for all my ways are before thee.

XXII. *Appropinquet deprecatio.*

Let my cry come near before thee, O Lord: give me understanding according to thy word.

Let my supplication come before thee: deliver me according to thy word.

My lips shall utter praise: when thou hast taught me thy statutes.

My tongue shall speak of thy word: for all thy commandments are righteousness.

Let thine hand help me: for I have chosen thy precepts.

I have longed for thy salvation, O Lord: and thy law is my delight.

Let my soul live, and it shall praise thee: and let thy judgments help me.

I have gone astray like a lost sheep, seek thy servant: for I do not forget thy commandments.

Psalm cxxi. *Levavi oculos.*

I will lift up mine eyes unto the hills: from whence cometh mine help.

My help cometh from the Lord: which made heaven and earth.

He will not suffer thy foot to be moved: he that keepeth thee will not slumber.

Behold, he that keepeth Israel: shall neither slumber nor sleep.

The Lord is thy keeper: the Lord is thy shade upon the right hand.

The sun shall not smite thee by day: nor the moon by night.

The Lord shall preserve thee from all evil: he shall preserve thy soul.

The Lord shall preserve thy going out and thy coming in: from this time forth, and even for evermore.

Psalm cxxii. *Laetatus sum.*

I was glad when they said unto me: Let us go into the house of the LORD.

Our feet shall stand within thy gates: O Jerusalem.

Jerusalem is builded: as a city that is compact together.

Whither the tribes go up, the tribes of the LORD: unto the testimony of Israel, to give thanks unto the name of the Lord.

For there are set thrones of judgment: the thrones of the house of David.

Pray for the peace of Jerusalem: they shall prosper that love thee,

Peace be within thy walls: and prosperity within thy palaces.

For my brethren and companions' sakes: I will now say, Peace be within thee.

Because of the house of the LORD our God: I will seek thy good.

Psalm cxxiv. *Nisi quia Dominus.*

If it had not been the LORD who was on our side: now may Israel say;

If it had not been the LORD who was on our side: when men rose up against us;

Then they had swallowed us up quick: when their wrath was kindled against us;

Then the waters had overwhelmed us: the stream had gone over our soul.

Then the proud waters: had gone over our soul.

Blessed be the LORD: who hath not given us as a prey to their teeth.

Our soul is escaped as a bird out of a snare of the fowlers: the snare is broken, and we are escaped.

Our help is in the name of the LORD: who made heaven and earth.

Psalm cxxv. *Qui confidunt.*

They that trust in the LORD: shall be as mount Zion: which cannot be removed, but abideth forever.

As the mountains are round about Jerusalem: so the LORD is round about his people from henceforth even forever.

For the rod of the wicked shall not rest upon the lot of the righteous: lest the righteous put forth their hands unto iniquity.

Do good, O LORD, unto those that be good: and to them that are upright in their hearts.

As for such as turn aside unto their crooked ways: the LORD shall lead them forth with the workers of iniquity; but peace shall be upon Israel.

Psalm cxxvi. *In convertendo.*

When the LORD turned again the captivity of Zion: we were like them that dream.

Then was our mouth filled with laughter: and our tongue with singing.

Then said they among the heathen: The LORD hath done great things for them.

The LORD hath done great things for us: whereof we are glad.

Turn again our captivity, O LORD: as the streams in the south.

They that sow in tears: shall reap in joy.

He that goeth forth and weepeth, bearing precious seed: shall doubtless come again with rejoicing, bringing his sheaves with him.

Psalm cxxx. *De profundis.*

Out of the depths: have I cried unto thee, O LORD.

Lord, hear my voice: let thine ears be attentive to the voice of my supplications.

If thou, LORD, shouldest mark iniquities: O Lord, who shall stand?

But there is forgiveness with thee: that thou mayest be feared.

I wait for the LORD, my soul doth wait: and in his word do I hope.

My soul waiteth for the Lord more than they that watch for the morning: I say, more than they that watch for the morning.

Let Israel hope in the LORD, for with the LORD there is mercy: and with him is plenteous redemption.

And he shall redeem Israel: from all his iniquities.

Psalm cxxxii. *Memento Domine.*

LORD, remember David: and all his afflictions;

How he sware unto the LORD: and vowed unto the mighty God of Jacob;

Surely I will not come into the tabernacle of my house: nor go up into my bed;

I will not give sleep to mine eyes: or slumber to mine eyelids,

Until I find out a place for the LORD: a habitation for the mighty God of Jacob.

Lo, we heard of it at Ephratah: we found it in the fields of the wood.

We will go into his tabernacles: we will worship at his footstool.

Arise, O LORD, into thy rest: thou, and the ark of thy strength.

Let thy priests be clothed with righteousness: and let thy saints shout for joy.

For thy servant David's sake: turn not away the face of thine anointed.

The LORD hath sworn in truth unto David: he will not turn from it;

Of the fruit of thy body: will I set upon thy throne.

If thy children will keep my covenant and my testimony that I shall teach them: their children shall also sit upon thy throne for evermore.

For the LORD hath chosen Zion: he hath desired it for his habitation.

This is my rest for ever: here will I dwell; for I have desired it.

I will abundantly bless her provision: I will satisfy her poor with bread.

I will also clothe her priests with salvation: and her saints shall shout aloud for joy.

There will I make the horn of David to bud: I have ordained a lamp for mine anointed.

His enemies will I clothe with shame: but upon himself shall his crown flourish.

Psalm cxxxvi. *Confitemini.*

O give thanks unto the LORD; for he is good: for his mercy endureth for ever.

O give thanks unto the God of gods: for his mercy endureth for ever.

O give thanks to the Lord of lords: for his mercy endureth for ever.

To him who alone doeth great wonders: for his mercy endureth for ever.

To him that by wisdom made the heavens: for his mercy endureth for ever.

To him that made great lights: for his mercy endureth for ever:

The sun to rule by day: for his mercy endureth for ever;

The moon and stars to rule by night: for his mercy endureth for ever.

To him that smote Egypt in their firstborn: for his mercy endureth for ever:

And brought out Israel free among them: for his mercy endureth for ever;

With a strong hand, and with a stretched-out arm: for his mercy endureth for ever.

To him which divided the Red sea into parts: for his mercy endureth for ever;

And made Israel to pass through the midst of it: for his mercy endureth for ever;

But overthrew Pharaoh and his host in the Red sea: for his mercy endureth for ever.

To him which led his people through the wilderness: for his mercy endureth for ever.

To him which smote great kings: for his mercy endureth for ever.

And slew famous kings: for his mercy endureth for ever;

Sihon king of the Amorites: for his mercy endureth for ever.

And Og the King of Bashan: for his mercy endureth for ever;

And gave their land for a heritage: for his mercy endureth for ever.

Even a heritage unto Israel his servant: for his mercy endureth for ever.

Who remembered us in our low estate: for his mercy endureth for ever;

And hath redeemed us from our enemies: for his mercy endureth for ever.

Who giveth food to all flesh: for his mercy endureth for ever.

O give thanks unto the God of heaven: for his mercy endureth for ever.

Psalm cxxxviii. *Confitebor tibi.*

I will praise thee with my whole heart: before the gods will I sing praise unto thee.

I will worship toward thy holy temple, and praise thy name for thy loving-kindness and for thy truth: for thou hast magnified thy word above all thy name.

In the day when I cried thou answeredst me: and strengthenedst me with strength in my soul.

All the kings of the earth shall praise thee, O Lord: when they hear the words of thy mouth.

Yea, they shall sing in the ways of the Lord: for great is the glory of the Lord.

Though the Lord be high, yet hath he respect unto the lowly: but the proud he knoweth afar off.

Though I walk in the midst of trouble, thou wilt revive me: thou shalt stretch forth thine hand against the wrath of mine enemies, and thy right hand shall save me.

The Lord will perfect that which concerneth me: thy mercy, O Lord, endureth for ever; forsake not the works of thine own hands.

Psalm cxxxix. *Domine, probasti.*

O Lord, thou hast searched me, and known me: thou knowest my downsitting and mine uprising; thou understandest my thought afar off.

Thou compassest my path and my lying down: and art acquainted with all my ways.

For there is not a word in my tongue: but lo, O Lord, thou knowest it altogether.

Thou hast beset me behind and before: and laid thine hand upon me.

Such knowledge is too wonderful for me: it is high, I cannot attain unto it.

Whither shall I go from thy Spirit: or whither shall I flee from thy presence?

If I ascend up into heaven, thou art there: if I make my bed in hell, behold thou art there.

If I take the wings of the morning: and dwell in the uttermost parts of the sea;

Even there shall thy hand lead me: and thy right hand shall hold me.

If I say, Surely the darkness shall cover me: even the night shall be light about me.

Yea, the darkness hideth not from thee; but the night shineth as the day: the darkness and the light are both alike to thee.

For thou hast possessed my reins: thou hast covered me in my mother's womb.

I will praise thee; for I am fearfully and wonderfully made: marvellous are thy works; and that my soul knoweth right well.

My substance was not hid from thee, when I was made in secret: and curiously wrought in the lowest parts of the earth.

Thine eyes did see my substance yet being unperfect: and in thy book all my members were written.

Which in continuance were fashioned: when as yet there was none of them.

How precious also are thy thoughts unto me, O God: how great is the sum of them!

If I should count them, they are more in number than the sand: when I awake, I am still with thee.

Surely thou wilt slay the wicked, O God: depart from me, therefore, ye bloody men.

For they speak against thee wickedly: and thine enemies take thy name in vain.

Do not I hate them, O LORD, that hate thee: and am not I grieved with those that rise up against thee?

I hate them with perfect hatred: I count them mine enemies,

Search me, O God, and know my heart: try me, and know my thoughts;

And see if there be any wicked way in me: and lead me in the way everlasting.

Psalm cxliii. *Domine exaudi.*

Hear my prayer, O LORD, give ear to my supplications: in thy faithfulness answer me, and in thy righteousness.

And enter not into judgment with thy servant: for in thy sight shall no man living be justified.

For the enemy hath persecuted my soul; he hath smitten my life down to the ground: he hath made me to dwell in darkness, as those that have been long dead.

Therefore is my spirit overwhelmed within me: my heart within me is desolate.

I remember the days of old; I meditate on all thy works: I muse on the work of thy hands.

I stretch forth my hands unto thee: my soul thirsteth after thee, as a thirsty land.

Hear me speedily, O LORD; my spirit faileth: hide not thy face from me, lest I be like unto them that go down into the pit.

Cause me to hear thy loving-kindness in the morning: for in thee do I trust: cause me to know the way wherein I should walk; for I lift up my soul unto thee.

Deliver me, O LORD, from mine enemies: I flee unto thee to hide me.

Teach me to do thy will; for thou art my God: thy Spirit is good; lead me into the land of uprightness.

Quicken me, O Lord, for thy name's sake: for thy righteousness' sake bring my soul out of trouble.

And of thy mercy cut off mine enemies: and destroy all them that afflict my soul; for I am thy servant.

Psalm cxlv. *Exaltabo te, Deus.*

I will extol thee, my God, O King: and I will bless thy name for ever and ever.

Every day will I bless thee: and I will praise thy name for ever and ever.

Great is the LORD, and greatly to be praised: and his greatness is unsearchable.

One generation shall praise thy works to another: and shall declare thy mighty acts.

I will speak of the glorious honour of thy majesty: and of thy wondrous works.

And men shall speak of the might of thy terrible acts: and I will declare thy greatness.

They shall abundantly utter the memory of thy great goodness: and shall sing of thy righteousness.

The LORD is gracious and full of compassion: slow to anger, and of great mercy.

The LORD is good to all: and his tender mercies are over all his works.

All thy works shall praise thee, O Lord: and thy saints shall bless thee.

They shall speak of the glory of thy kingdom: and talk of thy power;

To make known to the sons of men his mighty acts: and the glorious majesty of his kingdom.

Thy kingdom is an everlasting kingdom: and thy dominion endureth throughout all generations.

The LORD upholdeth all that fall: and raiseth up all those that be bowed down.

The eyes of all wait upon thee: and thou givest them their meat in due season.

Thou openest thine hand: and satisfiest the desire of every living thing.

The LORD is righteous in all his ways: and holy in all his works.

The LORD is nigh unto all them that call upon him: to all that call upon him in truth.

He will fulfill the desire of them that fear him: he also will hear their cry, and will save them.

The LORD preserveth all them that love him: but all the wicked will he destroy.

My mouth shall speak the praise of the LORD: and let all flesh bless his holy name for ever and ever.

Psalm cxlvi. *Lauda, anima mea.*

Praise ye the LORD: Praise the LORD, O my soul.

While I live will I praise the LORD: I will sing praises unto my God while I have any being.

Put not your trust in princes: nor in the son of man, in whom there is no help.

His breath goeth forth, he returneth to his earth: in that very day his thoughts perish.

Happy is he that hath the God of Jacob for his help: whose hope is in the LORD his God;

Which made heaven and earth, the sea, and all that therein is: which keepeth truth for ever:

Which executeth judgment for the oppressed: which giveth food to the hungry.

The LORD looseth the prisoners: the LORD openeth the eyes of the blind.

The LORD raiseth them that are bowed down: the LORD loveth the righteous.

The LORD preserveth the strangers; he relieveth the fatherless and widow: but the way of the wicked he turneth upside down.

The LORD shall reign for ever, even thy God, O Zion, unto all generations: Praise ye the LORD.

Psalm cxlvii. *Laudate Dominum.*

Praise ye the LORD, for it is good to sing praises unto our God: for it is pleasant; and praise is comely.

The LORD doth build up Jerusalem: he gathereth together the outcasts of Israel.

He healeth the broken in heart: and bindeth up their wounds.

He telleth the number of the stars: he calleth them all by their names.

Great is our Lord, and of great power: his understanding is infinite.

The LORD lifteth up the meek: he casteth the wicked down to the ground.

Sing unto the LORD with thanksgiving: sing praise upon the harp unto our God.

Who covereth the heaven with clouds, who prepareth rain for the earth: who maketh grass to grow upon the mountains.

He giveth to the beast his food: and to the young ravens which cry.

He delighteth not in the strength of the horse: he taketh not pleasure in the legs of a man.

The LORD taketh pleasure in them that fear him: in those that hope in his mercy.

Praise the LORD, O Jerusalem: praise thy God, O Zion.

For he hath strengthened the bars of thy gates: he hath blessed thy children within thee.

He maketh peace in thy borders: and filleth thee with the finest of the wheat.

He sendeth forth his commandment upon earth: his word runneth very swiftly.

He giveth snow like wool: he scattereth the hoar frost like ashes.

He casteth forth his ice like morsels: who can stand before his cold?

He sendeth out his word, and melteth them: he causeth his wind to blow, and the waters flow.

He sheweth his word unto Jacob: his statutes and his judgments unto Israel.

He hath not dealt so with any nation: and as for his judgments, they have not known them. Praise ye the LORD.

Psalm cxlviii. *Laudate Dominum.*

Praise ye the LORD. Praise ye the LORD from the heavens: praise him in the heights.

Praise ye him, all his angels: praise ye him, all his hosts.

Praise ye him, sun and moon: praise him all ye stars of light.

Praise him ye heaven of heavens: and ye waters that be above the heavens.

Let them praise the name of the LORD: for he commanded, and they were created.

He hath also stablished them for ever and ever: he hath made a decree which shall not pass.

Praise the LORD from the earth: ye dragons and all deeps;

Fire, and hail; snow and vapour: stormy wind fulfilling his word;

Mountains, and all hills: fruitful trees, and all cedars;

Beasts, and all cattle: creeping things, and flying fowl;

Kings of the earth, and all people: princes and all judges of the earth;

Both young men, and maidens: old men and children;

Let them praise the name of the LORD: for his name alone is excellent; his glory is above the earth and heaven.

He also exalteth the horn of his people, the praise of all his saints: even of the children of Israel, a people near unto him. Praise ye the LORD,

Psalm cl. *Laudate Dominum.*

Praise ye the LORD. Praise God in his sanctuary: praise him in the firmament of his power.

Praise him for his mighty acts: praise him according to his excellent greatness.

Praise him with the sound of the trumpet: praise him with the psaltery and harp.

Praise him with the timbrel and dance: praise him with stringed instruments and organs.

Praise him upon the loud cymbals: praise him upon the high sounding cymbals.

Let every thing that hath breath praise the LORD: Praise ye the LORD.

The Beginning of Worship

1 Herr Jesu Christ, Dich zu uns wend L. M.

Mel. 1648
Harm, Can. Goth. I. 1651

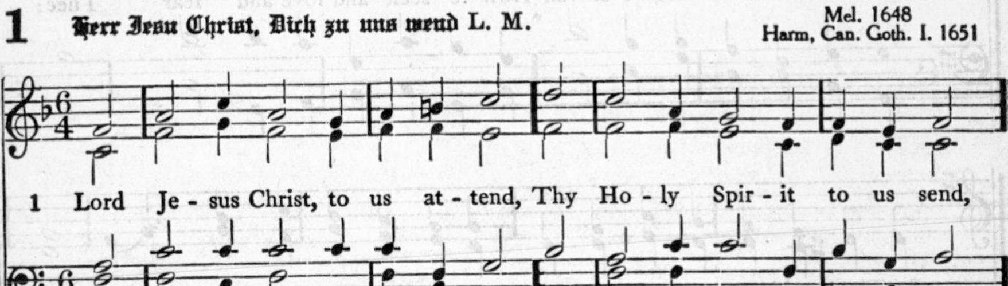
1 Lord Je - sus Christ, to us at - tend, Thy Ho - ly Spir - it to us send,

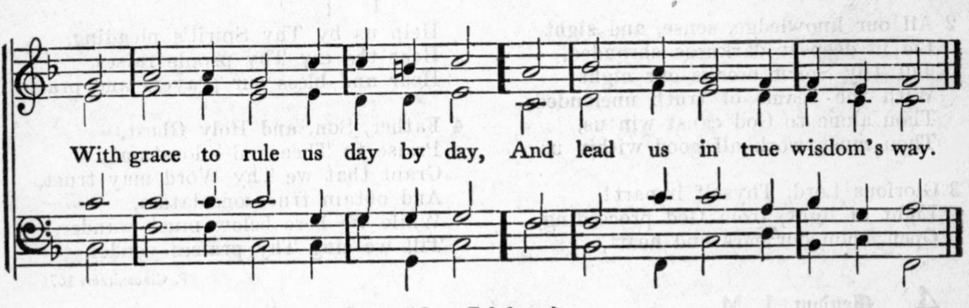
With grace to rule us day by day, And lead us in true wisdom's way.

(Or to Erhalt uns)

2 Unseal our lips to sing Thy praise,
Our hearts in true devotion raise,
Our faith increase, and grant us light,
That we may know thy name aright;

3 Until we join the hosts that cry,
"Holy art Thou, O Lord most high!"
And 'mid the light of that blest place
Shall gaze upon Thee face to face.

4 Glory to God, the Father, Son,
And Holy Spirit, Three in One!
To Thee, O Holy Trinity,
Be praise throughout eternity!

Anon.

2 L. M.

1 LORD, open Thou my heart to hear,
And by Thy Word to me draw near,
Let me Thy Word still pure retain,
Let me Thy child and heir remain.

2 Thy Word doth move the inmost heart,
Thy Word doth perfect health impart,
Thy Word my soul with joy doth bless,
Thy Word brings peace and blessedness.

3 Glory to God, the Father, Son,
And Holy Spirit, Three in One!
To Thee, O blessed Trinity,
Be praise throughout eternity!

Dr. J. Olearius, 1671

The Beginning of Worship

3 **Liebster Jesu, wir sind hier** 7, 8, 7, 8, 8, 8 R. AHLE, 1664.

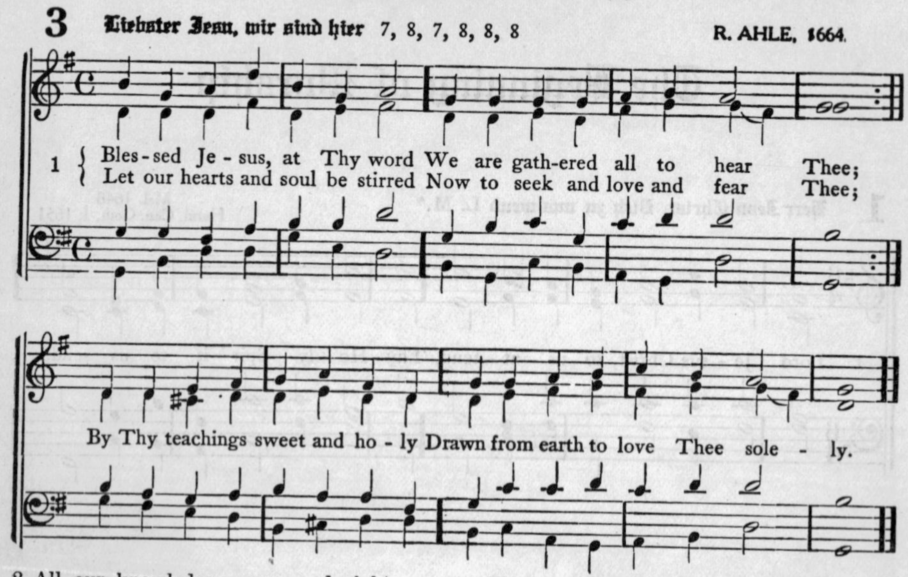
1 Bles-sed Je-sus, at Thy word We are gath-ered all to hear Thee;
Let our hearts and soul be stirred Now to seek and love and fear Thee;
By Thy teachings sweet and ho-ly Drawn from earth to love Thee sole-ly.

2 All our knowledge, sense, and sight
Lie in deepest darkness shrouded,
Till Thy Spirit breaks our night
With the beams of truth unclouded;
Thou alone to God canst win us,
Thou must work all good within us.

3 G[illegible]ious Lord, Thyself impart!
Ligh[illegible] of light, from God proceeding,
Open Thou our ears and heart,
Help us by Thy Spirit's pleading,
Hear the cry Thy people raises,
Hear and bless our prayers and praises.

4 Father, Son, and Holy Ghost,
Praise to Thee and adoration!
Grant that we Thy Word may trust,
And obtain true consolation,
While we here below must wander,
Till we sing Thy praises yonder.

F. Clausnitzer, 1671

4 **Mendon** L. M. German, arr. by LOWELL MASON

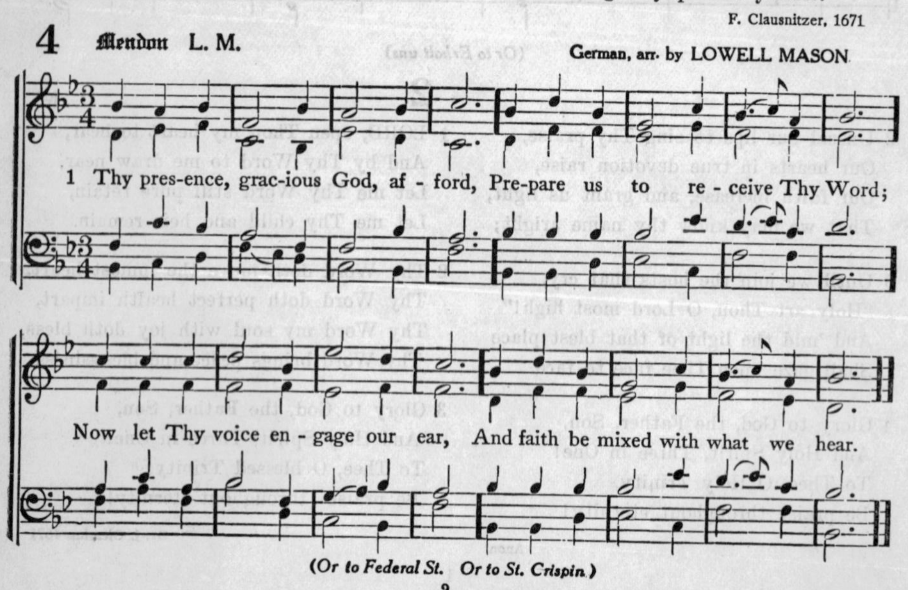
1 Thy pres-ence, grac-ious God, af-ford, Pre-pare us to re-ceive Thy Word;
Now let Thy voice en-gage our ear, And faith be mixed with what we hear.

(Or to Federal St. Or to St. Crispin.)

2 Distracting thoughts and cares remove,
And fix our hearts and hopes above;
With food divine may we be fed,
And satisfied with living bread.

3 To us the sacred Word apply
With sovereign power and energy;
And may we, in Thy faith and fear,
Reduce to practice what we hear.

4 Father, in us Thy Son reveal;
Teach us to know and do Thy will;
Thy saving power and love display,
And guide us to the realms of day.

J. Fawcett

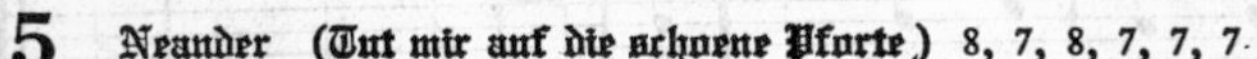

5 Neander (Tut mir auf die schoene Pforte) 8, 7, 8, 7, 7, 7. J. NEANDER 1680

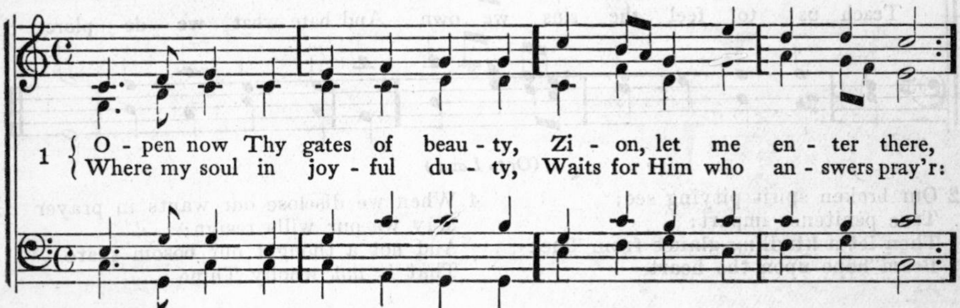
1 { O - pen now Thy gates of beau - ty, Zi - on, let me en - ter there,
Where my soul in joy - ful du - ty, Waits for Him who an - swers pray'r:

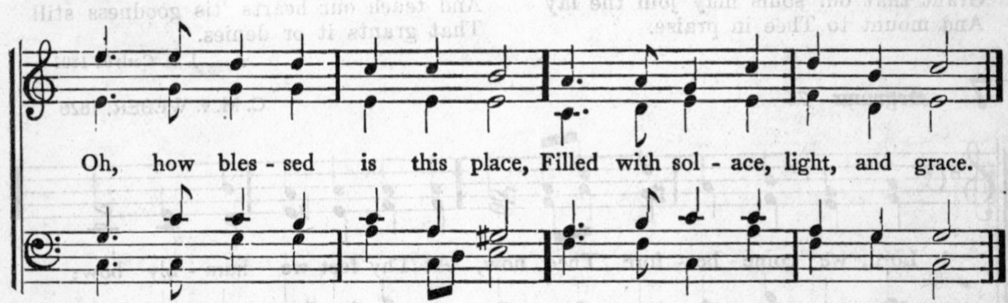
Oh, how bles - sed is this place, Filled with sol - ace, light, and grace.

2 Yes, my God, I come before Thee,
Come Thou also down to me;
Where we find Thee and adore Thee,
There a heaven on earth must be.
To my heart, oh, enter Thou,
Let it be Thy temple now.

3 Here Thy praise is gladly chanted,
Here Thy seed is duly sown;
Let my soul, where it is planted,
Bring forth precious sheaves alone,
So that all I hear may be
Fruitful unto life in me.

4 Thou my faith increase and quicken,
Let me keep Thy Gift divine,
Howsoe'er temptations thicken;
May Thy Word still o'er me shine,
As my pole-star through my life,
As my comfort in my strife.

5 Speak, O God, and I will hear Thee,
Let Thy will be done indeed;
May I undisturbed draw near Thee
Whilst Thou dost Thy people feed.
Here of life the fountain flows,
Here is balm for all our woes.

B. Schmolck, 1732. C. Winkworth, Tr. 1863.

The Beginning of Worship

6 Liberation C. M. German, ad. by H. A. POLACK, 1910

1 Lord, when we bend be - fore Thy throne And our con - fes - sions pour,
Teach us to feel the sins we own And hate what we de - plore.

(Or to Laud)

2 Our broken spirit pitying see;
True penitence impart;
Then let a kindling glance from Thee
Beam hope upon the heart.

3 When our responsive tongues essay
Their grateful hymns to raise,
Grant that our souls may join the lay
And mount to Thee in praise.

4 When we disclose our wants in prayer
May we our wills resign;
And not a thought our bosom share
That is not wholly Thine.

5 May faith each meek petition fill
And waft it to the skies,
And teach our hearts 'tis goodness still
That grants it or denies.

J. D. Carlyle, 1802

7 Seymour 7s C. M. v. WEBER, 1826

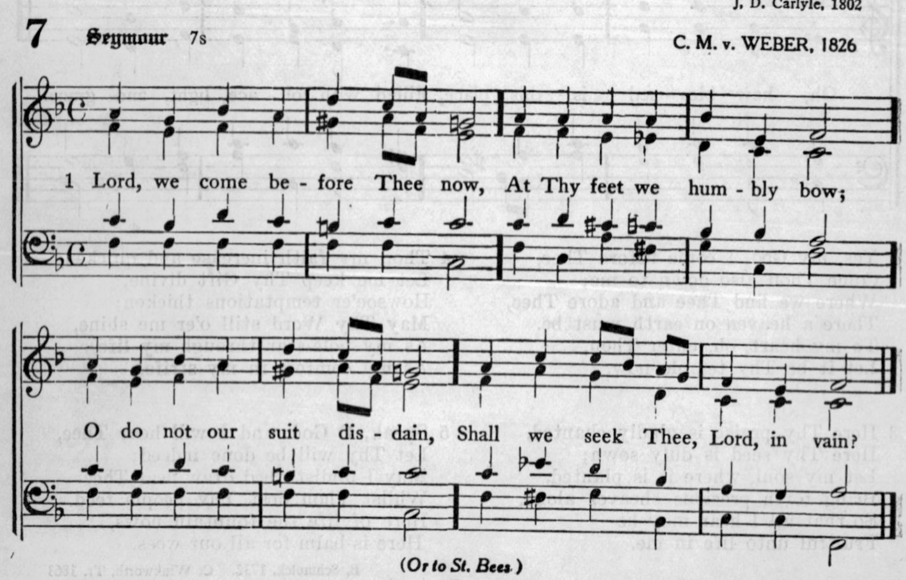
1 Lord, we come be - fore Thee now, At Thy feet we hum - bly bow;
O do not our suit dis - dain, Shall we seek Thee, Lord, in vain?

(Or to St. Bees)

2 Lord, on Thee our souls depend;
In compassion, now descend,
Fill our hearts with Thy rich grace,
Tune our lips to sing Thy praise.

3 In Thine own appointed way,
Now we seek Thee, here we stay;
Lord, we know not how to go,
Till a blessing Thou bestow.

4 Send some message from Thy Word,
That may joy and peace afford;
Let Thy Spirit now impart
Full salvation to each heart.

5 Comfort those who weep and mourn,
Let the time of joy return;
Those that are cast down lift up,
Strong in faith, in love, and hope.

6 Grant that those who seek may find
Thee a God sincere and kind;
Heal the sick, the captive free,
Let us all rejoice in Thee.

W. Hammond, 1745

8 Pruen 7s

F. A. G. OUSELEY, 1825—1889

1 To Thy tem-ple I re - pair; Lord, I love to wor - ship there,

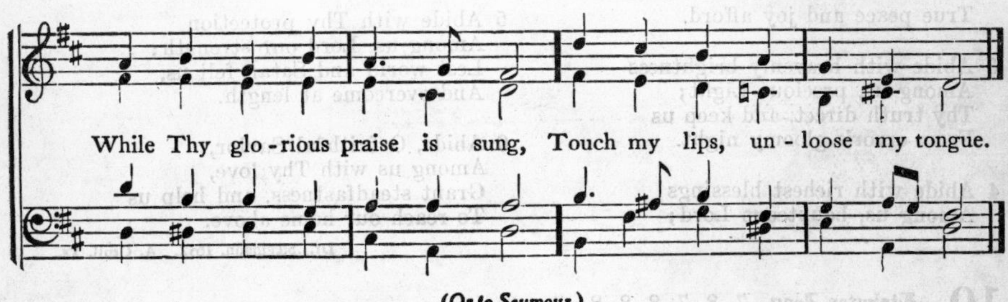
While Thy glo - rious praise is sung, Touch my lips, un - loose my tongue.

(Or to Seymour)

2 While the prayers of saints ascend,
God of love, to mine attend;
Hear me, for Thy Spirit pleads;
Hear, for Jesus intercedes.

3 While I hearken to Thy Law,
Fill my soul with humble awe,
Till Thy Gospel bring to me
Life and immortality.

4 While Thy ministers proclaim
Peace and pardon in Thy Name,
Through their voice, by faith, may I
Hear Thee speaking from the sky.

5 From Thy house when I return,
May my heart within me burn;
And at evening let me say,
"I have walked with God today."

J. Montgomery, 1812

The Close of Worship

9 Christus der ist mein Leben 7, 6, 7, 6 VULPIUS, 1609

1 A - bide, O dear - est Je - sus, A - mong us with Thy
grace, That Sa - tan may not harm us, Nor we to sin give place.

2 Abide, O dear Redeemer,
Among us with Thy Word,
And thus now and hereafter
True peace and joy afford.

3 Abide with heavenly brightness
Among us, precious Light;
Thy truth direct, and keep us
From error's gloomy night.

4 Abide with richest blessings
Among us, bounteous Lord;
Let us in grace and wisdom
Grow daily through Thy Word.

5 Abide with Thy protection
Among us, Lord our strength;
Lest world and Satan fell us,
And overcome at length.

6 Abide, O faithful Savior,
Among us with Thy love,
Grant steadfastness, and help us
To reach our home above.

Dr. J. Stegmann, 1632. A. Crull, Tr.

10 Liebster Jesu 7, 8, 7, 8, 8, 8

1 NOW our worship sweet is o'er—
Singing, praying, teaching, hearing;
Let us gladly God adore
For His gracious strength and cheering.
Praise our God, who now would save us,
For the rich repast He gave us.

2 Now the Blessing cheers our heart,
And the service all is ended,
Let us joyfully depart,—
Be our souls to God commended.
May His Spirit ever guide us,
And with all things well provide us.

3 Let our going out be blest,
Bless our entrance in like measure;
Bless, O Lord, our toil and rest,
Bless our bread, our grief and pleasure,
Be in death Thy blessing given,
And make us blest heirs of heaven.

M. Hartmann Schenck, 1680. M. Loy, Tr.

The Close of Worship

11 Zebulon H. M. 6, 6, 6, 6, 8, 8 L. MASON

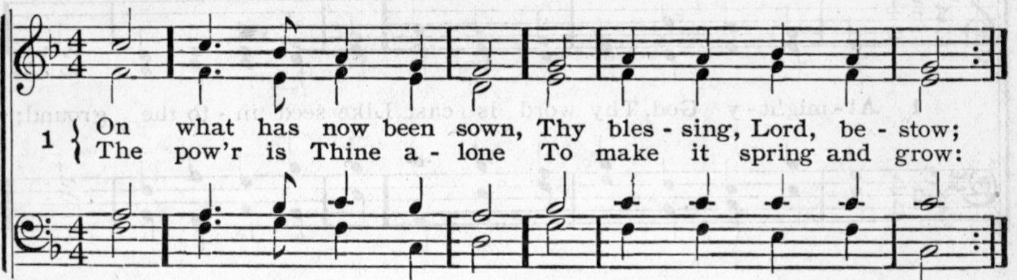
1 On what has now been sown, Thy bles - sing, Lord, be - stow;
The pow'r is Thine a - lone To make it spring and grow:

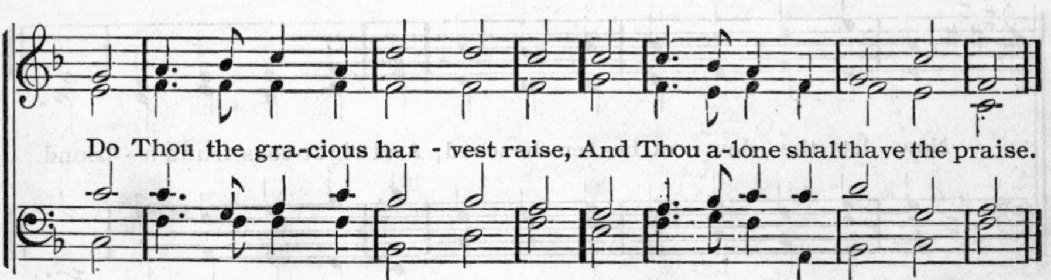
Do Thou the gra-cious har - vest raise, And Thou a-lone shalt have the praise.

2 To Thee our wants are known,
From Thee are all our powers,
Accept what is Thine own,
And pardon what is ours:
Our praises, Lord, and prayers receive,
And to Thy Word a blessing give.

3 O grant that each of us
Who meet before Thee here,
May meet together thus
When Thou and Thine appear,
And follow Thee to heaven our home;
E'en so, Amen, Lord Jesus, come!

John Newton, 1779

12 Melita L. M. 6 l

1 SWEET Savior, bless us ere we go;
Thy Word into our minds instil;
And make our luke-warm hearts to glow
With lowly love and fervent will.
Through life's long day and death's dark night,
O gentle Jesus, be our light.

2 The day is gone, its hours have run,
And Thou hast taken count of all,
The scanty triumphs grace hath won,
The broken vow, the frequent fall.
Through life's long day, etc.

3 Grant us, dear Lord, from evil ways
True absolution and release,
And bless us, more than in past days,
With purity and inward peace.
Through life's long day, etc.

4 For all we love, the poor, the sad,
The sinful, unto Thee we call;
O let Thy mercy make us glad;
Thou art our Savior, and our all.
Through life's long day, etc.

5 Sweet Savior, bless us; night is come;
Thro' night and darkness near us be;
Good angels watch about our home,
And we are one day nearer Thee.
Through life's long day, etc.

F. W. Faber, 1852

The Close of Worship

13 Dundee C. M.

Arr. from CHRISTOPHER TYE, 1553

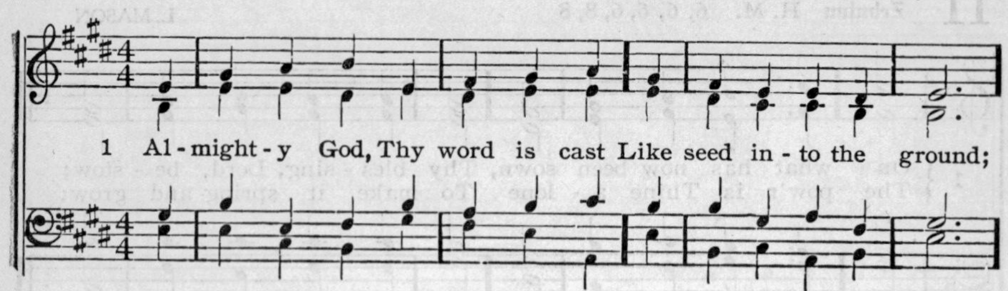
1 Al-might-y God, Thy word is cast Like seed in-to the ground;

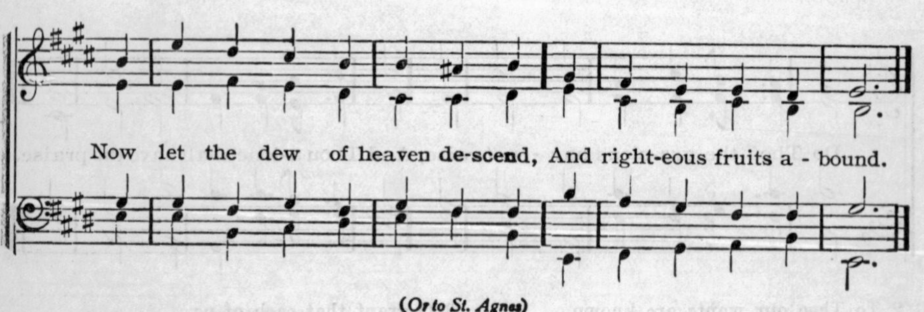
Now let the dew of heaven de-scend, And right-eous fruits a-bound.

(Or to St. Agnes)

2 Let not the foe of Christ and man
This holy seed remove;
But give it root in every heart,
To bring forth fruits of love.

3 Let not the world's deceitful cares
The rising plant destroy;
But let it yield a hundred fold
The fruits of peace and joy.

4 Oft as the precious seed is sown,
Thy quickening grace bestow,
That all whose souls the truth receive,
Its saving power may know.

J. Cawood

14 Merton 8, 7, 8, 7

W. H. MONK (P)

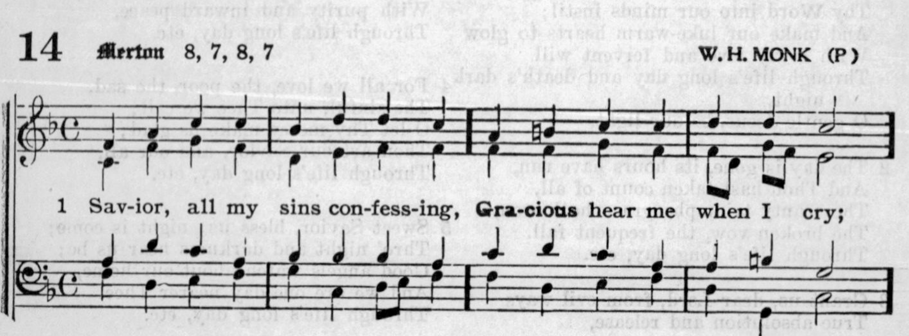
1 Sav-ior, all my sins con-fess-ing, Gra-cious hear me when I cry;

Give through faith the prom-ised blessing, Free-ly, ful-ly jus-ti-fy.

(Or to Batty)

2 By Thy Holy Spirit's leading,
Bring me to Thy bosom nigh;
In Thy blessed footsteps treading,
Soul and body *sanctify.*

3 So, the days of conflict ended,
In the mansions of the sky,
Whither, Lord, Thou art ascended,
With Thyself, me *glorify.*

Thomas Haweis, 1808, a

15 Burkland 7s

L. G. HAYNE

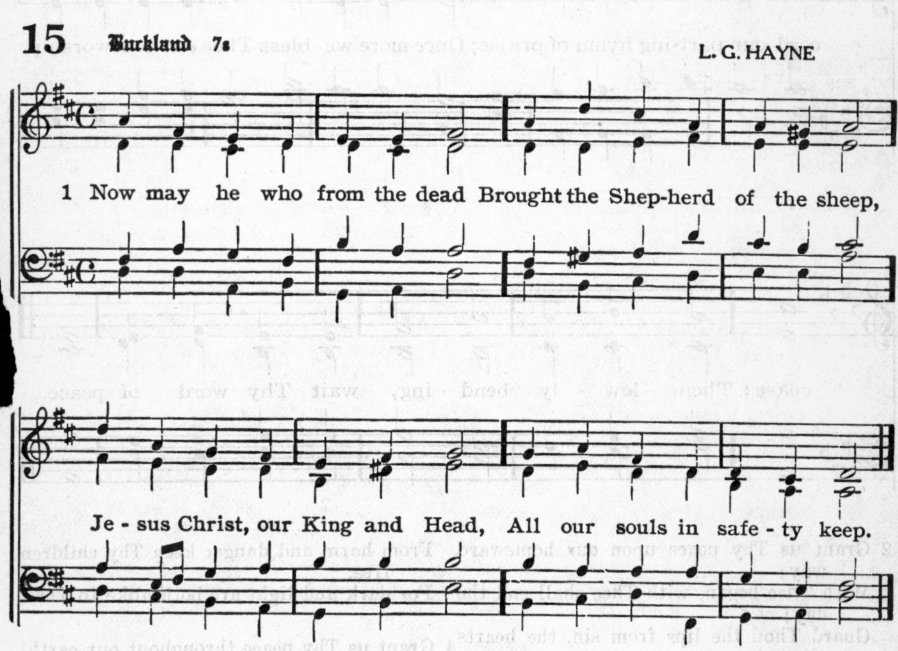
1 Now may he who from the dead Brought the Shep-herd of the sheep,
Je-sus Christ, our King and Head, All our souls in safe-ty keep.

(Or to Solitude. Or to Gott sei Dank.)

2 May He teach us to fulfil
What is pleasing in His sight;
Perfect us in all His will,
And preserve us day and night.

3 To that dear Redeemer's praise,
Who the covenant sealed with blood,
Let our hearts and voices raise
Loud thanksgivings to our God.

John Newton, 1779

The Close of Worship

16 Ellers (Benediction) 10s E. J. HOPKINS, 1867 (P)

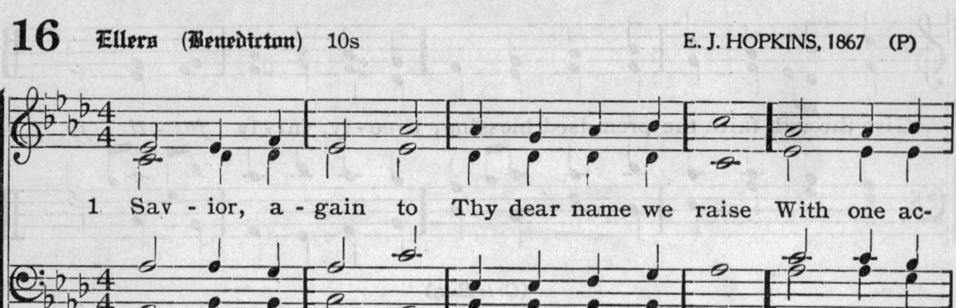
1 Sav - ior, a - gain to Thy dear name we raise With one ac-

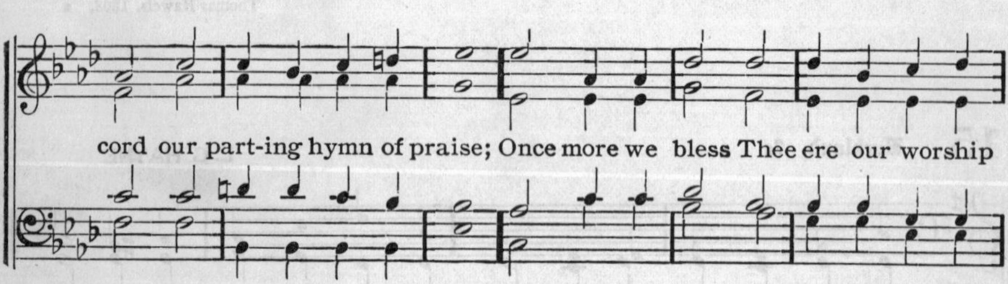
cord our part-ing hymn of praise; Once more we bless Thee ere our worship

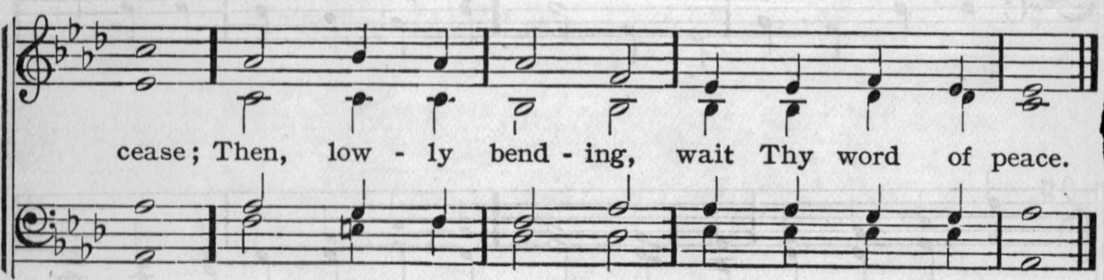
cease; Then, low - ly bend - ing, wait Thy word of peace.

2 Grant us Thy peace upon our homeward way;
With Thee began, with Thee shall end the day;
Guard Thou the lips from sin, the hearts from shame,
That in this house have called upon Thy name.

3 Grant us Thy peace, Lord, through the coming night;
Turn Thou for us its darkness into light;
From harm and danger keep Thy children free,
For dark and light are both alike to Thee.

4 Grant us Thy peace throughout our earthly life,
Our balm in sorrow, and our stay in strife;
Then, when Thy voice shall bid our conflict cease,
Call us, O Lord, to Thine eternal peace.

J. Ellerton, 1866

The Close of Worship

17 Sicilian Hymn 8, 7, 4, 7

1 { Lord, dis - miss us with Thy bless - ing, Fill our hearts with
Let us each, Thy love pos - sess - ing, Tri-umph in re-

joy and peace! }
deem - ing grace. }
O re - fresh us, O re-

fresh us, Trav'l -ing thro' this wil - der - ness.

2 Thanks we give and adoration
For Thy Gospel's joyful sound.
May the fruits of Thy salvation
In our hearts and lives abound:
|: May Thy presence :|
With us evermore be found.

3 So, whene'er the signal's given
Us from earth to call away,
Borne on angels' wings to heaven,
Glad the summons to obey,
|: May we, ready, :|
Rise and reign in endless day.

J. Fawcett, 1773

The Close of Worship

18 Wessex 8, 6, 8, 6, 8, 8 E. J. HOPKINS, Mus. D.

1 Lord of my life, Whose ten-der care Hath led me on till now,

Here low - ly at the hour of prayer Be - fore Thy Throne I bow;

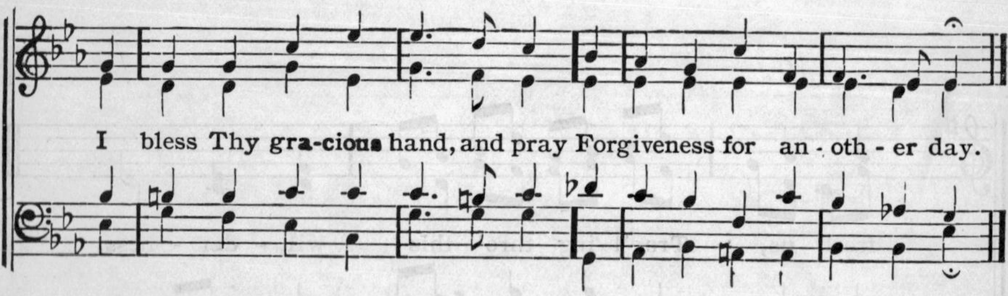
I bless Thy gra-cious hand, and pray Forgiveness for an - oth - er day.

2 O may I daily, hourly, strive
In heavenly grace to grow;
To Thee and to Thy glory live,
Dead else to all below;
Tread in the path my Savior trod,
Though thorny, yet the path to God!

3 With prayer my humble praise I bring,
For mercies day by day:
Lord, teach my heart Thy love to sing,
Lord, teach me how to pray!
All that I have, I am, to Thee
I offer through Eternity!

"Chelsea" 1838

Morning

19 Melita L. M. 61

J. B. DYKES, 1861 (P)

1 When streaming from the east - ern skies, The morning light sa-lutes my eyes,

O Sun of right-eous-ness di-vine, On me with beams of mer-cy shine,

Chase the dark clouds of sin a-way, And turn my darkness in - to day.

2 When to heaven's great and glorious King
My morning sacrifice I bring:
And grieving o'er my guilt and shame,
Ask mercy, Savior, in Thy name;
My conscience sprinkle with Thy blood,
And be my advocate with God.

3 When each day's scenes and labors close,
And wearied nature seeks repose,
With pardoning mercy richly blest,
Guard me, my Savior, while I rest;
And as each morning's sun shall rise,
O lead me onward to the skies.

4 And at my life's last setting sun,
My conflict o'er, my labors done,
Jesus, Thy heavenly radiance shed,
To cheer and bless my dying bed;
And from death's gloom my spirit raise,
To see Thy face and sing Thy praise.

William Shrubsole, 1813 a

20 O heilige Dreifaltigkeit L. M. 1558

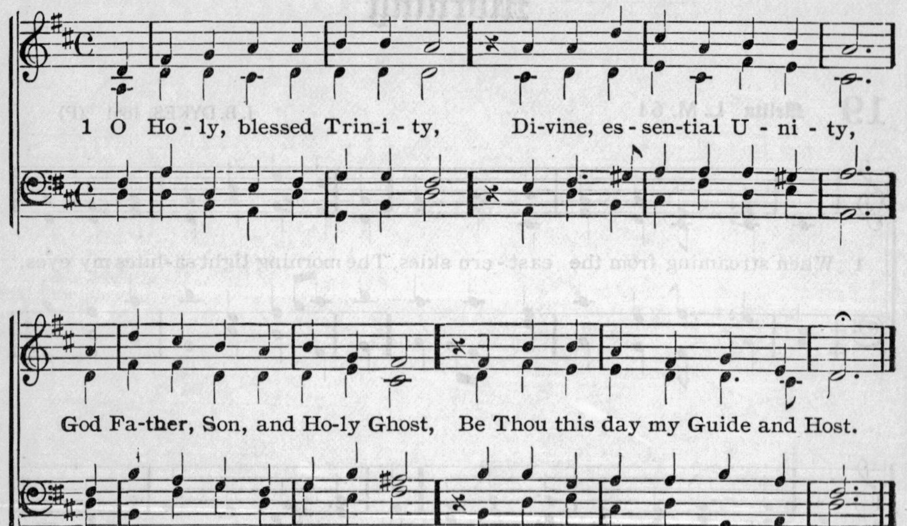
1 O Ho-ly, blessed Trin-i-ty, Di-vine, es-sen-tial U-ni-ty,
God Fa-ther, Son, and Ho-ly Ghost, Be Thou this day my Guide and Host.

2 My soul and body keep from harm,
O'er all I have extend Thine arm,
That Satan may not cause distress,
Nor bring me shame and wretchedness.

3 The Father's love shield me this day,
The Son's pure wisdom cheer my way,
The Holy Spirit's light divine,
Illume my heart's benighted shrine.

4 My Maker, strengthen Thou my heart,
O my Redeemer, help impart,
Blest Comforter, keep at my side,
That faith and love in me abide.

5 Lord, bless and keep Thou me as Thine!
Lord, make Thy face upon me shine!
Lord, lift Thy countenance on me,
And give me peace, sweet peace from Thee.

Martin Behm, 1608. C. H. L. Schuette, Tr. a

21 Geduld die soll'n wir haben 7, 6 8 1 BARTH. GESIUS, 1605

1. While yet the morn is break-ing, I thank my God once more,
Be-neath whose care a-wak-ing, I find the night is o'er;

Morning

I thank Him that He calls me to life and health a - new;

I know what-e'r be - falls me, His care will still be true.

(Or to Ich dank dir, lieber Or to Webb)

2 Guardian of Israel, hear me,
Watch o'er me through the day,
In all I do be near me:
For others, too, I pray;
To Thee I would commend them,
Our Church, our school, our land,
Direct them and defend them,
When dangers are at hand.

3 O gracious Lord, direct us,
Thy doctrine pure defend,
From heresies protect us,
And for Thy Word contend,
That we may praise Thee ever,
O God, with one accord,
Saying: The Lord our Savior
Be evermore adored!

4 O grant us peace and gladness,
Give us our daily bread,
Shield us from grief and sadness,
On us Thy blessings shed;
Grant that our whole behavior
In truth and righteousness
May praise Thee, Lord our Savior,
Whose holy name we bless.

5 And gently grant Thy blessing,
That we may do Thy will,
No more Thy ways transgressing,
Our proper task fulfill;
With Peter's full affiance
Let down our nets again;
If Thou art our Reliance,
Our toil will not be vain.

6 With craftiness unceasing
Strives Satan to restrain
What in Thy sight is pleasing
And for Thy Church is gain;
Yet vain is his endeavor,
For Thou, O Christ our Lord,
Dost rule all things forever
By Thine almighty Word.

7 Thou art the Vine,—O nourish
The branches graft in Thee,
And let them grow and flourish
A fair and fruitful tree;
Thy Spirit pour within us,
And let His gifts of grace
To all good actions win us,
That best may show Thy praise.

Johann Muehlmann, † 1613

Morning

22 Aus meines Herzens Grunde 7, 6, 7, 6, 6, 7, 7, 6 EISLEBEN H. B. 1598

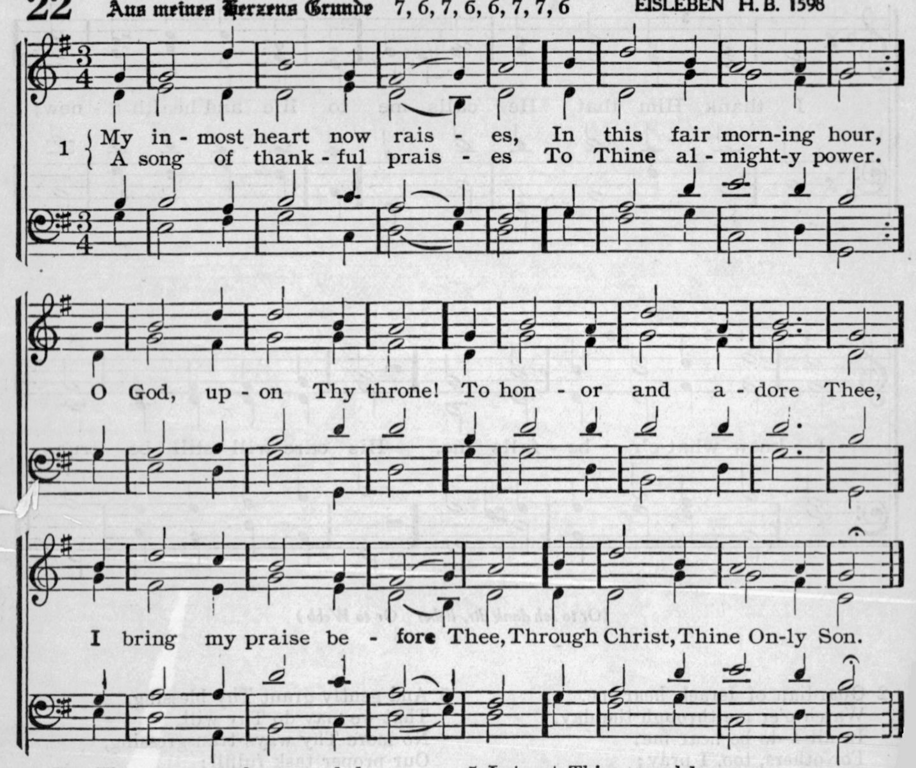

1 { My in - most heart now rais - es, In this fair morn-ing hour,
A song of thank - ful prais - es To Thine al - might-y power.
O God, up - on Thy throne! To hon - or and a - dore Thee,
I bring my praise be - fore Thee, Through Christ, Thine On-ly Son.

2 For Thou from me hast warded
All perils of the night;
From every harm hast guarded
My soul till morning's light,
Humbly to Thee I cry:
O Savior, have compassion,
And pardon my transgression;
Have mercy, Lord most high!

3 And shield me from all evil,
O gracious God, this day,
From sin, and from the Devil,
From shame and from dismay,
From fire's consuming breath,
From water's devastation,
From need and consternation,
From evil, sudden death.

4 My life, my soul—defend them!
My wife, child, goods, and home,—
To Thy hand I commend them,
From Thee these blessings come;
Thy bounteous hand bestows
My household and my treasures,
My parents, friends, and pleasures;
My cup with good o'erflows.

5 Let not Thine angel leave me,
While here on earth I stay,
Lest Satan's arts deceive me,
And lead my soul astray!
Then keep Thine angel near
At night and each new morrow,
Lest soul and body sorrow,
And faltering cost me dear.

6 God shall do my advising,
Whose might with wisdom blends;
May He bless rest and rising,
My efforts, means, and ends!
To God, forever blessed,
Will I with mine confide me,
And suffer Him to guide me
As seemeth to Him best.

7 Amen! I say, not fearing
That God rejects my prayer;
I doubt not He is hearing
And granting me His care.
So I put forth my hands,
And look not long behind me,
But ply the task assigned me
By God, as He commands.

Anon

Morning

23 Gott des Himmels und der Erden 8, 7, 8, 7, 7, 7 H. ALBERT, 1642

1 { God who ma-dest earth and heav-en, Fa - ther, Son, and Ho - ly Ghost,
Who the day and night hast giv - en, Sun and moon and star-ry host,

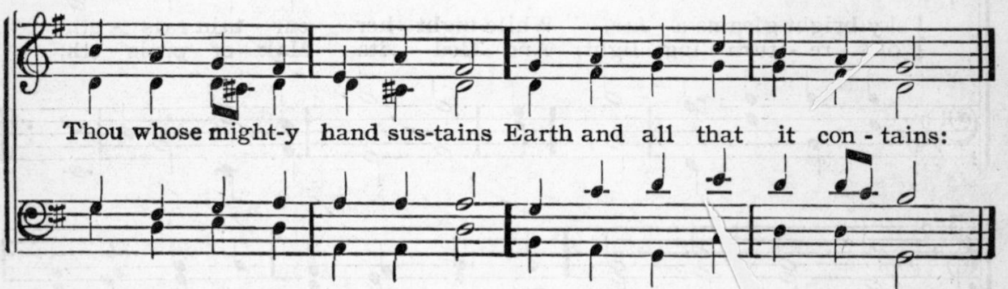
Thou whose might-y hand sus-tains Earth and all that it con - tains:

2 Praise to Thee my soul shall render,
  Who this night hast guarded me;
My omnipotent Defender,
  Who from ill dost set me free,
Free from danger, anguish, woe,
Free from the infernal Foe.

3 Let the night of my transgression
  With night's darkness pass away;
Jesus, into Thy possession
  I resign myself to-day;
In Thy wounds I find relief
From my greatest sin and grief.

4 Grant that I may rise this morning
  From the lethargy of sin,
So my soul, through Thy adorning,
  Shall be glorious within;
And I at the judgment day
Shall not be a cast-away.

5 Let my life and conve tion
  Be directed by Thy d;
Lord, Thy constant pres tion
  To Thine erring child a ;
Nowhere but alone in The
From all harm can I be f

6 Wholly to Thy blest protectio
  I commit my heart and mind.
Mighty God! to Thy direction
  Wholly may I be resigned.
Lord, my Shield, my Light divine,
O accept and own me Thine!

7 Lord, to me Thine angel sending,
  Keep me from the subtle foe;
From his craft and might defending,
  Never let Thy wanderer go,
Till my final rest shall come,
And Thine angel bear me home.

H. Albert, 1642. John Christian Jacobi, Tr. 1822. And Arthur Tozer Russell, 1848. a

Morning

24 Wie schoen leuchtet der Morgenstern 8,8,7,8,8,7.4,8,4,8 PH. NICOLAI, 1599

1 { How love - ly now the morn - ing star In twi - light sky bright gleams a - far, While night her cur - tain rais - eth;
Each crea - ture hails, with rav - ished sight, The glo - ries of re - turn - ing light, And God its Mak - er prais - eth.
Both far, And near, All things liv - ing Thanks are giv - ing,
There high soar - ing, Here through earth's wide field a - dor - ing.

2 Then haste, my soul, thy song to raise
Nor spare in thy Redeemer's praise
To pour thy due oblation;
For glory, Lord, to Thee belongs,
Thy praise resounds in grateful songs,
With pious emulation,
Joy rings Glad strings;
Voices sounding, Hearts rebounding,
Thus all nature
Sings Thy praise, O great Creator.

3 Unconscious, I securely slept,
Nor saw the cruel foes which kept
Close watch about my slumber;
Though evil spirits, through the night,
With hellish craft and watchful spite,
Came round me without number;
Whose hands In bands,
Mischief brewing For my ruin,
Had enslaved me,
Hadst not Thou stood by and saved me.

2 Preserved by Thine almighty arm,
I pass the shades of night,
Serene and safe from every harm,
And see returning light.

3 When sleep, death's semblance, o'er me spread,
And I unconscious lay;
Thy watchful care was round my bed
To guard my feeble clay.

4 O let the same almighty care
My waking hours attend:
From every trespass, every snare,
My heedless steps defend.

5 Smile on my minutes as they roll,
And guide my future days;
And let Thy goodness fill my soul
With gratitude and praise.

Anne Steele, 1760

28 Nicht so traurig, nicht so sehr 7s, 6 l

EBELING, 1666

1 { Ev - ry morn-ing mer - cies new Fall as fresh as morn - ing dew;
Ev - ry morn-ing let us pay Trib-ute with the ear - ly day;

For Thy mer - cies, Lord, are sure, Thy com - pas -sion doth en - dure.

2 Still the greatness of Thy love
Daily doth our sins remove;
Daily, far as east from west,
Lifts the burden from the breast;
Gives unbought, to those who pray,
Strength to stand in evil day.

3 Let our prayers each morn prevail,
That these gifts may never fail;
And, as we confess the sin
And the tempter's power within,
Feed us with the Bread of Life,
Fit us for our daily strife.

4 As the morning light returns,
As the sun with splendor burns,
Teach us still to turn to Thee,
Ever blessèd Trinity,
With our hands our hearts to raise,
In unfailing prayer and praise.

G. Phillimore, 1863

Morning

29 Morning Hymn L. M. F. H. BARTHELEMON, 1741—1808

1 A - wake my soul, and with the sun Thy dai - ly

stage of du - ty run; Shake off dull sloth, and

joy - ful rise To pay thy morn - ing sac - ri - fice.

(*Or to Die helle Sonn*)

2 All praise to Thee, who safe hast kept,
And has refreshed me while I slept:
Grant, Lord, when I from death shall wake,
I may of endless life partake!

3 Lord, I my vows to Thee renew;
Disperse my sins as morning dew;
Guard my first springs of thought and will,
And with Thyself my spirit fill.

4 Direct, control, suggest, this day,
All I design, or do, or say;
That all my powers, with all their might,
In Thy sole glory may unite.

5 Praise God, from whom all blessings flow;
Praise Him, all creatures here below;
Praise Him, above, ye heavenly host,
Praise Father, Son, and Holy Ghost!

Bp. Thomas Ken, 1695

Evening

30 Nun sich der Tag geendet hat C. M. A. KRIEGER, 1667

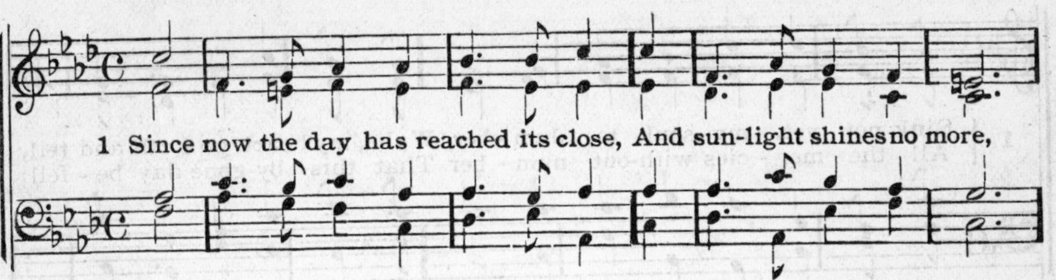
1 Since now the day has reached its close, And sun-light shines no more,

In sleep the toil-worn find re - pose, And all who wept be - fore.

2 But Thou, my God, no rest dost know,
No slumber dims Thy sight.
Thou hatest darkness as Thy foe,
For Thou Thyself art light.

3 O Lord, I pray remember me
Throughout the shades of night,
And grant to me most graciously
The shield of Thy great might.

4 Turn from me Satan's tyranny
Through many an angel arm,
Then shall I be from danger free,
And safe from every harm.

5 I know the evil I have done
Doth cry aloud to Thee;
But yet the mercy of Thy Son
Hath full atoned for me.

6 Him I present Thee as my bail,
While suppliant at Thy feet;
With such a[illegible]rance I'll not fail
Before Thy [illegible]dgment seat.

7 And therefore no[illegible] close my eyes,
And sleep with[illegible]quil breast;
Why waste the tim[illegible] fears or sighs?
God watches o'er [illegible]est.

8 Away, vain, idle though[illegible]epart!
Roam not my soul ab[illegible]
For now I build within m[illegible]art
A temple to my God.

9 Should this night prove the last for me
In this dark vale of tears,
Then lead me, Lord, in heaven to Thee
And my elect compeers.

10 And thus I live and die to Thee,
Strong Lord of hosts, indeed!
In life and death Thou helpest me
From every fear and need.

Joh. Friedr. Herzog, circa 1670

Evening

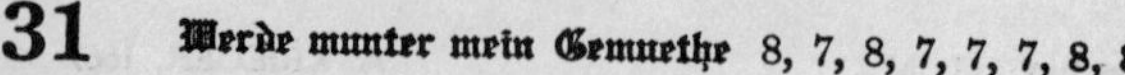

31 **Werde munter mein Gemuethe** 8, 7, 8, 7, 7, 7, 8, 8 J. SCHOP. 1642

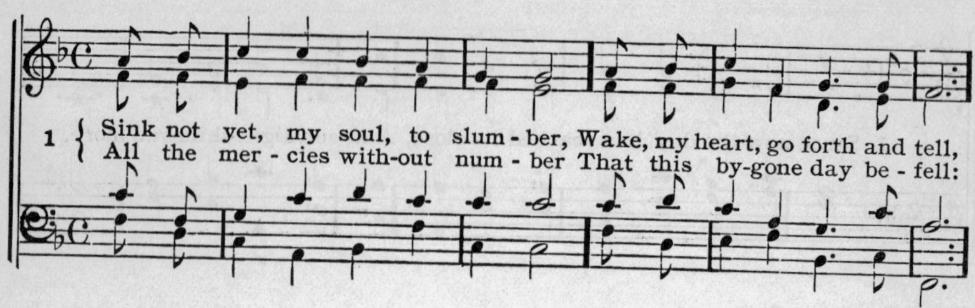
1 Sink not yet, my soul, to slum - ber, Wake, my heart, go forth and tell,
All the mer - cies with-out num - ber That this by-gone day be - fell:

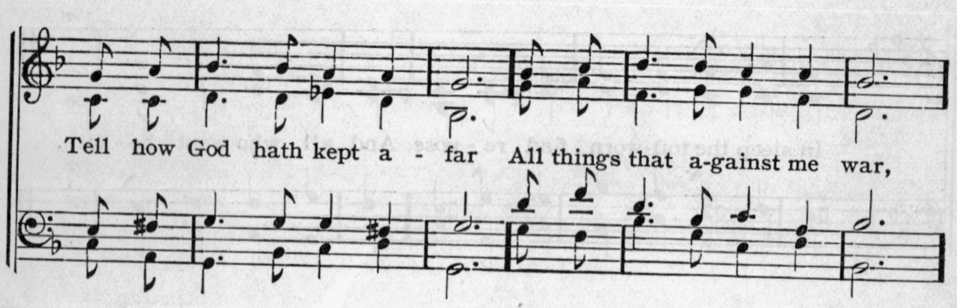
Tell how God hath kept a - far All things that a-gainst me war,

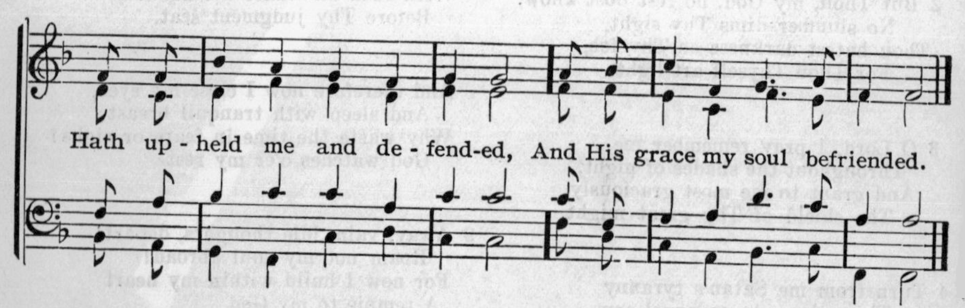
Hath up - held me and de - fend-ed, And His grace my soul befriended.

2 Father, merciful and holy,
  Thee to-night I praise and bless,
Who to labor true and lowly,
  Grantest ever meet success;
Many a sin and many a woe,
Many a fierce and subtle foe
Hast Thou checked that once alarmed me,
So that naught today has harmed me.

3 Yes, our wisdom vainly ponders,
  Fathoms not Thy loving thought.
Never tongue can tell the wonders
  That Thy hand for me hath wrought;
Thou hast guided me today,
That no ill hath crossed my way;
There is neither bound nor measure
In Thy love's o'erflowing treasure.

4 Now the light that nature gladdens,
And the pomp of day is gone,
And my heart is tired and saddens,
As the gloomy night comes on;
Ah, then with Thy changeless light
Warm and cheer my heart to-night;
As the shadows round me gather,
Keep me close to Thee, my Father

5 Of Thy grace, I pray Thee, pardon
All my sins, and heal their smart;
Sore and heavy is their burden,
Sharp their sting within my heart;
And my Foe lays many a snare
But to tempt me to despair;
Thou alone canst help me, Savior,
Punish not my ill behavior.

6 Though I have from Thee departed,
Now I seek Thy face again,
For Thy Son, the loving-hearted,
Made our peace through bitter pain.
Yes, far greater than our sin,
Though it still be strong within,
Is Thy love that fails us never,
Mercy that endures forever.

7 Brightness of th' eternal city!
Light of every faithful soul!
Safe beneath Thy sheltering pity
Let the tempests past me roll;
Now it darkens far and near,
Still, my God, still be Thou here;
Thou canst comfort, and Thou only,
When the night is long and lonely.

8 From the power of darkness save me,
And from Satan's hellish snares,
Who endeavors to enslave me,
And assails me unawares;
Let me never lose the sight
Of Thy good and gracious light;
Thou canst fill my heart with gladness,
That it feel no pain in sadness.

9 Though my weary eyes are closing,
And my senses fall asleep,
Still my soul, on Thee reposing,
Ever must its vigils keep.
Let my spirit longingly
Always dream, my God, of Thee.
Firmly unto Thee e'er cleaving,
E'en in sleep Thy grace receiving.

10 Lord, the twilight now hath vanishe
Send Thy blessing on my sleep,
Every sin and terror banished,
Let my rest be calm and deep.
Soul and body, mind and health,
Wife and children, house and wealth,
Friend and foe, the sick, the stranger,
Keep Thou safe from harm and danger.

11 O Thou mighty God, now hearken
To the prayer Thy child hath made;
Jesus, while the night-hours darken,
Be Thou still my hope, my aid;
Holy Ghost, on Thee I call,
Friend and Comforter of all,
Hear my earnest prayer, O hear me!
Lord, Thou hearest, Thou art near me.

Johann Rist, 1642

32 Spiritus Sancti gratia L. M.

TRILLER, 1555

1 The hap-py sun-shine now is gone, The gloom-y night comes swiftly on;

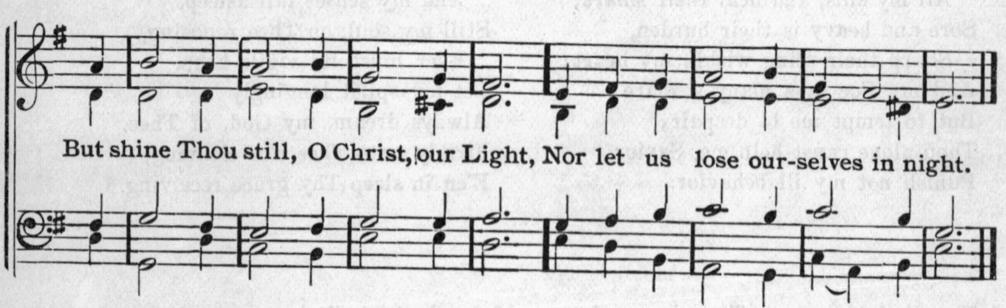
But shine Thou still, O Christ, our Light, Nor let us lose our-selves in night.

2 We thank Thee that throughout the day
Thy angels watched around our way,
And free from harm and vexing fear
Have led us on in safety here.

3 Whate'er of wrong we've done or said,
Let not the charge on us be laid;
That, through Thy free forgiveness blest,
In peaceful slumber we may rest.

4 Thy guardian angels round us place,
All evil from our couch to chase;
Our soul and body, while we sleep,
In safety, gracious Father, keep.

Nikolaus Hermann, 1560

33 O Welt, ich muss dich lassen 7, 7, 6, 7, 7, 8

H. ISAAC, † 1519

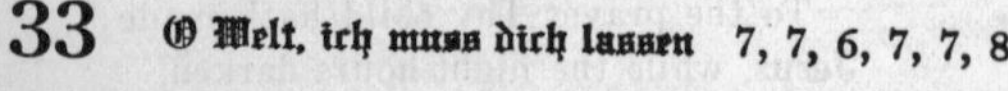
1 Now rest be-neath night's shadows, Man, beast, town, woods and meadows,

Evening

The world in slum-ber lies, But thou, my heart, a - wake thee,

To prayer and song be - take thee, Let praise to thy Cre - a - tor rise.

2 O sun, where art thou vanished?
The night Thy reign hath banished,
The foe of day, the night,
Farewell, for now appeareth
Another Sun and cheereth
My heart—'tis Jesus Christ my Light!

3 The last faint beam is going,
The golden stars are glowing
In yonder dark-blue deep;
Such is the glory given,
When called of God to heaven,
On earth no more we pine and weep.

4 To rest my body hasteth,
Aside its garments casteth,
Types of mortality;
These I put off and ponder
How Christ shall give me yonder
A robe of glorious majesty.

5 Head, hands, and feet reposing
Are glad the day is closing,
That work came to an end;
Cheer up my heart, with gladness!
For God from all earth's sadness
And from sin's toil relief will send.

6 Ye weary limbs! now rest you,
For toil hath sore oppressed you,
And quiet sleep ye crave;
A sleep shall once o'ertake you
From which no man can wake you,
In your last narrow bed—the grave.

7 My heavy eyes are closing:
When I lie deep reposing,
Soul, body, where are ye?
To helpless sleep I yield them,
O let Thy mercy shield them,
Thou sleepless Eye, their Guardian be!

8 Lord Jesus, who dost love me,
O spread Thy wings above me,
And shield me from alarm!
Though Satan would devour me;
Let angel-guards sing o'er me:
"This child of God shall meet no harm!"

9 My loved ones, rest securely,
From every peril surely
Our God will guard your heads.
May He sweet slumbers send you,
And bid His hosts attend you,
And golden-armed, watch o'er your beds!

Paul Gerhardt, 1653

Evening

34 Christe, der du bist Tag und Licht L. M. KOEPHL., 1537

1 Christ, ev - er - last - ing Source of light, All things are

o - pen to Thy sight; Thou Splendor of Thy Fa - ther's face,

Show us the path of truth and grace.

(Or to Herr Jesu Christ, dich.)

2 We now implore Thy sovereign might
To keep us, Lord, the coming night;
Preserve us, Lord, from all distress;
O God, Thy mercy we address.

3 Remove our sinful drowsiness;
Let Satan not our soul oppress;
Our feeble flesh keep chaste and pure,
And let us rest in Thee secure.

4 And when our eyes are bound in sleep,
The lamp of faith still burning keep;
Thy hand sustain us, while we rest;
Remove our sin, and we are blest.

5 Great Guardian of Thy Christian flock,
Thy presence be our saving rock;
Thine agony and holy blood
Be always our support, O God!

6 Remember, Lord, the woes and pains
Which here our body hold in chains;
Our soul, which Thou hast ransomed, Lord,
O comfort with Thy holy Word.

7 To God the Father, and the Son,
And Holy Spirit, Three in One,
Be glory, praise, and majesty
Now, ever, and eternally.

Christe qui lux es et dies. Wolfgang Meusslin, 1527

Evening

35 Christe, der du bist Tag und Licht L. M. KOEPHL. 1537

1 BEFORE Thy throne I now appear,
O Lord, bow down Thy gracious ear
To me, and cast not from Thy face
Thy sinful child that sues for grace.

2 Thou Father of eternity,
Thine image hast impressed on me;
In Thee I am, and live, and move,
Nor can exist without Thy love.

3 Oft hast Thou snatched me from distress,
And raised me oft when comfortless,
When but a step, nay, one hair's breadth,
Was 'twixt my tottering life and death.

4 My sense and reason come from Thee,
And sustenance Thou givest me;
A faithful friend Thou dost bestow,
To prove his love in weal and woe.

5 Thou hast redeemed me, Son of God,
Hast shed for me Thy precious blood,
The Law for my sake hast fulfilled,
And thus Thy Father's wrath hast stilled.

6 When sin and Satan witness bear
Against me, that I must despair,
As Mediator Thou stepst in,
And sav'st me from the curse of sin.

7 Thou art my Advocate for aye,
My Savior, Comfort, and my Stay!
Thine all-sufficient merit is
On earth, my peace; in heaven, my bliss.

8 God, Holy Spirit, Power divine!
Thou workest in this heart of mine;
Naught can be counted good in me,
But what proceeds alone from Thee.

9 Through Thee, I now my God adore,
And call Him Father evermore;
Through Thee, His Word and Sacrament
I love and hold, till life is spent.

10 Through Thee, I'm in temptation free
From fear and sad despondency;
Through Thee, I'm quickened oft to taste
The sweets of Thine eternal rest.

11 I, therefore, now give thanks to Thee
With heart and tongue most joyfully
For all Thy mercies, Lord, my God,
Which on my soul Thou hast bestowed.

12 Beseeching Thine almighty grace
To aid me, till I've run my race;
Soul, body, honor, house, and friend,
To Thy protection I commend.

13 Give me a heart that is sincere,
To love Thy truth, and persevere
In real Christian piety,
And shun all foul hypocrisy.

14 My sins and trespasses forgive;
Have patience with me, while I live;
O give me faith and charity,
And let my hope rest but in Thee.

15 Grant that in peace I close mine eyes,
But, on the last day, bid me rise,
And let me see Thy face fore'er—
Amen, Amen, Lord, hear my prayer!

Bodo von Hodenberg, 1640
Justus Gesenius, a. 1650

Evening

36 Gounod's Evening Hymn L. M. — C. F. GOUNOD (P)

1 Glo - ry to Thee, my God, this night, For all the bles - sings
3 Teach me to live, that I may dread The grave as lit - tle
of the light; Keep me, O keep me, King of kings,
as my bed; Teach me to die, that so I may
Be-neath Thine own al - might-y wings. 2. For-give me, Lord, for
With joy be - hold the judg-ment day. 4. O may my soul on
Thy dear Son, The ill that I this day have done,
Thee re - pose, And may sweet sleep my eye - lids close!

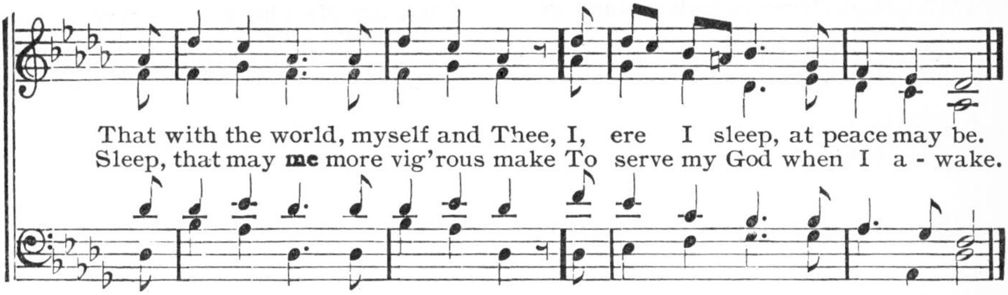

That with the world, myself and Thee, I, ere I sleep, at peace may be.
Sleep, that may me more vig'rous make To serve my God when I a - wake.

36 b Tallis' Canon L. M.

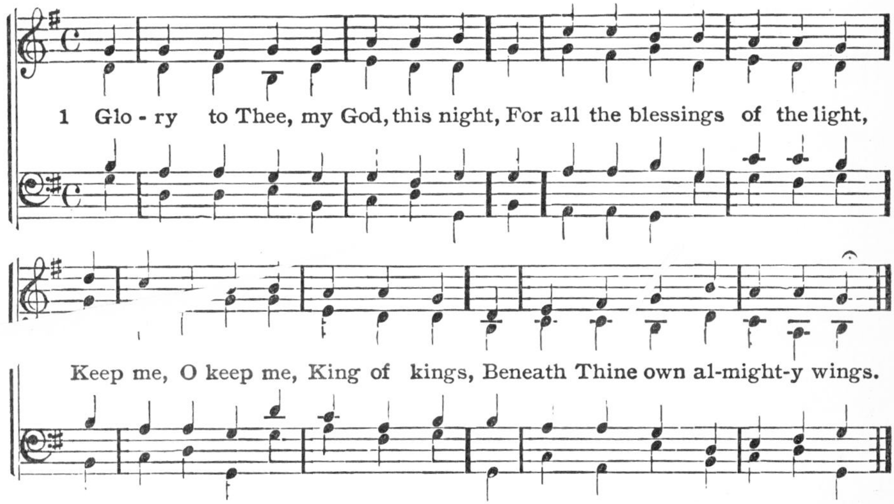

1 Glo - ry to Thee, my God, this night, For all the blessings of the light,

Keep me, O keep me, King of kings, Beneath Thine own al-might-y wings.

37 Evening Prayer 8, 7, 8, 7

GEORGE C. STEBBINS, 1878

1 Sav - ior, breathe an evening blessing, Ere re-pose our spir - its seal;

Sin and want we come con - fes-sing: Thou canst save, and Thou canst heal.

(Or to Batty)

He who, never weary,
h where Thy people be.

ift death this night o'ertake us
couch become our tomb,
morn in heaven awake us,
light and deathless bloom.

James Edmeston, 1820

J. BARNBY, 1872 (P)

is clos - ing The
- pos - ing, And 'neath His

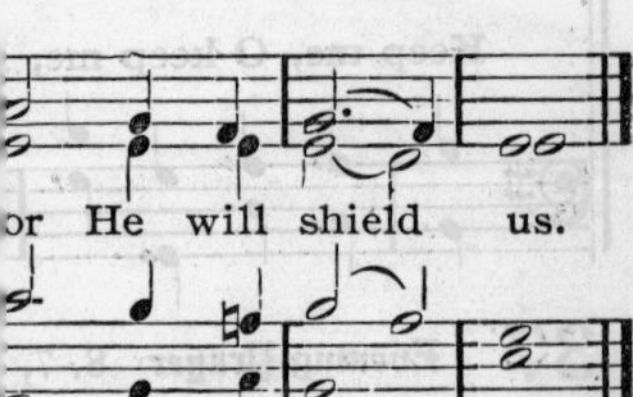

or He will shield us.

and orphans, we to Thee com-
hem,
befriend them.

no refuge, none on earth to aid

e, O Father, who Thine own
ade us;
dear presence will not leave
onely
Thee only.

Thy name be praised, Thy king-
ven,
be done on earth as 'tis in

y bread, forgive our sins,

nd ever.

ethren, 1566. C. Winkworth, Tr. 1863. a

Evening

39 Hebron L. M.

LOWELL MASON, 1830

1 Thus far the Lord has led me on; Thus far His

pow'r pro - longs my days; And ev - 'ry eve - ning

shall make known Some fresh me - mo - rial of His grace.

2 Much of my time has run to waste,
And I, perhaps, am near my home;
But He forgives my follies past,
And gives me strength for days to come.

3 I lay my body down to sleep;
Peace is the pillow for my head;
His ever-watchful eye will keep
Its constant guard around my bed.

4 Faith in Thy name forbids my fear;
O may Thy presence ne'er depart!
And in the morning may I bear
Thy loving-kindness on my heart!

Rev. Issac Watts, 1709, alt and ab.

40 Eventide 10s

W. H. MONK, 1861

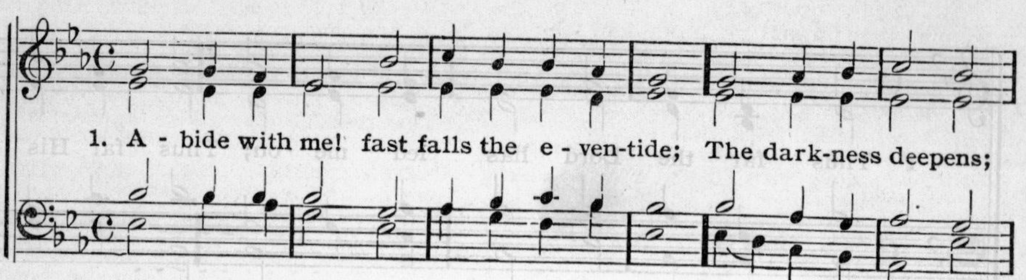
1. A - bide with me! fast falls the e - ven-tide; The dark-ness deepens;

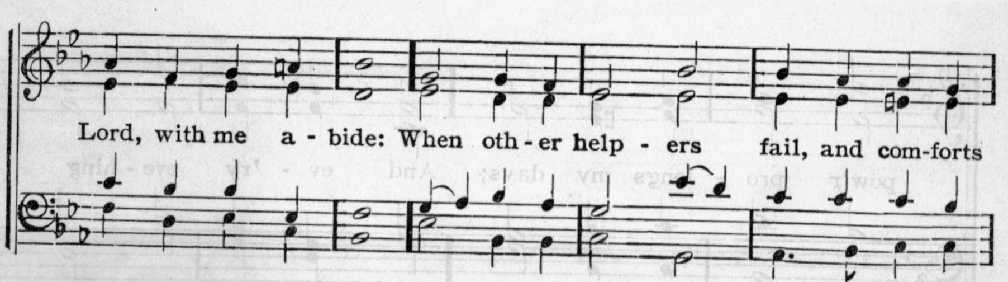
Lord, with me a - bide: When oth - er help - ers fail, and com-forts

flee, Help of the help-less, Oh, a - bide with me.

2 Swift to its close ebbs out life's little day;
Earth's joys grow dim, its glories pass away;
Change and decay in all around I see;
O Thou who changest not, abide with me!

3 Not a brief glance I beg, a passing word
But as Thou dwell'st with Thy disciples, Lord,
Familiar, condescending, patient, free,
Come, not to sojourn, but abide with me.

4 Come not in terrors as the King of kings,
But kind and good, with healing in Thy wings;
Tears for all woes, a heart for every plea;
O Friend of sinners, thus abide with me!

5 Thou on my head in early youth didst smile,
And, though rebellious and perverse meanwhile,
Thou hast not left me, oft as I left Thee:
On to the close, O Lord, abide with me!

6 I need Thy presence every passing hour:
What but Thy grace can foil the Tempter's power?
Who like Thyself my guide and stay can be?
Through cloud and sunshine, O abide with me!

7 I fear no foe, with Thee at hand to bless:
Ills have no weight, and tears no bitterness.
Where is death's sting? where, grave, thy victory?
I triumph still, if Thou abide with me!

8 Hold Thou Thy cross before my closing eyes,
Shine through the gloom, and point me to the skies:
Heaven's morning breaks, and earth's vain shadows flee;
In life, in death, O Lord, abide with me!

Henry F. Lyte, 1847

41 Schumann (Heath) S. M.

An. fr. R. SCHUMANN, 1810—1856

1. The day is past and gone, The eve - ning shades ap - pear;

O may I ev - er keep in mind The night of death draws near.

2 Lord, keep me safe this night,
Secure from all my fears;
May angels guard me while I sleep,
Till morning light appears.

3 And when I early rise,
And view the unwearied sun,
May I set out to win the prize,
And after glory run:

4 That when my days are past,
And I from time remove,
Lord, I may in Thy bosom rest,
The bosom of Thy love.

John Leland, 1792

Evening

42 Hursley L. M. P. RITTER, 1792. Arr. by W. H. MONK, 1861

1. Sun of my soul, Thou Sav - ior dear, It is not

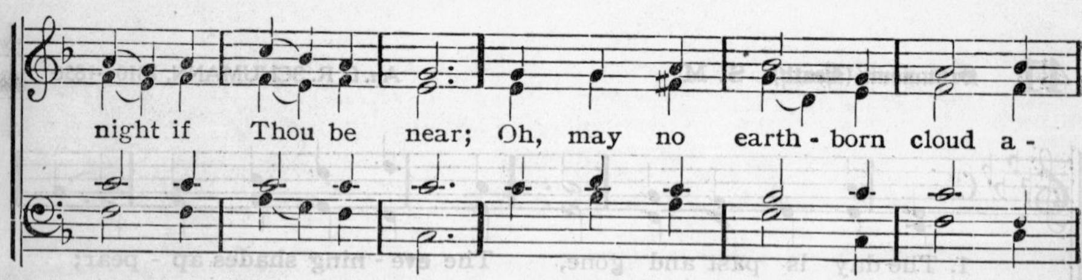
night if Thou be near; Oh, may no earth - born cloud a -

rise, To hide Thee from Thy ser - vant's eyes.

2 When the soft dews of kindly sleep
My wearied eyelids gently steep,
Be my last thought, how sweet to rest
Forever on my Savior's breast.

3 Abide with me from morn till eve,
For without Thee I cannot live;
Abide with me when night is nigh,
For without Thee I dare not die.

4 If some poor wandering child of Thine
Has spurned to-day the voice divine,
Now, Lord, the gracious work begin;
Let him no more lie down in sin.

5 Watch by the sick; enrich the poor
With blessings from Thy boundless store;
Be every mourner's sleep to-night,
Like infant's slumbers, pure and light.

6 Come near and bless us when we wake,
Ere through the world our way we take;
And lead us by Thy hand of love,
Until we reach our home above.

J. Keble, 1820

Evening

43 Through the Day 8, 7, 8, 7, 7, 7 — Sir JOSEPH BARNBY, 1872

1. Through the day Thy love has spared us, Now we lay us down to rest;

Through the si - lent watches guard us; Let no foe our peace mo - lest:

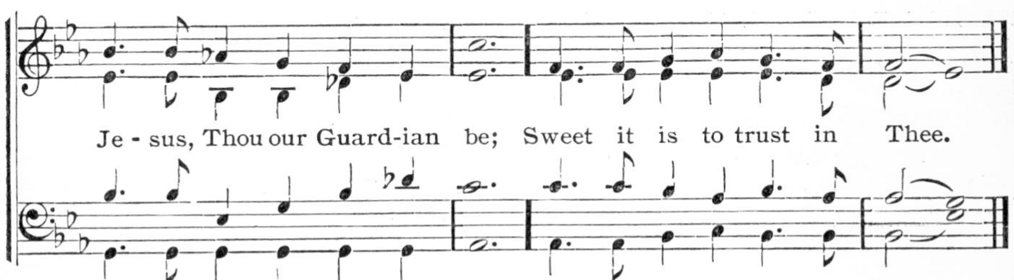
Je - sus, Thou our Guard-ian be; Sweet it is to trust in Thee.

(*Or to Gott des Himmels*)

2 Pilgrims here on earth, and strangers,
  Dwelling in the midst of foes,
Us and ours preserve from dangers;
  In Thine arms may we repose;
And, when life's sad day is past,
Rest with Thee in heaven at last.

3 Triune God, let all adore Thee,
  Saints on earth, and saints in heaven;
Every creature bow before Thee,
  Who hast all their being given;
Who dost seek and save the lost;
Father, Son, and Holy Ghost.

Rev. Thomas Kelly, 1806

Evening

44 Temple 8, 4, 8, 4, 8, 8, 8, 4 E. J. HOPKINS, 1867 (P)

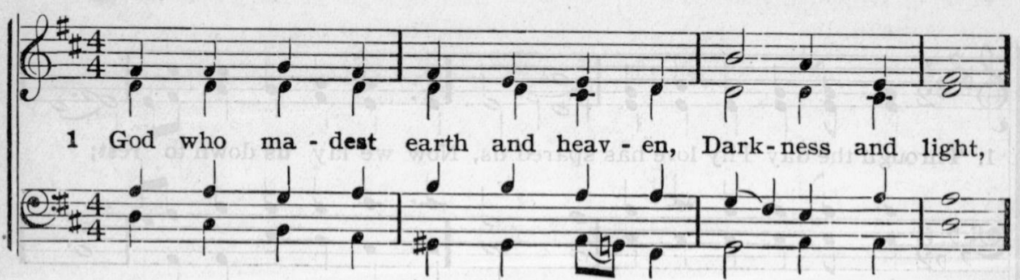
1 God who ma - dest earth and heav - en, Dark - ness and light,

Who the day for toil hast giv - en, For rest the night,

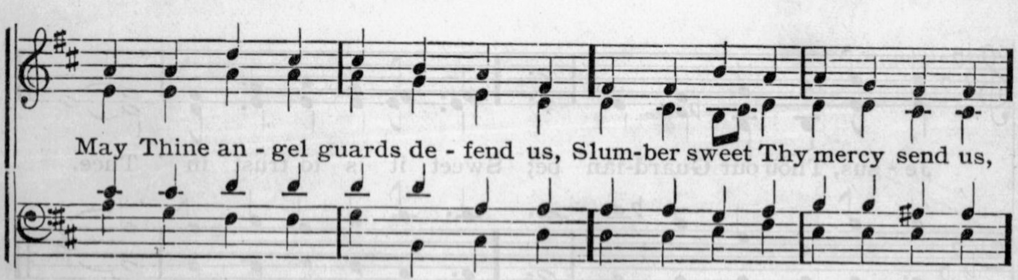
May Thine an - gel guards de - fend us, Slum - ber sweet Thy mercy send us,

Ho - ly dreams and hopes at - tend us, This live - long night.

2 Guard us waking, guard us sleeping,
And when we die,
Let us in Thy mighty keeping
All peaceful lie.
When the trumpet's call shall wake us,
Do not Thou, blest Lord, forsake us,
But to reign in glory take us
With Thee on high!

Reginald Heber, 1827; 2d stanza, Richard Whately, 1860

45 Merrial 6, 5, 6, 5

BARNBY

1. Now the day is o - ver, Night is draw - ing nigh;

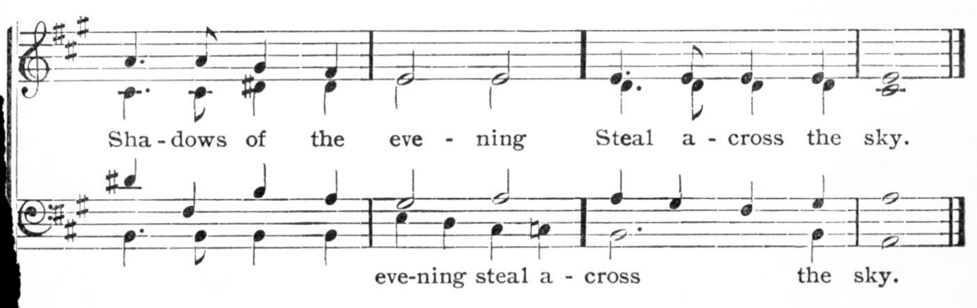
Sha - dows of the eve - ning Steal a - cross the sky.
eve-ning steal a - cross the sky.

2 Now the darkness gathers,
Stars begin to peep,
Birds, and beasts, and flowers
Soon will be asleep.

3 Jesus, give the weary
Calm and sweet repose,
With Thy tenderest blessing
May my eyelids close.

4 Through the long night-watches
May Thine Angels spread
Their white wings above me,
Watching round by bed.

5 When the morning wakens,
Then may I arise
Pure and fresh and sinless
In Thy Holy Eyes.

6 Glory to the Father,
Glory to the Son,
And to Thee, blest Spirit,
While all ages run.

S. Baring-Gould, 1865. ab

Invitation

46 Vox Dilecti C. M. 81 Mel. J B. DYKES (P)

1 I heard the voice of Je - sus say, "Come un - to me and rest;
Lay down, thou wear - y one, lay down Thy head up - on my breast."
I came to Je - sus as I was, Wear - y and worn and sad;
2d v, Of that life - giv - ing stream;
3d v, In Him my star, my sun,
I found in Him a rest ing-place, And He has made me glad.

2 I heard the voice of Jesus say,
"Behold, I freely give
The living water; thirsty one,
Stoop down, and drink, and live!"
I came to Jesus and I drank
Of that life-giving stream;
My thirst was quenched, my soul revived,
And now I live in Him.

3 I heard the voice of Jesus say,
"I am this dark world's Light;
Look unto me, thy morn shall rise,
And all thy day be bright!"
I looked to Jesus, and I found
In Him my star, my Sun;
And in that Light of life I'll walk,
Till traveling days are done.

47 Azmon C. M.

LOWELL MASON, 1828. Arr. by CARL GLAESER

1 The Sav-ior calls; let ev -'ry ear At - tend the heaven-ly sound.

Ye doubt-ing souls, dis - miss your fear; Hope smiles re - viv - ing round.

2 For every thirsty, longing heart,
Here streams of bounty flow,
And life, and health, and bliss impart,
To banish mortal woe.

3 Here springs of sacred pleasure rise
To ease your every pain;
Immortal fountain! full supplies!
Nor shall you thirst in vain.

4 Ye sinners come, 'tis mercy's voice;
The gracious call obey:
Mercy invites to heavenly joys,
And can you yet delay?

5 Dear Savior, draw reluctant hearts;
To Thee let sinners fly,
And take the bliss Thy love imparts,
And drink and never die.

Anne Steele, 1760

48 Heinlein (Aus der Tiefe) 7s

M. HEINLEIN, 1676

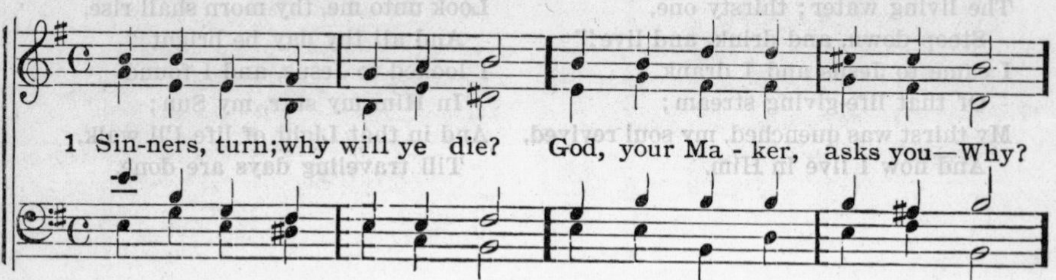
1 Sin-ners, turn; why will ye die? God, your Ma - ker, asks you—Why?

God, who did your be - ing give, Made you with Him - self to live.

2 He the fatal cause demands,
Asks the work of His own hands,
Why, ye thankless creatures, why
Will ye cross His love and die?

3 Sinners, turn; why will ye die?
God, your Savior, asks you—Why?
He, who did your souls retrieve,
Died Himself that you might live.

4 Will ye let Him die in vain?
Crucify your Lord again?
Why, ye ransomed sinners, why
Will ye slight His grace, and die?

5 Sinners, turn; why will ye die?
God, the Spirit asks you—Why?
He who all your life-time strove,
Wooed you to embrace His love.

6 Will ye not His grace receive?
Will ye still refuse to live?
O ye long-sought sinners, why
Will ye grieve your God and die?

Charles Wesley 1741

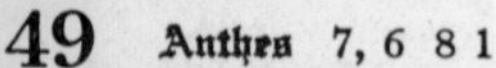

49 Anthes 7, 6 8 1

ANTHES, 1847

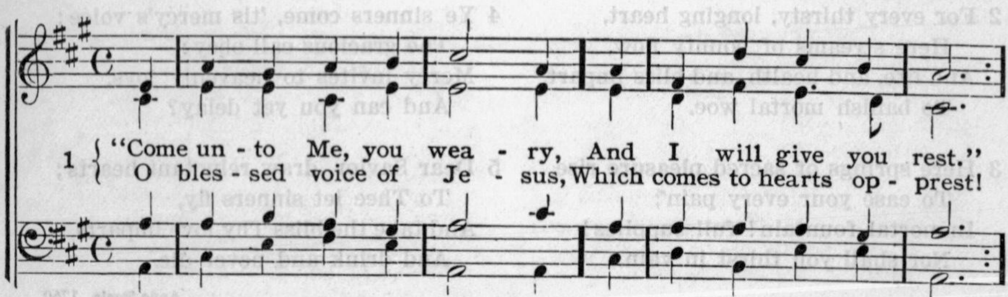
1 { "Come un - to Me, you wea - ry, And I will give you rest."
O bles - sed voice of Je - sus, Which comes to hearts op - prest!

Invitation

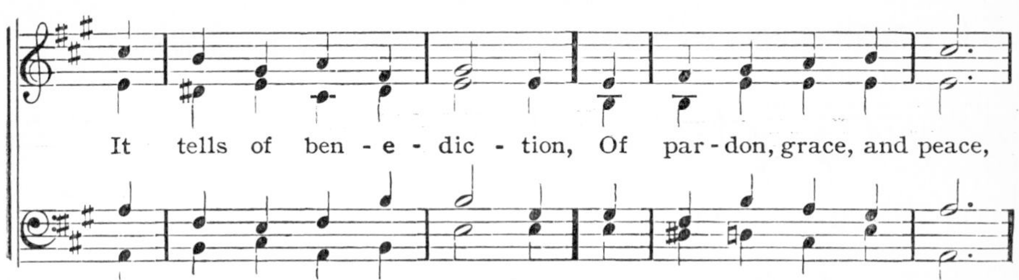
It tells of ben - e - dic - tion, Of par - don, grace, and peace,

Of joy that hath no end - ing, Of love which can - not cease.

2 "Come unto Me, dear children,
And I will give you light."
O loving voice of Jesus,
Which comes to cheer the night.
Our hearts were filled with sadness,
And we had lost our way;
But He has brought us gladness
And songs at break of day.

3 "Come unto Me, ye weary,
And I will give you life."
O cheering voice of Jesus,
Which comes to aid our strife,
The foe is stern and eager,
The fight is fierce and long;
But Thou hast made us mighty
And stronger than the strong.

4 "And whosoever cometh
I will not cast him out."
O welcome voice of Jesus,
Which drives away our doubt,
Which calls us, very sinners,
Unworthy though we be
Of love so free and boundless,
To come, dear Lord, to Thee.

W. C. Dix, 1867

50 7, 6

1 TODAY Thy mercy calls us
To wash away our sin,
However great our trespass,
Whatever we have been;
However long from mercy
Our hearts have turn'd away,
Thy precious blood can cleanse us,
And make us white today.

2 Today Thy gate is open,
And all who enter in
Shall find a Father's welcome,
And pardon for their sin.
The past shall be forgotten,
A present joy be given,
A future grace be promised,
A glorious crown in heaven.

3 Today our Father calls us,
His Holy Spirit waits;
His blessed angels gather
Around the heavenly gates.
No question will be asked us
How often we have come;
Although we oft have wandered,
It is our Father's home.

4 O all-embracing mercy!
O ever-open door!
What should we do without Thee
When heart and eye run o'er?
When all things seem against us,
To drive us to despair,
We know one gate is open,
One ear will hear our prayer.

O. Allen, 1862

51 Zephyr L. M. W. B. BRADBURY, 1844 (P)

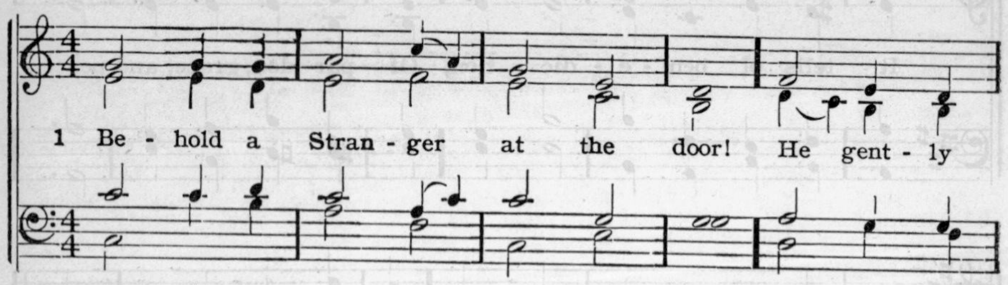
1 Be - hold a Stran - ger at the door! He gent - ly

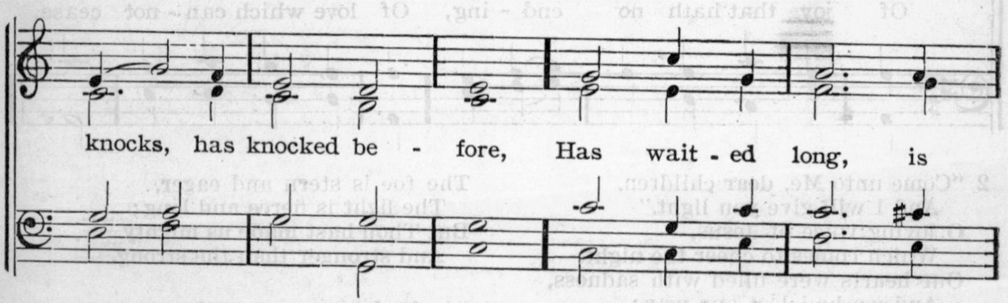
knocks, has knocked be - fore, Has wait - ed long, is

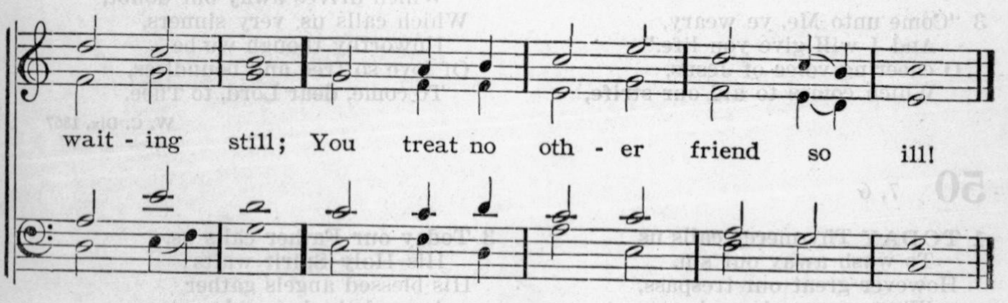
wait - ing still; You treat no oth - er friend so ill!

(Or to Rivaulx)

2 But will He prove a friend indeed?
He will; the very friend you need:
The friend of sinners—yes, 'tis He,
With garments dyed on Calvary.

3 O lovely attitude! He stands
With melting heart and laden hands;
O matchless kindness! and He shows
This matchless kindness to His foes.

4 Admit Him, lest His anger burn,
And He, departing, ne'er return:
Admit Him, or the hour's at hand,
When, at His door, denied you'll stand.

Rev. Joseph Grigg, 1765. a

52 Monsell (St. Andrew) S. M.

J. BARNBY, 1866 (P)

1 The Spir - it, in our hearts, Is whispering, "Sin-ner, come!"

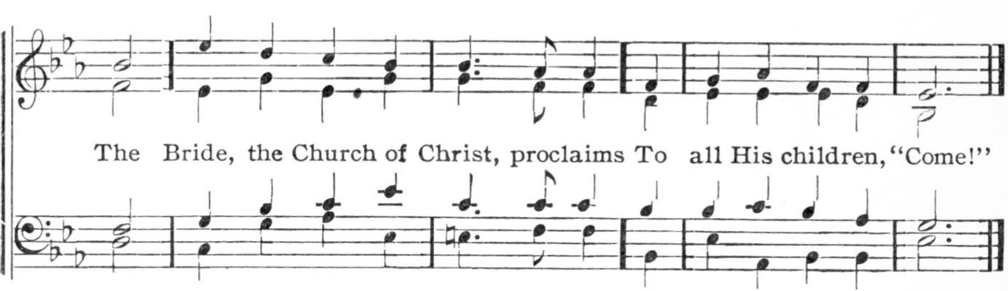
The Bride, the Church of Christ, proclaims To all His children, "Come!"

(*Or to Schumann Or to St. Thomas*)

2 Let him that heareth say
To all about him, "Come!"
Let him that thirsts for righteousness,
To Christ, the Fountain, come!

3 Yes, whosoever will,
O let him freely come,
And freely drink the stream of life;
'Tis Jesus bids him come.

4 Lo, Jesus, who invites,
Declares, "I quickly come;"
Lord, even so! I wait Thine hour;
Jesus, my Savior, come.

H. U. Onderdonk, 1826

53 Monsell S. M.

1 Let every ear attend,
And every heart rejoice;
The trumpet of the Gospel sounds
With an inviting voice.

2 Ho! all ye starving souls,
That feed upon the wind,
And vainly strive with earthly toys
To fill an empty mind.

3 Here Wisdom has prepared
A soul-reviving feast,
And bids your longing appetites
The rich provision taste.

4 Ho! ye that pant for streams,
And pine away and die,
Here you may quench your raging thirst
With springs that never dry.

5 Rivers of mercy here
In a rich ocean join;
Salvation in abundance flows,
Like floods of milk and wine.

6 The gates of Gospel grace
Stand open night and day:
Lord! we are come to seek supplies,
And drive our wants away.

Isaac Watts, 1707

Invitation

54 Abends L. M. H. S. OAKELEY, 1873 (P)

1 Re - turn, O wan - der - er, re - turn, And seek an

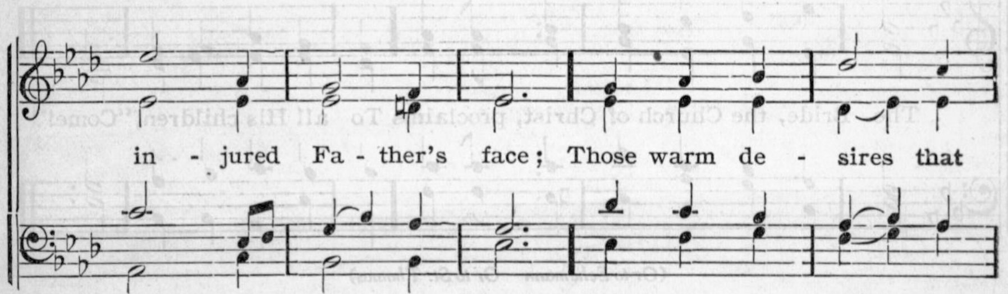
in - jured Fa - ther's face; Those warm de - sires that

in thee burn Were kin - dled by re - claim - ing grace.

(Or to Hebron)

2 Return, O wanderer, return,
And seek a Father's melting heart;
His pitying eyes thy grief discern,
His hand shall heal thine inward smart.

3 Return, O wanderer, return,
Thy Savior bids thy spirit live;
Go to His bleeding feet, and learn
How freely Jesus can forgive.

4 Return, O wanderer, return,
And wipe away the falling tear;
'Tis God who says, "No longer mourn,"
'Tis mercy's voice invites thee near.

55 Abends L. M.

1 Hasten, O sinner, to be wise,
And stay not for the morrow's sun,
The longer wisdom you despise,
The harder is she to be won.

2 O hasten, mercy to implore,
And stay not for the morrow's sun,
For fear thy season should be o'er
Before this evening's course be run.

3 Hasten, O sinner, to return,
And stay not for the morrow's sun,
For fear thy lamp should fail to burn
Before the needful work is done.

4 Hasten, O sinner, to be blest,
And stay not for the morrow's sun,
For fear the curse should thee arrest
Before the morrow is begun.

Thomas Scott, 1773

56 Brasted 7s

P. WEIMER

1 Come, my soul, thy suit pre - pare, Je - sus loves to an - swer prayer;

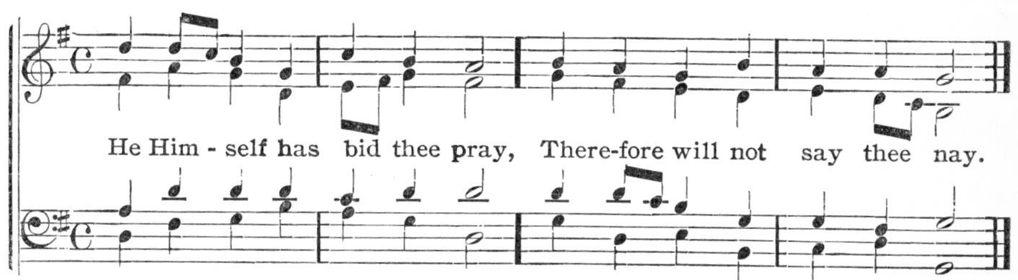
He Him - self has bid thee pray, There-fore will not say thee nay.

2 Thou art coming to a King:
Large petitions with thee bring;
For His grace and power are such,
None can ever ask too much.

3 With my burden I begin:
Lord, remove this load of sin ;
Let Thy blood, for sinners spilt,
Set my conscience free from guilt.

4 Lord, I come to Thee for rest,
Take possession of my breast;
There Thy blood-bought right maintain,
And without a rival reign.

5 While I am a pilgrim here,
Let Thy love my spirit cheer;
As my guide, my guard, my friend,
Lead me to my journey's end.

6 Show me what I have to do,
Every hour my strength renew;
Let me live a life of faith,
Let me die Thy people's death.

John Newton, 1779

Invitation

57 Delay Not 11s, 4 1

WM. CROFT (?), 1708. HAENDEL (?)

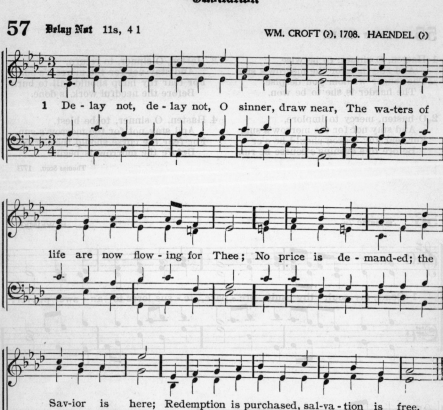

1 De - lay not, de - lay not, O sinner, draw near, The wa-ters of

life are now flow - ing for Thee; No price is de - mand-ed; the

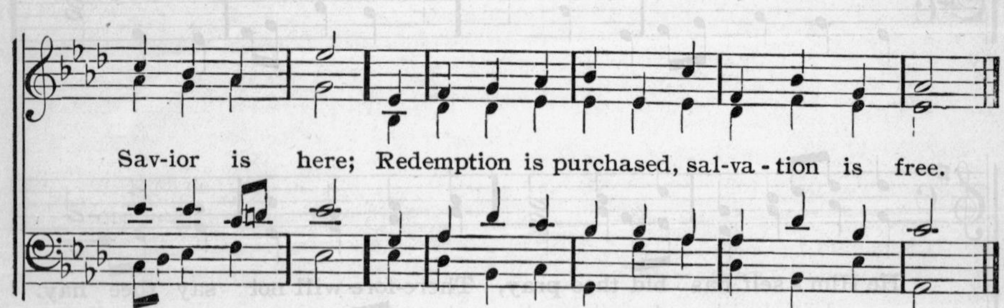
Sav-ior is here; Redemption is purchased, sal-va - tion is free.

2 Delay not, delay not, why longer abuse
The love and compassion of Jesus, thy God?
A fountain is opened; how canst thou refuse
To wash and be cleansed in His pardoning blood?

3 Delay not, delay not, O sinner, to come,
For mercy still lingers, and calls thee today;
Her voice is not heard in the vale of the tomb;
Her message, unheeded, will soon pass away.

4 Delay not, delay not, the Spirit of grace,
Long grieved and resisted, may take its sad flight,
And leave thee in darkness to finish thy race,
To sink in the gloom of eternity's night.

5 Delay not, delay not, the hour is at hand;
The earth shall dissolve, and the heavens shall fade;
The dead, small and great, in the judgment shall stand;
What power then, O sinner, shall lend thee its aid?

Thomas Hastings, 1831

58 Ach, wann werd ich dahin kommen 7s

WITT, 1715

1 Come, ye wear-y sin - ners come, All who feel your heav - y load;

Je - sus calls His wand-'rers home; Has - ten to your pardoning God.

(Or to Seymour)

2 Come, ye guilty souls oppressed,
Answer to the Savior's call:
"Come, and I will give you rest;
Come, and I will save you all."

3 Jesus, full of truth and love,
We Thy gracious call obey;
Faithful let Thy mercies prove,
Take our load of guilt away.

4 Fain we would on Thee rely,
Cast on Thee our sin and care:
To Thine arms of mercy fly,
Find our lasting quiet there.

5 Lo, we come to Thee for ease:
True and gracious as Thou art,
Now our weary souls release,
Write forgiveness on our heart.

Charles Wesley. a

Praise

59 Nun lob' mein Seel' den Herren 7,8,7,8,7,6,7,6,7,6,6,7,6 BABST, 1557

1 { My soul, now bless thy Mak - er! Let all with-
Who mak - eth thee par - tak - er Of mer - cies

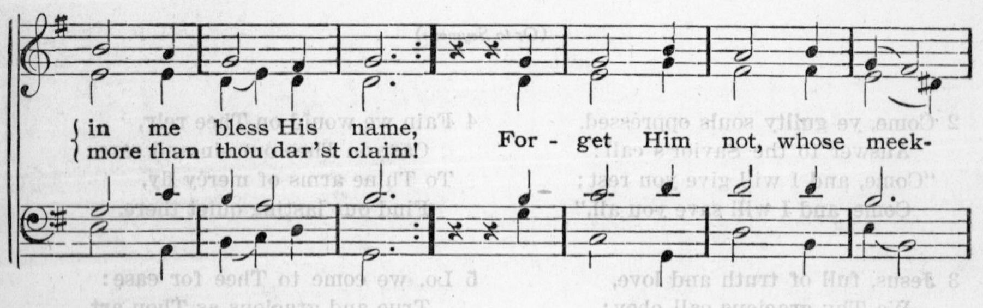
{ in me bless His name,
more than thou dar'st claim! For - get Him not, whose meek-

ness, For - giv - eth all thy sin; Who heal - eth all thy

weak - ness, Re - news thy life with - in; Whose grace and

care are end - less, And saved thee through the past; Who

leaves no suffer - er friend - less, But rights the wronged at last.

2 He shows to man His treasure
  Of judgment, truth, and righteousness,
His love beyond all measure,
  His yearning pity o'er distress;
Nor treats us as we merit,
  But lays His anger by,
The humble, contrite spirit
  Finds His compassion nigh;
Far as the heavens above us,
  As break from close of day,
So far, since He doth love us,
  He casts our sins away.

3 For as a tender father
  Hath pity on his children here,
He in His arms will gather
  All who are His in childlike fear.
He knows how frail our powers,
  Who but from dust are made,
We flourish as the flowers,
  And even so we fade,
The wind but o'er them passes,
  And all their bloom is o'er,—
We wither like the grasses,
  Our place knows us no more.

4 His grace alone endureth,
  And children's children yet shall prove
How God with strength assureth
  The hearts of all that seek His love.
In heaven is fixed His dwelling,
  His rule is over all;
Angels in might excelling,
  Bright hosts, before Him fall!
Praise Him who ever reigneth,
  All ye who hear His Word,
Nor our poor hymns disdaineth;—
  My soul, O bless the Lord!

Johann Graumann, 1525; C. Winkworth, Tr. a

60 Lobet den Herrn, ihr Heiden all 8, 7, 8, 7, 8, 8, 7

VULPIUS, 1609 [I]

1 To God, the Fa - ther of all love, The God of earth and heav - en,
The might - y God who reigns a - bove, Be praise and glo - ry giv - en!
With heal-ing balm my soul He fills, And ev-'ry pain and sor - row stills: To God all praise and glo - ry!

(Or to Nun freut euch lieben)

2 The angel host, O King of kings,
Thy praise forever telling,
In earth and sky all living things
Beneath Thy shadow dwelling,
Adore and praise their Maker's might,
Whose wisdom orders all things right;
To God all praise and glory!

3 What God's almighty power hath made,
His gracious mercy keepeth;
By morning glow or evening shade
His watchful eye ne'er sleepeth;
Within the kingdom of His might,
Lo! all is just and all is right;
To God all praise and glory!

4 I cried to God in my distress,
His mercy heard me calling;
My Savior saw my helplessness,
And kept my feet from falling;
For this, Lord, praise and thanks to Thee!
Praise God most high, praise God with me!
To God all praise and glory!

5 The Lord forsaketh not His flock,
His chosen generation;
He is their Refuge and their Rock,
Their Peace and their Salvation,
And with a mother's watchful love
He guides them wheresoe'er they rove;
To God all praise and glory!

6 When earth can comfort us no more,
Nor human help availeth,
The Maker comes Himself, whose store
Of blessing never faileth,
And bends on them a Father's eyes
Whom earth all rest and hope denies;
To God all praise and glory!

7 Thus all my pilgrim way along
I'll sing aloud Thy praises,
That men may hear the grateful song
My voice unwearied raises;
Be joyful in the Lord, my heart!
Both soul and body, bear your part!
To God all praise and glory!

8 Ye who confess Christ's holy name,
To God give praise and glory!
Ye who the Father's power proclaim,
To God give praise and glory!
All idols under foot be trod,
The Lord is God! The Lord is God!
To God all praise and glory!

9 Then come before His presence now,
And banish fear and sadness;
To your Redeemer pay your vow,
And sing with joy and gladness:
Though great distress my soul befell,
The Lord my God did all things well;
To God all praise and glory!

Johann Jakob Schuetz, 1673

61 Nun danket all und bringet Ehr C. M.

J. CRUEGER, 1656

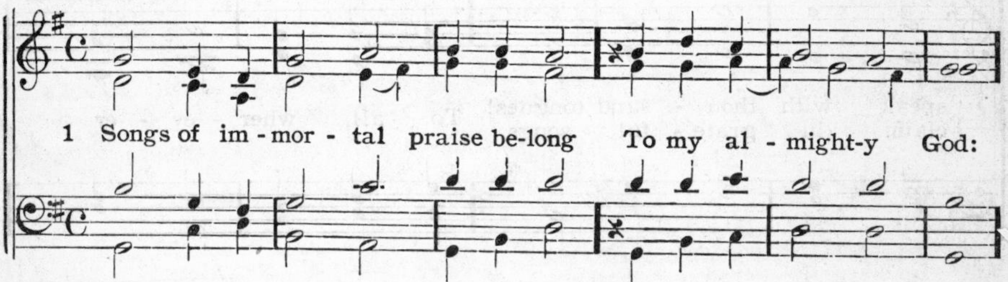
1 Songs of im-mor-tal praise be-long To my al-might-y God:

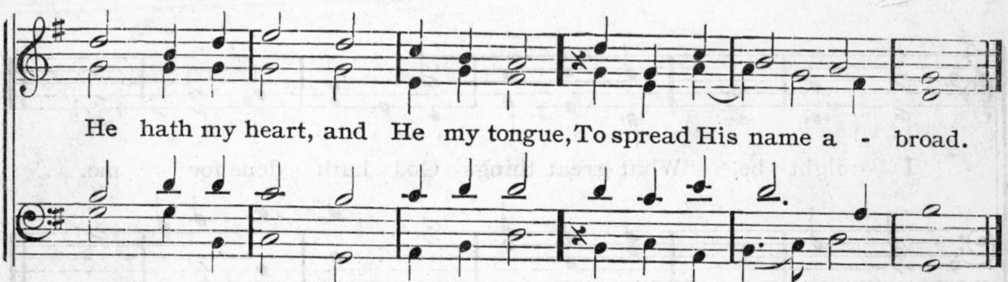
He hath my heart, and He my tongue, To spread His name a - broad.

2 How great the works His hand hath wrought!
How glorious in our sight!
And men in every age have sought
His wonders with delight.

3 How most exact is nature's frame!
How wise th' eternal Mind!
His counsels never change the scheme
That His first thoughts designed.

4 When He redeemed the sons of men,
He fixed His covenant sure;
The orders that His lips pronounce
To endless years endure.

5 Nature and time and earth and skies
Thy heavenly skill proclaim.
What shall we do to make us wise,
But learn to read Thy name!

6 To fear Thy power, to trust Thy grace,
Is our divinest skill;
And He's the wisest of our race,
Who best obeys Thy will.

Rev. Issac Watts

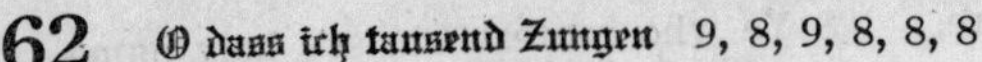
62 O dass ich tausend Zungen 9, 8, 9, 8, 8, 8

DRETZEL, 1731

1 O that I had a thou - sand voic - es! A mouth to
My heart which in the Lord re - joic - es, Then would pro -

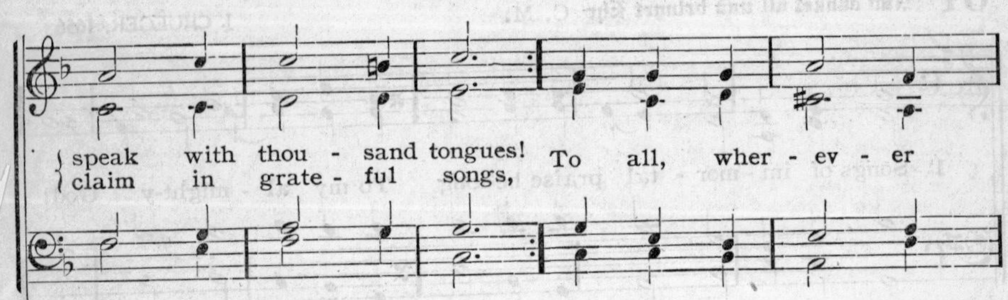
speak with thou - sand tongues! To all, wher - ev - er
claim in grate - ful songs,

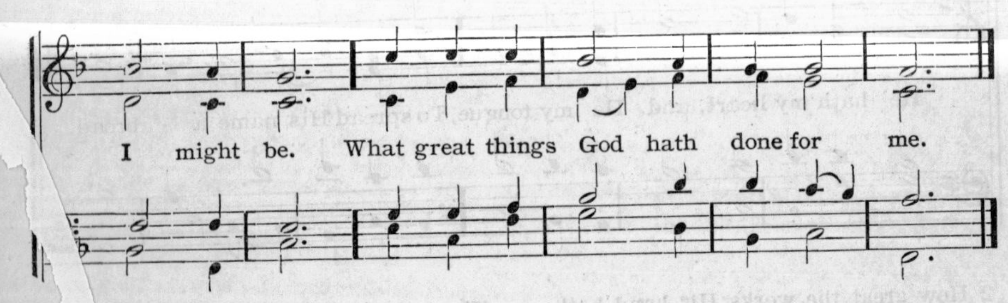
I might be. What great things God hath done for me.

2 O that my voice might high be sounding,
Far as the widely distant poles;
My blood run quick with rapture bounding,
Long as its vital current rolls,
And every pulse thanksgiving raise,
And every breath a hymn of praise!

3 O all ye powers that God implanted,
Arise, keep silence thus no more,
Put forth the strength that He hath granted,
Your noblest work is to adore;
My soul and body make ye meet
With heartfelt praise your Lord to greet!

4 Ye forest leaves so green and tender,
That dance for joy in summer air;
Ye meadow grasses bright and slender,
Ye flowers so wondrous sweet and fair;
Ye live to show His praise alone,
Help me to make His glory known!

5 O all things that have breath and motion
That throng with life earth, sea, and sky,
Now join me in my heart's devotion,
Help me to raise His praises high;
My utmost powers can ne'er aright
Declare the wonders of His might.

6 Dear Father, endless praise I render
For soul and body strangely joined;
I praise Thee, guardian kind and tender,
For all the noble joys I find
So richly spread on every side,
And freely for my use supplied.

7 What equal praises can I offer,
Dear Jesus, for Thy mercy shown?
What pangs, my Savior, didst Thou suffer,
And thus for all my sins atone!
Thy death alone my soul could free
From Satan, to be blest with Thee.

8 Honor and praise, still onward reaching,
Be Thine too, Spirit of all grace,
Whose holy power and faithful teaching
Give me among Thy saints a place:
Whate'er of good in me may shine
Comes only from Thy light divine.

9 Who grants abundant gifts to bless me?
Who, but Thyself, O God of love?
Who guards my ways lest fears oppress me
'Tis Thou, Lord God of hosts, above!
And when my sins Thy wrath provoke,
Thy patience, Lord, forbears the stroke.

10 I kiss the rod, too, unrepining,
When God His chastening makes me feel,
My graces call for His refining,
The trial works no lasting ill:
It purifies and makes it known
That He regards me as a son.

11 In life I often have discovered,
With gratitude and glad surprise,
When clouds of sorrows o'er me hovered,
God sent from them my best supplies:
In troubles He is ever near,
And shows me all a Father's care.

12 Why not, then, with a faith unbounded,
Forever in His love confide?
Why not, with earthly griefs surrounded,
Rejoicing still in hope abide?
Until I reach that blissful home
Where doubt and sorrow never come?

13 No more low vanities regarding,
To Thee, in whom I find my rest,
I cry—my inmost soul according,—
"My God, Thou art the highest, best;
Strength, honor, praise, and thanks, and power
Be Thine, both now and evermore!"

14 Lord, I will tell, while I am living,
Thy goodness forth with every breath,
And greet each morning with thanksgiving,
Until my heart is still in death,
Yea, when at last my lips grow cold,
Thy praise shall in my sighs be told.

15 O Father, deign Thou, I beseech Thee,
To listen to my earthly lays;
A nobler strain in heaven shall reach Thee,
When I with angels hymn Thy praise,
And learn amid their choirs to sing
Loud hallelujahs to my King.

Joh. Menzer, 1704

63 Lobe den Herren, den maechtigen 14, 14, 4, 7, 8 STRALSUND H. B. 1665

1
Praise to the Lord, the Al - might - y, the King of cre-
O my soul, praise Him, for He is thy Health and Sal-

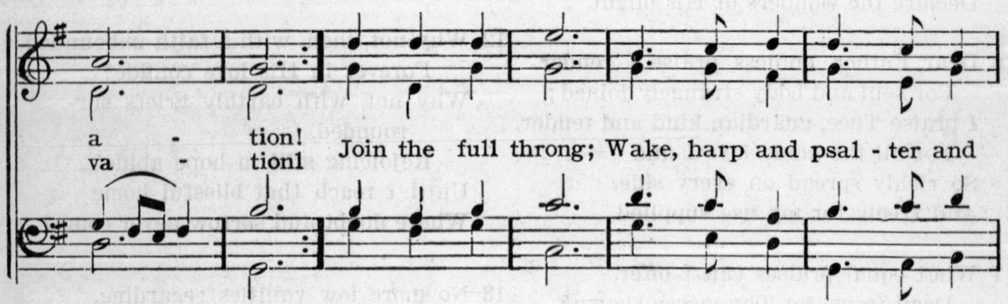
a - tion! Join the full throng; Wake, harp and psal - ter and
va - tion!

song; Sound forth in glad a - do - ra - - - tion.

2 Praise to the Lord, who o'er all things so wondrously reigneth,
Who, as on wings of an eagle, uplifteth, sustaineth;
Hast thou not seen
How thy desires all have been
Granted in what He ordaineth?

3 Praise to the Lord, who hath fearfully, wondrously made thee;
Health hath vouchsafed, and when heedlessly falling hath stayed thee;
What need or grief
Ever hath failed of relief?—
Wings of His mercy did shade thee.

4 Praise to the Lord, who doth visibly bless and defend thee;
Who, from the heavens, the streams of His mercy doth send thee;
Ponder anew
What the Almighty can do,
If with His love He befriend thee!

5 Praise to the Lord! O let all that is in me adore Him!
All that hath life and breath, come now with praises before Him!
He is thy Light;
Soul, keep it always in sight,
Gladly forever adore Him!

Joachim Neander, 1679

64 Nun danket alle Gott 6, 7, 6, 7, 6, 6, 6, 6 J. CRUEGER, 1648

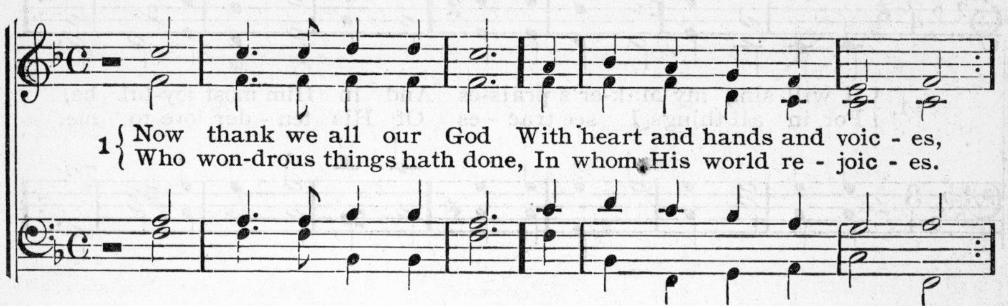
1 { Now thank we all our God With heart and hands and voic - es,
Who won-drous things hath done, In whom His world re - joic - es.

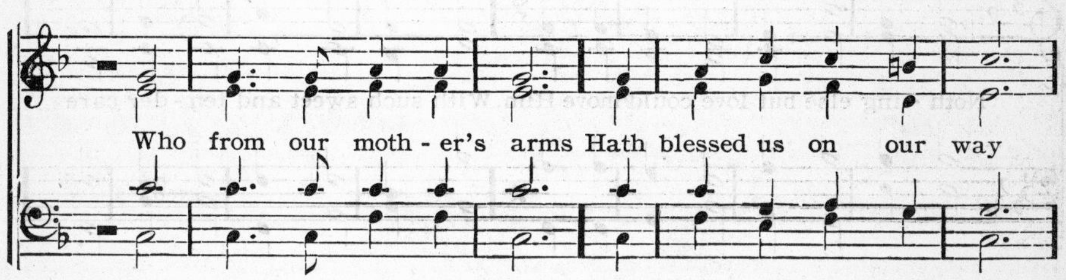
Who from our moth - er's arms Hath blessed us on our way

With count-less gifts of love, And still is ours to - day.

2 O may this bounteous God
  Through all this life be near us,
With ever joyful hearts
  And blessed peace to cheer us;
And keep us in His grace,
  And guide us when perplexed,
And free us from all ills
  In this world and the next.

3 All praise and thanks to God
  The Father now be given
The Son, and Him who reigns
  With them in highest heaven:
The One eternal God,
  Whom earth and heaven adore;
For thus it was, is now,
  And shall be evermore!

Martin Rinkart, 1644. C. Winkworth, Tr. 1858

Praise

65 Sollt' ich meinem Gott nicht singen 8, 7, 8, 7, 8, 7, 7, 8, 7, 7 J. SCHOP, 1640

1. I will sing my Mak-er's prais-es And in Him most joy-ful be,
For in all things I see trac - es Of His ten - der love to me.
Noth - ing else but love could move Him, With such sweet and ten - der care
Ev - er - more to raise and bear All who try to serve and love Him.
All things else have but their day, God's great love a - bides for aye.

2 As an eagle spreadeth over
Her young brood her sheltering wings,
So the arm of God did cover
Me against affliction's stings.
He who life and being gave me,
Even in my mother's womb,
From the cradle to the tomb
He shall ever guard and save me.
All things else have but their day,
God's great love abides for aye.

3 Yea, so dear did He esteem me,
That His Son He loved so well
He hath given to redeem me
From the quenchless flames of hell.
O Thou Spring of boundless blessing,
How could e'er my feeble mind
Of Thy depth the bottom find,
Though my efforts were unceasing?
All things else have but their day,
God's great love abides for aye.

4 God His Spirit to instruct me
In His holy Word hath given,
That He safely may conduct me
Through this weary world to heaven.
He my heart's dark cnamber filleth
With the clear pure light of faith,
Which destroys the power of death,
Yea, e'en hell itself it stilleth.
All things else have but their day,
God's great love abides for aye.

5 All which for my soul is needful
He doth carefully provide,
Nor of that is He unheedful
Which my body needs beside.
When my strength can not avail me,
When my powers can do no more,
Doth my God His strength outpour,
In my need He doth not fail me.
All things else have but their day,
God's great love abides for aye.

6 All the hosts of earth and heaven
Wheresoe'er I turn mine eye,
For my benefit are given,
That they may my need supply.
All that's living, all that's growing,
On the heights or in the woods,
In the vales or in the floods,
God is for my good bestowing,
All things else have but their day,
God's great love abides for aye.

7 When I sleep, He still is near me,
O'er me rests His guardian eye;
And new gifts and blessings cheer me,
When the morning streaks the sky.
Were it not for God's protection,
Had His countenance not been
Here my guide, I had not seen
E'er the end of my affliction.
All things else have but their day,
God's great love abides for aye.

8 Ah! how often doth the Devil
Cause some great calamity!
But my life from all such evil
Till this moment has been free.
For the angel whom God sendeth,
Wardeth off each threatening hurt.
Every evil doth avert
That mine enemy intendeth.
All things else have but their day,
God's great love abides for aye.

9 As a father never turneth
Wholly from a wayward child,
For the prodigal still yearneth,
Longing to be reconciled:
So my many sins and errors
Find a tender pardoning God,
Chastening frailty with His rod,
Not, in vengeance, with His terrors.
All things else have but their day,
God's great love abides for aye.

10 All His strokes and scourges truly
For the moment grievous prove,
And yet, when I weigh them duly,
Are but tokens of His love:
Proofs that He is watching o'er me,
And by crosses to His fold,
From the world that fain would hold
Soul and body, would restore me.
All things else have but their day,
God's great love abides for aye.

11 On this thought I dwell with pleasure;
For it granteth joy and peace.
Christ's cross hath its time and measure,
And at last will wholly cease.
When the winter disappeareth,
Lovely summer comes again;
Joy is given for woe and pain
Who His cross in patience beareth.
All things else have but their day,
God's great love abides for aye.

12 Since, then, neither change nor coldness
In my Father's love can be,
Lo! I lift my hands with boldness,
As Thy child I come to Thee.
Grant me grace, O God, I pray Thee,
That I may with all my might,
All my life-time, day and night,
Love and trust Thee, and obey Thee;
And when this brief life is o'er,
Praise and love Thee evermore.

Paul Gerhardt, 1659

Praise

66 Gottlob es geht nunmehr zu Ende L. M. Mel. J. S. BACH, 1736

1 Thee we a - dore, e - ter - nal Lord! We praise Thy name with one ac-cord.

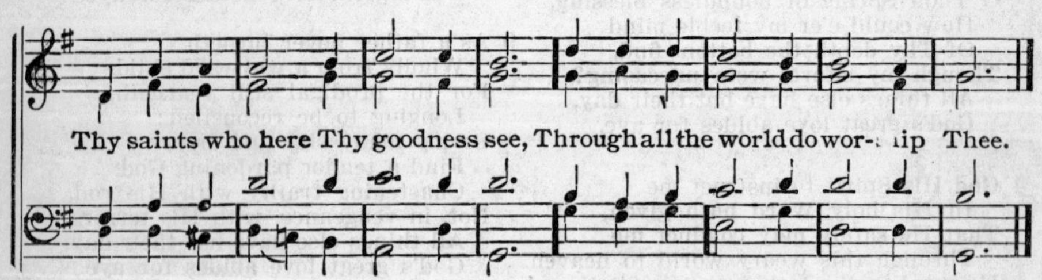
Thy saints who here Thy goodness see, Through all the world do wor-ship Thee.

2 To Thee aloud all angels cry,
The heavens and all the power on high;
Thee, "Holy, Holy, Holy King,
Lord God of hosts!" they ever sing.

3 Th' Apostles join the glorious throng;
The Prophets swell the immortal song;
Thy Martyrs' noble army raise
Eternal anthems to Thy praise.

4 From day to day, O Lord, do we
Highly exalt and honor Thee!
Thy name we worship and adore,
World without end, forevermore!

5 Vouchsafe, O Lord, we humbly pray,
To keep us safe from sin this day;
Have mercy, Lord! we trust in Thee;
O let us ne'er confounded be!

John Gambold, 1754. Thomas Cotterill, 1815. a

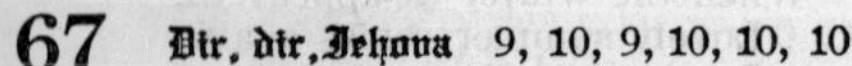

67 Dir, dir, Jehova 9, 10, 9, 10, 10, 10 FREYLINGHAUSEN, 1704

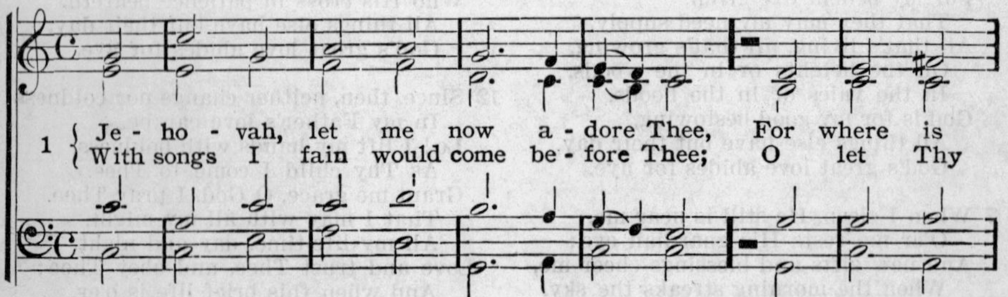
1 { Je - ho - vah, let me now a - dore Thee, For where is
With songs I fain would come be - fore Thee; O let Thy

there a God such, Lord, as Thou?
Ho-ly Spir-it teach me now
To praise Thee in His
name, through whom alone Our songs can please Thee, through Thy bles-sed Son.

2 O Father, draw me to my Savior,
That Thy dear Son may draw me unto Thee;
Thy Spirit guide my whole behavior
And rule both sense and reason thus in me,
That, Lord, Thy peace I taste may ne'er depart
But wake sweet melodies within my heart.

3 Grant that Thy Spirit prompt my praises,
Then shall my singing surely please Thine ear;
Sweet are the sounds my heart then raises,
My prayer in truth and spirit Thou wilt hear.
Then shall Thy Spirit raise my heart to Thee,
To sing Thee psalms of praise in high degree.

4 For He can plead for me with sighings
That are unspeakable to lips like mine;
He bids me pray with earnest cryings,
Bears witness with my soul that I am Thine,
Joint-heir with Christ, and thus may dare to say:
O Abba, Father! hear me, when I pray.

5 When thus my heart in prayer ascendeth
Through Thine own Holy Spirit unto Thee,
Thy heart, O Father, kindly bendeth
Its fervent love and favor unto me,
Rejoicing my petition to fulfill
Which I have made according to Thy will.

6 And what Thy Spirit thus hath taught me
To seek from Thee, must needs be such a prayer
As Thou wilt grant, through Him who bought me,
And raised me up to be Thy child and heir;
In Jesus' name I fearless seek Thy face,
And take from Thee, my Father, grace for grace.

7 O joy! my hope and trust are founded
On His sure Word, and witness in the heart;
I know Thy mercies are unbounded,
And all good gifts Thou freely wilt impart,
Nay, more is lavished by Thy bounteous hand
Than I can ask, or seek, or understand.

8 O bliss! in Jesus' name I've tendered
My prayer; He pleads at Thy right hand for me.
Yea and Amen in Him is rendered
What I in faith and spirit ask of Thee.
O joy for me! and praise be ever Thine
Whose wondrous love has made such blessings mine!

Bartholomaeus Crasselius, 1697. C. Winkworth, Tr. a

68 Innocents 7s OLD FRENCH MELODY

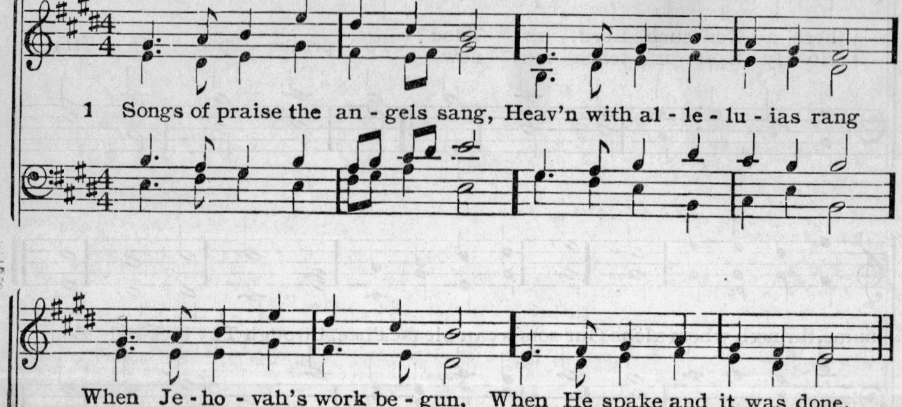
1 Songs of praise the an - gels sang, Heav'n with al - le - lu - ias rang
When Je - ho - vah's work be - gun, When He spake and it was done.

(Or to Vienna)

2 Songs of praise awoke the morn,
When the Prince of peace was born;
Songs of praise arose when He
Captive led captivity.

3 Heaven and earth must pass away;
Songs of praise shall crown that day:
God will make new heavens and earth;
Songs of praise shall hail their birth.

4 And shall man alone be dumb,
Till that glorious kingdom come?
No;—the Church delights to raise
Psalms, and hymns, and songs of praise.

5 Saints below, with heart and voice,
Still in songs of praise rejoice;
Learning here, by faith and love,
Songs of praise to sing above.

6 Borne upon their latest breath,
Songs of praise shall conquer death;
Then amidst eternal joy
Songs of praise their powers employ.

James Montgomery, 1819

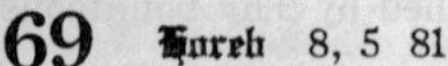
69 Horeb 8, 5 81 H. A. POLACK, 1910

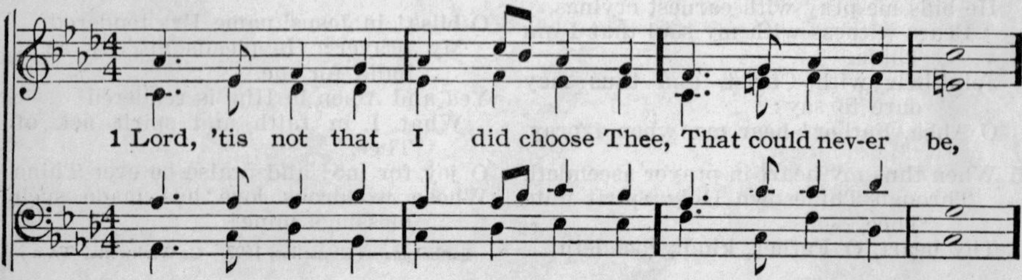
1 Lord, 'tis not that I did choose Thee, That could nev-er be,

Praise

For this heart would still re - fuse Thee, Thou hast cho - sen me:

Hast from all the sin that staind me. Washed and set me free;

rit.
And un - to this end or - dained me, That I live to Thee.

2 'Twas Thy sovereign mercy called me,
Taught my opening mind;
Else the world had yet enthralled me,
To Thy glories blind.
Now my heart owns none above Thee;
For Thy grace I thirst;
Knowing well that, if I love Thee,
Thou didst love me first.

3 Praise the God of all creation,
For His boundless love;
Praise the Lamb, our Expiation,
Priest enthroned above,
Praise the Spirit of salvation,
Him by whom we live;
Undivided adoration
To the Godhead give!

Josiah Condor

70 Laaus (Norwich) L. M.

A. H. MANN, 1850

1 Give to our God im - mor - tal praise! Mer - cy and
truth are all His ways. Won - ders of grace to
God be - long: Re - peat His mer - cies in your song.

2 Give to the Lord of lords renown,
The King of kings with glory crown.
His mercies ever shall endure,
When lords and kings are known no more.

3 He built the earth, he spread the sky,
And fixed the starry lights on high.
Wonders of grace to God belong:
Repeat His mercies in your song.

4 He fills the sun with morning light;
He bids the moon direct the night:
His mercies ever shall endure,
When suns and moons shall shine no more.

5 He sent His Son with power to save
From guilt and darkness and the grave;
Wonders of grace to God belong:
Repeat His mercies in your song.

6 Through this vain world He guides our feet,
And leads us to His heavenly seat.
His mercies ever shall endure,
When this vain world shall be no more.

Rev. Issac Watts

71 Fred til Bod 7s 6 1

J. P. HARTMAN (I)

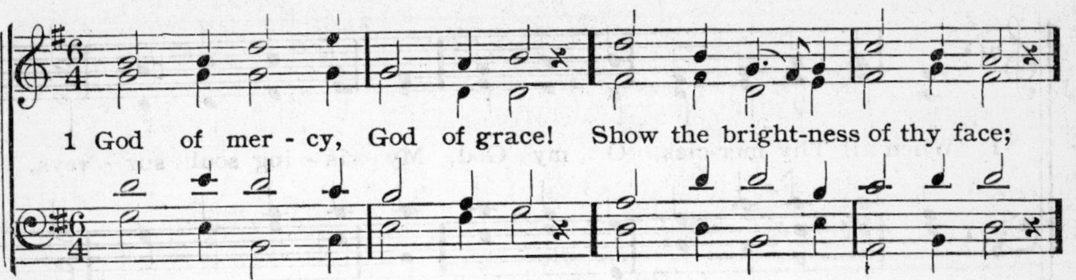
1 God of mer - cy, God of grace! Show the bright-ness of thy face;

Shine up - on us, Sav - ior, shine; Fill Thy Church with light di-vine,

And Thy sav - ing health ex - tend Un - to earth's re - mot - est end.

2 Let the people praise Thee, Lord!
Be by all that live adored;
Let the nations shout and sing
Glory to their Lord and King;
At Thy feet their tribute pay,
And Thy holy will obey.

3 Let the people praise Thee, Lord!
Earth shall then her fruits afford,
God to man His blessing give,
Man to God devoted live;
All below and all above
One in joy, and light and love.

Henry F. Lyte, 1834

72 Winchester Old C. M.

ESTE'S PSALTER, 1592

1 When all Thy mer-cies, O my God, My ris - ing soul sur - veys,

Trans-port - ed with the view, I'm lost In won - der love and praise.

(Or to Nun danket all und Or to Belmont)

2 Ten thousand thousand precious gifts
My daily thanks employ;
Nor is the least a cheerful heart
That tastes those gifts with joy.

3 Through every period of my life
Thy goodness I'll pursue;
And after death, in distant worlds,
The glorious theme renew.

4 When nature fails, and day and night
Divide Thy works no more,
My ever grateful heart, O Lord,
Thy mercies shall adore.

5 Through all eternity to Thee
A joyful song I'll raise;
But oh! eternity's too short
To utter all Thy praise.

J. Addison, 1712. ab.

73 Swiss Tune L. M. 6 l

WUERTEMB, H. B. (I and P)

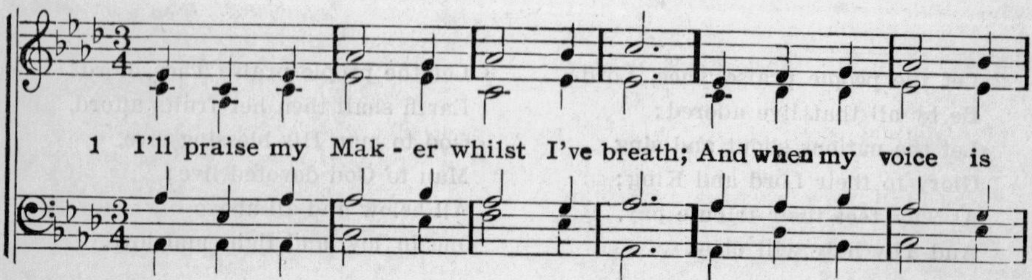
1 I'll praise my Mak - er whilst I've breath; And when my voice is

Praise

lost in death, praise shall em - ploy my no - bler powers.

My days of praise shall ne'er be past, While life and thought and

be - ing last, Or im - mor - tal - i - ty en - dures.

2 Happy the man whose hopes rely
On Israel's God, who made the sky,
And earth, and seas, with all their train;
His truth forever stands secure;
He saves th' oppressed, He feeds the poor;
And none shall find His promise vain.

4 The Lord gives eyesight to the blind;
The Lord supports the sinking mind;
He sends the laboring conscience peace;
He helps the stranger in distress,
The widow and the fatherless,
And grants the prisoner sweet release.

5 I'll praise Him while He lends me breath;
And when my voice is lost in death,
Praise shall employ my nobler powers:
My days of praise shall ne'er be past,
While life and thought and being last,
Or immortality endures.

Isaac Watts

74 St. Osmin C. M.

J. B. DYKES

1 To God be glo - ry, peace on earth, To all man - kind good will!

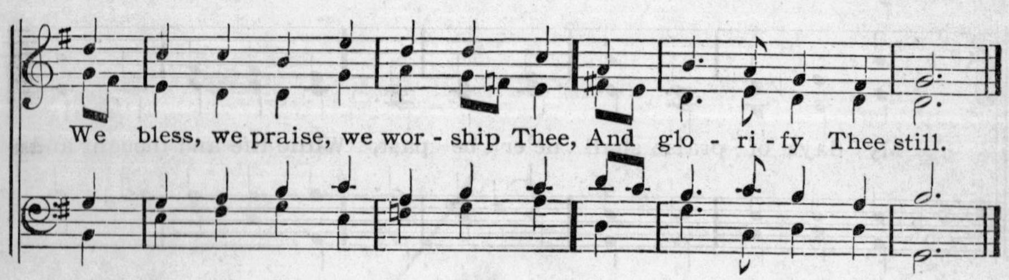
We bless, we praise, we wor - ship Thee, And glo - ri - fy Thee still.

(Or to Laud)

2 And thanks for Thy great glory give,
That fills our soul with light;
O Lord, our heavenly King, the God
And Father of all might!

3 And Thou, begotten Son of God,
Before all time begun;
O Jesus Christ, Thou Lamb of God,
The Father's only Son:

4 Have mercy, Thou that tak'st the sins
Of all the world away!
Have mercy, Savior of mankind,
And hear us when we pray!

5 O Thou, who sitt'st at God's right hand,
Upon the Father's throne,
Have mercy on us, Thou, O Christ,
Who art the Holy One!

6 Thou only, with the Holy Ghost,
Whom earth and heaven adore,
In glory of the Father art
Most high forevermore.

Tate and Brady's, Sup. a.

75 St. Osmin C. M.

1 Through all the changing scenes of life,
In trouble and in joy,
The praises of my God shall still
My heart and tongue employ.

2 Of His deliverance I will boast,
Till all that are distrest
From my example comfort take,
And charm their griefs to rest.

3 O magnify the Lord with me,
With me exalt His name!
When in distress on Him I called,
He to my rescue came.

4 The hosts of God encamp around
The dwellings of the just;
Deliverance He affords to all
Who on His succor trust.

5 O make but trial of His love:
Experience will decide
How blest are they and only they,
Who in His truth confide.

6 Fear Him, ye Christians, you will then
Have nothing else to fear;
Make you His service your delight,
Your wants shall be His care.

Nicholas Brady and Nahum Tate, 1696 a.

76 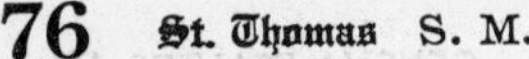 St. Thomas S. M. A. WILLIAMS, 1762

1 O bless the Lord, my soul! Let all with - in me join,

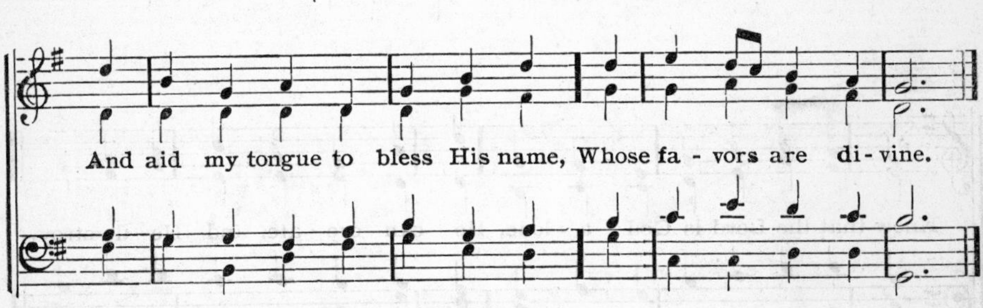
And aid my tongue to bless His name, Whose fa - vors are di - vine.

(Or to Boylston)

2 O bless the Lord, my soul!
Nor let His mercies lie
Forgotten in unthankfulness,
And without praises die.

3 'Tis He forgives thy sins;
'Tis He relieves thy pain;
'Tis He that heals thy sicknesses,
And gives thee strength again.

4 He crowns thy life with love,
When ransomed from the grave;
He that redeemed my soul from death
Hath sovereign power to save.

5 He fills the poor with good;
He gives the sufferers rest:
The Lord hath judgments for the proud,
And justice for th' oppressed.

6 His wondrous works and ways
He made by Moses known;
But sent the world His truth and grace
By His beloved Son.

Isaac Watts 1719, a

77 St. Thomas S. M.

1 My soul, repeat His praise,
Whose mercies are so great;
Whose anger is so slow to rise,
So ready to abate.

2 God will not always chide;
And, when His wrath is felt,
His strokes are fewer than our crimes,
And lighter than our guilt.

3 High as the heavens are raised
Above the ground we tread,
So far the riches of His grace
Our highest thoughts exceed.

4 His grace subdues our sins;
And His forgiving love,
Far as the east is from the west,
Doth all our guilt remove.

5 The pity of the Lord,
To those who fear His name,
Is such as tender parents feel;
He knows our feeble frame.

6 Our days are as the grass,
Or like the morning flower;
If one sharp blast sweep o'er the field,
It withers in an hour.

7 But Thy compassions, Lord,
To endless years endure;
And children's children ever find
Thy words of promise sure.

Isaac Watts, 1719

78 Old Hundredth L. M.

GENEVA PSALTER, 1551

1 Be-fore Je - ho-vah's aw - ful throne, Ye na - tions bow with sa-cred joy;

Know that the Lord is God a - lone, He can cre - ate, and He de-stroy.

(Or to Duke St.)

2 His sov'reign power, without our aid,
Made us of clay, and formed us men;
And when like wandering sheep we strayed,
He brought us to His fold again.

3 We are His people, we His care,
Our souls and all our mortal frame:
What lasting honors shall we rear,
Almighty Maker, to Thy name?

4 We'll crowd Thy gates with thankful songs,
High as the heavens our voices raise:
And earth, with her ten thousand tongues,
Shall fill Thy courts with sounding praise.

5 Wide as the world is Thy command,
Vast as eternity Thy love;
Firm as a rock Thy truth must stand,
When rolling years shall cease to move.

Isaac Watts, 1719 a

79 Old Hundredth L. M.

1 From all that dwell below the skies
Let the Creator's praise arise;
Let the Redeemer's name be sung,
Through every land, by every tongue.

2 Eternal are Thy mercies, Lord;
Eternal truth attends Thy Word,
Thy praise shall sound from shore to shore,
Till suns shall rise and set no more.

3 Your lofty themes, ye mortals, bring;
In songs of praise divinely sing;
The great salvation loud proclaim,
And shout for joy the Savior's name.

4 In every land begin the song;
To every land the strains belong;
In cheerful sounds all voices raise,
And fill the world with loudest praise.

Isaac Watts, 1719

80 Allein Gott in der Höh' 8, 7, 8, 7, 8, 8, 7 N. DECIUS, 1539

1 The Lord hath helped me hith - er - to by His sur-pass - ing fa - vor;
His mer - cies ev - 'ry morn were new, His kind - ness did not wa - ver.
God hith - er - to hath been my guide, hath pleas-ures hith - er - to sup-plied, and hith - er - to hath helped me.

2 I praise and thank Thee, Lord, my God,
For Thine abundant blessing,
Which heretofore Thou hast bestowed
And I am still possessing.
Inscribe this on my memory:
The Lord hath done great things for me,
And graciously hath helped me.

3 Help me in future, God of grace,
Help me on each occasion,
Help me in each and ev'ry place,
Help me through Jesus' passion;
Help me in life and death, O God,
Help me through Jesus' dying blood,
Help me as Thou hast helped me!

Emilia Juliana, Countess of Schwarzburg † 1706. A. Crull, Tr. 1882

81 Trust 8, 7, 8, 7 — Arr. fr. MENDELSSOHN, 1840 [P]

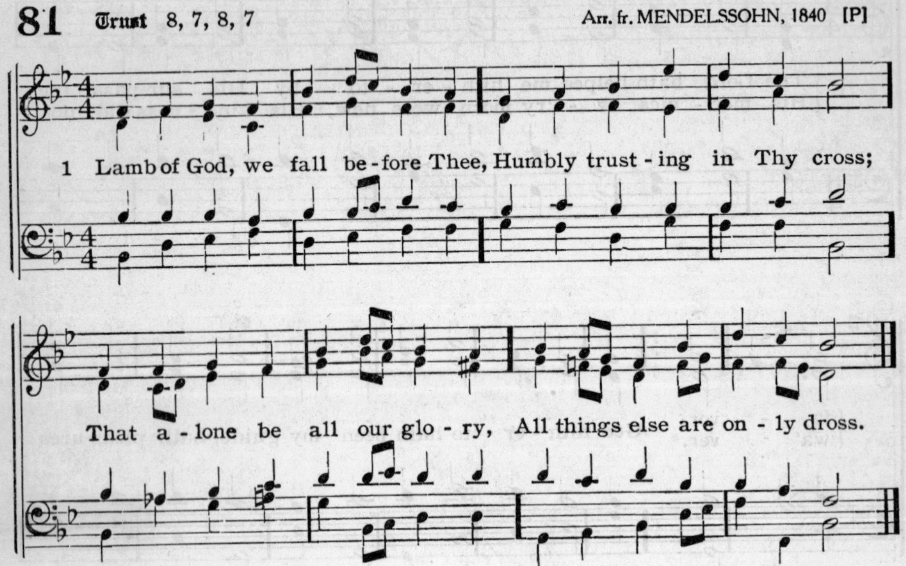
1 Lamb of God, we fall be - fore Thee, Humbly trust - ing in Thy cross;
That a - lone be all our glo - ry, All things else are on - ly dross.

2 Thee we own a perfect Savior,
Only Source of all that's good.
Every grace and every favor
Comes to us through Jesus' blood.

3 Jesus gives us true repentance,
By His Spirit sent from heaven;
Whispers this transporting sentence,
"Son, thy sins are all forgiven."

4 Faith He grants us to believe it,
Grateful hearts His love to prize;
Want we wisdom?—He must give it;
Hearing ears, and seeing eyes.

5 Jesus gives us pure affections,
Wills to do what He requires,
Makes us follow His directions,
And what He commands, inspires.

6 All our prayers, and all our praises,
Rightly offered in His name,—
He that dictates them is Jesus;
He that answers is the same.

Joseph Hart, 1759

82 Jesu, meine Freude 6, 6, 5, 6, 6, 5, 7, 8, 6 — J. CRUEGER, 1649

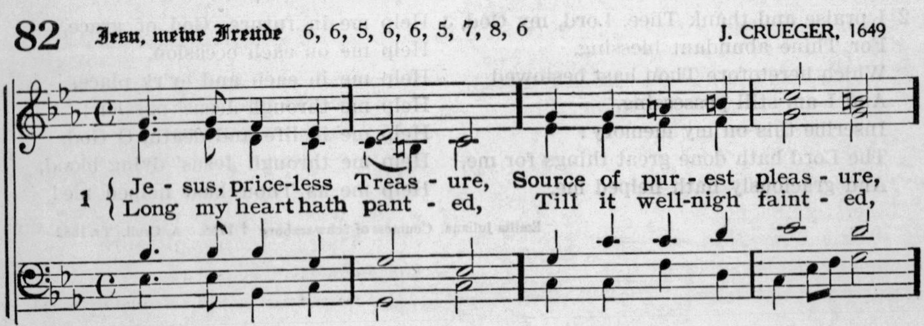
1 { Je - sus, price-less Treas - ure, Source of pur - est pleas - ure,
Long my heart hath pant - ed, Till it well-nigh faint - ed,

The Redeemer

Tru - est friend to me!
Thirst - ing af - ter Thee!
Thine I am, O spot-less Lamb! I will

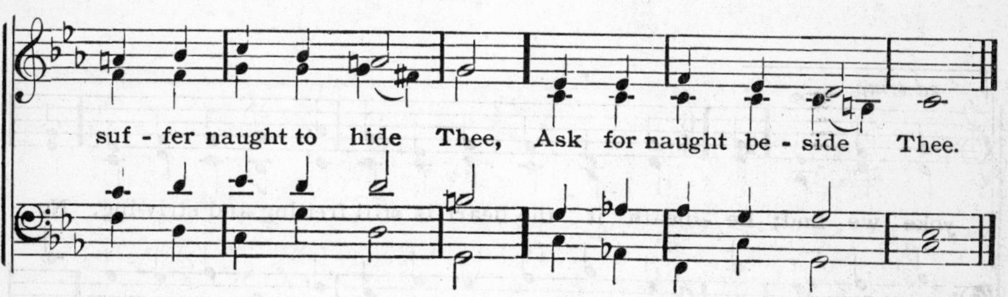

suf - fer naught to hide Thee, Ask for naught be - side Thee.

2 In Thine arms I rest me,
Foes who would molest me
Cannot reach me here;
Though the earth be shaking,
Every heart be quaking,
Jesus calms my fear;
Sin and hell, in conflict fell,
With their heaviest storms assail me,
Jesus will not fail me.

3 Satan, I defy thee;
Death, I need not fly thee;
Fear, I bid thee cease!
Rage, O world, thy noises
Cannot drown our voices
Singing still of peace,
For God's power guards every hour;
Earth and all its depths adore Him,
Silent bow before Him.

4 Wealth, I will not heed thee,
Wherefore should I need thee?
Jesus is my Joy!
Honors, ye may glisten,
But I will not listen,
Ye the soul destroy!
Want or loss or shame or cross
Ne'er to leave my Lord shall move me,
Since He deigns to love me.

5 Farewell, thou who choosest
Earth and heaven refusest,
Thou wilt tempt in vain;
Farewell, sins, nor blind me,
Get ye far behind me,
Come not forth again;
Past your hour, O pomp and power;
Godless life, thy bonds, I sever,
Farewell now forever!

6 Hence, all fears and sadness!
For the Lord of gladness,
Jesus, enters in;
Those who love the Father,
Though the storms may gather,
Still have peace within;
Yea, whate'er I here must bear,
Still in Thee lies purest pleasure,
Jesus, priceless Treasure!

Johann Franck, c. 1652 C. Winkworth, Tr.

83
Eins ist not 8, 7, 12, 11, 12, 12, 11, 11
Dr. F. LAYRIZ, 1849
1st time
1 { One thing's need-ful! then Lord Je - sus, Keep this one thing in my mind;
All be-side, though first it please us, Soon a grie-vous
2d time
yoke we find; Be - neath it the heart is still fretting and striv-ing, No
true, last-ing hap - pi - ness ev - er de - riv - ing. The gain of this
one thing all loss can re-quite, And teach me in all things to find true delight.

2 Soul, wilt thou this one thing find thee?
Seek not 'midst created things;
What is earthly, leave behind thee,
Over nature stretch thy wings.
For where God and Man both in One are united,
With God's perfect fulness the heart is delighted,
There, there is the worthiest lot and the best,
My One and my All, and my Joy and my Rest.

3 How were Mary's thoughts devoted
Her eternal joy to find,
As intent each word she noted,
At her Savior's feet reclined!
How kindled her heart, how devout was its feeling,
While hearing the lessons that Christ was revealing!
For Jesus all earthly concerns she forgot,
And all was repaid in that one happy lot.

4 Thus my longings, heavenward tending,
Jesus, rest alone on Thee;
Help me, thus on Thee depending,
Savior, come and dwell in me!
Although all the world should forsake and forget Thee,
In love I will follow Thee, ne'er will I quit Thee;
Lord Jesus, both spirit and life is Thy Word;
And is there a joy which Thou dost not afford?

5 Wisdom's highest, noblest treasure,
Jesus, lies concealed in Thee;
Grant that this may still the measure
Of my will and actions be.
Humility there, and simplicity, reigning,
My steps shall in wisdom forever be training.
Oh! if I of Christ have this knowledge divine,
The fulness of heavenly wisdom is mine.

6 Christ, Thou art the sole oblation
That I'll bring before my God;
In His sight I've acceptation
Only Through Thy streaming blood.
Immaculate righteousness I have acquired,
Since Thou on the tree of the cross hast expired;
The robe of salvation for ever is mine,
In this shall my faith through eternity shine.

7 Let my soul, in full exemption,
Wake up in Thy likeness now;
Thou art made to me redemption,
My sanctification Thou.
Whatever I need for my journey to heaven,
In Thee, O my Savior, is unto me given;
O let me all perishing pleasure forego,
And Thy life, O Jesus, alone let me know.

8 Where should else my hopes be centered?
Grace o'erwhelms me with its flood;
Thou, my Savior, once hast entered
Holiest heaven through Thy blood.
Eternal redemption for sinners there finding,
From hell's dark dominion my spirit unbinding,
To me perfect freedom Thy entrance has brought,
And childlike to cry "Abba, Father," I'm taught.

9 Christ Himself, my Shepherd, feeds me,
Peace and joy my spirit fill;
In a pasture green, He leads me
Forth beside the waters still.
Oh! naught to my soul is so sweet and reviving,
As thus unto Jesus alone to be living;
True happiness this, and this only, supplies,
Through faith on my Savior to fasten, mine eyes.

10 Therefore, Jesus, my Salvation,
Thou my One, my All, shalt be;
Prove my fixed determination,
Root out all hypocrisy;
Look well if on sin's slippery paths I am hasting,
And lead me, O Lord, in the way everlasting!
This one thing is needful, all others are vain;
I count all but lost that I Christ may obtain.

Johann Heinrich Schroeder, 1697 F. E. Cox, Tr. a

84 St. Petersburg L. M. 6 l DIMITRI S. BORTNIANSKY, 1751–1825

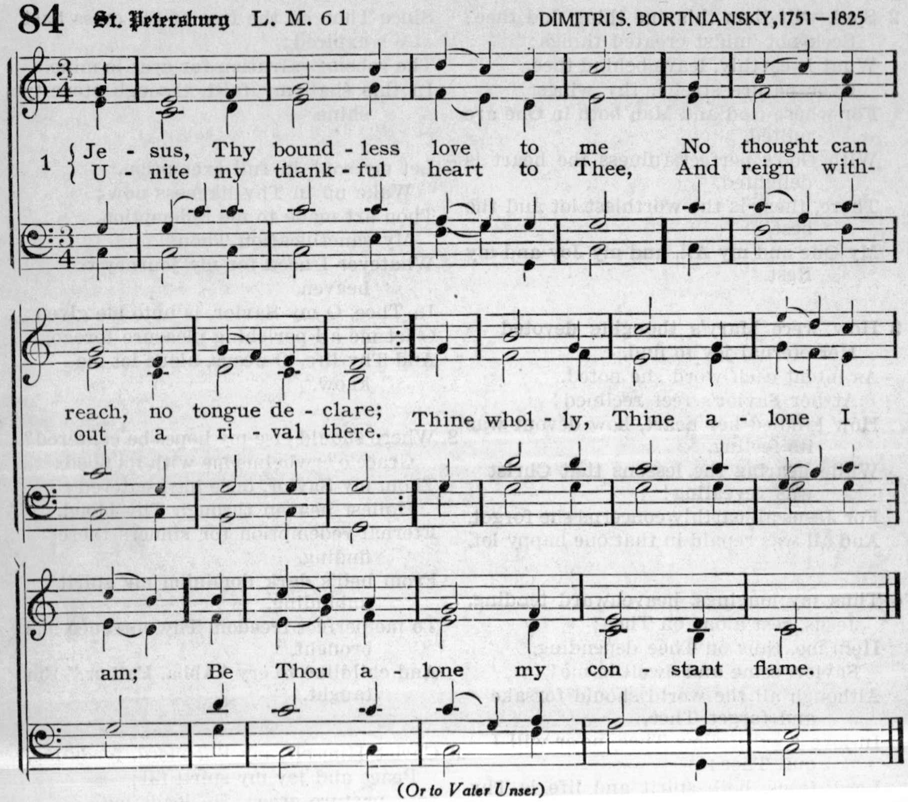
1 { Je - sus, Thy bound - less love to me No thought can reach, no tongue de - clare; Thine whol - ly, Thine a - lone I am; Be Thou a - lone my con - stant flame.
U - nite my thank - ful heart to Thee, And reign with - out a ri - val there.

(*Or to Vater Unser*)

2 O grant that nothing in my soul
May dwell but Thy pure love alone;
O may Thy love possess me whole,
My Joy, my Treasure, and my Crown:
Strange flames far from my heart remove;
My every act, word, thought, be love!

3 O Love, how cheering is Thy ray!
All pain before Thy presence flies;
Care, anguish, sorrow, melt away,
Where'er Thy healing beams arise:
O Jesus, nothing may I see,
Nothing desire or seek but Thee.

4 Unwearied, may I this pursue,
Dauntless to the high prize aspire;
Hourly within my soul renew
This holy flame, this heavenly fire;
And day and night be all my care
To guard this sacred treasure there.

5 O draw me, Savior, after Thee!
So shall I run and never tire.
With gracious words still comfort me;
Be Thou my Hope, my sole Desire.
Free me from every weight: nor fear
Nor sin can come, if Thou art here.

6 From all eternity, with love
Unchangeable Thou hast me viewed,
Ere knew this beating heart to move,
Thy tender mercies me pursued.
Ever with me may they abide,
And close me in on every side.

7 Still let Thy love point out my way;
How wondrous things Thy love hath wrought!
Still lead me, lest I go astray;
Direct my work, inspire my thought;
And if I fall, soon may I hear
Thy voice, and know that love is near.

8 In suffering be Thy love my peace,
In weakness be Thy love my power;
And when the storms of life shall cease,
Jesus, in that important hour,
In death as life be Thou my Guide,
And save me, who for me hast died!

Paul Gerhardt, 1666 John Wesley, Tr. a

85 St. Petersburg C. M. 61

1 The Lord my pasture shall prepare,
And feed me with a shepherd's care;
His presence shall my wants supply,
And guard me with a watchful eye,
My noonday walks he shall attend,
And all my midnight hours defend.

2 While on the sultry glebe I faint,
Or on the thirsty mountain pant,
To fertile vales and dewy meads
My every wandering steps He leads,
Where peaceful rivers soft and slow,
Amid the verdant landscape flow.

3 Though in a bare and rugged way,
Through devious lonely wilds I stray,
Thy bounty shall my pains beguile;
The barren wilderness shall smile,
With sudden greens and herbage crowned,
And streams shall murmur all around.

4 Though in the paths of death I tread,
With gloomy horrors overspread,
My steadfast heart shall fear no ill,
For Thou, O Lord, art with me still;
Thy friendly crook shall give me aid,
And guide me through the dreadful shade.

J. Addison, 1712

86 Jesus, Jesus, nichts als Jesus 8, 7, 8, 7, 7, 7

B. KOENIG, 1738

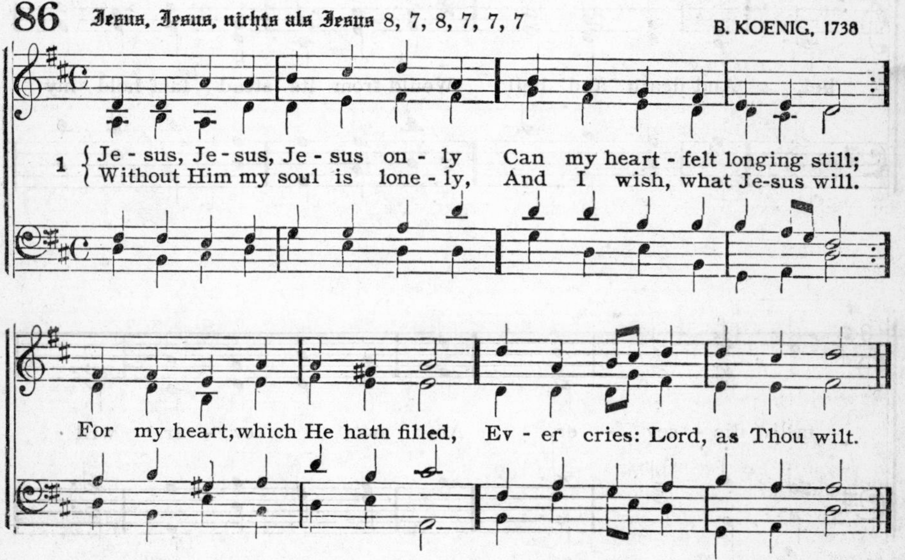
1 Je - sus, Je - sus, Je - sus on - ly Can my heart - felt longing still;
Without Him my soul is lone - ly, And I wish, what Je-sus will.
For my heart, which He hath filled, Ev - er cries: Lord, as Thou wilt.

(*Or to Consolation Or to Gott des Himmels*)

2 One it is for whom I'm living,
Whom I'm loving faithfully;
Jesus, unto whom I'm giving
What in love He gave to me.
Jesus' blood hides all my guilt;
Lord, O lead me as Thou wilt.

3 Seems a thing to me a treasure,
Which displeasing is to Thee,
Then remove such dangerous pleasure;
Give instead what profits me.
Let my heart by Thee be stilled,
Make me Thine, Lord, as Thou wilt.

4 Grant that always I endeavor
Thy good pleasure to fulfill,
In me, through me, with me ever,
Lord, accomplish Thou Thy will.
Let me die, Lord, on Thee built,
When, and where, and as Thou wilt.

5 Lord, my praise shall be unceasing,
For Thou gav'st Thyself to me,
And besides so many a blessing,
That I sing now joyfully:
Be it unto me, my Shield,
As Thou wilt, Lord, as Thou wilt.

Ludaemilie Elisabeth, Graefin zu Schwarzburg, 1668 A. Crull, Tr.

87 Ich lass dich nicht 11, 4, 4, 11, 6, 6, 6, 7, 8
J. F. DOLES, 1780
1 I leave Thee not! Thou art my Je - sus ev - er, Though earth re -
bel, And death and hell Would from its stead - fast hold my
faith dis - sev - er. Ah, no! I ev - er will
Cling to my Help - er still. Hear what my love is taught: Thou

The Redeemer

art my Je - sus ev - er, I leave Thee not, I leave Thee not!

2 I leave Thee not, O Love! of love the highest,
Though doubt display
Its battle-day;
I own the power which Thou, my Lord, appliest.
Thou didst bear guilt and woe;
Shall I to torment go,
When into judgment brought?
O Love! of love the highest,
I leave Thee not, I leave Thee not!

3 I leave Thee not, O Thou who sweetly cheerest!
Whose fresh supplies
Cause strength to rise,
Just in the hour when faith's decay is nearest.
If sickness chill the soul,
And nights of languor roll,
My heart one hope hath caught;
O Thou who sweetly cheerest,
I leave Thee not, I leave Thee not!

4 I leave Thee not, Thou Help in tribulation!
Heap ill on ill,
I trust Thee still,
I hope when all seems near to desolation,
Do what Thou wilt with me,
I yet will cling to Thee;
Thy grace I have besought;
Thou Help in tribulation,
I leave Thee not, I leave Thee not!

5 I leave Thee not: shall I forsake salvation?
No, Jesus, no!
Thou shalt not go;
Mine still Thou art, to free from condemnation.
After this fleeting night,
Thy presence brings me light,
Whose ray my soul hath sought;
Shall I forsake salvation?
I leave Thee not, I leave Thee not!

6 I leave Thee not; Thy Word my way shall brighten:
With Thee I go
Through weal and woe,
Thy precept wise shall every burden lighten.
My Lord, on Thee I hang,
Nor heed the journey's pang,
Though thorny be my lot;
Let but Thy Word enlighten,
I leave Thee not, I leave Thee not!

7 I leave Thee not, e'en in the lap of pleasure;
For when I stray
Without Thy ray,
My richest joy must cease to be a treasure.
I shudder at the glee,
When no delight from Thee
Has heartfelt peace begot;
E'en in the lap of pleasure,
I leave Thee not, I leave Thee not!

8 I leave Thee not! I fear no condemnation,
For how could share
Thy child and heir
The lot of those who spurn their soul's salvation?
Thy blood, Lord, cleanseth me,
And therefore I am free
From hell, the sinner's lot.
I fear no condemnation;
I leave Thee not, I leave Thee not!

9 I leave Thee not, my God, my Lord, my Heaven!
Nor death shall rend
From Thee, my Friend,
Who for my sake Thyself to death hast given.
Thou diedst for love to me,
And love goes back to Thee;
My heart has but one thought:
My God, my Lord, my Heaven,
I leave Thee not, I leave Thee not!

W. C. Dessler, 1692. Dr. Alexander, Tr. a

88 Meinen Jesum lass 7, 8, 7, 8, 7, 7 A. HAMMERSCHMIDT, 1858

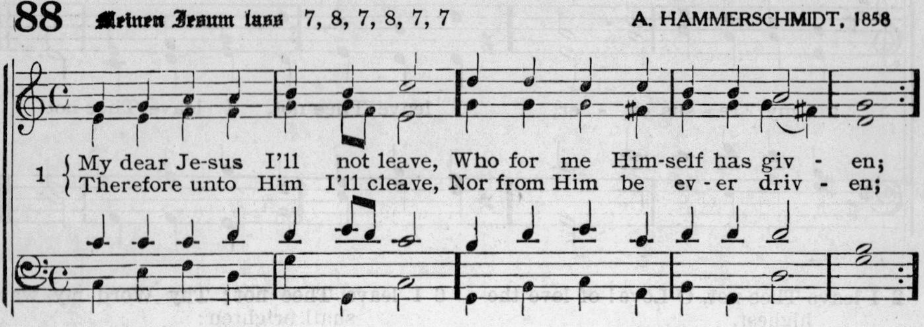
1 { My dear Je-sus I'll not leave, Who for me Him-self has giv - en;
Therefore unto Him I'll cleave, Nor from Him be ev - er driv - en;

Life from Him doth light re - ceive; My dear Je - sus I'll not leave.

(Or to Meinen Jesum, by Witt)

2 Jesus I will never leave,
While on earth I am abiding;
My full trust He shall receive;
What I have, without dividing,
All to Him I freely give;
My dear Jesus I'll not leave.

3 Though my eyesight pass away,
Hearing, taste and feeling fail me;
Though the earth's last light of day
Shall o'ertake and sore assail me;
E'en when my last sigh I heave
My dear Jesus I'll not leave.

4 Nor will I my Jesus leave
When at length I shall come thither
Where His saints He will receive,
That in bliss they live together;
Endless joy to me He'll give;—
My dear Jesus I'll not leave.

5 Not for earth's vain joys I crave,
Not for heaven's glorious pleasure;
Jesus who my soul did save
Shall be my Desire and Treasure:
He redemption did achieve;—
My dear Jesus I'll not leave.

6 Jesus I shall never leave,
To His side still firmly clinging.
Christ leads all who Him receive
To life's waters ever springing.
Blessed they who to Him cleave!—
My dear Jesus I'll not leave.

Chr. Keymann, 1656 or 1658

The Redeemer

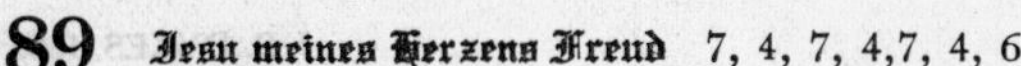

89 Jesu meines Herzens Freud

7, 4, 7, 4,7, 4, 6 LUENEBURGER H. B. 1886

1 Je - sus, Thou my heart's de - light, Sweet - est Je - sus!

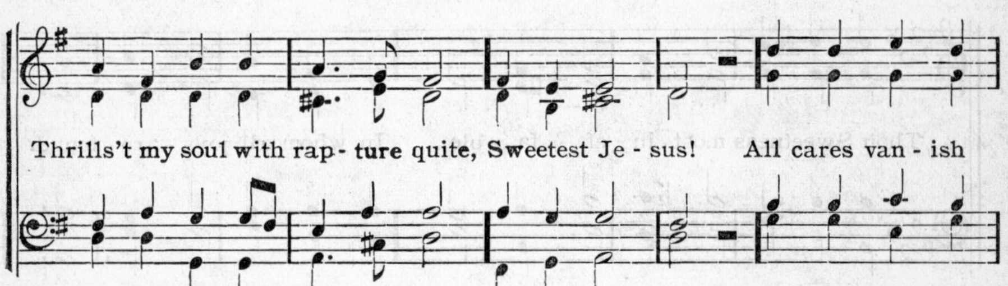

Thrills't my soul with rap - ture quite, Sweetest Je - sus! All cares van - ish

at Thy sight, Sweet-est Je - sus, Je - sus, sweet-est Je - sus!

2 Evermore I think of Thee,
My Redeemer!
And I long for none but Thee,
My Redeemer!
Yearns my soul with Thee to be,
My Redeemer,
Jesus, my Redeemer!

3 Feed Thou me and fill my soul,
Heavenly Manna!
Quench my thirst, my heart make whole,
Help, Hosanna!
Be the rest unto my soul,
Rest of weary,
Jesus, Rest of weary!

4 Naught is lovelier than Thou,
Fairest Lover!
Naught is friendlier than Thou,
Gentle Lover!
And naught sweeter is than Thou,
Sweetest Lover,
Jesus, sweetest Lover!

5 I am weak, come, strengthen me.
Strength in weakness!
Faint am I, refresh Thou me,
Sweetest Jesus!
When I die, console Thou me,
Thou Consoler,
Jesus, my Consoler.

Johann Flittner, 1661 J. A. Rimbach, Tr. 1903. a

90

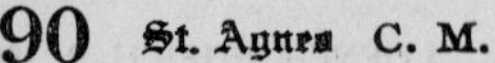

St. Agnes C. M. J. B. DYKES, 1866

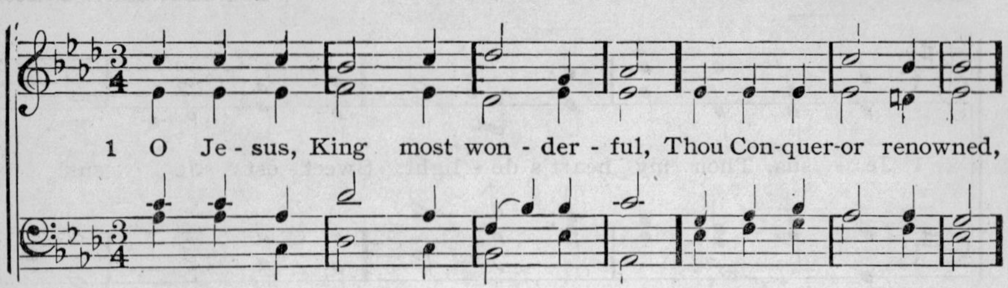
1 O Je - sus, King most won - der - ful, Thou Con-quer-or renowned,

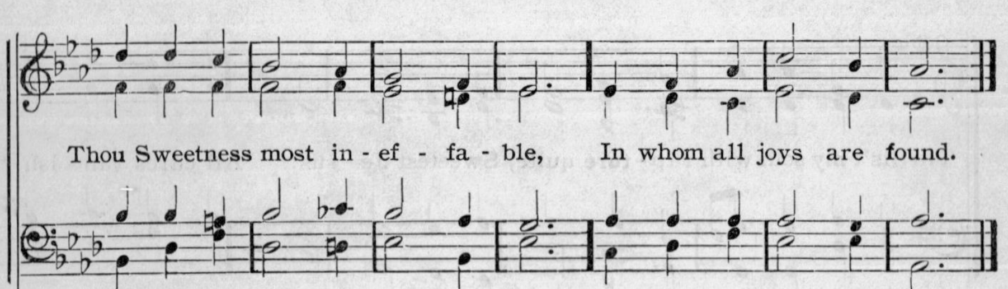
Thou Sweetness most in - ef - fa - ble, In whom all joys are found.

2 When once Thou visitest the heart,
Then truth begins to shine,
Then earthly vanities depart,
Then kindles love divine.

3 O Jesus, Light of all below,
Thou Fount of life and fire!
Surpassing all the joys we know,
All that we can desire,—

4 May every heart confess Thy name,
And ever Thee adore;
And, seeking Thee, itself inflame
To seek Thee more and more.

5 Thee may our tongues forever bless;
Thee may we love alone,
And ever in our lives express
The image of Thine own.

Bernard of Clairvaux, 1091—1153 Edw. Caswell, Tr. 1848

91

Federal Street L. M. HENRY K. OLIVER, 1832

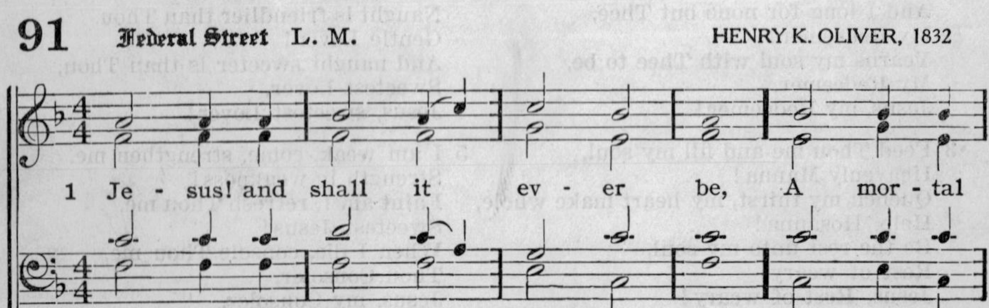
1 Je - sus! and shall it ev - er be, A mor - tal

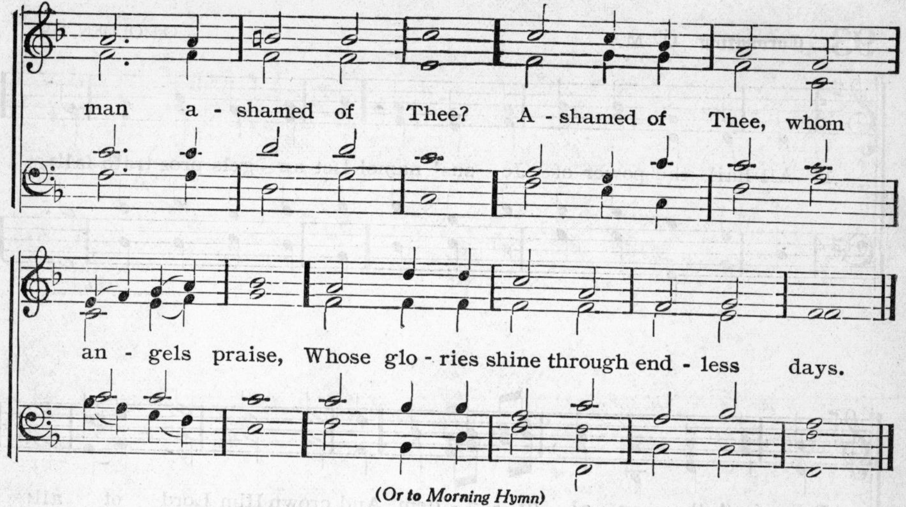
man a - shamed of Thee? A - shamed of Thee, whom
an - gels praise, Whose glo - ries shine through end - less days.

(Or to Morning Hymn)

2 Ashamed of Jesus! sooner far
Let evening blush to own a star;
He sheds the beams of light divine
O'er this benighted soul of mine.

3 Ashamed of Jesus! just as soon
Let midnight be ashamed of noon:
'Tis midnight with my soul, till He,
Bright Morning-star, bids darkness flee.

4 Ashamed of Jesus! that dear Friend
On whom my hopes of heaven depend!
No; when I blush, be this my shame,
That I no more revere His name.

5 Ashamed of Jesus! yes, I may,
When I've no guilt to wash away,
No tear to wipe, no good to crave,
No fears to quell, no soul to save.

6 Till then—nor is my boasting vain—
Till then I boast a Savior slain;
And oh, may this my glory be,
That Christ is not ashamed of me.

Joseph Grigg, 1765. Benjamin Francis, 1787

92 Federal Street L. M.

1 Awake, my soul, to joyful lays,
And sing Thy great Redeemer's praise,
He justly claims a song from me—
His loving-kindness, O how free!

2 He saw me ruined in the fall,
Yet loved me notwithstanding all,
He saved me from my lost estate—
His loving-kindness, O how great!

3 When I was Satan's easy prey,
And deep in debt and bondage lay,
He paid His life for my discharge—
His loving-kindness, O how large!

4 Though numerous hosts of mighty foes,
Though earth and hell my way oppose,
He safely leads my soul along—
His loving-kindness, O how strong!

5 When trouble, like a gloomy cloud,
Has gathered thick and thundered loud,
He near my soul has always stood—
His loving-kindness, O how good!

6 When earthly friends forsake me quite,
And I have neither skill nor might,
He's sure my Helper to appear—
His loving-kindness, O how near!

7 Often I feel my sinful heart
Prone from my Jesus to depart;
But though I have Him oft forgot
His loving-kindness changes not.

8 When I shall pass death's gloomy vale,
And all my mortal power must fail;
O may my last expiring breath
His loving-kindness sing in death!

9 Then shall I mount and soar away
To the bright world of endless day;
And sing, with rapture and surprise,
His loving kindness in the skies.

S. Medley, 1782

93 Coronation C. M. O. HOLDEN, 1793

1 All hail the power of Je - sus' name! Let an - gels pros-trate fall;
Bring forth the roy - al di - a - dem, And crown Him Lord of all;
Bring forth the roy - al di - a - dem, And crown Him Lord of all!

(*Or to Laud*)

2 Crown Him, ye martyrs of our God,
Who from His altar call;
Extol the Stem of Jesse's rod,
And crown Him Lord of all!

3 Ye seed of Israel's chosen race,
Ye ransomed from the fall,
Hail Him, who saves you by His grace,
And crown Him Lord of all!

4 Hail Him, ye heirs of David's line,
Whom David Lord did call;
The God incarnate, Man divine:
And crown Him Lord of all!

5 Sinners, whose love can ne'er forget
The wormwood and the gall,
Go spread your trophies at His feet,
And crown Him Lord of all!

6 Let every kindred, every tribe,
On this terrestrial ball,
To Him all majesty ascribe,
And crown Him Lord of all!

7 O that with yonder sacred throng
We at His feet may fall,
Join in the everlasting song,
And crown Him Lord of all!

E. Perronet, 1779--80; J. Rippon, 1787

94 Bedham C. M.

W. GARDINER, 1830

1 Thou art the Way: to Thee a - lone From

sin and death we flee, And he who would the

Fa - ther seek, Must seek Him, Lord, by Thee.

2 Thou art the Truth: Thy Word alone
True wisdom can impart:
Thou only canst inform the mind,
And purify the heart.

3 Thou art the Life: the rending tomb
Proclaims Thy conquering arm:
And those who put their trust in Thee,
Nor death nor hell shall harm.

4 Thou art the Way, the Truth, the Life:
Grant us that Way to know,
That Truth to keep, that Life to win,
Whose joys eternal flow.

G. W. Doane, 1824

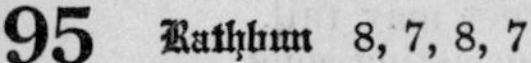
95 Rathbun 8, 7, 8, 7

I. CONKEY, 1851

1 In the cross of Christ I glo - ry, Tow-'ring o'er the wrecks of time;

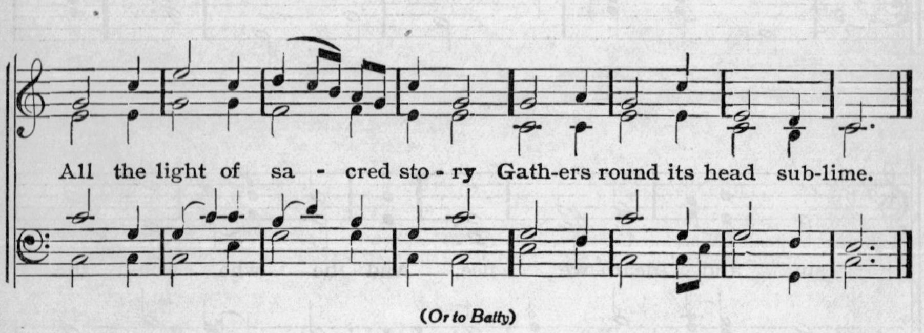
All the light of sa - cred sto - ry Gath-ers round its head sub-lime.

(*Or to Batty*)

2 When the woes of life o'ertake me,
Hopes deceive, and fears annoy,
Never shall the cross forsake me:
Lo! it glows with peace and joy.

3 When the sun of bliss is beaming
Light and love upon my way,
From the cross the radiance streaming
Adds new lustre to the day.

4 Bane and blessing, pain and pleasure,
By the cross are sanctified;
Peace is there that knows no measure,
Joys that through all time abide.

Sir John Bowring, 1825

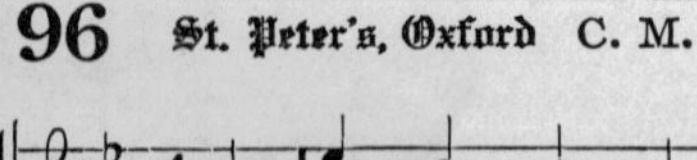
96 St. Peter's, Oxford C. M.

ALEX. R. REINAGLE, 1826

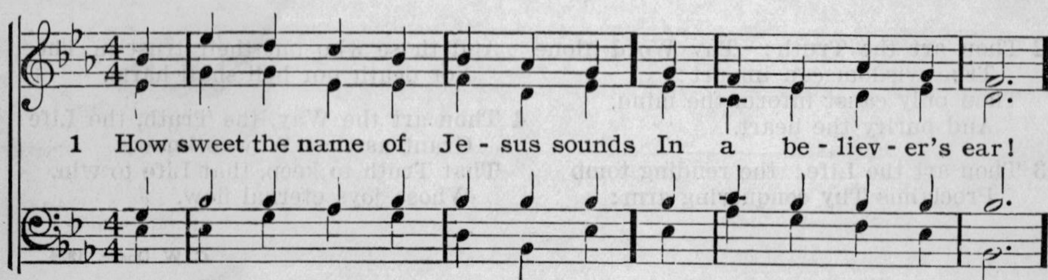
1 How sweet the name of Je - sus sounds In a be - liev - er's ear!

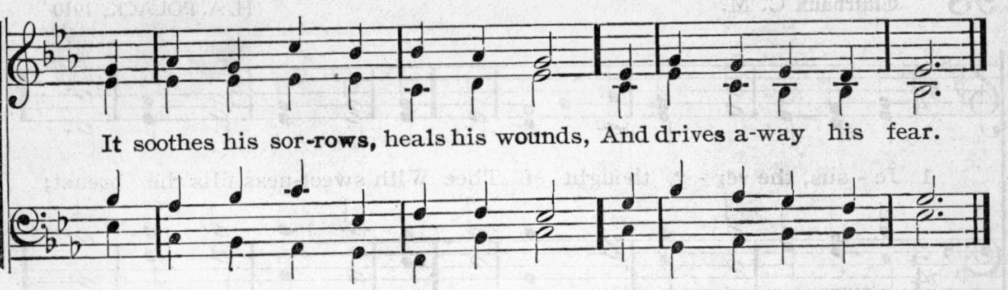
It soothes his sor-rows, heals his wounds, And drives a-way his fear.

(*Or to Heber*)

2 It makes the wounded spirit whole,
And calms the troubled breast;
'Tis manna to the hungry soul,
And to the weary rest.

3 Dear name! the Rock on which I build,
My Shield and Hiding-place;
My never-failing Treasury, filled
With boundless stores of grace.

4 By Thee my prayers acceptance gain,
Although with sin defiled:
Satan accuses me in vain,
And I am owned a child.

5 Jesus! my Shepherd, Guardian, Friend,
My Prophet, Priest, and King,
My Lord, my Life, my Way, my End,
Accept the praise I bring.

6 Weak is the effort of my heart,
And cold my warmest thought;
But, when I see Thee as Thou art,
I'll praise Thee as I ought.

7 Till then, I would Thy love proclaim
With every fleeting breath;
And may the music of Thy name
Refresh my soul in death.

John Newton, 1779

97 Rathbun 8, 7, 8, 7

1 Jesus, Thou art mine forever,
Dearer far than earth to me;
Neither life nor death shall sever
Those sweet ties which bind to Thee.

2 All were drear to me and lonely,
If Thy presence gladdened not;
While I sing to Thee—Thee only,
Mine's an ever blissful lot.

3 Thou alone art all my Treasure,
Who hast died that I may live,
Thou conferrest noblest pleasure,
Who dost all my sins forgive.

4 Brightest gems and fairest flowers,
Lose their beauty in Thy frown;
Joy and peace, like balmy showers,
In Thy smile come gently down.

5 Jesus, thou art mine forever,
Suffer not myself to stray;
Let me in my weakness never
Cast my priceless pearl away.

6 Lamb of God! I do implore Thee,
Guard, support me, lest I fall;
Let me evermore adore Thee,
Be my everlasting All.

M. Loy

98 Clairvaux C. M.

H. A. POLACK, 1910

1 Je - sus, the ver - y thought of Thee With sweet-ness fills the breast;

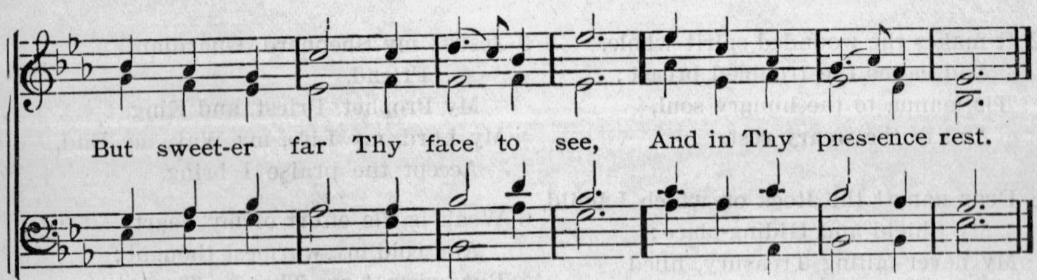
But sweet-er far Thy face to see, And in Thy pres-ence rest.

(*Or to St. Agnes or to Evan*)

2 Nor voice can sing, nor heart can
frame,
Nor can the memory find
A sweeter sound than Thy blest name,
O Savior of mankind!

3 O Hope of every contrite heart,
O Joy of all the meek!
To those who fall, how kind Thou art,
How good to those who seek!

4 But what to those who find? Ah! this
Nor tongue nor pen can show;
The love of Jesus, what it is,
None but His loved ones know.

5 Jesus, our only Joy be Thou!
As Thou our Prize wilt be;
Jesus, be Thou our Glory now,
And through eternity!

Bernard of Clairvaux, 1091—1153 Edward Caswall, Tr. 1849 a

99 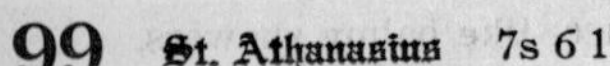 St. Athanasius 7s 6 l

E. J. HOPKINS, 1872 (P)

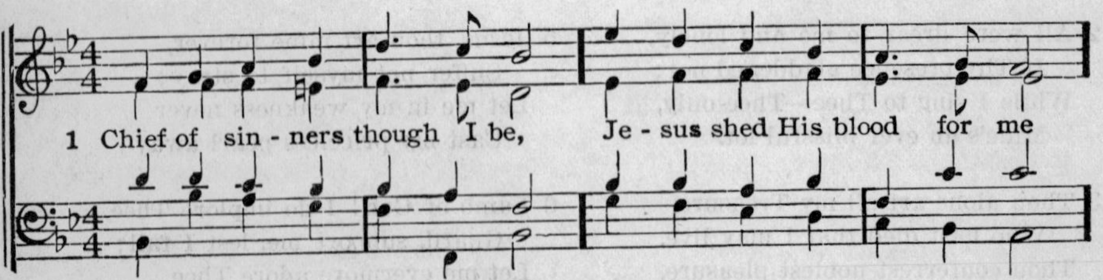
1 Chief of sin - ners though I be, Je - sus shed His blood for me

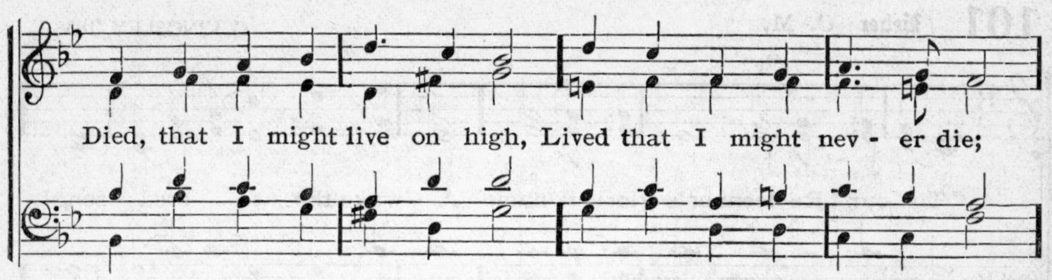
Died, that I might live on high, Lived that I might nev - er die;

As the branch is to the vine, I am His, and He is mine.

(*Or to Toplady*)

2 O the height of Jesus' love!
Higher than the heavens above,
Deeper than the depths of sea,
Lasting as eternity;
Love that found me,—wondrous thought!—
Found me when I sought Him not.

3 Jesus only can impart
Balm to heal the smitten heart;
Peace that flows from sin forgiven,
Joy that lifts the soul to heaven;
Faith and hope to walk with God,
In the way that Enoch trod.

4 Chief of sinners though I be,
Christ is all in all to me;
All my wants to Him are known,
All my sorrows are His own;
Safe with Him from earthly strife,
He sustains the hidden life.

5 O my Savior, help afford
By Thy Spirit and Thy Word!
When my wayward heart would stray,
Keep me in the narrow way;
Grace in time of need supply,
While I live, and when I die.

William McComb, 1864

100 St. Athanasius 7s 61

1 Christ, whose glory fills the skies,
Christ, the true, the only Light,
Sun of righteousness, arise,
Triumph o'er the shades of night;
Day-spring from on high, be near,
Day-star, in my heart appear.

2 Dark and cheerless is the morn
Unaccompanied by Thee;
Joyless is the day's return,
Till Thy mercy's beams I see;
Till they inward light impart,
Cheer my eyes, and warm my heart.

3 Visit, then, this soul of mine,
Pierce the gloom of sin and grief;
Fill me, Radiancy divine,
Scatter all my unbelief,
More and more Thyself display,
Shining to the perfect day.

Charles Wesley, 1740

(*Or to Dix*)

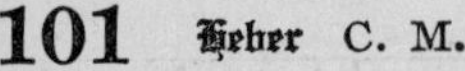

101 Heber C. M.

G. KINGSLEY, 1838

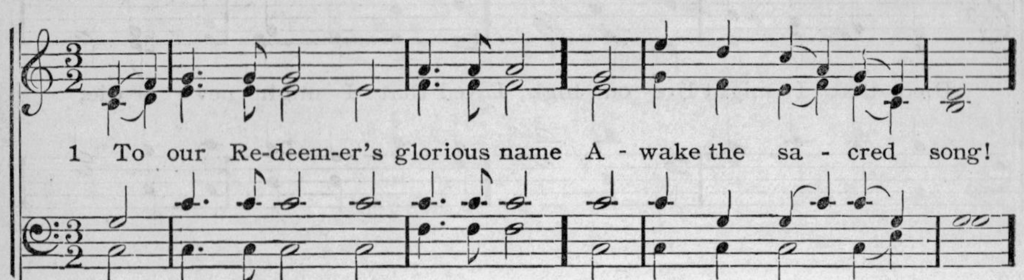
1 To our Re-deem-er's glorious name A - wake the sa - cred song!

O may His love, im - mor- tal flame, Tune ev - 'ry heart and tongue.

2 His love, what mortal thought can reach!
What mortal tongue display!
Imagination's utmost stretch
In wonder dies away.

3 He left His radiant throne on high,
Left the bright realms of bliss,
And came to earth to bleed and die!
Was ever love like this?

4 Dear Lord, while we adoring pay
Our humble thanks to Thee,
May every heart with rapture say,
"The Savior died for me."

5 O may the sweet, the blissful theme
Fill every heart and tongue,
Till strangers love the charming name,
And join the sacred song.

H. Steele, 1760.

102 Land C. M.

J. B. DYKES, 1862

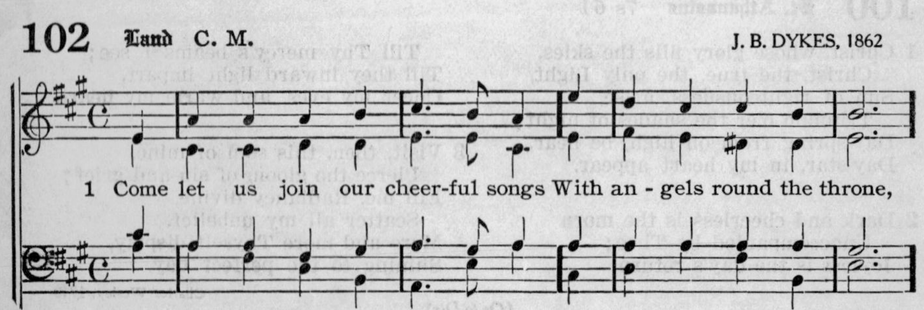
1 Come let us join our cheer-ful songs With an - gels round the throne,

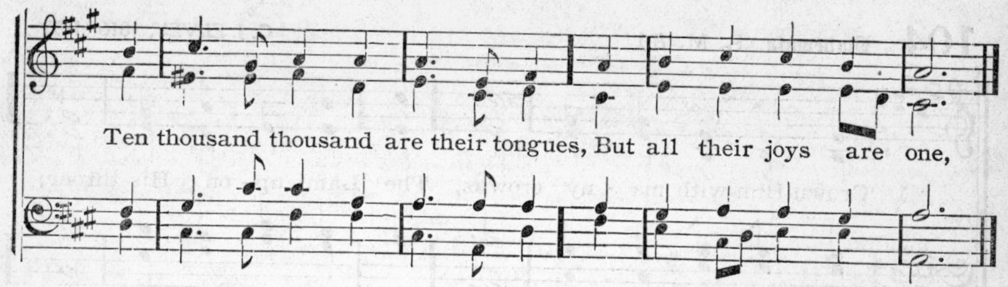
Ten thousand thousand are their tongues, But all their joys are one,

2 "Worthy the Lamb that died," they cry,
"To be exalted thus."
"Worthy the Lamb," our lips reply,
For He was slain for us.

3 Jesus is worthy to receive
Honor and power divine;
And blessings more than we can give,
Be, Lord, forever Thine.

4 Let all that dwell above the sky,
And air, and earth, and seas,
Conspire to lift Thy glories high,
And speak Thine endless praise!

5 The whole creation join in one,
To bless the sacred name
Of Him that sits upon the throne,
And to adore the Lamb.

Isaac Watts, 1707

103 Wie schoen leuchtet 8,8,7,8,8,7,4,8,4,8

1 O morning star, how fair and bright
Thou beamest forth in truth and light!
O Sovereign meek and lowly!
Sweet Root of Jesse, David's Son,
My King and Bridegroom, Thou hast won
My heart to love Thee solely!
Lovely art Thou, fair and glorious,
All victorious, Rich in blessing,
Rule and might o'er all possessing.

2 O King high-born, Pearl dearly won,
True Son of God and Mary's Son,
Crown of exceeding glory!
My heart calls Thee a Lily, Lord,
Pure milk and honey is Thy Word,
Thy sweetest Gospel-story.
Rose of Sharon, hail! hosanna!
Heavenly Manna, Feed us ever;
Lord, I can forget Thee never!

3 Clear Jasper, Ruby fervent red,
Deep, deep into my heart now shed
Thy love's pure fire forever;
Fill me with joy, grant me to be
Thy member closely joined to Thee,
Whom naught from Thee may sever;
Toward Thee longing doth possess me:
Come and bless me, For Thy gladness
Eye and heart here pine in sadness.

4 But if Thou look on me in love,
There straightway falls from God above
A ray of purest pleasure;
Thy Word and Spirit, flesh and blood,
Refresh myself with heavenly food,
Thou art my hidden Treasure.
Let Thy grace, Lord, warm and cheer me,
O draw near me; Thou hast taught us
Thee to seek, since Thou hast sought us.

5 Lord God, my Father, mighty Shield,
Thou in Thy Son art all revealed
As Thou hast loved and known me:
Thy Son hath me with Him betrothed,
In His own whitest raiment clothed,
He for His bride will own me.
Hallelujah! Life in heaven
Hath He given, With Him dwelling,
Still shall I His praise be telling.

6 Then touch the chords of harp and lute,
Let no sweet music now be mute,
But joyously resounding,
Tell of the marriage-feast, the bride,
The heavenly Bridegroom at her side,
'Mid love and joy abounding;
Shout for triumph, loudly sing ye,
Praises bring ye, Fall before Him,
King of kings, let all adore Him!

7 Here rests my heart, and holds it fast;
The Lord I love is First and Last,
The End and the Beginning!
I welcome death, for I shall rise
Through Him to His own Paradise
Above all tears and sinning,
Amen! Amen! Come, Lord Jesus,
Soon release us! With deep yearning
Lord, we look for Thy returning!

Dr. Philipp Nicolai, 1597 C. Winkworth, Tr. a

104 Diademata S. M. 81

G. J. ELVEY, 1816–1893

1 Crown Him with ma - ny crowns, The Lamb up - on His throne;
Hark! how the heav'n-ly an - them drowns All mu - sic but its own;
A - wake, my soul, and sing Of Him who died for thee,
And hail Him as thy match-less King Thro' all e - ter - ni - ty.

2 Crown Him the Virgin's Son,
The God incarnate born,
Whose arm those crimson trophies won
Which now His brow adorn;
Fruit of the mystic rose,
As of that rose the stem;
The root whence mercy ever flows,
The Babe of Bethlehem.

3 Crown Him the Lord of love;
Behold His hands and side,
Rich wounds, yet visible above
In beauty glorified:
No angel in the sky
Can fully bear that sight,
But downward bends his wond'ring eye
At mysteries so bright.

4 Crown Him the Lord of peace,
Whose power a sceptre sways
From pole to pole, that wars may cease,
And all be prayer and praise.
His reign shall know no end,
And round His pierced feet
Fair flowers of Paradise extend
Their fragrance ever sweet.

5 Crown Him the Lord of years,
The Potentate of time,
Creator of the rolling spheres,
Ineffably sublime.
All hail, Redeemer, hail!
For Thou hast died for me;
Thy praise shall never, never fail
Throughout eternity.

M. Bridges, 1848

105 Diadremata S. M. 81

1 I was a wandering sheep,
  I did not love the fold;
I did not love my Shepherd's voice
  I would not be controlled.
I was a wayward child,
  I did not love my home;
I did not love my Father's voice,
  I loved afar to roam.

2 The Shepherd sought His sheep,
  The Father sought His child;
They followed me o'er vale and hill,
  O'er deserts waste and wild;
They found me nigh to death,
  Famished, and faint, and lone;
They bound me with the bands of love,
  They saved the wandering one.

3 Jesus my Shepherd is,
  'Twas He that loved my soul,
'Twas He that washed me in His blood,
  'Twas He that made me whole;
'Twas He that sought the lost,
  That found the wandering sheep;
'Twas He that brought me to the fold,
  'Tis He that still doth keep.

4 I was a wandering sheep,
  I would not be controlled;
But now I love my Shepherd's voice,
  I love, I love the fold.
I was a wayward child,
  I once preferred to roam,
But now I love my Father's voice,
  I love, I love His home.

H. Bonar

106 Gott sei Dank durch alle Welt 7s

J. A. FREYLINGHAUSEN, 1704

1 Je - sus, Sav - ior, come to me! Let me ev - er be with Thee;
Come, and nev - er - more de - part, Thou who reign-est in my heart.

(*Or to Nun komm der Heiden Heiland Or to Solitude*)

2 Lord, for Thee I ever sigh,
Nothing else can satisfy,
'Tis my constant cry to Thee:
Jesus, Jesus, come to me!

3 Earthly joys can give no peace
Cannot bid my longing cease;
But to have my Jesus near,
This is all my pleasure here.

4 All that makes the angels glad,
In their garb of glory clad,
Only fills me with distress,
If Thy presence do not bless.

5 Take Thou all away from me,
I shall still thus minded be;
Thou who madest me Thine own
Shalt be e'er my joy alone.

6 Lord, to none on earth, beside
Thee, my heart I open wide;
Enter Thou, possess it all,
Thee alone mine own I call.

7 Thou alone, my God and Lord,
Art my Glory and Reward;
Thou hast bled for me and died,
I will be no other's bride.

8 Come then, Lamb for sinners slain,
Come and ease me of my pain;
Evermore I cry to Thee:
Jesus, Jesus, come to me!

9 Patiently I wait Thy day;
For this gift yet, Lord, I pray,
That, when death shall come to me,
My sweet Jesus Thou wilt be.

Johann Scheffler (Angelus), 1657 or 1668

107 Martyn 7s 8 l

S. B. MARSH, 1834

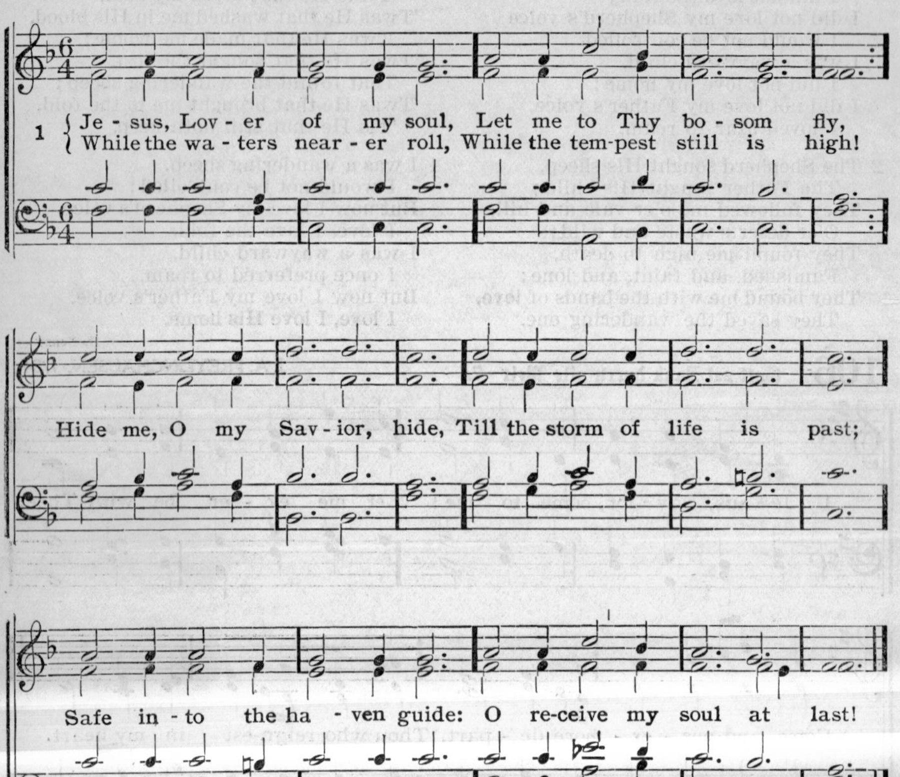
1 { Je - sus, Lov - er of my soul, Let me to Thy bo - som fly,
While the wa - ters near - er roll, While the tem - pest still is high!
Hide me, O my Sav - ior, hide, Till the storm of life is past;
Safe in - to the ha - ven guide: O re - ceive my soul at last!

2 Other refuge have I none;
  Hangs my helpless soul on Thee;
Leave, ah, leave me not alone,
  Still support and comfort me!
All my trust on Thee is stayed,
  All my help from Thee I bring:
Cover my defenceless head
  With the shadow of Thy wing.

3 Wilt Thou not regard my call?
  Wilt thou not accept my prayer?
Lo! I sink, I faint, I fall;
  Lo! on Thee I cast my care.
Reach me out Thy gracious hand!
  While I of Thy strength receive,
Hoping against hope I stand,
  Dying, and behold, I live!

4 Thou O Christ, art all I want;
  More than all in Thee I find:
Raise the fallen, cheer the faint,
  Heal the sick, and lead the blind.
Just and holy is Thy name;
  I am all unrighteousness:
False and full of sin I am;
  Thou art full of truth and grace.

5 Plenteous grace with Thee is found,
  Grace to cover all my sin;
Let the healing streams abound;
  Make and keep me pure within.
Thou of life the Fountain art,
  Freely let me take of Thee:
Spring Thou up within my heart,
  Rise to all eternity.

Charles Wesley, 1740

108 Beatitudo C. M.

J. B. DYKES, 1875

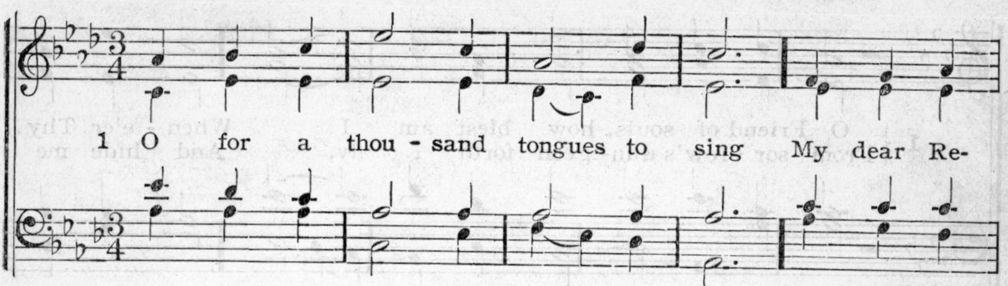
1 O for a thou - sand tongues to sing My dear Re-

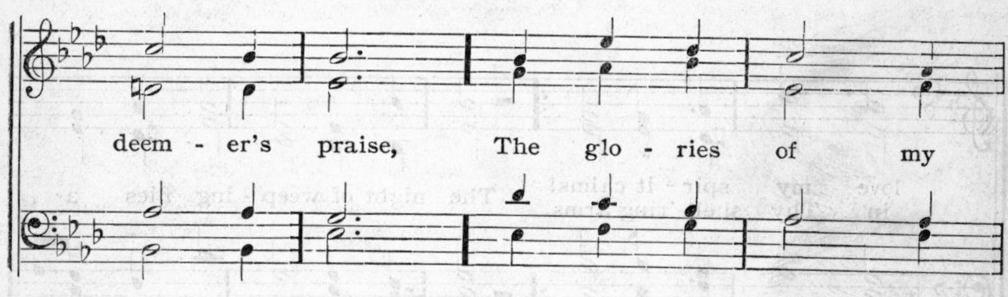
deem - er's praise, The glo - ries of my

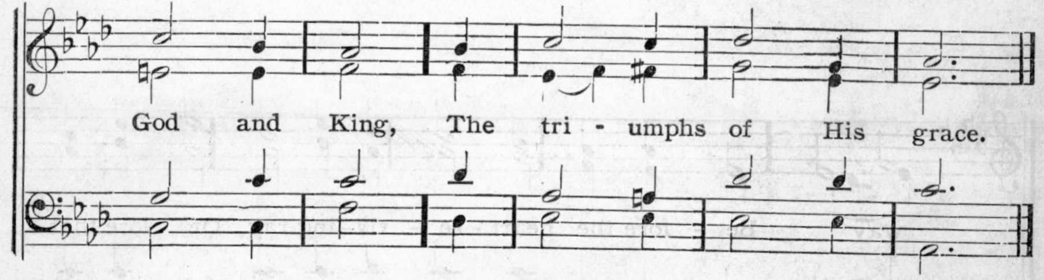
God and King, The tri - umphs of His grace.

(*Or to Lobt Gott ihr*)

2 My gracious Master and my God,
Assist me to proclaim,
To spread through all the earth abroad
The honors of Thy name.

3 Jesus! the name that charms our fears,
That bids our sorrows cease;
'Tis music in the sinner's ears,
'Tis life, and health, and peace.

4 He breaks the power of canceled sin,
He sets the prisoner free;
His blood can make the foulest clean;
His blood avails for me.

5 Look unto Him, ye nations; own
Your God, ye fallen race;
Look, and be saved through faith alone,
Be justified by grace.

6 See all your sins on Jesus laid;
The Lamb of God was slain:
His soul was once an offering made
For every soul of man.

7 Glory to God, and praise, and love,
Be ever, ever given
By saints below and saints above,
The Church in earth and heaven.

C. Wesley, 1739

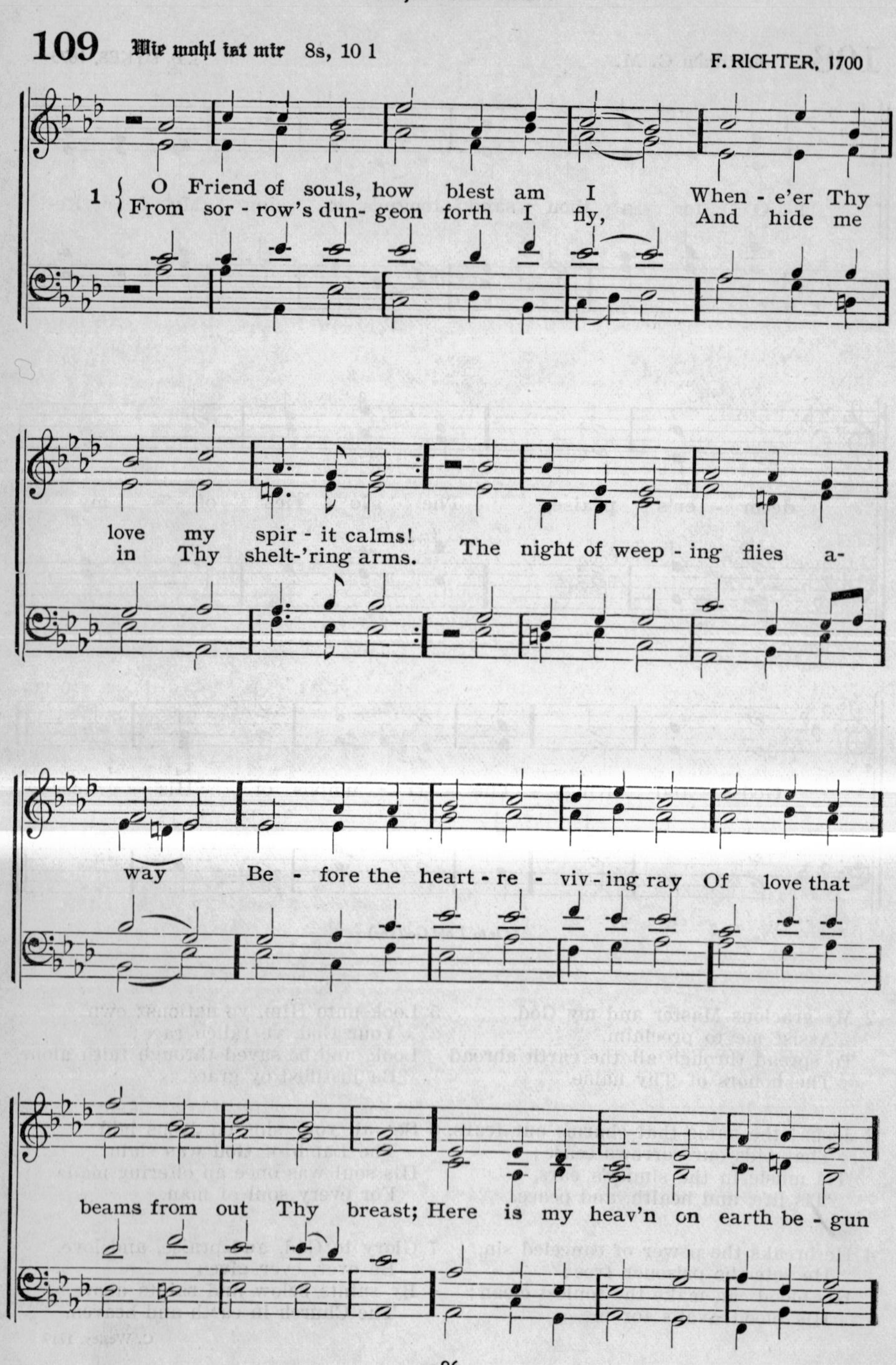
109 Wie wohl ist mir 8s, 10 1
F. RICHTER, 1700
1 { O Friend of souls, how blest am I When - e'er Thy love my spir - it calms!
From sor - row's dun - geon forth I fly, And hide me in Thy shelt-'ring arms.
The night of weep - ing flies a - way Be - fore the heart - re - viv - ing ray Of love that beams from out Thy breast; Here is my heav'n on earth be - gun

The Redeemer

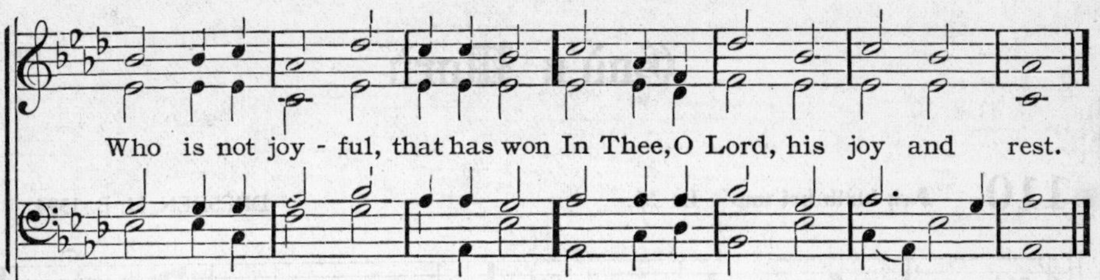
Who is not joy - ful, that has won In Thee, O Lord, his joy and rest.

2 The world may call herself my foe,
So be it; for I trust her not,
E'en though a friendly face she show,
And heap with her good things my lot.
In Thee alone will I rejoice,
Thou art the Friend, Lord, of my choice,
For Thou art true when friendships fail;
'Mid storms of woe Thy truth is still
My anchor; hate me as she will,
The world shall o'er me ne'er prevail.

3 The Law may threaten endless death
From awful Sinai's burning hill,
Straightway from its consuming breath
My soul through faith mounts higher still;
She throws herself at Jesus' feet
And finds with Him a safe retreat
Where curse and death can never come.
Though all things threaten condemnation,
Yet Jesus, Thou art my Salvation,
For in Thy love I find my home.

4 Through deserts of the cross Thou leadest,
I follow leaning on Thy hand;
From out the clouds Thy child Thou feedest,
And giv'st him water from the sand.
I know Thy wonderous ways will end
In love and blessing, Thou true Friend;
Enough, if Thou art ever near.
I know whom thou wilt glorify,
And raise o'er sun and stars on high,
Thou lead'st through depths and darkness here.

5 To others death seems dark and grim,
But not, Thou Life of life, to me,
I know Thou ne'er forsakest him
Whose heart and spirit rest in Thee.
Oh! who would fear his journey's close,
If from dark woods and lurking foes,
He then find safety and release?
Nay, rather, with a joyful heart
From this dark region I depart
To Thy eternal light and peace.

6 O Friend of souls, then blest indeed
Am I when on Thy love I lean!
The world, nor pain, nor death I heed,
Since Thou, my God, my Joy hast been.
O let this peace that Thou hast given,
Be but a foretaste of Thy heaven,
For goodness infinite is Thine.
Hence, world with all Thy flattering toys!
In God alone lie all my joys;
O rich delight, my Friend is mine!

Wolfgang Christoph Dessler, 1692 C. Winkworth, Tr. a

God's Word

110 Ach bleib bei uns L. M. DRESDEN, H. B. 1594

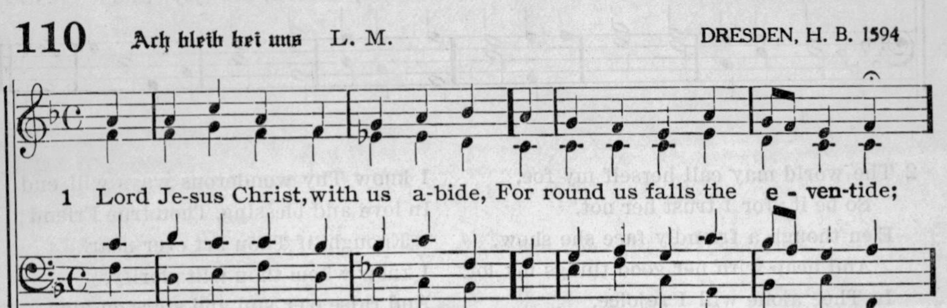
1 Lord Je-sus Christ, with us a-bide, For round us falls the e-ven-tide;

Let not Thy Word, that heav'nly light, For us be ev-er veiled in night.

2 In these last days of sore distress
Grant us, dear Lord, true steadfastness,
That pure we keep, till life is spent,
Thy holy Word and Sacrament.

3 Lord Jesus, help, Thy Church uphold,
For we are sluggish, thoughtless, cold;
Indue Thy Word with power and grace,
And spread its truth in every place.

4 O keep us in Thy Word, we pray;
The guile and rage of Satan stay;
Unto Thy Church grant, Lord, Thy grace,
Peace, concord, patience, fearlessness.

5 O God! how sin's dread works abound!
Throughout the earth no rest is found.
And wide has falsehood's spirit spread,
And error boldly rears its head.

6 Those haughty spirits, Lord, restrain,
Who o'er Thy Church with might would reign,
And always set forth something new,
Devised to change Thy doctrine true.

7 And since the cause and glory, Lord,
Are Thine, not ours, do Thou afford
Us help and strength and constancy;
With all our heart we trust in Thee.

8 A trusty weapon is Thy Word,
Thy Church's buckler, shield, and sword;
Lord, let us in this Word abide,
That we may seek no other guide.

9 O grant that in Thy holy Word
We here may live and die, dear Lord;
And when our journey endeth here,
Receive us into glory there.

Dr. N. Selnecker, 1587   3—9 by unknown author

111 Wolder C. M.

J. J. WOLDER, 1788

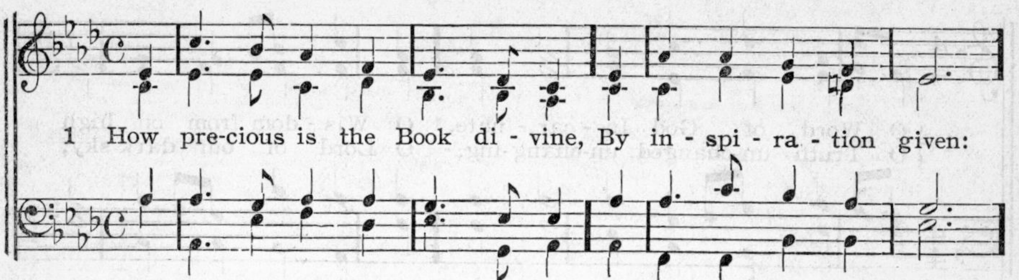
1 How pre-cious is the Book di - vine, By in - spi - ra - tion given:

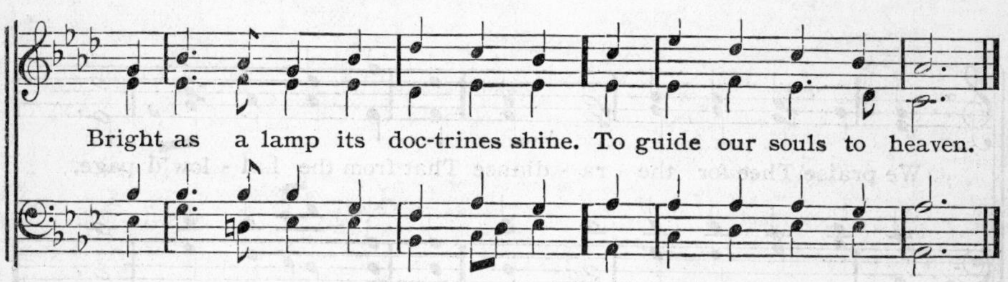
Bright as a lamp its doc-trines shine. To guide our souls to heaven.

(*Or to Dundee Or to Beatitudo Or to St. Stephen*)

2 Its light, descending from above,
Illumes this world so drear,
Displays a Savior's boundless love,
And brings His glories near.

3 It shows to man his wandering ways,
And where his feet have trod;
And brings to view the matchless grace
Of a forgiving God.

4 O'er all the straight and narrow way
Its radiant beams are cast;
A light whose never weary ray
Grows brightest at the last.

5 It sweetly cheers our drooping hearts
In this dark vale of tears;
Life, light, and joy it still imparts,
And quells our rising fears.

6 This lamp, through all the tedious night
Of life, shall guide our way,
Till we behold the clearer light
Of an eternal day.

John Fawcett, 1782 a

112 Wolder C. M.

1 How shall the young secure their hearts,
And guard their lives from sin?
Thy Word the choicest rules imparts
To keep the conscience clean.

2 'Tis like the sun, a heavenly light,
That guides us all the day;
And through the dangers of the night
A lamp to lead our way.

3 The starry heavens Thy rule obey,
The earth maintains her place;
And these Thy servants, night and day,
Thy skill and power express.

4 But still Thy Law and Gospel, Lord,
Have lessons more divine;
Not earth stands firmer than Thy Word.
Nor stars so nobly shine.

5 Thy Word is everlasting truth:
How pure is every page!
That holy Book shall guide our youth,
And well support our age.

Rev. Isaac Watts

113 Munich 7s, 6s 8 1 — J. G. STOERL'S CHORALBUCH, 1710

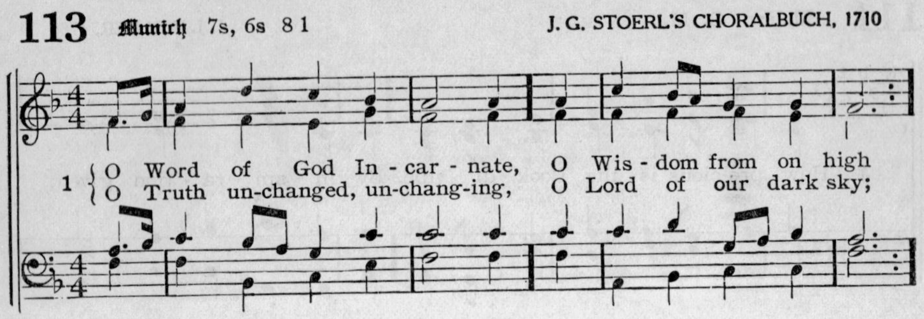
1 { O Word of God In-car-nate, O Wis-dom from on high
O Truth un-changed, un-chang-ing, O Lord of our dark sky;

We praise Thee for the ra-diance That from the hal-low'd page,

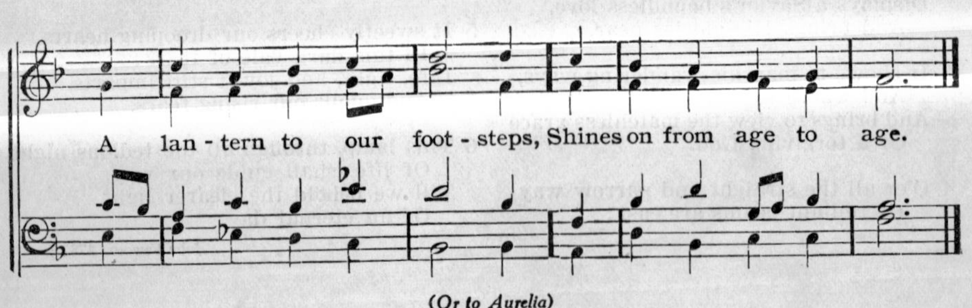
A lan-tern to our foot-steps, Shines on from age to age.

(Or to Aurelia)

2 The Church from her dear Master
Received the gift divine,
And still that light she lifteth
O'er all the earth to shine.
It is the golden casket
Where gems of truth are stored,
It is the heaven-drawn picture
Of Christ, the living Word.

3 It floateth like a banner
Before God's host unfurled;
It shineth like a beacon
Above the darkling world;
It is the chart and compass
That o'er life's surging sea,
'Mid mists and rocks and quicksands,
Still guides, O Christ, to Thee.

4 Oh, make Thy Church, dear Savior,
A lamp of burnished gold,
To bear before the nations
Thy true light as of old;
O teach Thy wandering pilgrims
By this their path to trace,
Till, clouds and darkness ended,
They see Thee face to face.

W. W. How, 1867, a

Gods's Word

114 **Creation** L. M. Arr. from F. J. Haydn, 1798

1 The heavens de-clare Thy glo - ry, Lord, In ev - 'ry

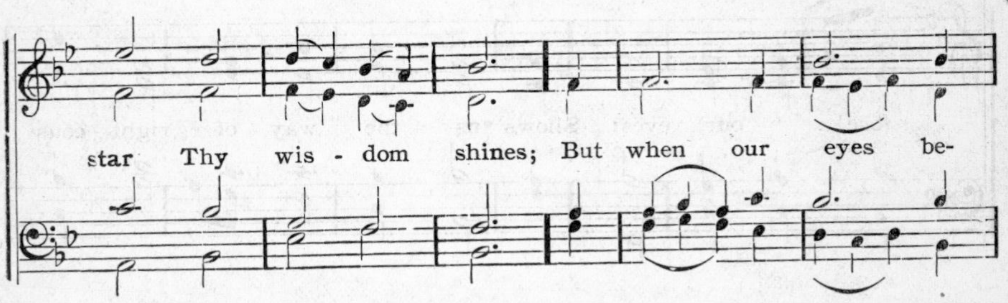
star Thy wis - dom shines; But when our eyes be-

hold Thy Word, We read Thy name in fair - er lines.

(*Or to Uxbridge*)

2 The rolling sun, the changing light,
And nights and days, Thy power confess;
But the blest volume Thou didst write
Reveals Thy justice and Thy grace.

3 Thy Gospel-heralds dare not rest,
Till through the world Thy truth has run;
Till Christ has all the nations blest
That see the light, or feel the sun.

4 Great Sun of righteousness, arise;
Bless the dark world with heavenly light;
The Gospel makes the simple wise,
Thy laws are pure, Thy judgments right.

5 Thy noblest wonders here we view,
In souls renewed, and sins forgiven;
Lord, cleanse our sins, our souls renew,
And make Thy Word our guide to heaven.

I. Watts, 1719. ab.

God's Word

115 Germany L. M.

L. v. BEETHOVEN

1 The Law of God is good and wise, And sets His will be-

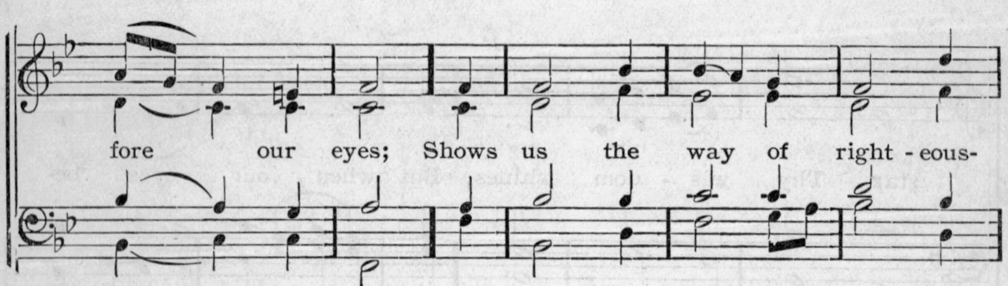
fore our eyes; Shows us the way of right - eous-

ness, And dooms to death when we trans - gress.

(Or to Wo Gott zum)

2 Its light of holiness imparts
The knowledge of our sinful hearts,
That we may see our lost estate,
And seek deliv'rance ere too late.

3 To those who help in Christ have found,
And would in works of love abound,
It shows what deeds are His delight,
And should be done as good and right.

4 When men the offered help disdain,
And willfully in sin remain,
Its terror in their ear resounds
And keeps their wickedness in bounds.

5 The Law is good; but since the fall
Its holiness condemns us all;
It dooms us for our sin to die,
And has no power to justify.

6 To Jesus we for refuge flee,
Who from the curse has set us free,
And humbly worship at His throne,
Saved by His grace through faith alone.

M. Loy

116 Es kam die gnadenvolle L. M.

H. EGLI, 1790

1 The Gos - pel shows the Fath - er's grace, Who

sent His Son to save our race: Pro - claims how Je - sus

lived and died That man might thus be jus - ti - fied.

2 It sets the Lamb before our eyes
Who made th' atoning sacrifice,
And calls the souls with guilt oppressed
To come and find eternal rest.

3 It brings the Savior's righteousness
Our souls to robe in royal dress;
From all our guilt it brings release,
And gives the troubled conscience peace.

4 It is the power of God to save
From sin and Satan and the grave;
It works the faith which firmly clings
To all the treasures which it brings.

5 It bears to all the tidings glad,
And bids their hearts no more be sad:
The heavy laden soul it cheers,
And banishes their guilty fears.

6 May we in faith its tidings learn,
Nor thanklessly its blessings spurn;
May we in faith its truth confess,
And praise the Lord our righteousness.

M. Loy

God's Word

117 Bedford C. M. WHEALL, 1729

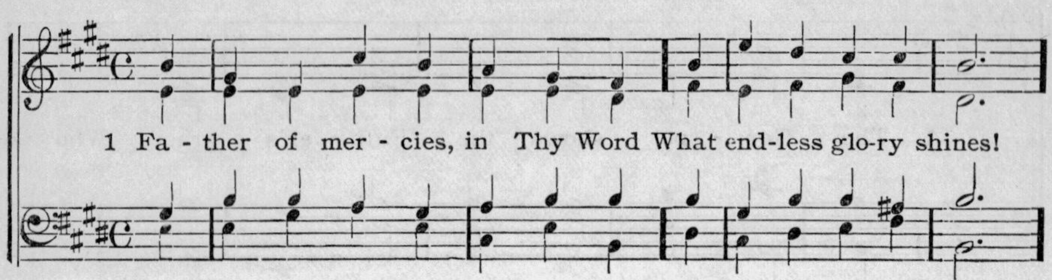

1 Fa - ther of mer - cies, in Thy Word What end-less glo-ry shines!

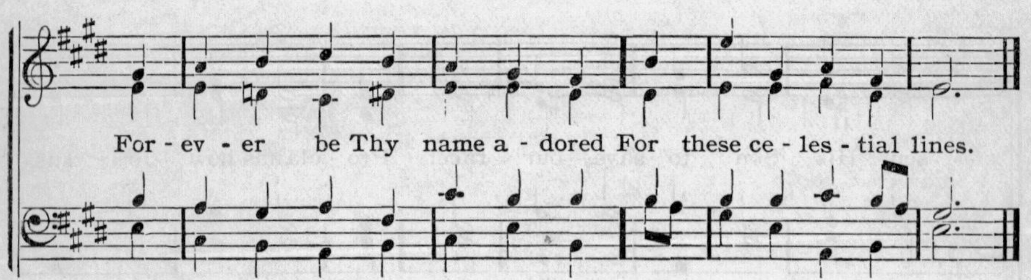

For - ev - er be Thy name a - dored For these ce - les - tial lines.

(Or to Nun danket all)

2 Here the Redeemer's welcome voice
Spreads heavenly peace around;
And life and everlasting joys
Attend the blissful sound.

3 O may these heavenly pages be
My ever dear delight;
And still new beauties may I see,
And still increasing light!

4 Divine Instructor, gracious Lord!
Be Thou forever near;
Teach me to love Thy sacred Word,
And view my Savior there.

Anne Steele, 1760

118 Thanksgiving L. M. DYKES (P)

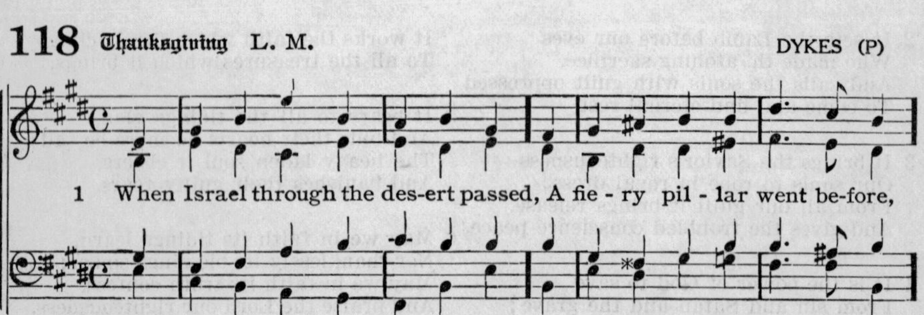

1 When Israel through the des-ert passed, A fie - ry pil - lar went be-fore,

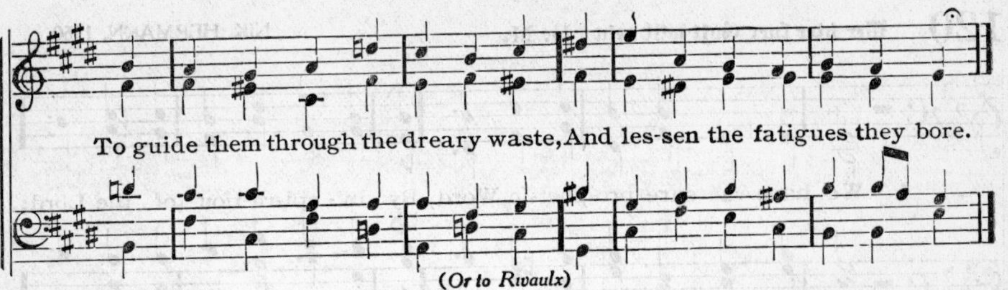

To guide them through the dreary waste, And les-sen the fatigues they bore.
(Or to Rivaulx)

2 Such is Thy glorious Word, O God!
'Tis for our light and guidance given;
It sheds its luster all abroad,
And points the path to bliss and heaven.

3 It fills the soul with sweet delight,
And quickens its inactive powers;
It sets our wand'ring footsteps right,
Displays Thy love, and kindles ours.

4 Its promises rejoice our hearts;
Its doctrines are divinely true;
While highest wisdom it imparts,
It comforts and instructs us, too.

5 Ye favored lands, that have this Word,
Ye saints, who feel its saving power,
Unite your tongues to praise the Lord,
And His distinguished grace adore!

B. Beddome

119 Nox Praecessit C. M.

J. B. CALKIN. 1875

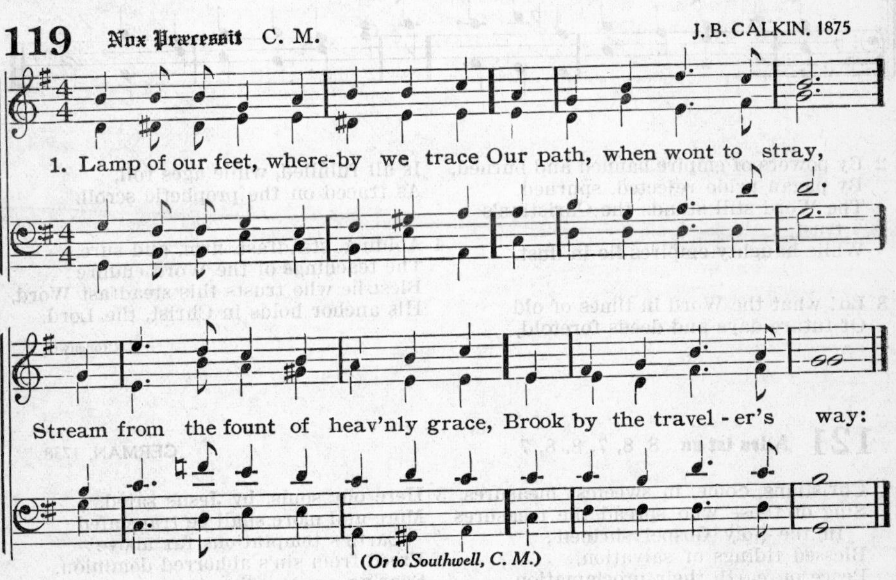

1. Lamp of our feet, where-by we trace Our path, when wont to stray,
Stream from the fount of heav'nly grace, Brook by the travel-er's way:
(Or to Southwell, C. M.)

2 Bread of our souls, whereon we feed,
True manna from on high;
Our guide and chart, wherein we read
Of realms beyond the sky:

3 Pillar of fire, through watches dark,
Or radiant cloud by day;
When waves would break our tossing bark,
Our anchor and our stay:

4 Word of the ever-living God,
Will of His glorious Son;
Without Thee how could earth be trod,
Or heaven itself be won?

5 Lord, grant us all aright to learn
The wisdom it imparts;
And to its heavenly teaching turn,
With simple, childlike hearts.

B. Barton, 1827

120 Wer hier fuer Gott will sein L. M.

NIK. HERMANN, 1560

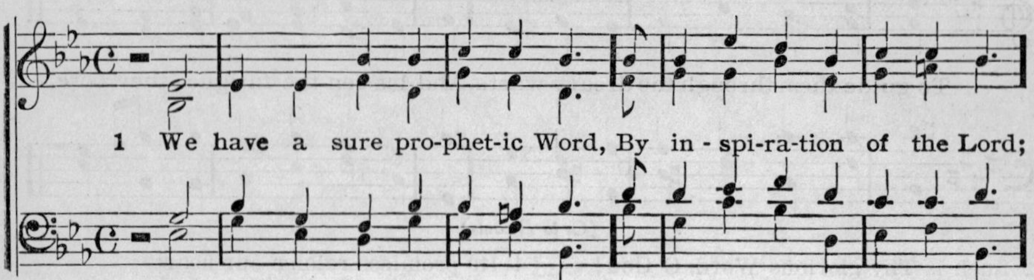
1 We have a sure pro-phet-ic Word, By in - spi-ra-tion of the Lord;

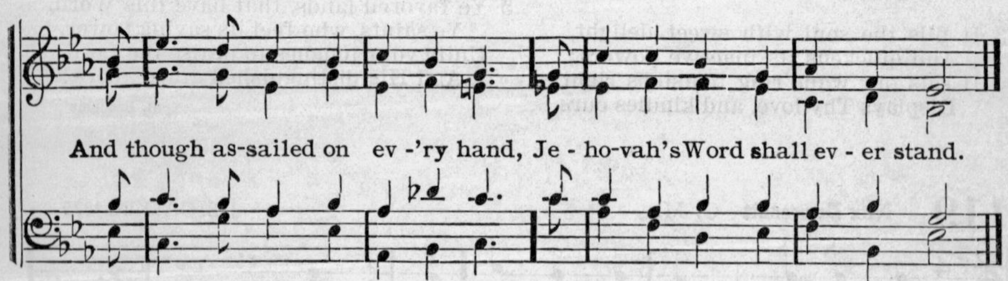
And though as-sailed on ev -'ry hand, Je - ho-vah's Word shall ev - er stand.

2 By powers of empire banned and burned,
By pagan pride rejected, spurned,
The Word still stands the Christian's trust,
While haughty empires lie in dust.

3 Lo! what the Word in times of old
Of future days and deeds foretold,
Is all fulfilled, while ages roll,
As traced on the prophetic scroll.

4 Abiding, steadfast, firm, and sure,
The teachings of the Word endure:
Blest he who trusts this steadfast Word,
His anchor holds in Christ, the Lord.

E. Cronenwett

121 Alles ist an 8, 8, 7, 8, 8, 7

GERMAN, 1738

1 Christians, come, in sweetest measures,
Sing of those who spread the treasures
In the holy Gospel shrined;
Blessed tidings of salvation,
Peace on earth their proclamation,
Love from God to lost mankind.

2 See the rivers four that gladden
With their streams the better Eden,
Planted by our Savior dear:
Christ the fountain, these the waters;
Drink, O Zion's sons and daughters,
Drink, and find salvation here.

3 Here our souls, by Jesus sated,
More and more shall be translated
Earth's temptations far above:
Freed from sin's abhorred dominion,
Soaring on angelic pinion,
They shall reach the source of love.

4 Then shall thanks and praise ascending,
For Thy mercies without ending,
Rise to Thee, O Savior blest:
With Thy gracious aid defend us;
Let Thy guiding light attend us;
Bring us to Thy place of rest.

Adam of St. Victor, 1150. Tr. R. Campbell, 1850. a

God's Word

122 Harmony Grove L. M. H. K. OLIVER

1 In vain would boast - ing rea - son find The path to
hap - pi - ness and God; Her weak di - rec - tions leave the
mind Be - wil - dered in a doubt - ful road.

(Or to Hursley)

2 Jesus, Thy words alone impart
Eternal life; on these I live;
Here sweeter comforts cheer my heart
Than all the powers of nature give.

3 Here let my constant feet abide;
Thou art the true, the living Way;
Let Thy good Spirit be my guide
To the bright realms of endless day.

4 The various forms that men devise,
To shake my faith with treacherous art,
I scorn as vanity and lies,
And bind Thy Gospel to my heart.

Anne Steele, 1760. a

The Lord's Day

123 Fred til Bod 7s 6 1 L. M. LINDEMAN, 1812—'87 (P)

1 Fa-ther, who the light this day Out of dark-ness didst cre - ate,
Shine up-on us now, we pray, While with-in Thy courts we wait.
Wean us from the works of night, Make us chil - dren of the light.

2 Savior, who this day didst break
From the bondage of the tomb,
Bid our slumbering souls awake,
And dispel their doubt and gloom;
Let us, from our bonds set free,
Rise from sin and live to Thee.

3 Blessed Spirit, Comforter,
Sent this day from Christ on high,
Lord, on us Thy gifts confer,
Cleanse, illumine, sanctify;
All Thine influence shed abroad;
Lead us to the truth of God.

Julia A. Elliott

124 Croft 6, 6, 6, 6, 8, 8 (H. M.)

WM. CROFT, 1700 (P)

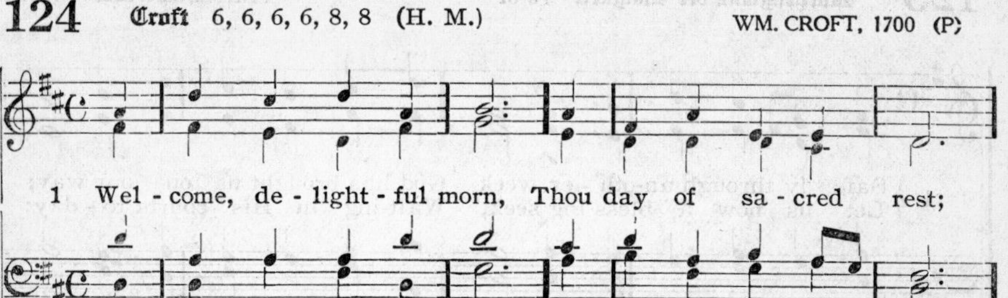
1 Wel - come, de - light - ful morn, Thou day of sa - cred rest;

I hail Thy kind re - turn: Lord, make these mo - ments blest. From

the low train of mor - tal toys I soar to reach im - mor - tal joys.

(*Or to Bevan*)

2 Now may the King descend,
And fill His throne of grace;
Thy sceptre, Lord, extend,
While saints address Thy face;
Let sinners feel Thy quickening word
And learn to know and fear the Lord.

3 Descend, O heavenly Dove,
With all Thy quickening powers,
Disclose a Savior's love,
And bless these sacred hours:
Then shall my soul new life obtain,
Nor Lord's Days e'er be spent in vain.

Hayward, in J. Dobell's Coll., 1806

125 Morgenglanz der Ewigkeit 7s 61

FREYLINGHAUSEN, 1704

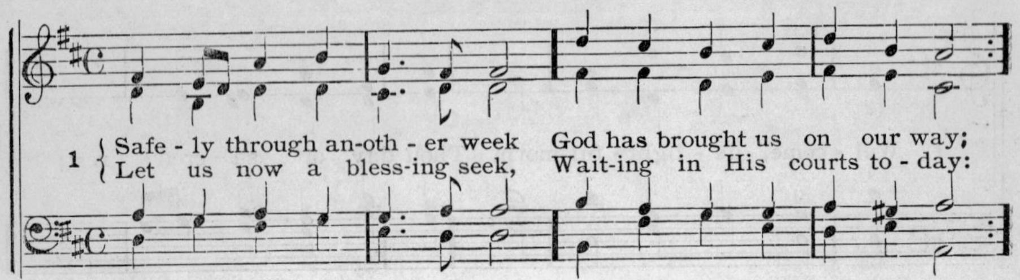
1 { Safe - ly through an-oth - er week God has brought us on our way;
Let us now a bless-ing seek, Wait-ing in His courts to - day:

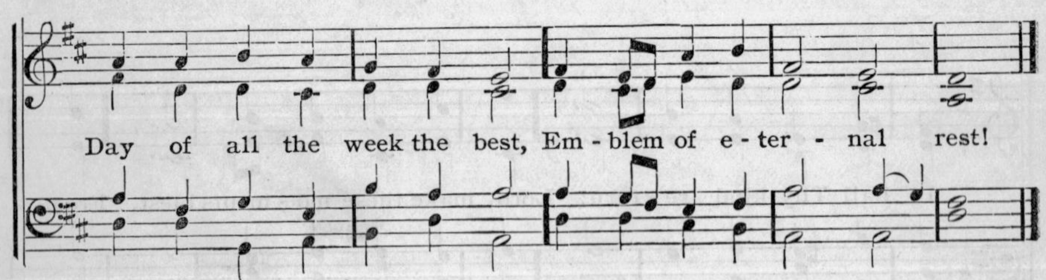
Day of all the week the best, Em - blem of e - ter - nal rest!

(Or to Fred til Bod Or to Dix)

2 Mercies multiplied each hour
 Through the week our praise demand;
Guarded by almighty power,
 Fed and guided by His hand,
Though ungrateful we have been,
And repaying love with sin.

3 While we pray for pardoning grace,
 Through the dear Redeemer's name,
Show Thy reconciled face,
 Take away our sin and shame:
From our worldly cares set free,
May we rest this day in Thee.

4 As we come Thy name to praise
 May we feel Thy presence near;
May Thy glory meet our eyes,
 While we in Thy house appear:
Here afford us, Lord, a taste
Of our everlasting feast.

5 May Thy Gospel's joyful sound
 Conquer sinners, comfort saints;
Make the fruits of grace abound,
 Bring relief for all complaints:
Thus may all our Sabbaths prove
Till we join the Church above.

J. Newton 1779

126 Solitude 7s

L. T. DOWNES, 1851

1 On this day, the first of days, God the Fa-ther's name we praise,

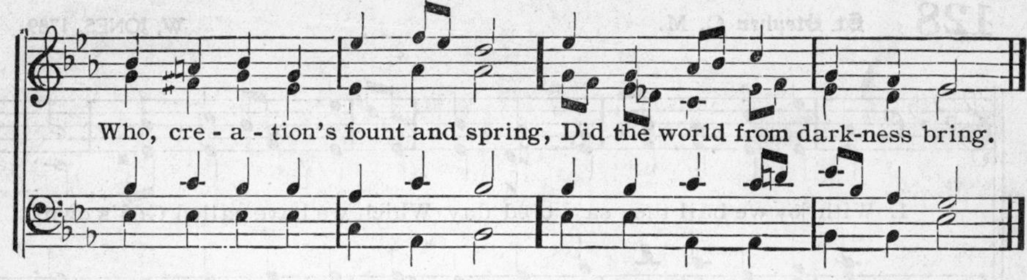
Who, cre - a - tion's fount and spring, Did the world from dark-ness bring.

(Or to Jesu komm [Gott sei])

2 On this day the eternal Son
Over death His triumph won;
On this day the Spirit came
With His gifts of living flame.

3 Oh, that fervent love today
May in every heart have sway,
Teaching us to praise aright
God, the source of life and light!

4 Father, who didst fashion me
Image of Thyself to be,
Fill me with Thy love divine,
Let my every thought be Thine.

5 Holy Jesus, may I be
Dead and buried here with Thee,
And, by love inflamed, arise
Unto Thee a sacrifice.

H. W. Baker, Tr, 1861

127 Waltham L. M.

J. B. CALKIN, 1872 [P]

1 This day at Thy cre - at - ing word First o'er the earth the light was poured:
O Lord, this day up - on us shine, And fill our souls with light di-vine.

2 This day the Lord for sinners slain
In might victorious rose again:
O Jesus, may we raised be
From death of sin, to life in Thee.

3 This day the Holy Spirit came
With fiery tongues of cloven-flame:
O Spirit, fill our hearts this day
With grace to hear, and grace to pray.

4 O day of light, and life, and grace,
From earthly toils sweet resting-place,
Thy hallowed hours, best gift of love,
Give we again to God above!

W. W. How, 1854

The Lord's Day

128 St. Stephen C. M.

W. JONES, 1789

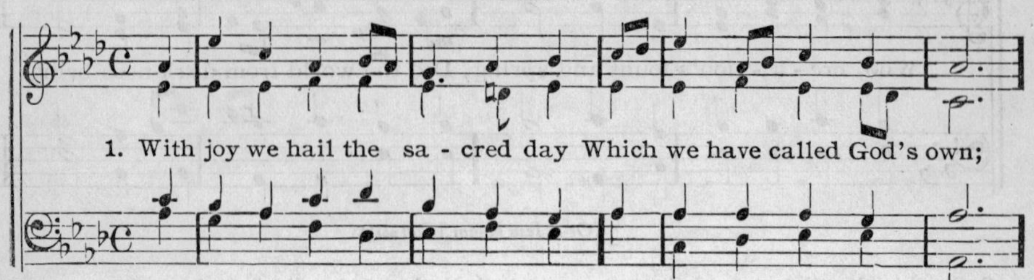
1. With joy we hail the sa - cred day Which we have called God's own;

With joy the sum-mons we o - bey To wor - ship at His throne.

2 Thy chosen temple, Lord, how fair!
As here Thy servants throng
To breathe the humble, fervent prayer,
And pour the choral song.

3 Spirit of grace, O deign to dwell
Within Thy Church below;
Make her in holiness excel,
With pure devotion glow.

4 Let peace within her walls be found;
Let all her sons unite
To spread with holy zeal around
Her clear and shining light.

5 Great God, we hail the sacred day
Which we have called Thine own;
With joy the summons we obey
To worship at Thy throne.

H. Auber. 1833 a

129 Colchester C. M.

AARON WILLIAM'S COLL., CIR., 1760 [P]

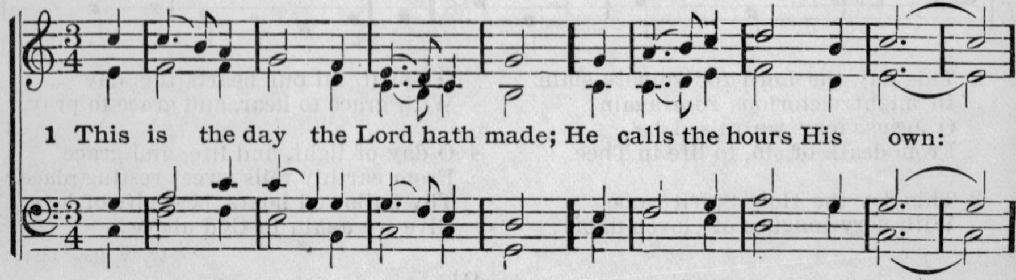
1 This is the day the Lord hath made; He calls the hours His own:

The Lord's Day

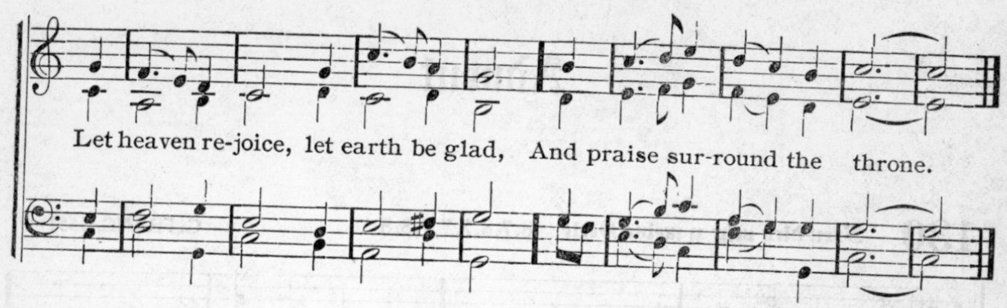
Let heaven re-joice, let earth be glad, And praise sur-round the throne.

(*Or to Azmon or to Ich singe dir*)

2 Today He rose and left the dead,
And Satan's empire fell;
Today the saints His triumph spread
And all His wonders tell.

3 Hosanna, to th' anointed King,
To David's holy Son:
Help us, O Lord; descend and bring
Salvation from Thy throne.

4 Blest be the Lord, who comes to men
With messages of grace;
Who comes in God His Father's name,
To save our sinful race.

5 Hosanna, in the highest strains
The Church on earth can raise!
The highest heavens, in which He reigns,
Shall give Him nobler praise.

Isaac Watts, 1719

Advent

130 Freu dich sehr, o meine Seele 8,7,8,7,7,7,8,8 G. FRANC, 1551

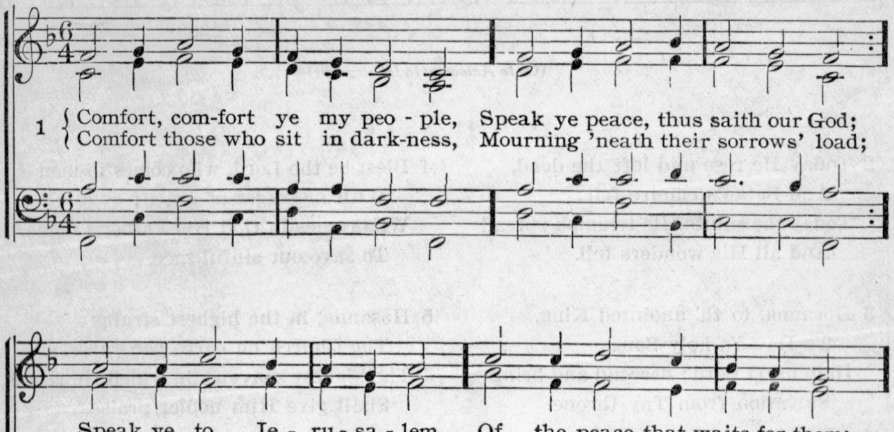

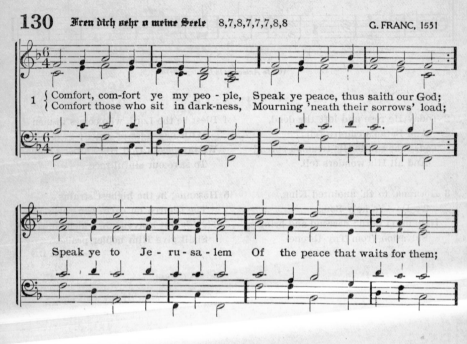

1 { Comfort, com-fort ye my peo - ple, Speak ye peace, thus saith our God;
{ Comfort those who sit in dark-ness, Mourning 'neath their sorrows' load;

Speak ye to Je - ru - sa - lem Of the peace that waits for them;

Tell her that her sins I cov - er, And her war-fare now is o - ver.

2 For the Herald's voice is crying
In the desert far and near,
Bidding all men to repentance,
Since the kingdom now is here.
O, that warning cry obey!
Now prepare for God a way!
Let the valleys rise to meet Him,
And the hills bow down to greet Him.

3 Make ye straight what long was crooked,
Make the rougher places plain:
Let your hearts be true and humble,
As befits His holy reign;
For the glory of the Lord
Now o'er earth is shed abroad,
And all flesh shall see the token
That His Word is never broken.

John Olearius (Oelschlaeger), 1671 Miss Cath. Winkworth, Tr. 1862

Advent

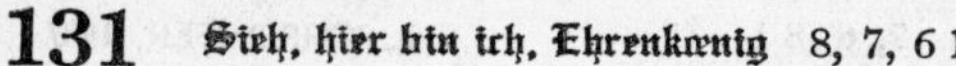
131 Sieh, hier bin ich, Ehrenkönig

8, 7, 6 1 DARMST. H. B., 1698 (P)

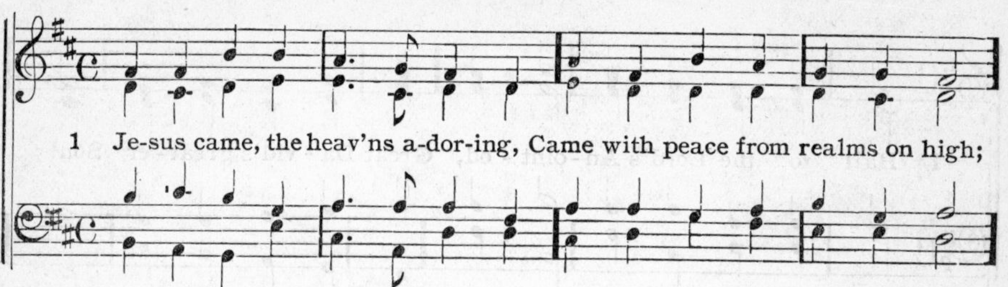
1 Je-sus came, the heav'ns a-dor-ing, Came with peace from realms on high;

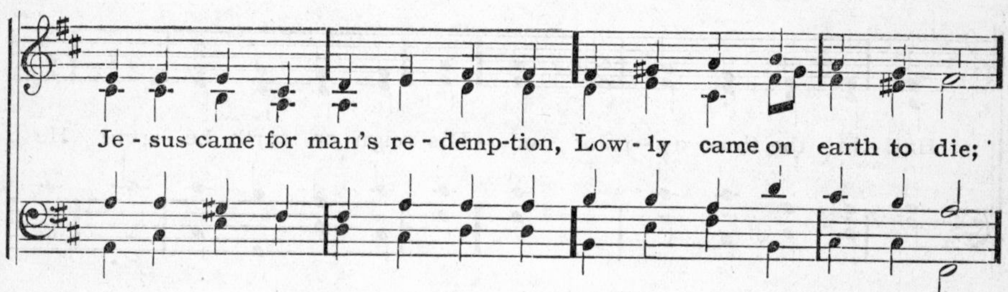
Je - sus came for man's re - demp-tion, Low - ly came on earth to die;

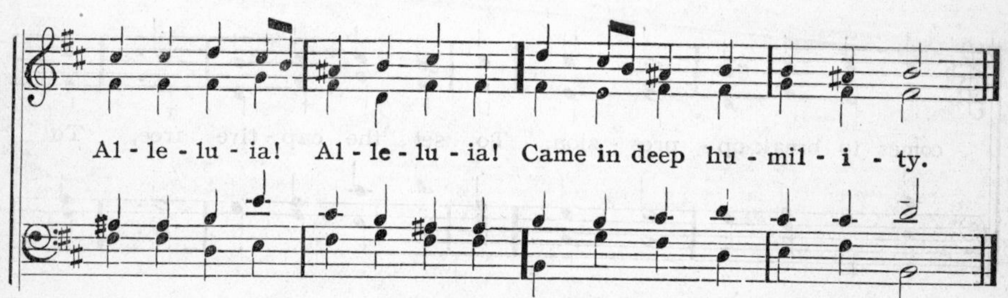
Al - le - lu - ia! Al - le - lu - ia! Came in deep hu - mil - i - ty.

(Or to Her vil ties)

2 Jesus comes again in mercy,
When our hearts are bowed with care;
Jesus comes again in answer
To an earnest, heartfelt prayer;
Alleluia! Alleluia!
Comes to save us from despair.

3 Jesus comes to hearts rejoicing,
Bringing news of sins forgiven;
Jesus comes in sounds of gladness,
Leading souls redeemed to heaven:
Alleluia! Alleluia!
Now the gate of death is riven.

4 Jesus comes in joy and sorrow,
Shares alike our hopes and fears;
Jesus comes, whate'er befalls us,
Glads our hearts, and dries our tears;
Alleluia! Alleluia!
Cheering e'en our failing years.

5 Jesus comes on clouds triumphant,
When the heavens shall pass away;
Jesus comes again in glory,
Let us then our homage pay,
Alleluia! Ever singing,
Till the dawn of endless day.

G. Thring, 1864

Advent

132 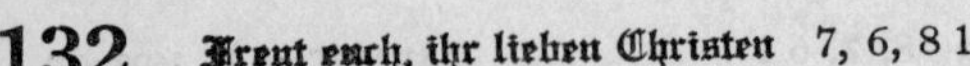
Freut euch, ihr lieben Christen
7, 6, 8 1 L. SCHROETER, 1587

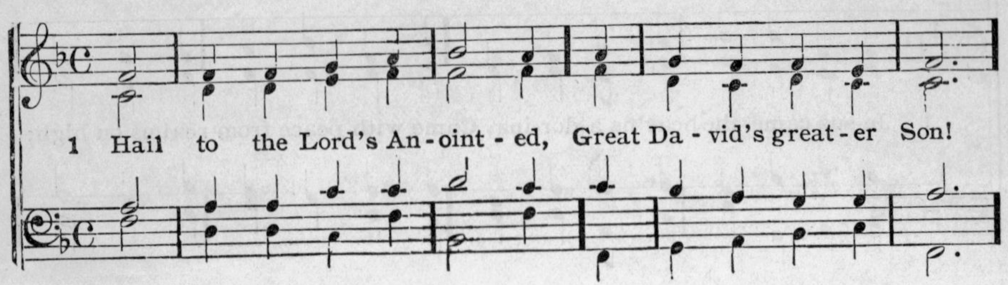
1 Hail to the Lord's An - oint - ed, Great Da - vid's great - er Son!

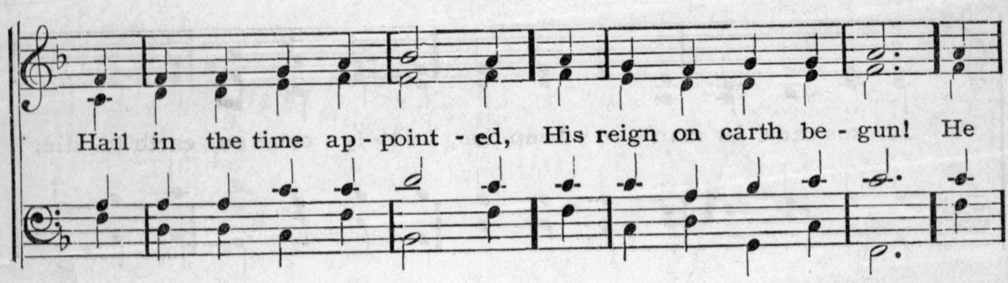
Hail in the time ap - point - ed, His reign on earth be - gun! He

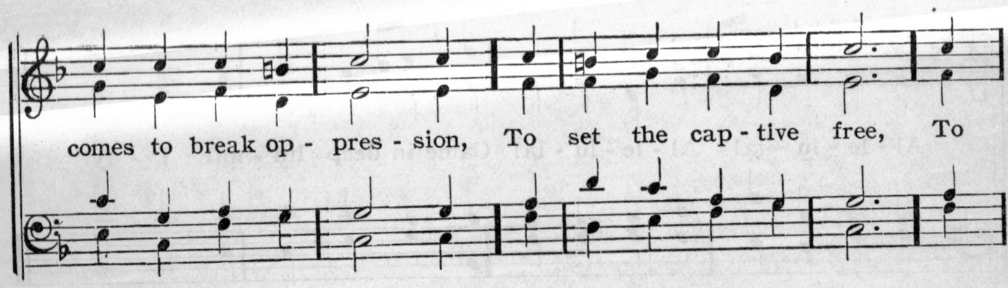
comes to break op - pres - sion, To set the cap - tive free, To

take a - way trans-gres - sion, And rule in e - - qui - ty.

(Or to Webb Or to Valet will ich)

2 He comes with succor speedy
To those who suffer wrong;
To help the poor and needy,
And bid the weak be strong;
To give them songs for sighing,
Their darkness turn to light,
Whose souls, condemned and dying,
Were precious in His sight.

3 He shall come down like showers
Upon the fruitful earth;
And love, joy, hope like flowers,
Spring in His path to birth.
Before Him, on the mountains
Shall peace, the herald, go;
And righteousness, in fountains,
From hill to valley flow.

4 To Him shall prayer unceasing
And daily vows ascend;
His kingdom still increasing,
A kingdom without end.
The tide of time shall never
His covenant remove;
His name shall stand forever;
That name to us is Love.

J. Montgomery, 1821

133 O der alles hätt verloren 8, 7, 8, 7 FREYLINGHAUSEN, 1705

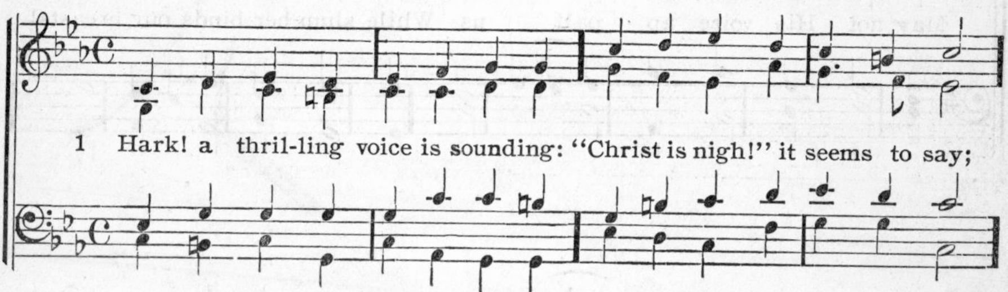
1 Hark! a thril-ling voice is sounding: "Christ is nigh!" it seems to say;

"Cast a - way the dreams of dark-ness, O ye chil-dren of the day!"

(*Or to Batty*)

2 Startled at the solemn warning,
Let the earth-bound soul arise;
Christ, her Sun, all sloth dispelling,
Shines upon the morning skies.

3 Lo, the Lamb, so long expected,
Comes with pardon down from heaven.
Let us haste, with tears of sorrow,
One and all, to be forgiven.

4 So, when next He comes with glory,
Wrapping all the earth in fear,
With His mercy He may shield us,
And with words of love draw near.

Edward Caswall, Tr. 1848 a

Advent

134 Ach Gott vom Himmelreiche 7, 6, 8 1
M. PRAETORIUS, 1609
1 The Bridegroom soon will call us: Come, all ye wed-ding guests!
May not His voice ap - pall us While slum-ber binds our breasts!
May all our lamps be burn - ing, And oil be found in store,
That we with Him re - turn - ing, May o - pen find the door!

(*Or to Ich dank dir lieber Herre*)

2 There shall we see delighted
  Our dear Redeemer's face,
Who leads our souls benighted
  To glory by His grace;
The patriarchs shall meet us,
  The prophets' holy band,
Apostles, martyrs, greet us
  In that celestial land.

3 They will not blush to own us
  As brothers, sisters dear,
Love ever will be shown us
  When we with them appear
We all shall come before Him,
  Who for us man became,
As Lord and God adore Him,
  And ever bless His name.

4 Our Father, rich in blessing,
  Will give us crowns of gold,
And to His bosom pressing,
  Impart a bliss untold,
Will welcome with embraces
  Of never-ending love,
And deck us with His graces
  In blissful realms above.

5 In yonder home shall never
  Be silent music's voice;
With hearts and lips forever
  We shall in God rejoice;
The angels shall adore Him,
  All saints shall sing His praise,
And bring with joy before Him
  Their sweetest heavenly lays.

6 In mansions fair and spacious
  Will God the feast prepare,
And, ever kind and gracious,
  Bid us its riches share;
There bliss that knows no measure
  From springs of love shall flow,
And never-changing pleasure
  His bounty will bestow.

7 Thus God shall from all evil
  Forever make us free,
From sin and from the Devil,
  From all adversity,
From sickness, pain and sadness,
  From troubles, cares and fears,
And grant us heavenly gladness,
  And wipe away our tears.

Johann Walther, 1555

135 Meinen Jesum 7, 8, 7, 8, 7, 7

1 Come, Thou precious Ransom, come!
Only Hope for sinful mortals!
Come, O Savior of the world!
Open are to Thee all portals;
Come in wonted suavity,
Anxiously we wait for Thee.

2 O great King of glory, come!
Let me be Thy living temple;
Enter Thou into my heart;
Though I am but poor and simple,
Yet my riches then shall be,
That Thou reignest, Lord, in me.

3 My hosannas and my palms
Graciously receive, I pray Thee;
Evermore, as best I can,
Savior, I will homage pay Thee,
And in faith I will embrace,
Lord, Thy merit through Thy grace.

4 Hail! Hosanna! David's Son,
Help, Lord, hear our supplication!
Let Thy kingdom, scepter, crown
Bring us blessing and salvation,
That forever we may sing:
Hail! Hosanna to our king.

J. G. Olearius, 1644 A. Crull, Tr.

136 Wie soll ich dich empfangen 7, 6, 8 1 J. CRUEGER, 1653

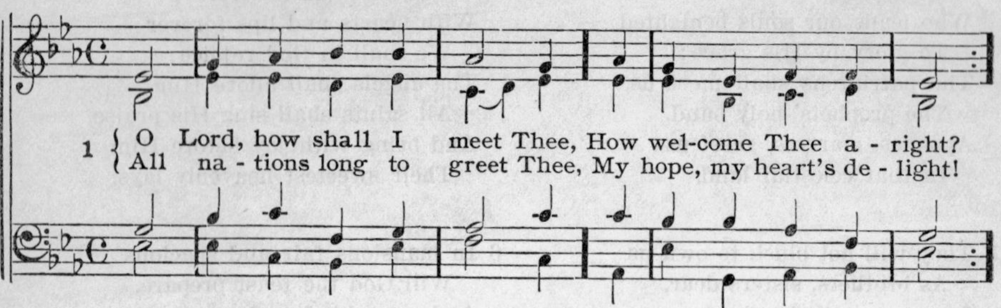
1 { O Lord, how shall I meet Thee, How wel-come Thee a - right?
All na - tions long to greet Thee, My hope, my heart's de - light!

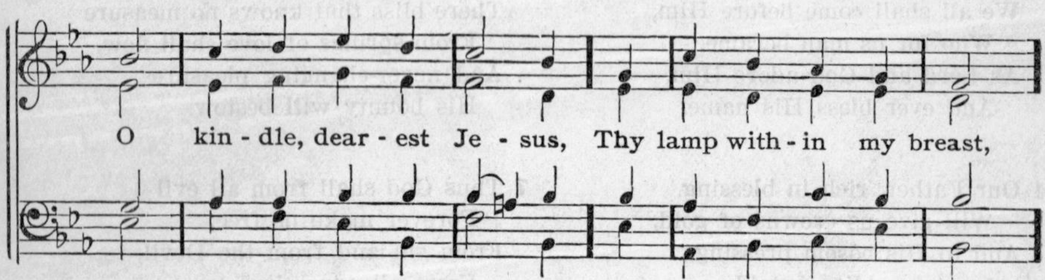
O kin - dle, dear - est Je - sus, Thy lamp with - in my breast,

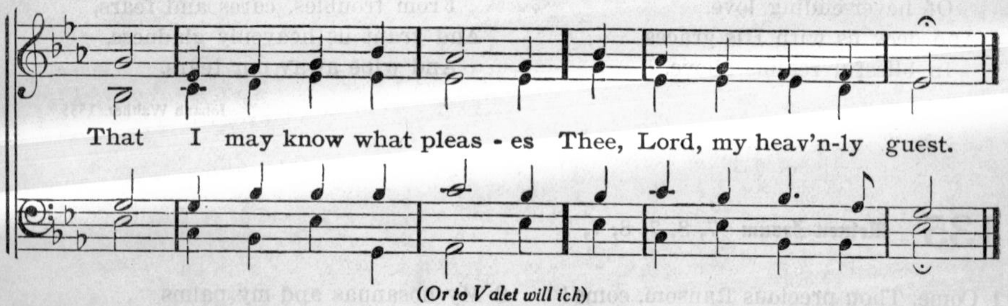
That I may know what pleas - es Thee, Lord, my heav'n-ly guest.

(*Or to Valet will ich*)

2 Thy Zion strews before Thee
Green boughs and fairest palms,
And I, too, will adore Thee
With sweetest songs and psalms.
My heart shall bloom forever
For Thee with praises new,
And from Thy name shall never
Withhold the honor due.

3 What hast Thou left ungranted
To give me glad relief?
When soul and body panted
In utmost depth of grief,
In deepest degradation,
Devoid of joy and peace,
Then, Thou, my soul's Salvation,
Didst come to bring release.

4 I lay in fetters groaning,
Thou com'st to set me free;
I stood, my shame bemoaning,
Thou com'st to honor me;
A glory Thou dost give me,
A treasure safe on high,
That will not fail or leave me
As earthly riches fly.

5 Naught, naught, dear Lord, could move Thee
To leave Thy rightful place
Save love, for which I love Thee;
A love that could embrace
A world where sorrow dwelleth,
Which sin and suffering fill,
More than the tongue e'er telleth;—
Yet Thou couldst love it still!

6 Rejoice, then, ye sad-hearted,
Who sit in deepest gloom,
Who mourn o'er joys departed,
And tremble at your doom;
Despair not, He is near you,
Yea, standing at the door,
Who best can help and cheer you,
And bid you weep no more.

7 No care nor effort either
Is needed day or night,
How ye may draw Him hither
In your own strength and might.
He comes, He comes with gladness,
Moved by His love alone,
To calm your fear and sadness,
Which unto Him are known.

8 Sin's debt, that fearful burden,
Let not your souls distress;
Your guilt the Lord will pardon
And cover with His grace.
He comes, He comes procuring
The peace of sin forgiven,
To all God's sons securing
Their part and lot in heaven.

9 Why should the wicked move you?
Heed not their craft and spite!
Your Savior who doth love you,
Will scatter all their might.
He comes, a King most glorious,
And all His earthly foes
In vain His course victorious
Endeavor to oppose.

10 He comes to judge the nations,
A terror to His foes,
A light of consolations
And blessed hope to those
Who love the Lord's appearing.
O glorious Sun, now come,
Send forth Thy beams so cheering,
And guide us safely home!

Paul Gerhardt, 1653

137 St. Helena S. M. HAR. W. H. MONK

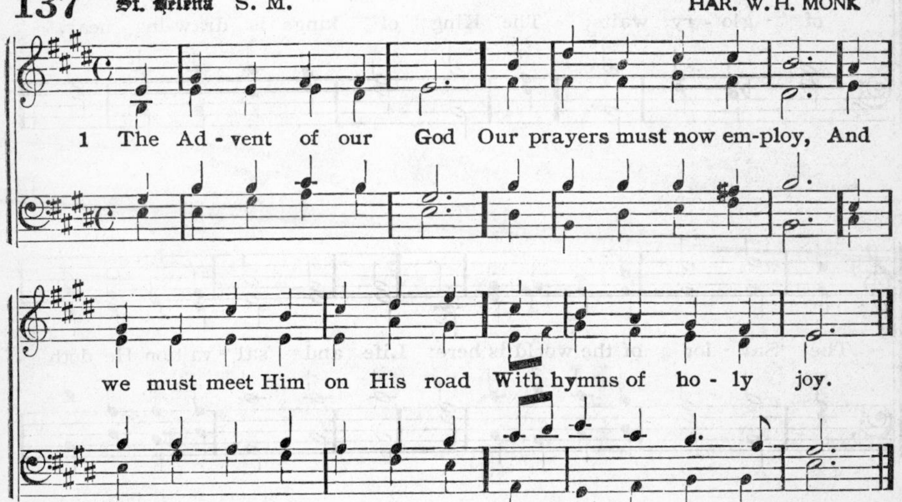
1 The Ad - vent of our God Our prayers must now em-ploy, And
we must meet Him on His road With hymns of ho - ly joy.

2 The everlasting Son
Incarnate deigns to be:
Himself a servant's form puts on,
To set His people free.

3 Daughter of Zion, rise
And greet thy lowly King,
And do not wickedly despise
The mercies He will bring.

4 As judge, in clouds of light,
He will come down again,
And all His scattered saints unite
With Him in Heaven to reign.

5 Before that dreadful day
May all our sins be gone;
May the old man be put away,
And the new man put on!

6 Praise to the Savior Son
From the created host:
Like praise be to the Father done,
And to the Holy Ghost.

John Chandler. 1837 a

Advent

138 Macht hoch die Thuer 8, 8, 8, 8, 8, 8, 6, 6 — J. STOBAEUS, 1634

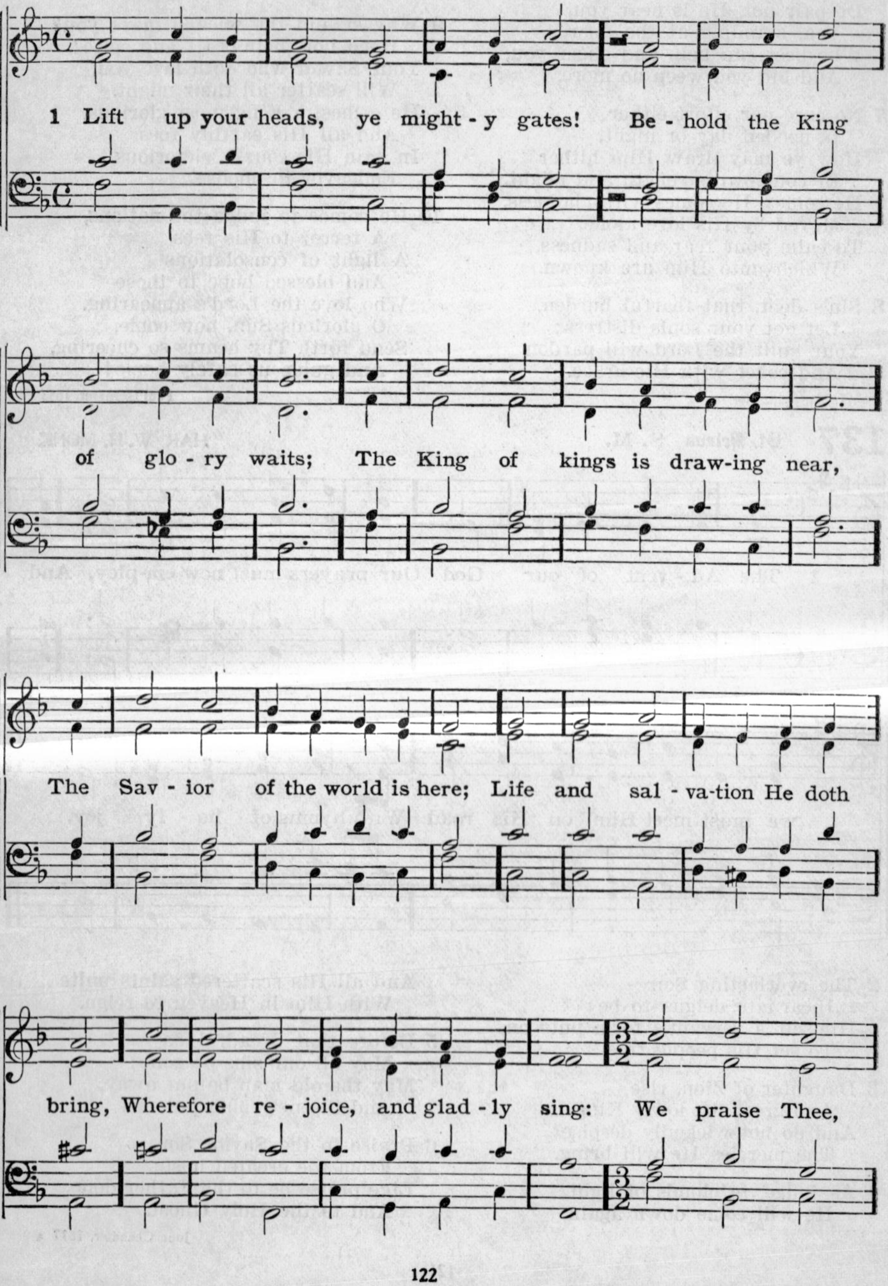

1 Lift up your heads, ye might-y gates! Be-hold the King of glo-ry waits; The King of kings is draw-ing near, The Sav-ior of the world is here; Life and sal-va-tion He doth

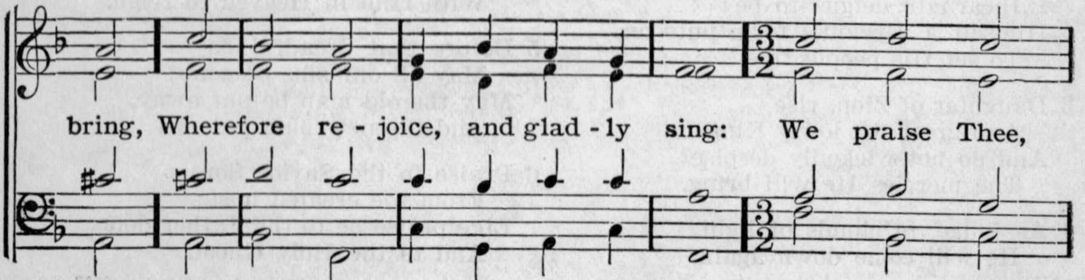
bring, Wherefore re-joice, and glad-ly sing: We praise Thee,

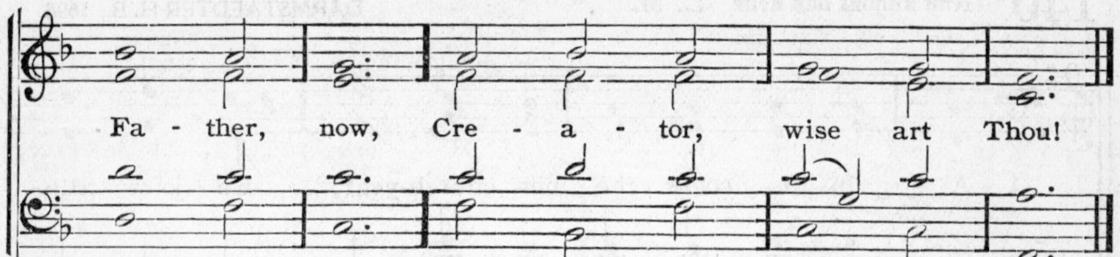
Fa - ther, now, Cre - a - tor, wise art Thou!

2 The Lord is just, a Helper tried,
Mercy is ever at His side,
His kingly crown is holiness,
His scepter, pity in distress,
The end of all our woe He brings;
Wherefore the earth is glad and sings:
We praise Thee, Savior, now,
Mighty in deed art Thou!

3 O blest the land, the city blest,
Where Christ the Ruler is confessed!
O happy hearts and happy homes
To whom this King in triumph comes!
The cloudless Sun of joy He is,
Who bringeth pure delight and bliss.
We praise Thee, Spirit, now,
Our Comforter art Thou.

4 Fling wide the portals of your heart;
Make it a temple set apart
From earthly use for heaven's employ,
Adorned with prayer, and love, and joy;
So shall your Sovereign enter in,
And new and nobler life begin;
To Thee, O God, be praise,
For word, and deed, and grace!

5 Redeemer, come! I open wide
My heart to Thee; here, Lord, abide!
Let me Thy inner presence feel,
Thy grace and love in me reveal;
Thy Holy Spirit guide us on,
Until our glorious goal be won!
Eternal praise and fame
We offer to Thy name.

Georg Weissel, 1633 C. Winkworth, Tr. a

139 Chesterfield C. M. T. HAWEIS, 1733—1820 (P)

1 Hark, the glad sound! the Sav - ior comes, The Sav - ior prom - ised long;
Let ev - 'ry heart pre - pare a throne, And ev - 'ry voice a song.

(*Or to Lobt Gott ihr*)

2 He comes the prisoners to release,
In Satan's bondage held;
The gates of brass before Him burst,
The iron fetters yield.

3 He comes, from thickest films of vice
To clear the mental ray,
And on the eyeballs of the blind
To pour the heav'nly day.

4 He comes, the broken heart to bind,
The bleeding soul to cure,
And with the treasures of His grace
T' enrich the humble poor.

5 Our glad hosannas, Prince of peace,
Thy welcome shall proclaim;
And heaven's eternal arches ring
With Thy beloved name.

Philip Doddridge, 1735

140 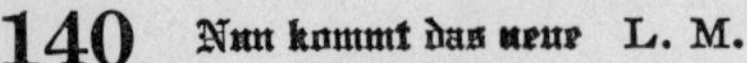
Nun kommt das neue
L. M. DARMSTAEDTER H. B., 1698

1 A - gain is come the new church-year; Re - joice all

Christ-ians, far and near! Thy King, O Zi - on, comes to Thee,

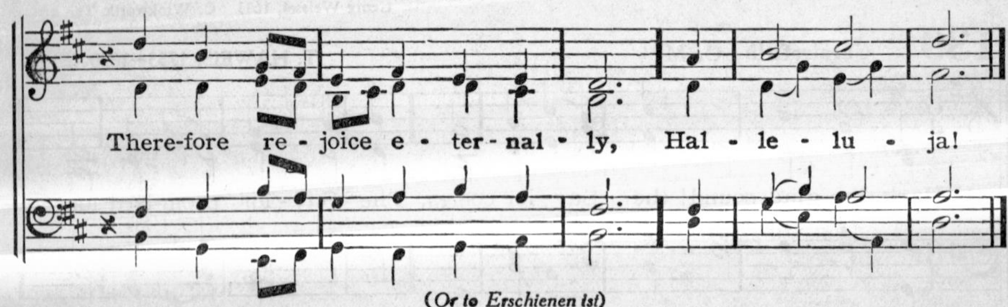
There-fore re - joice e - ter - nal - ly, Hal - le - lu - ja!

(Or to Erschienen ist)

2 Amongst us now anew are heard
The lessons of God's gracious Word,
Which shows the way to life in heaven.
For this all praise to God be given!
Hallelujah!

3 May what is taught in Thy true Word,
Increase our faith in Thee, O Lord,
And so abide in us that we
May render endless praise to Thee!
Hallelujah!

Johann Olearius, 1671

141 Nun komm, der Heiden Heiland 7s

ERFURT ENCHIRIDION, 1524

1 Sav - ior of the heath-en, come, Vir-gin's Son, here make Thy home;

Won-der at it, heav'n and earth, That the Lord chose such a birth.

2 Not by human flesh and blood,
By the Spirit of our God
Was the Word of God made flesh—
Woman's blossom, sweet and fresh.

3 Though the virgin was with child,
Chastity proved undefiled;
Many a virtue rare forth shone,
God was there upon His throne.

4 From the Father forth He came,
And returned unto the same,
Down to hell He went alone,
And again to God's high throne.

5 Thou, the Father's equal, win
Victory in the flesh o'er sin,
By Thy strength divine, O Lord,
Help to our frail flesh afford.

6 Lord, Thy manger is so bright,
Night sends forth a novel light;
Darkness must not enter there,
Faith abides in light fore'er.

7 Praise to God the Father sing,
Praise to God the Son, our King,
Praise to God the Spirit be
Ever and eternally.

Dr. Martin Luther, 1524 ab.

142 Aus meines Herzens Grunde 7, 6, 7, 6, 6, 7, 7, 6

1 Arise, sons of the kingdom!
The King is drawing nigh;
Arise, and hail with gladness
The Ruler from on high.
Ye Christians, hasten forth!
Your praise and homage bring Him,
And glad hosannas sing Him;
Naught else your love is worth.

2 Arise, ye drooping mourners!
The King is very near;
Away with grief and sorrow,
For lo! your Help is here.
Behold, in many a place—
O blessed consolation!—
We find Him, our Salvation,
In His pure means of grace.

3 Now hear, ye bold transgressors,
The King does well give heed
To all that ye are doing,
And to the life ye lead,
Enthralled by sin and hell;
Nothing in all Creation
Escapes His observation,
He marketh all things well.

4 Be righteous, ye His subjects,
The King is just and true;
Prepare for Him a high-way,
Make all things straight and new.
He means all for our good;
Then let us bear the crosses
Which He Himself imposes,
In an undaunted mood.

5 He nevermore forsaketh
A child that feels the rod,
Who Him his refuge maketh,
And puts his trust in God.
He is our sovereign King;
E'en death itself shall never
Those from their Master sever
Who to His mercy cling.

6 Arise, ye faint and fearful!
The King now comes with might;
His heart hath long since loved us,
He makes our darkness light.
Now are our sorrows o'er;
No wrath shall e'er befall us,
Since God in grace doth call us
His children evermore.

7 The King in grace remembers
His loved ones here below
With gifts of royal treasures,
Yea, doth Himself bestow
Through His blest Word and grace.
O King, arrayed in splendor,
To Thee all praise we'll render
Here and there face to face.

8 O rich the gifts Thou bring'st us,
Thyself made poor and weak;
O Love beyond expression
That thus can sinners seek!
For this, O Lord, will we
Our joyous tribute bring Thee,
And glad hosannas sing Thee,
And ever grateful be.

Johann Rist, 1651 ab.

143

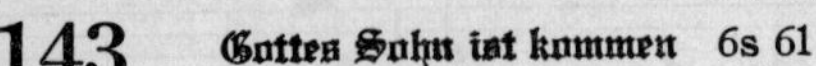
Gottes Sohn ist kommen

6s 61

M. WEISS, 1531
Harm. by CH. HEINROTH, 1910

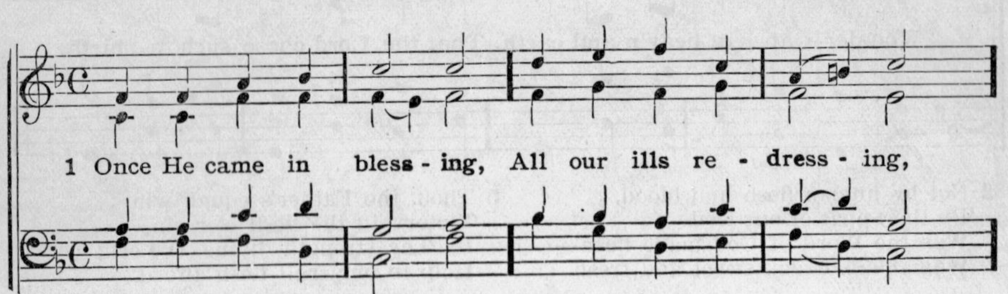
1 Once He came in bless - ing, All our ills re - dress - ing,

Came in like - ness low - ly, Son of God most ho - - - - ly;

Bore the Cross to save us Hope and free-dom gave us.

2 Still He comes within us,
Still His voice would win us
From the sins that hurt us;
Would to Truth convert us
From our foolish errors,
Ere He comes in terrors.

3 Thus if thou hast known Him,
Not ashamed to own Him,
Nor dost love Him coldly,
But will trust Him boldly,
He will now receive thee,
Heal thee, and forgive thee.

4 He who well endureth,
Bright reward secureth;
Come then, O Lord Jesus,
From our sins release us;
Let us here confess Thee,
Till in heaven we bless Thee.

John Horn, 1544 Miss Cath. Winkworth, Tr. 1862 a

144 Luton L. M.

GEO. BURDER. 1780

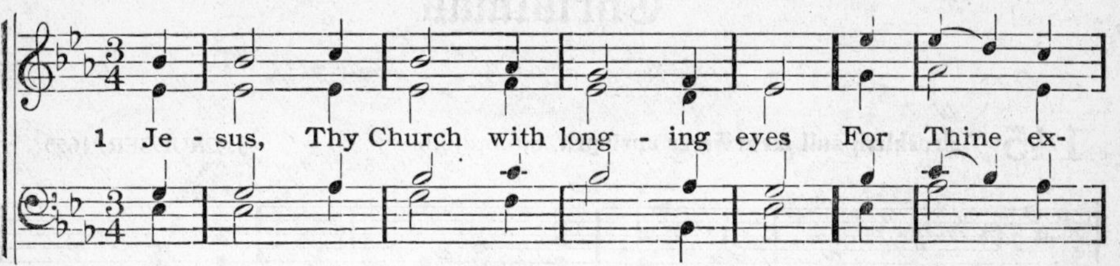
1 Je - sus, Thy Church with long - ing eyes For Thine ex-

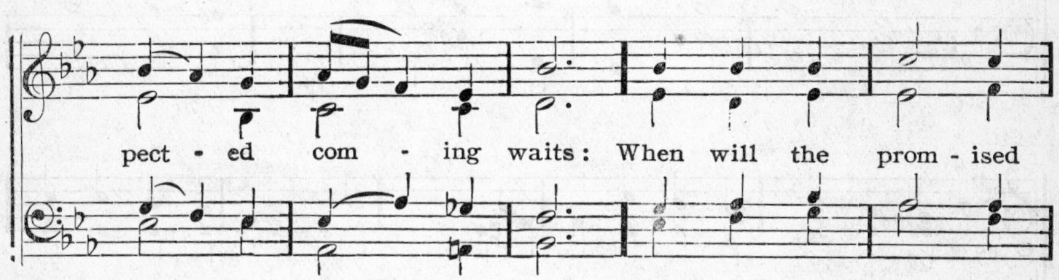
pect - ed com - ing waits: When will the prom - ised

light a - rise, And glo - ry beam from Zi - on's gates?

(*Or to Zephyr*)

2 E'en now, when tempests round us fall,
And wintry clouds o'ercast the sky,
Thy words with pleasure we recall,
And deem that our redemption's nigh.

3 Come, gracious Lord, our hearts renew,
Our foes repel, our wrongs redress,
Man's rooted enmity subdue,
And crown Thy Gospel with success.

4 O come, and reign o'er every land;
Let Satan from his throne be hurled.
All nations bow to Thy command,
And grace revive a dying world.

5 Teach us in watchfulness and prayer
To wait for the appointed hour;
And fit us by Thy grace to share
The triumphs of Thy conquering power.

Wm. Hiley Bathhurst, 1831

Christmas

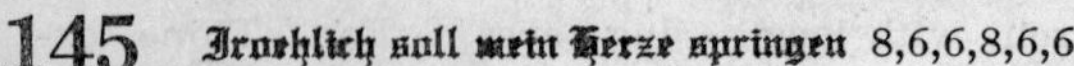

145 Fröhlich soll mein Herze springen 8,6,6,8,6,6 J. CRUEGER, 1653

1 All my heart this night re - joic - es, As I hear

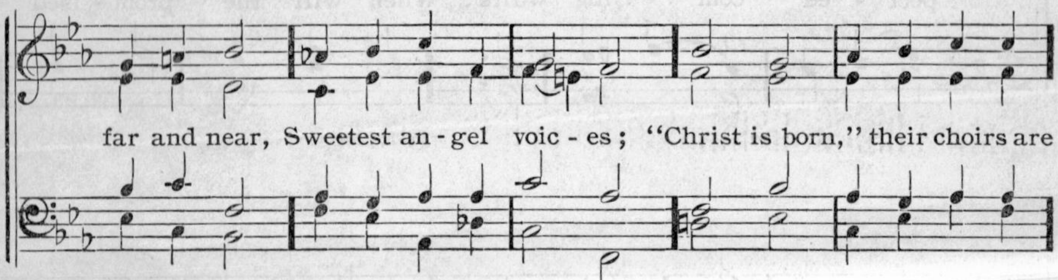
far and near, Sweetest an - gel voic - es; "Christ is born," their choirs are

sing - ing, Till the air ev -'ry-where Now with joy is ring - ing.

2 Forth today the Conqu'ror goeth,
Who the foe, | Sin and woe,
Death and hell o'erthroweth,
God is man, man to deliver,
His dear Son | Now is one
With our blood forever.

3 Shall we still dread God's displeasure,
Who to save | Freely gave
Us His dearest treasure?
To redeem us, He hath given
His own Son | From the throne
Of His might in heaven.

4 Should He, who Himself imparted,
Aught withhold | From the fold,
Leave us broken-hearted?
Should the Son of God not love us,
Who to cheer | Sufferers here
Left His throne above us?

5 If our blessed Lord and Maker
Hated men, | Would He then
Be of flesh partaker?
If He in our woe delighted,
Would He bear | All the care
Of our race benighted?

6 He becomes the Lamb that taketh
Sin away, | And for aye
Full atonement maketh.
For our life His own He tenders,
And our race, | By His grace,
Meet for glory renders.

7 Hark! a voice from yonder manger,
Soft and sweet, | Doth entreat:
"Flee from woe and danger;
Brethren, from all ills that grieve you,
You are freed | All you need
I will surely give you."

8 Come, then, banish all your sadness,
One and all, | Great and small,
Come with songs of gladness;
Love Him who with love is glowing.
Hail the Star | Near and far
Light and joy bestowing!

9 Ye whose anguish knew no measure,
Weep no more, | See the door
To celestial pleasure.
Cling to Him, for He will guide you
Where no cross, | Pain or loss,
Can again betide you.

10 Hither come, ye heavy-hearted,
Who for sin, | Deep within,
Long and sore have smarted;
For the poisoned wounds you're feeling
Help is near, | One is here
Mighty for their healing.

11 Hither come, ye poor and wretched,
Know His will | Is to fill
Every hand outstretched;
Here are riches without measure,
Here forget | All regret,
Fill your hearts with treasure.

12 Let me in my arms receive Thee,
On Thy breast | Let me rest,
Savior, ne'er to leave Thee!
Since Thou hast Thyself presented
Now to me, | I shall be
Evermore contented.

13 Guilt no longer can distress me;
Son of God, | Thou my load
Bearest to release me.
Stain in me Thou findest never;
I am clean, | All my sin
Is removed forever.

14 I am pure, In Thee believing,
From Thy store | Evermore
Righteous robes receiving.
In my heart I will enfold Thee,
Treasure rare, | Let me there
Loving ever hold Thee!

15 Thee, O Lord, with heed I'll cherish,
While I've breath, | E'en in death
Shall my faith not perish.
I shall dwell with Thee forever,
Far on high, | In the joy
That can alter never.

Paul Gerhardt, 1666

146 Nun komm der Heiden Heiland 7s

1 Let the earth now praise the Lord,
Who hath truly kept His word,
And the sinners' Help and Friend
Now at last to us doth send.

2 What the fathers most desired,
What the prophets' heart inspired,
What they longed for many a year,
Stands fulfilled in glory here.

3 Abram's promised great Reward,
Zion's Helper, Jacob's Lord,
Him of twofold race behold,
Truly came, as long foretold.

4 Welcome, O my Savior, now!
Hail! my portion, Lord, art thou!
Here, too, in my heart, I pray,
O prepare Thyself a way.

5 King of glory, enter in!
Cleanse it from the filth of sin,
As Thou hast so often done;
It belongs to Thee alone.

6 As Thy coming was in peace,
Noiseless, full of gentleness,
Let the same mind dwell in me
That was ever found in Thee.

7 Comfort my desponding heart;
Thou my strength and refuge art.
I am weak, and cunningly
Satan lays his snares for me.

8 Bruise for me the Serpent's head,
That, set free from doubt and dread,
I may cleave to Thee in faith,
Safely kept through life and death:

9 And when Thou dost come again
As a glorious King to reign,
I with joy may see Thy face,
Truly ransomed by Thy grace.

From the Latin of Ambrosius Dr. Martin Luther, 1524 C. Winkworth, Tr. a

Christmas

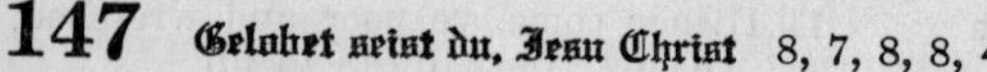
147 Gelobet seist du, Jesu Christ

8, 7, 8, 8, 4 Ancient. J. WALTHER, 1524

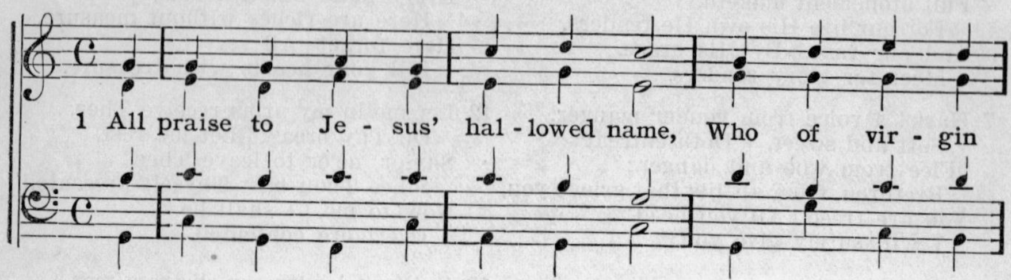
1 All praise to Je - sus' hal - lowed name, Who of vir - gin

pure be - came True man for us! The an - gels sing, As

the glad news to earth they bring, Hal - le - lu - jah.

2 Th' eternal Father's only Son
For a manger leaves His throne;
Disguised in our poor flesh and blood
Is now the everlasting Good.
Hallelujah.

3 He whom the world could not inclose
Doth in Mary's lap repose,
He is become an infant small,
Who by His might upholdeth all.
Hallelujah.

4 Th' eternal Light, come down from heaven,
Hath to us new sunshine given;
It shineth in the midst of night,
And maketh us the sons of light.
Hallelujah.

5 The Father's Son, God ever blest,
In the world became a guest;
He leads us from this vale of tears,
And makes us in His kingdom heirs.
Hallelujah.

6 He came to earth despised and poor,
Man to pity and restore,
And make us rich in heaven above,
Equal with angels through His love.
Hallelujah.

7 All this He did, that He might prove
To us sinners His great love;
For this let Christendom adore
And praise His name for evermore.
Hallelujah.

Dr. Martin Luther, 1524 R. Massie, Tr. a

148 Christum wir sollen loben schon L. M. ERFURT ENCHIRIDION, 1524

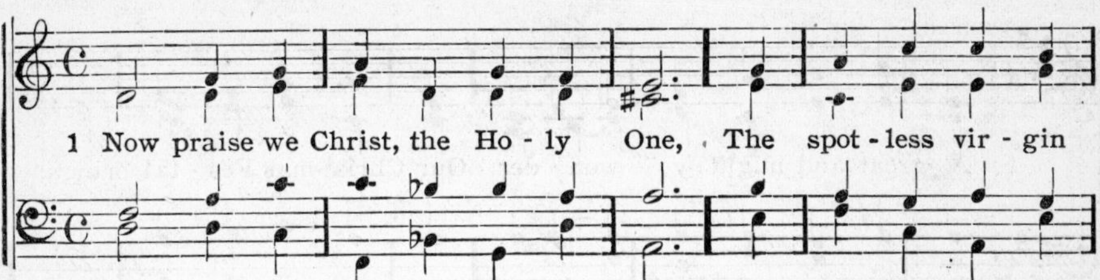
1 Now praise we Christ, the Ho - ly One, The spot - less vir - gin

Ma - ry's Son, Far as the bless - ed sun doth shine,

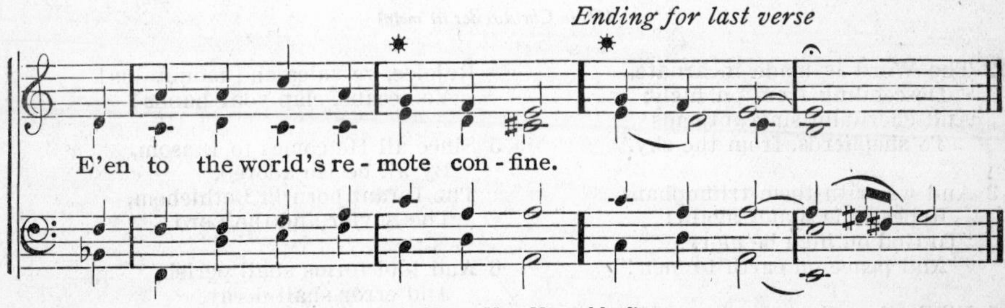
Ending for last verse
E'en to the world's re - mote con - fine.

(Or to Vom Himmel hoch)

2 He who Himself all things did make,
A servant's form vouchsafed to take,
That He as man mankind might win,
And save His creatures from their sin.

3 The grace of God, the mighty Lord,
On the chaste mother was outpoured;
A virgin pure and undefiled
In wondrous wise conceived a child.

4 The noble mother bare a Son,
For so did Gabriel's promise run,
Whom John confessed, and leapt with joy,
Ere yet the mother knew her boy.

5 In a rude manger, stretched on hay,
In poverty content He lay;
With milk was fed the Lord of all,
Who feeds the ravens when they call.

6 The heavenly choirs rejoice, and raise
Their voice to God in songs of praise;
To humble shepherds is proclaimed
The Shepherd who the world hath framed.

7 All honor unto Christ be paid,
Pure offspring of the holy maid,
With Father and with Holy Ghost,
Till time in endless time be lost.

From the Latin of Sedulius Dr. Martin Luther Tr. 1524 R. Massie, Tr. a. and ab.

149 Rejoicing 7, 6, 7, 6 J. J. WOLDER, 1788

1 A great and might-y won-der Our Christ-mas Fes-tal brings:

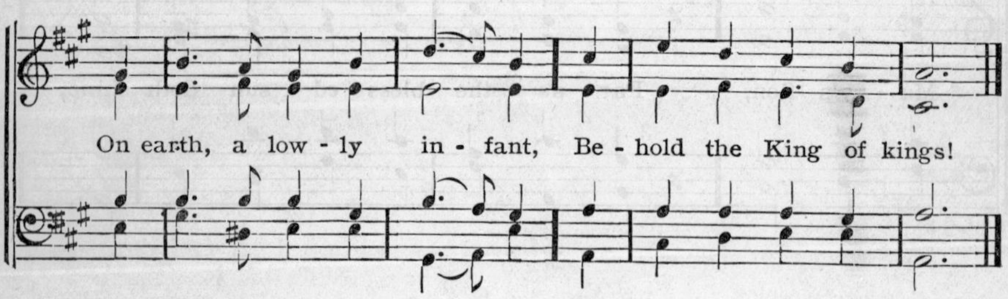
On earth, a low-ly in-fant, Be-hold the King of kings!

(Or to Christus der ist mein)

2 The Word is made incarnate,
Descending from on high;
And cherubim sing anthems
To shepherds, from the sky.

3 And we with them triumphant,
Repeat the hymn again:
"To God on high be glory,
And peace on earth to men!"

4 While thus they sing your Monarch,
Those bright angelic bands,
Rejoice, ye vales and mountains!
Ye oceans, clap your hands!

5 Since all He comes to ransom,
By all be He adored,
The Infant born in Bethlehem,
The Savior and the Lord!

6 And idol forms shall perish,
And error shall decay,
And Christ shall wield His scepter,
Our Lord and God for aye.

Anatolius, c. 450. John Mason Neale, Tr. 1862 a

150 Vom Himmel hoch L. M. SCHUMANN 1539

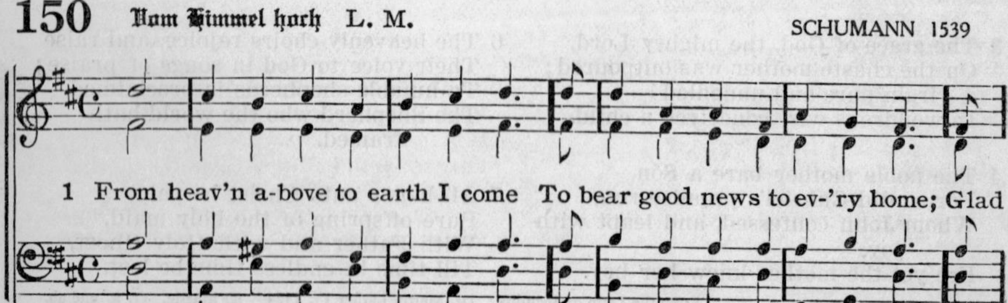
1 From heav'n a-bove to earth I come To bear good news to ev-'ry home; Glad

ti-dings of great joy I bring, Where-of I now will say and sing.

2 To you this night is born a child
Of Mary, chosen virgin mild;
This little child, of lowly birth,
Shall be the joy of all the earth.

3 This is the Christ, our God and Lord,
Who in all need shall aid afford;
He will Himself your Savior be,
From all your sins to make you free.

4 He brings those blessings, long ago
Prepared by God for all below,
That in His heavenly Kingdom blest
You may with us forever rest.

5 These are the tokens ye shall mark;
The swaddling-clothes and manger dark;
There shall ye find the young child laid,
By whom the heavens and earth were made.

6 Now let us all with gladsome cheer,
Follow the shepherds, and draw near,
To see the wondrous gift of God,
Who hath His own dear Son bestowed.

7 Give heed, my heart, lift up thine eyes!
What is it in yon manger lies?
Who is this child, so young and fair?
Dear little Jesus lieth there.

8 Welcome to earth, Thou noble Guest,
Through whom the sinful world is blest!
Thou com'st to share my misery,
What thanks shall I return to Thee?

9 Ah! Lord, who hast created all,
How hast Thou made Thee weak and small,
That Thou must choose Thy infant bed,
Where humble cattle lately fed.

10 And were the world ten times as wide,
With gold and jewels beautified,
It would be far too small to be
A narrow cradle, Lord, for Thee.

11 For velvets soft and silken stuff
Thou hast but hay and straw so rough,
Whereon Thou King, so rich and great,
As 'twere Thy heaven, art throned in state.

12 And thus, dear Lord, it pleased Thee,
To make this truth quite plain to me,
That this world's honor, wealth, and might
Are naught and worthless in Thy sight.

13 Ah! dearest Jesus, holy Child,
Make Thee a bed, soft, undefiled,
Within my heart, that it may be
A quiet chamber kept for Thee.

14 My heart for very joy doth leap,
My lips no more can silence keep;
I, too, must sing with joyful tongue
That sweetest ancient cradle-song:

15 Glory to God in highest heaven,
Who unto man His Son hath given!
While angels sing with pious mirth,
A glad New Year to all the earth.

Dr. Martin Luther, 1535

151 Vom Himmel hoch L. M.

1 Rejoice, ye sons of men alway!
God comes to you from heaven today;
The Lord is born a little child
Of Mary, virgin undefiled.

2 He is the Branch of Jesse's tree,
The Lion out of Judah, He
The Gentiles' Light, the promised Seed
Who was to bruise the Serpent's head.

3 He brings us peace and happiness,
And heals all sorrow and distress
Which on account of Adam's fall
Forever weighed upon us all.

4 Through His low birth and holy blood
We all are saved by Christ, true God;
The angel's glory we shall share,
And in His kingdom live fore'er.

Cornelius Freund, † 1591 A. Crull, Tr. a

152 Freuet euch, ihr Christen 8, 7, 7, 8, 7, 7, 8, 8, 8, 8 A. HAMMERSCHMIDT, 1646

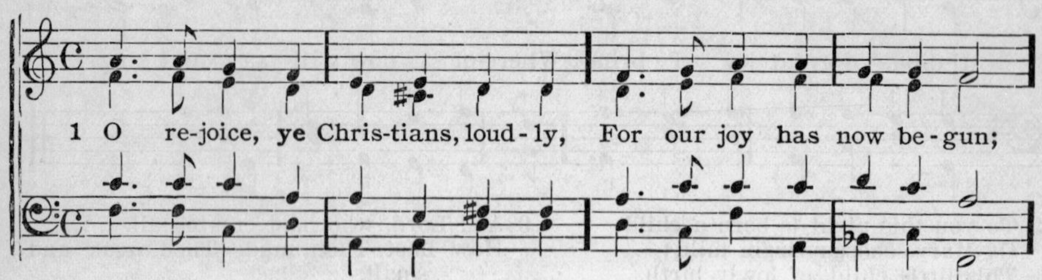
1 O re-joice, ye Chris-tians, loud-ly, For our joy has now be-gun;

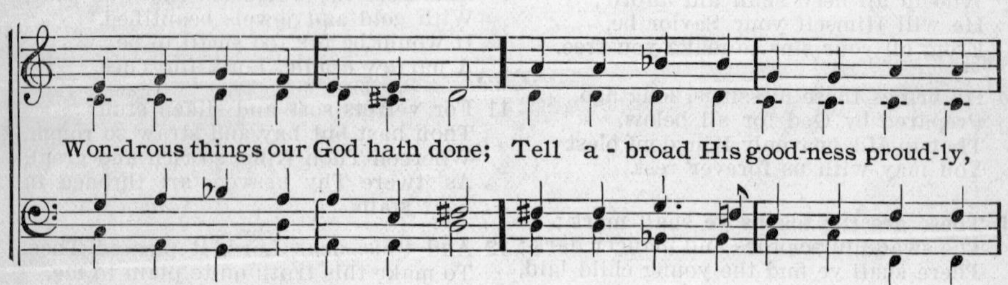
Won-drous things our God hath done; Tell a-broad His good-ness proud-ly,

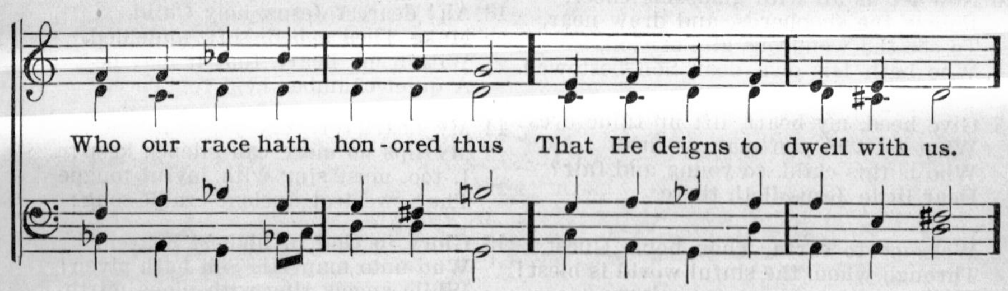
Who our race hath hon-ored thus That He deigns to dwell with us.

Joy, O Joy, be-yond all gladness! Christ hath done a-way with sad-ness!

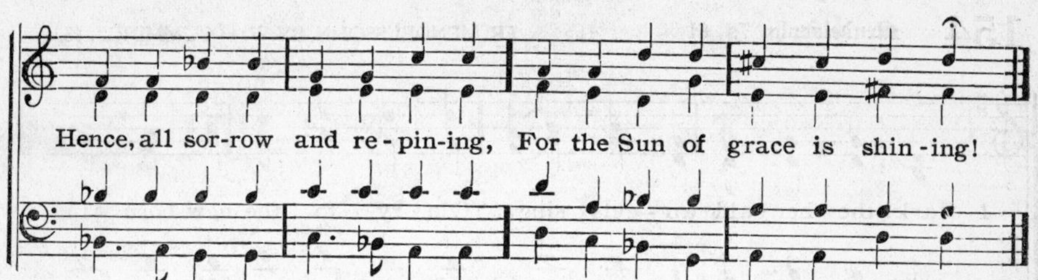
Hence, all sor-row and re-pin-ing, For the Sun of grace is shin-ing!

2 See, my soul, thy Savior chooses
Weakness here and poverty,
In such love He comes to thee,
Nor the hardest couch refuses;
All he suffers for thy good,
To redeem thee by His blood.
Joy, O Joy, etc.

3 Lord, how shall I thank Thee rightly!
I acknowledge that by Thee
I am saved eternally,
Let me not forget it lightly,
But to Thee through all things cleave,
And my heart true peace receive.
Joy, O Joy, etc.

4 Jesus, guard and guide Thy members,
Fill Thy brethren with Thy grace,
Hear their prayers in every place,
Quicken now life's faintest embers;
Grant all Christians, far and near,
Holy peace, a glad New Year!
Joy, O Joy, etc.

Christian Keymann, 1646 C. Winkworth, Tr. a

153 Lasst uns alle froehlich sein 7, 6, 7, 6

DRESDEN H. B., 1656

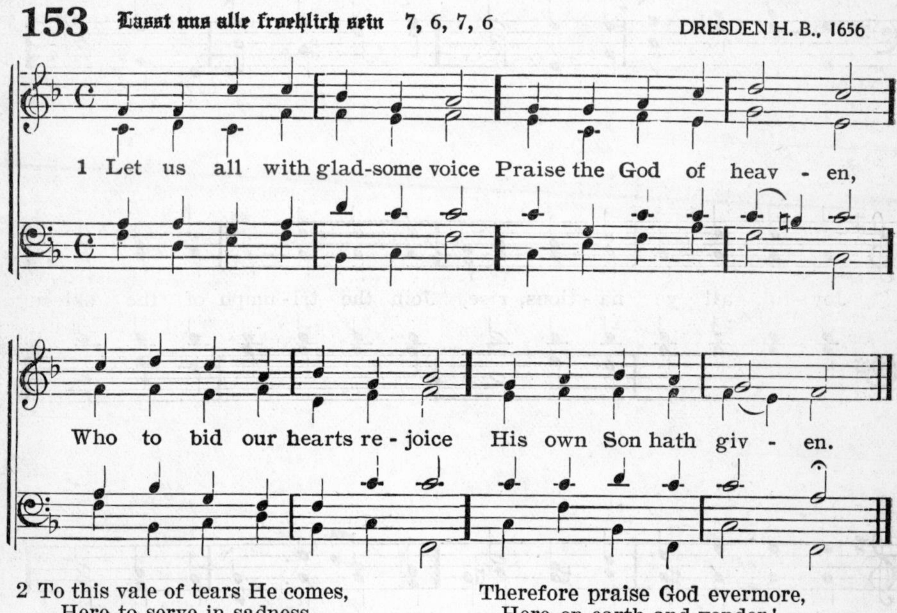
1 Let us all with glad-some voice Praise the God of heav - en,
Who to bid our hearts re - joice His own Son hath giv - en.

2 To this vale of tears He comes,
Here to serve in sadness,
That with Him in heaven's fair homes
We may reign in gladness.

3 We are rich, for He was poor;
Is not this a wonder!
Therefore praise God evermore,
Here on earth and yonder!

4 O Lord Christ, our Savior dear,
Be Thou ever near us.
Grant us now a glad New Year;
Amen, Jesus, hear us!

Urban Langhanns, c. 1560

154 Mendelssohn 7s 81

FR. MENDELSSOHN, BY W. H CUMMINGS, 1855

1 Hark! the her-ald an-gels sing, "Glo-ry to the new-born King;
Peace on earth, and mer-cy mild, God and sin-ners rec-on-ciled!"
Joy-ful, all ye na-tions, rise, Join the tri-umph of the skies;
With th' an-gel-ic hosts pro-claim, "Christ is born in Beth-le-hem!"

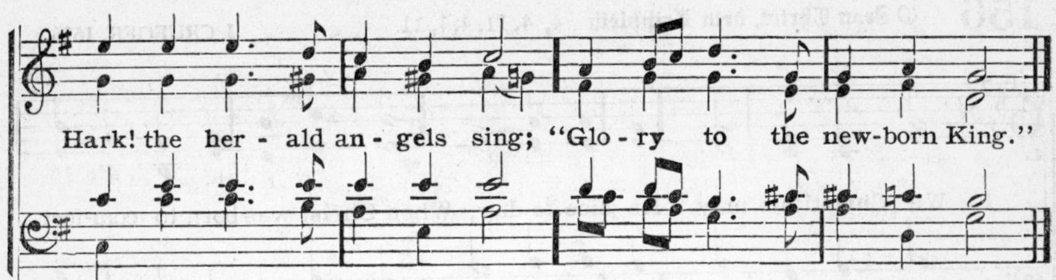
Hark! the her - ald an - gels sing; "Glo - ry to the new-born King."

(Or to Gott sei dank)

2 Joyful, all ye nations, rise,
Join the triumph of the skies;
With th' angelic hosts proclaim,
"Christ is born in Bethlehem!"

3 Veiled in flesh, the Godhead see;
Hail, th' incarnate Deity,
Pleased as man with men to dwell;
Jesus, our Emmanuel!

4 Hail, the heavenly Prince of peace!
Hail, the Sun of righteousness!
Light and life to all He brings,
Ris'n with healing in His wings.

5 Mild He lays His glory by,
Born that man no more may die,
Born to raise the sons of earth,
Born to give them second birth.

6 Come, Desire of nations, come,
Fix in us Thy humble home;
O, to all Thyself impart,
Formed in each believing heart!

Charles Wesley, 1739 a.

155 Canaan C. M.

A. S. BAKER, 1868–1896

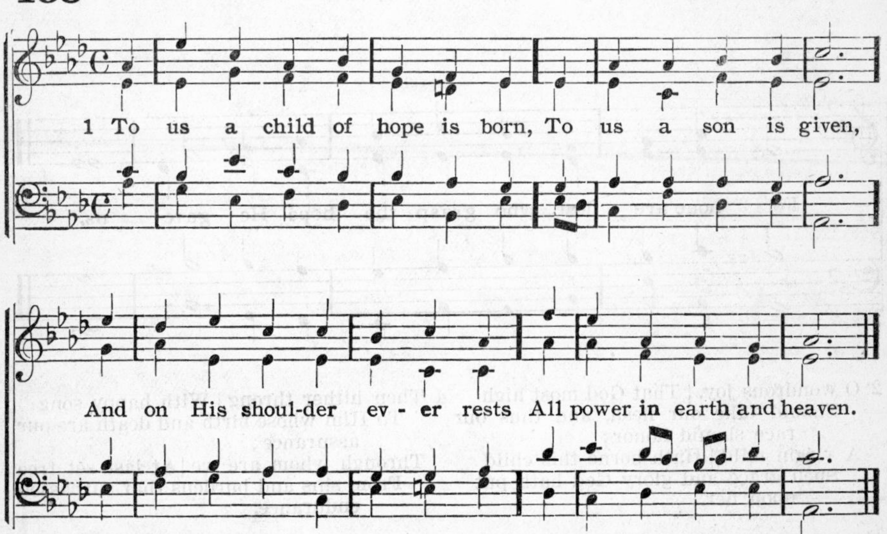
1 To us a child of hope is born, To us a son is given,
And on His shoul-der ev - er rests All power in earth and heaven.

2 His name shall be the Prince of Peace,
The everlasting Lord,
The Wonderful, the Counsellor,
The God by all adored.

3 His righteous government and power
Shall over all extend;
On judgment and on justice based,
His reign shall have no end.

4 Lord Jesus, reign in us, we pray,
And make us Thine alone,
Who with the Father ever art
And Holy Spirit, one.

J. Morison, 1781 Version of Hs. A. and M., Ab.

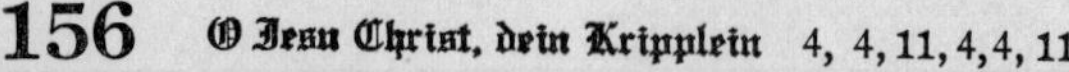

156 O Jesu Christ, dein Kripplein 4, 4, 11, 4, 4, 11 J. CRUEGER, 1656

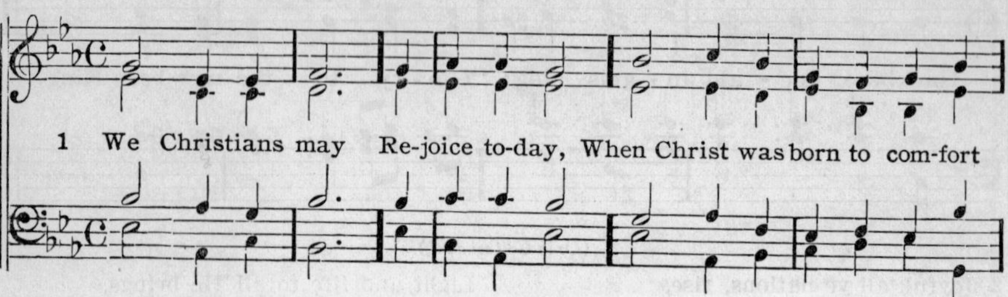
1 We Christians may Re-joice to-day, When Christ was born to com-fort

and to save us; Who thus be-lieves No lon-ger grieves,

For none are lost who grasp the hope He gave us.

2 O wondrous joy, | That God most high
Should take our flesh, and thus our race should honor;
A virgin mild | Hath borne this child
Such grace and glory God hath put upon her.

3 Sin brought us grief; | But Christ, relief,
When down to earth He came for our salvation;
Since God with us | Is dwelling thus,
Who dares to speak the Christian's condemnation?

4 Then hither throng | With happy song
To Him whose birth and death are our assurance;
Through whom are we | At last set free
From sins and burdens that surpassed endurance.

5 Yes, let us praise | Our God, and raise
Loud *hallelujahs* to the skies above us;
The bliss, bestowed | Today by God,
To ceaseless thankfulness and joy should move us.

Caspar Fugger. 1592 C. Winkworth. Tr. a

157 Lobt Gott, ihr Christen allzugleich C. M. N. HERMANN, 1554

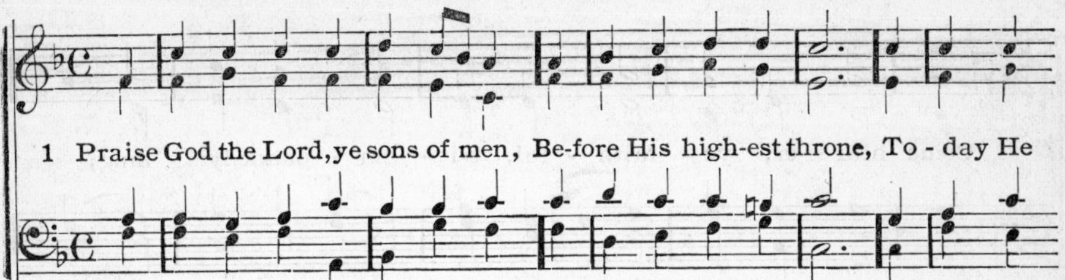
1 Praise God the Lord, ye sons of men, Be-fore His high-est throne, To - day He

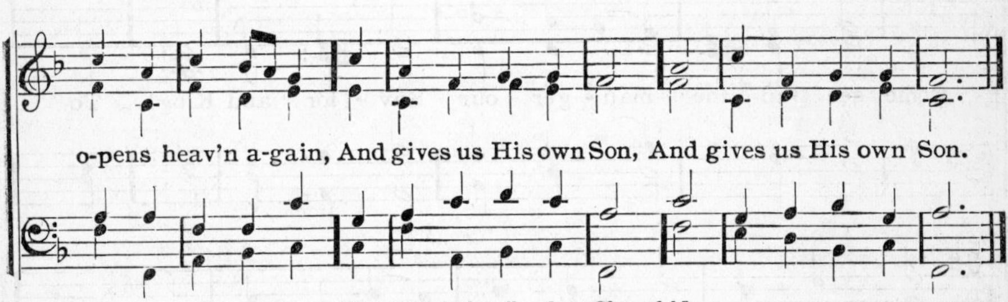
o-pens heav'n a-gain, And gives us His own Son, And gives us His own Son.

(Or to Nun danket all Or to Chesterfield)

2 He leaves His heavenly Father's throne,
Is born an infant small,
And in a manger poor and lone
Lies in an humble stall.

3 He lays aside His power divine,
A servant's form doth take,
In want and lowness He doth pine
Who heaven and earth did make.

4 He nestles at His mother's breast,
Her milk His food must be,
Whom saints and angels call the Blest,
Of David's house is He.

5 'Tis He who in these latter days
From Judah's tribe should come,
By whom the Lord again would raise
His Church, His Christendom.

6 A wondrous change which He doth make
He takes our flesh and blood,
And lays aside for sinners' sake,
His majesty of God.

7 He serves, that I a lord may be;
A great exchange, indeed!
Could Jesus' love do more for me,
To help me in my need?

8 He opens us again the door
Of Paradise today;
The cherub guards the gate no more.
To God our thanks we pay.

Nik. Hermann, 1560 A. Crull, Tr. a

158 Lobt Gott, ihr Christen C. M.

1 Joy to the world! the Lord is come:
Let earth receive her King;
Let every heart prepare Him room,
And heaven and nature sing.

2 Joy to the earth! the Savior reigns:
Let men their songs employ,
While fields and floods, rocks, hills and plains
Repeat the sounding joy.

3 No more let sins and sorrows grow,
Nor thorns infest the ground;
He comes to make His blessings flow
Far as the curse is found.

4 He rules the world with truth and grace,
And makes the nations prove
The glories of His righteousness,
And wonders of His love.

Isaac Watts, 1719

159 Portuguese Hymn 11s

J. READING. 1692

1 Come hith - er, ye faith - ful, tri - um - phant-ly sing;
Come see in the man - ger our Sav - ior and King! To
Beth - le - hem has - ten with joy - ful ac - cord;
O come, ye, come hith - er O come ye, come hith - er;
O come ye, come hith - er to wor - ship the Lord!

2 True Son of the Father, He comes from the skies;
To be born of a virgin He does not despise;
To Bethlehem hasten with joyful accord;
O come ye, come hither to worship the Lord!

3 Hark, hark to the angels all singing in heaven,
"To God in the highest all glory be given!"
To Bethlehem hasten with joyful accord;
O come ye, come hither to worship the Lord!

4 To Thee, then, O Jesus, this day of Thy birth,
Be glory and honor through heaven and earth,
True Godhead incarnate, omnipotent Word!
O come, let us hasten to worship the Lord!

Latin, 17th Cent. E. Caswall, Tr. 1848

160 Lobt den Herrn, die Morgensonne 8, 7, 8, 7 NAUE'S CHORALBOOK. 1892

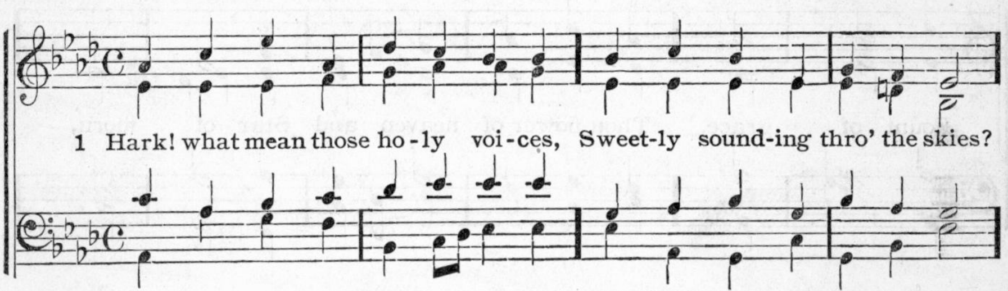
1 Hark! what mean those ho-ly voi-ces, Sweet-ly sound-ing thro' the skies?

Lo! th' an-gel-ic host re-joi-ces, Heaven-ly hal-le-lu-jahs rise.

(Or to Rathbun)

2 Listen to the wondrous story,
Which they chant, in hymns of joy,
"Glory in the highest, glory!
Glory be to God most high!

3 Peace on earth, good will from heaven,
Reaching far as man is found;
Souls redeemed, and sins forgiven!
Loud our golden harps shall sound.

4 Christ is born, the great Anointed;
Heaven and earth, His praises sing!
O receive whom God appointed
For your Prophet, Priest, and King.

5 Hasten, mortals, to adore Him;
Learn His name and taste His joy;
Till in heaven ye sing before Him,
Glory be to God most high!"

6 Let us learn the wondrous story
Of our great Redeemer's birth;
Spread the brightness of His glory,
Till it cover all the earth.

J. Cawood, 1819

161 Erschienen ist der herrlich Tag L. M. N. HERMANN, 1560

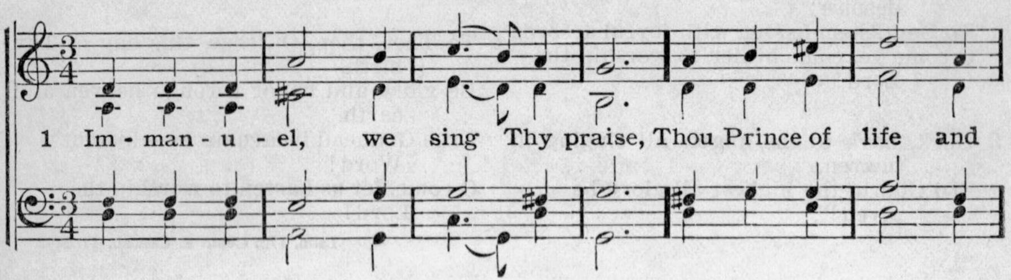
1 Im - man - u - el, we sing Thy praise, Thou Prince of life and

Fount of grace, Thou flower of heaven and Star of morn,

Thou Lord of lords, Thou Vir - gin - born. Hal - le - lu - jah.

2 With all Thy saints Thee, Lord, we sing,
Praise, honor, thanks to Thee we bring,
That Thou, O long-expected Guest,
Hast come at last to make us blest!
Hallelujah!

3 For Thee, since first the world was made,
So many hearts have watched and prayed;
The patriarchs' and prophets' throng
For Thee have hoped and waited long.
Hallelujah.

4 Above all others longed for Thee
Thy people's king and shepherd, he
With whom Thou, Lord, so well wert pleased,
When with His harp Thy name he praised.
Hallelujah.

5 O that the Savior soon would come
To break our bonds and lead us home!
O that He might salvation bring,
Then Jacob would rejoice and sing.
Hallelujah.

6 Now Thou art here, Thou ever Blest!
In lowly manger Thou dost rest;
Who makest all things great, art small;
Naked Thyself, who clothest all.
Hallelujah.

7 All heavens are Thine, yet Thou dost come
To sojourn in a stranger's home;
A mother's milk dost not despise,
Who art the joy of angels' eyes.
Hallelujah.

8 Thou hast set bounds to earth and sea,
Yet swaddling-bands encircle Thee;
Thou'rt God—a bed of straw Thou hast;
Thou'rt man—yet art the First and Last.
Hallelujah.

9 From Thee above all gladness flows,
Yet Thou must bear such bitter woes;
The Gentiles' Light and Hope Thou art,
Yet findest none to soothe Thy heart.
Hallelujah.

10 The sweetest Friend of man Thou art.
Yet many hate Thee in their heart;
By Herod's heart Thou art abhorred,
Yet Thou art our Salvation, Lord.
Hallelujah.

11 But I, Thy humblest servant, may
Confess my love and freely say,
I love Thee truly, but I would
That I might love Thee as I should.
Hallelujah.

12 I have the will, the power is weak,
Yet, Lord, my humble offering take
And graciously the love receive
Which my poor heart to Thee can give.
Hallelujah.

13 Thou to be weak dost not disdain,
Dost choose the things the world deems vain,
Art poor and needy, and content
To suffer poverty and want.
Hallelujah.

14 Thou sleepest on the lap of earth;
The manger where Thou at Thy birth
Wastlaid to rest, the hay, the stall
Were mean and miserable all.
Hallelujah.

15 And therefore doth my courage rise,
Me also Thou wilt not despise;
O dearest Lord, Thy tender grace
Fills me with hope and happiness.
Hallelujah.

16 Although I've passed in sin my days,
And wandered far from wisdom's ways,
Yet thou for this to earth hast come,
To bring the wand'ring sinner home.
Hallelujah.

17 Had I no load of sin to bear,
Thy grace, O Lord, I could not share;
In vain had'st Thou been born for me,
If from God's wrath I had been free.
Hallelujah.

18 Now fearlessly I come to Thee,
From every grief Thou mak'st me free;
Thou bear'st the wrath, dost death destroy,
And turnest sorrow into joy.
Hallelujah.

19 Thou art my Head, my Lord divine,
I am Thy member, wholly Thine,
And by Thy Spirit's gracious power
Will seek to serve Thee evermore.
Hallelujah.

20 I'll sing loud hallelujahs here.
With joyful spirit year by year;
And in Thy courts of joy above
Forever I will sing Thy love.
Hallelujah!

Paul Gerhardt, 1656 C. Winkworth, Tr. a

162 Vom Himmel kam der Engel Schar L. M. DAVID WOLDER, 1598

1 To shepherds, as they watched by night, Ap-peared a troop of an-gels

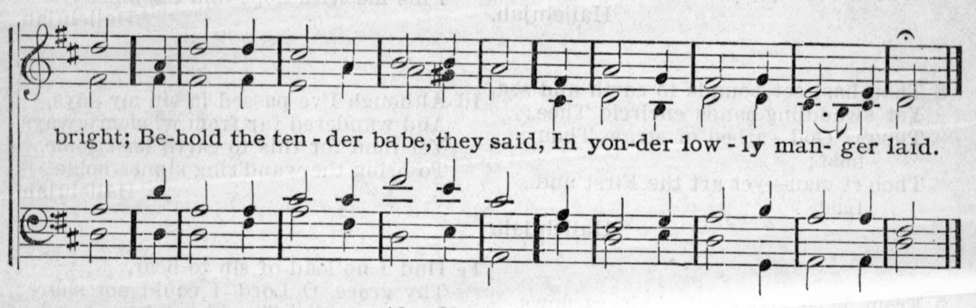
bright; Be-hold the ten - der babe, they said, In yon-der low - ly man- ger laid.

(Or to Vom Himmel hoch)

2 At Bethlehem, in David's town,
As Micah did of old make known;
'Tis Jesus Christ, your Lord and King,
Who doth to all salvation bring.

3 Rejoice ye, then, that through His Son
God is with sinners now at one;
Made like yourselves of flesh and blood,
Your brother is th' eternal God.

4 What harm can sin and death then do?
The true God now abides with you.
Let hell and Satan rage and chafe,
God is your brother—ye are safe.

5 Not one He will, nor can, forsake
Who Him his confidence doth make;
E'en if their worst your en'mies try,
Ye may their pow'rless rage defy.

6 Ye must prevail at last, for ye
Have now become God's family;
To God forever give ye praise,
Patient and cheerful all your days.

Dr. Martin Luther 1543 R. Massie, Tr. a.

End of Year

163 Wachet doch; erwacht 7s 8 l PRAXIS PIETATIS, 1662

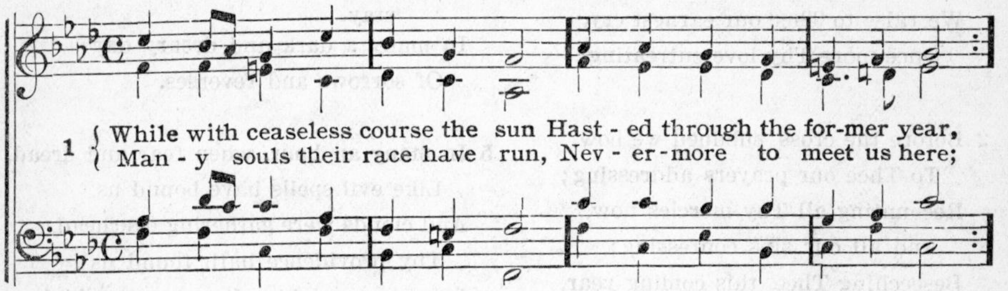
1 { While with ceaseless course the sun Hast - ed through the for-mer year,
Man - y souls their race have run, Nev - er-more to meet us here;

Fixed in an e - ter - nal state, They have done with all be - low;

We a lit-tle lon - ger wait, But how lit - tle, none can know.

(Or to Spanish Chant)

2 As the winged arrow flies
Speedily, the mark to find;
As the lightning from the skies
Darts, and leaves no trace behind;
Swiftly thus our fleeting days
Bear us down life's rapid stream:
Upward, Lord, our spirits raise;
All below is but a dream.

3 Thanks for mercies past receive,
Pardon of our sins renew,
Teach us henceforth how to live
With eternity in view.
Bless Thy Word to young and old,
Fill us with a Savior's love;
And when life's short tale is told,
May we dwell with Thee above.

J. Newton, 1774

End of Year

164 Allein Gott 8, 7, 8, 7, 8, 8, 7 (Iambic)

1 Across the sky the shades of night
This winter's eve are fleeting:
We deck Thine altar, Lord, with light,
In solemn worship meeting;
And as the year's last hours go by,
We raise to Thee our earnest cry,
Once more Thy love entreating.

2 Before the cross subdued we bow,
To Thee our prayers addressing;
Recounting all Thy mercies now,
And all our sins confessing;
Beseeching Thee, this coming year,
To keep us in Thy faith and fear,
And crown us with Thy blessing.

3 And while we pray, we lift our eyes
To dear ones gone before us,
Safe home with Thee in Paradise,
Whose peace descendeth o'er us:
And beg of Thee, when life is past
To re-unite us all at last
With those who've gone before us.

4 We gather up, in this brief hour,
The memory of Thy mercies:
Thy wondrous goodness, love, and power,
Our grateful song rehearses:
For Thou hast been our strength and stay
In many a dark and dreary day
Of sorrows and reverses.

5 In many an hour, when fear and dread,
Like evil spells have bound us,
And clouds were gathering overhead,
Thy providence hath found us:
In many a night, when seas ran high,
Thy gracious presence, drawing nigh,
Hath made all calm around us.

6 Then, O great God, in years to come,
Whatever may betide us,
Right onward through our journey home
Be Thou at hand to guide us:
Nor leave us till, at close of life,
Safe from all perils, toil, and strife,
Heaven shall enfold and hide us.

James Hamilton, 1882

165 Heinlein 7, 7, 7, 7

1 Thou who roll'st the year around,
Crowned with mercies large and free,
Rich Thy gifts to us abound,
Warm our praise shall rise to Thee.

2 Kindly to our worship bow,
While our grateful thanks we tell,
That, sustained by Thee, we now
Bid the parting year—farewell!

3 All its numbered days are sped,
All its busy scenes are o'er,
All its joys for ever fled,
All its sorrows felt no more.

4 Mingled with the eternal past,
Its remembrance shall decay;
Yet to be revived at last
At the solemn judgment-day.

5 All our follies, Lord, forgive!
Cleanse us from each guilty stain;
Let Thy grace within us live,
That we spend not years in vain.

6 Then, when life's last eve shall come,
Happy spirits, may we fly
To our everlasting home,
To our Father's house on high!

Ray Palmer, 1858

New Year

166 Glorification 7, 5, 8 1 J. H. TSCHERLITZKY, ad. by H. I. 1910

1 Fa-ther, let me ded - i - cate All this year to Thee, In what-ev - er
earth-ly state Thou wilt have me be. Not from sor-row, pain or care,
Free-dom dare I claim; This a-lone shall be my prayer: Glorify Thy name.

2 Can a child presume to choose
Where or how to live?
Can a Father's love refuse
All the best to give?
More Thou givest every day
Than the best can claim,
Nor withholdest aught that may
Glorify Thy name.

3 If in mercy Thou wilt spare
Joys that yet are mine;
If on life, serene and fair,
Brighter rays may shine,—
Let my glad heart, while it sings,
Thee in all proclaim,
And, whate'er the future brings,
Glorify Thy name.

4 If Thou callest to the cross,
And its shadow come,
Turning all my gain to loss,
Shrouding heart and home,—
Let me think how Thy dear Son
To His glory came,
And in deepest woe pray on:
"Glorify Thy name."

L. Tuttiett, 1825

New Year

167 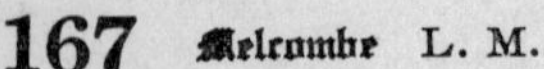 L. M. S. WEBBE, 1740–1816

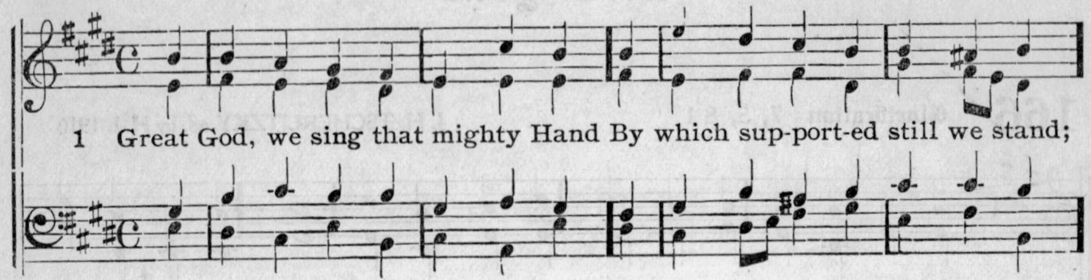
1 Great God, we sing that mighty Hand By which sup-port-ed still we stand;

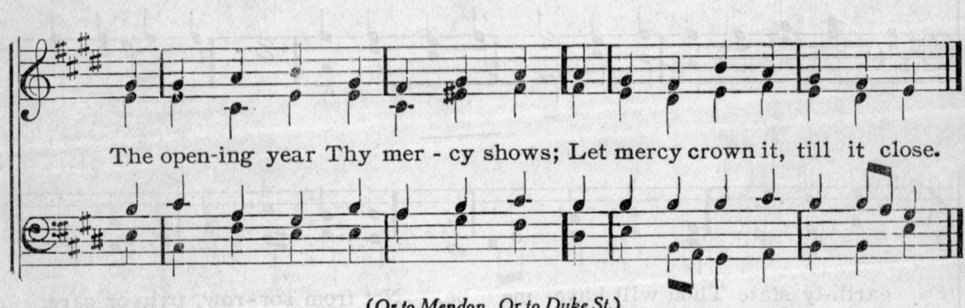
The open-ing year Thy mer - cy shows; Let mercy crown it, till it close.

(*Or to Mendon Or to Duke St.*)

2 By day, by night, at home, abroad,
Still we are guarded by our God;
By His incessant bounty fed,
By His unerring counsel led.

3 With grateful hearts the past we own;
The future, all to us unknown,
We to Thy guardian care commit,
And, peaceful, leave before Thy feet.

4 In scenes exalted or depressed,
Be Thou our Joy, and Thou our Rest,
Thy goodness all our hopes shall raise,
Adored through all our changing days.

5 When death shall interrupt our songs,
And seal in silence mortal tongues;
Our helper, God, in whom we trust,
In better worlds our soul shall boast.

P. Doddridge, 1755

168 Heinlein 7, 7, 7, 7

1 For Thy mercy and Thy grace,
Constant through another year,
Hear our song of thankfulness;
Jesus, our Redeemer, hear.

2 Lo! our sins on Thee we cast,
Thee, our perfect sacrifice;
And, forgetting all the past,
Press unto our glorious prize.

3 Dark the future; let Thy light
Guide us, bright and morning star:
Fierce our foes, and hard the fight;
Arm us, Savior, for the war.

4 In our weakness and distress,
Rock of strength, be Thou our stay;
In the pathless wilderness
Be our true and living way.

5 Who of us death's awful road
In the coming year shall tread?
With Thy rod and staff, O God,
Comfort Thou his dying bed.

6 Keep us faithful, keep us pure,
Keep us evermore Thine own;
Help, O help us to endure;
Fit us for the promised crown.

7 So within Thy palace gate
We shall praise, on golden strings,
Thee the only Potentate,
Lord of lords, and King of kings.

H. Downton, 1841 a

(*Or to Vienna*)

New Year

169 Christum wir sollen loben schon L. M.

15th CENTURY

1 The new-born Child this ear - ly morn, The dear Christ-child of vir-gin born,

A-gain brings from His heavenly home A new year to all Christendom.

(*Or to Vom Himmel hoch*)

2 This causes joy to angels fair,
Who love to keep us in their care;
They sing that in this wondrous Child
God now with man is reconciled.

3 Since God is reconciled with men,
What harm can Satan do us then?
O'er Satan and the gates of hell
This Christ-child shall for us prevail.

4 He brings the year of jubilee!
Why doubt we yet despondently?
Cheer up! This is a joyous day,
The Christ-child drives all care away.

Cyriacus Schneegas, † 1597 E. Cronenwett, Tr. a

170 Nun freut euch 8, 7, 8, 7, 8, 8, 7

1 O Lord our Father, thanks to Thee
In this new year we render,
For Thou hast been from misery
And dangers our defender;
Through all the year that now has fled
Hast given us life and daily bread,
And peace within our borders.

2 Lord Jesus Christ, our thanks to Thee
In this new year we render,
For Thou still rulest zealously
Thy fold, with mercy tender;
Thou hast redeemed us with Thy blood,
Thou art our only Trust and Good,
In life and death our Savior.

3 Lord Holy Ghost, our thanks to Thee
In this new year we render,
For by Thy grace it is that we
Enjoy Thy Word's pure splendor;
Thus Thou hast kindled from above
Within our hearts true faith and love,
And other Christian virtues.

4 Our faithful God, we cry to Thee:
Still bless us with Thy favor;
Blot out all our iniquity,
And hide our sins forever;
Grant us a happy, good New Year,
And when the hour of death draws near,
A blest departure. Amen.

Cyriacus Schneegas, 1597 A. Crull, Tr.

171 Ich sterbe täglich 9, 8, 9, 8, 8, 8 1756

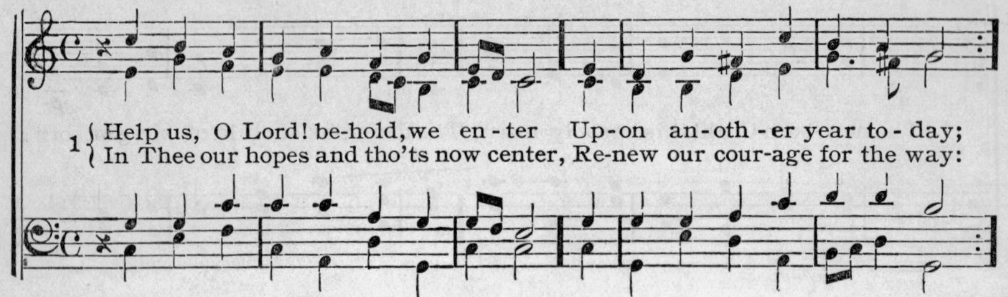
1 { Help us, O Lord! be-hold, we en - ter Up-on an-oth - er year to - day;
In Thee our hopes and tho'ts now center, Re-new our cour-age for the way:

New life, new strength, new happiness We ask of Thee, O hear and bless!

(Or to Wer nur)

2 May every plan and undertaking
 This year be all begun with Thee;
When I am sleeping or am waking,
 Still let me know Thou art with me;
Abroad do Thou my footsteps guide,
 At home be ever at my side.

3 Be this a time of grace and pardon;
 Thy rod I take with willing mind,
But suffer naught my heart to harden;
 O let me now Thy mercy find;
In Thee alone, my God, I live,
 Thou only canst my sins forgive.

4 And may this year to me be holy;
 Thy grace so fill my every thought
That all my life be pure and lowly
 And truthful as a Christian's ought;
So make me, while yet dwelling here,
Pious and blest from year to year.

5 And grant, Lord, when the year is over,
 That it for me in peace may close;
In all things care for me, and cover
 My head in time of fear and woes;
So may I, when my years are gone,
Appear with joy before Thy throne.

Johann Rist 1642 C. Winkworth, Tr.

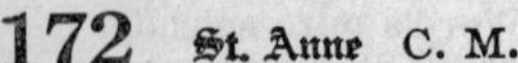

172 St. Anne C. M. W. CROFT, 1708 (P)

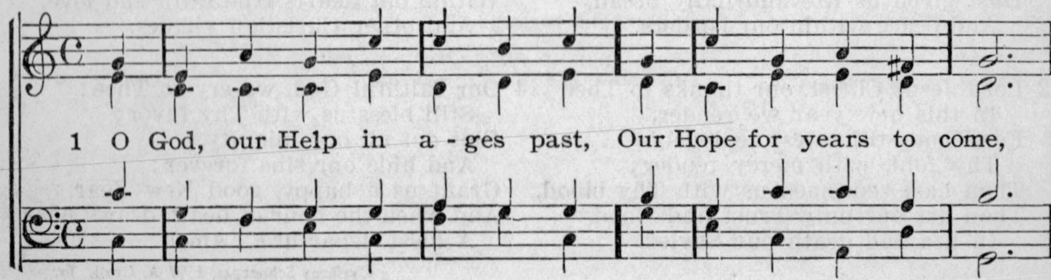
1 O God, our Help in a - ges past, Our Hope for years to come,

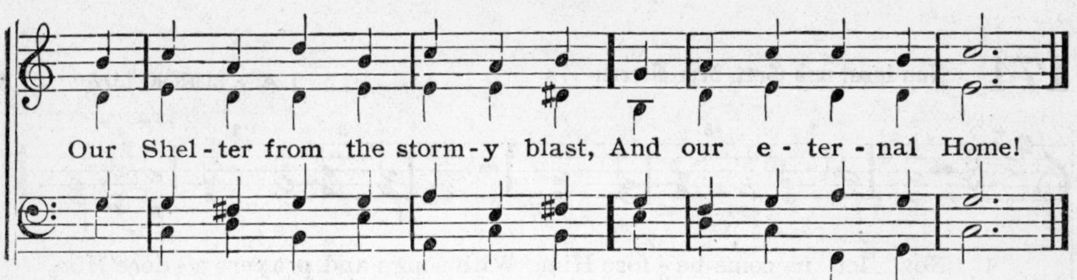
Our Shel-ter from the storm-y blast, And our e-ter-nal Home!

(*Or to Evan*)

2 Under the shadow of Thy throne
Thy saints have dwelt secure;
Sufficient is Thine arm alone,
And our defence is sure.

3 Before the hills in order stood,
Or earth received her frame,
From everlasting Thou art God,
To endless years the same.

4 A thousand ages, in Thy sight,
Are like an evening gone;
Short as the watch that ends the night
Before the rising sun.

5 Thy word commands our flesh to dust:
"Return, ye sons of men;"
All nations rose from earth at first,
And turn to earth again.

6 Time, like an ever-rolling stream,
Bears all its sons away;
They fly forgotten, as a dream
Dies at the opening day.

7 Like flowery fields the nations stand,
Pleased with the morning light;
The flowers beneath the mower's hand
Lie withering ere 'tis night.

8 O God, our Help in ages past,
Our Hope for years to come,
Be Thou our Guard while troubles last,
And our eternal Home.

Isaac Watts, 1719.

173 Das alte Jahr ist nun dahin L. M. M. PRAETORIUS, 1609

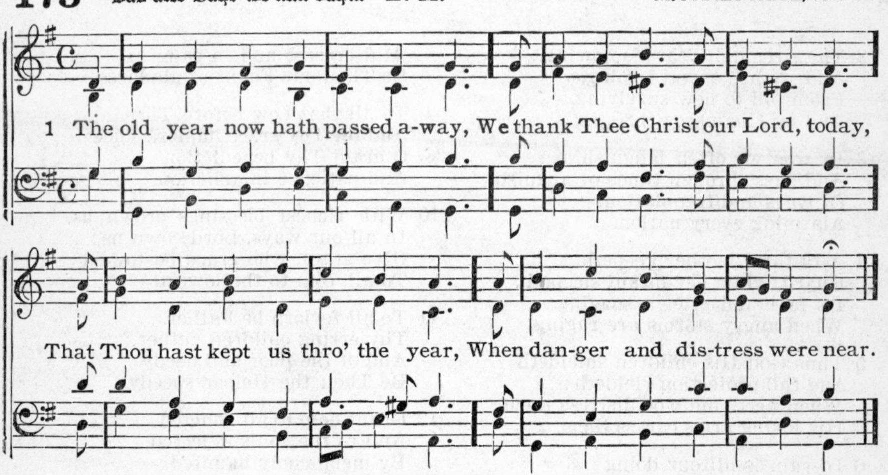
1 The old year now hath passed a-way, We thank Thee Christ our Lord, today,
That Thou hast kept us thro' the year, When dan-ger and dis-tress were near.

(*Or to Herr Jesu Christ, dich*)

2 We pray Thee, O Eternal Son,
Who with the Father reign'st as one,
To guard and rule Thy Christendom
Through all the ages yet to come.

3 Take not Thy saving Word away,
Our souls' true comfort, staff, and stay;
Abide with us, and keep us free
From all false doctrines graciously.

4 O help us to forsake all sin,
A new and holier course begin;
From last year's sins, Lord, hide Thy face,
In this new year grant us Thy grace:

5 That as true Christians we may live,
Or die in peace that Thou wilt give,
To rise again when Thou shalt come,
And enter our eternal home.

Johann Steuerlein, 1588 C. Winkworth, Tr. a

174 Nun lasst uns Gott, dem Herren 7s

J. A. v. BURGK. 1577

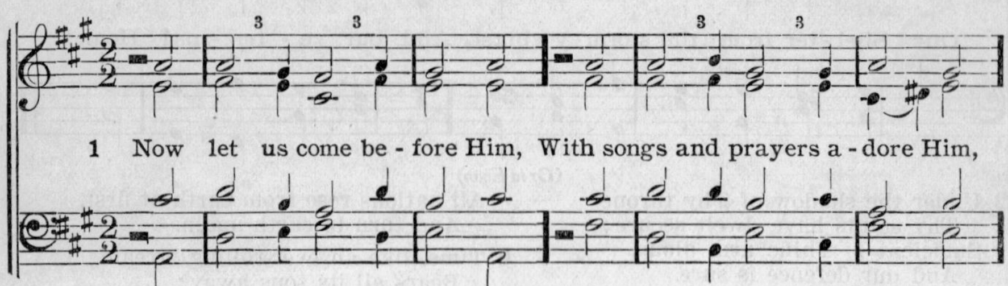
1 Now let us come be - fore Him, With songs and prayers a - dore Him,

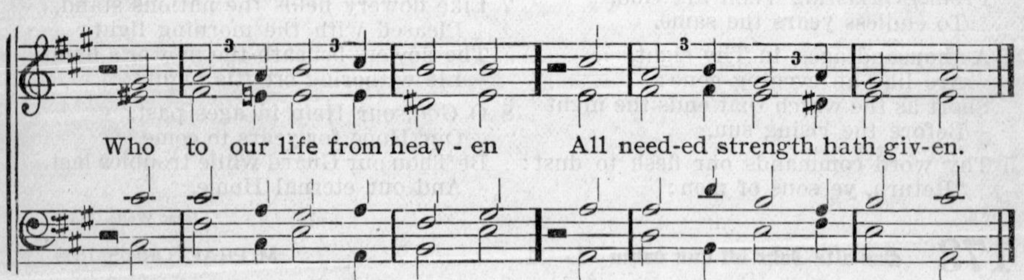
Who to our life from heav - en All need-ed strength hath giv-en.

2 The stream of years is flowing,
And we are onward going,
From old to new surviving,
And by His mercy thriving.

3 In woe we often languish,
And pass through times of anguish,
Of wars and trepidation,
Alarming every nation.

4 A faithful mother keepeth
Guard, while her infant sleepeth,
Its fear and grief assuaging,
When angry storms are raging.

5 Thus God His children shieldeth
And full protection yieldeth;
When need and woe distress them,
His loving arms caress them.

6 In vain is all our doing;
The labor we're pursuing
In our hands prospers never,
Unless God watches ever.

7 Our song to Thee ascendeth,
Whose mercy never endeth;
Our thanks to Thee we render,
Who art our strong Defender.

8 O God of mercy! hear us,
Our Father! be Thou near us;
'Mid crosses and in sadness
Be Thou our Fount of gladness.

9 To all that bow before Thee
And for Thy grace implore Thee
O grant Thy benediction
And patience in affliction.

10 With richest blessings crown us,
In all our ways, Lord! own us;
Give grace, who grace bestowest
To all, e'en to the lowest.

11 To all forlorn be Father,
Thy erring children gather,
And of the poor and needy
Be Thou the Helper speedy.

12 Grant help to all afflicted;
And to the souls dejected,
By melancholy haunted,
May cheerful thoughts be granted.

13 O Lord! assistance lend us,
Thy holy Spirit send us,
That He may make us glorious,
And lead to Thee victorious.

14 All this Thy hand bestoweth,
Thou Life, whence our life floweth;
To me and all believers
Grant, Lord, these New Year's favors.

Ludwig Helmbold, 1584 J. Kelly. Tr. a

Circumcision of Christ

175 Potsdam S. M.

Ad. from BACH

1 The year be-gins with Thee, And Thou be-gin'st with woe,

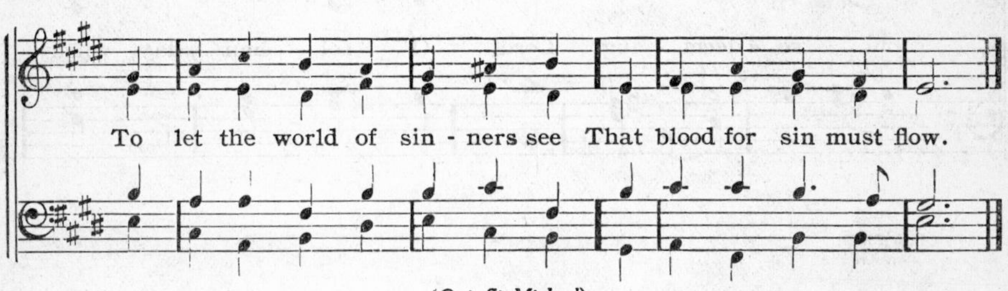
To let the world of sin-ners see That blood for sin must flow.

(Or to St. Michael)

2 Thine infant cries, O Lord,
Thy tears upon the breast
Are not enough, the legal sword
Must do its stern behest.

3 Seemeth it strange to me
My own will to deny?
Seemeth it sad, my soul, to Thee
Under the yoke to lie?

4 I look, and hold my peace:
The Giver of all good
E'en from His birth takes no release
From suffering, tears, and blood.

5 That I may reap in love,
Help me to sow in fear:
So life a winter's morn may prove
To a bright endless year.

J. Keble, a

176 Potsdam S. M.

1 The ancient Law departs,
And all its terrors cease;
For Jesus makes with faithful hearts
A covenant of peace.

2 The Light of light divine,
True brightness undefiled,
He bears for us the shame of sin,
A holy, spotless Child.

3 His infant body now
Begins our pain to feel;
Those precious drops of blood that flow
For death the victim seal.

4 Today the Name is Thine,
At which we bend the knee;
They call Thee Jesus, Child divine;
Our Jesus deign to be.

5 All praise, eternal Son,
For Thy redeeming love,
With Father, Spirit, ever one,
In glorious might above.

(Or to Monsell [St. Andrew])

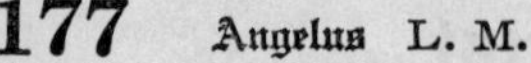

177 Angelus L. M.

G. JOSEPHI, 1657 (P and I)

1 O sa - cred day, when first was poured The blood of

our re - deem - ing Lord, O sol - emn day, when

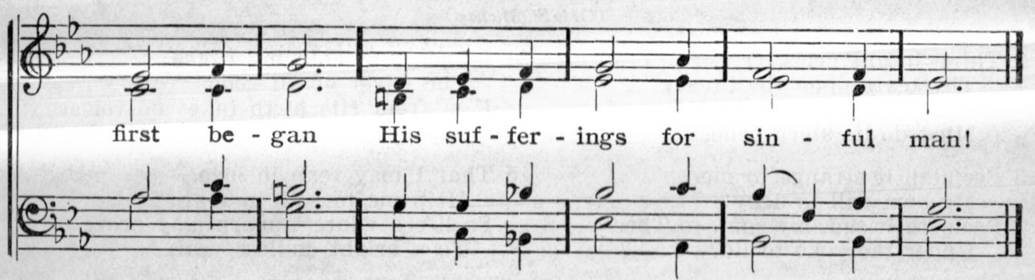
first be - gan His suf - fer - ings for sin - ful man!

2 Just born into this world of woe,
His blood for man was made to flow;
His future death was thus expressed,
Thus, too, His early love confessed.

3 From heaven descending, to fulfil,
The mandates of His Father's will,
E'en now behold the Victim lie,
The Lamb of God prepared to die.

4 Beneath the knife behold the Child,
The innocent, the undefiled:
For captives He the ransom pays,
For lawless man the Law obeys.

5 Lord, circumcise our hearts, we pray,
Our fleshly natures purge away;
Thy name, Thy likeness, may we bear;
O stamp Thy holy image there.

a. and ab.

Circumcision of Christ

178 St. Bees 7s J. B. DYKES, 1874 (P)

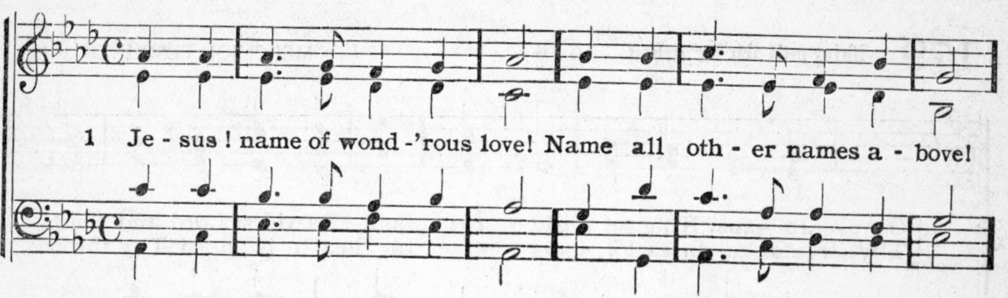
1 Je - sus ! name of wond - 'rous love! Name all oth - er names a - bove!

Un - to which must ev - 'ry knee, Bow in deep hu - mil - i - ty.

(Or to Gud, var Gud)

2 Jesus! Name decreed of old:
To the maiden-mother told,
Kneeling in her lowly cell,
By the angel Gabriel.

3 Jesus! Name of priceless worth
To the fallen sons of earth,
For the promise that it gave,—
"Jesus shall His people save."

4 Jesus! Name of mercy mild,
Given to the holy Child,
When the cup of human woe
First He tasted here below.

5 Jesus! only Name that's given
Under all the mighty heaven,
Whereby man, to sin enslaved,
Bursts his fetters, and is saved.

6 Jesus! Name of wondrous love!
Human name of God above;
Pleading only this we flee,
Helpless, O our God, to Thee.

W. W. How, 1854 a

Epiphany

179 Valet will ich dir geben 7, 6, 8 l MELCHIOR TESCHNER, 1613

1 { O Je - sus, King of glo - ry! Both Da-vid's Lord and Son!
Thy realm en-dures for - ev - er In heav'n is fixed Thy throne;
Help, that in earth's do - min - ions, Through-out from pole to pole,
Thy realm may spread sal - va - tion To each be-night-ed soul.

2 The eastern sages, bringing
Their tribute-gifts to Thee,
Bear witness to Thy kingdom,
And humbly bow the knee;
To Thee the star is pointing,
To Thee th' inspired Word;
Hence joyously we hail Thee:
Our Savior and our Lord!

3 Thou art a mighty Monarch,
As by the Word we're told,
Yet carest Thou but little
For earthly goods or gold;
On no proud steed Thou ridest,
Thou wear'st no jewelled crown,
Nor dwell'st in lordly castle,
But bearest scoff and frown.

4 Yet art Thou decked with beauty,
With rays of glorious light;
Thou ever teem'st with goodness,
And all Thy ways are right.
Vouchsafe to shield Thy people
With Thine almighty arm,
That they may dwell in safety
From those who mean them harm.

5 Ah look on me with pity,
Though I am weak and poor,
Admit me to Thy kingdom,
To dwell there, blest and sure.
I pray Thee, guide and keep me
Safe from my bitter foes,
From sin, and death, and Satan;
Free me from all my woes.

6 And bid Thy Word within me
Shine as the fairest star;
Keep sin and all false doctrine
Forever from me far;
Help me confess Thee truly,
And with Thy Christendom
Here own Thee King and Savior
And in the world to come.

Martin Behm, 1606

180 Was fuerchtst du Feind Herodes L. M. MELCHIOR FRANK, 1616

1 The Star proclaims the King is here; But, Her - od, why this sense-less

fear? He takes no realms of earth a-way Who gives the realms of heavenly day.

2 The wiser Magi see from far
And follow on His guiding star;
And led by light to light they press,
And by their gifts their God confess.

3 Within the Jordan's crystal flood
In meekness stands the Lamb of God,
And sinless sanctifies the wave,
Mankind from sin to cleanse and save.

4 At Cana first His power is shown;
His might the blushing waters own,
And changing, as He speaks the word,
Flow wine, obedient to their Lord.

5 All glory, Jesus, be to Thee
For this Thy glad Epiphany:
Whom with the Father we adore,
And Holy Ghost for evermore.

Latin, (5th Cent.) J. M. Neale, Tr. 1852 a

181 Morning Star 11, 10, 11, 10 J. P. HARDING

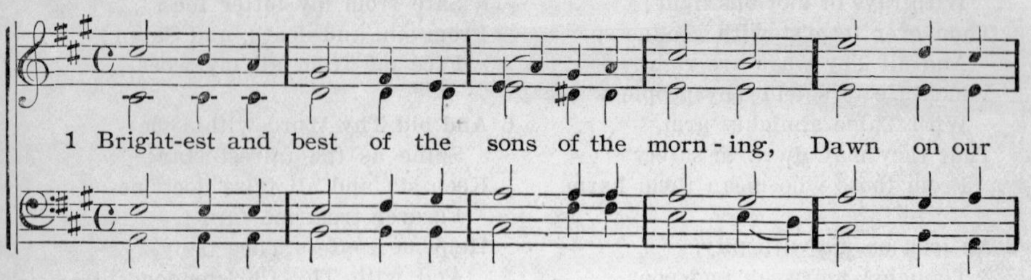
1 Bright-est and best of the sons of the morn-ing, Dawn on our

dark-ness, and lend us Thine aid; Star of the East, the ho-

ri - zon a-dorn-ing, Guide where our in - fant Re - deem-er is laid.

2 Cold on His cradle the dewdrops are shining;
Low lies His head with the beasts of the stall:
Angels adore Him in slumber reclining,
Maker, and Monarch, and Savior of all!

3 Say, shall we yield Him, in costly devotion,
Odors of Edom, and offerings divine?
Gems of the mountain, and pearls of the ocean,
Myrrh from the forest, or gold from the mine?

4 Vainly we offer each ample oblation;
Vainly with gifts would His favor secure:
Richer by far is the heart's adoration;
Dearer to God are the prayers of the poor.

5 Brightest and best of the sons of the morning,
Dawn on our darkness, and lend us Thine aid;
Star of the East, the horizon adorning,
Guide where our infant Redeemer is laid.

Reginald Heber, 1811

182 O Durchbrecher aller Bande 8, 7, 8 1 FREYLINGHAUSEN. 1704

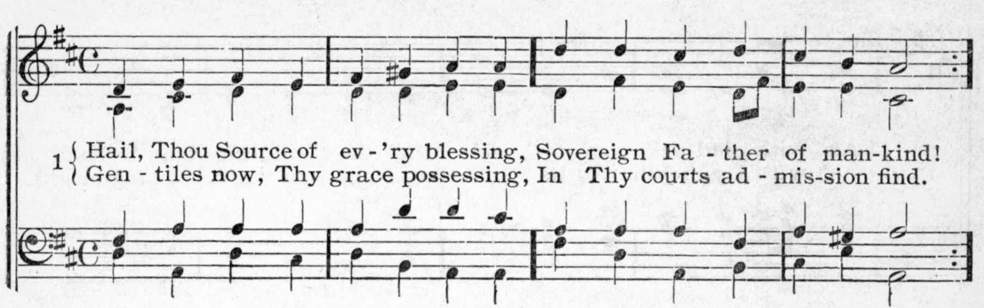
1 { Hail, Thou Source of ev - 'ry blessing, Sovereign Fa - ther of man-kind!
Gen - tiles now, Thy grace possessing, In Thy courts ad - mis-sion find.

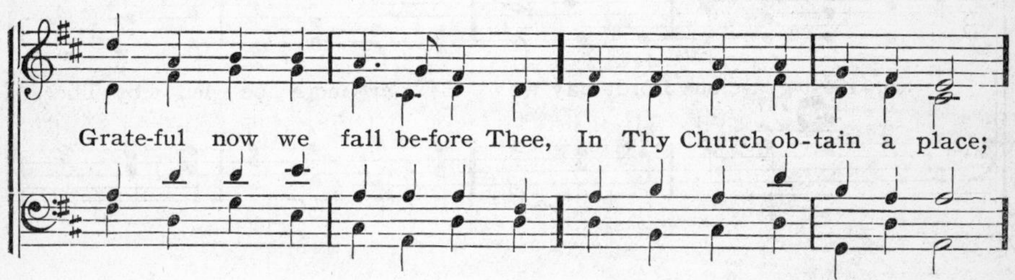
Grate-ful now we fall be-fore Thee, In Thy Church ob-tain a place;

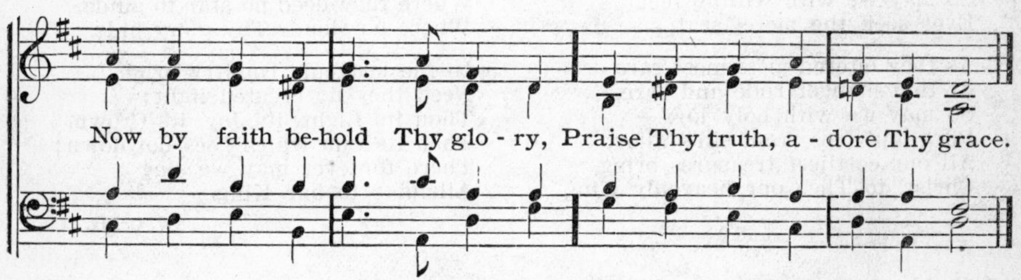
Now by faith be-hold Thy glo - ry, Praise Thy truth, a - dore Thy grace.

2 Once far off, but now invited,
We approach Thy sacred throne;
In Thy covenant united,
Reconciled, redeemed, made one.
Now revealed to Eastern sages,
See the star of mercy shine;
Mystery hid in former ages,
Mystery great of love divine.

3 Hail, Thou all-inviting Savior!
Gentiles now their offerings bring;
In Thy temple seek Thy favor,
Jesus Christ, our Lord and King,
May we, body, soul, and spirit,
Live devoted to Thy praise,
Glorious realms of bliss inherit,
Grateful anthems ever raise.

Basil Wood, 1799

183 Dix (Treuer Heiland, wir sind hier) 7s 61

Arr. fr. C. KOCHER, 1786—1872

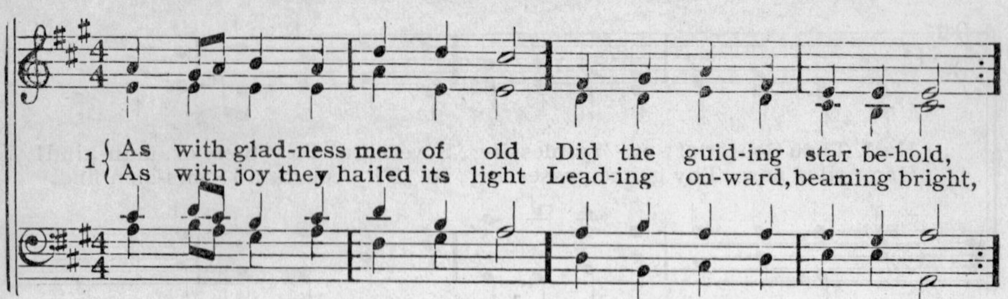
1 { As with glad-ness men of old Did the guid-ing star be-hold,
As with joy they hailed its light Lead-ing on-ward, beaming bright,

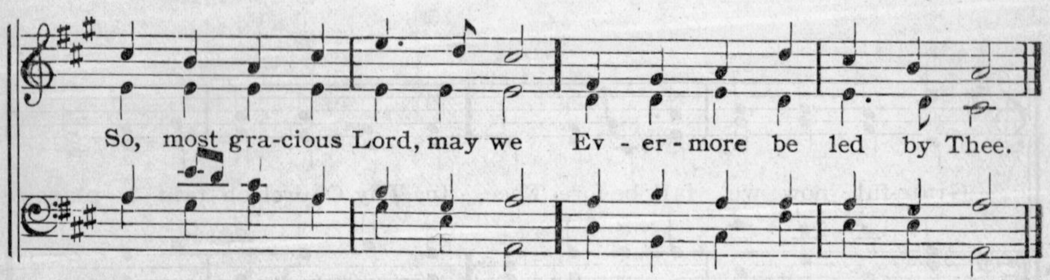
So, most gra-cious Lord, may we Ev - er - more be led by Thee.

2 As with joyful steps they sped
To that lowly manger-bed,
There to bend the knee before
Him whom heaven and earth adore,
So may we with willing feet
Ever seek the mercy-seat.

3 As they offered gifts most rare
At that manger rude and bare,
So may we with holy joy,
Pure and free from sin's alloy,
All our costliest treasures bring,
Christ, to Thee our heavenly King.

4 Holy Jesus, every day
Keep us in the narrow way;
And, when earthly things are past,
Bring our ransomed souls at last
Where they need no star to guide,
Where no clouds Thy glory hide.

5 In the heavenly country bright,
Need they no created light;
Thou its Light, its Joy, its Crown,
Thou its Sun which goes not down;
There for ever may we sing
Alleluias to our King.

W. C. Dix, 1856

184 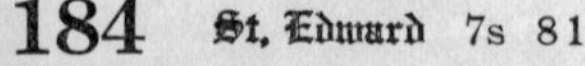 St. Edward 7s 81

C. STEGGALL, 1826

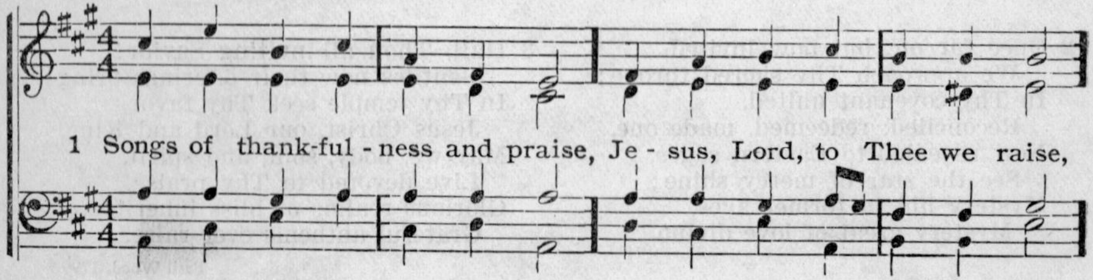
1 Songs of thank-ful - ness and praise, Je - sus, Lord, to Thee we raise,

Epiphany

Man - i - fest - ed by the star To the sa - ges from a - far;

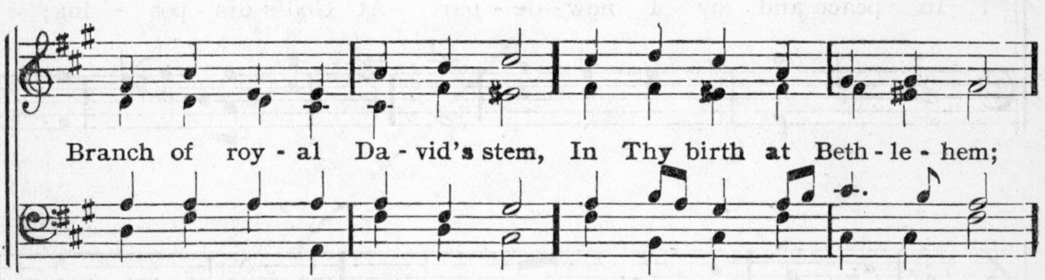
Branch of roy - al Da - vid's stem, In Thy birth at Beth - le - hem;

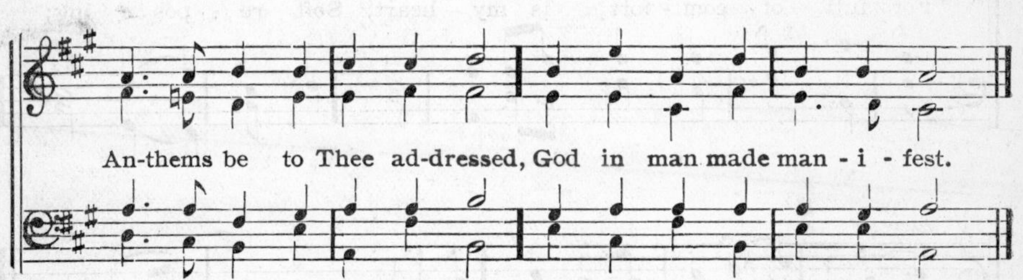
An-thems be to Thee ad-dressed, God in man made man - i - fest.

2 Manifest at Jordan's stream,
Prophet, Priest, and King supreme,
And at Cana, wedding-guest,
In Thy Godhead manifest;
Manifest in power divine,
Changing water into wine;
Anthems be to Thee addressed,
God in man made manifest.

3 Manifest in making whole
Palsied limbs and fainting soul;
Manifest in valiant fight,
Quelling all the devil's might;
Manifest in gracious will,
Ever bringing good from ill;
Anthems be to Thee addressed,
God in man made manifest.

4 Sun and moon shall darkened be,
Stars shall fall, the heavens shall flee;
Christ will then like lightning shine,
All will see His glorious sign;
All will then the trumpet hear,
All will see the Judge appear;
Thou by all wilt be confessed,
God in man made manifest.

5 Grant us grace to see Thee, Lord,
Present in Thy holy Word;
May we imitate Thee now,
And be pure, as pure art Thou,
That we like to Thee may be
At Thy great Epiphany;
And may praise Thee, ever blest,
God in man made manifest.

C. Wordsworth, 1862

The Presentation of Christ

185 Mit Fried und Freud ich fahr dahin 8,5,8,4,7,7 J. WALTHER, 1524

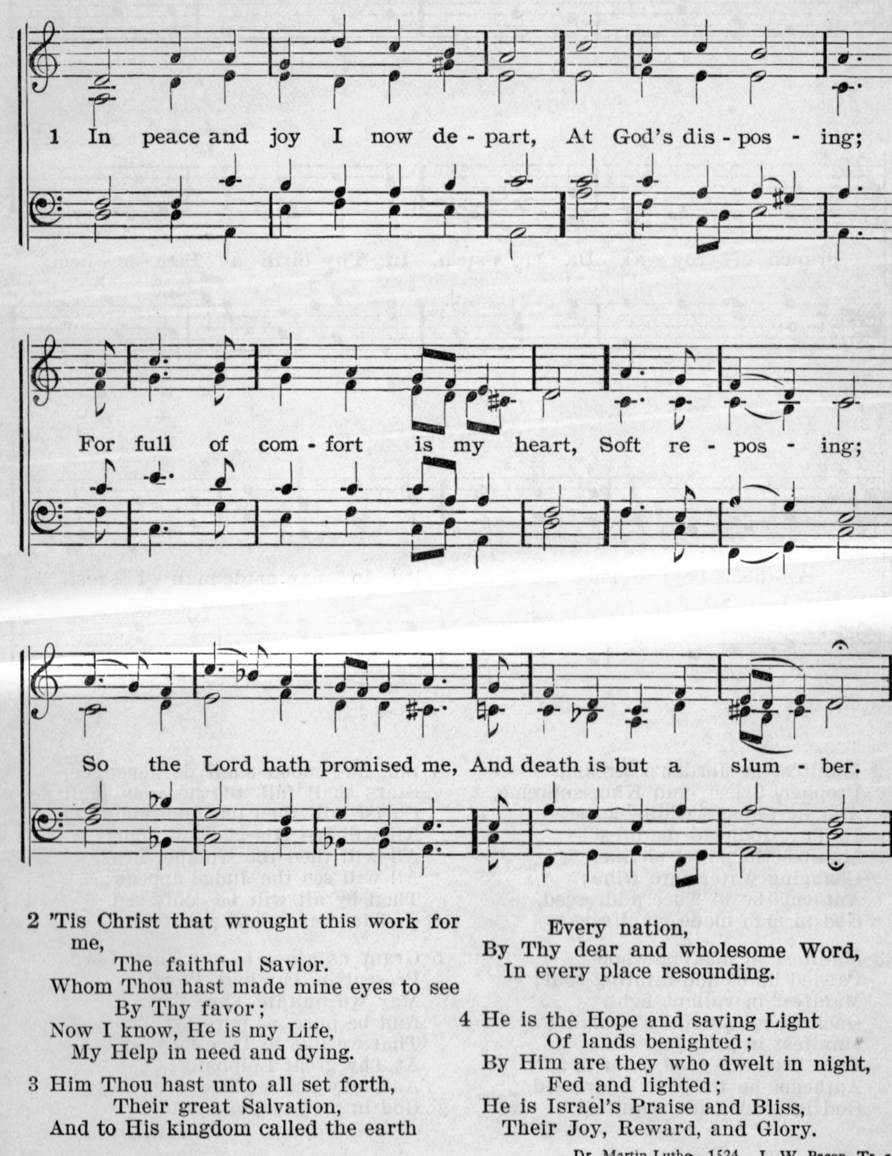
1 In peace and joy I now de - part, At God's dis - pos - ing;
For full of com - fort is my heart, Soft re - pos - ing;
So the Lord hath promised me, And death is but a slum - ber.

2 'Tis Christ that wrought this work for me,
The faithful Savior.
Whom Thou hast made mine eyes to see
By Thy favor;
Now I know, He is my Life,
My Help in need and dying.

3 Him Thou hast unto all set forth,
Their great Salvation,
And to His kingdom called the earth
Every nation,
By Thy dear and wholesome Word,
In every place resounding.

4 He is the Hope and saving Light
Of lands benighted;
By Him are they who dwelt in night,
Fed and lighted;
He is Israel's Praise and Bliss,
Their Joy, Reward, and Glory.

Dr. Martin Luther, 1524. L. W. Bacon, Tr. a

186 Bist willkommen, Licht der Heiden 8, 7, 6 1

J. CHR. KITTEL 1790

1 In His tem - ple now be - hold Him, See the long ex - pect - ed Lord;
An-cient pro-phets had fore - told Him, God has now ful-filled His word.

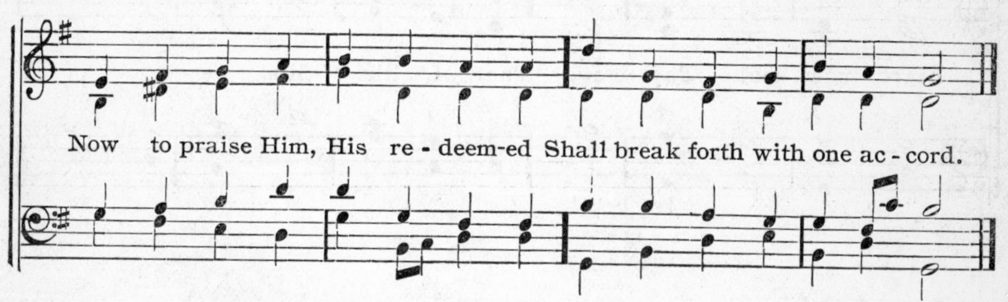
Now to praise Him, His re - deem-ed Shall break forth with one ac - cord.

2 In the arms of her who bore Him,
Virgin pure, behold Him lie,
While His aged saints adore Him,
Ere in perfect faith they die.
Hallelujah! Hallelujah!
Lo, the incarnate God most high.

3 Jesus, by Thy presentation,
Thou who didst for us endure,
Make us see our great salvation,
Seal us with Thy promise sure;
And present us, in Thy glory,
To Thy Father, cleansed and pure.

Henry John Pye, 1853

187 Regent Square 8, 7, 61

1 Angels, from the realms of glory,
Wing your flight o'er all the earth;
Ye who sang creation's story,
Now proclaim Messiah's birth:
Come and worship,
Come and worship:
Worship Christ, the new-born King.

2 Shepherds, in the fields abiding,
Watching o'er your flocks by night;
God with man is now residing,
Yonder shines the heav'nly Light:
Come and worship,
Come and worship:
Worship Christ, the new-born King.

3 Sages, leave your contemplations;
Brighter visions beam afar:
Seek the great Desire of nations,
Ye have seen His natal star:
Come and worship,
Come and worship:
Worship Christ, the new-born King.

4 Saints, before the altar bending,
Watching long in hope and fear,
Suddenly the Lord descending,
In His temple shall appear:
Come and worship,
Come and worship:
Worship Christ, the new-born King.

James Montgomery, 1819 a

Presentation of Christ

188 Dich bitt ich, trautes Jesulein L. M.

B. HELDER, 1651

1 O dear - est Je - sus, Thee I pray: With - in my
heart now make Thy stay, That I, like Sim - e - on of
old, By faith may glad - ly Thee en - fold.

(Or to Herr Jesu Christ, dich)

2 Thou art my Life and Happiness,
Whom God hath sent, my soul to bless:
O cleanse and purify my heart,
That from Thy paths I ne'er depart.

3 Lord, with Thy light show me the way,
That never I may go astray;
Ward off all sorrow and despair,
And let me be Thine own fore'er.

4 Lift up Thy face upon me, Lord,
In life and death Thy help afford;
Then I'll depart most cheerfully
This life, whene'er it pleaseth Thee.

Barth. Helder, 1614. A. Crull, Tr.

189 Es ist das Heil 8, 7, 8, 7, 8, 8, 7 (Iambic)

1 Thank God! my Jesus cleanseth me
From all sins I committed,
He paid my debt and set me free,
I, therefore, am acquitted
Of sin's and Satan's bondage fell;
My faith now laughs at death and hell,
Because my life is Jesus.

2 Why should I grieve? He who fulfilled
The Law, thus to release us,
He who His Father's wrath has stilled
By His own death, this Jesus
Still liveth, and all that He hath
He giveth unto me through faith;
Is there a greater treasure?

3 Because my Jesus cleanseth me
From sin by His own merit,
I am from pain and fear set free,
Death cannot daunt my spirit;
I trust in Jesus' righteousness,
His innocence and blessedness
Are now my life and treasure.

4 Now I, like Simeon, can end
My life in peace and gladness,
And to my God I can commend
My spirit without sadness;
For when my weary eyes I close,
My death becomes a sweet repose,
I see the joys of heaven.

5 How happy, therefore, shall I be,
When life's frail thread is broken;
When holy angels carry me
To joys that ne'er were spoken;
When I behold Him face to face,
When I have gained that blessed place,
Prepared for me by Jesus.

6 Lord, grant that e'er prepared I be,
That naught from Thee me sever.
And when I die, let me with Thee
In glory live forever;
Come quickly to delivér me
Lord, by Thy death and agony,
Yea, come, Lord Jesus! Amen.

Dr. Johann Olearius, 1671. A. Crull, Tr.

190 Valet will ich 7, 6, 8 1

1 Light of the Gentile nations,
Thy people's Joy and Love!
Drawn by Thy Spirit hither,
We gladly come to prove
Thy presence in Thy temple,
And seek with earnest mind,
As Simeon once had waited
His Savior God to find.

2 Yea, Lord, Thy servants meet Thee,
E'en now, in every place
Where Thy true Word hath promised
That they should see Thy face.
Thou yet wilt gladly grant us,
Who gather round Thee here,
In faith's strong arms to bear Thee,
As did that aged seer.

3 Be Thou our Joy, our Brightness,
That shines 'mid pain and loss,
Our Sun in times of terror,
The Glory round our cross;
A Glow in sinking spirits,
A Sunbeam in distress,
Physician, Friend in sickness;
In death, our Happiness.

4 Let us, O Lord, be faithful
Like Simeon to the end,
So that his dying song may
From all our hearts ascend:
"O Lord, now let Thy servant
Depart in peace, I pray,
Since I have seen my Savior,
Have here beheld His day."

5 My Savior, I behold Thee
Now with the eye of faith;
No foe of Thee can rob me,
Though bitter words he saith.
Within Thy heart abiding,
As thou dost dwell in me,
No pain, no death has terrors
To part my soul from Thee.

6 Lord, here on earth Thou seemest
At times to frown on me,
And through my tears I often
Can scarce distinguish Thee;
But in the heavenly mansions
Shall nothing dim my sight,
And I shall see forever
Thine always glorious light.

Johann Franck, 1674 C. Winkworth, Tr. a

Passion of Christ

General

191 An Wasser fluessen Babylon 8, 7, 8, 7, 8, 8, 7, 8, 8, 7 STRASSBURGER K. A. 1525

1 { A Lamb goes un-com-plain-ing forth, The guilt of all men bear-ing;
'Tis la-den with the sin of earth, None else the bur-den shar-ing:
It goes its way, grows weak and faint, To slaugh-ter led without com-plaint, Its spot-less life to of-fer; Bears shame, and
stripes, and wounds, and death, An-guish and mock-er-

Passion of Christ

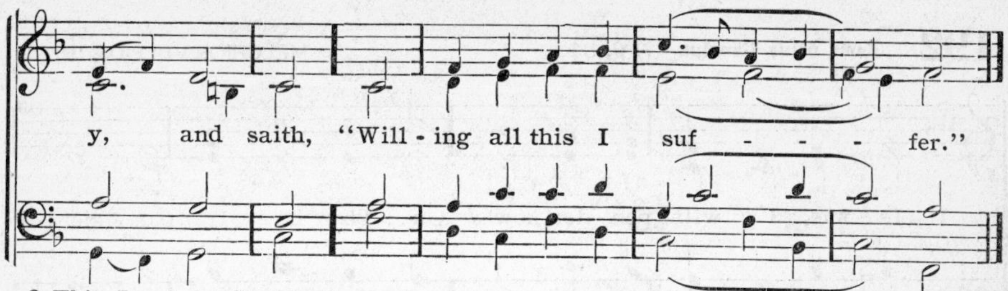

y, and saith, "Will - ing all this I suf - - - fer."

2 This Lamb is Christ, the soul's great friend
And everlasting Savior;
Him, Him God chose, sin's reign to end
And bring us to His favor
"Go forth, my Son!" He said, "and bail
The children, who are doomed to hell
But for Thine intercession.
The punishment is great, and dread
The wrath, but Thou Thy blood shalt shed,
And save them from perdition."

3 "Yea, Father, yea, most willingly
I'll bear what Thou commandest;
My will conforms to Thy decree,
I do what Thou demandest."
O wondrous Love! what hast Thou done!
The Father offers up His Son,
The Son content descendeth!
O Love! O Love! how strong art Thou!
In shroud and grave Thou lay'st Him low
Whose word the mountains rendeth!

4 Thou lay'st Him, Love, upon the cross,
With nails and spear Him bruising;
Thou slay'st Him as a lamb, His loss
From soul and body oozing;
From body 'tis the crimson flood
Of precious sacrificial blood,
From soul, the strength of anguish:
My gain it is; sweet Lamb to Thee
What can I give, whose love to me
For me doth make Thee languish?

5 Lord, all my life I'll cleave to Thee,
Thy love fore'er beholding,
Thee ever, as Thou ever me,
With loving arms enfolding.
Yea, Thou shalt be my Beacon-light,
To guide me safe through death's dark night,
And cheer my heart in sorrow;
Henceforth myself and all that's mine
To Thee, my Savior, I consign,
From whom all things I borrow.

6 By morn and eve my theme shall be
Thy mercy's wondrous measure;
To sacrifice myself to Thee,
My foremost aim and pleasure.
My stream of life shall flow for Thee,
Its steadfast current ceaselessly
In praise to Thee outpouring;
And all that Thou hast done for me,
I'll treasure in my memory,
Thy gracious love adoring.

7 Enlarge, shrine of my heart, and swell,
To Thee shall now be given
A treasure that doth far excel
The worth of earth and heaven.
Away with the Arabian gold,
With treasures of an earthly mold!
I've found a better jewel.
My priceless treasure, Lord my God,
Is Thy most holy, precious blood,
Which flowed from wounds so cruel.

8 This treasure ever I'll employ,
This ever aid shall yield me;
In sorrow it shall be my joy,
In conflict it shall shield me;
In joy, the music of my feast,
And when all else has lost its zest,
This manna still shall feed me;
In thirst my drink; in want my food;
My company in solitude,
To comfort and to lead me.

9 Death's poison cannot harm me now,
Thy blood new life bestoweth;
My Shadow from the heat art Thou,
When noonday's sunlight gloweth.
When I'm by inward grief oppress,
On Thee my weary soul shall rest,
As sick men on their pillows.
Thou art my Anchor, when by woe
My bark is driven to and fro
On trouble's restless billows.

10 And when Thy glory I shall see
And taste Thy kingdom's pleasure,
Thy blood my royal robe shall be,
And joy beyond all measure;
It then shall be my glorious crown
Thus I'll appear before the throne
Of God, and need not hide me;
And shall, by Him to Thee betrothed,
By Thee in bridal garments clothed,
Stand as a bride beside Thee.

Paul Gerhardt, 1653

Passion of Christ

192 Jesu, deine Passion 7, 6, 8l MELCHIOR VULPIUS, 1609

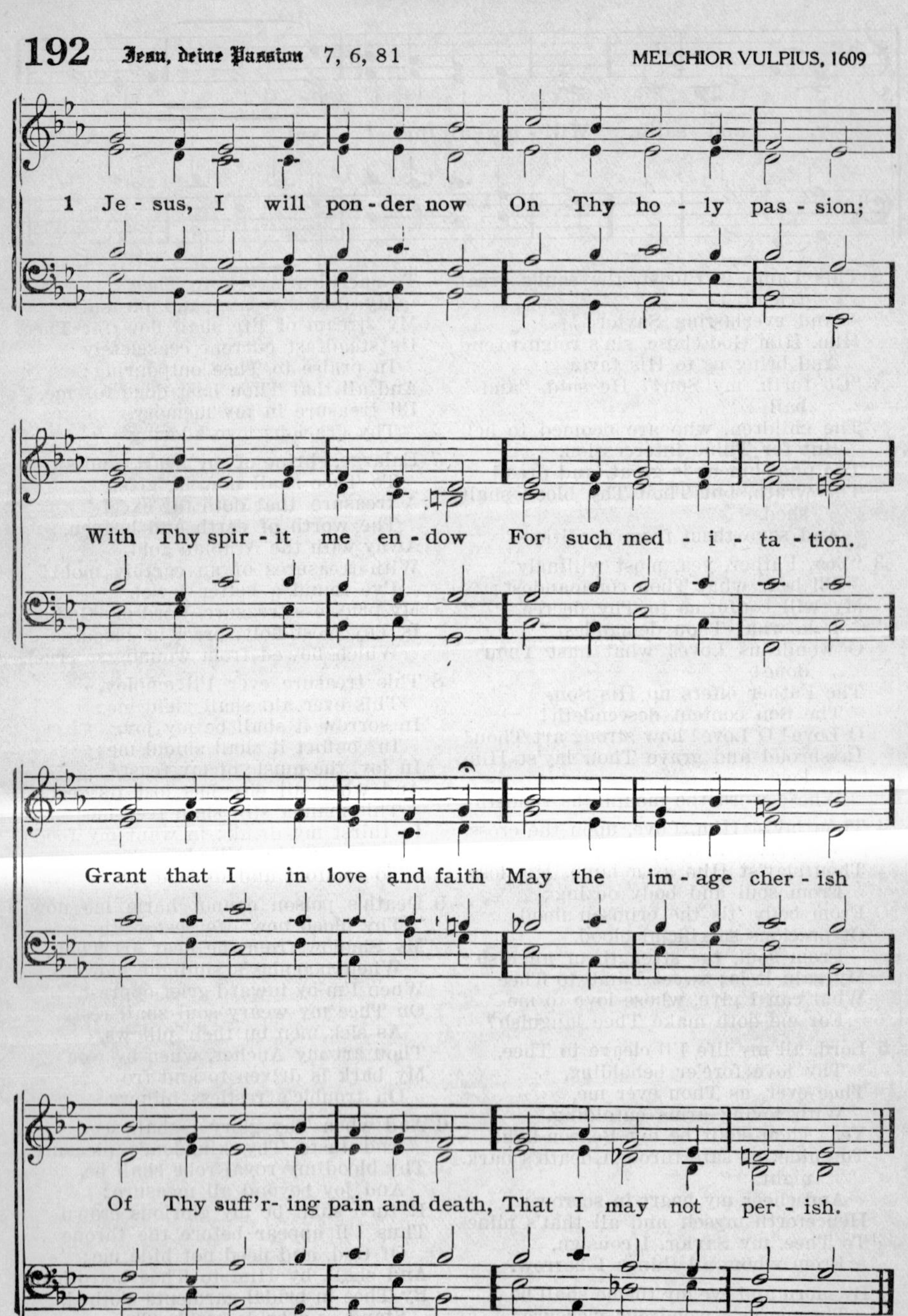
1 Je - sus, I will pon - der now On Thy ho - ly pas - sion;
With Thy spir - it me en - dow For such med - i - ta - tion.
Grant that I in love and faith May the im - age cher - ish
Of Thy suff'r - ing pain and death, That I may not per - ish.

2 Make me see Thy great distress,
 Anguish and affliction,
Bonds and stripes, and wretchedness,
 And Thy crucifixion;
Make me see how scourge and rod,
 Spear and nails did wound Thee,
How for man Thou diedst, O God,
 Who with thorns had crowned Thee.

3 Yet, O Lord, not thus alone
 Make me see Thy passion,
But its cause to me make known,
 And its termination.
Ah! I also and my sin
 Wrought thy deep affliction;
This the real cause hath been
 Of Thy crucifixion.

4 Grant that I Thy passion view
 With repentant grieving,
Nor Thee crucify anew
 By unholy living.
How could I refuse to shun
 Every sinful pleasure,
Since for me God's only Son
 Suffered without measure?

5 If my sins give me alarm
 And my conscience grieve me,
Let Thy cross my fear disarm,
 Peace of conscience give me.
Grant that I may trust in Thee
 And Thy holy passion;
If His Son so loveth me,
 God must have compassion.

6 Grant that I may willingly
 Bear with Thee my crosses.
Learning humbleness of Thee.
 Peace 'mid pain and losses.
May I give Thee love for love.
 Hear me, O my Savior,
That I may in heaven above
 Sing Thy praise forever.

Sigmund v. Birken (Betulius) 1653. A. Crull, Tr. a

193 Wir danken dir, Herr Jesu Christ L. M. "BERGKREYEN," 1551

1 To Thee, Lord Je-sus, thanks we give, Who diedst for us, that we might live,

And thro' Thy ho-ly pre-cious blood Hast made us right-eous be - fore God.

(Or to Nun lasst uns den Leib)

2 We pray Thee, O true God and Man,
Who wast for our offences slain:
Save us from everlasting death,
And cheer us, when we yield our breath.

3 Defend us, Lord, from sin and shame;
Help us by Thine almighty name
To bear our crosses patiently,
To trust in Thy great agony.

4 And thence the full assurance gain,
That Thou wilt e'er our Friend remain,
And not forsake us in our strife,
Until we enter into life.

Christoph Vischer c 1568 A. Crull, Tr. a

194 Der am Kreuz ist meine Liebe 8,7,8,7,7,7,8,8

KOENIG, 1738

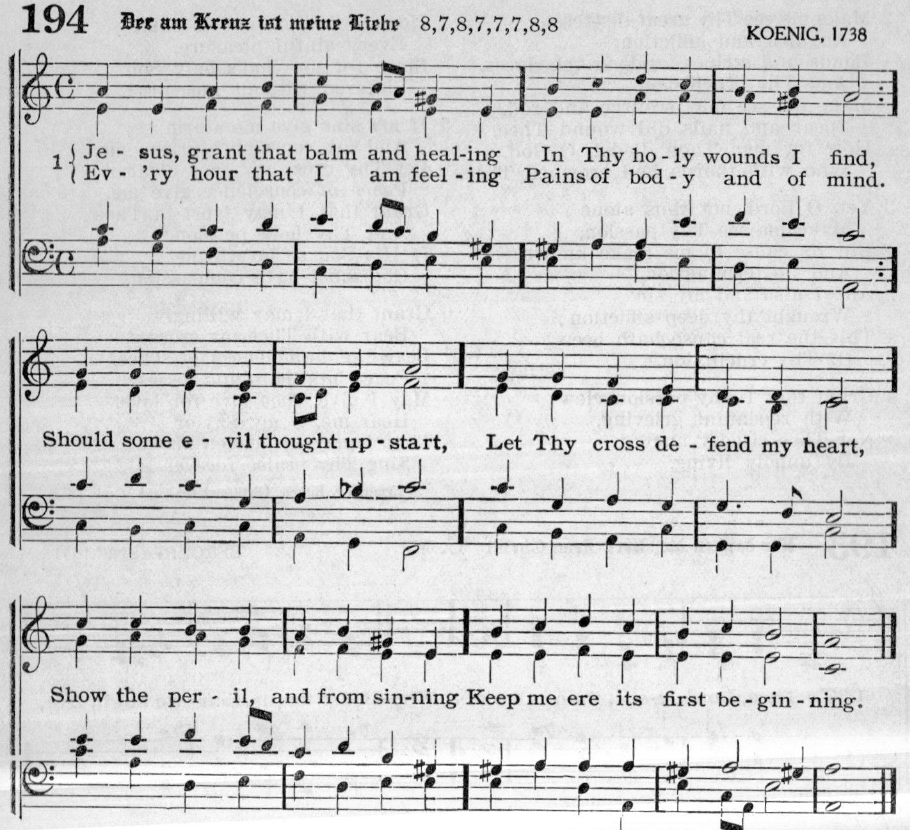
1 { Je - sus, grant that balm and heal-ing In Thy ho - ly wounds I find,
Ev - 'ry hour that I am feel - ing Pains of bod - y and of mind.
Should some e - vil thought up - start, Let Thy cross de - fend my heart,
Show the per - il, and from sin-ning Keep me ere its first be - gin - ning.

(*Or to Werde munter Or to Freu dich sehr*)

2 Should some lust or sharp temptation
Prove too strong for flesh and blood,
Let me think upon Thy passion,
And the breach is soon made good.
Or should Satan make his way
To my heart, O let me say:
"Jesus Christ for me was wounded,"
And the Tempter flees confounded.

3 If the world my heart entices
On the broad and easy road,
Filled with mirth and pleasant vices,
Let me think upon the load
Thou didst once for me endure,
That I flee all thoughts impure,
Banishing each wild emotion,
Calm and blest in my devotion.

4 Yes, whate'er may pain or grieve me,
Let Thy wounds, Lord, make me whole.
When I'm faint, let them revive me,
Granting new life to my soul.
May Thy comfort render sweet
Every bitter cup I meet,
Thou who by Thy death and passion
Hast procured my soul's salvation!

5 O my God, my rock and tower!
Grant that in Thy death I trust,
Knowing death has lost his power
Since Thou trod'st him in the dust.
Savior, let Thine agony
Ever help and comfort me;
Let Thy death be my protection,
Safety, life, and resurrection.

6 Jesus, grant that balm and healing
In Thy holy wounds I find,
Every hour that I am feeling
Pains of body and of mind;
And when I this world must leave,
Grant that, Lord, to Thee I cleave,
In Thy wounds find consolation,
And obtain my soul's salvation.

From J. Heermann, 1644. Hannoversches Gesangbuch, 1657

195 O Jesu Christ, meins Lebens Licht L. M. NUERNBERG H. B. 1676

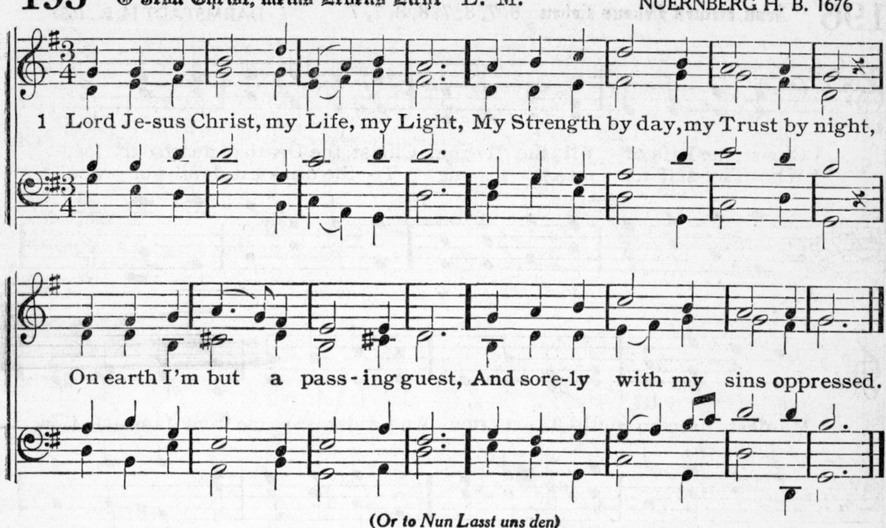
1 Lord Je-sus Christ, my Life, my Light, My Strength by day, my Trust by night,
On earth I'm but a pass-ing guest, And sore-ly with my sins oppressed.

(Or to Nun Lasst uns den)

2 Far off I see my fatherland,
Where through Thy blood I hope to stand,
But ere I reach that Paradise,
A weary way before me lies.

3 My heart sinks at the journey's length,
My wasted flesh has little strength,
Only my soul still cries in me:
"Lord, take me home, take me to Thee!"

4 O let Thy sufferings give me power
To meet the last and darkest hour;
Thy sweat refresh and comfort me,
Thy bonds and fetters make me free!

5 The blows and stripes that fell on Thee
Heal up the wounds of sin in me;
Thy crown of thorns, Thy foes' mad spite
Let be my glory and delight!

6 That thirst and bitter draught of Thine
Let help me bear with patience mine;
Thy piercing cry uphold my soul,
When floods of anguish o'er me roll!

7 O let Thy holy wounds for me
Clefts in the rock forever be,
Where as a dove my soul can hide
And safe from Satan's rage abide.

8 And when my lips grow white and chill,
Thy Spirit cry within me still,
And help my soul Thy heaven to find,
When these poor eyes grow dark and blind!

9 And when my spirit flies away,
Thy parting words shall be my stay,
Let me depart with peaceful brow,
When I in death my head shall bow.

10 Thy cross shall be my staff in life,
Thy holy grave my rest from strife;
The winding-sheet that covered Thee,
O let it be a shroud for me.

11 Lord, from Thy nail-prints let me read
That Thou to save me hast decreed,
And grant that in Thy opened side
My troubled soul may ever hide.

12 Since Thou hast died, the Pure, the Just,
I take my homeward way in trust,
The gates of heaven, Lord, open wide,
When here I may no more abide.

13 And when the last great day shall come,
And Thou, our Judge, shalt speak the doom,
Let me with joy behold the light,
And set me then upon Thy right.

14 Renew this wasted flesh of mine,
That like the sun it there may shine
Among the angels pure and bright,
Yea, like Thyself in glorious light.

15 Ah, then I have my heart's desire,
When singing with the angels' choir,
Among the ransomed of Thy grace,
Forever I behold Thy face!

M. Behm, 1608

196 Jesu, meines Lebens Leben 8, 7, 8, 7, 8, 8, 7, 7 DARMSTADT H. B., 1687

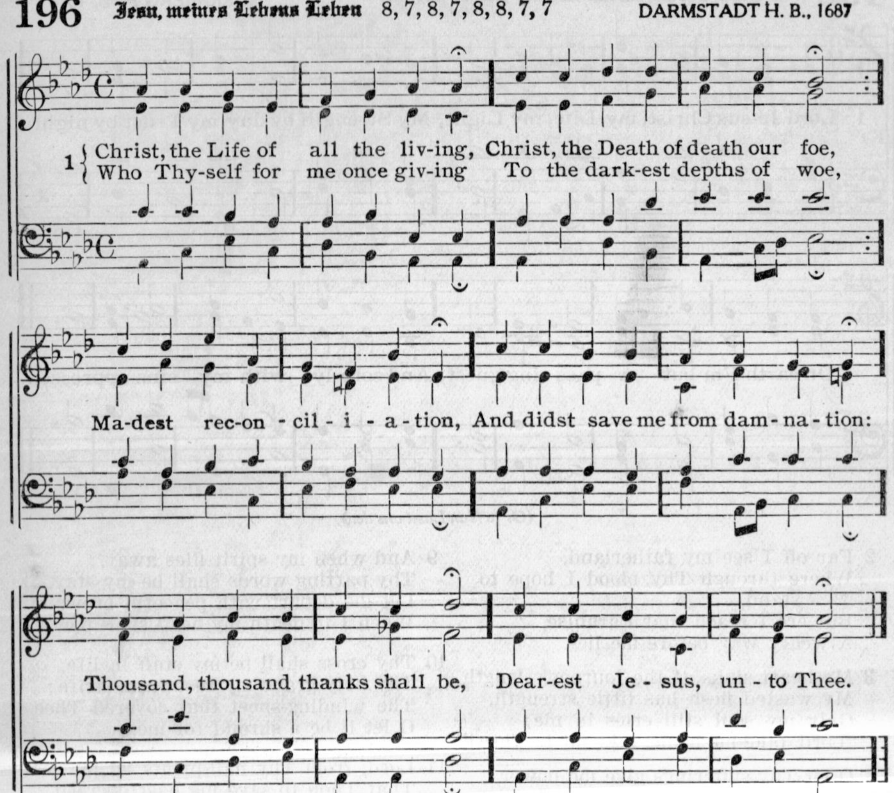
1 { Christ, the Life of all the liv-ing, Christ, the Death of death our foe,
Who Thy-self for me once giv-ing To the dark-est depths of woe,
Ma-dest rec-on-cil-i-a-tion, And didst save me from dam-na-tion:
Thousand, thousand thanks shall be, Dear-est Je-sus, un-to Thee.

2 Thou, ah! Thou, hast taken on Thee
Bonds and stripes, a cruel rod;
Pain and scorn were heaped upon Thee,
O Thou sinless Son of God!
Thus didst Thou my soul deliver
From the bonds of sin forever.
Thousand, thousand thanks shall be,
Dearest Jesus, unto Thee.

3 Thou hast borne the smiting only
That my wounds might all be whole;
Thou hast suffered, sad and lonely,
Rest to give my weary soul;
Yea, the curse of God enduring,
Blessing unto me securing.
Thousand, thousand thanks shall be,
Dearest Jesus, unto Thee.

4 Heartless scoffers did surround Thee,
Treating Thee with cruel scorn,
E'en with piercing thorns they crowned Thee;
All disgrace Thou, Lord, hast borne,
That as Thine Thou mightest own me,
And with heavenly glory crown me.
Thousand, thousand thanks shall be,
Dearest Jesus, unto Thee.

5 Thou hast suffered men to bruise Thee,
That from pain I might be free;
Falsely did Thy foes accuse Thee—
Thence I gain security;
Comfortless once Thou didst languish,
Me to comfort in my anguish.
Thousand, thousand thanks shall be,
Dearest Jesus, unto Thee.

6 Thou hast suffered great affliction,
And has borne it patiently,
Even death by crucifixion,
That Thou might'st atone for me;
Thou didst choose to be tormented,
That my doom should be prevented.
Thousand, thousand thanks shall be,
Dearest Jesus, unto Thee.

Ernst Christoph Homburg, 1659

197 Herr Christ, der einig Gott's Sohn 7, 6, 7, 6, 8, 7, 6 J. WALTHER, 1524

1 When o'er my sins I sor - row, Lord, I will look to Thee,
And hence my com - fort bor - row, That Thou wast slain for me.
Yea, Lord, Thy pre - cious blood was spilt For me,
O most un - worth - y, To take a - way my guilt.

2 O what a marvelous offering!
Behold! the Master spares
His servants, and their suffering
And grief for them He bears.
God stoopeth from His throne on high,
For me, His guilty creature,
He deigns as man to die.

3 My manifold transgression
Henceforth can harm me none,
Since Jesus' bloody passion
For me God's grace hath won;
His precious blood my debts hath paid;
Of hell and all its torments
I am no more afraid.

4 Therefore, I will forever
Give glory unto Thee,
O Jesus, loving Savior,
For what Thou'st borne for me.
I'll spend my breath in songs of thanks
For Thy sad cry, Thy sufferings,
Thy wrongs, Thy guiltless death.

5 Lord, let Thy woes, Thy patience,
My heart with strength inspire
To vanquish all temptations,
And spurn all base desire;
This thought I fain would cherish most—
What pain my soul's redemption
Hath Thee, O Savior cost!

6 Whate'er may be the burden,
The cross here on me laid;
Be shame or want my guerdon,
I'll bear it with Thine aid;
Give patience, give me strength to take
Thee for my bright example,
And all the world forsake.

7 And let me do to others
As Thou hast done to me:
Love all men as my brothers,
And serve them willingly,
With ready heart, nor seek my own,
But as Thou, Lord, hast helped us,
From purest love alone.

Dr. J. Gesenius, 1646 C. Winkworth, Tr. a

198 Herzliebster Jesu, was hast du verbrochen 11,11,11,5 J. CRUEGER, 1640

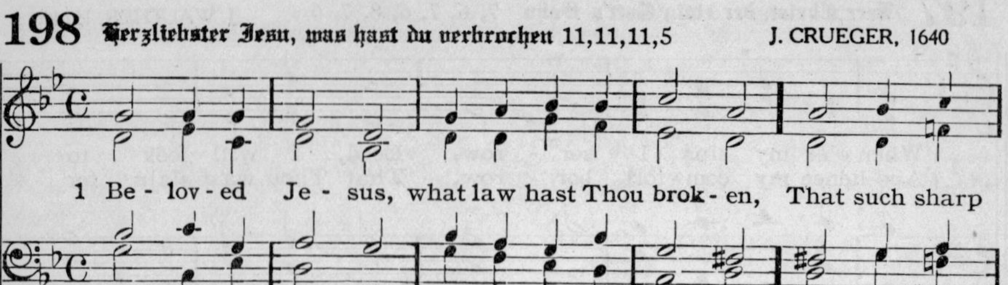
1 Be - lov - ed Je - sus, what law hast Thou brok - en, That such sharp

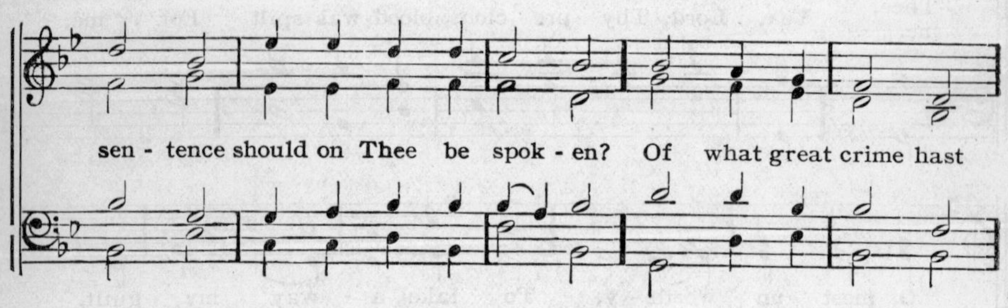
sen - tence should on Thee be spok - en? Of what great crime hast

Thou to make con - fes - sion, Of what trans - gres - sion?

2 They crown Thy head with thorns, they smite, they scourge Thee,
With cruel mockings to the cross they urge Thee,
They give Thee gall to drink, they still decry Thee,
They crucify Thee.

3 Whence come these sorrows, whence this mortal anguish?
It is my sins for which Thou, Lord, must languish;
Yea, all the wrath, the woe Thou dost inherit,
'Tis I do merit.

4 What strangest punishment is suffered yonder?
The Shepherd dies for sheep that love to wander,
The Master pays the debt His servants owe Him,
Who would not own Him.

5 The sinless Son of God must die in sadness;
The sinful child of man may live in gladness;
Man forfeited his life, and is acquitted—
God is committed.

6 There was no spot in me by sin untainted,
Sick with sin's poison all my heart had fainted;
My heavy guilt to hell had well nigh brought me,
Such woe it wrought me.

7 O wondrous love, whose depth no heart hath sounded,
That brought Thee here by foes and thieves surrounded,
All worldly pleasures, heedless, I was trying,
While Thou wert dying!

8 O mighty King, no time can dim Thy glory!
How shall I spread abroad Thy wondrous story?
How shall I find some worthy gifts to proffer?
What dare I offer?

9 For vainly doth our human wisdom ponder
Thy woes, Thy mercy still transcends our wonder.
O how should I do aught that could delight Thee!
Can I requite Thee?

10 Yet unrequited, Lord, I would not leave Thee;
I will renounce whate'er doth vex or grieve Thee,
And quench with thoughts of Thee and prayers most lowly
All fires unholy.

11 But since my own strength never will suffice me
To crucify desires that still entice me,
To all good deeds, O let Thy Spirit win me,
And reign within me!

12 I'll think upon Thy mercy without ceasing,
That earth's vain joys to me no more be pleasing;
To do Thy will shall be my sole endeavor
Henceforth forever.

13 Whate'er of earthly good this life may grant me
I'll risk for Thee; no shame, no cross shall daunt me;
I shall not fear what man can do to harm me,
Nor death alarm me.

14 But, worthless is my sacrifice, I own it;
Yet Lord, for love's sake Thou wilt not disown it;
Thou wilt accept my gift in Thy great meekness,
Nor shame my weakness.

15 And when, dear Lord, before Thy throne in heaven,
To me the crown of joy at last is given,
Where sweetest hymns Thy saints forever raise Thee,
I too shall praise Thee.

Johann Heerman, 1630 C. Winkworth, Tr. a

199 Gethsemane 7s 61

R. REDHEAD, 1853

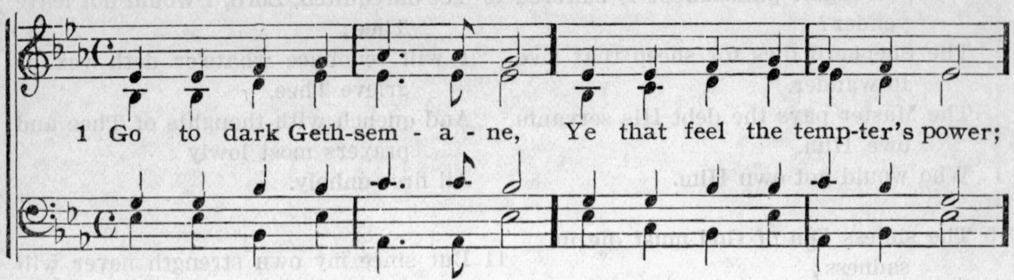
1 Go to dark Geth-sem - a - ne, Ye that feel the temp-ter's power;

Your Re-deem-er's con - flict see, Watch with Him one bit - ter hour;

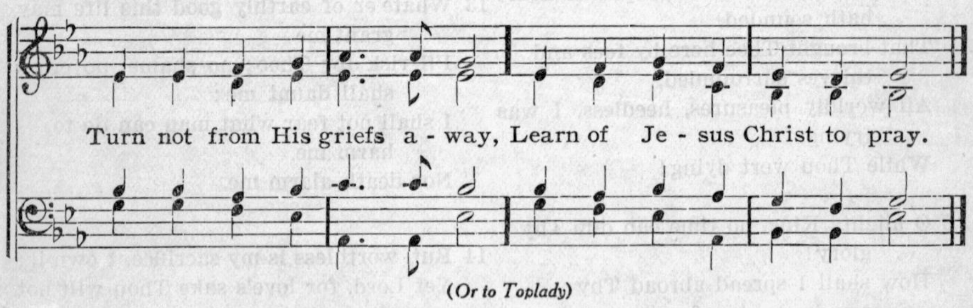
Turn not from His griefs a - way, Learn of Je - sus Christ to pray.

(*Or to Toplady*)

2 Follow to the judgment-hall,
View the Lord of life arraigned;
Oh, the wormwood and the gall!
Oh, the pangs His soul sustained!
Shun not suffering, shame or loss,
Learn of Him to bear the cross.

3 Calvary's mournful mountain climb,
There, adoring at His feet,
Mark that miracle of time,
God's own sacrifice complete;
"It is finished," hear the cry,
Learn of Jesus Christ to die.

4 Early hasten to the tomb
Where they laid His breathless clay;
All is solitude and gloom,
Who hath taken Him away?
Christ is risen! He meets our eyes.
Savior, teach us so to rise.

J. Montgomery, 1820

200 Cowper C. M. L. MASON, 1830

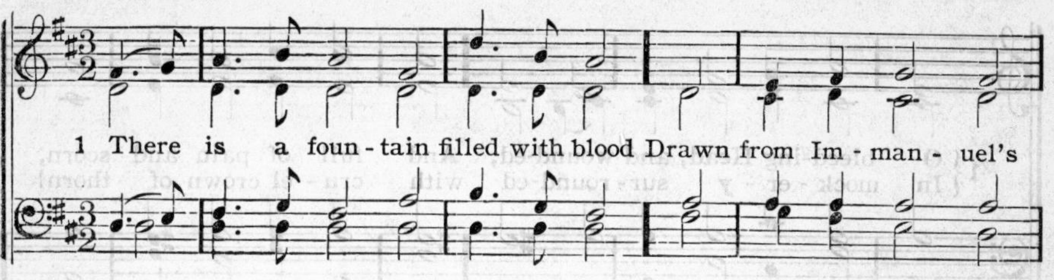
1 There is a foun - tain filled with blood Drawn from Im - man - uel's

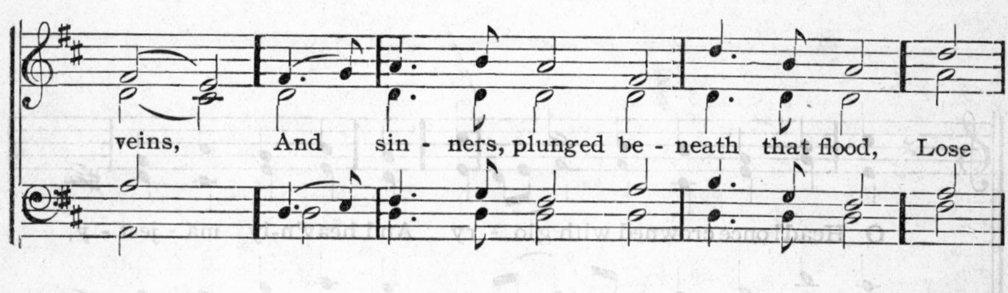
veins, And sin - ners, plunged be - neath that flood, Lose

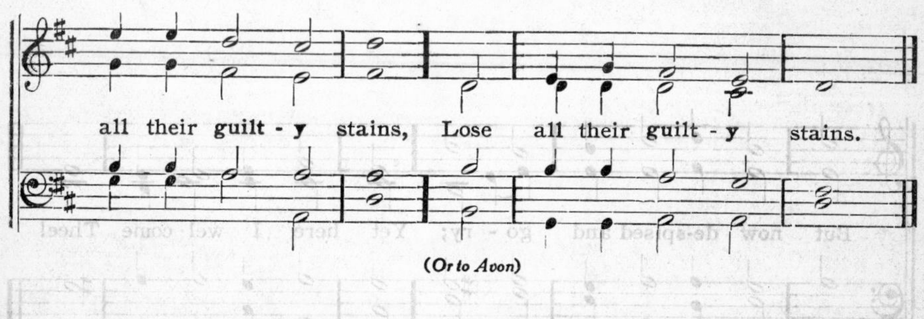
all their guilt - y stains, Lose all their guilt - y stains.

(Or to Avon)

2 The dying thief rejoiced to see
That fountain in his day;
And there have I, as vile as he,
Washed all my sins away.

3 Dear dying Lamb, Thy precious blood
Shall never lose its power,
Till all the ransomed Church of God
Be saved to sin no more.

4 E'er since, by faith, I saw the stream
Thy flowing wounds supply,
Redeeming love has been my theme,
And shall be, till I die.

5 Then in a nobler, sweeter song
I'll sing Thy power to save,
When this poor lisping, stammering tongue
Lies silent in the grave.

W. Cowper, 1771

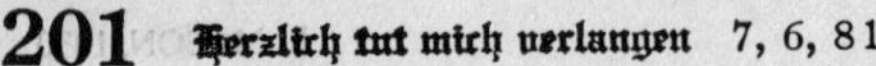

201 Herzlich tut mich verlangen 7, 6, 8l — HANS LEO HASSLER, 1601

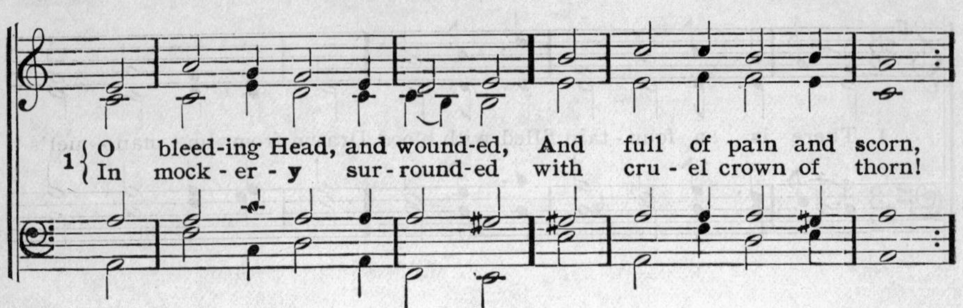
1 O bleed-ing Head, and wound-ed, And full of pain and scorn,
In mock-er-y sur-round-ed with cru-el crown of thorn!

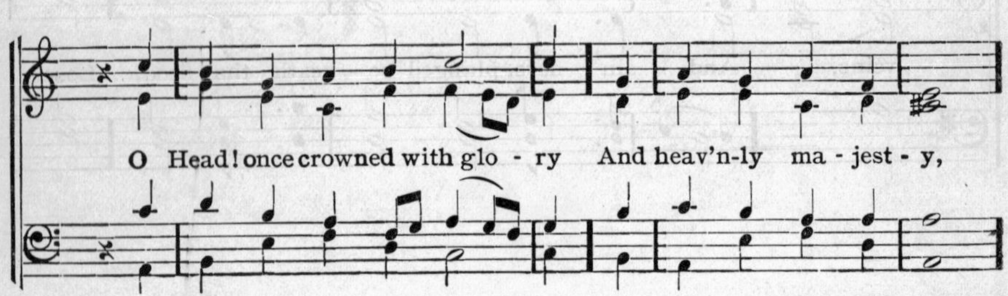
O Head! once crowned with glo-ry And heav'n-ly ma-jest-y,

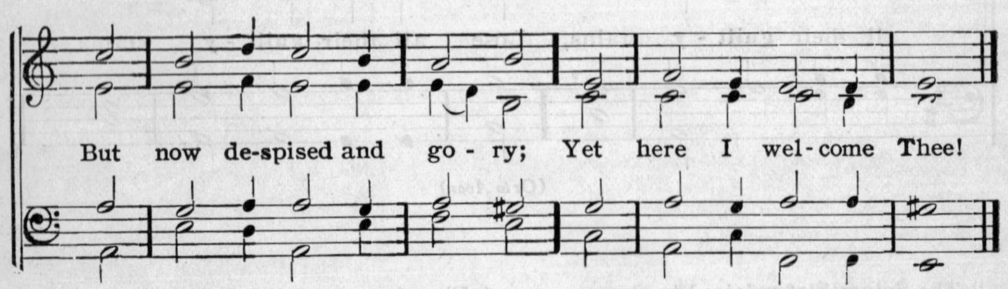
But now de-spised and go-ry; Yet here I wel-come Thee!

2 Men spit upon and jeer Thee,
Thou noble countenance,
Though mighty worlds shall fear Thee,
And flee before Thy glance!
How art Thou pale with anguish,
With sore abuse and scorn!
How does Thy visage languish,
Which once was bright as morn!

3 Now from Thy cheeks has vanished
Their color once so fair;
From Thy red lips is banished
The splendor that was there.
Pale Death with cruel rigor
Bereaveth Thee of life;
Thus losest Thou Thy vigor
And strength in this sad strife.

4 My burden, in Thy passion,
Lord, Thou hast borne for me,
For it was my transgression,
Which brought this woe on Thee.
I cast me down before Thee,
Wrath were my rightful lot,
Have mercy, I implore Thee,
Redeemer, spurn me not!

5 My Shepherd, now receive me!
My Guardian, own me Thine!
Great blessings Thou didst give me,
O Source of gifts divine!
Thy lips have often fed me
With milk and sweetest food;
Thy Spirit oft has led me
To stores of heavenly good.

6 Here I will stand beside Thee,
From Thee I will not part;
O Savior, do not chide me!
When breaks Thy loving heart,
When soul and body languish
In death's last fatal grasp,
Then, in Thy deepest anguish,
Thee in mine arms I'll clasp.

7 Naught ever so much blesses,
So much rejoices me,
As when in Thy distresses
I take a part with Thee.
Ah, well for me, if lying
Here at Thy feet, my life,
I too with Thee were dying,
And thus might end my strife!

8 Thanks from my heart I offer
Thee, Jesus, dearest Friend,
For all that Thou didst suffer;
My good didst Thou intend.
Ah! grant that I may ever.
To Thy truth faithful be;
When soul and body sever,
May I be found in Thee!

9 When hence I must betake me,
Lord, do not Thou depart!
O nevermore forsake me,
When death is at my heart!
When soul and body languish,
O leave me not alone,
But take away mine anguish,
By virtue of Thine own!

10 Be Thou my Consolation
And Shield when I must die;
Remind me of Thy passion,
When my last hour draws nigh.
Mine eyes shall then behold Thee,
Upon Thy cross shall dwell,
My heart by faith enfold Thee,
Who dieth thus, dies well!

Paul Gerhardt, 1659

202 Wenn wir in hoechsten Noeten L. M.

1 Enslaved by sin, and bound in chains,
Beneath its dreadful tyrant sway,
And doomed to everlasting pains,
We wretched, guilty captives lay.

2 Nor gold nor gems could buy our peace,
Nor the whole world's collected store
Suffice to purchase our release;
A thousand worlds were all too poor.

3 Jesus, the Lord, the mighty God,
An all-sufficient ransom paid:
O matchless price! His precious blood
For vile, rebellious traitors shed.

4 Jesus the sacrifice became
To rescue guilty souls from hell;
The spotless, bleeding, dying Lamb,
Beneath avenging justice fell.

5 Amazing goodness! love divine!
O may our grateful heart adore
The matchless grace; nor yield to sin,
Nor wear its cruel fetters more!

Anne Steele

Good Friday

203 O Lamm Gottes unschuldig 7,7,7,7,7,7,8 N. DECIUS, 1529

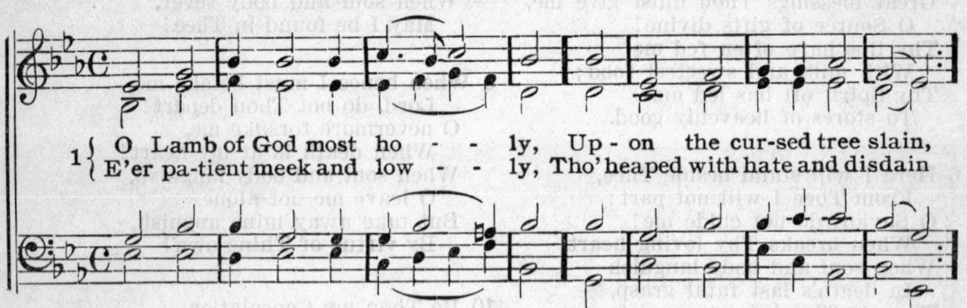
1 { O Lamb of God most ho - - ly, Up - on the cur-sed tree slain,
E'er pa-tient meek and low - - ly, Tho' heaped with hate and disdain

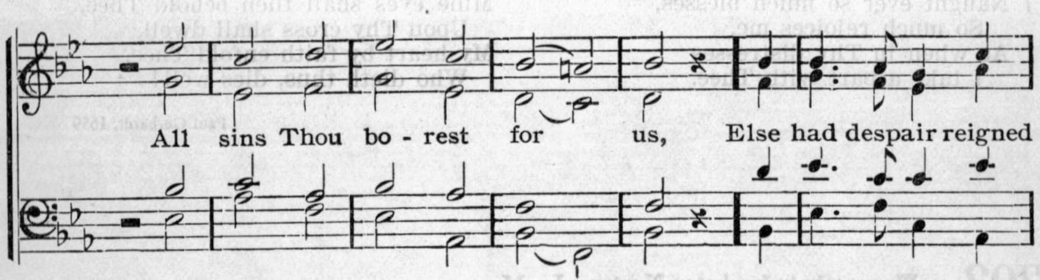
All sins Thou bo - rest for us, Else had despair reigned

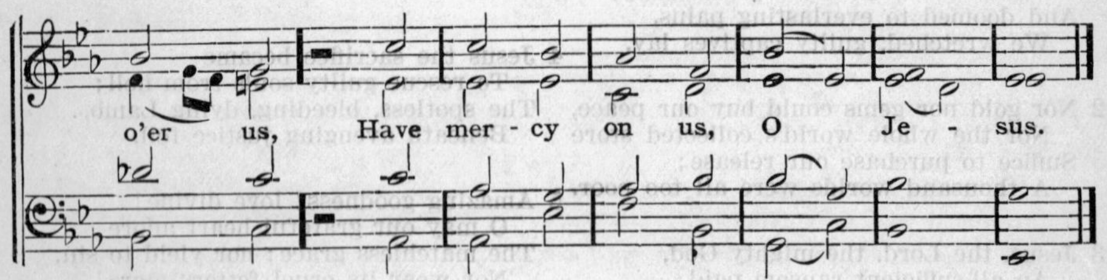
o'er us, Have mer - cy on us, O Je - sus.

2 O Lamb of God, most holy, etc.
Have mercy on us, O Jesus!

3 O Lamb of God, most holy, etc.
Thy peace be with us, O Jesus!

N. Decius, 1528. C Winkworth, Tr. a

204 Marburg L. M. Ad. fr. J. CRUEGER, by H. ILSE, 1910

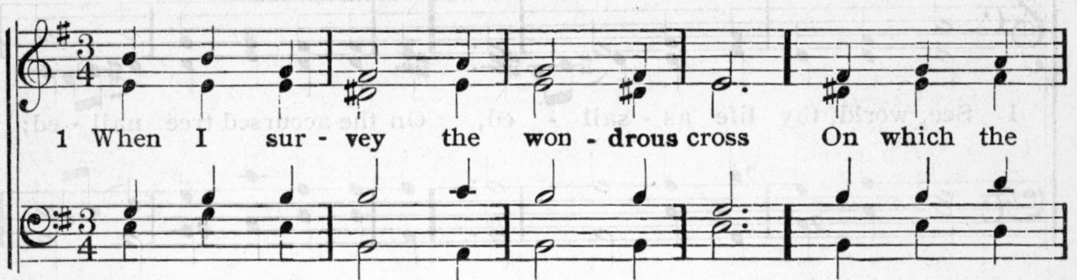
1 When I sur - vey the won - drous cross On which the

Prince of glo - ry died, My rich - est gain I

count but loss, And pour con - tempt on all my pride.

(Or to O Jesu Christ meins)

2 Forbid it, Lord, that I should boast,
Save in the death of Christ, my God;
All the vain things that charm me most,
I sacrifice them to His blood.

3 See, from His head, His hands, His feet,
Sorrow and love flow mingled down!
Did e'er such love and sorrow meet,
Or thorns compose so rich a crown?

4 Were the whole realm of nature mine,
That were a tribute far too small;
Love so amazing, so divine,
Demands my soul, my life, my all.

Isaac Watts, 1709 a

205 O Welt, sieh hier dein Leben 7, 7, 6, 7, 7, 8

H. FRIESE, 1703

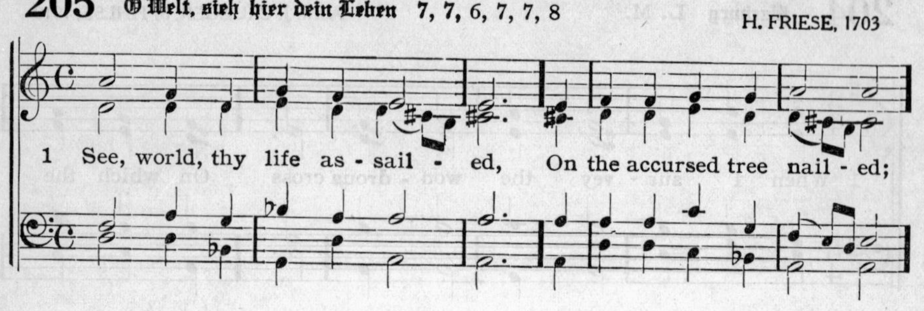
1 See, world, thy life as-sail - ed, On the accursed tree nail - ed;

Thy Sav-iour sinks in death! The might-y prince from heav - en

Himself hath freely giv - en To shame, and blows and cru - el wrath!

(*Or to O Welt ich muss dich lassen*)

2 Come hither now and ponder,
'Twill fill thy soul with wonder,
Blood streams from every pore.
Through grief whose depth none knoweth,
From His great heart there floweth
Sigh after sigh of anguish o'er!

3 Who is it that afflicts Thee?
My Savior, what dejects Thee
And causeth all Thy woe?
Sin Thou committed'st never,
As we and our seed ever,
Of deeds of evil naught dost know.

4 I many times transgressing,
In number far surpassing
The sand upon the coast,
I thus the cause have given,
That Thou with grief art riven,
And with afflictions' scourging host.

5 I've done it, and deliver
Me hand and foot forever,
Thou justly might'st to hell.
The mocking to Thee offered,
The scourging Thou hast suffered,
My soul it was deserved it well.

6 The load Thou takest on Thee,
That pressed so sorely on me,
Than stone more heavily.
A curse, Lord, Thou becamest,
Thus blessings for me claimest,
Thy pain must all my comfort be.

7 Not death itself Thou fearest,
As surety Thou appearest
For all my debts and me.
For me Thy brow is crowned
With thorns, and Thou'rt disowned
By men, and bear'st all patiently.

8 Into death's jaws Thou springest,
Deliverance to me bringest
From such a monster dire.
My death away Thou takest,
Thy grave its grave Thou makest;
O love, O unexampled fire!

9 I'm bound, my Savior ever,
By ties most sacred never
Thy service to forsake;
With soul and body ever,
With all my powers t' endeavor,
In praise and service joy to take.

10 Not much can I be giving
In this poor life I'm living,
But one thing do I say:
Thy death and sorrows ever,
Till soul from body sever,
My heart remember shall for aye.

11 Before mine eyes I'll place them,
And joyfully embrace them,
Wherever I may be,
They'll be a glass revealing
Pure innocence, and sealing
Love and unfeigned sincerity.

12 Of sin how great the danger;
How it excites God's anger;
How doth His vengeance burn;
How sternly He chastiseth;
How His wrath's flood ariseth:—
Shall I from all Thy suff'rings learn.

13 From them shall I be learning,
How I may be adorning,
My heart with quietness,
And how I still should love them
Whose malice aye doth move them
To grieve me by their wickedness.

14 When tongues of bad men grieve me,
Of peace and name deprive me,
My restive heart I'll still;
Their evil deeds enduring,
Of pardon free assuring
My neighbor for his every ill.

15 I'll on the cross unite me
To Thee, what doth delight me
I'll there renounce for aye.
Whate'er Thy Spirit's grieving,
There I'll for aye be leaving
As much as in my strength doth lay.

16 Thy groaning and Thy sighing,
Thy thousand tears and crying,
That once were heard from Thee.
They'll lead me to Thy glory,
Where I shall joy before Thee,
And evermore at rest shall be!

Paul Gerhardt, 1653. J. Kelly, Tr. a

206 Nun laßt uns den Leib L. M.

1 Thy soul, O Jesus, hallow me,
Thy Spirit steep me all in Thee,
Thy body, pierced by ruthless steel,
My wretched soul and body heal.

2 The water from Thy side that poured
For me a cleansing bath afford,
And all Thy blood, with life divine,
Revive this weakened heart of mine.

3 The sweat of death upon Thy face
Deliver me from death's embrace,
And all Thy passion, cross, and pain,
With strength my feebleness sustain.

4 O Christ, turn not away from me,
Receive and hide me all in Thee,
Within Thy holy wounds inclose,
And keep me safe from all my foes.

5 In death's dark hour with me abide,
And place me, Savior, at Thy side,
Where with Thy saints I shall adore
And praise Thee, Lord, forevermore.

Scheffler (Angelus), † 1677 M. Loy, Tr. a

207 Da Jesus an des Kreuzes Stamm

8, 8, 7, 8, 7 — ANCIENT, 1537

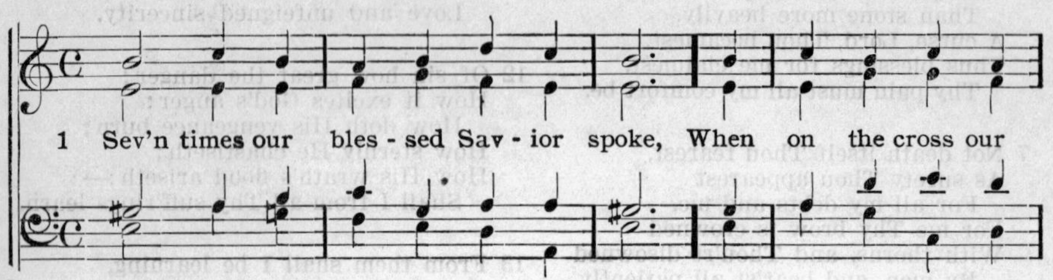
1 Sev'n times our bles - sed Sav - ior spoke, When on the cross our

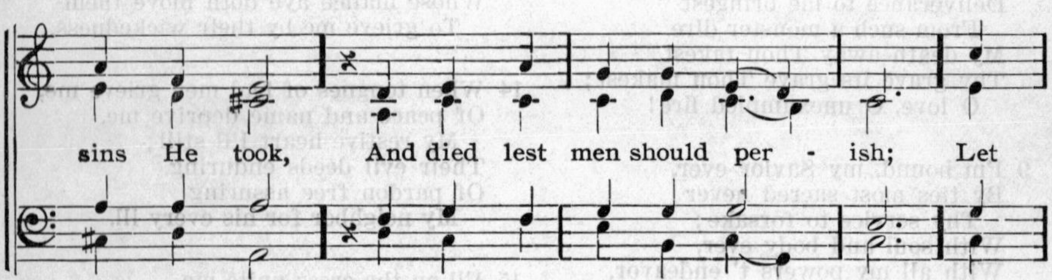
sins He took, And died lest men should per - ish; Let

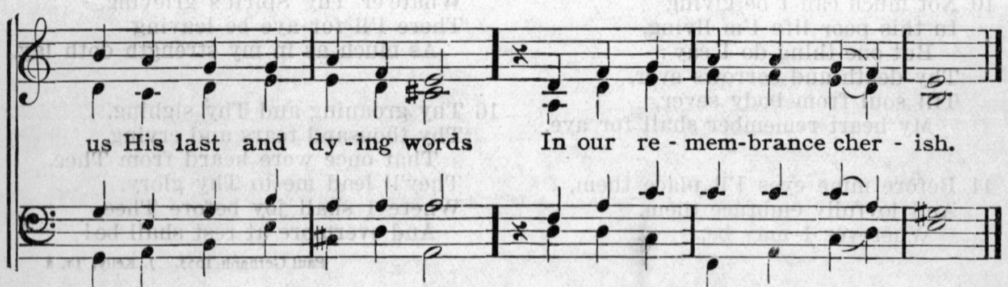
us His last and dy - ing words In our re - mem - brance cher - ish.

2 "Father, forgive these men, for lo!
They truly know not what they do!"
So far His love extended:
Forgive us, Lord, for we, too, have
Through ignorance offended.

3 Now to the contrite thief He cries:
"Thou, verily, in Paradise
Shalt meet me ere tomorrow:"
Lord, take us to Thy kingdom soon,
Who linger here in sorrow.

4 To weeping Mary, standing by,
"Behold thy Son!" now hear Him cry;
To John, "Behold thy mother!"
Provide, O Lord, for those we leave,
Let each befriend the other.

5 The Savior's fourth word was, "I thirst!"
O mighty Prince of Life, Thy thirst
For us and our salvation
Is truly great: do help us then
That we escape damnation.

6 The fifth, "My God, my God, O why
Forsake me?" Hark, the awful cry!
Lord, Thou wast here forsaken,
That we might be received on high;
Let this hope not be shaken.

7 The sixth, when victory was won,
"'Tis finished!" for Thy work was done.
Grant, Lord, that onward pressing
We may the work Thou dost impose
Fulfill with Thine own blessing.

8 The last, as woe and sufferings end,
"O God my Father, I commend
Into Thy hands my spirit:"
Be this, dear Lord, my dying wish;
O heavenly Father, hear it.

9 Whoe'er, by sense of sin oppressed,
Upon these words his thoughts will rest,
He joy and hope obtaineth,
And, through God's love and boundless grace,
A peaceful conscience gaineth.

10 O Jesus Christ, Thou Crucified,
Who hast for our offences died,
Grant that we e'er may ponder
Thy wounds, Thy cross, Thy bitter death,
Both here below and yonder.

Hannoversches Gesangbuch, 1646

208 Caswall (Wenn in Leidenstagen) 6,5,6,5 FR. FILITZ

1 Glo - ry be to Je - sus, Who, in bit - ter pains,

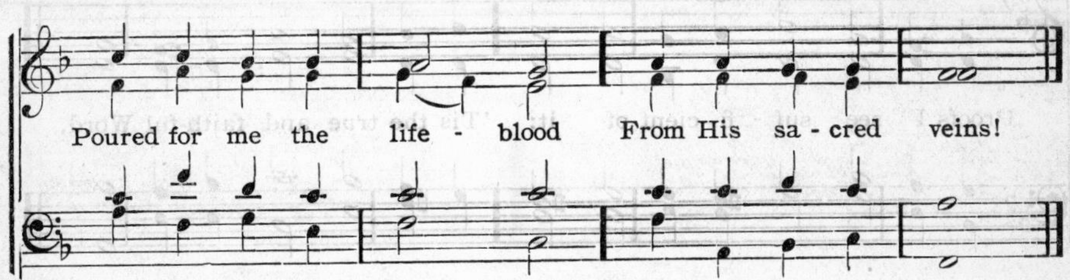
Poured for me the life - blood From His sa - cred veins!

2 Grace and life eternal
In that blood I find;
Blest be His compassion,
Infinitely kind!

3 Blest through endless ages
Be the precious stream,
Which from endless torments
Did the world redeem!

4 Abel's blood for vengeance
Pleaded to the skies;
But the blood of Jesus
For our pardon cries!

5 Oft as earth exulting
Wafts its praise on high,
Angel hosts rejoicing
Make their glad reply.

6 Lift we then our voices,
Swell the mighty flood;
Louder still, and louder,
Praise the precious blood!

From the Italian by E. Caswall

Passion of Christ

209 O mein Jesu, ich muss sterben 8, 7. 8 l PADERBORN MEL. 1850

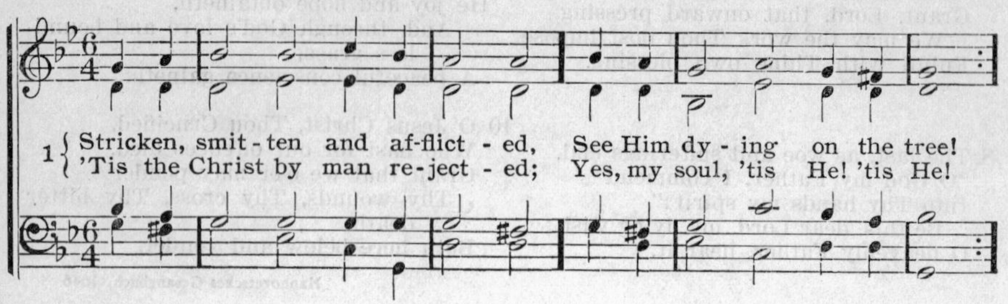
1 { Stricken, smit - ten and af-flict - ed, See Him dy - ing on the tree!
'Tis the Christ by man re-ject - ed; Yes, my soul, 'tis He! 'tis He!

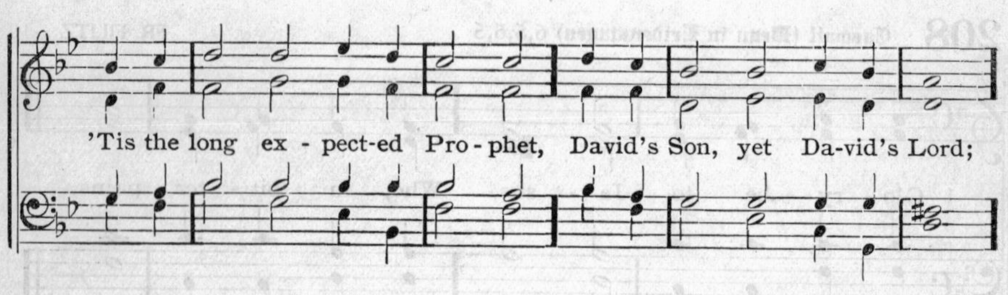
'Tis the long ex - pect-ed Pro - phet, David's Son, yet Da-vid's Lord;

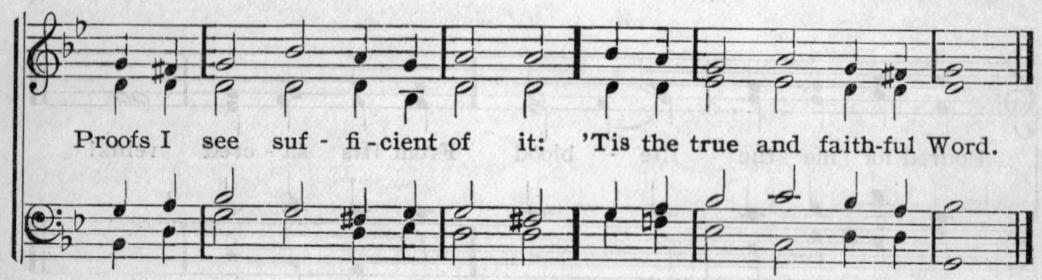
Proofs I see suf - fi - cient of it: 'Tis the true and faith-ful Word.

(Or to Autumn)

2 Tell me, ye who hear Him groaning,
Was there ever grief like His?
Friends through fear His cause disowning,
Foes insulting His distress;
Many hands were raised to wound Him,
None would interpose to save;
But the deepest stroke that pierced Him
Was the stroke that Justice gave.

3 Ye who think of sin but lightly,
Nor suppose the evil great,
Here may view its nature rightly,
Here its guilt may estimate.
Mark the Sacrifice appointed!
See who bears the awful load;
'Tis the WORD, the LORD'S ANOINTED,
Son of man, and Son of God.

4 Here we have a firm foundation;
Here the refuge of the lost;
Christ's the Rock of our salvation:
His the name of which we boast;
Lamb of God, for sinners wounded!
Sacrifice to cancel guilt!
None shall ever be confounded
Who on Him their hope have built.

Thomas Kelley, 1804

210 O mein Jesu, ich muss 8, 7, 8 1

1 Jesus, Refuge of the weary,
Object of the spirit's love,
Fountain in life's desert dreary,
Savior from the world above;
O how oft Thine eyes offended,
Gaze upon the sinner's fall!
Yet upon the cross extended
Thou didst bear the pain of all.

2 Do we pass that cross unheeding,
Breathing no repentant vow,
Though we see Thee wounded bleeding,
See Thy thorn-encircled brow?
Yet Thy sinless death hath brought us
Life eternal, peace and rest;
Only what Thy grace hath taught us
Calms the sinner's stormy breast.

3 Jesus, may our hearts be burning,
With more fervent love for Thee;
May our eyes be ever turning
To Thy cross of agony;
Till in glory, parted never
From the blessed Savior's side,
Graven in our hearts forever,
Dwell the cross, the Crucified.

Jerome Savonarola, 1498

211 Ach wie sehnlich wart ich C. M. WOLFG. BRIEGEL 1687

1 Be - hold the Sav - ior of man-kind Nailed to the shame-ful tree!

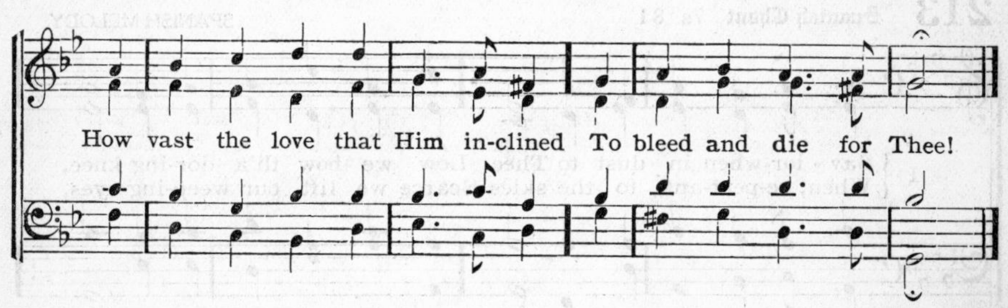
How vast the love that Him in-clined To bleed and die for Thee!

(Or to Dundee)

2 Hark, how He groans! while nature shakes,
And earth's strong pillars bend!
The temple's veil in sunder breaks,
The solid marbles rend.

3 'Tis done; the precious ransom's paid;
"Receive my soul!" He cries:
See where He bows His sacred head!
He bows His head and dies.

4 But soon He'll break death's envious chain,
And in full glory shine.
O Lamb of God! was ever pain,
Was ever love like Thine?

Samuel Wesley, Sr., 1700

212 Consolation (Nar mit Öie) 8, 8, 7, 7, 7 L. M. LINDEMAN, 1812—1887

1 { Come to Cal-vary's ho - ly moun-tain, Sin-ners ru-ined by the fall;
Here a pure and heal - ing foun-tain Flows to you, to me, to all;
In a full per-pet - ual tide, O-pened when our Sav - ior died.

2 Come in poverty and meanness,
Come defiled, without, within;
From infection and uncleanness,
From the leprosy of sin,
Wash your robes and make them white;
Ye shall walk with God in light.

3 Come in sorrow and contrition,
Wounded, impotent, and blind;
Here the guilty free remission,
Here the troubled peace, may find:
Health this fountain will restore;
He that drinks shall thirst no more.

4 He that drinks shall live forever;
'Tis a soul-renewing flood:
God is faithful; God will never
Break His covenant of blood,
Signed when our Redeemer died,
Sealed when He was glorified.

J. Montgomery, 1819

213 Spanish Chant 7s 81 SPANISH MELODY

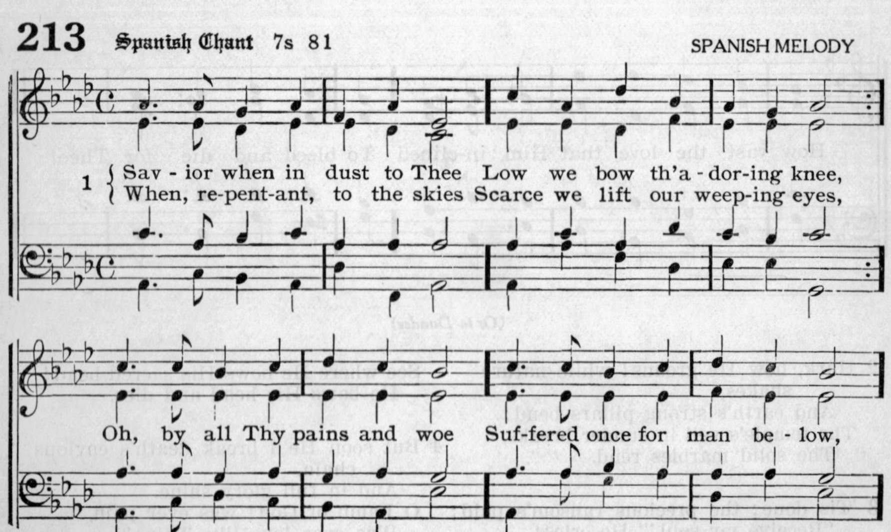
1 { Sav - ior when in dust to Thee Low we bow th'a - dor-ing knee,
When, re-pent-ant, to the skies Scarce we lift our weep-ing eyes,
Oh, by all Thy pains and woe Suf-fered once for man be - low,

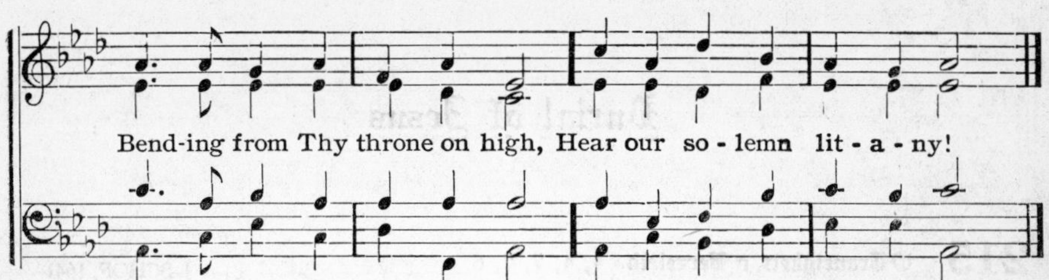
Bend-ing from Thy throne on high, Hear our so - lemn lit - a - ny!

2 By Thy helpless infant years,
By Thy life of want and tears,
By Thy days of sore distress
In the savage wilderness,
By the dread mysterious hour
Of th' insulting Tempter's power:
Turn, O turn a favoring eye,
Hear our solemn litany!

3 By Thine hour of dire despair,
By Thine agony of prayer,
By the cross, the nail, the thorn,
Piercing spear, and torturing scorn;
By the gloom that veiled the skies
O'er the dreadful sacrifice:
Listen to our humble cry,
Hear our solemn litany!

4 By Thy deep expiring groan;
By the sad sepulchral stone;
By the vault, whose dark abode
Held in vain the rising God:
O from earth to heaven restored,
Mighty, reascended Lord,
Listen, listen to the cry
Of our solemn litany!

Robert Grant, 1815 a

214 Avon C. M.

H. WILSON, 1764–1824

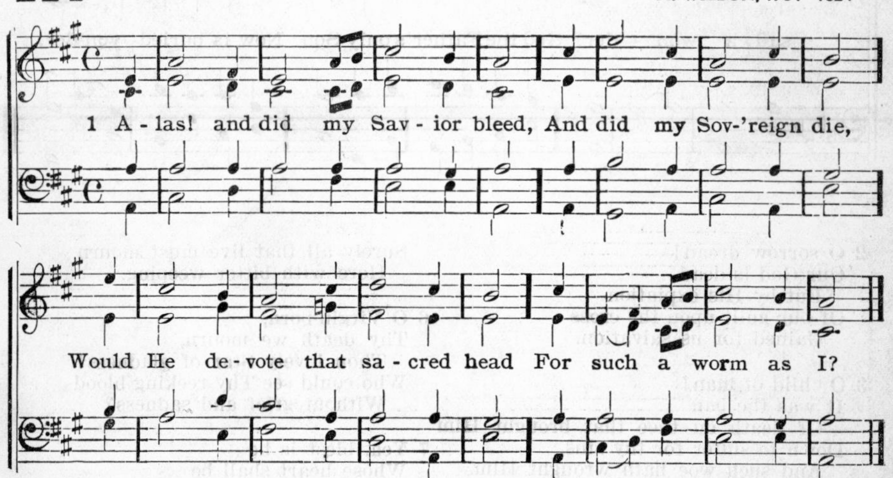
1 A - las! and did my Sav - ior bleed, And did my Sov-'reign die,
Would He de - vote that sa - cred head For such a worm as I?

2 Was it for crimes that I had done
He groaned upon the tree?
Amazing pity, grace unknown,
And love beyond degree!

3 Well might the sun in darkness hide,
And shut his glories in,
When God, the mighty Maker, died
For man the creature's sin.

4 Thus might I hide my blushing face
While His dear Cross appears,
Dissolve my heart in thankfulness,
And melt my eyes in tears.

5 But drops of grief can ne'er repay
The debt of love I owe;
Here, Lord, I give myself away,
'Tis all that I can do.

Isaac Watts, 1707

Burial of Jesus

215 O Traurigkeit, o Herzeleid 4, 4, 7, 7, 6 J. SCHOP, 1641

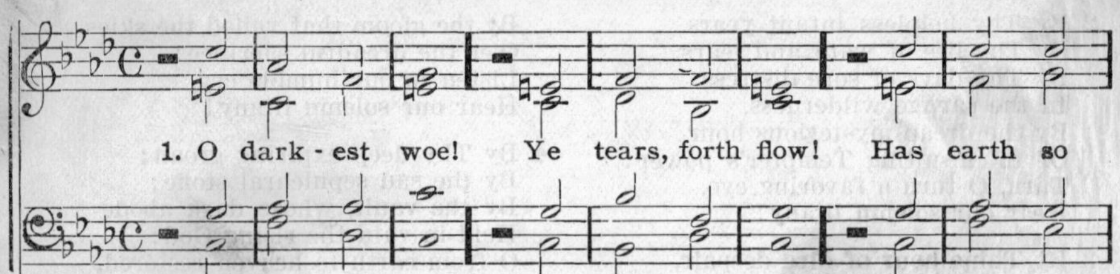
1. O dark - est woe! Ye tears, forth flow! Has earth so

sad a won - der? God the Father's only Son Now is buried yon-der.

2 O sorrow dread!
Our God is dead.
But by His expiation
Of our guilt upon the cross
Gained for us salvation.

3 O child of man!
It was the ban
Of death on thee that brought Him
Down to suffer for thy sins,
And such woe hath wrought Him.

4 See, stained with blood,
The Lamb of God,
The Bridegroom, lies before thee,
Pouring out His life that He
May to life restore thee.

5 O Ground of faith,
Laid low in death!
Sweet lips now silent sleeping!
Surely all that live must mourn
Here with bitter weeping.

6 O Virgin-born,
Thy death we mourn,
Thou lovely Star of gladness!
Who could see Thy reeking blood
Without grief and sadness?

7 Yea, blest is he
Whose heart shall be
Fixed here, who apprehendeth
Why the Lord of glory thus
To the grave descendeth.

8 O Jesus blest,
My Help and Rest,
With tears I now entreat Thee:
Make me love Thee to the last,
Till in heaven I greet Thee!

V. 1 Anon. Johann Rist, 1641

216 O Traurigkeit, o Herzeleid 4, 4, 7, 7, 6

1 So rest, my Rest!
Thou ever Blest!
Thy grave with sinners making;
By Thy precious death from sin
My dead soul awaking.

2 After Thy strife,
Life of my life,
Thou'rt in the tomb reposing,
Round Thee now a rock-hewn grave,
Rock of ages, closing.

3 How cold art Thou,
My Savior, now!
Thy fervent love hath driven
Thee into the cold, dark grave,
That I might gain heaven.

4 Breath of all breath!
I know, from death
Thou wilt my dust awaken;
Wherefore should I dread the grave,
Or my faith be shaken?

5 To me the tomb
Shall be a room,
Where I lie down on roses;
Who by faith hath conquered death,
Sweetly there reposes.

6 The body dies—
Naught else— and lies
In dust, until victorious
From the grave it shall arise
Beautiful and glorious.

7 Meantime I will,
My Savior, still
Deep in my bosom lay Thee,
Ever musing on Thy death:
Leave me not, I pray Thee!

Sal. Franck, 1716

217 Wir danken dir, Herr Jesu Christ L. M. ERFURT H. B. 1663

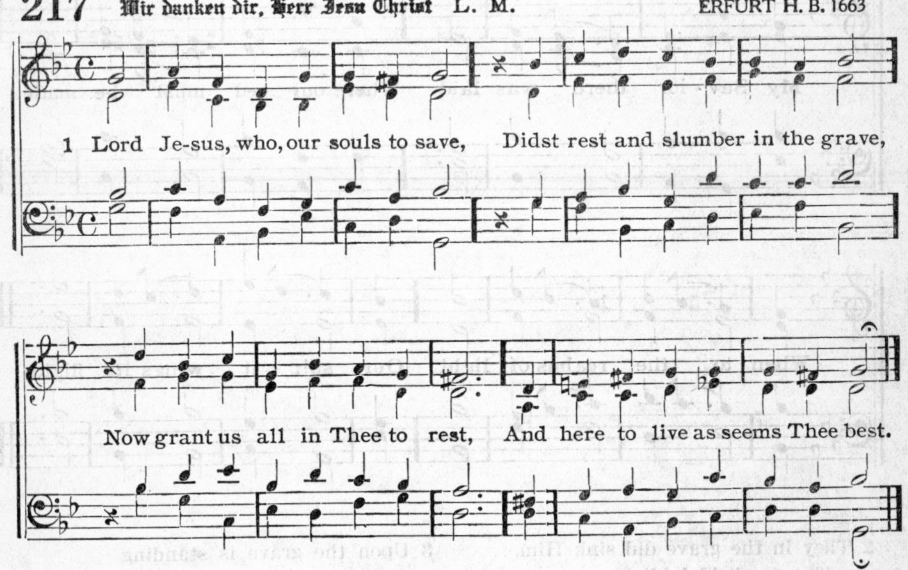
1 Lord Je-sus, who, our souls to save, Didst rest and slumber in the grave,
Now grant us all in Thee to rest, And here to live as seems Thee best.

(*Or to Nun lasst uns den Leib*)

2 Give us the strength, the dauntless faith,
That Thou hast purchased with Thy death,
And lead us to that glorious place,
Where we shall see the Father's face.

3 O Lamb of God, who once wast slain,
We thank Thee for that bitter pain.
Let us share in Thy death, that we
May enter into life with Thee.

George Werner, 1638 C. Winkworth, Tr. a

Easter

218 Auf, auf, mein Herz, mit Freuden 7,6,7,6,6,6,6,6 J. CRUEGER, 1648

1 { A-wake, my heart, with glad - ness, See what to - day is done!
How af-ter gloom and sad - ness Comes forth the glo-rious Sun!
My Sav - ior there was laid Where our bed must be made,
When to the realms of light Our spir - it wings its flight.

2 They in the grave did sink Him,
The foe held jubilee;
Before he can bethink him,
Lo! Christ again is free,
And "Victory!" He cries,
And waveth toward the skies
His banner, for the field
Is by the Hero held.

3 Upon the grave is standing
The Hero, looking round;
The foe, no more withstanding,
His weapons on the ground
Throws down, his hellish power
To Christ he must give o'er,
And to the Victor's bands
Must yield his feet and hands.

4 This is a sight that gladdens
And fills my heart with glee;
Now, naughtsoever saddens
My soul, nor takes from me
My trust or fortitude.
Or any precious good
Which by His victory
My Savior gained for me.

5 Hell and its prince, the Devil,
Now of their power are shorn,
I now am safe from evil,
And sin I laugh to scorn;
Grim death with all his might
Cannot my soul affright;
He is a powerless form,
Howe'er he rage and storm.

6 The world against me rageth,
Its fury I disdain;
Though bitter war it wageth,
Its work is all in vain.
My heart from care is free,
Misfortune now is play,
No trouble troubles me,
And night is bright as day.

7 I cleave now and forever,
To Christ, a member true;
My Head will leave me never,
Whate'er He passeth through;
He treads the world beneath
His feet, and conquers death
And hell, and breaks sin's thrall
I'm with Him through it all.

8 To glory He ascendeth,
I follow Him fore'er,
For Christ, my Head, defendeth
His member from all care:
No enemy I fear,
Because my Head is near;
My Savior is my Shield,
By Him all rage is stilled.

9 He brings me to the portal
That opens into bliss,
Where graved in words immortal
This golden scripture is:
"Who there are scorned with me,
Here with me crowned shall be;
Who there with me shall die,
Shall here be raised as I!"

Paul Gerhardt, 1644. J. Kelly, Tr. a

219 Dedham C. M.

1 Father of Jesus Christ, my Lord,
My Savior, and my Head,
I trust in Thee, whose powerful word
Hath raised Him from the dead.

2 Thou know'st for my offence He died,
And rose again for me;
Fully and freely justified,
That I might live to Thee.

3 Eternal life to all mankind
Thou hast in Jesus given;
And all who seek, in Him, shall find
The happiness of heaven.

4 Obedient faith, that waits on Thee,
Thou never wilt reprove;
But Thou wilt form Thy Son in me,
And perfect me in love.

5 To Thee the glory of Thy power
And faithfulness I give.
I shall in Christ, at that glad hour,
And Christ in me shall live.

C. Wesley, 1742

220 Jesus, meine Zuversicht 7,8,7,8,7,7 J. CRUEGER, 1656

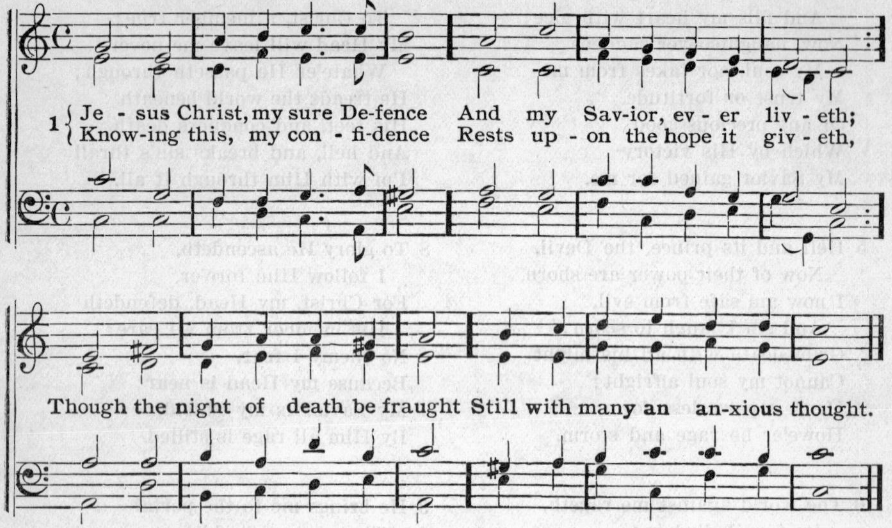
1 { Je - sus Christ, my sure De-fence And my Sav-ior, ev - er liv - eth;
Know-ing this, my con - fi-dence Rests up - on the hope it giv - eth,
Though the night of death be fraught Still with many an an-xious thought.

2 Jesus, my Redeemer, lives!
I, too, unto life must waken;
Endless joy my Savior gives;
Shall my courage then be shaken?
Shall I fear? or could the Head
Rise and leave His members dead?

3 Nay, too closely am I bound
Unto Him by hope forever;
Faith's strong hand the Rock hath found,
Grasped it, and will leave it never;
Even death now cannot part
From its Lord the trusting heart.

4 I am only flesh and blood,
And on this corruption seizeth;
But I know my Lord and God
From the grave my body raiseth,
That with Him eternally
In His glory I may be.

5 Glorified I shall again
With this skin then be enshrouded,
In this body I shall then
See my God with eyes unclouded,
In this flesh I then shall see
Jesus Christ eternally.

6 Then these eyes my Lord shall know,
My Redeemer and my Brother;
In His love my soul shall glow,—
I myself, and not another!
Only there shall disappear
Weakness in and round me here.

7 What now sickens, mourns, and sighs,
Christ with Him in glory bringeth;
Earthly is the seed and dies,
Heavenly from the grave it springeth;
Natural is the death we die,
Spiritual our life on high.

8 Then take comfort, nay, rejoice!
For His members Christ will cherish;
Fear not, they will know His voice,
Though awhile they seem to perish,
When the final trump is heard,
And the deaf, cold grave is stirred.

9 Laugh to scorn the gloomy grave,
And at death no longer tremble,
For the Lord, who comes to save,
Round Him shall His saints assemble,
Raising them o'er all their foes,
Mortal weakness, fear, and woes.

10 Only draw away your heart
Now from pleasures base and hollow;
Would ye there with Christ have part,
Here His footsteps ye must follow;
Fix your hearts beyond the skies,
Whither ye yourselves would rise!

Anon. C. Winkworth, Tr. a

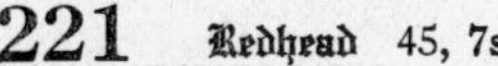

221 Redhead 45, 7s REDHEAD

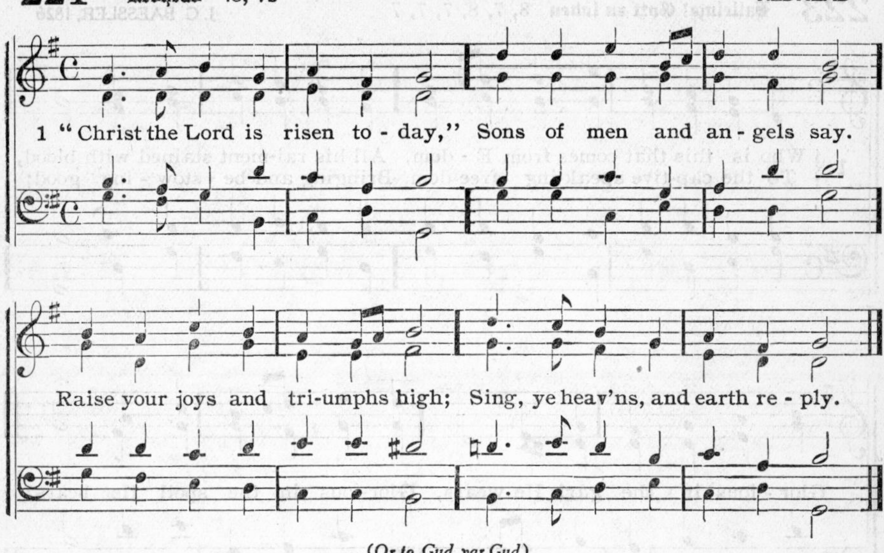
1 "Christ the Lord is risen to-day," Sons of men and an-gels say.
Raise your joys and tri-umphs high; Sing, ye heav'ns, and earth re-ply.

(Or to Gud, var Gud)

2 Love's redeeming work is done,
Fought the fight, the battle won;
Lo! our Sun's eclipse is o'er;
Lo! He sets in blood no more.

3 Vain the stone, the watch, the seal;
Christ has burst the gates of hell.
Death in vain forbids Him rise;
Christ has opened Paradise.

4 Lives again our glorious King;
Where, O death, is now thy sting?
Dying once, He all doth save;
Where thy victory, O grave?

5 Soar we now where Christ has led,
Following our exalted Head;
Made like Him, like Him we rise;
Ours the cross, the grave, the skies!

6 Hail the Lord of earth and heaven!
Praise to Thee by both be given:
Thee we greet triumphant now;
Hail, the Resurrection Thou!

Charles Wesley

222 Jesus, meine Zuversicht 7,8,7,8,7,7

1 Jesus lives! no longer now
Can thy terrors, Death, appall me;
Jesus lives! by this I know,
From the grave He will recall me.
Brighter scenes will then commence;
This shall be my confidence.

2 Jesus lives! to Him the throne
High o'er heaven and earth is given:
I shall go where He is gone,
Live and reign with Him in heaven.
God is pledged; weak doubtings, hence!
This shall be my confidence.

3 Jesus lives! for me He died,
Hence will I, to Jesus living,
Pure in heart and act abide,
Praise to Him and glory giving.
Freely God doth aid dispense;
This shall be my confidence.

4 Jesus lives! I know full well,
Naught from me His love shall sever;
Life, nor death, nor powers of hell,
Part me now from Christ forever.
God will be a sure defence:
This shall be my confidence.

5 Jesus lives! henceforth is death
But the gate of life immortal;
This shall calm my trembling breath,
When I pass its gloomy portal.
Faith shall cry, as fails each sense,
"Jesus is my confidence!"

Christian F. Gellert, 1757 Frances Elizabeth Cox, Tr. 1841—64 a

223 Halleluja! Gott zu loben 8, 7, 8, 7, 7, 7

J. G. BAESSLER, 1826

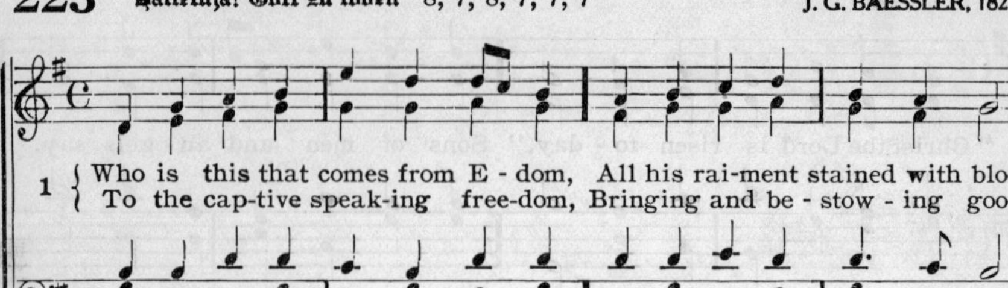
1 { Who is this that comes from E - dom, All his rai-ment stained with blood,
To the cap-tive speak-ing free-dom, Bringing and be - stow - ing good;

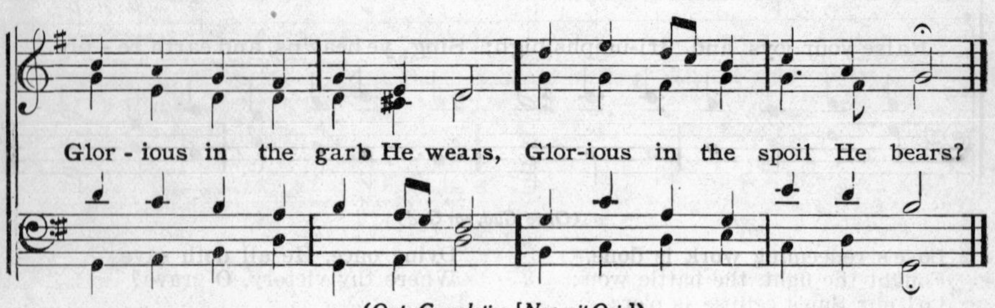
Glor - ious in the garb He wears, Glor-ious in the spoil He bears?

(Or to Consolation [Nar mit Oeie])

2 'Tis the Savior, now victorious,
Traveling onward in His might;
'Tis the Savior; O how glorious
To His people is the sight!
Satan conquered and the grave,
Jesus now is strong to save.

3 Why that blood His raiment staining?
'Tis the blood of many slain;
Of His foes there's none remaining,
None the contest to maintain.
Fall'n they are, no more to rise;
All their glory prostrate lies.

4 Mighty Victor, reign forever,
Wear the crown so dearly won;
Never shall Thy people, never,
Cease to sing what Thou hast done;
Thou hast fought Thy people's foes;
Thou hast healed Thy people's woes.

Thomas Kelly, 1809 a

224 Christ lag in Todes Banden 8,7,8,7,7,8,7,4

DR. MARTIN LUTHER, 1524

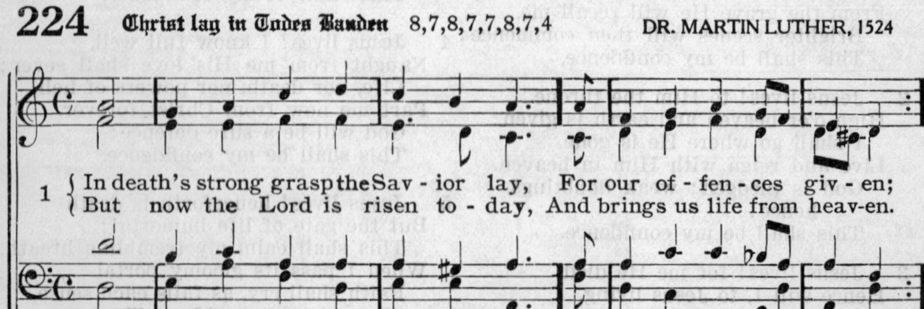
1 { In death's strong grasp the Sav - ior lay, For our of - fen - ces giv - en;
But now the Lord is risen to - day, And brings us life from heav-en.

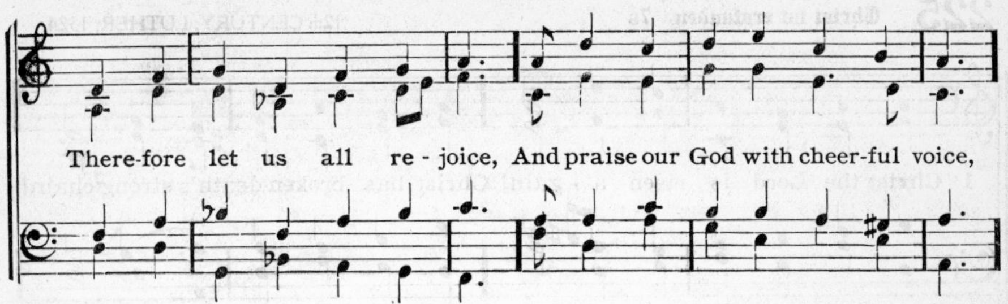
There-fore let us all re-joice, And praise our God with cheer-ful voice,

And sing loud hal-le-lu-jahs. Hal-le-lu-jah!

2 No son of man could conquer Death,
Such mischief sin had wrought us,
For innocence dwelt not on earth,
And, therefore, Death had brought us
Into thraldom from of old,
And ever grew more strong and bold,
And kept us in his bondage.
Hallelujah!

3 But Jesus Christ, God's only Son,
To our low state descended,
The cause of Death he has undone,
His power forever ended,
Ruined all his right and claim,
And left him nothing but the name,—
His sting is lost forever.
Hallelujah!

4 It was a strange and dreadful fray,
When Death and Life contended;
But it was Life that won the day,
The reign of Death was ended.
Holy Scripture plainly saith,
That Death is swallowed up by Death,
Made henceforth a derision.
Hallelujah!

5 Here the true Paschal Lamb we see,
Whom God so freely gave us;
He died on the accursed tree,
So strong His love! to save us.
See! His blood doth mark our door,
Faith points to it, Death passes o'er,
The Murderer can not harm us.
Hallelujah!

6 So let us keep the festival
With heartfelt exultation.
Christ is Himself the Joy of all,
The Sun of our salvation.
By His grace He doth impart
Eternal sunshine to the heart;
The night of sin is ended.
Hallelujah!

7 Then let us feast this Easter-day
On Christ, the Bread of heaven;
The Word of grace hath purged away
The old and evil leaven;
Christ alone our souls will feed,
He is our meat and drink indeed,
Faith lives upon no other.
Hallelujah!

Dr. Martin Luther, 1524

225 Christ ist erstanden 7s

12th CENTURY. LUTHER, 1524

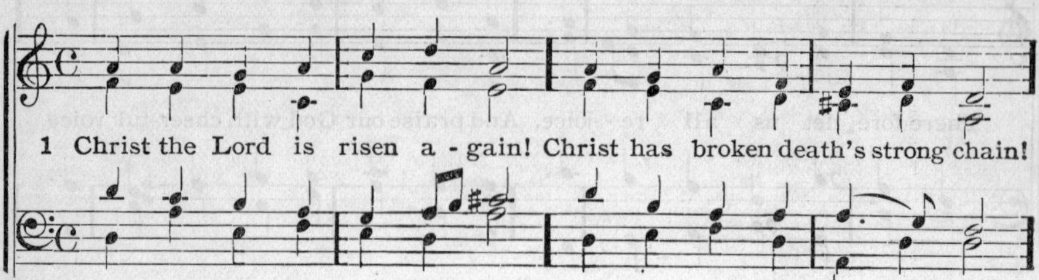
1 Christ the Lord is risen a - gain! Christ has broken death's strong chain!

Hark, the angels shout for joy, Singing ev-er-more on high: Hal - le - lu - jah!

2 He who gave for us His life,
Who for us endured the strife,
Is our Paschal Lamb today!
We, too, sing for joy, and say:
Hallelujah!

3 He who bore all pain and loss
Comfortless upon the cross,
Lives in glory now on high,
Pleads for us and hears our cry:
Hallelujah!

4 He whose path no records tell,
Who descended into hell,
Who the strong man armed hath bound,
Now in highest heaven is crowned:
Hallelujah!

5 He who slumbered in the grave,
Is exalted now to save;
Now through Christendom it rings
That the Lamb is King of kings!
Hallelujah!

6 Now He bids us tell mankind
How all may salvation find,
How poor sinners are forgiven,
And through faith may enter heaven:
Hallelujah!

7 Thou our Paschal Lamb indeed,
Christ, today Thy people feed;
Take our sins and guilt away,
That we all may sing for aye:
Hallelujah!

Bohemian Brethren, M. Weiss, 1531. C. Winkworth, Tr. a

226 Es ist genug 10, 6, 10, 9, 9, 4

RUD. AHLE 1560

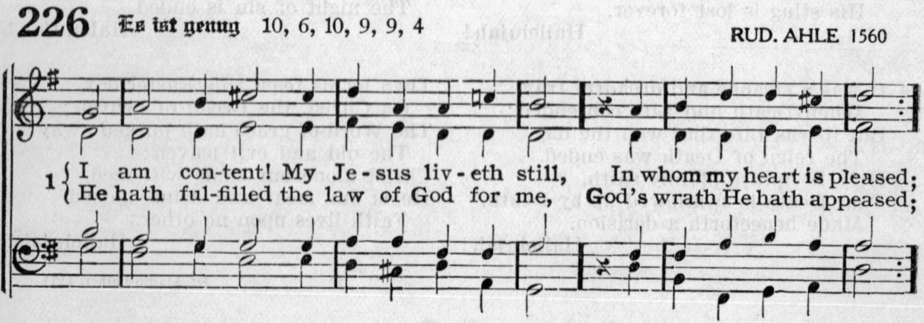
1 { I am con-tent! My Je-sus liv-eth still, In whom my heart is pleased;
He hath ful-filled the law of God for me, God's wrath He hath appeased;

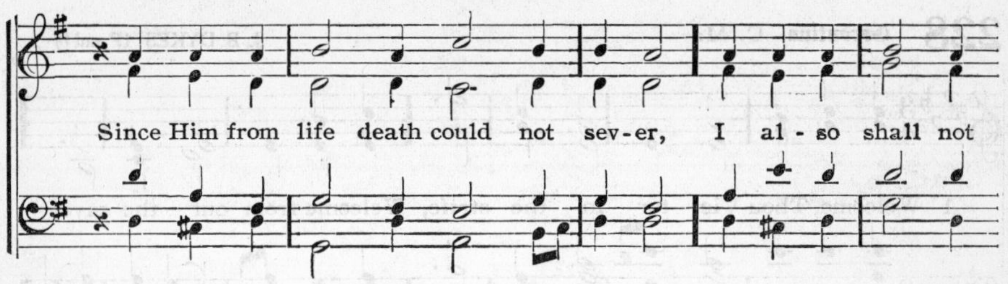
Since Him from life death could not sev - er, I al - so shall not

die for - ev - er. I am con - tent! I am con - tent!

2 I am content! My Jesus is my Head,
His member I will be;
He bowed His head, when on the cross
He died,
With cries of agony;
Now death is brought into subjection
For me, too, by His resurrection.
I am content!

3 I am content! My Jesus is my Lord,
My Prince of life and peace;
His loving heart is thirsting after man's
Welfare and future bliss.
Where He, my Lord and Master, liveth,
His servant also He receiveth.
I am content!

4 I am content! My Jesus is my Light,
My radiant Sun of grace.
His cheering rays beam blessings forth
for all;
Sweet comfort, hope, and peace.
This Easter-sun brings life, salvation,
And everlasting exultation.
I am content!

5 I am content! Lord, draw me but to
Thee,
That from the dead I rise
With Thee, my Head, and enter
cheerfully
Into Thy heavenly joys.
The fetters of my body sever,
Then shall my soul rejoice forever.
I am content!

Franz Joachim Burmeister, 1662 A. Crull, Tr.

227 Ach bleib bei uns L. M.

1 Where wilt Thou go, since night draws
near,
O Jesus Christ, Thou Pilgrim dear?
Lord, make me happy, be my Guest,
And in my heart, O deign to rest.

2 Grant my request, O dearest Friend,
For truly I Thy best intend;
Thou knowest that Thou ever art
A welcome Guest unto my heart.

3 The day is now far spent and gone,
The shades of night come quickly on;
Then stay with me, Thou heavenly Light,
And do not leave me in this night.

4 Enlighten me that from the way
That leads to heaven, I may not stray,
That I may never be misled,
Though night of sin is round me spread.

5 And when I on my death-bed lie,
Help me, and let me gently die.
Abide! I will not let Thee go!
Thou wilt not leave me, Lord, I know.

E. C. Homburg, † 1681. A. Crull, Tr. a

228 Gerontius C. M. J. B. DYKES (P and !)

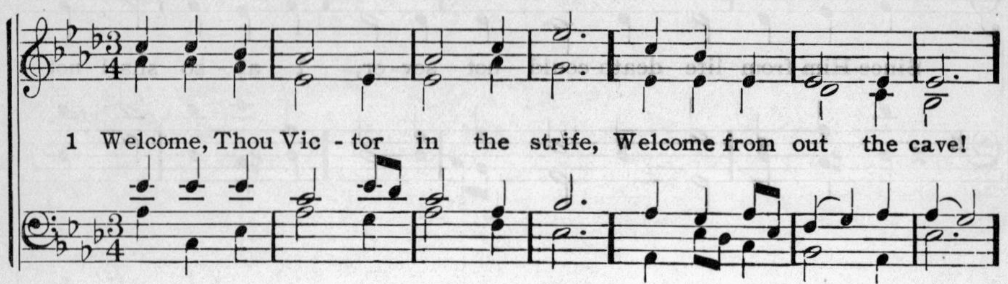
1 Welcome, Thou Vic - tor in the strife, Welcome from out the cave!

To-day we tri - umph in Thy life Around Thine emp - ty grave.

(Or to Nun danket all und)

2 Our enemy is put to shame,
His short-lived triumph o'er;
Our God is with us, we exclaim,
We fear our foe no more.

3 The dwellings of the just resound
With songs of victory;
For in their midst Thou, Lord, art found,
And bringest peace with Thee.

4 O let Thy conquering banner wave
O'er hearts Thou makest free;
And point the path that from the grave
Leads heavenward up to Thee.

5 We bury all our sin and crime
Deep in our Savior's tomb,
And seek the treasure there, that time
Nor change can e'er consume.

6 Fearless we lay us in the tomb,
And sleep the night away,
For Thou art there to break the gloom,
And call us back today.

Benjamin Schmolk, 1712 C. Winkworth, 1855 Tr. ab. a

229 Duke Street L. M. JOHN HATTON, 1790

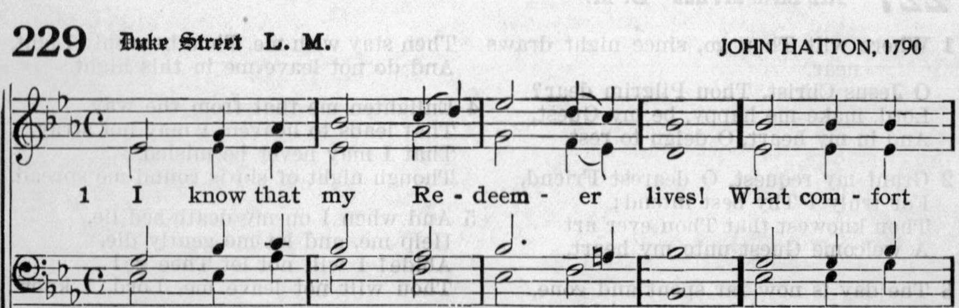
1 I know that my Re - deem - er lives! What com - fort

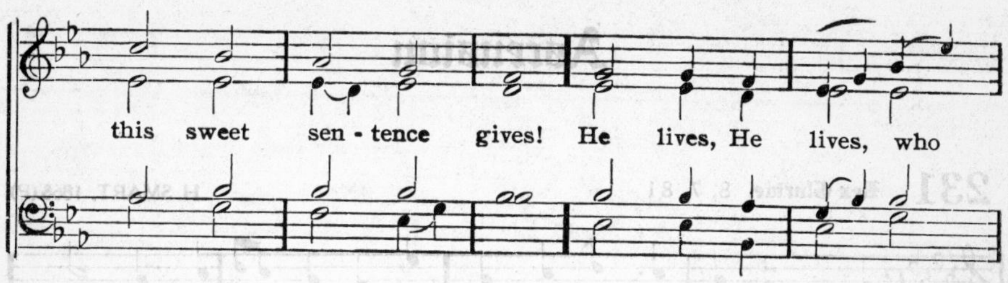
this sweet sen - tence gives! He lives, He lives, who

once was dead, He lives my ev - er - liv - ing Head.

2 He lives triumphant from the grave,
He lives eternally to save;
He lives all-glorious in the sky,
He lives exalted there on high.

3 He lives to bless me with His love,
He lives to plead for me above,
He lives my hungry soul to feed,
He lives to help in time of need.

4 He lives to grant me rich supply,
He lives to guide me with His eye,
He lives to comfort me when faint,
He lives to hear my soul's complaint.

5 He lives to silence all my fears,
He lives to wipe away my tears,
He lives to calm my troubled heart,
He lives, all blessings to impart.

6 He lives, my kind, wise, heavenly Friend,
He lives and loves me to the end;
He lives, and while He lives, I'll sing;
He lives, my Prophet, Priest, and King!

7 He lives, and grants me daily breath;
He lives, and I shall conquer death;
He lives my mansion to prepare;
He lives to bring me safely there.

8 He lives, all glory to His name!
He lives, my Jesus, still the same;
O the sweet joy this sentence gives,
"I know that my Redeemer lives!"

Samuel Medley, 1800

230 Old Hundredth L. M.

1 Lord Jesus Christ, strong Hero Thou,
Grim death Thou hast o'erpowered now,
Thou dost destroy hell's gate and chain,
Dost on the third day rise again.

2 Thou grantest to Thy friends the grace
To look again upon Thy face,
And showest them the glorious prize,
Won when from death Thou didst arise.

3 Grant that we and all Christians may
Partake of this great joy today,
Which by Thy resurrection Thou
To all men freely givest now.

4 Grant us that we may rise from sin,
A holy life to lead begin,
Till we, from sin and pain set free,
In endless Easter live with Thee.

Barthold Helder, 1620. A. Crull, Tr. a

Ascension

231 Rex Gloriae 8, 7, 8 1
H. SMART, 1868 (P)
1 See the Conqueror mounts in tri-umph; See the King in roy - al state,
Rid-ing on the clouds His char-iot To His heav'n-ly pal-ace gate!
Hark! the choirs of an - gel - voic - es Joy - ful al - le - lu - ias sing,
And the por - tals high are lift - ed To re - ceive their heav'nly King.

2 Who is this that comes in glory
With the trump of jubilee?
Lord of battles, God of armies,
He hath gained the victory.
He who on the cross did suffer,
He who from the grave arose,
He has vanquished sin and Satan;
He by death has spoiled His foes.

3 While He raised His hands in blessing,
He was parted from His friends,
While their eager eyes behold Him,
He upon the clouds ascends;
He who walked with God and pleased Him,
Preaching truth and doom to come,
He, our Enoch, is translated,
To His everlasting home.

4 Now our heav'nly Aaron enters,
With His blood, within the veil;
Joshua now is come to Canaan,
And the kings before Him quail;
Now He plants the tribes of Israel
In their promised resting-place;
Now our great Elijah offers
Double portion of His grace.

5 Thou hast raised our human nature
On the clouds to God's right hand:
There we sit in heav'nly places,
There with Thee in glory stand.
Jesus reigns, adored by angels;
Man with God is on the throne;
Mighty Lord, in Thine ascension,
We by faith behold our own.

Wordsworth, 1868

232 Duke Street L. M.

1 Our Lord is risen from the dead,
Our Jesus is gone up on high;
The powers of hell are captive led,
The Victor rises to the sky.

2 There His triumphal chariot waits,
And angels chant the solemn lay:
"Lift up your heads, ye heavenly gates!
Ye everlasting doors, give way!"

3 Loose all your bars of massy light,
And wide unfold the radiant scene;
He claims these mansions as His right;
Receive the King of glory in.

4 Who is the King of glory, who?
The Lord, that all His foes o'ercame,
The world, sin, death, and hell o'erthrew;
And Jesus is the Conqueror's name.

5 Lo! His triumphal chariot waits,
And angels chant the solemn lay;
"Lift up your heads, ye heavenly gates;
Ye everlasting doors, give way!"

6 Who is the King of glory, who?
The Lord, of glorious power possessed,
The King of saints and angels too,
God over all, forever blest!

Charles Wesley, 1741

(Or to Old Hundredth)

233 Von Gott will ich nicht lassen 7,6,7,6,6,7,7,6 J. CRUEGER, 1540

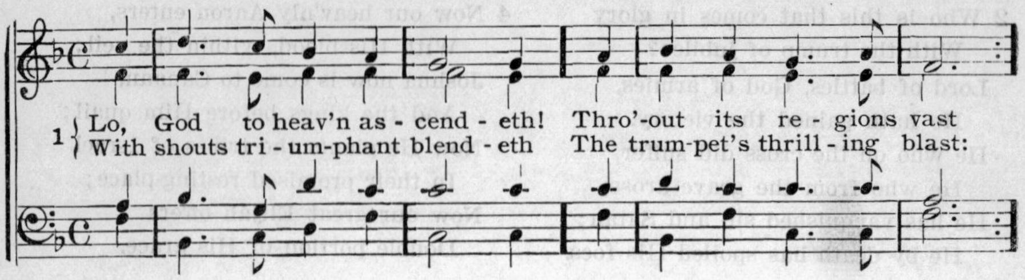
1 { Lo, God to heav'n as - cend - eth! Thro'-out its re - gions vast
With shouts tri - um-phant blend - eth The trum-pet's thrill - ing blast:

Sing praise to Christ the Lord! Sing praise with ex - ul - ta - tion,

King of each heath - en na - tion The God of hosts a - dored!

(*Or to Aus meines Or to Zeuch ein* [*German*])

2 With joy is heaven resounding,
Christ's glad return to see;
Behold the saints surrounding
The Lord who set them free:
Bright myriads thronging come;
The cherub band rejoices,
And loud seraphic voices
Welcome Messiah home.

3 No more the way is hidden,
Since Christ, our Head, arose;
No more to man forbidden
The road to heaven that goes.
Our Lord is gone before,
But here He will not leave us,
In heaven He'll soon receive us;
He opens wide the door.

4 Christ is our place preparing,
To heaven we, too, shall rise,
And, joys angelic sharing,
Be where our Treasure lies;
There may each heart be found,
Where Jesus Christ has entered;
There let our hopes be centered,
Our course still heavenward bound!

5 May we, His servants, thither
In heart and mind ascend;
And let us sing together:
"We seek Thee, Christ our Friend,
Thee, God's anointed Son,
Our Life, and Way to heaven,
To whom all power is given,
Our Joy, and Hope, and Crown!"

6 Farewell with all thy treasures,
O world, to falsehood given!
Thy dross gives no true pleasures;
We seek the joys of heaven:
The Savior is our Prize;
He comforts us in sadness,
And fills our hearts with gladness;
To Him we lift our eyes.

7 When, on our vision dawning,
Will break the wished-for hour
Of that all-glorious morning,
When Christ shall come with power?
O come, thou welcome day!
When we, our Savior meeting,
His second advent greeting,
Shall hail the heaven-sent ray.

Dr. Gottfr. Wilh. Sacer, 1661 Frances Elizabeth Cox, Tr. a

234 Ach Gott und Herr 4, 4, 7, 4, 4, 7 C. PETER, 1655

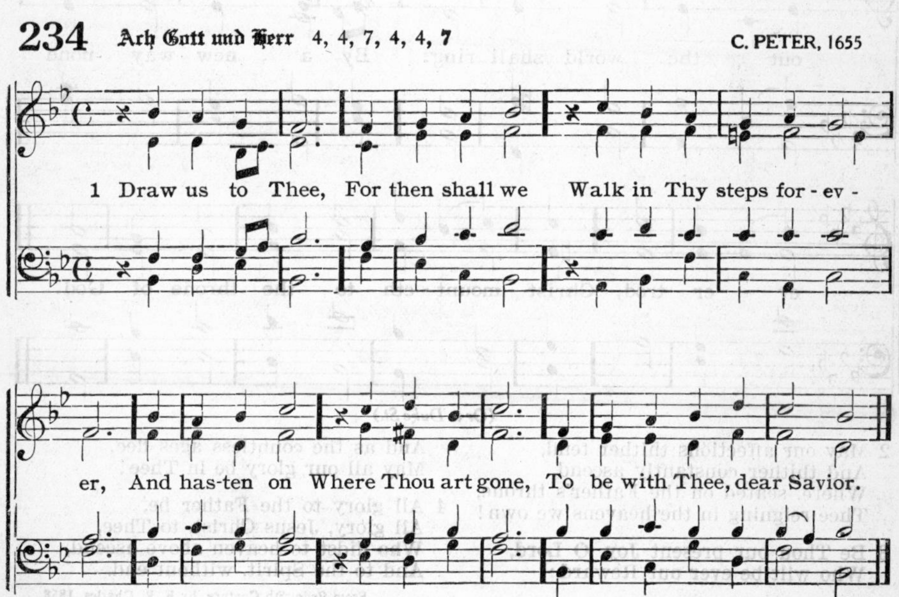
1 Draw us to Thee, For then shall we Walk in Thy steps for - ev -
er, And has-ten on Where Thou art gone, To be with Thee, dear Savior.

2 Draw us to Thee,
Lord, lovingly;
Let us depart with gladness,
That we may be
Forever free
From sorrow, grief, and sadness.

3 Draw us to Thee,
O grant that we
May find the road to heaven;
Direct our way,
Lest we should stray,
And from Thy paths be driven.

4 Draw us to Thee,
That also we
Thy heavenly bliss inherit,
And ever dwell
Where sin and hell
No more can vex our spirit.

5 Draw us to Thee
Unceasingly,
Into Thy kingdom take us;
Let us fore'er
Thy glory share,
Thy saints and joint-heirs make us.

F. Fabricius, 1668 A. Crull, Tr.

235 Louvan L. M. V. C. TAYLOR, 1847

1 A hymn of glo - ry let us sing; New songs thro'-
out the world shall ring: By a new way none
ev - er trod, Christ mount - eth to the throne of God.

(Or to Duke St.)

2 May our affections thither tend,
And thither constantly ascend,
Where, seated on the Father's throne,
Thee reigning in the heavens we own!

3 Be Thou our present Joy, O Lord,
Who wilt be ever our Reward:
And as the countless ages flee,
May all our glory be in Thee!

4 All glory to the Father be,
All glory, Jesus Christ, to Thee,
Who didst to heaven above ascend,
And to the Spirit, without end.

From Bede, 8th Century, by E. R. Charles, 1858

236 Nun freut euch 8, 7, 8, 7, 8, 8, 7

1 Since Christ has gone to heaven, His home,
I, too, that home one day must share;
And in this hope I overcome
All doubt, all anguish, and despair;
For where the Head is, well we know,
The members He has left below
In time He surely gathers.

2 Since Christ has reached His glorious throne,
And mighty gifts henceforth are His,
My heart can rest in heaven alone,
On earth my Lord I always miss;
I long to be with Him on high,
My heart and thoughts forever fly
Where is my only Treasure.

3 From Thy ascension let such grace,
Dear Lord, be ever found in me,
That steadfast faith may guide my ways
With step unfalt'ring up to Thee,
And at Thy voice I may depart
With joy to dwell where Thou, Lord, art;
Lord, hear my supplication!

J. Wegelius, 1637 C. Winkworth, Tr.

Session

237 St. Magnus C. M. — J. CLARKE, (1670—1707)

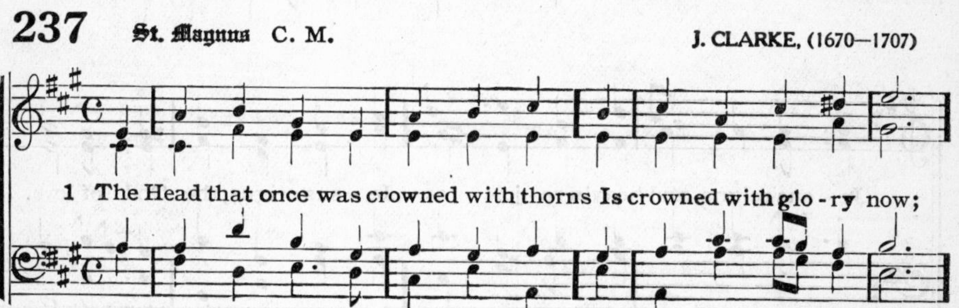
1 The Head that once was crowned with thorns Is crowned with glo - ry now;

A roy - al di - a - dem a - dorns The might-y Vic - tor's brow.

(Or to Bedford)

2 The highest place that heaven affords
Is His by sovereign right,
The King of kings and Lord of lords,
And heaven's eternal Light.

3 The Joy of all who dwell above,
The Joy of all below,
To whom He manifests His love
And grants His name to know.

4 To them the cross, with all its shame,
With all its grace, is given;
Their name an everlasting name,
Their joy the joy of heaven.

5 They suffer with their Lord below,
They reign with Him above,
Their profit and their joy to know
The mystery of His love.

6 The cross He bore is life and health,
Though shame and death to Him:
His people's hope, His people's wealth,
Their everlasting theme.

T. Kelly, 1820

Session

238 Prescott 8, 7, 8, 7, 7, 7 — R. P. STEWART, 1868

1 Hark! ten thou-sand harps and voic - es Sound the note of praise a-bove;
Je - sus reigns, and heav'n re - joic - es,—Je - sus reigns, the God of love.
See, He sits on yon - der throne: Je - sus rules the world a-lone.

(Or to Consolation [Naar mit Oeie])

2 Christians, come, unite your praises
With the angels round His throne;
Soon, we hope, our God will raise us
To the place where He is gone.
Meet it is that we should sing,
"Glory, glory to our King!"

3 Sing how Jesus came from heaven,
How He bore the cross below,
How all power to Him is given,
How He reigns in glory now;
'Tis a great and endless theme
O 'tis sweet to sing of Him.

4 Jesus, hail! whose glory brightens
All above, and makes it fair:
Lord of life, Thy smile enlightens,
Cheers and charms Thy people here.
When we think of love like Thine,
Lord, we own it love divine.

5 King of glory, reign forever,
Thine an everlasting crown;
Nothing from Thy love shall sever
Those whom Thou hast made Thine own,
Happy objects of Thy grace,
Destined to behold Thy face.

6 Savior, hasten Thine appearing;
Bring, O bring the glorious day
When, the awful summons hearing,
Heaven and earth shall pass away;
Then, with golden harps, we'll sing,
"Glory, glory to our King!"

Thomas Kelly, 1804 a

239 Der heilge Geist hernieder kam 8, 8, 8, 8, 4 JOH. HEINR. SCHEIN, 1627

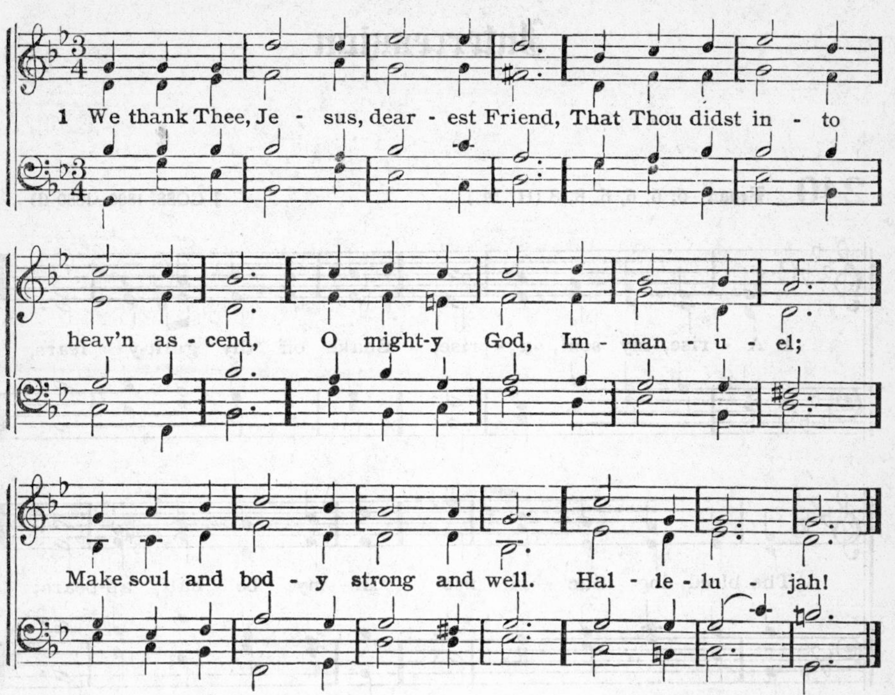
1 We thank Thee, Je - sus, dear - est Friend, That Thou didst in - to
heav'n as - cend, O might - y God, Im - man - u - el;
Make soul and bod - y strong and well. Hal - le - lu - jah!

2 Now all His Christians can rejoice,
And sing His praise with cheerful voice:
Glory to God in heaven's high throne,
Our Brother is God's only Son.
Hallelujah!

3 Ascended to His throne on high,
He yet to us is always nigh;
Thus God and man He ever reigns,
And infinite in power remains.
Hallelujah!

4 Above all heavens in glory raised,
Forever by all angels praised,
All human beings rules our Lord,
All creatures must obey His word.
Hallelujah!

5 He rules and reigns at God's right hand,
And has all power at His command,
All things are subject to His rod—
The Son of man and Son of God.
Hallelujah!

6 The world, sin, Satan, death, and hell
Are vanquished by Immanuel,
Dispute who will His mighty reign,
He still the Victor must remain.
Hallelujah!

7 The man who trusts in Him is blest,
And finds in Him eternal rest;
This world's allurements we despise
And fix on Christ alone our eyes.
Hallelujah!

8 We trust in Him, our Lord and God,
Who hath redeemed us by His blood;
He captive led captivity,
From bitter death to set us free.
Hallelujah!

9 We, therefore, heartily rejoice,
And sing His praise with cheerful voice:
Our Brother, our own flesh and blood,
Is God and King, our greatest Good.
Hallelujah!

10 Through Him we heirs of heaven are made;
O Brother, Christ, extend Thine aid,
That we may firmly trust in Thee,
And live through Thee eternally.
Hallelujah!

11 Amen, Amen, O Lord! we cry;
Do Thou, who art exalted high,
In Thy pure doctrine keep our hearts,
And shield us from the Devil's arts.
Hallelujah!

Dr. Nik. Selnecker, 1587

Intercession

240 Bevan 6, 6, 6, 6, 8, 8 (H. M.) J. GOSS. 1800—1880 (I)

1 A - rise, my soul, a - rise, Shake off thy guilt-y fears,
The bleed - ing Sac - ri - fice In my be - half ap-pears;
Be-fore the throne my Surety stands, My name is writ-ten on His hands.

2 He ever lives above,
For me to intercede,
His all-redeeming love,
His precious blood to plead;
His blood atoned for all our race,
And sprinkles now the throne of grace.

3 Five bleeding wounds He bears,
Received on Calvary;
They pour effectual prayers,
They strongly speak for me;
Forgive him, O forgive, they cry,
Nor let that ransomed sinner die!

4 The Father hears Him pray,
His dear Anointed One;
He cannot turn away,
Cannot refuse His Son;
His Spirit answers to the blood,
And tells me I am born of God.

5 My God is reconciled,
His pardoning voice I hear;
He owns me for His child,
I can no longer fear;
With confidence I now draw nigh,
And "Father, Abba Father!" cry.

Charles Wesley. 1742 a

241 St. Godric 6, 6, 6, 6, 8, 8 (H. M.) J. B. DYKES, 1862 (P)

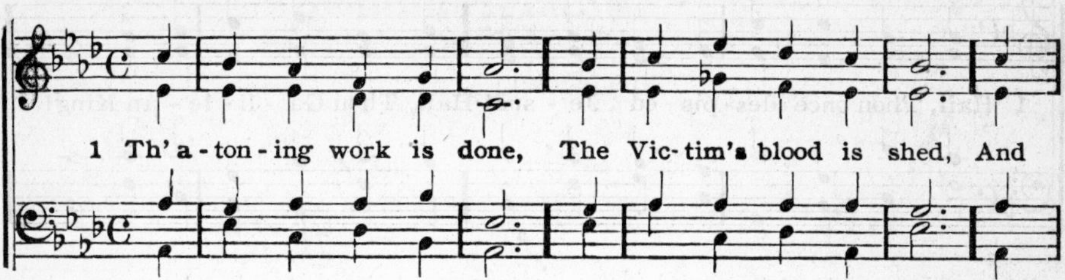
1 Th' a-ton-ing work is done, The Vic-tim's blood is shed, And

Je - sus now is gone His peo-ple's cause to plead: He

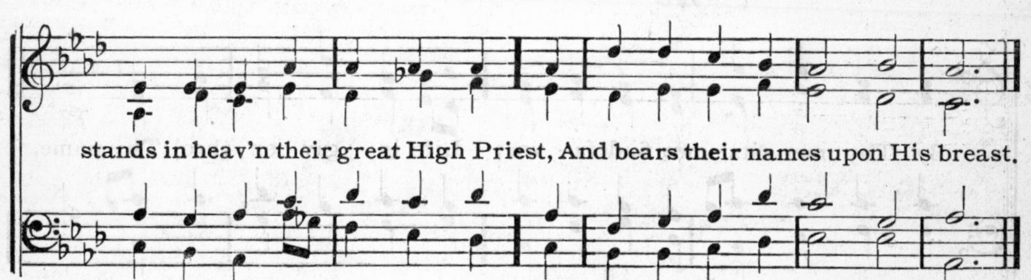
stands in heav'n their great High Priest, And bears their names upon His breast.

2 He sprinkled with His blood
The mercy-seat above;
For justice had withstood
The purposes of love;
But justice now withstands no more,
And mercy yields her boundless store.

3 No temple made with hands
His place of service is;
In heaven itself He stands,
A heavenly priesthood His:
In Him the shadows of the Law
Are all fulfilled, and now withdraw.

4 And though awhile He be
Hid from the eyes of men,
His people look to see
Their great High Priest again:
In brightest glory He will come,
And take His waiting people home.

Thomas Kelly, 1806

242 St. Hilary 8, 7 81 GANTHER

1 Hail, Thou once des-pis-ed Je-sus! Hail, Thou Ga-li-le-an King!
Thou didst suf-fer to re-lease us; Thou didst free sal-va-tion bring.
Hail, Thou ag-o-niz-ing Sav-ior, Bear-er of our sin and shame!
By Thy mer-its we find fa-vor; Life is giv-en thro' Thy name.

(Or to Autumn)

2 Paschal Lamb, by God appointed,
All our sins on Thee were laid;
By almighty love anointed,
Thou hast full atonement made.
All Thy people are forgiven
Through the virtue of Thy blood;
Open is the gate of heaven;
Peace is made 'twixt man and God.

3 Jesus, hail! enthroned in glory,
There forever to abide;
All the heavenly host adore Thee,
Seated at Thy Father's side.
There for sinners Thou art pleading,
There Thou dost our place prepare,
Ever for us interceding,
Till in glory we appear.

4 Worship, honor, power, and blessing,
Thou art worthy to receive;
Loudest praises, without ceasing,
Meet it is for us to give.
Help, ye bright angelic spirits,
Bring your sweetest, noblest lays;
Help to sing our Savior's merits,
Help to chant Immanuel's praise.

John Bakewell, 1760, v. 3 a by M. Toplady, 1776

243 Horton 7s

X. S. Von WARTENSEE

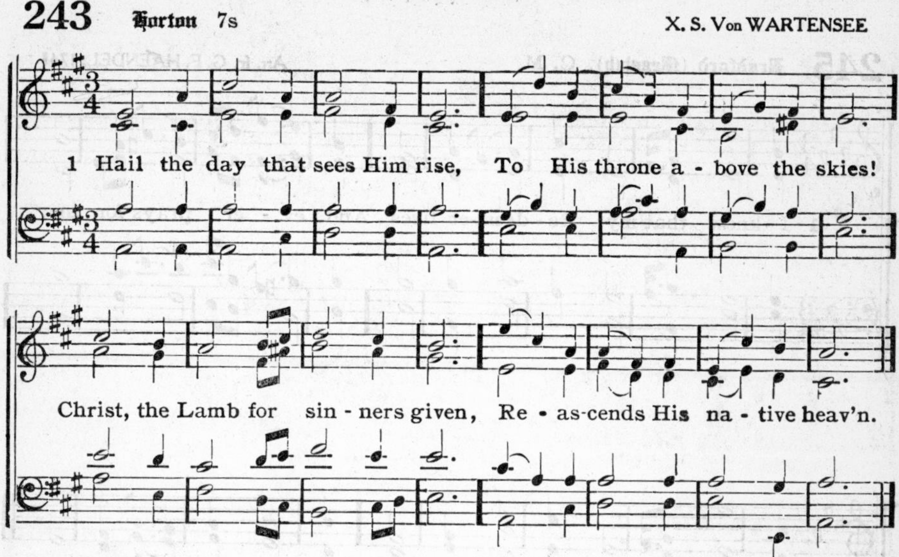
1 Hail the day that sees Him rise, To His throne a - bove the skies!
Christ, the Lamb for sin - ners given, Re - as-cends His na - tive heav'n.

(*Or to Solitude*)

2 There the glorious triumph waits:
Lift your heads, eternal gates;
He hath conquered death and sin;
Take the King of glory in!

3 Him though highest heaven receives,
Still He loves the earth He leaves;
Though returning to His throne,
Still He calls mankind His own.

4 See, He lifts His hands above,
See, He shows the prints of love,
Hark! His gracious lips bestow
Blessings on His Church below!

5 Still for us His death He pleads;
Prevalent, He intercedes;
Near Himself prepares our place,
Harbinger of human race.

6 There we shall with Thee remain,
Partners of Thy endless reign;
There Thy face unclouded see,
Find our heaven of heavens in Thee.

Charles Wesley, 1739

244 Bevan 6,6,6,6,8,8 (H. M.)

1 Jesus, my great High Priest,
Offered His blood and died;
My guilty conscience seeks
No sacrifice beside.
His powerful blood did once atone,
And now it pleads before the throne.

2 To this dear Surety's hand
Will I commit my cause;
He answers and fulfills
His Father's broken laws.
Behold my soul at freedom set;
My Surety paid the dreadful debt.

3 My Advocate appears
For my defence on high;
The Father bows His ears,
And lays His thunder by.
Not all that hell or sin can say,
Shall turn His heart, His love away.

4 Should all the hosts of death,
And powers of hell unknown,
Put their most dreadful forms
Of rage and mischief on,
I shall be safe, for Christ displays
Superior power and guardian grace.

Isaac Watts, 1709

245 Bradford (Messiah) C. M.

An. fr. G. F. HAENDEL, 1741

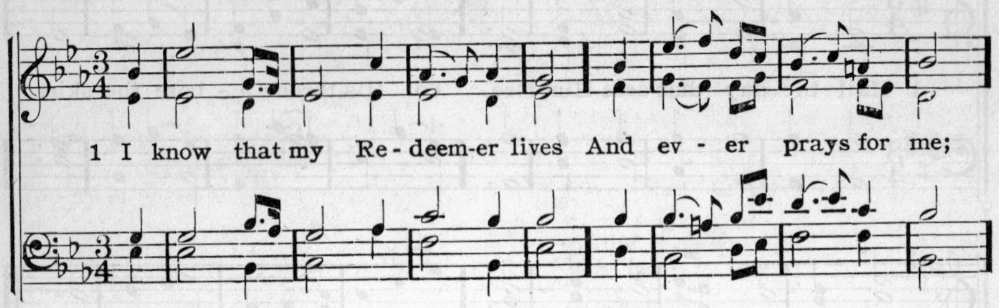
1 I know that my Re-deem-er lives And ev - er prays for me;

A tok - en of His love He gives, A pledge of lib - er - ty.

2 I find Him lifting up my head;
He brings salvation near;
His presence makes me free indeed,
And He will soon appear.

3 He wills that I should holy be:
What can withstand His will?
The counsel of His grace in me
He surely shall fulfill.

4 Jesus, I hang upon Thy word:
I steadfastly believe
Thou wilt return, and claim me, Lord,
And to Thyself receive.

5 When God is mine, and I am His,
Of Paradise possessed,
I taste unutterable bliss
And everlasting rest.

C. Wesley, 1742 ab.

Pentecost

246 Komm, o komm du Geist des Lebens 8,7,8,7,7,7 J. C. BACH, 1680

1 { Come, O come, Thou quick'ning Spir-it, True God from e - ter-ni - ty!
Let us Thy blest grace in - her - it, And our souls be filled with Thee;
Then shall spir - it, life, and light Drive a - way our in - ner night.

(*Or to Gott des Himmels*)

2 Grant our hearts Thy heavenly treasure:
Wisdom, counsel, purity;
That in naught we may take pleasure
Save in that which pleaseth Thee.
Let Thy knowledge spread and grow,
Working error's overthrow.

3 Lead us to our soul's salvation,
Keep us in the paths of grace,
Shield us from the world's temptation
That might foil us in the race;
When we stumble, hear our call,
Work repentance for our fall.

4 Let us trust Thy witness wholly
That we children are of God,
Who rely upon Him solely,
When they pass beneath the rod;
For the Father's chastenings
Bless above all earthly things.

5 Prompt us, that we come before Him
Joyously with hope in view,
Sigh in us, when we implore Him,
Ever plead for us anew;
Then our prayer shall not be vain,
And our faith new strength shall gain.

6 If our soul for comfort languish,
And despondency grow strong,
That the heart must cry in anguish:
"O my God, my God, how long!"
Comfort then the aching breast,
Grant us courage, patience, rest.

7 Mighty Spirit of reliance,
Sure Defence in all our need!
When the foe bids us defiance,
Bid Thy work in us Godspeed!
Grant us weapons for the strife,
And with victory crown our life.

8 Guard, O God, our faith forever;
Let not Satan, death or shame
Ever part us from our Savior;
Lord, our Refuge is Thy name.
Though our flesh would fain say Nay,
Be Thy Word to us still Yea.

9 And when death life's thread is rending,
Then assure us yet the more,
As the heirs of life unending,
Of the glory there in store
Which can never be expressed,
But with which we shall be blest.

Joachim Neander, 1679

247 Wie schoen leuchtet der 8,8,7,8,8,7,4,8,4,8 PH. NICOLAI, 1599

1 { O Ho-ly Spir-it, en-ter in, And in our hearts Thy work be-gin, Thy tem-ple deign to make us;
Sun of the soul, Thou Light di-vine, A-round and in us bright-ly shine, To joy and gladness wake us. }
That we to Thee Tru-ly liv-ing,
To Thee giving Prayer unceasing, Still may be in love in-creas-ing.

2 Give to Thy Word impressive power,
That in our hearts, from this good hour,
As fire it may be glowing;
That we confess the Father. Son,
And Thee, the Spirit, Three in One,
Thy glory ever showing.
O stay and sway
Our souls ever, That they never
May forsake Thee,
But by faith their refuge make Thee.

3 Thou Fountain, whence all wisdom flows,
Which God on pious hearts bestows,
Grant us Thy consolation,
That in our pure faith's unity
We faithful witnesses may be
Of grace that brings salvation.
Hear us, Cheer us
By Thy teaching; Let our preaching
And our labor
Praise Thee, Lord, and bless our neighbor.

4 Left to ourselves we shall but stray;
O lead us on the narrow way,
With wisest counsel guide us,
And give us steadfastness, that we
May ever faithful prove to Thee,
Whatever woes betide us.
Lord, now Heal Thou
All hearts broken, And betoken
Thou art near us,
Whom we trust to light and cheer us.

5 Thy heavenly strength sustain our heart
That we may act the valiant part
With Thee as our reliance;
Be Thou our refuge and our shield,
That we may never quit the field,
Bidding all foes defiance.
Descend, Defend
From all errors And earth's terrors:
Thy salvation
Be our constant consolation.

6 O mighty Rock, O Source of life,
Let Thy dear Word, 'mid doubt and strife,
Be so within us burning,
That we be faithful unto death,
In Thy pure love and holy faith,
From Thee true wisdom learning!
Thy grace And peace
On us shower; By Thy power
Christ confessing,
Let us win our Savior's blessing.

7 O gentle Dew, from heaven now fall
With power upon the hearts of all,
Thy tender love instilling:
That heart to heart more closely bound,
Fruitful in kindly deeds be found,
The law of love fulfilling;
Then, Lord, Discord
Shall not grieve Thee; We receive Thee;
Where Thou livest,
Peace, and love, and joy Thou givest.

8 Grant that our days, while life shall last,
In purest holiness be passed,
Be Thou our strength forever;
Grant that our hearts henceforth be free
From sinful lust and vanity,
Which us from Thee must sever.
Keep Thou Pure now
From offences Heart and senses.
Blessed Spirit!
Let us heavenly life inherit.

Michael Schirmer, 1650, Stanza 2 by unknown author

248 Werde munter 8, 7, 8, 7, 7, 7, 8, 8

1 Send, O God, a gentle shower,
For my heart is dry as sand;
Father, bathe Thy drooping flower,
Water Thou Thy thirsty land;
Let Thy Holy Spirit's boon
O'er me from Thy heavenly throne
Like abundant streams be flowing,
Blessings on my heart bestowing.

2 By a human father, even
Though he is by sin defiled,
Only good gifts will be given
Unto a beloved child;
How much more dost Thou the same
For "Good Father" is Thy name!
Thou wilt send to me Thy Spirit,
Thy good gifts I shall inherit.

3 Jesus, who for my salvation
To the Father didst ascend,
Hear my earnest supplication,
Unto me Thy Spirit send;
Let the Comforter for aye
Bide with me, my strength and stay,
That in faith I may not waver,
Steadfast in the truth forever.

4 Holy Ghost, strength of the simple,
O make Thine abode with me,
Let me ever be Thy temple;
Cheerfully I welcome Thee.
Do Thou purify my heart,
Cast out all things that might part
Me from those sweet joys of heaven
Which by Thee to faith are given.

5 With Thy gifts my heart endowing,
Make it new and clean and fair;
Let it in true love be glowing,
Living in Thy grace fore'er;
Give me courage bold and good,
Sanctify my flesh and blood,
Let me, trusting in Christ's merit,
Worship God in truth and spirit.

6 Thus myself I will deliver,
Lord, to Thee; my soul shall strive
Only after heaven forever,
Until there I shall arrive.
Where the Father, and the Son,
And Thyself in heaven's high throne,
I shall praise and all Thy treasures
In angelic, heavenly measures.

Mauritius Kramer, 1683 A. Crull, Tr.

249 Komm, Gott Schœpfer Heiliger Geist 8,8,8,7

ERFURT ENCHIRIDION, 1524

1 Come, God Cre - a - tor, Ho - ly Ghost, And vis - it Thou the souls of men;

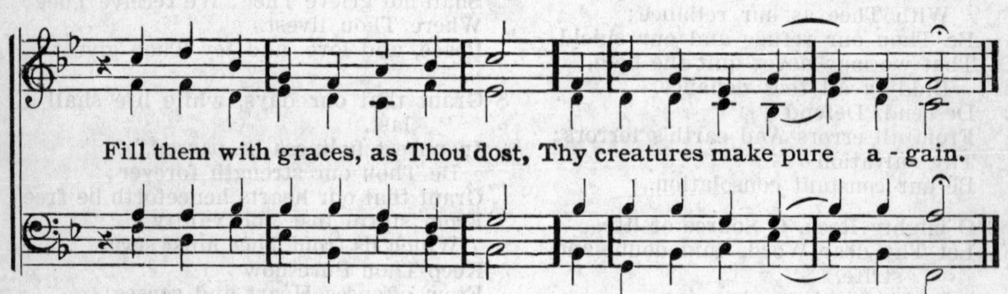
Fill them with graces, as Thou dost, Thy creatures make pure a - gain.

2 For Comforter Thy name we call,
Sweet Gift of God most high above
A holy Unction to us all,
A living Fount, Fire, and Love.

3 Our minds enlighten and refresh,
Deep in our hearts let love burn bright;
Thou know'st the weakness of our flesh;
O strengthen us with Thy might.

4 Thou with Thy wondrous sevenfold gifts,
The Finger art of God's right hand;
The Father's Word Thou sendest swift
On tongues of fire to each land.

5 Drive far from us our wily foe,
Grant us Thy blessed peace within,
That in Thy footsteps we may go,
And shun the dark ways of sin.

6 Teach us to know the Father well
And Jesus Christ, His Son, our Lord,
That in our hearts true faith may dwell,
Spirit of both, aye adored!

7 To God the Father, God the Son
Who from the dead is risen again,
And God the Spirit, Three in One,
Be evermore praise. Amen.

Dr. Martin Luther, 1524 L. W Bacon, Tr. a

250 Redemption L. M.

CHERUBINI

1 Spir - it of mer - cy, truth and love, O shed Thine

in - fluence from a - bove: And still from age to

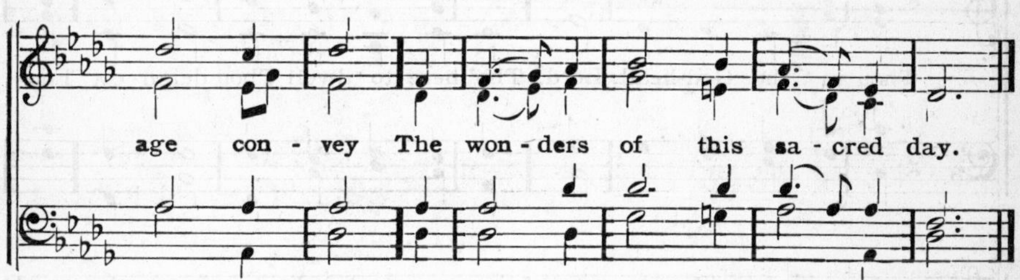
age con - vey The won - ders of this sa - cred day.

(Or to Hursley Or to Melcombe)

2 In every clime, by every tongue,
Be God's surpassing glory sung;
Let all the listening earth be taught
The wonders by our Savior wrought.

3 Unfailing Comfort, heavenly Guide,
Still o'er Thy holy Church preside;
Still let mankind Thy blessings prove,
Spirit of mercy, truth, and love.

Found. Hosp. Coll. 1774

251 Redemption L. M.

1 O Holy Ghost, eternal God,
Blest Comfort for life's rugged road,
With all my heart I pray to Thee;
Hear my entreaty graciously.

2 O Lord, be Thou my Comforter,
Lest in my sins I might despair;
Protect me from the snares of hell,
Grant that in Jesus Christ I dwell.

3 That always I may ready be
To serve this Master faithfully,
And own Him in true living faith
My Lord and Savior unto death.

4 O lead me in the narrow way,
And from the fold let me not stray,
That when this mortal frame I leave,
The crown of life I may receive.

Barthold Helder, 1635 A. Crull, Tr.

(Or to Wenn wir im hoechsten Or to Federal St.)

252 Zeuch ein zu meinen Toren 7,6,7,6,6,7,7,6 J. CRUEGER, 1653

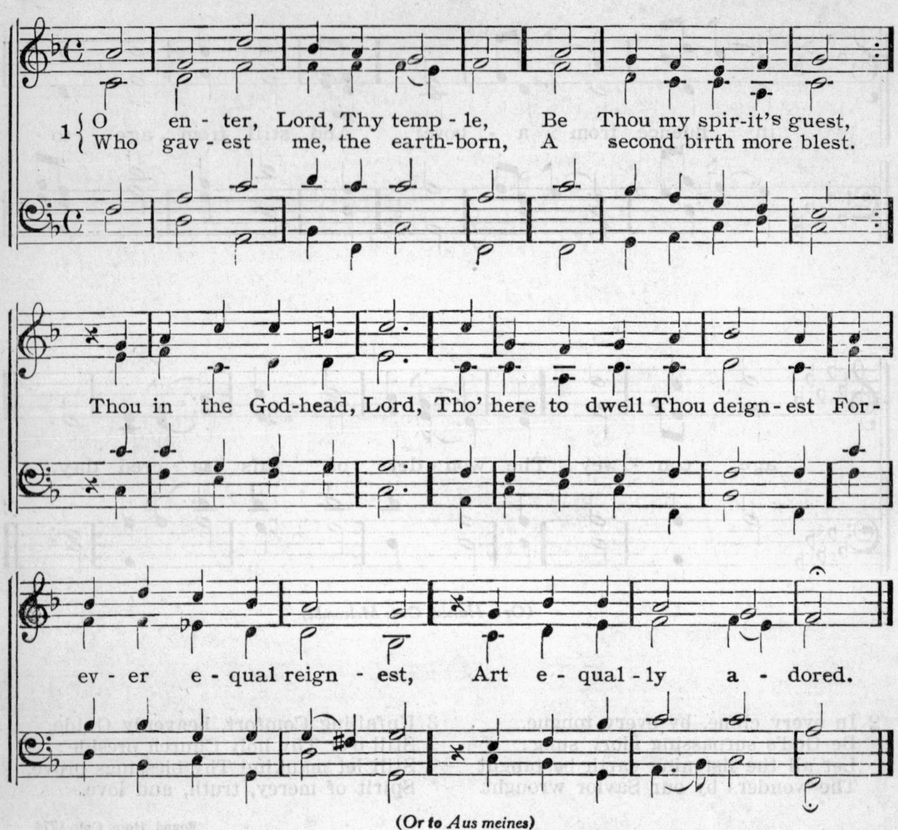
1 { O en - ter, Lord, Thy temp - le, Be Thou my spir - it's guest,
Who gav - est me, the earth - born, A second birth more blest.
Thou in the God - head, Lord, Tho' here to dwell Thou deign - est For -
ev - er e - qual reign - est, Art e - qual - ly a - dored.

(Or to Aus meines)

2 O enter, let me know Thee,
And feel Thy power within,
The power that breaks our fetters,
And rescues us from sin;
So wash and cleanse Thou me
That I may serve Thee truly,
And render honor duly
With perfect heart to Thee.

3 An olive wild by nature
Thou graftedst me anew;
Death preyed upon my vitals,
And claimed me as his due:
But Christ's atoning blood,
In death true comfort granting,
Drowned death with all his vaunting,
In His baptismal flood.

4 Thou art, O Holy Spirit.
The true anointing Oil,
Through which are consecrated
Soul, body, ease, and toil
To Christ, whose guardian wings,
Where'er their lot appointed,
Protect His own anointed,
His prophets, priests, and kings.

5 'Tis Thou, O Spirit, teachest
The soul to pray aright;
Thy songs have sweetest music,
Thy prayers have wondrous might:
They pierce the highest heaven,
Unheard they cannot fall,
Till He His help hath given
Who surely helpeth all.

6 Joy is Thy gift, O Spirit,
Thou wouldst not have us pine;
In darkest hours Thy comfort
Doth aye most brightly shine;
And, oh, how oft Thy voice
Hath shed its sweetness o'er me,
And opened heaven before me,
And bid my heart rejoice!

7 All love is Thine, O Spirit;
Thou hatest enmity;
Thou lovest peace and friendship,
All strife wouldst have us flee;
Where wrath and discord reign
Thy whisper inly pleadeth,
And to the heart that heedeth
Brings love and light again.

8 The whole wide world, O Spirit!
Upon Thy hands doth rest;
Our wayward hearts Thou turnest
As it may seem Thee best;
Once more Thy power make known,
As Thou hast done so often,
Convert the wicked, soften
Thyself the hearts of stone.

9 O Holy Spirit, hear us
And make our sorrow cease;
Thy scattered flock restore now
To union, joy, and peace;
Bid flourish once again
The lands by men forsaken,
The churches spoiled and shaken
By war's unhallowed train.

10 On those that rule our country
O shower Thy blessings down,
And in Thy loving-kindness
Adorn, as with a crown,
With piety our youth,
With godliness our nation,
That all, to gain salvation,
May know Thy heavenly truth.

11 With holy zeal then fill us,
To keep the faith still pure;
And bless our lands and houses
With wealth that may endure;
And make the Foe to flee,
Who in us with Thee striveth,
From out our heart he driveth
Whate'er delighteth Thee.

12 Grant steadfastness and courage,
That bravely we contend
Against the wiles of Satan;
O Lord, Thy flock defend!
Help us to battle well,
To triumph o'er the Devil,
To overcome the evil
And all the powers of hell.

13 Order our path in all things
According to Thy mind,
And when this life is over,
And all must be resigned,
O grant us then to die
With calm and fearless spirit,
And after death inherit
Eternal life on high.

Paul Gerhardt, 1653

253 Schoenste Sonne 7s FR. ENCKHAUSEN (P)

1 Gra-cious Spir - it, Dove di - vine! Let Thy light with-in me shine;
All my guilt - y fears re - move, Fill me with Thy heaven-ly love.
(Or to Mercy)

2 Speak Thy pardoning grace to me,
Set the burdened sinner free;
Lead me to the Lamb of God,
Wash me in His precious blood.

3 Life and peace to me impart;
Seal salvation on my heart;
Dwell Thyself within my breast,
Earnest of eternal rest.

4 Let me never from Thee stray,
Keep me in the narrow way;
Fill my soul with joy divine,
Keep me, Lord, forever Thine.

John Stockton, 1777 a

254 Erfurt 8,6,8,6,8.8 H. ILSE, 1910

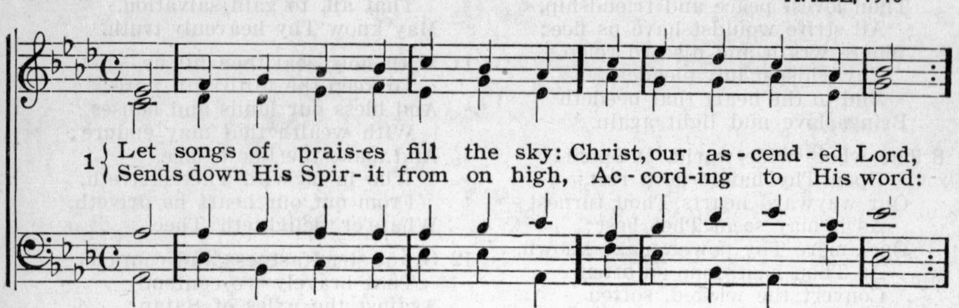
1 { Let songs of prais-es fill the sky: Christ, our as-cend-ed Lord,
Sends down His Spir-it from on high, Ac-cord-ing to His word:

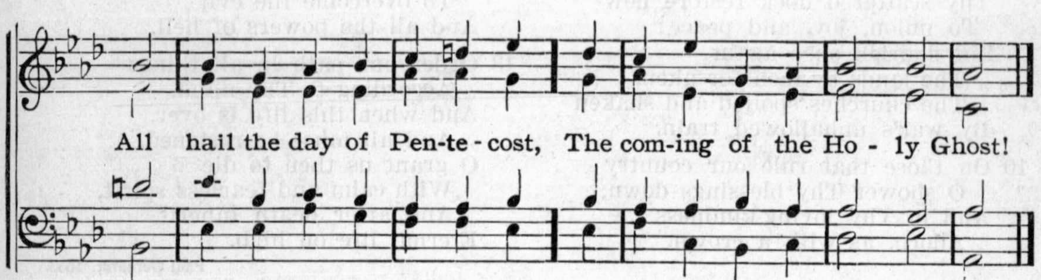
All hail the day of Pen-te-cost, The com-ing of the Ho-ly Ghost!

2 The Spirit by His heavenly breath,
Creates new life within;
He quickens sinners from the death
Of trespasses and sin:
All hail the day of Pentecost,
The coming of the Holy Ghost!

3 The things of Christ the Spirit takes,
And shows them unto men;
The fallen soul His temple makes;
God's image stamps again:
All hail the day of Pentecost,
The coming of the Holy Ghost!

4 Come, Holy Spirit, from above,
With Thy celestial fire;
Come, and with flames of zeal and love
Our hearts and tongues inspire!
Be this our day of Pentecost,
The coming of the Holy Ghost!

Thos. Cotterill, 1819

255 Peterborough C. M. R. HARRISON

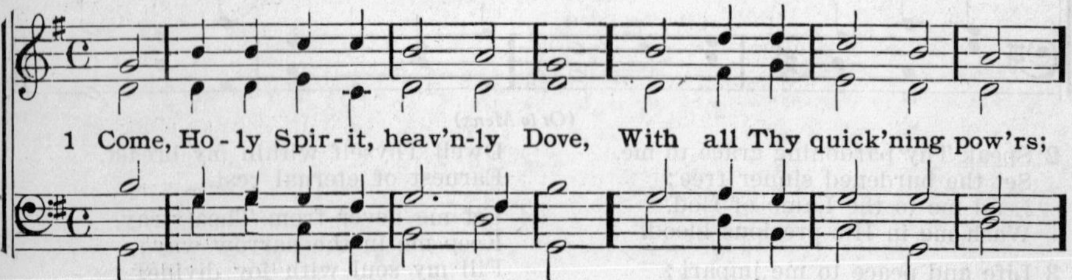
1 Come, Ho-ly Spir-it, heav'n-ly Dove, With all Thy quick'ning pow'rs;

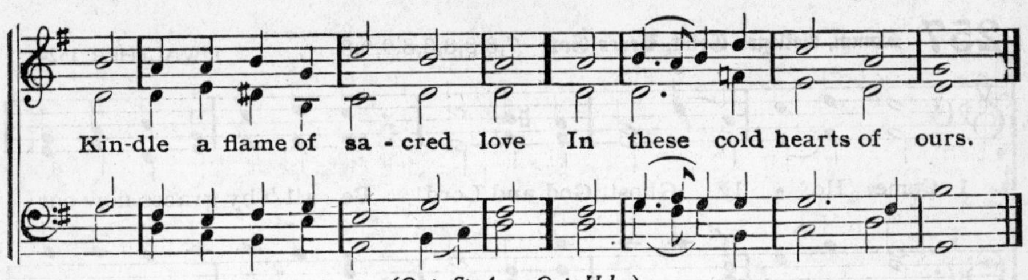
Kin-dle a flame of sa - cred love In these cold hearts of ours.

(Or to St. Agnes Or to Heber)

2 See, how we grovel here below,
Fond of these earthly toys;
Our souls, how heavily they go,
To reach eternal joys!

3 In vain we tune our formal songs,
In vain we strive to rise;
Hosannas languish on our tongues,
And our devotion dies.

4 Dear Lord, and shall we ever live
At this poor, dying rate—
Our love so cold, so faint to Thee,
And Thine to us so great?

5 Come, Holy Spirit, heavenly Dove,
With all Thy quickening powers,
Come, shed abroad a Savior's love,
And that shall kindle ours.

Isaac Watts, 1707

256 St. Constantine 6, 5, 6, 5 W. H. MONK, 1861

1 Ho - ly Spir - it! hear us On this sa - cred day;
Come to us with bless - ing, Come with us to stay.

(Or to Caswall)

2 Come, as once Thou camest
To the faithful few,
Patiently awaiting
Jesus' promise true.

3 Up to heaven ascending
Our dear Lord has gone;
Yet His little children
Leaves He not alone.

4 To His blessed promise
Now in faith we cling:—
Comforter, most holy!
Spread o'er us Thy wing.

5 Lighten Thou our darkness,
Be Thyself our light;
Strenghten Thou our weakness,
Spirit of all might!

6 Spirit of adoption!
Make us overflow
With Thy sevenfold blessing,
And in grace to grow.

7 Into Christ baptized
Grant that we may be,
Day and night, dear Spirit,
Perfected by Thee!

J. Mohr, 1818 Claudia F. Hernamann, Tr.

Pentecost

257 Komm, Heiliger Geist, Herre Gott 7,8,8,8,8,8,9,9,8 J. WALTHER, 1524

1 Come, Ho - ly Ghost, God and Lord! Be all Thy graces now out -
poured On each be-liev-er's mind and heart; Thy fer-vent love to them im -
part. Lord, by the brightness of Thy light Thou in the faith dost men u -
nite Of ev-'ry tongue and ev-'ry na - tion; We, there-fore, sing with ex-ul -

ta - tion: Hal - le - lu - jah! Hal - le - lu - jah!

2 Thou holy Light, Guide divine,
O cause the Word of life to shine;
Teach us to know our God aright,
And call Him Father with delight,
From error, Lord, our souls defend,
That they on Christ alone attend,
In Him with living faith abiding,
In Him with all their might confiding.
Hallelujah! Hallelujah!

3 Thou holy Fire, Source of rest,
Grant that, with joy and hope possessed
We always in Thy service stay,
And trouble drive us not away.
Lord, by Thy power prepare each heart
To our weak nature strength impart,
That firmly here we be contending,
Through life and death to Thee ascending.
Hallelujah! Hallelujah!

Dr. Martin Luther, 1524

258 Mornington S. M.

EARL of MORNINGTON, 1760 (P)

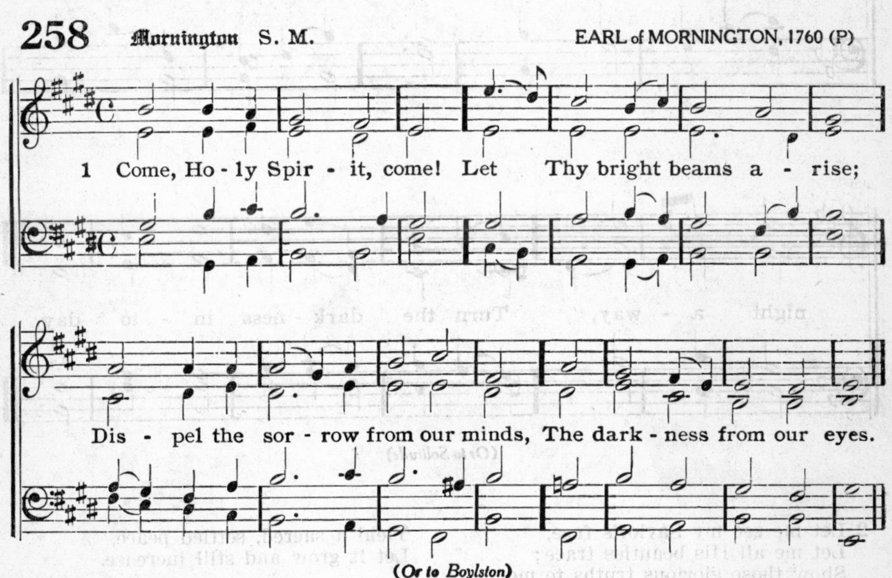
1 Come, Ho - ly Spir - it, come! Let Thy bright beams a - rise;
Dis - pel the sor - row from our minds, The dark - ness from our eyes.

(Or to Boylston)

2 Revive our drooping faith,
Our doubts and fears remove,
And kindle in our breasts the flame
Of never-dying love.

3 Convince us of our sin;
Then lead to Jesus' blood,
And to our wondering view reveal
The mercies of our God.

4 'Tis Thine to cleanse the heart,
To sanctify the soul,
To pour fresh life on every part,
And new-create the whole.

5 Dwell, therefore, in our hearts;
Our minds from bondage free;
Then shall we know, and praise, and love,
The Father, Son, and Thee.

Joseph Hart, a

259 Mercy 7s LOUIS M. GOTTSCHALK, Arr. by EDWIN P. PARKER

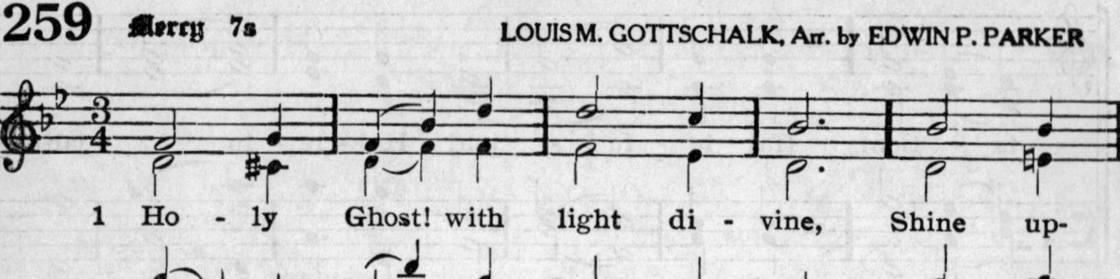
1 Ho - ly Ghost! with light di - vine, Shine up-

on this heart of mine; Chase the shades of

night a - way, Turn the dark - ness in - to day.

(Or to Solitude)

2 Let me see my Savior's face,
Let me all His beauties trace;
Show those glorious truths to me,
Which are only known to Thee.

3 Holy Ghost, with power divine,
Cleanse this guilty heart of mine;
In Thy mercy pity me,
From sin's bondage set me free.

4 Holy Ghost, with joy divine,
Cheer this saddened heart of mine;
Yield a sacred, settled peace,
Let it grow and still increase.

5 Holy Spirit, all divine,
Dwell within this heart of mine;
Cast down every idol-throne,
Reign supreme and reign alone.

6 See, to Thee I yield my heart,
Shed Thy life through every part;
A pure temple I would be,
Wholly dedicate to Thee.

Andrew Reed, 1817

260 Nun bitten wir den heiligen Geist 9,9,11,10,4 13th CENTURY, WALTHER, 1524

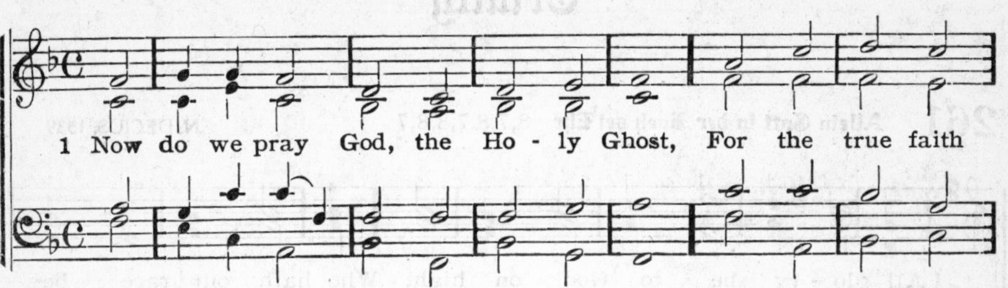
1 Now do we pray God, the Ho - ly Ghost, For the true faith

which we need the most, And that He de - fend us, when life is end-ing,

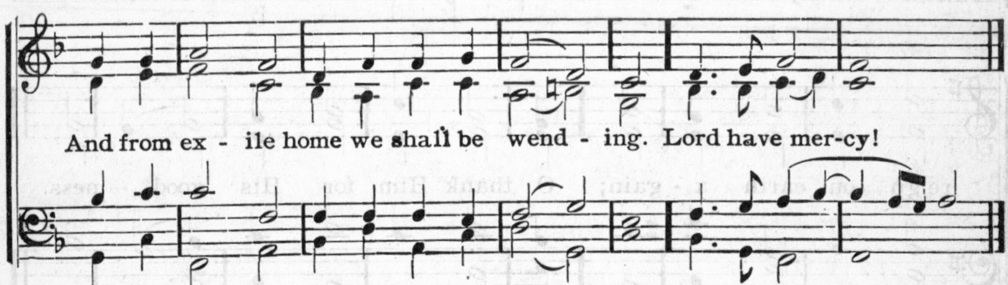
And from ex - ile home we shall be wend - ing. Lord have mer-cy!

2 Shine in our hearts, O most precious
Light,
That we Jesus Christ may know aright,
Clinging to our Savior, whose blood has
bought us,
Who again to our true home has
brought us.
Lord, have mercy!

3 Thou sweetest Love, grace on us bestow,
Set our hearts with heavenly fire aglow,
That with hearts united we love each
other,
Of one mind, in peace with every
brother.
Lord, have mercy!

4 Thou highest Comfort in every need!
Grant that neither shame nor death we
heed,
That e'en then our courage may never
fail us,
When at last th' Accuser shall assail us.
Lord, have mercy!

Dr. Martin Luther, 1525

Trinity

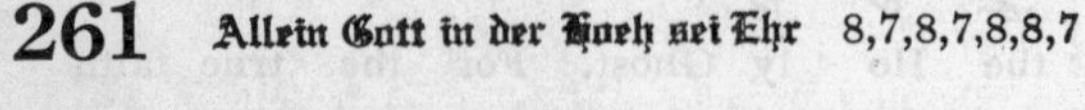

261 Allein Gott in der Höh sei Ehr 8,7,8,7,8,8,7

N. DECIUS, 1539

1 { All glo - ry be to God on high, Who hath our race be- friend - ed!
To us no harm shall now come nigh, The strife at last is end - ed; }
God show - eth His goodwill to men, And peace shall reign on earth a - gain; O thank Him for His good - ness.

2 We praise, we worship Thee, we trust,
And give Thee thanks forever,
O Father that Thy rule is just,
And wise, and changes never:
Thy boundless power o'er all things
reigns,
Done is whate'er Thy will ordains:
Well for us that Thou rulest!

3 O Jesus Christ, Thou only Son
Of God, Thy heavenly Father,
Who didst for all our sins atone
And the lost sheep dost gather,
Thou Lamb of God, to Thee on high,
From out our depths, we sinners cry,
Have mercy on us, Jesus!

4 O Holy Ghost, Thou precious gift,
Thou Comforter unfailing,
O'er Satan's snares our souls uplift,
And let Thy power availing
Avert our woes and calm our dread;
For us the Savior's blood was shed,
We trust in Thee to save us!

N. Decius, 1529 C. Winkworth, Tr. a

Trinity

262 Italian Hymn 6,6,4,6,6,6,4

FELICE de GIARDINI, 1769 (P)

1 Come, Thou al - might - y King, Help us Thy name to

sing, Help us to praise! Fa - ther all glo - ri - ous, O'er all vic -

to - ri - ous, Come and reign o - ver us, An - cient of days.

2 Jesus, our Lord, arise;
Scatter our enemies,
And make them fall;
Let Thine almighty aid
Our sure defence be made;
Our souls on Thee be stayed;
Lord, hear our call!

3 Come, Thou incarnate Word,
Gird on Thy mighty sword,
Our prayer attend:
Come, and Thy people bless,
And give Thy Word success;
Spirit of holiness,
On us descend.

4 Come, holy Comforter,
Thy sacred witness bear
In this glad hour:
Thou who almighty art,
Now rule in ev'ry heart,
And ne'er from us depart,
Spirit of power!

5 To the great One in Three
The highest praises be,
Hence, evermore!
His sovereign majesty
May we in glory see,
And to eternity
Love and adore!

Charles Wesley, 1757

263 Nicaea 11, 12, 12, 10 J. B. DYKES, 1861

1 Ho - ly, ho - ly, ho - ly, Lord, God Al - might - y!

Ear - ly in the morn - ing our song shall rise to Thee;

Ho - ly, ho - ly, ho - ly! mer - ci - ful and might - y!

God in Three Per - sons, bles - sed Trin - i - ty!

2 Holy, holy, holy! all the saints adore Thee,
Casting down their golden crowns around the glassy sea,
Cherubim and seraphim falling down before Thee,
Which wert and art and evermore shalt be.

3 Holy, holy, holy! though the darkness hide Thee,
Though the eye of sinful man Thy glory may not see,
Only Thou art holy; there is none beside Thee,
Perfect in power, in love and purity.

4 Holy, holy, holy! Lord God Almighty!
All Thy works shall praise Thy name, in earth, and sky, and sea;
Holy, holy, holy! merciful and mighty!
God in Three Persons, blessed Trinity!

R. Heber 1827

264 Es wollt uns Gott genaedig 8, 7, 8, 7, 8, 7, 8, 7, 7

1 The mystery hidden from the eyes
Of learned men and sages,
God hath revealed us from the skies,
In Scriptures holy pages,
That He alone is King above
All other gods whatever,
Great, mighty, faithful, full of love,
His people's Shield and Savior;
One Essence, but three Persons.

2 As Father, Son, and Holy Ghost,
The righteous seed adore Him;
So named, so praised, He is the boast
Of all who bow before Him;
He's Abraham's and Isaac's God,
And Jacob's whom He knoweth,
The Lord of hosts, who every good,
Both night and day, bestoweth;
Who only worketh wonders.

3 The Father hath the Son begot,
First-born of every creature;
The Son took our weak flesh, but not
Our sinfulness of nature;
Both from the Father and the Son
The Holy Ghost proceedeth
From all eternity; yet none
In might and power exceedeth;
All equal, co-eternal.

4 Be glad, my heart, thy Portion see,
Thy priceless Pearl and Treasure!
He is thy Friend, supply will He
Thy needs with bounteous measure;
He made thee in His image, was
For thy offences smitten,
With true faith fill thee, through His grace
Doth all thy crosses sweeten
With His dear word of promise.

5 Rise, then, to Him, the Ever-blest,
And learn to know Him rightly;
Such knowledge can alone bring rest,
And make thy soul burn brightly
With the pure flame of holy love,
Which cheers thy course to heaven;
For God will show thee things above,
Which here 'tis only given
To hear of, and see darkly.

6 But woe to the ungodly race
In willful blindness living,
Rejecting God and His dear grace,
Their heart to creatures giving.
On them, alas! the hellish gates
Ere long will close forever;
For him who God rejects and hates
God will reject and sever
From His eternal kingdom.

7 O Prince of might! Thy mercy show,
Thou God of earth and heaven;
To every sinner here below
Thy saving grace be given!
Bring back Thy sheep that go astray,
And blinded eyes enlighten,
And turn Thou everything away
That wickedly might frighten
Thine own, whose faith is feeble.

8 Grant this, that we Thy people may
All reach the heavenly portals,
And in Thy kingdom sing for aye
'Mid all the blest immortals:
That Thou, O Lord, art King alone,
Above all gods whatever,
The Father, Son, and Spirit, One,
Thy people's Shield and Savior,
One Essence, but three Persons!

Paul Gerhardt, 1666

(Or to Christ unser Herr zum)

265 Clinging 8, 8, 8, 6 — G. W. TORRANCE, 1835

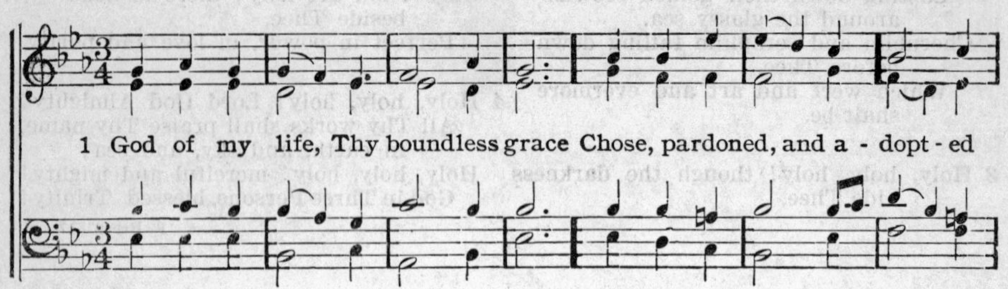
1 God of my life, Thy boundless grace Chose, pardoned, and a - dopt - ed

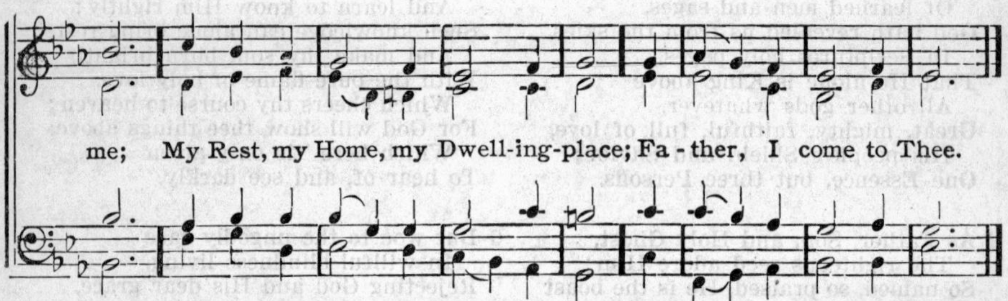
me; My Rest, my Home, my Dwell-ing-place; Fa - ther, I come to Thee.

2 Jesus, my Hope, my Rock, my Shield,
Whose precious blood was shed for me,
Into Thy hands my soul I yield:
Savior, I come to Thee.

3 Spirit of glory and of God,
Long hast Thou deigned my guide to be;
Now be Thy comfort sweet bestowed:
My God, I come to Thee.

4 I come to join that countless host,
Who praise Thy name unceasingly;
Blest Father, Son, and Holy Ghost,
My God, I come to Thee.

C. Elliott. 1841

266 Die helle Sonn leucht't jetzt L. M. — VULPIUS, 1609

1 Thou who art Three in u - ni - ty, True God from all e - ter - ni - ty,

Trinity

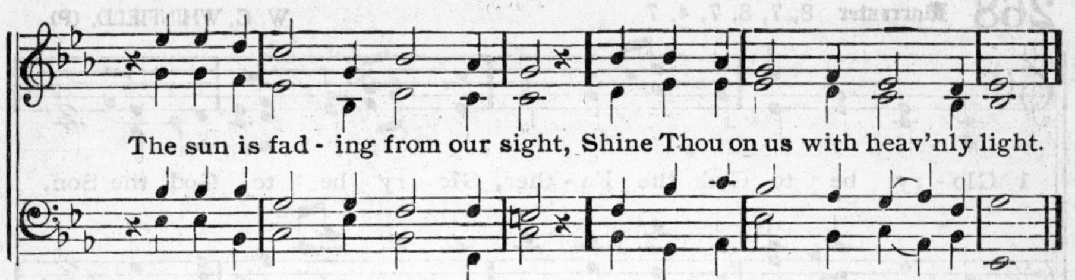
The sun is fad - ing from our sight, Shine Thou on us with heav'nly light.

2 We praise Thee with the dawning day,
To Thee at even also pray;
With our poor song we worship Thee
Now, ever, and eternally.

3 Let God the Father be adored,
And God the Son, the only Lord,
And God the Holy Spirit be
Adored throughout eternity!

Dr. Martin Luther, 1543 R. Massie, Tr.

267 Sursum Corda C. M. HAENDEL

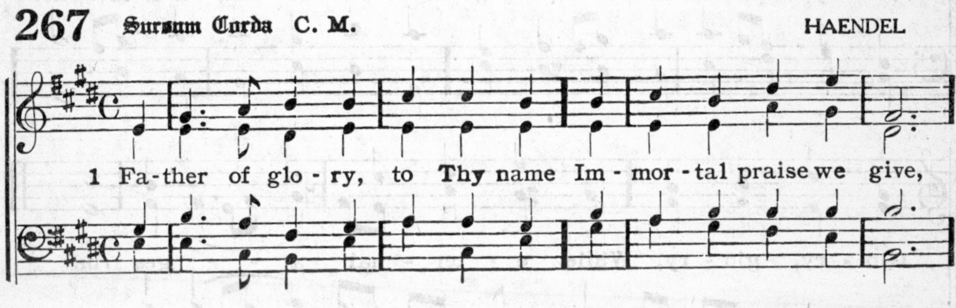
1 Fa - ther of glo - ry, to Thy name Im - mor - tal praise we give,

Who dost an act of grace pro - claim, And bid us reb - els live.

(Or to Dedham)

2 Immortal honor to the Son,
Who makes Thine anger cease;
Our lives He ransomed with His own,
And died to make our peace.

3 To Thine almighty Spirit be
Immortal glory given,
Whose teachings bring us near to Thee,
And train us up for heaven.

4 Let men with their united voice
Adore th' eternal God,
And spread His honors and their joys
Through nations far abroad.

5 Let faith, and love, and duty, join
One grateful song to raise;
Let saints in earth and heaven combine
In harmony, and praise.

Isaac Watts

Trinity

268 Worcester 8, 7, 8, 7, 4, 7 — W. G. WHINFIELD, (P)

1 Glo - ry be to God the Fa - ther, Glo - ry be to God the Son,

Glo - ry be to God the Spir - it, Great Je - ho - vah, Three in One!

Glo - ry, glo - ry, While e - ter - nal a - - ges run!

2 Glory be to Him who loved us,
Washed us from each spot and stain;
Glory be to Him who bought us,
Made us kings with Him to reign!
Glory, glory,
To the Lamb that once was slain!

3 Glory to the King of angels,
Glory to the Church's King,
Glory to the King of nations,
Heaven and earth your praises bring!
Glory, glory,
To the King of glory bring!

4 Glory, blessing, praise eternal!
Thus the choir of angels sings;
Honor, riches, power, dominion!
Thus its praise creation brings;
Glory, glory,
Glory to the King of kings!

H. Bonar, 1866

269 Rivaulx L. M. — J. B. DYKES, 1875

1 Father of heav'n whose love pro-found A ransom for our souls hath found,

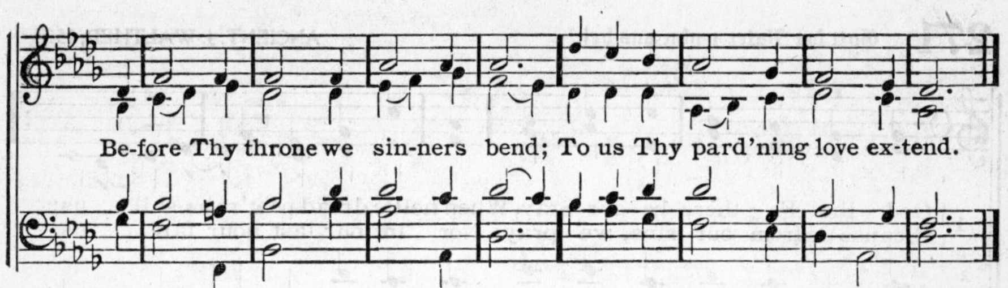
Be-fore Thy throne we sin-ners bend; To us Thy pard'ning love ex-tend.

2 Almighty Son, Incarnate Word,
Our Prophet, Priest, Redeemer, Lord,
Before Thy throne we sinners bend;
To us Thy saving grace extend.

3 Eternal Spirit, by whose breath
The soul is raised from sin and death,
Before Thy throne we sinners bend;
To us Thy quickening power extend.

4 Jehovah, Father, Spirit, Son,
Eternal Godhead, Three in One,
Before Thy throne we sinners bend;
Grace, pardon, life, to us extend.

E. Cooper, 1805

270 Dover S. M. — ENGLISH, harm. by GOSS

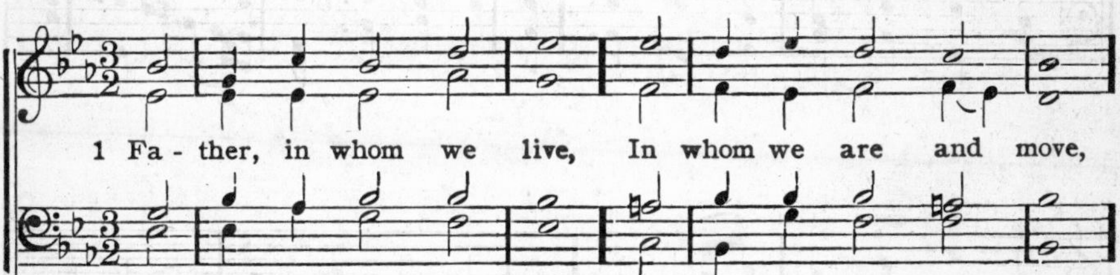
1 Fa - ther, in whom we live, In whom we are and move,

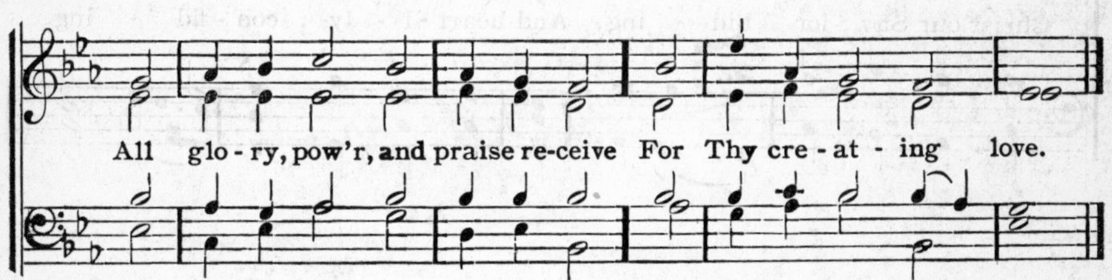
All glo - ry, pow'r, and praise re-ceive For Thy cre - at - ing love.

2 O Thou incarnate Word,
Let all Thy ransomed race
Unite in thanks, with one accord,
For Thy redeeming grace.

3 Spirit of holiness,
Let all Thy saints adore
Thy sacred gifts, and join to bless
Thy heart-renewing power.

4 Eternal, triune Lord,
Let all the hosts above,
Let all the sons of men record
And dwell upon Thy love.

Charles Wesley, 1746

271 Gott der Vater wohn uns bei
ANCIENT, J. WALTHER, 1524
1 { God the Fa - ther, be our Stay, When hell's dread pow'rs as-sail us;
Cleanse us from our sins, we pray, Nor in our last hour fail us.
Keep us from the E - vil One: Firm in the faith a - bid - ing, In
Christ our Sav - ior hid - ing, And heart - i - ly con - fid - ing.
Let us put God's ar-mor on: With all true Christians run - ning Our

heav'n-ly race, and shun - ning The Dev-il's wiles and cun - ning.

A-men, A-men, this be done, So sing we Hal - le - lu-jah!

2 Jesus Christ, be Thou our Stay, etc.

3 Holy Ghost, be Thou our Stay, etc.

15th Century Litany, adapted by Dr. Martin Luther, 1524

272 Nun danket alle Gott 6,7,6,7,6,6,6,6

1 The Lord my God be praised,
My Light, my Life from heaven,
My Maker, who to me
Hath soul and body given,
My Father, who protects
My life from infancy,
And mighty gifts of love
Hath e'er bestowed on me.

2 The Lord my God be praised,
My Trust, my Life from heaven,
The Father's own dear Son,
Whose life for me was given,
Who thus atoned for me
With His most precious blood,
Who giveth to my faith
The greatest heavenly good.

3 The Lord my God be praised,
My Hope, my Life from heaven,
The Father's Spirit, whom
The Son to me hath given:
He who revives my heart,
And gives me strength and power,
Help, comfort and support
In sorrow's gloomy hour.

4 The Lord my God be praised,
He who forever liveth,
To whom the heavenly host
E'er praise and honor giveth;
The Lord my God be praised,
In whose great name I boast,
God Father, God the Son,
And God the Holy Ghost.

5 To Him we now sing praise,
With joy our offering bringing,
And with the angel host,
The "Holy! Holy!" singing;
To Him all Christendom
Sings praises joyfully;
The Lord my God be praised
Throughout eternity!

J. Olearius, 1671 A. Crull, Tr.

Festival of the Reformation

273 Ein feste Burg ist unser Gott 8,7,8,7,5,5,5,6,7 DR. MARTIN LUTHER

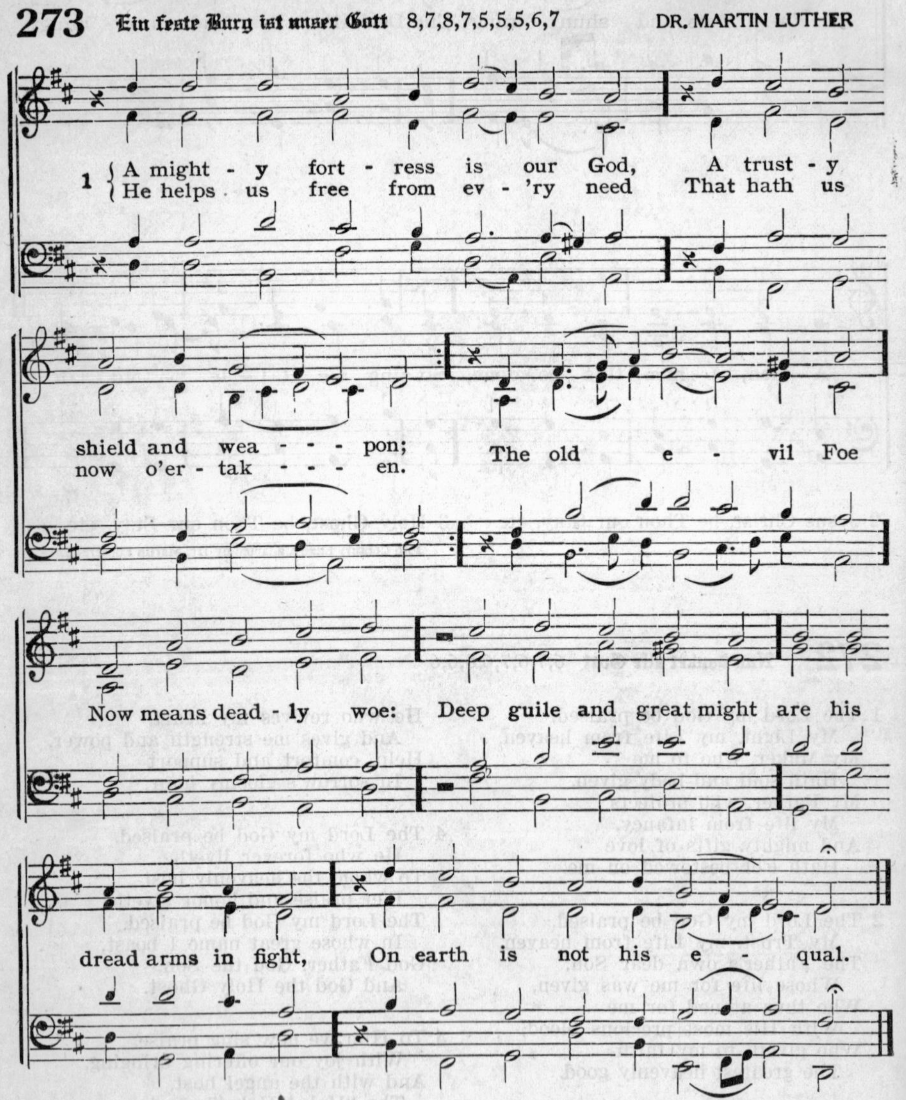
1 { A might - y fort - ress is our God, A trust - y shield and wea - - - pon;
He helps us free from ev - 'ry need That hath us now o'er - tak - - - en.
The old e - vil Foe Now means dead - ly woe: Deep guile and great might are his dread arms in fight, On earth is not his e - qual.

2 With might of ours can naught be done,
Soon were our loss effected;
But for us fights the Valiant One,
Whom God Himself elected.
Ask ye, Who is this?
Jesus Christ, it is,
Of Sabaoth Lord,
And there's none other God,
He holds the field forever.

3 Though devils all the world should fill,
All eager to devour us,
We tremble not, we fear no ill,
They shall not overpower us.
This world's prince may still
Scowl fierce as he will,
He can harm us none,
He's judged; the deed is done;
One little word can fell him.

4 The Word they still shall let remain,
And not a thank have for it;
He's by our side upon the plain
With His good gifts and Spirit.
And take they our life,
Goods, fame, child, and wife:
Let these all be gone,
They yet have nothing won;
The kingdom ours remaineth.

Dr. Martin Luther, 1529

274 Erhalt uns Herr bei deinem L. M.

KLUGE, 1543

1 Lord, keep us in Thy Word and work, Restrain the murd'rous Pope and Turk,
Who fain would tear from off Thy throne Christ Jesus, Thy be-lov - ed son.

2 Lord Jesus Christ, Thy power make known
For Thou art Lord of lords alone;
Shield Thy poor Christendom, that we
May evermore sing praise to Thee.

3 Thou Comforter of priceless worth,
Give one mind to Thy flock on earth,
Stand by us in our final strife,
And lead us out of death to life.

4 Destroy their counsels, Lord our God,
And smite them with an iron rod,
And let them fall into the snare
Which for Thy Christians they prepare.

5 So that at last they may perceive
That, Lord our God, Thou still dost live,
And dost deliver mightily
All those who put their trust in Thee.

Dr. Martin Luther, 1541 Stanzas 4 & 5 by Justus Jonas, 1544

275 Erhalt uns Herr bei deinem Wort L. M.

1 Thine honor rescue, Christ our Lord!
Hear Zion's sighs, and help afford;
Destroy the wiles of mighty foes,
Who now Thy Word and truth oppose.

2 Their craft and vaunting pomp is great;
High beat their hearts, with power elate;
Our dearest hopes they but deride,
They deem us nothing in their pride.

3 Forgive, O Lord, our sins forgive,
Grant us Thy grace and let us live;
Convince Thy foes throughout the land
That godless counsels shall not stand.

4 Preserve Thy little flock in peace,
Nor let Thy boundless mercy cease;
Let it to all the world appear
That Thy true Church indeed is here.

5 That Thou art with us, loud proclaim,
Who put'st our enemies to shame,
Dost all their haughtiness suppress,
And help Thine own in their distress.

Joh. Heermann, 1630 M. Loy, Tr. a

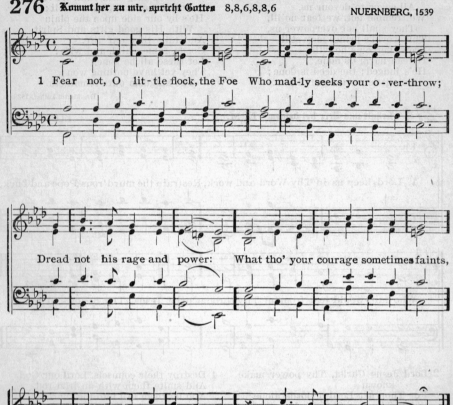

276 Kommt her zu mir, spricht Gottes 8,8,6,8,8,6 NUERNBERG, 1539

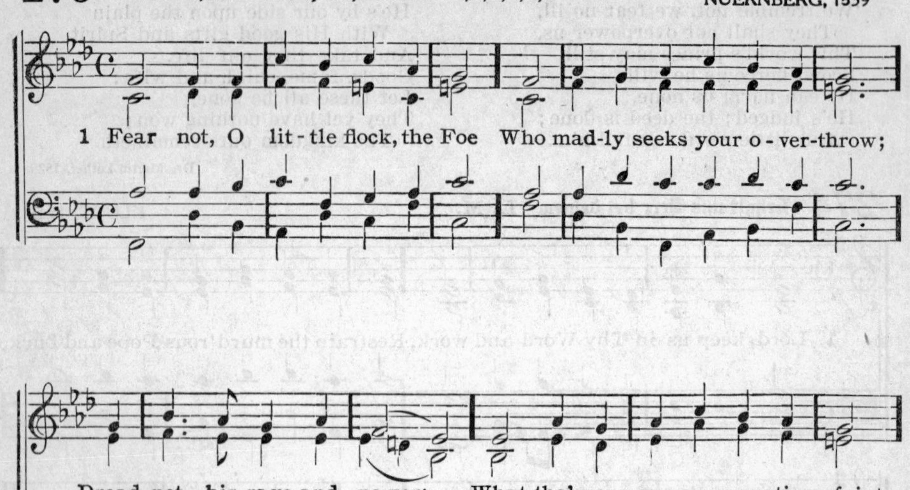
1 Fear not, O lit-tle flock, the Foe Who mad-ly seeks your o-ver-throw;
Dread not his rage and power: What tho' your courage sometimes faints,

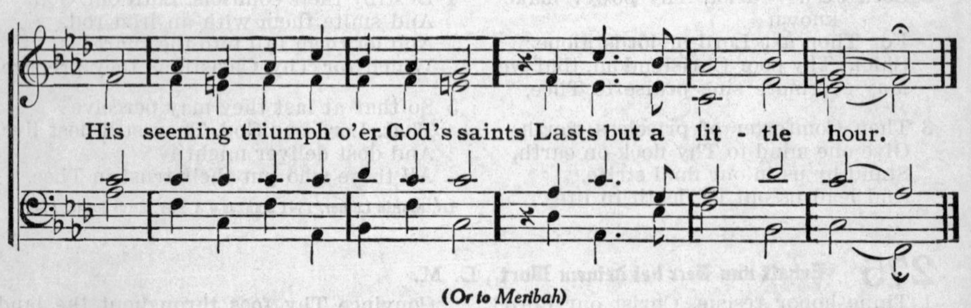
His seeming triumph o'er God's saints Lasts but a lit-tle hour.

(*Or to Meribah*)

2 Be of good cheer; your cause belongs
To Him who can avenge your wrongs;
Leave it to Him, our Lord.
Though hidden yet from mortal eyes,
His Gideon shall for you arise,
Uphold you and His Word.

3 As true as God's own Word is true,
Not earth nor hell with all their crew
Against us shall prevail.
A jest and byword are they grown;
God is with us; we are His own;
Our victory cannot fail.

4 Amen, Lord Jesus, grant our prayer!
Great Captain, now thine arm make bare,
Fight for us once again!
So shall Thy saints and martyrs raise
A mighty chorus to Thy praise,
World without end: Amen!

King Gustavus Adolphus of Sweden and J. Fabricius, 1631 C. Winkworth, Tr. 1855 a

277 Es spricht der Unweisen Mund 8,7,8,7,8,8,7

J. WALTHER, 1524

1 { The mouth of fools doth God con - fess, But while their lips draw nigh Him,
Their heart is full of wick - ed - ness, And all their deeds de - ny Him,
Cor - rupt are they, and ev - 'ry one A - bom - i - na - ble works hath done; There is not one well - do - er.

(Or to Es ist gewisslich)

2 The Lord looked from His heavenly throne
On all mankind below Him,
To see if there were any one
Who truly sought to know Him,
And all his understanding bent
To search His holy Word, intent
To do His will in earnest.

3 But none there was who walked with God
For all aside had slidden,
Delusive paths of folly trod,
And followed lusts forbidden;
Not one there was who practiced good,
Though many deemed, in haughty mood,
Their deeds to God were pleasing.

4 How long, by folly blindly led,
Will they oppress the needy,
And eat my people up like bread?
So fierce are they and greedy!
In God they put no trust at all,
Nor will on Him in trouble call,
But be their own providers.

5 Therefore their heart is never still,
A constant fear dismays them,
God is with him who doth His will,
Who trusts Him and obeys Him;
Ye shame the counsel of the poor,
And mock him when he doth assure
That God is e'er his refuge.

6 Who shall to Israel's outcast race
From Zion bring salvation?
God will Himself at length show grace
And loose the captive nation;
That will He do by Christ their King;
Let Jacob then be glad and sing,
And Israel be joyful.

Dr. Martin Luther 1524. Richard Massie, Tr. a

278 Ach Gott, vom Himmel 8,7,8,7,8,8,7 ERFURT ENCHIRIDION, 1524

1 { O God from heav'n look down and see A sight which well may move Thee:
Of god - ly men how few there be, For - sa - ken we who love Thee!
With - held is Thy pure Word, the light Of faith it - self extinguished quite In all the sons of Ad - am. . . . .

(Or to Es ist gewisslich)

2 Fictions they teach with cunning art,
And lies of man's invention;
Not grounded on God's Word, their heart
Breeds naught but strange dissension;
One chooses this, another that,
Untold division they create
Though saint-like in appearance.

3 May God root out all heresy,
And of false teachers rid us,
Who proudly say: "Now where is he
That shall our speech forbid us!
We have the right and might alone,
And what we say must stand, we own
None as our Lord and master."

4 Therefore saith God, "I must arise,
The poor suffer wrong-doing;
To me ascend my people's sighs,
And I have heard their suing:
My saving Word shall take the field,
Shall be the poor man's strength and shield,
Shall conquer all opposers."

5 As silver seven times furnace-tried
Is pure from all its drosses,
So doth the Word of God abide
The brighter for its crosses;
For trial shows its worth aright,
And manifests its strength, and light,
That through all lands it shineth.

6 O God, preserve it pure and free
From this vile generation,
And let us be preserved by Thee
From their abomination;
The wicked walk on every side,
When 'mid Thy flock the vile abide
In power and are exalted.

Dr. Martin Luther, 1524

279 Herzliebster Jesu 10,10,10,4

J. CRUEGER, 1640

1 Christ, Thou the Cham - pion of the band who own
Thy cross, O make Thy suc - cor quick - ly known! The schemes of
those who long our blood have sought Bring Thou to nought.

2 Do Thou Thyself for us Thy children fight,
Withstand the Devil, quell his rage and might,
Whate'er assails Thy members left below,
Do Thou o'erthrow.

3 And give us Thy peace: peace in Church and school,
Peace to the powers who o'er our country rule,
Peace to the conscience, peace within the heart
Do Thou impart.

4 So shall Thy goodness here be still adored,
Thou Guardian of Thy little flock, dear Lord;
And heaven and earth through all eternity
Shall worship Thee.

Math. Apelles v. Loewenstern, 1644 C. Winkworth, Tr.

280 Herzliebster Jesu 11,11,11,5

1 Ah! Lord our God, let them not be confounded
Who, though by want, and woe, and pain surrounded,
Yet day and night still for Thy hope are sighing,
To Thee are crying.

2 But put to shame Thy foes, who breathe defiance,
And make their own vain might their sole reliance;
O turn in mercy to Thy generation,
Lord have compassion!

3 We stand bereft of help, and poor and lonely.
'Twere vain to trust in man;—with Thee, Lord, only
We may defeat the enemies around us
Who seek to wound us.

4 Thou art our Champion who canst overthrow them,
And save the little flock now crushed below them,
We trust in Thee; for Jesus' sake be near us!
Help, Helper hear us!

Joh. Heermann, 1630 C. Winkworth, Tr.

Festival of the Reformation

281 Blendon L. M.

FELICE de GIARDINI, 1719—1796 (I and P)

1 No change of time shall ev - er shock My firm af-
fec - tion, Lord, to Thee; For Thou hast al - ways
been a Rock, A Fort - ress and De - fence to me.

2 Thou my Deliverer art, my God;
My trust is in Thy mighty power:
Thou art my Shield from foes abroad;
At home, my Safeguard and my Tower.

3 To Thee I will address my prayer,
To whom all praise we justly owe;
So shall I, by Thy watchful care,
Be guarded safe from every foe.

4 Let the eternal Lord be praised,
The Rock on whose defence I rest:
O'er highest heavens His name be raised,
Who me with His salvation blest.

Tate and Brady ab.

282 War Gott nicht mit uns diese Zeit 8,7,8,7,8,8,7

J. WALTHER, 1537

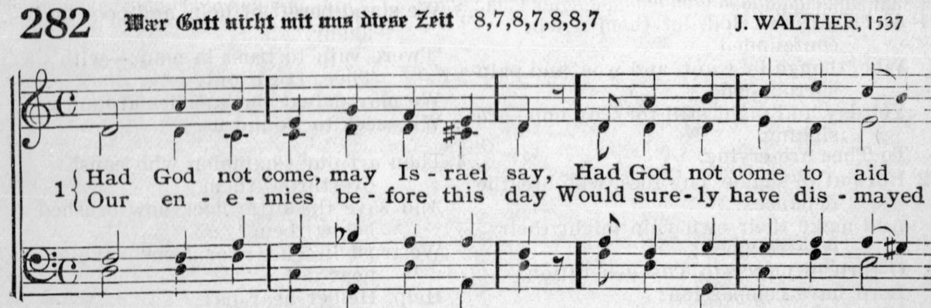
1 { Had God not come, may Is - rael say, Had God not come to aid
Our en - e - mies be - fore this day Would sure - ly have dis - mayed

1
2
us,
(Omit.) us; For we are but a hand-ful small Held in con-

tempt and scorn by all, All men rise up a - gainst us.

(Or to Nun freut)

2 Their furious wrath, did God permit,
Would surely have consumed us,
And in the deep and yawning pit
With life and limb entombed us;
Like men o'er whom dark waters roll,
The streams had gone e'en o'er our soul,
And mightily o'erwhelmed us.

3 Blest be the Lord, who from the pit
Snatched us, when it was gaping;
Our souls, like birds that break the net,
To the blue skies escaping;
The snare is broken—we are free!
Our help is ever, Lord, in Thee,
The God of earth and heaven.

Dr. Martin Luther 1525. Richard Massie, Tr. a

283 Blendon L. M.

1 When Rome had shrouded earth in night,
God said again, Let there be light!
And Luther with the Gospel came
To spread the truth in Jesus' name.

2 When Rome the saints of God oppressed,
And burdened souls could find no rest,
Through Luther God deliv'rance sent
By His pure Word and Sacrament.

3 Though hosts against us stand arrayed,
Christ bids us still, Be not afraid;
Though all its powers the truth assail,
The gates of hell shall not prevail.

4 Today with joyful hearts we sing
The guardian care of Christ our King,
Who through His chosen instrument
To us hath this salvation sent.

5 O Lord, whose mercies still endure,
Preserve to us Thy Gospel pure;
Let it alone within us reign,
That Thine the glory may remain.

M. Loy

(Or to Rockingham)

Festival of the Reformation

284 Wo Gott der Herr nicht bei uns hält 8,7,8,7,8,8,7 KLUGE, 1535

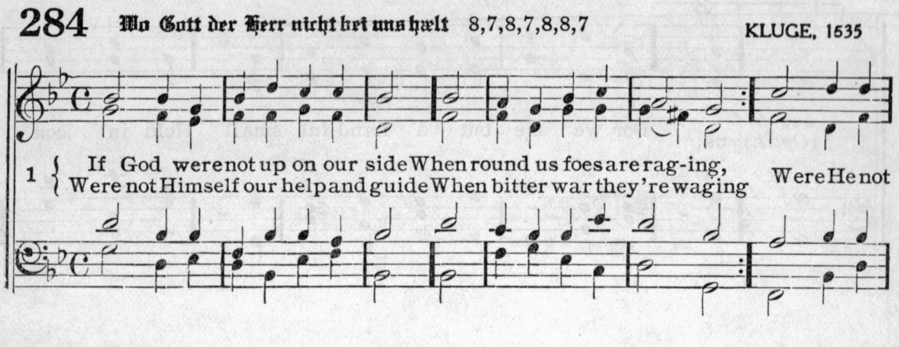

1 { If God were not up on our side When round us foes are rag-ing,
Were not Himself our help and guide When bitter war they're waging
Were He not

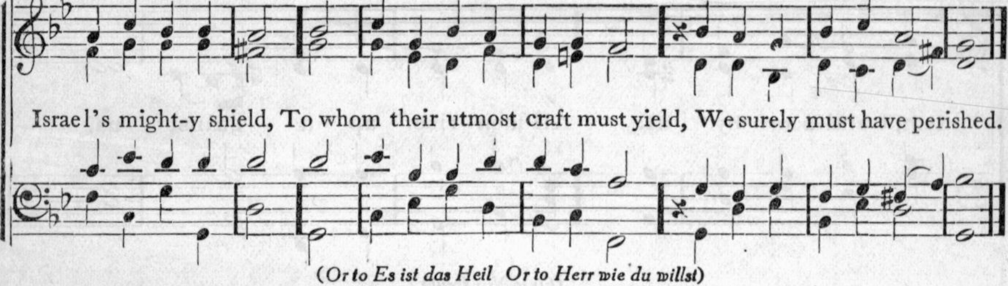

Israel's might-y shield, To whom their utmost craft must yield, We surely must have perished.

(Or to Es ist das Heil Or to Herr wie du willst)

2 But now no human wit or might
  His chosen people frighteth,
God sitteth in the highest height,
  And He their counsels blighteth;
When craftiest snares and nets they lay,
God doth His work another way,
  And makes a path before us.

3 Against our souls they rage and mock,
  Exciting great commotion:
As billows meet with angry shock
  Out on the stormy ocean,
So they our lives with fury seek;
But God hath pity on the weak,
  And Him they have forgotten.

4 They call us heretics, and aye
  Their Christian name are flaunting;
They seek to spill our blood, while they
  Their fear of God are vaunting.
Ah, God! that precious name of Thine
O'er many a wicked deed must shine,
  But Thou wilt once avenge it.

5 They open wide their ravenous jaws,
  And threaten to devour us,
But thanks to God, who rules our cause,
  They shall not overpower us;
Their snares He yet will bring to naught,
And overthrow what they have taught;
  God is too mighty for them.

6 How richly He consoleth those
  Whom no one else befriendeth!
The door of grace doth never close;
  Sense cannot comprehend it,
How this may be, and deems all lost,
When through this very cross a host
  Of champions God is raising.

7 Our foes, O God, are in Thy hand,
  Thou knowest their endeavor;
But only give us strength to stand,
  And let us waver never,
Though reason strives with faith, and still
It fears to wholly trust Thy will,
  And sees not Thy salvation.

8 But heaven and earth, O Lord, are Thine,
  For Thou alone hast made them;
Thy light let on Thy people shine,
  And in their sorrows aid them;
Kindle our hearts to love and faith
That shall be steadfast e'en to death,
  Howe'er the world may murmur!

Justus Jonas, 1524 C, Winkworth Tr. a

285 Trisagion 10s 4 1 HENRY SMART, 1868

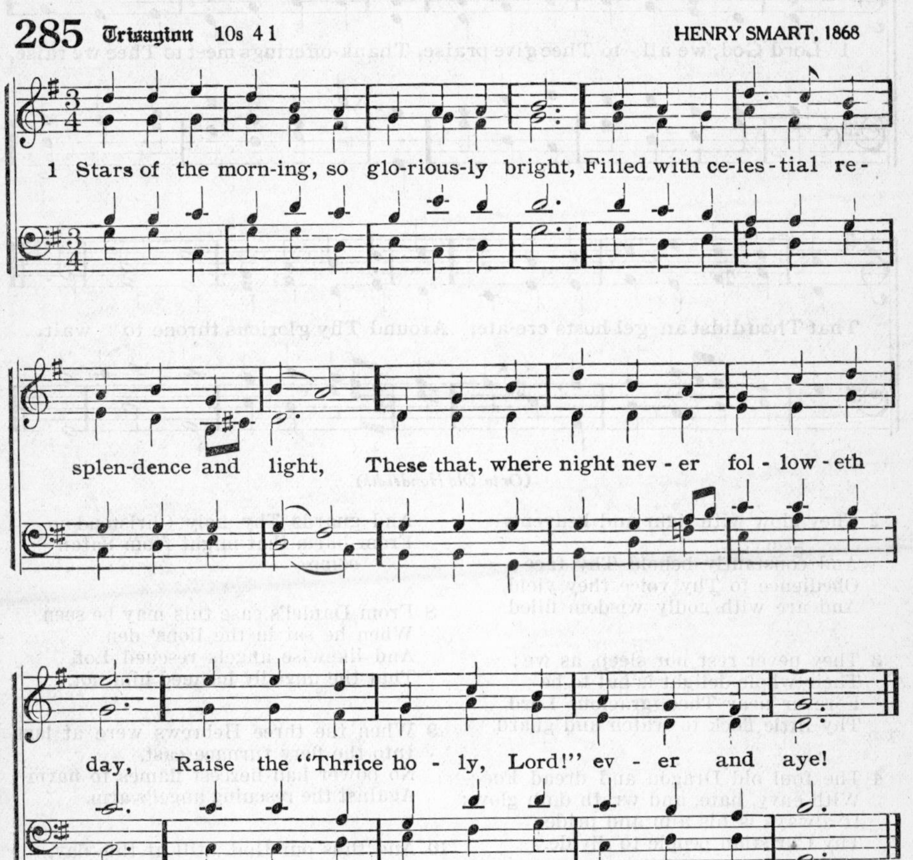
1 Stars of the morn-ing, so glo-rious-ly bright, Filled with ce-les-tial re-
splen-dence and light, These that, where night nev-er fol-low-eth
day, Raise the "Thrice ho-ly, Lord!" ev-er and aye!

2 These are Thy ministers, these dost Thou own,
Lord God of Sabaoth! nearest Thy throne.
These are Thy messengers; these dost Thou send,
Help of the helpless ones, man to defend.

3 When by Thy word earth was first poised in space,
When the far planets first sped on their race,
When was completed the six days' employ,
Then "all the sons of God shouted for joy."

4 Still let them succor us; still let them fight,
Lord of angelic hosts! battling for right;
Till, where their anthems they ceaselessly pour,
We with the angels may bow and adore.

Joseph of the Studium, c. 850 John Mason Neale, Tr. 1862 a

St. Michael and All Angels

286 Angels L. M.

ORLANDO GIBBONS, 1623 (P)

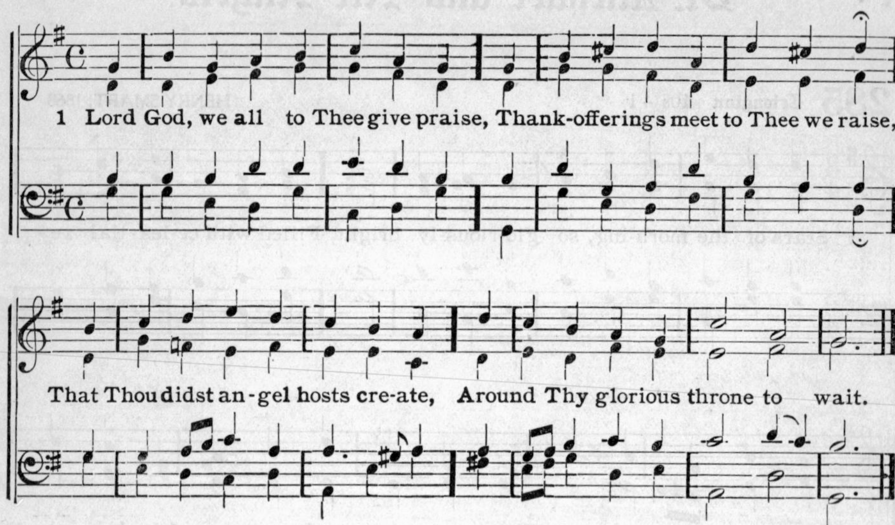

1 Lord God, we all to Thee give praise, Thank-offerings meet to Thee we raise,
That Thou didst an-gel hosts cre-ate, Around Thy glorious throne to wait.

(Or to Old Hundredth)

2 They glow with light and heavenly grace,
And constantly behold Thy face;
Obedience to Thy voice they yield,
And are with godly wisdom filled.

3 They never rest nor sleep, as we;
Their whole delight is but to be
Forever near Thee, gracious Lord,
Thy little flock to watch and guard.

4 The foul old Dragon and dread Foe
With envy, hate, and wrath doth glow;
It always is his aim and pride
Thy Christian people to divide.

5 As he has blighted earth of old,
He keeps e'en now his deathly hold,
Chafes madly to annihilate
All virtue, honor, Church, and State.

6 Therefore, no halt nor rest he knows;
A roaring lion round he goes,
Or lies in wait with baneful snare
To drive the Christians to despair.

7 But watchful is the angel-band,
That follows Christ on every hand,
And guards Thy holy Christendom
From harm that might from Satan come,

8 From Daniel's case this may be seen,
When he sat in the lions' den,
And likewise angels rescued Lot,
That the ungodly harmed him not.

9 When the three Hebrews were at last
Into the fiery furnace cast,
No power had fiercest flames to harm
Against the rescuing angel's arm.

10 And thus our God, still at this day,
From harm and many an evil way
Keeps us by His dear angel-guard,
Placed o'er us as our watch and ward.

11 For this, now and eternally,
Our praise shall rise, O God, to Thee,
Whom all the angel-hosts adore
With joy now and forevermore.

12 We also pray Thee to defend
By them unto the latter end,
Thy fold, that little flock, O Lord,
That holds in honor Thy blessed Word.

From the Latin of Philip Melanchthon Paul Eber, 1566

St. Michael and All Angels

287 Irby 8,7,8,7,7,7 H. J. GAUNTLETT

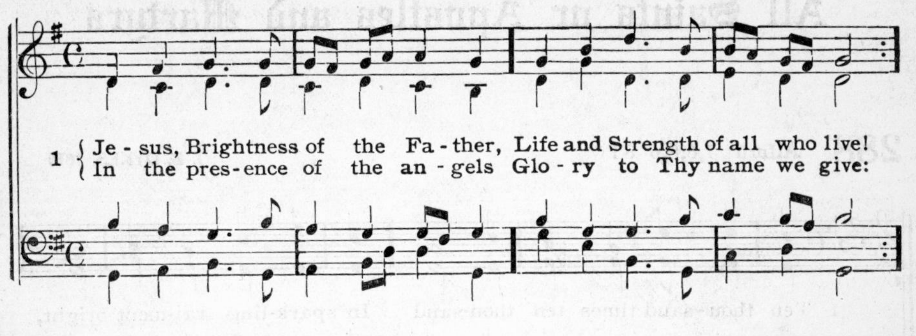

1 { Je - sus, Brightness of the Fa - ther, Life and Strength of all who live!
In the pres - ence of the an - gels Glo - ry to Thy name we give:

And Thy won - drous praise re - hearse, Sing-ing in har - mo-nious verse.

(*Or to Gott des Himmels*)

2 Blessed Lord, by their protection
Shelter us from harm this day:
Keep us pure in flesh and spirit;
Save us from the Foe we pray:
And vouchsafe us by Thy grace
In Thy paradise a place.

3 Glory to the almighty Father,
Sing we with the heavenly host;
Glory to the great Redeemer,
Glory to the Holy Ghost;
Three in One, and One in Three,
Throughout all eternity!

Rhabanus Maurus, †856, Edward Caswall Tr. 1848 a

All Saints or Apostles and Martyrs

288 Alford 7,6,8,6 8 1 J. B. DYKES, 1875

1 Ten thou-sand times ten thou-sand In spark-ling rai-ment bright,
The ar-mies of the ransomed saints Throng up the steeps of light:
'Tis fin-ished! all is fin-ished, Their fight with death and sin:
Fling o-pen wide the gold-en gates, And let the vic-tors in.

2 What rush of alleluias
Fills all the earth and sky!
What ringing of a thousand harps
Bespeaks the triumph nigh!
Oh, day, for which creation
And all its tribes were made;
Oh, joy, for all its former woes
A thousand-fold repaid!

3 Oh, then what raptured greetings
On Canaan's happy shore;
What knitting severed friendships up,
Where partings are no more!
Then eyes with joy shall sparkle
That brimmed with tears of late;
Orphans no longer fatherless,
Nor widows desolate.

4 Bring near Thy great salvation,
Thou Lamb for sinners slain;
Fill up the roll of Thine elect,
Then take Thy power, and reign:
Appear, Desire of nations,
Thine exiles long for home:
Show in the heav'ns Thy promised sign;
Thou Prince and Savior, come!

H. Alford, 1867

289 Carlisle S. M.

C. LOCKHART, 1745–1815

1 For all Thy saints, O Lord, Who strove in Thee to live,

Who fol-lowed Thee, o-beyed, a-dored, Our grate-ful hymn re-ceive.

2 For all Thy saints, O Lord,
Accept our thankful cry,
Who counted Thee their great reward,
And strove in Thee to die.

3 They all in life and death,
With Thee, their Lord, in view,
Learned from Thy Holy Spirit's breath
To suffer and to do.

4 For this Thy name we bless,
And humbly pray that we
May follow them in holiness,
And live and die in Thee.

R. Mant, 1837 ab.

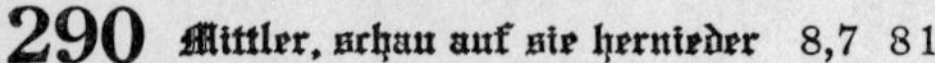
290 Mittler, schau auf sie hernieder 8,7 81

J. G. SCHICHT, 1819

1 Hark! the sound of ho - ly voi - ces Chant-ing o'er the crys - tal sea,
Al - le - lu - ia, Al - le - lu - ia, Al - le - lu - ia, Lord, to Thee;

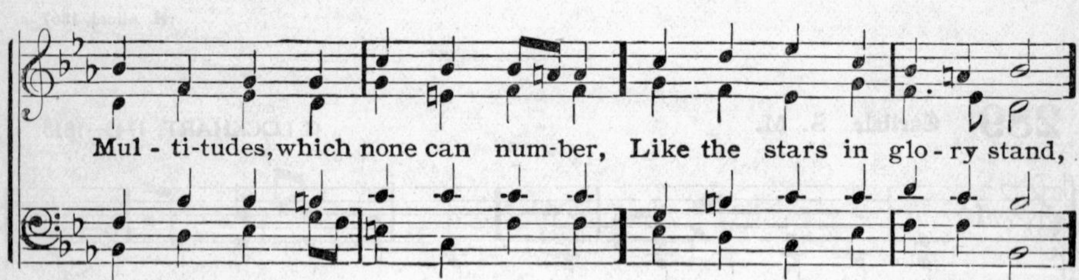
Mul - ti-tudes, which none can num-ber, Like the stars in glo - ry stand,

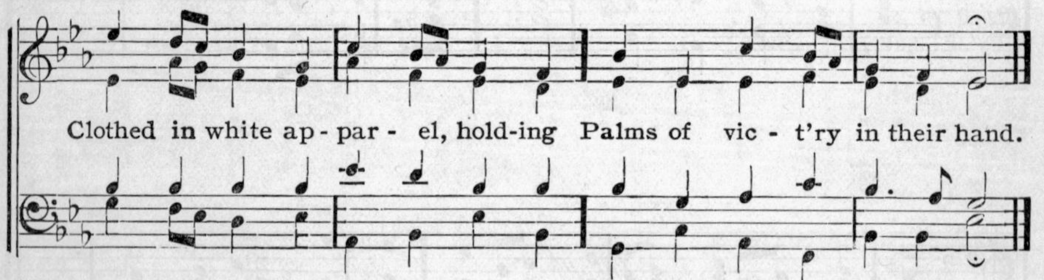
Clothed in white ap - par - el, hold-ing Palms of vic - t'ry in their hand.

2 Patriarch, and Holy Prophet,
Who prepared the way of Christ,
King, Apostle, Saint, Confessor,
Martyr and Evangelist,
Saintly Maiden, Godly Matron,
Widows who have watched to prayer,
Joined in holy concert, singing
To the Lord of all, are there.

3 They have come from tribulation,
And have washed their robes in blood,
Washed them in the blood of Jesus;
Tried they were, and firm they stood;
Mocked, imprisoned, stoned, tormented,
Sawn asunder, slain with sword,
They have conquered death and Satan
By the might of Christ the Lord.

4 Marching with Thy cross their banner,
They have triumphed, following
Thee, the Captain of salvation,
Thee, their Savior and their King.
Gladly, Lord, with Thee they suffered,
Gladly, Lord, with Thee they died;
And by death to life immortal
They were born and glorified.

5 Now they reign in heavenly glory
Now they walk in golden light,
Now they drink, as from a river,
Holy bliss and infinite:
Love and peace they taste forever,
And all truth and knowledge see
In the beatific vision
Of the Blessed Trinity.

C. Wordsworth, 1862

291 St. Werburgh L. M. 61 J. B. DYKES

1 O Lord, whose bounteous hand a-gain Hath poured Thy gifts in plenty down.
Who all cre - a - tion dost sus-tain And all the earth with goodness crown:
Lord of the har - vest here we own Our joy Thy gift, and Thine a-lone.

(*Or to Vater unser im*)

2 O may we ne'er with thankless heart
Forget from whom our blessings flow:
Still, Lord, Thy heavenly grace impart;
Still teach us what to Thee we owe.
Lord, may our lives with fruit divine
Return Thy care, and prove us Thine.

3 Lord, grant that each may sow to Thee;
Grant us in endless life to reap:
Of every heart the Guardian be:
By day and night Thy servants keep,
That all to Thee may joy afford
On Thy great harvest-day, O Lord.

292 Ich singe dir mit Herz C. M.

J. L. KOENIG, 1739

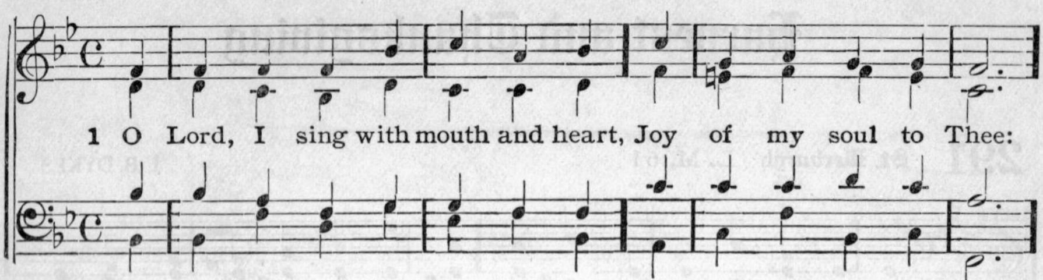
1 O Lord, I sing with mouth and heart, Joy of my soul to Thee:

To earth Thy knowledge I im - part, As it is known to me.

(*Or to Lobt Gott ihr Christen Or to Sursum Corda*)

2 Thou art the Fount of grace, I know,
And Spring so full and free,
Whence saving health and goodness flow
Each day so bounteously.

3 For what have all that live and move
Through this wide world below,
That does not from Thy bounteous love,
O heavenly Father, flow?

4 Who built the lofty firmament?
Who spread th' expanse of blue?
By whom are to our pastures sent
Refreshing rain and dew?

5 Who warmeth us in cold and frost?
Who shields us from the wind?
Who orders it that oil and must
We in their season find?

6 Who is it life and health bestows?
Who keeps us with His hand
In golden peace wards off war's woes
From our dear native land?

7 O Lord, of this and all our store
Thou art the author blest;
Thou keepest watch before our door,
While we securely rest.

8 Thou feedest us from year to year.
And constant dost abide:
With ready help in time of fear,
Thou standest at our side.

9 With patience dost Thou ever chide,
And chasten'st sparingly;
Thou castest all our sins aside,
And drown'st them in the sea.

10 When silent woe our bosom rends,
Thy pity sees our grief,
And gives what to our glory tends
No less than our relief.

11 Thou knowest when a Christian weeps,
And why his tear-drops fall;
And in the book Thy mercy keeps
These things are noted all.

12 Our deepest needs dost Thou supply,
Thou giv'st what lasts for aye,
Thou lead'st us to our home on high,
When hence we pass away.

13 Cheer up! my heart, rejoice and sing,
A cheerful trust maintain!
For God, the source of everything,
Thy portion will remain.

14 He is thy treasure, He thy joy,
Thy life, and light and Lord,
Thy counsellor when doubts annoy,
Thy shield and great reward.

15 In restless thought or blank despair,
Why spend each day and night?
On Him who made thee cast thy care;
He makes our burdens light.

16 Did not His love, and truth, and power
Watch o'er thy childhood's day?
Has He not oft in threatening hour,
Turned dreaded ills away?

17 His wisdom never plans in vain,
Ne'er falters or mistakes;
All that His counsels did ordain
A happy ending makes.

18 Upon thy lips, then, lay thy hand,
And trust His guiding love;
Then firm as rock thy peace shall stand,
Here and in heaven above.

Paul Gerbardt, 1653

293 Ich singe dir mit Herz C. M.

1 We sing th' almighty power of God,
Who bade the mountains rise,
Who spread the flowing seas abroad,
And built the lofty skies.

2 We sing the wisdom that ordained
The sun to rule the day,
The moon shines, too, at His command,
And all the stars obey.

3 We sing the goodness of the Lord,
Who fills the earth with food;
Who formed His creatures by a word,
And then pronounced them good.

4 Lord, how Thy wonders are displayed,
Where'er we turn our eyes,
Whether we view the ground we tread,
Or gaze upon the skies!

5 There's not a plant nor flower below,
But makes Thy glories known;
And clouds arise and tempests blow,
By order from Thy throne.

6 On Thee each moment we depend:
If Thou withdraw, we die.
O may we ne'er that God offend,
Who is forever nigh!

Minstrel

(Or to Azmon Or to Nun danket all und)

294 O Herre Gott, dein 8,7 81

1 To Thee, O Lord, our hearts we raise
In hymns of adoration,
To Thee bring sacrifice of praise
With shouts of exultation:
Bright robes of gold the fields adorn,
The hills with joy are ringing,
The valleys stand so thick with corn
That even they are singing.

2 And now on this our festal day,
Thy bounteous hand confessing,
Upon Thine altar, Lord, we lay
The first-fruits of Thy blessing.
By Thee the souls of men are fed
With gifts of grace supernal,
Thou who dost give us earthly bread,
Give us the Bread eternal.

3 We bear the burden of the day,
And often toil seems dreary;
But labor ends with sunset ray,
And rest comes for the weary.
May we, the angel-reaping o'er,
Stand at the last accepted,
Christ's golden sheaves for evermore
To garners bright elected.

4 Oh, blessed is that land of God,
Where saints abide forever;
Where golden fields spread fair and broad,
Where flows the crystal river:
The strains of all its holy throng
With ours today are blending;
Thrice blessed is that harvest-song
Which never hath an ending.

W. C. Dix, 1864

295 St George's Windsor 7s 8l G. J. ELVEY, 1858

1 Come, ye thank-ful peo - ple, come, Raise the song of Har-vest-home:
All is safe - ly gath - ered in, Ere the win - ter storms be - gin;
God, our Mak - er, doth pro - vide For our wants to be sup-plied;
Come to God's own tem - ple, come, Raise the song of Har - vest-home.

(*Or to Ebeling*)

2 We ourselves are God's own field,
Fruit unto His praise to yield;
Wheat and tares together sown,
Unto joy or sorrow grown;
First the blade, and then the ear,
Then the full corn shall appear:
Lord of harvest, grant that we
Wholesome grain and pure may be.

3 For the Lord, our God, shall come,
And shall take His harvest home;
From His field shall purge away
All that doth offend, that day;
Give His angels charge at last
In the fire the tares to cast,
But the fruitful ears to store
In His garner evermore.

4 Come, Thou Lord of harvest, come
To Thy final Harvest-home;
Gather Thou Thy people in,
Free from sorrow, free from sin;
There, forever purified,
In Thy garner to abide;
Come with all Thine angels, come,
Raise the glorious Harvest-home!

H. Alford, 1845

296 Ebeling 7s 81 — Ad. fr. EBELING, by H. I.

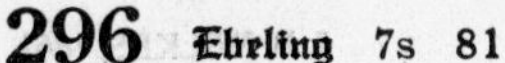

1 { Christ, by heav'n-ly hosts a - dored, Gra-cious, might-y, sov-'reign Lord,
God of na-tions, King of kings, Head of all cre - at - ed things,

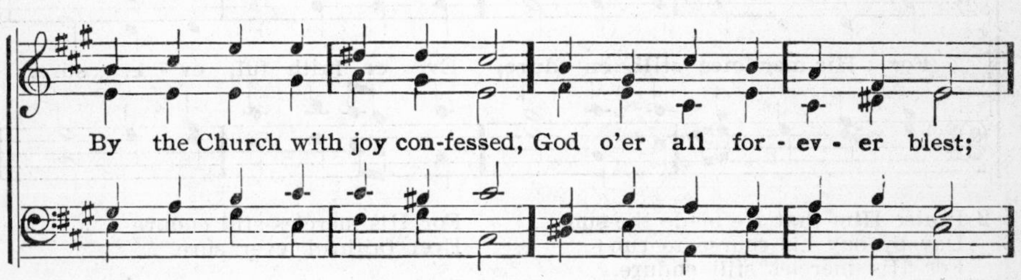
By the Church with joy con-fessed, God o'er all for - ev - er blest;

Plead-ing at Thy throne we stand, Save Thy peo - ple, bless our land.

2 On our fields of grass and grain
Send, O Lord, the kindly rain;
O'er our wide and goodly land
Crown the labors of each hand.
Let Thy kind protection be
O'er our commerce on the sea:
Open, Lord, Thy bounteous hand,
Bless Thy people, bless our land.

3 Let our rulers ever be
Men that love and honor Thee;
Let the powers by Thee ordained
Be in righteousness maintained;
In the people's hearts increase
Love of piety and peace;
Thus united we shall stand
One wide, free, and happy land.

H. Harbaugh, 1860

297 Monkland 7s

J. B. WILKES, 1861

1 Praise, O praise our God and King! Hymns of ad - o - ra - tion sing;

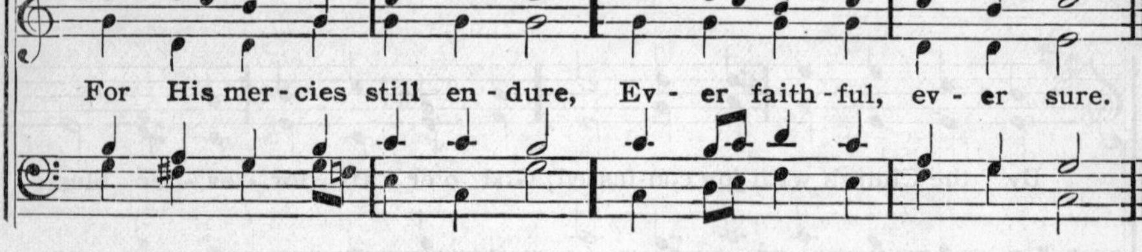
For His mer - cies still en - dure, Ev - er faith - ful, ev - er sure.

2 Praise Him that He made the sun
Day by day his course to run;
For His mercies still endure,
Ever faithful, ever sure.

3 And the silver moon by night,
Shining with her gentle light;
For His mercies still endure,
Ever faithful, ever sure.

4 Praise Him that He gave the rain
To mature the swelling grain;
For His mercies still endure,
Ever faithful, ever sure.

5 And hath bid the fruitful field
Crops of precious increase yield;
For His mercies still endure,
Ever faithful, ever sure.

6 Praise Him for our harvest store,
He hath filled the garner floor;
For His mercies still endure,
Ever faithful, ever sure.

7 And for richer food than this,
Pledge of everlasting bliss;
For His mercies still endure,
Ever faithful, ever sure.

8 Glory to our bounteous King,
Glory let creation sing;
Glory to The Father, Son,
And the Spirit, Three in One!

H. W. Baker, 1861

298 Dix 7s 61

1 Praise to God, immortal praise,
For the love that crowns our days;
Bounteous source of ev'ry joy,
Let Thy praise our tongues employ;
All to Thee, our God, we owe,
Source whence all our blessings flow.

2 All the plenty summer pours;
Autumn's rich o'erflowing stores;
Flocks that whiten all the plain;
Yellow sheaves of ripened grain:
Lord, for these our souls shall raise
Grateful vows and solemn praise.

3 Peace, prosperity, and health,
Private bliss, and public wealth,
Knowledge with its gladdening streams,
Pure religion's holier beams:
Lord, for these our souls shall raise
Grateful vows and solemn praise.

4 As Thy prospering hand hath blest,
May we give Thee of our best;
And by deeds of kindly love
For Thy mercies grateful prove;
Singing thus through all our days,
Praise to God, immortal praise.

(Or to Coburg Or to Fred til Bod)

Mrs. A. L. Barbauld, 1772 a ab.

299 Thanksgiving 7s 81 W. B. GILBERT, 1965 (P)

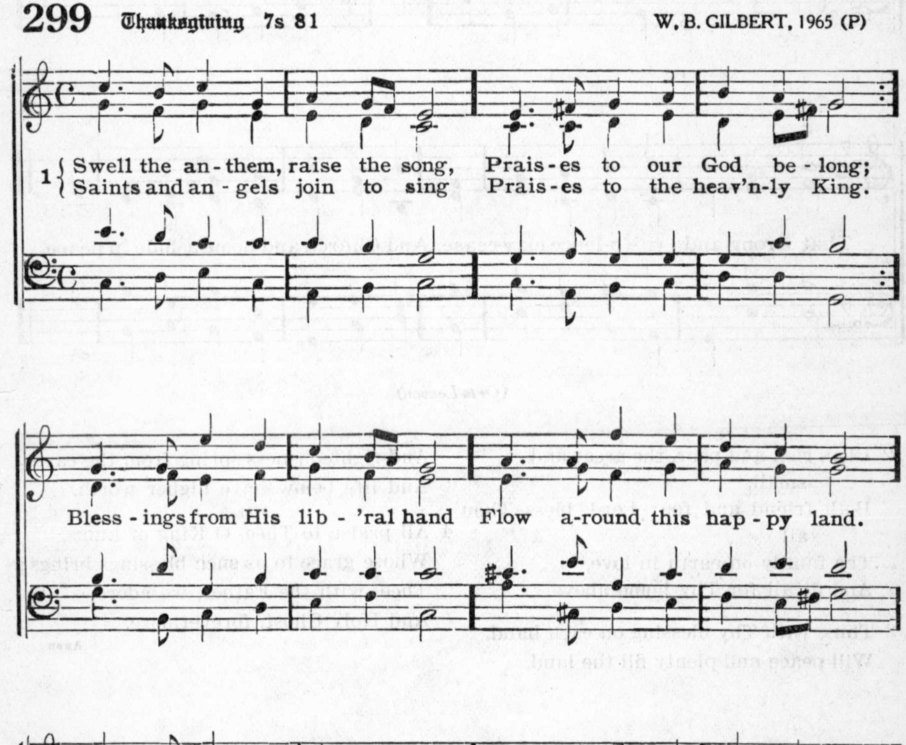
1 { Swell the an-them, raise the song, Prais-es to our God be-long;
Saints and an-gels join to sing Prais-es to the heav'n-ly King.
Bless-ings from His lib-'ral hand Flow a-round this hap-py land.
Kept by Him, no foes an-noy; Peace and free-dom we en-joy.

2 Here, beneath a virtuous sway
May we cheerfully obey;
Never feel oppression's rod,
Ever own and worship God.

Hark! the voice of nature sings
Praises to the King of kings;
Let us join the choral song,
And the grateful notes prolong.

Nathan Strong

National and Day of Humiliation and Prayer

300 Das walt Gott Vater L. M.

J. S. BACH, 1736

1 O bless, Thou heav'nly Po-tentate With wisdom, strength, the pow'rs of state,
That wrong and vi - o-lence may cease, And Church and home a-bide in peace.

(*Or to Louvan*)

2 Bless rich and poor, the great and small,
Both friend and foe; Lord, bless Thou all
The family on earth in love,
And fit all for Thy home above.

3 Thus, with Thy blessing on each hand,
Will peace and plenty fill the land,
And righteousness spring from the earth,
And life below have higher worth.

4 All praise to Thee, O King of kings,
Whose grace to us such blessings brings;
Thee, with the Father, we adore,
And Holy Ghost, forevermore.

Amen

301 Coburg 7s 61

FRDR. ENCKHAUSEN, 1868

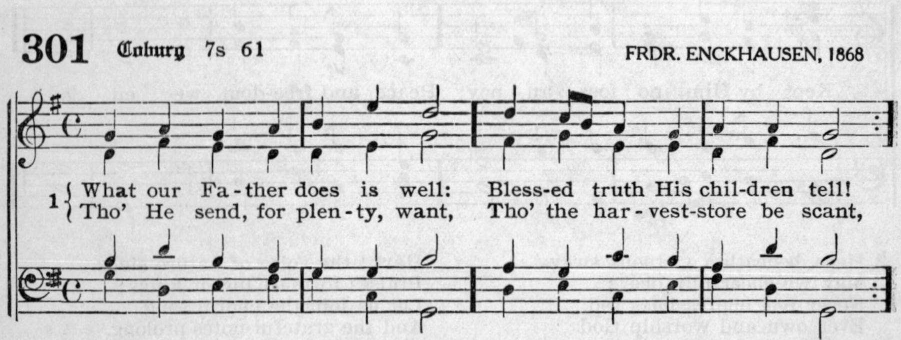
1 { What our Fa - ther does is well: Bless-ed truth His chil-dren tell!
Tho' He send, for plen - ty, want, Tho' the har - vest-store be scant,

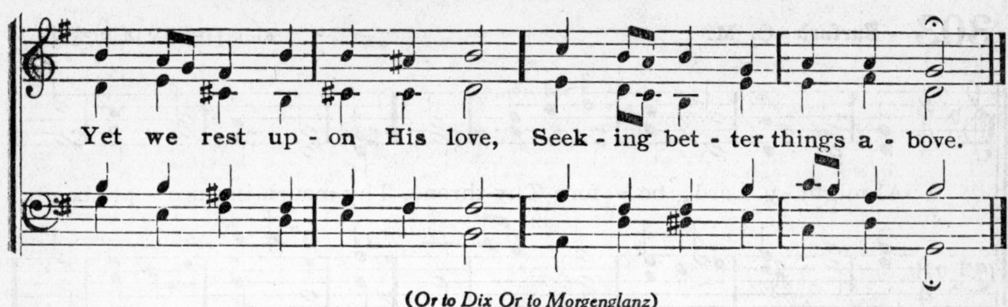
Yet we rest up - on His love, Seek - ing bet - ter things a - bove.

(Or to Dix Or to Morgenglanz)

2 What our Father does is well:
Shall the willful heart rebel
If a blessing He withhold
In the field, or in the fold?
Is He not Himself to be
All our store eternally?

3 What our Father does is well:
Though He sadden hill and dell,
Upward yet our praises rise
For the strength His Word supplies.
He has called us sons of God;—
Can we murmur at His rod?

4 What our Father does is well:
May the thought within us dwell;
Though nor milk nor honey flow,
In our barren Canaan now,
God can save us in our need,
God can bless us, God can feed.

5 Therefore unto Him we raise
Hymns of glory, songs of praise;
To the Father and the Son
And the Spirit, Three in One,
Honor, might, and glory be,
Now and through eternity.

B. Schmolk, 1720 H. W. Baker, Tr. 1861

302 Nox Praecessit C. M.

J. B. CALKIN, 1875

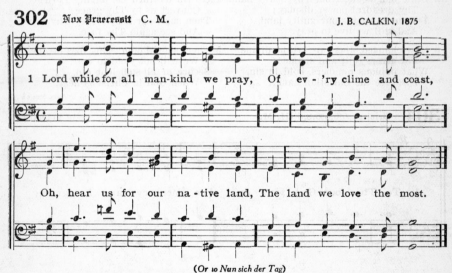

1 Lord while for all man-kind we pray, Of ev - 'ry clime and coast,
Oh, hear us for our na - tive land, The land we love the most.

(Or to Nun sich der Tag)

2 Oh, guard our shores from every foe,
With peace our borders bless,
With prosperous times our cities crown,
Our fields with plenteousness.

3 Unite us in the sacred love
Of knowledge, truth and Thee;
And let our hills and valleys shout
The songs of liberty.

4 Here may religion, pure and mild,
Smile on our Sabbath hours;
And piety and virtue bless
The home of us and ours.

5 Lord of the nations, thus to Thee
Our country we commend;
Be Thou her Refuge and her Trust,
Her everlasting Friend.

John R. Wreford

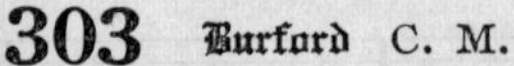

303 Burford C. M.

Att. to HENRY PURCELL

1 Al-might - y Lord, be - fore Thy throne, Thy mourn-ing peo - ple bend:

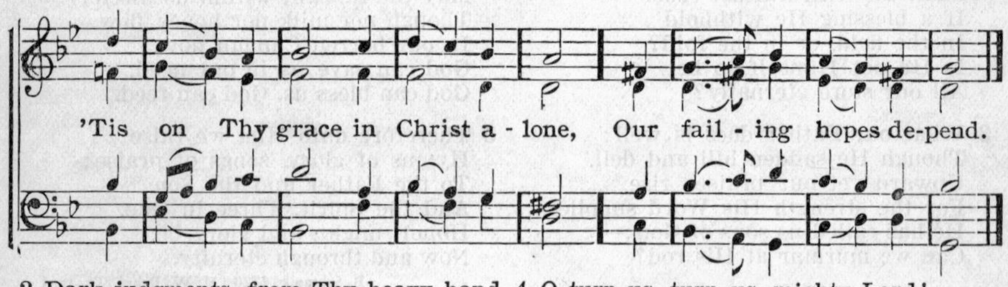
'Tis on Thy grace in Christ a - lone, Our fail - ing hopes de-pend.

2 Dark judgments, from Thy heavy hand,
Thy dreadful power display;
Yet mercy spares our guilty land,
And still we live to pray.

3 How changed, alas! are truths divine
For error, guilt and shame!
What impious numbers, bold in sin,
Disgrace the Christian name!

4 O turn us, turn us, mighty Lord!
Convert us by Thy grace;
Then shall our hearts obey Thy word,
And see again Thy face.

5 Then, should oppressing foes invade,
We will not yield to fear,
Secure of all-sufficient aid,
When God in Christ is near.

Anne Steele a

304 Belsize 6,6,6,6,8,8 (H. M.)

J. W. ELLIOTT

p
1 To Thee our God we fly For mer - cy and for grace;
Oh, hear our lone - ly cry, And hide not Thou Thy face. O
cresc.

dim.
Lord, stretch forth Thy mighty hand, And guard and bless our Fa - ther - land.

2 Arise, O Lord of hosts,
Be jealous for Thy name,
And drive from out our coasts
The sins that put to shame:
O Lord, stretch forth Thy mighty hand,
And guard and bless our Fatherland.

3 Thy best gifts from on high
In rich abundance pour,
That we may magnify
And praise Thee more and more:
O Lord, stretch forth Thy mighty hand,
And guard and bless our Fatherland.

4 The powers ordained by Thee
With heavenly wisdom bless;
May they Thy servants be,
And rule in righteousness:
O Lord, stretch forth Thy mighty hand,
And guard and bless our Fatherland.

5 The Church of Thy dear Son
Inflame with love's pure fire;
Bind her once more in one,
And life and truth inspire:
O Lord, stretch forth Thy mighty hand,
And guard and bless our Fatherland.

W. W. How 1871

305 America 6,6,4,6,6,6,4

H. CAREY, 1743

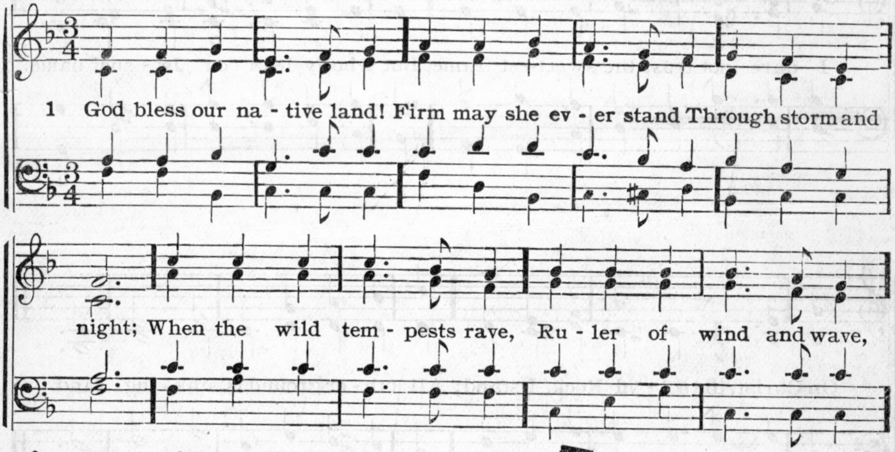

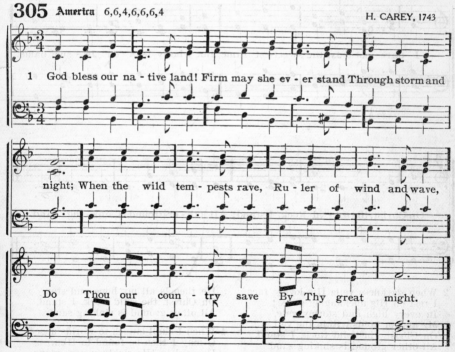

1 God bless our na - tive land! Firm may she ev - er stand Through storm and night; When the wild tem - pests rave, Ru - ler of wind and wave, Do Thou our coun - try save By Thy great might.

2 For her our prayer shall rise
To God above the skies;
On Him we wait:
Thou who art ever nigh,
Guarding with watchful eye,
To Thee aloud we cry,
God save the State!

C. T Brooks. 1834 J. S. Dwight, 1844

Faith and Justification

306 Magdalen (Rest) L. M. 61 SIR JOHN STAINER, 1875

1 My hope is built on noth-ing less Than Je - sus' blood and righteousness;

I dare not trust the sweet-est frame, But wholly lean on Je - sus' name.

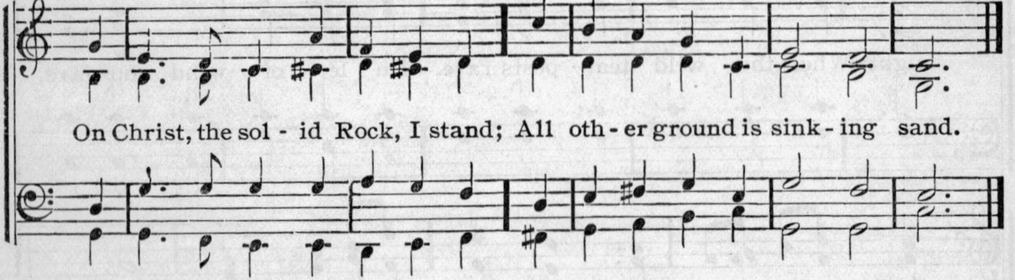

On Christ, the sol - id Rock, I stand; All oth - er ground is sink - ing sand.

2 When darkness veils His lovely face
I rest on His unchanging grace;
In every high and stormy gale,
My anchor holds within the veil.
On Christ, the solid Rock, I stand,
All other ground is sinking sand.

3 His oath, His covenant, and blood,
Support me in the sinking flood;
When every earthly prop gives way,
He then is all my hope and stay.
On Christ, the solid Rock, I stand,
All other ground is sinking sand.

4 When I shall launch to worlds unseen,
O may I then be found in Him,
Dressed in His righteousness alone,
Faultless to stand before the throne.
On Christ, the solid Rock, I stand;
All other ground is sinking sand.

Rev. Edward Mote, 1834

307 Palestrina C. M.

Arr. fr. PALESTRINA (P)

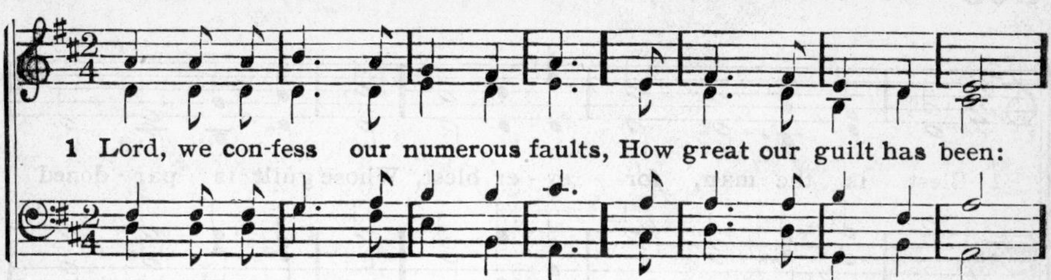
1 Lord, we con-fess our numerous faults, How great our guilt has been:

Fool - ish and vain were all our thoughts, And all our lives were sin.

2 But, O my soul, forever praise,
Forever love His name,
Who turns thy feet from dangerous ways
Of folly, sin, and shame.

3 'Tis not by works of righteousness
Which our own hands have done,
But we are saved by sovereign grace
Abounding through His Son.

4 'Tis from the mercy of our God
That all our hopes begin;
'Tis by the Water and the Blood
Our souls are washed from sin.

5 'Tis through the purchase of His death
Who hung upon the tree,
The Spirit is sent down to breathe
On such dry bones as we.

6 Raised from the dead, we live anew;
And justified by grace,
We shall appear in glory too,
And see our Father's face.

Isaac Watts, 1700 a

308 Palestrina C. M.

1 All that I was, my sin, my guilt,
My death, was all my own;
All that I am, I owe to Thee,
My gracious God, alone.

2 The evil of my former state
Was mine, and only mine;
The good in which I now rejoice
Is Thine, and only Thine.

3 The darkness of my former state,
The bondage, all was mine;
The light of life in which I walk,
The liberty, is Thine.

4 Thy grace first made me feel my sin,
It taught me to believe;
Then, in believing, peace I found,
And now I live, I live!

5 All that I am, even here on earth,
All that I hope to be
When Jesus comes and glory dawns,
I owe it, Lord, to Thee.

H. Bonar, 1853

(Or to Dundee Or to Evan)

309 Rockingham L. M. L. MASON

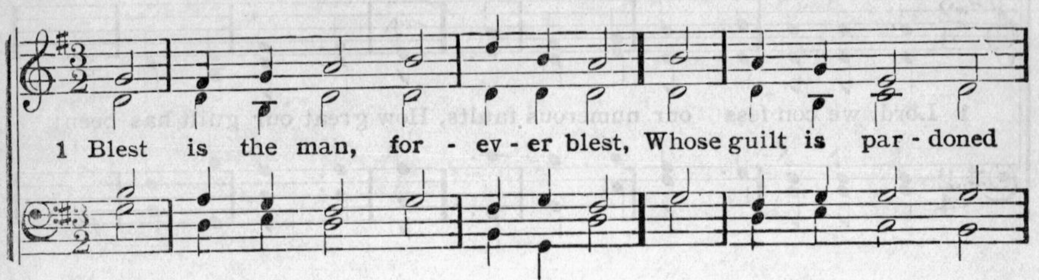
1 Blest is the man, for - ev - er blest, Whose guilt is par - doned

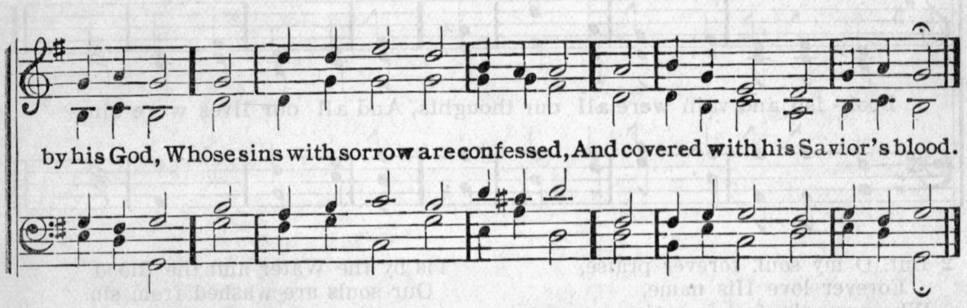
by his God, Whose sins with sorrow are confessed, And covered with his Savior's blood.

(Or to Federal St.)

2 Blest is the man to whom the Lord
Imputes not his iniquities;
He pleads no merit of reward,
And not on works, but grace relies.

3 From guile his heart and lips are free,
His humble joy, his holy fear,
With deep repentance well agree,
And join to prove his faith sincere.

4 How glorious is that righteousness
That hides and cancels all his sins!
While a bright evidence of grace
Through his whole life appears and shines.

Isaac Watts, 1719

310 Nun freut euch, lieben Christen 8,7,8,7,8,8,7 WITTENBERG H. B. 1524

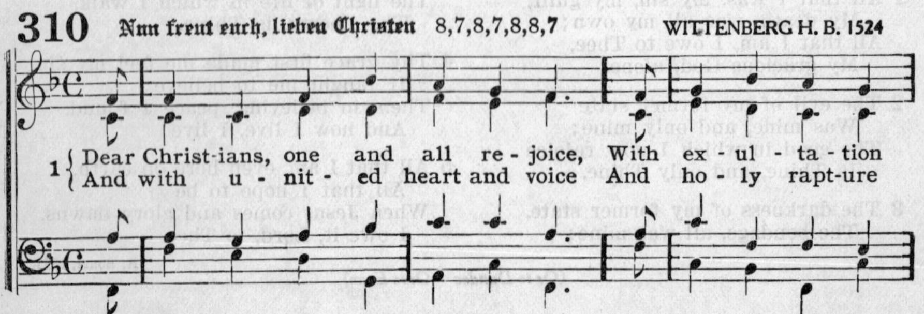
1 { Dear Christ-ians, one and all re - joice, With ex - ul - ta - tion
And with u - nit - ed heart and voice And ho - ly rapt-ure

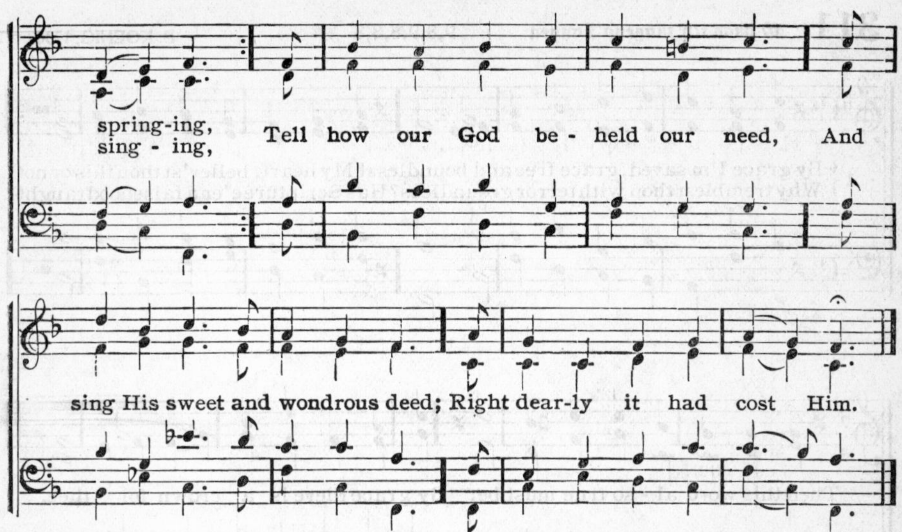
spring-ing, Tell how our God be - held our need, And
sing - ing,
sing His sweet and wondrous deed; Right dear-ly it had cost Him.

2 Fast bound in Satan's chains I lay,
Death brooded darkly o'er me,
My sin oppressed me night and day,
Therein my mother bore me;
Deeper and deeper still I fell,
Life had become a living hell,
So firmly sin possessed me.

3 My good works could avail me naught,
For they with sin were stained;
Free-will against God's judgment fought,
And dead to good remained;
Grief drove me to despair, and I
Had nothing left me but to die,
To hell I fast was sinking.

4 Then God beheld my wretched state
With deep commiseration;
He thought upon His mercy great,
And willed my soul's salvation;
He turned to me a Father's heart—
Not small the cost!—to heal my smart,
He gave His best and dearest.

5 He spake to His beloved Son:
'Tis time to take compassion;
Then go, my heart's most precious crown,
And bring to man salvation;
From sin and sorrow set him free,
Slay bitter death for him, that he
May live with Thee forever.

6 The Son His Father did obey,
And, born of virgin-mother,
He came awhile on earth to stay,
That He might be my brother.
His mighty power He hidden bore,
A servant's form like mine, He wore,
To lead the Devil captive.

7 He spake to me: "Hold fast by me,
I am thy rock and castle;
I wholly give myself for thee,
For thee I strive and wrestle;
For I am thine, and thou art mine,
Henceforth my place is also thine;
The foe shall never part us.

8 The foe shall shed my precious blood,
Me of my life bereaving;
All this I suffer for thy good;
Be steadfast and believing.
Life shall from death the victory win,
Mine innocence shall bear thy sin,
So art thou blest forever.

9 Now to my Father I depart,
From earth to heaven ascending,
Thence heavenly wisdom to impart,
The Holy Spirit sending;
He shall in trouble comfort thee,
Teach thee to know and follow me,
Into all truth shall guide thee.

10 What I have done and taught, do thou
To do and teach endeavor;
So shall my kingdom flourish now,
And God be praised forever;
Take heed lest men with base alloy
The heavenly treasure should destroy;
This counsel I bequeath thee."

Dr. Martin Luther, 1523

311 O dass ich tausend Zungen 9,8,9,8,8,8 B. KOENIG, 1738

1 { By grace I'm saved, grace free and boundless! My heart, believ'st thou this or not?
Why defendest thou with terror groundless? Has Scripture e'er a falsehood taught?

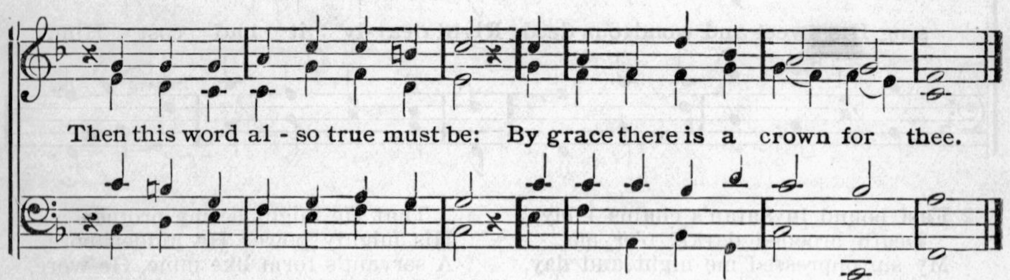
Then this word al - so true must be: By grace there is a crown for thee.

2 By grace! our works are all rejected,
All claims of merit pass for naught;
The mighty Savior, long expected,
To us this blissful truth has brought,
That He by death redeems our race,
And we are saved alone by grace.

3 By grace! mark well these words' true meaning,
When thou dost sorrow sin-oppressed,
When Satan threats with pride o'erweening,
When troubled conscience sighs for rest;
What reason cannot comprehend
It pleases God by grace to send.

4 By grace His Son, on earth appearing,
Vouchsafed beneath thy woe to bend;
Hadst thou, damnation justly fearing,
Done aught to render Him thy friend?
Was't not that He thy welfare sought,
And but by grace deliverance wrought?

5 By grace! this ground of our salvation,
As long as God is true, endures:
What saints have penned by inspiration,
What God by His own Word assures,
What all our faith must rest upon,
Is grace, free grace, through His dear Son.

6 By grace! but think not, thou who livest
Securely on in godless ways,
That thou,—though all are called,—receivest
The promised rest that wakes our praise;
By grace none find in heaven a place
Who live in sin in hope of grace.

7 By grace! they who have heard this sentence
Must bid hypocrisy farewell;
For only after deep repentance
The soul what grace imports can tell,
To sin while grace a trifle seems,
To faith it bright with glory beams.

8 By grace the timid hearts that languish,
Find access to the Father's heart,
When conflicts fierce and bitter anguish
Bid all their joy and hopes depart.
Where, ofttimes, should I strength obtain,
Did grace my anchor not remain!

9 By grace! on this in death I'll rest me,
Rejoicing e'en though feeling naught;
I know my sin—it oft oppressed me—
But Him, too, who salvation brought
My heart exults, grief flees apace,
Because my soul is saved by grace.

10 By grace! may sin and Satan hearken!
I bear my flag of faith in hand,
And pass—for doubts my joy can't darken—
The Red Sea to the Promised Land.
I cling to what my Savior taught,
And trust it, whether felt or not.

C. L. Scheidt, 1742 M. Loy, Tr. a

312 O dass ich tausend Zungen 9,8,9,8,8,8

1 Now I have found the sure foundation,
Where evermore my anchor grounds!
It lay there ere the world's creation,
Where else, but in my Savior's wounds?
Foundation, which unmoved shall stay,
When earth and heaven pass away.

2 It is that mercy never ending,
Which all conception far transcends,
Of Him, who, with love's arms extending,
To wretched sinners condescends;
Whose heart with pity still doth break,
Whether we seek Him, or forsake.

3 Our ruin God has not intended,
Salvation He would fain bestow;
For this the Son to earth descended,
And then to heaven again did go;
For this so loudly evermore
He knocketh at our heart's closed door.

4 O depth of love, in which, past finding,
My sins through Christ's blood disappear;
This is for wounds the safest binding,
There is no condemnation here;
For Jesus' blood through earth and skies
Forever Mercy! Mercy! cries.

5 I never will forget this crying,
In faith I'll trust it all my days,
And, when o'er all my sins I'm sighing,
I towards my Father's heart will gaze;
For there is always to be found
Free mercy without end and bound.

6 Though I be robbed of every pleasure
That soul and body can make glad,
Bereft of every earthly treasure,
Forlorn, forsaken, lone and sad:
However far His help may be,
His mercy yet is left to me.

7 Though earthly cares and want oppress me,
And cause me sorrow and regret
That things so vain can still distress me,
And give me so much trouble yet:
Though I am bowed down to the dust,
Still in His mercy I will trust.

8 Though in the best of all my actions,
In works that are admired the most,
I must perceive great imperfections,
I surely have no right to boast;
Yet this sweet comfort doth abide:
In mercy only I confide.

9 Be it with me as He is willing,
Whose mercy is a boundless sea;
May He Himself my heart be stilling,
That this may ne'er forgotten be;
Then it will rest, in joy and woe,
On mercy, while it beats below.

10 On this foundation I unshrinking
Will stand, while I on earth remain;
This shall engage my acting, thinking,
While I the breath of life retain;
Then I will sing eternally,
Unfathomed Mercy, still of Thee.

Johann Andreas Rothe, 1728

313 Rockingham L. M.

1 Who shall the Lord's elect condemn?
'Tis God who justifies their souls;
And mercy, like a mighty stream,
O'er all their sins divinely rolls.

2 He lives! He lives! and sits above,
Forever interceding there:
Who shall divide us from His love,
Or what should tempt us to despair?

3 Shall persecution, or distress,
Famine, or sword, or nakedness?
He who hath loved us bears us through,
And makes us more than conquerors too.

4 Not all that men on earth can do,
Nor powers on high, nor powers below,
Shall cause His mercy to remove,
Or wean our hearts from Christ, our Love.

I. Watts a

314 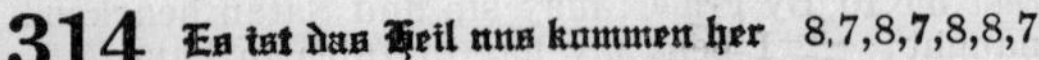
Es ist das Heil uns kommen her
8.7,8,7,8,8,7 J. WALTHER, 1524

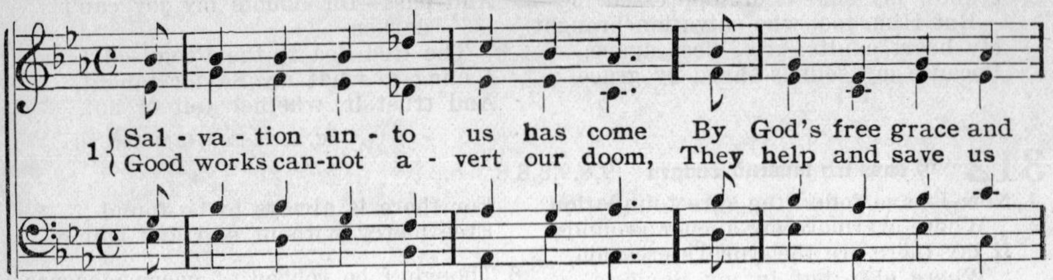
1 { Sal - va - tion un - to us has come By God's free grace and
Good works can-not a - vert our doom, They help and save us

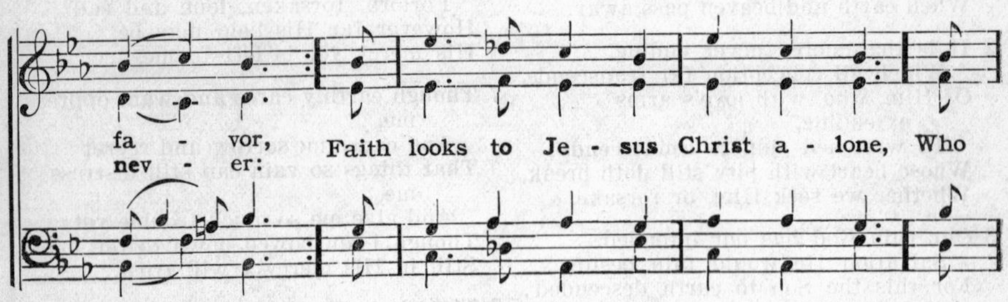
fa - vor, Faith looks to Je - sus Christ a - lone, Who
nev - er:

did for all the world a - tone; He is the Me - di - a - tor.

2 What God doth in His Law demand
No man to Him can render,
And so He draws His flaming brand
To punish the offender:
Our flesh has not those pure desires
Which first of all the Law requires,
So we're in condemnation.

3 It was a false, misleading dream
That God His Law had given
For us to keep and merit claim
And earn our way to heaven:
God's Law is but a mirror bright
To bring the inbred sin to sight,
That lurks within our nature.

4 By our own strength to put aside
God's wrath, and win His blessing,
Is useless task, by many tried,
Is only guilt increasing:
For God hypocrisy abhors;
Flesh with the spirit ever wars,
For 'tis by nature evil.

5 And yet, the Law fulfilled must be
Or we were lost forever;
Therefore God sent His Son that He
Might us from death deliver;
He all the Law for us fulfilled,
And thus His Father's anger stilled,
Which over us impended.

6 Since Christ hath full atonement made
And brought to us salvation,
Each Christian therefore may be glad
And build on this foundation:
Thy grace alone, dear Lord, I plead,
Thy death my life now is indeed,
For Thou hast paid my ransom.

7 Not doubting this, I trust in Thee,
Thy word cannot be broken;
Thou all dost call, "Come unto me!"
No falsehood hast Thou spoken:
"He that believes and is baptized,
He shall be saved," say'st Thou, O
Christ,
"And he shall never perish."

8 He's just 'fore God, and he alone,
Who by this faith is living;
This faith will by good works be
known,
To God the glory giving;
Faith gives thee peace with God above,
But thou thy neighbor too wilt love,
If thou art a new creature.

9 The Law reveals the guilt of sin
And makes man conscience-stricken;
The Gospel then doth enter in
The sinful soul to quicken.
Come to the Cross, trust Christ and
live;
The Law to you no peace can give
With all its good endeavors.

10 From faith in Christ, whene'er 'tis
right,
Good works are surely flowing;
The faith is dead that shuns the light,
No good works ever showing:
By faith alone the just shall live,
Good works alone the proof can give
Of love, which true faith worketh.

Paul Speratus, 1532 ab. Comp. Tr. 1910

315 Voller Wunder 7s 6 1

J. G. EBELING

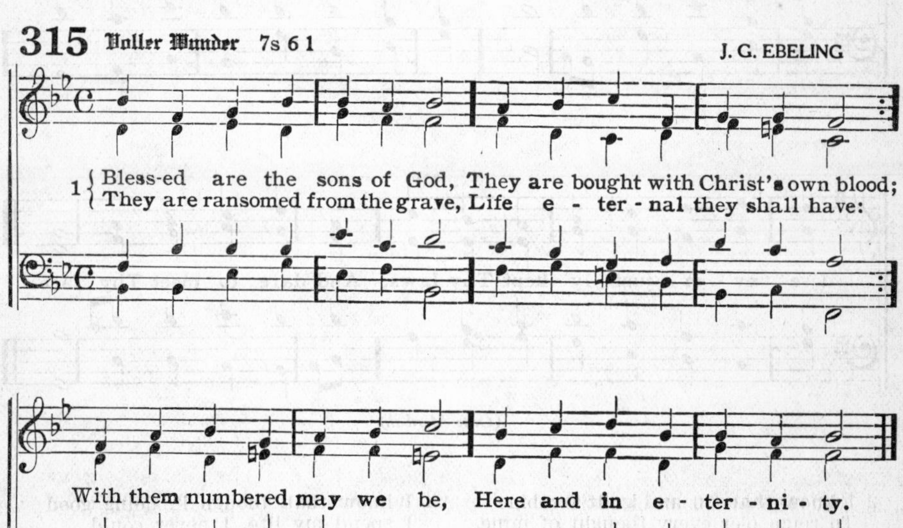
1 { Bless-ed are the sons of God, They are bought with Christ's own blood;
They are ransomed from the grave, Life e - ter - nal they shall have:
With them numbered may we be, Here and in e - ter - ni - ty.

(Or to Dix)

2 They are justified by grace,
They enjoy the Savior's peace;
All their sins are washed away,
They shall stand in God's great day:
With them numbered may we be,
Here and in eternity.

3 They are lights upon the earth,
Children of a heavenly birth;
One with God, with Jesus one,
Glory is in them begun:
With them numbered may we be,
Here and in eternity.

Rev. Joseph Humphreys, 1743; arr. and verse 2, l. 2 a

316 Wittenberg 8,8,6,8,8,6 (C. P. M.) H. ILSE, 1910

1 I do not come be-cause my soul Is free from sin, and pure, and whole,

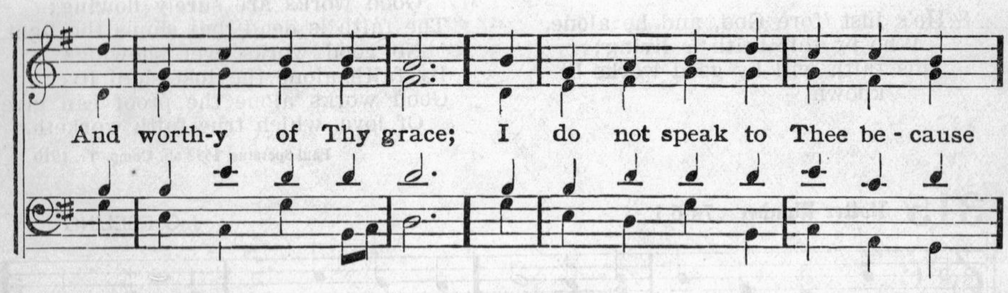
And worth-y of Thy grace; I do not speak to Thee be-cause

I've ev-er just-ly kept Thy laws, And dare to meet Thy face.

(*Or to Meribah*)

2 I know that sin and guilt combine
To reign o'er every thought of mine,
And turn from good to ill;
I know that when I try to be
Upright, and just, and true to Thee,
I am a sinner still!

3 I know that often when I strive
To keep a spark of love alive
For Thee, the powers within
Leap up in unsubmissive might,
And oft benumb my sense of right,
And pull me back to sin.

4 I know that, though in doing good
I spend my life, I never could
Atone for all I've done:
But though my sins are black as night,
I dare to come before Thy sight,
Because I trust Thy Son.

5 In Him alone my trust I place—
Come boldly to Thy throne of grace,
And there commune with Thee.
Salvation sure, O Lord, is mine,
And, all-unworthy, I am Thine,
For Jesus died for me!

F. B. St. John

317 Ach, was soll ich Suender machen 8,7,7,8,7,7 J. FLITTNER, 1653

1 O how great is Thy com-pas-sion, Faith-ful Fa-ther, God of grace,

That up-on man's wretch-ed-ness, That up-on man's dep-ra-va-tion

Thou took'st pit-y, so that we Might be saved e-ter-nal-ly!

2 Thy great love for this hath striven
That man from all pain shall free
And forever blessed be.
Yea, Thy Son Himself hath given,
And extends an earnest call
To His Supper unto all.

3 And for this our soul's salvation
Voucheth Thy good Spirit, Lord,
In Thy Sacraments and Word,
He doth prosper Thy vocation,
Granteth us the gift of faith,
That we fear nor hell nor death.

4 Lord, Thy mercy will not leave me—
Truth doth evermore abide—
Then in Thee I will confide;
Since Thy Word cannot deceive me,
My salvation is to me
Well assured eternally.

5 I will praise Thy great compassion,
Faithful Father, God of grace,
That upon my wretchedness,
That upon my depravation
Thou took'st pity graciously;
Evermore be praise to Thee!

Johann Olearius, 1671 A. Crull, Tr.

318 Woodworth L. M W. B. BRADBURY, 1849

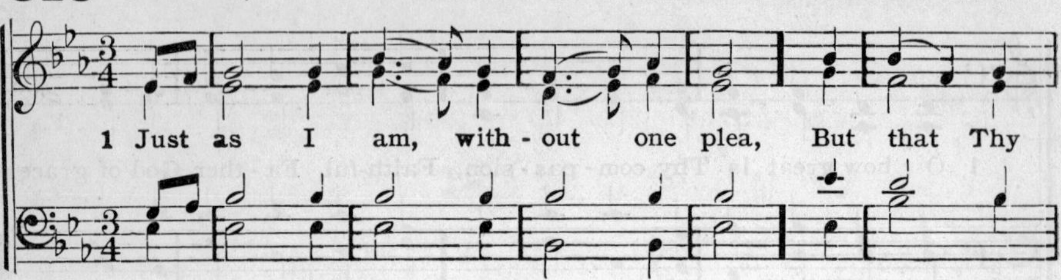
1 Just as I am, with-out one plea, But that Thy

blood was shed for me, And that Thou bid'st me come to

Thee, O Lamb of God, I come, I come.

2 Just as I am, and waiting not
To rid my soul of one dark blot,
To Thee, whose blood can cleanse each spot,
O Lamb of God, I come, I come.

3 Just as I am, though tossed about
With many a conflict, many a doubt,
Fightings and fears within, without,
O Lamb of God, I come, I come.

4 Just as I am, poor, wretched, blind;
Sight, riches, healing of the mind,
Yea, all I need, in Thee to find,
O Lamb of God, I come, I come.

5 Just as I am, Thou wilt receive,
Wilt welcome, pardon, cleanse, relieve;
Because Thy promise I believe,
O Lamb of God, I come, I come.

6 Just as I am, Thy love unknown
Has broken every barrier down;
Now to be Thine, yea, Thine alone,
O Lamb of God, I come, I come.

Ch. Elliott, 1836 a

319 Ben Rhydding S. M.

A. R. REINAGLE, 1799–1877

1 Not all the blood of beasts On Jew - ish al - tars slain,

Could give the guilt - y conscience peace, Or wash a - way the stain.

2 But Christ, the heavenly Lamb,
Takes all our sins away;
A sacrifice of nobler name,
And richer blood, than they.

3 My faith would lay her hand
On that dear head of Thine,
While like a penitent I stand,
And there confess my sin.

4 My soul looks back to see
The burdens Thou didst bear,
When hanging on the cursed tree,
And hopes her guilt was there.

5 Believing, we rejoice
To see the curse remove;
We bless the Lamb with cheerful voice,
And sing His bleeding love.

Isaac Watts, 1709

320 Ben Rhydding S. M.

1 Not what these hands have done
Can save this guilty soul;
Not what this toiling flesh has borne
Can make my spirit whole.

2 Not what I feel or do
Can give me peace with God;
Not all my prayers and sighs and tears
Can bear my awful load.

3 Thy work alone, O Christ,
Can ease this weight of sin;
Thy blood alone, O Lamb of God,
Can give me peace within.

4 Thy love to me, O God,
Not mine, O Lord, to Thee,
Can rid me of this dark unrest,
And set my spirit free.

5 Thy grace alone, O God,
To me can pardon speak;
Thy power alone, O Son of God,
Can this sore bondage break.

6 I bless the Christ of God;
I rest on love Divine;
And, with unfaltering lip and heart,
I call this Savior mine.

H. Bonar, 1861

(*Or to Monsell* [*St. Andrew*])

321 **Dunstan** 8,8,8,6 J. BARNBY, 1883 (P)

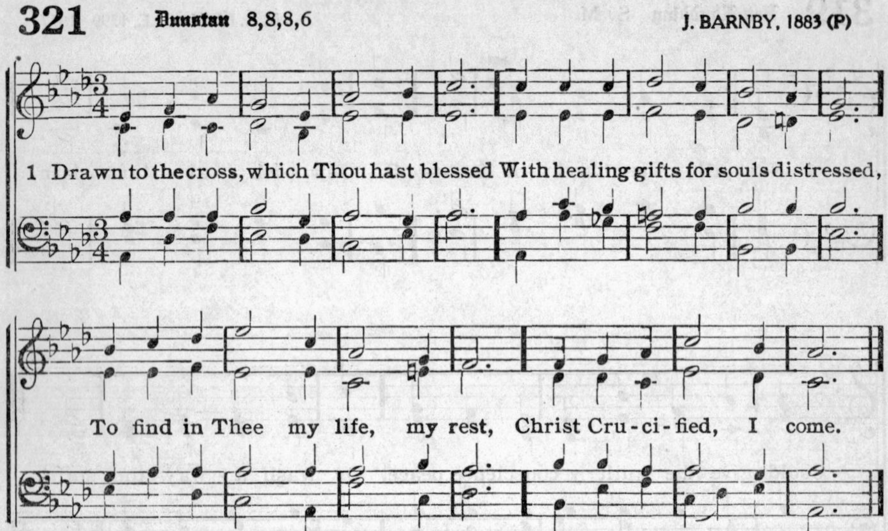
1 Drawn to the cross, which Thou hast blessed With healing gifts for souls distressed,
To find in Thee my life, my rest, Christ Cru-ci-fied, I come.

2 Thou knowest all my griefs and fears,
Thy grace abused, my misspent years;
Yet now to Thee, with contrite tears,
Christ Crucified, I come.

3 Wash me, and take away each stain;
Let nothing of my sin remain;
For cleansing, though it be through pain,
Christ Crucified, I come.

4 And then for work to do for Thee,
Which shall so sweet a service be
That angels well might envy me,
Christ Crucified, I come.

Miss G. M. Irons, 1880

322 **In Morgenrot gekleidet** 7,6 8 1 J. B. BEUTLER, 1799

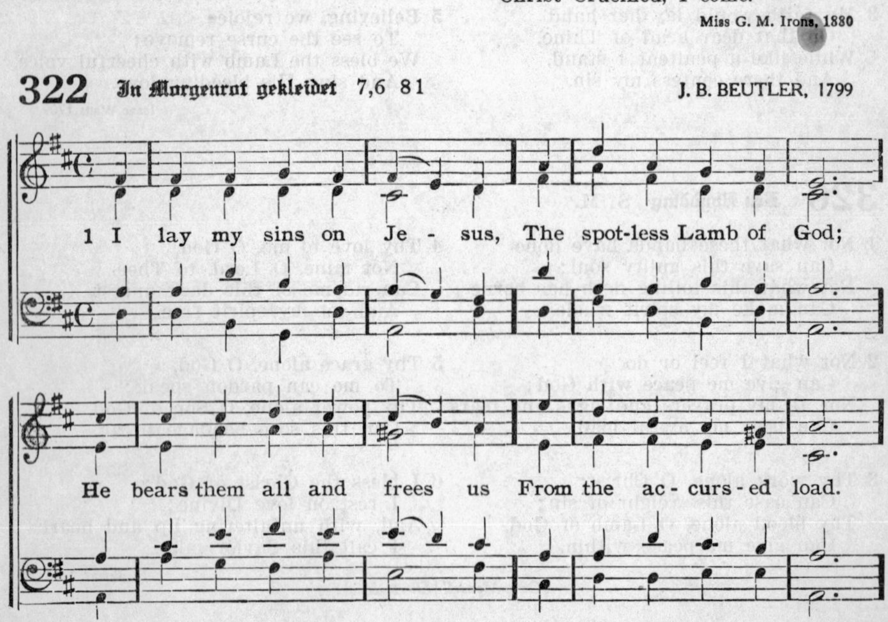
1 I lay my sins on Je - sus, The spot-less Lamb of God;
He bears them all and frees us From the ac - curs - ed load.

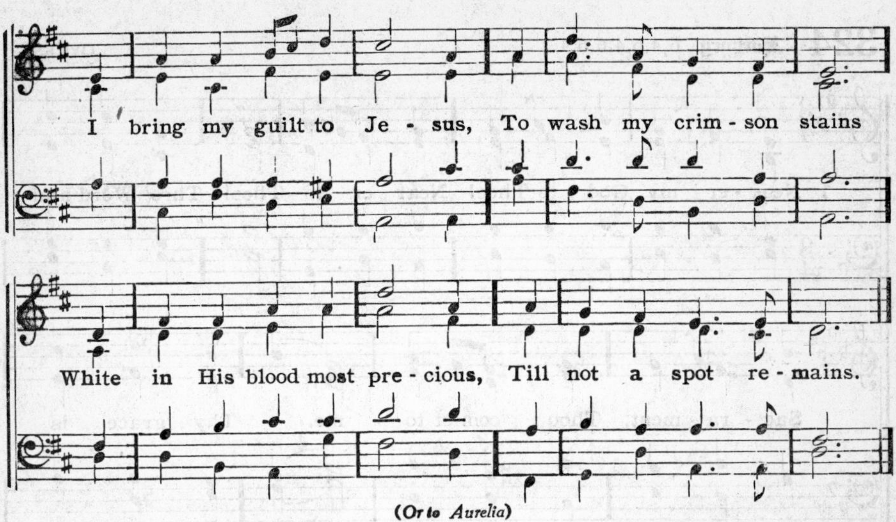
I bring my guilt to Je - sus, To wash my crim - son stains
White in His blood most pre - cious, Till not a spot re - mains.

(Or to Aurelia)

2 I lay my wants on Jesus;
All fullness dwells in Him;
He heals all my diseases,
He doth my soul redeem.
I lay my griefs on Jesus,
My burdens and my cares;
He from them all releases,
He all my sorrows shares.

3 I rest my soul on Jesus,
This weary soul of mine;
His right hand me embraces,
I on His breast recline.
I love the name of Jesus,
Immanuel, Christ, the Lord;
Like fragrance on the breezes
His name abroad is poured.

4 I long to be like Jesus,
Meek, loving, lowly, mild;
I long to be like Jesus,
The Father's holy child.
I long to be with Jesus,
Amid the heavenly throng,
To sing with saints His praises,
To learn the angels' song.

Horatius Bonar, 1849

323 Ich dank dir lieber 7,6 81

1 Through Jesus' bloody merit
I am at peace with God;
What, then, can daunt my spirit,
However dark my road?
My courage shall not fail me,
For God is on my side;
Though hell itself assail me,
Its rage I may deride.

2 There's nothing that can sever
Me from the love of God;
No want, no pain whatever,
No famine, peril, blood.
Though thousand foes surround me,
And in their base design
A sheep for slaughter count me,
The victory still is mine.

3 That neither life's temptation,
Nor death's terrific hour,
Nor angels of high station,
Nor any other power,
Nor things that now are present,
Nor things that are to come,
Nor height, however pleasant,
Nor depth of deepest gloom,

4 Nor any creature ever
Shall from the love of God
Me, the poor sinner, sever;
For in my Savior's blood
This love its fountain taketh;
He hears my faithful prayer,
And nevermore forsaketh
Me, his dear child and heir.

Simon Dach, 1651 A. Crull, Tr.

(Or to Valet will)

324 Horbury 6,4,6,4,6,6,4 DYKES

1 Near-er my God to Thee! Near-er to Thee! Thro' Word and
Sac-ra-ment, Thou com'st to me. Thy grace is
ev-er near, Thy Spir-it ev-er here, Draw-ing to Thee.

2 Ages on ages rolled,
  Ere earth appeared,
Yet Thine unmeasured love
  The way prepared;
E'en then Thou yearn'st for me
That I might nearer be,
  Nearer to Thee!

3 Thy Son has come to earth,
  My sin to bear,
My every wound to heal,
  My pain to share.
"God in the flesh" for me,
Brings me now nearer Thee,
  Nearer to Thee!

4 Lo! all my debt is paid,
  My guilt is gone.
See! He has risen for me,
  My throne is won.
Thanks, O my God, to Thee!
None now can nearer be,
  Nearer to Thee!

5 Welcome, then, to Thy home,
  Blest One in Three!
As Thou hast promised, come!
  Come, Lord, to me!
Work, Thou, O God, through me,
Live, Thou, O God, in me,
  Ever in me!

6 By the Baptismal stream,
  Which made me Thine,
By the dear flesh and blood,
  Thy love made mine,
Purge, Thou, all sin from me,
That I may nearer be,
  Nearer to Thee!

7 Surely it matters not
  What earth may bring,
Death is of no account,
  Grace will I sing.
Nothing remains for me,
Save to be nearer Thee,
  Nearer to Thee!

H. E. Jacobs, 1887

325 Toplady 7s 61 T. HASTINGS, 1830

1 Rock of a - ges, cleft for me, Let me hide my - self in Thee:

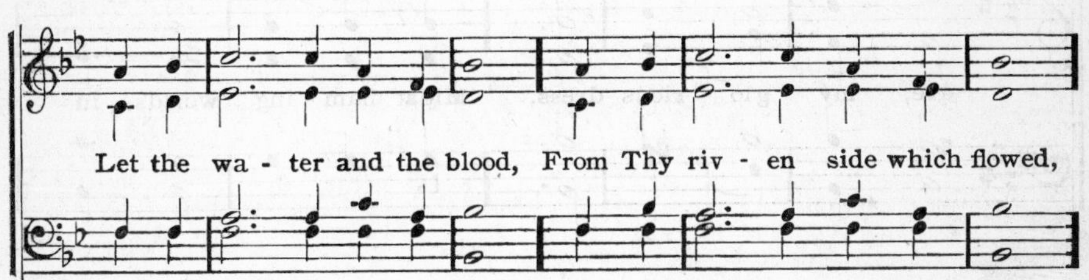
Let the wa - ter and the blood, From Thy riv - en side which flowed,

Be of sin the dou - ble cure, Cleanse me from its guilt and power.

2 Not the labors of my hands
Can fulfill Thy Law's demands;
Could my zeal no respite know,
Could my tears forever flow,
All for sin could not atone;
Thou must save, and Thou alone.

3 Nothing in my hand I bring,
Simply to Thy cross I cling;
Naked, come to Thee for dress;
Helpless, look to Thee for grace;
Foul, I to the fountain fly:
Wash me, Savior, or I die!

4 While I draw this fleeting breath,
When my eyelids close in death,
When I soar to worlds unknown,
See Thee on Thy judgment throne;
Rock of ages, cleft for me,
Let me hide myself in Thee!

Augustus M. Toplady, 1776 a

326 St. Crispin L. M.

SIR GEORGE JOB ELVEY, 1865

1 Je - sus, Thy blood and right - eous - ness, My beau - ty

are, my glo - rious dress, 'Midst flam - ing worlds, in

these ar - rayed, With joy shall I lift up my head.

2 Bold shall I stand in that great day,
For who aught to my charge shall lay?
Fully through these absolved I am
From sin and fear, from guilt and
shame.

3 The holy, meek, unspotted Lamb,
Who from the Father's bosom came,
Who died for me, e'en me to atone,
Now for my Lord and God I own.

4 Lord, I believe Thy precious blood,
Which at the mercy-seat of God
Forever doth for sinners plead,
For me—e'en for my soul—was shed.

5 Lord, I believe were sinners more
Than sands upon the ocean shore,
Thou hast for all a ransom paid,
For all a full atonement made.

6 When from the dust of death I rise
To claim my mansion in the skies,
E'en then, this shall be all my plea:
Jesus hath lived, and died for me.

7 Jesus, be endless praise to Thee,
Whose boundless mercy hath for me,
For me, and all Thy hands have made,
An everlasting ransom paid.

Count Zinzendorf, 1739 John Wesley, 1740

327 St. Crispin L. M.

1 Our God so loved the world that He
Gave His own Son, and did decree
That all who would in Him believe
Should everlasting life receive.

2 Christ Jesus is the ground of faith,
Who was made flesh and suffered death;
All that confide in Him alone
Are built on this chief Corner-stone.

3 God would not have the sinner die,
His Son with saving grace is nigh,
His Spirit in the Word doth teach
How man the blessed goal may reach.

4 Be of good cheer, for God's own Son
Forgives all sins which thou hast done;
Thou'rt justified by Jesus' blood,
Thy baptism grants the highest good.

5 If thou be sick, if death draw near,
This truth thy troubled heart can cheer;
Christ Jesus saves my soul from death,
That is the firmest ground of faith.

6 Glory to God the Father, Son,
And Holy Spirit, Three in One!
To Thee, O blessed Trinity,
Be praise now and eternally!

J. Olearius, 1671 A. Crull, Tr.

(Or to Herr Jesu Christ, meins)

328 Silver Street S. M.

I. SMITH, c. 1770

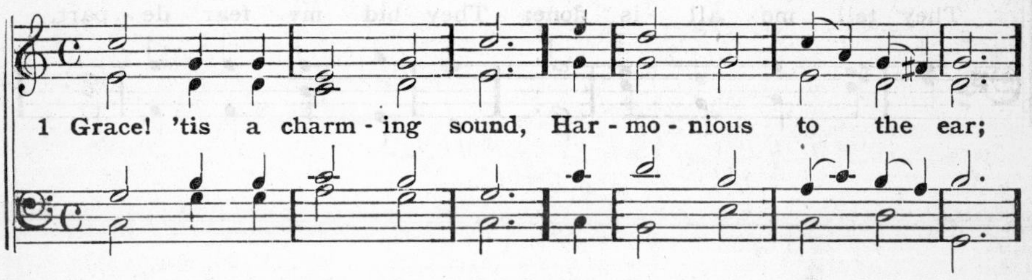
1 Grace! 'tis a charm - ing sound, Har - mo - nious to the ear;

Heav'n with the ech - o shall re - sound, And all the earth shall hear.

2 Grace first contrived the way
To save rebellious man;
And all the steps that grace display
Which drew the wondrous plan.

3 Grace first inscribed my name
In God's eternal book;
'Twas grace that gave me to the Lamb,
Who all my sorrows took.

4 Grace led my roving feet
To tread the heavenly road;
And new supplies each hour I meet,
While pressing on to God.

5 Grace taught my soul to pray,
And made my eyes o'erflow;
'Twas grace that kept me to this day,
And will not let me go.

6 Grace all the work shall crown,
Through everlasting days;
It lays in heaven the topmost stone,
And well deserves the praise.

Philip Doddridge, 1755

329 St. John 6,6,6,6,8,8 (H. M.) OLD ENGLISH: PARISH CHOIR, 1815 (P)

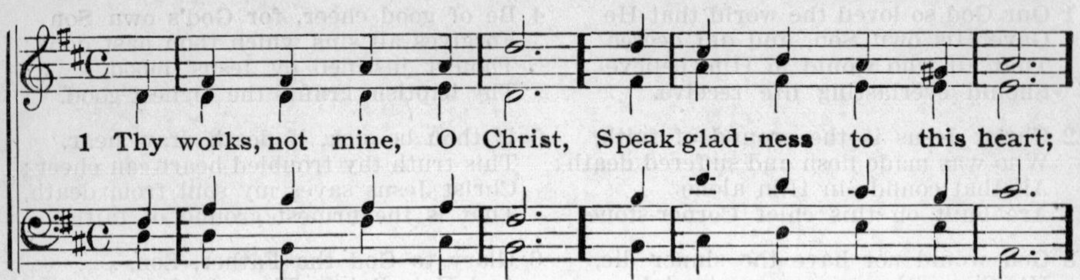
1 Thy works, not mine, O Christ, Speak glad-ness to this heart;

They tell me all is done; They bid my fear de-part,

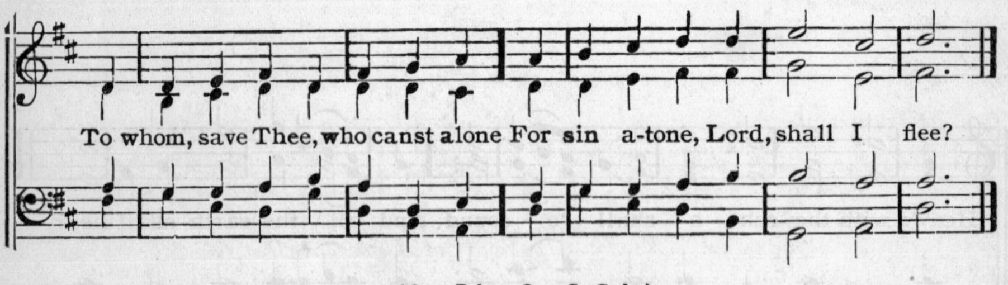
To whom, save Thee, who canst alone For sin a-tone, Lord, shall I flee?

(Or to Belsize Or to St. Godric)

2 Thy cross, not mine, O Christ,
Has borne the awful load
Of sins, that none in heaven
Or earth could bear but God.
To whom, save Thee, who canst alone
For sin atone, Lord, shall I flee?

3 Thy death, not mine, O Christ,
Has paid the ransom due;
Ten thousand deaths like mine
Would have been all too few.
To whom, save Thee, who canst alone
For sin atone, Lord, shall I flee?

4 Thy righteousness, O Christ,
Alone can cover me;
No righteousness avails
Save that which is of Thee.
To whom, save Thee, who canst alone
For sin atone, Lord, shall I flee?

H. Bonar, 1857

330 Albany C. M. VINCENT NOVELLO, 1868

1 O mys-ter - y of love Di - vine That thought and thanks o'er-powers!

Lord Je - sus, was our por - tion Thine, And is Thy por - tion ours?

2 Emmanuel, didst Thou take our place
To set us in Thine own?
Didst Thou our low estate embrace
To lift us to Thy throne?

3 Didst Thou fulfill each righteous deed,
God's perfect will express,
That we th' unfaithful ones might plead
Thy perfect faithfulness?

4 On Thy pure soul did dread and gloom
In that drear garden rise?
Are ours the brightness and the bloom
Of Thine own Paradise?

5 For Thee the Father's hidden face?
For Thee the bitter cry?
For us the Father's endless grace,
The song of victory?

6 Our load of sin and misery
Didst Thou, the Sinless, bear?
Thy spotless robe of purity
Do we, the sinners, wear?

7 Lord Jesus, is it even so?
Have we been loved thus?
What love can we on Thee bestow
Who hast exchanged with us?

8 Thou, who our very place didst take,
Dwell in our very heart:
Thou, who Thy portion ours dost make,
Thyself, Thyself, impart.

Thomas H. Gill, 1864

Sanctification

Obedience

331 Seelenbraeutigam 5,5,8,8,5,5 A. DRESE, 1698

1 Je - sus, still lead on Till our rest is won; And al-though the
way be cheer - less, We will fol - low calm and fear - less;
Guide us by Thy hand, To our fa - ther - land.

2 If the way be drear,
If the foe be near.
Let no faithless fears o'ertake us;
Let not faith and hope forsake us;
For through many a woe
To our home we go.

3 When we seek relief
From a long-felt grief:
When temptations come alluring,
Make us patient and enduring;
Show us that bright shore
Where we weep no more.

4 Jesus, still lead on,
Till our rest be won:
Heavenly Leader, still direct us,
Still support, control, protect us,
Till we safely stand
In our fatherland.

Count Zinzendorf, 1700—1760 Jane Borthwick, Tr. 1853

332 Larghetto (Bonn) L. M. BEETHOVEN (P)

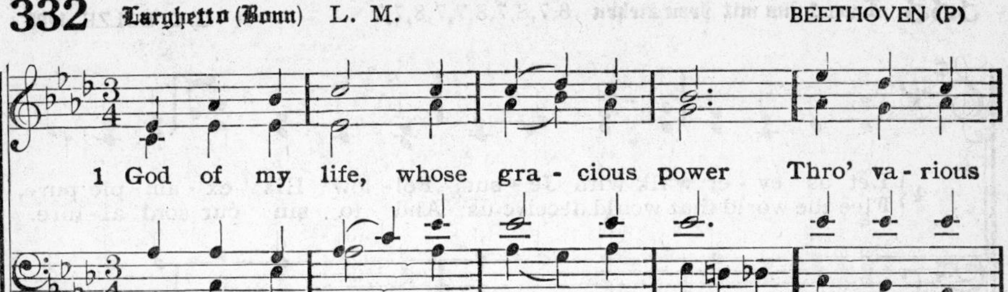
1 God of my life, whose gra - cious power Thro' va - rious

deaths my soul hath led; Or turned a - side the

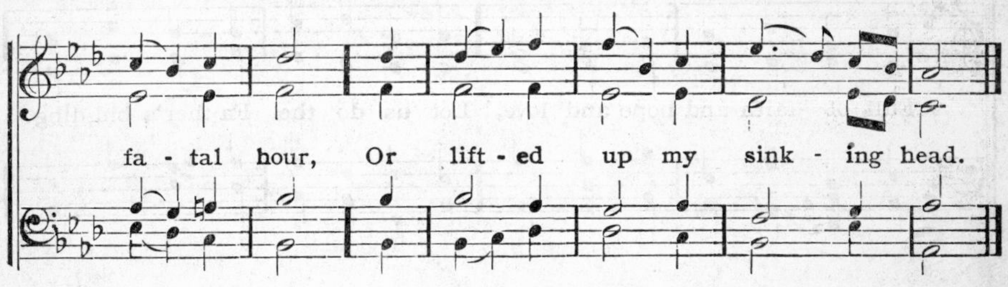
fa - tal hour, Or lift - ed up my sink - ing head.

(*Or to Grace Church*)

2 In all my ways Thy hand I own,
Thy ruling Providence I see:
O help me still my course to run,
And still direct my path to Thee.

3 Whither, O whither should I fly,
But to my loving Savior's breast?
Secure within Thine arms to lie,
And safe beneath Thy wings to rest!

4 I have no skill the snare to shun,
But Thou, O Christ, my Wisdom art!
I ever into ruin run;
But Thou art greater than my heart.

5 Foolish, and impotent, and blind,
Lead me a way I have not known;
Bring me where I my heaven may find,
The heaven of loving Thee alone.

6 Enlarge my heart to make Thee room;
Enter, and in me ever stay:
The crooked then shall straight become;
The darkness shall be lost in day.

Charles Wesley, 1740

333 Lasset uns mit Jesu ziehen 8,7,8,7,8,7,7,8,7,7 G. G. BOLZE, 1788

1 { Let us ev - er walk with Je - sus, Fol - low His ex - am - ple pure,
Flee the world that would deceive us And to sin our soul al - lure.
Ev - er in His foot-steps tread-ing, Bod - y here, yet soul a - bove,
Full of faith and hope and love, Let us do the Fa-ther's bid-ding.
Faith-ful Lord, a - bide with me, Sav - ior lead, I fol - low Thee.

(*Or to Sollt ich meinem Gott nicht singen*)

2 Let us suffer here with Jesus,
To His image e'er conform;
Heaven's glory soon will please us,
Sunshine follow on the storm.
Having sown in tears, in gladness
We shall reap. With patient cheer.
Let us hope and, void of fear,
Bid the turning of our sadness.
Christ, I suffer here with Thee,
There, oh, share Thy joy with me!

3 Let us also die with Jesus.
His death from the second death,
From our soul's destruction, frees us,
Quickens us with life's glad breath.
Let us mortify, while living,
Flesh and blood, and die to sin;
And the grave that shuts us in
Shall but prove the gate to heaven.
Jesus, here I die to Thee,
There to live eternally.

4 Let us also live with Jesus;
Since He's risen from the dead,
Must the conquered grave release us.
Jesus, Thou art now our Head,
We Thy body's cherished members,
Where Thou livest, live shall we;
Own us evermore to be,
Dearest Friend, Thy loved brethren.
Jesus, here I live to Thee,
Yonder, too, eternally.

Sigismund von Birken (Betulius), 1652. J. A. Rimbach, Tr. a

334 Mach's mit mir, Gott, nach deiner Güt 8,7,8,7,8,8 J. H. SCHEIN, 1628

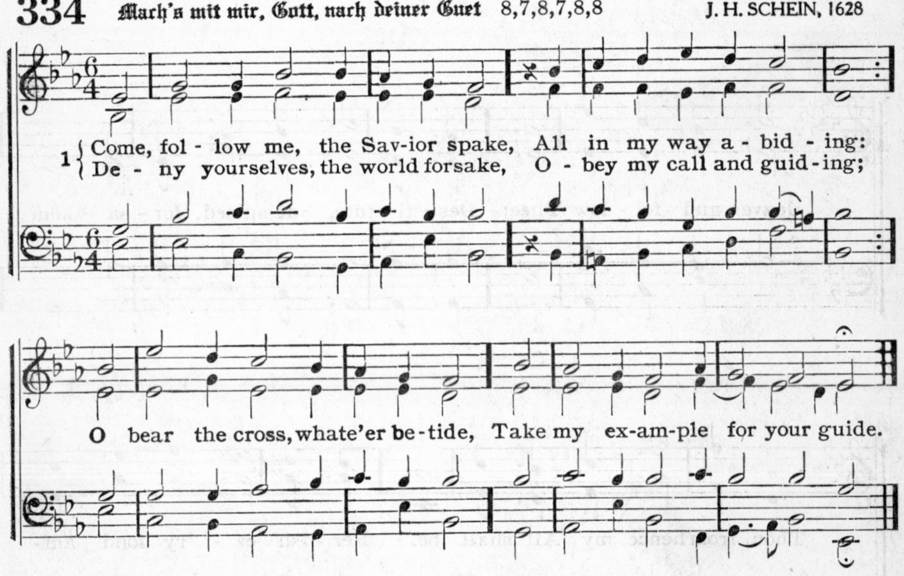
1 { Come, fol - low me, the Sav-ior spake, All in my way a - bid - ing:
De - ny yourselves, the world forsake, O - bey my call and guid - ing;
O bear the cross, whate'er be - tide, Take my ex-am-ple for your guide.

2 I am the Light, I light the way,
A virtuous life displaying;
Who comes to me and follows, aye,
I lead from his dark straying.
I am the Way, and well I show
How men should sojourn here below.

3 My heart in lowliness abounds,
My soul with love is glowing,
And from my mouth are words and sounds
Of meekness overflowing.
My heart, my mind, my strength, my all
To God I yield, on Him I call.

4 I teach you to avoid and flee
What harms your soul's salvation,
Your heart to purify and free
From sin's abomination.
Your Rock and Fortress e'er am I,
And lead you to the life on high.

5 But if too hot you find the fray,
I, at your side, stand ready;
I fight myself, I lead the way,
At all times firm and steady.
A coward he who will not heed
When the chief Captain takes the lead.

6 Who seeks to find his soul's welfare
Without me, he shall lose it;
But who to lose it may appear,
In God shall introduce it.
Who bears no cross, nor follows hard,
Deserves not me, nor my reward.

7 Then let us follow our dear Lord,
Bearing the cross appointed,
And bravely cleaving to His Word,
In suffering be undaunted.
Who has not stood the battle's strain
The crown of life shall ne'er obtain.

Johann Scheffler, (Angelus) 1668. C. W. Schaeffer, Tr a

335 Autumn 8, 7 8 1 F. H. BARTHELEMON

1 Je - sus, I my cross have ta - ken, All to
leave and fol - low Thee; Des - ti - tute, de-spised, for - sa - ken,
Thou, from hence, my All shalt be. Per - ish ev - 'ry fond am -
bi - tion, All I've sought, or hoped, or known; Yet how

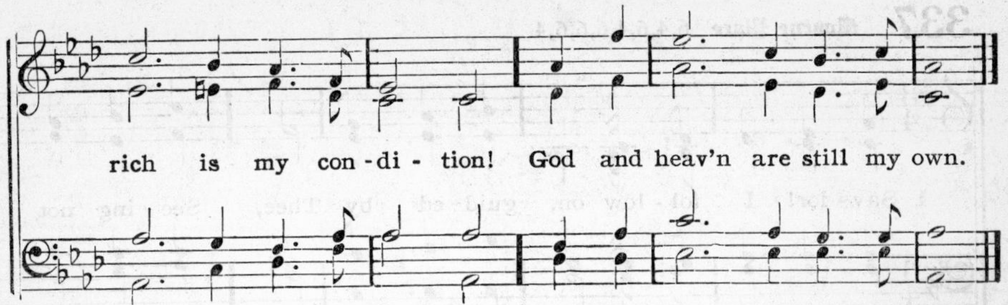
rich is my con-di-tion! God and heav'n are still my own.

2 Let the world despise and leave me,
They have left my Savior too:
Human hearts and looks deceive me
Thou art not, like them, untrue.
And while Thou shalt smile upon me,
God of wisdom, love, and might,
Foes may hate, and friends may shun me;
Show Thy face, and all is bright.

3 Go, then, earthly fame and treasure!
Come, disaster, scorn and pain!
In Thy service, pain is pleasure;
With Thy favor, loss is gain.
I have called Thee Abba, Father!
I have stayed my heart on Thee;
Storms may howl, and clouds may gather,
All must work for good to me.

4 Man may trouble and distress me,
'Twill but drive me to Thy breast;
Life with trials hard may press me,
Heaven will bring me sweeter rest.
O 'tis not in grief to harm me,
While Thy love is left to me;
O 'twere not in joy to charm me,
Were that joy unmixed with Thee.

5 Take, my soul, thy full salvation;
Rise o'er sin, and fear, and care;
Joy to find in every station,
Something still to do or bear.
Think what Spirit dwells within thee;
What a Father's smile is thine;
What a Savior died to win thee:
Child of heaven, shouldst thou repine?

6 Haste, then, on from grace to glory,
Armed by faith, and winged by prayer;
Heaven's eternal day's before thee,
God's own hand shall guide thee there.
Soon shall close thy earthly mission,
Swift shall pass thy pilgrim days:
Hope soon change to glad fruition,
Faith to sight, and prayer to praise.

Henry Francis Lyte, 1824

336 Autumn 8,7 8 1

1 Holy Father! Thou hast taught me
I should live to Thee alone;
Year by year Thy hand hath brought me
On through dangers oft unknown.
When I wandered, Thou hast found me;
When I doubted, sent me light;
Still Thine arm has been around me,
All my paths were in Thy sight.

2 In the world will foes assail me,
Crafty, stronger far than I;
And the strife will never fail me,
Well I know, before I die.
Therefore, Lord, I come, believing
Thou canst give the power I need,
Through the prayer of faith receiving
Strength—the Spirit's strength, indeed.

3 I would trust in Thy protecting,
Wholly rest upon Thine arm,
Follow wholly Thy directing,
Thou mine only Guard from harm!
Keep me from mine own undoing,
Help me turn to Thee when tried;
Still my footsteps, Father, viewing,
Keep me ever at Thy side.

John M. Neale, 1842 a

337 Monroe Place 6,4,6,4,6,6,6,4

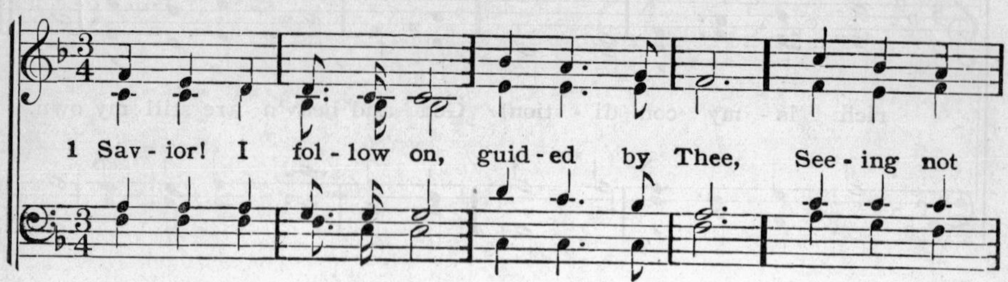
1 Sav - ior! I fol - low on, guid - ed by Thee, See - ing not

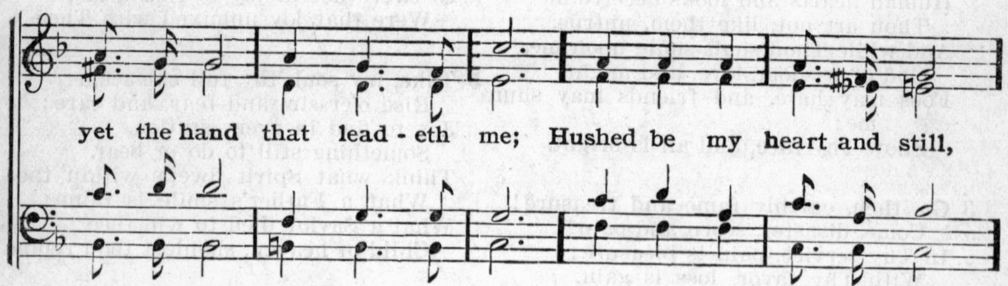
yet the hand that lead - eth me; Hushed be my heart and still,

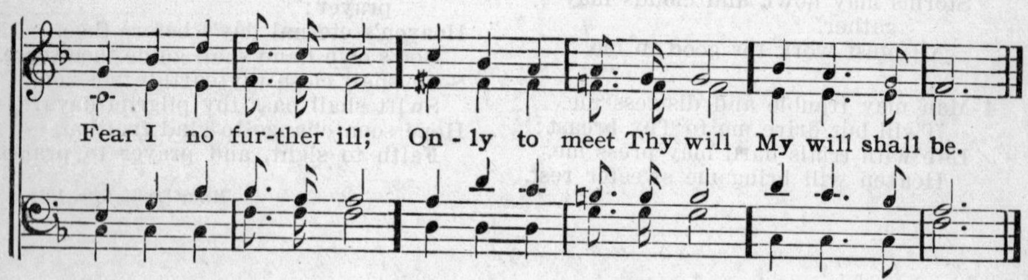
Fear I no fur-ther ill; On - ly to meet Thy will My will shall be.

(*Or to Winterton Or to Bethany*)

2 Riven the rock for me
  Thirst to relieve,
Manna from heaven falls
  Fresh every eve;
Never a want severe
Causeth my eye a tear,
But Thou dost whisper near,
  "Only believe!"

3 Often to Marah's brink
  Have I been brought;
Shrinking the cup to drink,
  Help I have sought;
And with the prayer's ascent,
Jesus the branch hath rent—
Quickly relief hath sent,
  Sweetening the draught.

4 Savior! I long to walk
  Closer with Thee;
Led by Thy guiding hand,
  Ever to be
Constantly near Thy side,
Quickened and purified,
Living for Him who died
  Freely for me!

C. S. Robinson

338 Goudimel S. M. 81

Ad. fr. GOUDIMEL by J. PEARCE

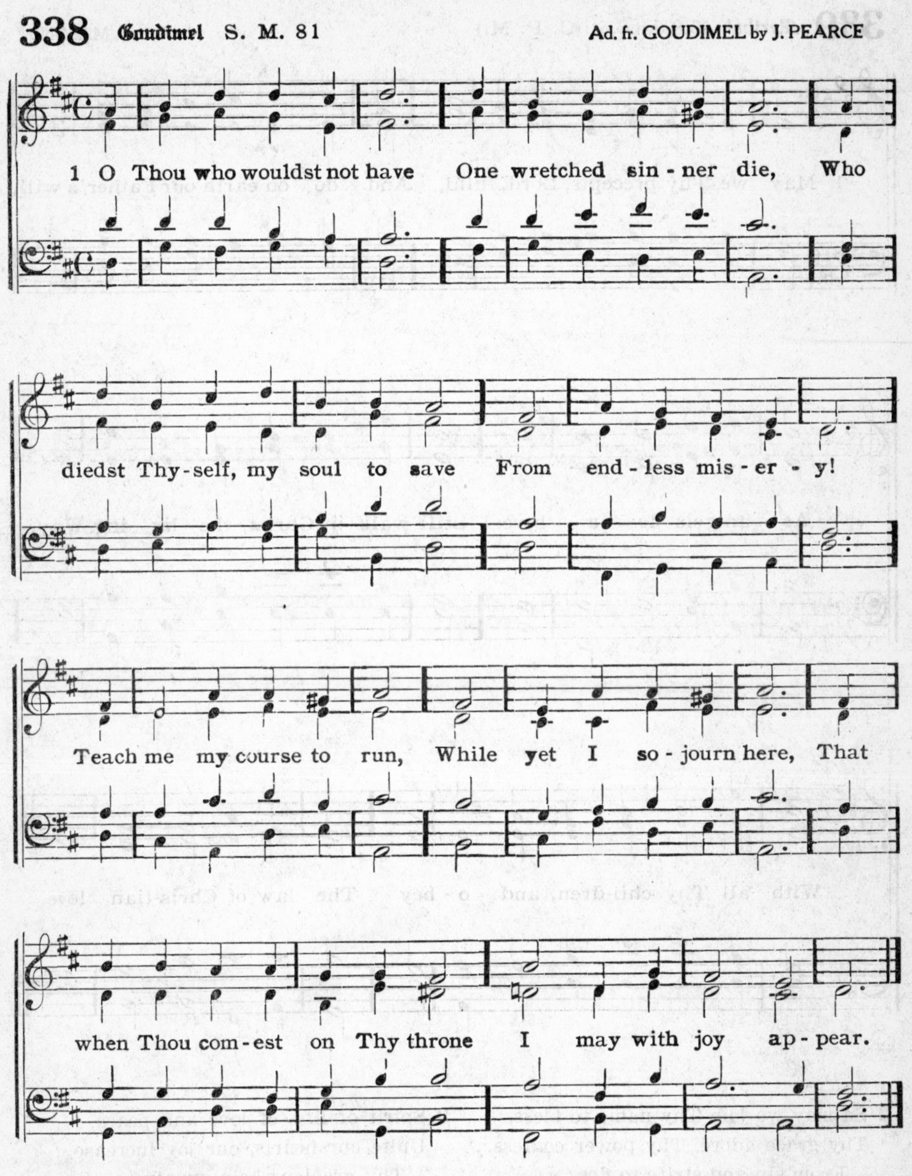
1 O Thou who wouldst not have One wretched sin - ner die, Who
diedst Thy-self, my soul to save From end - less mis - er - y!
Teach me my course to run, While yet I so - journ here, That
when Thou com - est on Thy throne I may with joy ap - pear.

2 Thou art Thyself the Way,
Thyself in me reveal;
So shall I pass my life's short day
Obedient to Thy will;

So shall I love my God,
Because He first loved me,
And praise Thee in Thy bright abode,
Through all eternity.

Charles Wesley. a

339 Meribah 8,8,6,8,8,6 (C. P. M.) L. MASON

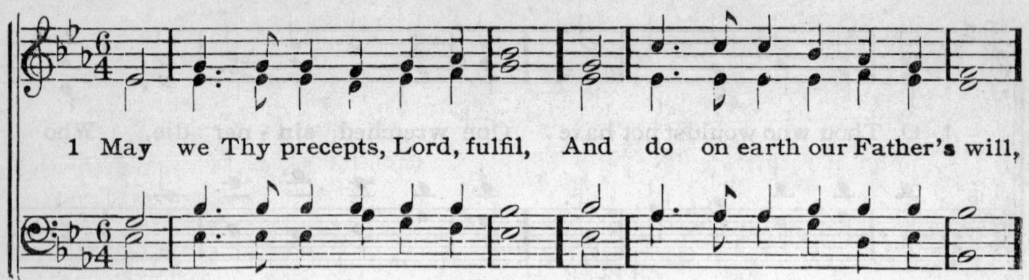
1 May we Thy precepts, Lord, fulfil, And do on earth our Father's will,

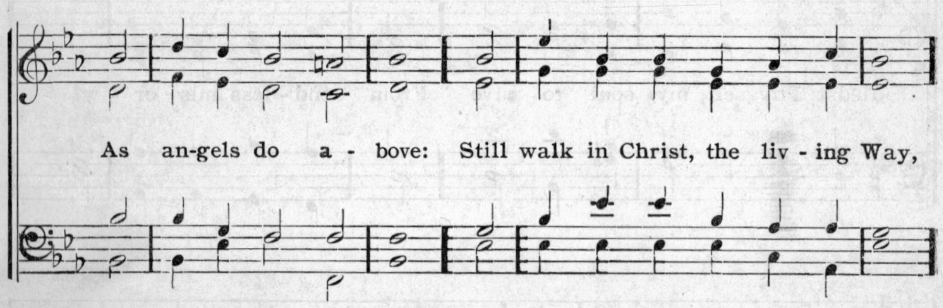
As an-gels do a - bove: Still walk in Christ, the liv - ing Way,

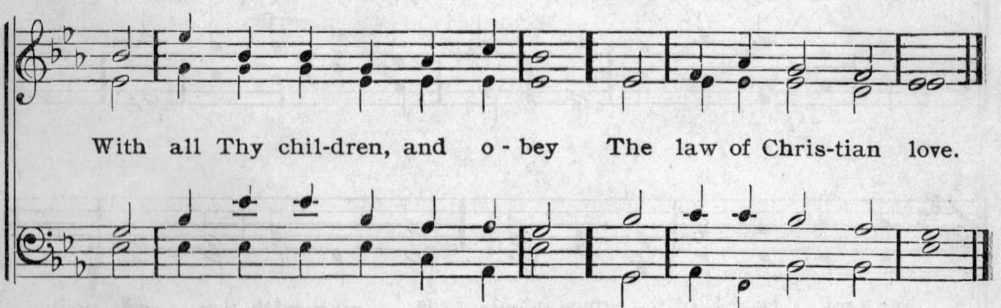
With all Thy chil-dren, and o - bey The law of Chris-tian love.

2 So may we join Thy name to bless,
Thy grace adore, Thy power confess,
From sin and strife to flee:
One is our calling, one our name,
The end of all our hopes the same,
A crown of life with Thee.

3 Spirit of life, of love and peace,
Unite our hearts, our joy increase,
Thy gracious help supply:
To each of us the blessing give,
In Christian fellowship to live,
In joyful hope to die.

Edward Osler 1836 a

340 Guide Me 8,7,8,7,4,7

G. W. WARREN, 1884 (P)

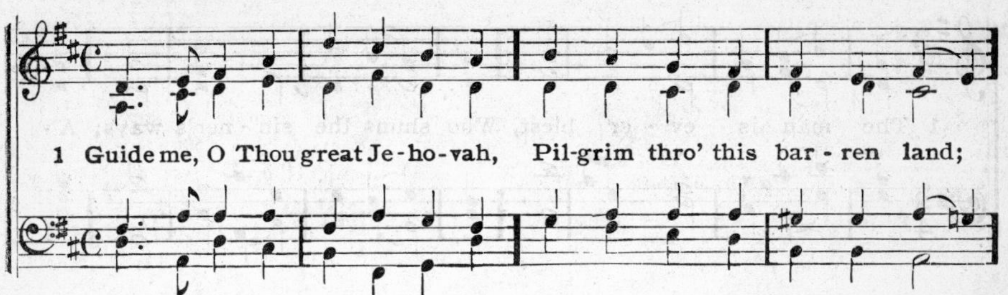
1 Guide me, O Thou great Je - ho - vah, Pil - grim thro' this bar - ren land;

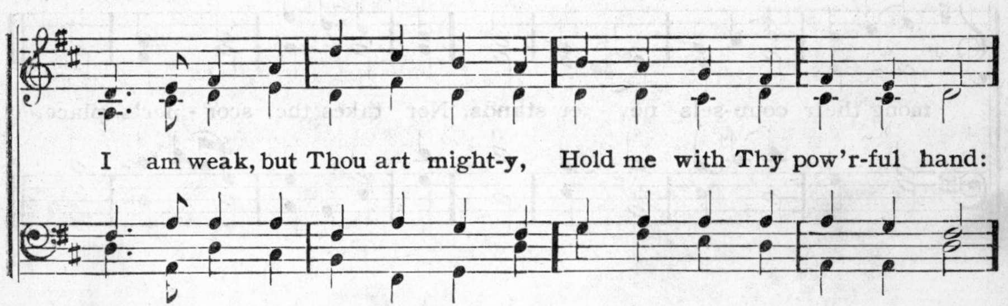
I am weak, but Thou art might - y, Hold me with Thy pow'r - ful hand:

Bread of heav - en, Feed me till I want no more.

(*Or to Regent Square*)

2 Open now the crystal fountain
Whence the healing streams do flow,
Let the fiery, cloudy pillar
Lead me all my journey through:
Strong Deliverer,
Be Thou still my Strength and Shield!

3 When I tread the verge of Jordan,
Bid my anxious fears subside;
Death of death, and hell's Destruction,
Land me safe on Canaan's side;
Songs of praises
I will ever give to Thee.

Wm. Williams, 1745. Peter Williams, Tr. 1771

341 Thatcher S. M.

Arr. fr. G. F. HAENDEL, 1732

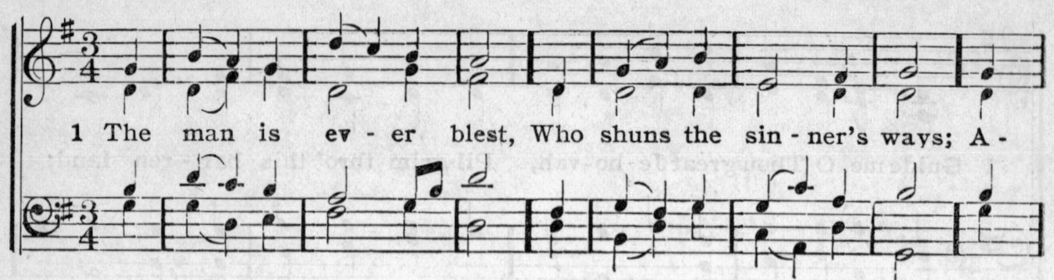
1 The man is ev - er blest, Who shuns the sin - ner's ways; A -

mong their coun-sels nev - er stands, Nor takes the scor - ner's place.

2 But makes the Law of God
His study and delight,
Amid the labors of the day,
And watches of the night.

3 He like a tree shall thrive,
With waters near the root;
Fresh as the leaf, his name shall live;
His works are heavenly fruit.

4 Not so the ungodly race,
They no such blessings find;
Their hopes shall flee like empty chaff
Before the driving wind.

5 How will they bear to stand
Before that judgment-seat,
Where all the saints at Christ's right hand
In full assembly meet?

6 He knows and He approves
The way the righteous go:
But sinners and their works shall meet
A dreadful overthrow.

Isaac Watts

342 Evan C. M.

W. H. HAVERGAL, 1846

1 O that the Lord would guide my ways, To keep His stat-utes still!

O that my God would grant me grace To know and do His will.

2 Order my footsteps by Thy Word,
And make my heart sincere;
Let sin have no dominion, Lord,
But keep my conscience clear.

3 Assist my soul, too apt to stray,
A stricter watch to keep;
And should I e'er forget Thy way,
Restore Thy wandering sheep.

4 Make me to walk in Thy commands—
'Tis a delightful road;
Nor let my head, or heart, or hands,
Offend against my God.

Isaac Watts, 1719 a

343 Liebster Jesu 7, 8, 7, 8, 8, 8

1 God, from all eternity
In Thy Son Thou didst elect me;
Therefore, Father, graciously
In my course to heaven direct me;
Send to me Thy Holy Spirit,
That His gifts I may inherit.

2 Though alive, I'm dead in sin,
To all good things lost by nature;
Holy Ghost, change me within,
Make of me a new-born creature;
For the flesh deserves damnation,
And can never gain salvation.

3 Drive away the gloomy night
Of erroneous reflection;
Quench all thoughts that are not right,
Hold my reason in subjection;
Grant that I from Thee with yearning
Wisdom may be always learning.

4 All desires and thoughts of mine,
From my youth, are only evil;
Save me by Thy power divine
From myself and from the Devil;
Give me strength in ample measure,
Both to will and do Thy pleasure.

5 A clean heart create in me,
Which in Thee, O God, believeth,
And at the iniquity
Of my sins sincerely grieveth;
And when hours of woe betide me,
In the wounds of Jesus hide me.

6 As a branchlet in the vine,
In my blessed Lord implant me;
Ever of my Head divine
To remain a member, grant me;
O let Him, my Lord and Savior,
Be my Life and Love forever.

7 Faith, and hope, and charity,
Graciously, O Father, give me;
Be my Guardian constantly,
That no devil e'er may grieve me,
Grant me humbleness, and gladness,
Peace, and patience, in my sadness.

8 Help me speak what's right and just,
And keep silence on occasion;
Help me pray, Lord, as I must;
Help me bear my tribulation;
Help me die, and let my spirit
Everlasting life inherit.

C. Neumann, 1680. A. Crull, Tr.

344 O Gott, du frommer 6,7,6,7,6,6,6,6

1 How can I thank Thee, Lord,
For all Thy loving-kindness?
Thou hast so long a time
Had patience with my blindness,
When dead in many sins
And trespasses I lay,
And kindled, holy God,
Thine anger every day.

2 Lord, Thou hast shown to me
Divine commiseration:
I persevered in sin,
But Thou in great compassion;
I did resist Thee, Lord,
Deferring to repent;
Thou didst defer Thy wrath
And instant punishment.

3 It is Thy work alone,
That now I am converted,
Thy power o'er Satan's work
In me Thou hast asserted;
Thy mercy, that doth reach
Unto the clouds, O Lord,
Did break my stony heart
By Thine own mighty Word.

4 Though able to offend
Thee, Lord, by sin and failing,
Still to regain Thy grace
My strength was unavailing.
Though I could fall from grace
And choose the way of sin,
I had no strength to rise,
A new life to begin.

5 But Thou hast raised me up,
And with divine compassion
Hast shown me, Lord, the way
That leadeth to salvation.
I thank Thee, Lord, that now
My former sins I hate,
And freely—not from fear—
Dead works abominate.

6 That I may not backslide,
But life in heaven inherit,
Grant me, while here I live,
O Lord, Thy holy Spirit,
That He may give me strength
In mine infirmity,
And e'er renew my heart,
To serve Thee willingly.

7 O guide and lead me, Lord,
While here below I wander;
Grant that I follow Thee,
My Guide, and my Commander.
For if I lead myself,
I soon am led astray,
But if Thou leadest me,
I do my duty aye.

8 O Father, God of love,
Hear now my supplication!
Lord Jesus, Son of God,
O grant me Thy salvation!
And Thou, O Holy Ghost,
Always abide with me,
That I may serve Thee here,
And there eternally!

Justus Gesenius c. 1647 A. Crull, Tr.

(Or to Nun danket alle Gott)

Sanctification

Consecration

345 O dass ich tausend Zungen hätte 9,8,9,8,8,8 DRETZEL, 1731

1 Soul, what re - turn has God thy Sav - ior For all He gives thee day by day? The best of off - 'rings He re - quires; Give Him thy heart with its de - sires.
O hast thou in thy gift a fa - vor That can de - light and please Him?—say!

2 Give God His own, if aught thou'rt giving;
Say, soul, to whom belongs the heart?
Can Satan, he who hates the living,
Or any creature claim a part?—
To Thee alone I will assign
O Lord, my heart and all that's mine.

3 Accept the gift which Thou requirest,
The first-fruits of my heart, O God!
The offerings Thou so much desirest,
And dearly paid'st for with Thy blood;
To Thee alone I now resign
My heart, to be forever Thine.

4 Whom should I give my heart's affection
But Thee, who givest Thine to faith?
Thy fervent love is my protection:
Lord, Thou hast loved me unto death.
My heart with Thine shall ever be
One heart throughout eternity.

Karl Friedr. Lochner, c. 1673

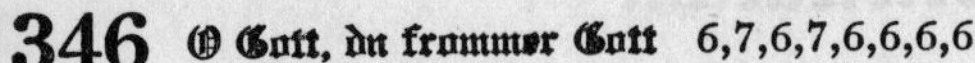

346 O Gott, du frommer Gott 6,7,6,7,6,6,6,6

J. G. CHR. STOERL, 1710

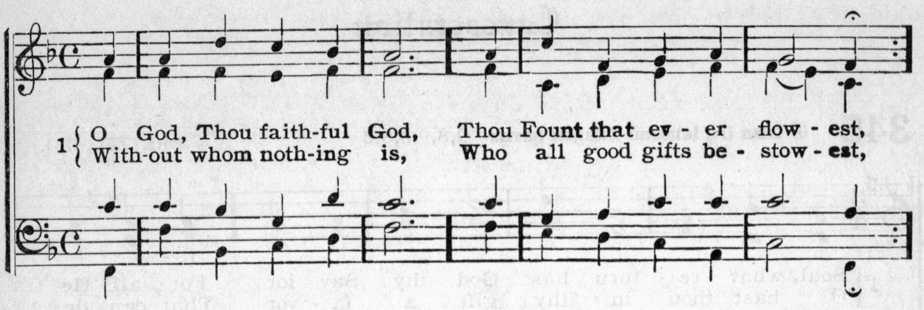
1 { O God, Thou faith-ful God, Thou Fount that ev - er flow - est,
With-out whom noth-ing is, Who all good gifts be - stow - est,

A pure and health - y frame O give me, and with - in

A con science free from blame, A soul un - hurt by sin.

2 And grant me, Lord, to do,
With ready heart and willing,
Whate'er Thou shalt command:
My calling here fulfilling;
To do it when I ought,
With all my strength; and bless
The work I thus have wrought,
For Thou must give success.

3 O let me never speak
What bounds of truth exceedeth:
Grant that no idle word
From out my mouth proceedeth;
And grant, when in my place
I must and ought to speak,
My words due power and grace,
Nor let me wound the weak.

4 If dangers gather round,
Still keep me calm and fearless;
Help me to bear the cross,
When life is dark and cheerless;
Let me subdue my foe
By words and actions kind;
When counsel I would know,
Good counsel let me find.

5 And let me with all men,
As far as in me lieth,
In peace and friendship live;
And if Thy gift supplieth
Me wealth and honor fair,
Then this refuse me not,
That naught be mingled there
Of goods unjustly got.

6 And if a longer life,
Be here on earth decreed me,
And Thou through many a strife
To age at last wilt lead me,
Thy patience in me shed,
Avert all sin and shame,
And crown my hoary head
With pure untarnished fame.

7 Let me depart this life
Confiding in my Savior;
Do Thou my soul receive,
That it may live forever;
And let my body have
A quiet resting-place
Beside a Christian's grave;
And let it sleep in peace.

8 And on that solemn day
When all the dead are waking,
Stretch o'er my grave Thy hand,
Thyself my slumbers breaking;
Then let me hear Thy voice,
Change Thou this earthly frame,
And bid me aye rejoice
With those who love Thy name.

Johann Heermann, 1630

347 O Gott, du frommer Gott 6,7,6,7,6,6,6,6

1 O God, forsake me not!
But lead, full of compassion,
With loving hands Thy child,
That I may gain salvation,
When here my course is run;
Be Thou my Light, my Lot,
My Staff, my Rock, my Shield,—
O God, forsake me not!

2 O God, forsake me not!
Take not Thy Spirit from me,
And suffer not the might
Of sin to overcome me;
Increase my feeble faith,
Which Thou Thyself hast wrought;
Be Thou my Strength and Power—
O God, forsake me not!

3 O God, forsake me not!
Lord, hear my supplication!
In every evil hour
Help me o'ercome temptation;
And when the Prince of hell
My conscience seeks to blot,
Be Thou not far from me—
O God, forsake me not!

4 O God, forsake me not!
Thy mercy I'm addressing;
O Father, God of love,
Grant me Thy heavenly blessing
To do the duty which
To me Thou didst allot,
To do what pleaseth Thee—
O God, forsake me not!

5 O God, forsake me not!
Lord, I am Thine forever,
Grant me true faith in Thee,
Grant that I leave Thee never;
Grant me a blessed end,
When my good fight is fought,
Help me in life and death—
O God, forsake me not!

Salomon Franck, † 1725 A. Crull, Tr

348

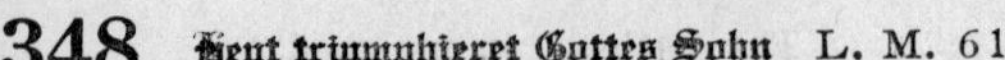

Heut triumphieret Gottes Sohn L. M. 61 S. CALVISIUS, 1597

1 O Love, who form-edst me to wear The im-age of Thy God-head here; Who sought-est me with ten-der care Thro' all my wan-d'rings wild and drear— O Love, I give my-self to Thee, Thine ev-er, on-ly Thine to be.

(Or to Vater Unser Or to St. Petersburg)

2 O Love, who ere life's earliest dawn
On me Thy choice hast gently laid;
O Love, who here as man wast born
And like to us in all things made—
O Love, I give myself to Thee,
Thine ever, only Thine to be.

3 O Love, who once in time wast slain,
Pierced through and through with bitter woe;
O Love, who wrestling thus didst gain
That we eternal joy might know—
O Love, I give myself to Thee,
Thine ever, only Thine to be.

4 O Love, of whom is truth and light,
The Word and Spirit, life and power,
Whose heart was bared to them that smite,
To shield us in our trial hour—
O Love, I give myself to Thee,
Thine ever, only Thine to be.

5 O Love, who thus hast bound me fast
Beneath that gentle yoke of Thine;
Love, who hast conquered me at last,
Enrapturing this heart of mine—
O Love, I give myself to Thee,
Thine ever, only Thine to be.

6 O Love, who lovest me for aye,
Who for my soul dost ever plead;
O Love, who didst my ransom pay,
Who for me e'er dost intercede—
O Love, I give myself to Thee,
Thine ever, only Thine to be.

7 O Love, who once shalt bid me rise
From out this dying life of ours;
O Love, who once above yon skies
Shalt set me in the fadeless bowers—
O Love, I give myself to Thee,
Thine ever, only Thine to be.

J. Scheffler (Angelus), 1657 C. Winkworth, Tr. a

349 Ich will dich lieben, meine Staerke 9,8,9,8,8,6

B. KOENIG, 1738

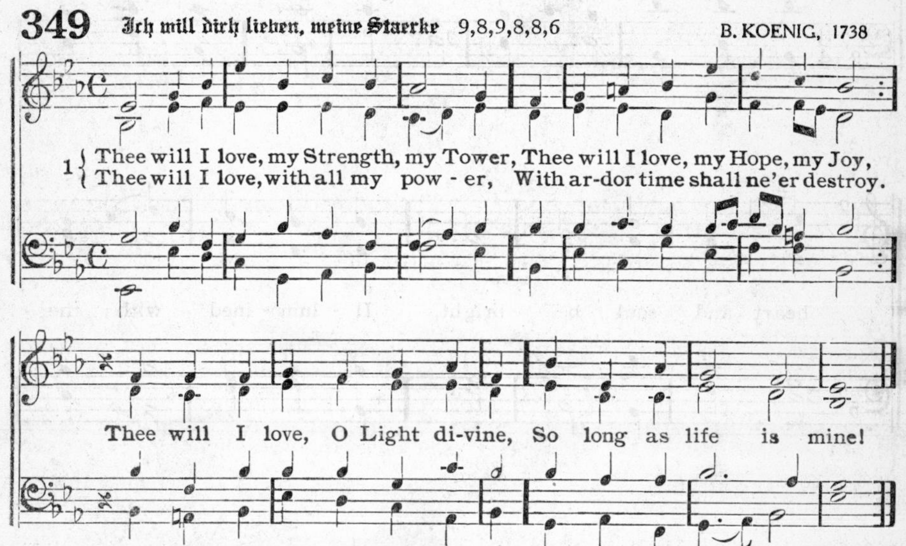
1 { Thee will I love, my Strength, my Tower, Thee will I love, my Hope, my Joy,
Thee will I love, with all my pow - er, With ar-dor time shall ne'er destroy.
Thee will I love, O Light di-vine, So long as life is mine!

2 Thee will I love, my Life, my Savior,
Who art my best and truest Friend;
Thee will I love and praise forever,
For never shall Thy kindness end;
Thee will I love with all my heart,
For Thou my Bridegroom art.

3 Alas! that I so late have known Thee,
Who art the Fairest and the Best;
Nor sooner for my Lord could own Thee,
Our highest Good, our only Rest!
Now bitter shame and grief I prove
O'er this my tardy love.

4 I wandered long in willing blindness,
I sought Thee, but I found Thee not,
For still I shunned Thy beams of kindness,
The creature-light filled all my thought.
And if at last I see Thee now,
'Twas Thou to me didst bow!

5 I thank Thee, Jesus, Sun from heaven,
Whose shining hath brought light to me;
I thank Thee, who hast richly given
All that could make me glad and free;
I thank Thee that my soul is healed
By what Thy lips revealed.

6 O keep me watchful, then, and humble,
And suffer me no more to stray;
Uphold me when my feet would stumble,
Nor let me loiter by the way;
Fill all my nature with Thy light,
O Radiance strong and bright!

7 O teach me Lord, to love Thee truly
With soul and body, head and heart,
And grant me grace that I may duly
Practice fore'er love's sacred art;
Grant that my every thought may be
Directed e'er to Thee.

8 Thee will I love, my Crown of gladness,
Thee will I love, my God and Lord,
Amid the darkest depths of sadness,
Not for the hope of high reward,
For Thine own sake, O Light divine,
So long as life is mine.

J. Scheffler (Angelus), 1657 C. Winkworth, Tr. a

350 Herr Jesu Christ, meins Lebens L. M. 1625

1 Re - new me, O e - ter - nal Light, And let my

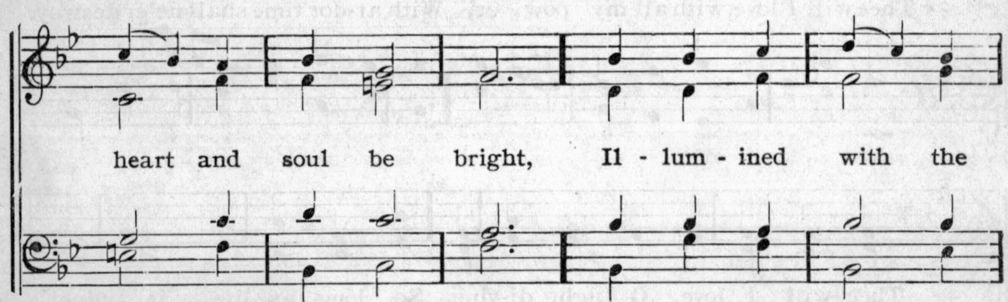
heart and soul be bright, Il - lum - ined with the

light of grace, That is - sues from Thy ho - ly face.

2 Destroy in me the lust of sin,
From all impureness make me clean,
O grant me power and strength, my God,
To strive against my flesh and blood.

3 Create in me a new heart, Lord,
That gladly I obey Thy Word,
And naught but what Thou wilt, desire;
With such new life my soul inspire.

4 Grant that I only Thee may love,
And seek those things which are above,
Till I behold Thee face to face,
O Light eternal, through Thy grace.

Joh. Friedr. Ruopp, 1704 A. Crull, Tr

351 Olivet 6,6,4,6,6,6,4

LOWELL MASON, 1831

1 My faith looks up to Thee, Thou Lamb of Cal - va - ry,

Sav - ior di - vine! Now hear me while I pray; Take all my

guilt a - way; O let me from this day Be whol - ly Thine.

2 May Thy rich grace impart
Strength to my fainting heart,
My zeal inspire;
As Thou hast died for me,
O may my love to Thee
Pure, warm, and changeless be,
A living fire.

3 While life's dark maze I tread,
And griefs around me spread,
Be Thou my Guide;
Bid darkness turn to day,
Wipe sorrow's tears away,
Nor let me ever stray
From Thee aside.

4 When ends life's transient dream,
When death's cold sullen stream
Shall o'er me roll;
Blest Savior, then, in love,
Fear and distrust remove;
O bear me safe above,
A ransomed soul!

Ray Palmer 1830

352 St. Olav 6s 6 1 BARNBY

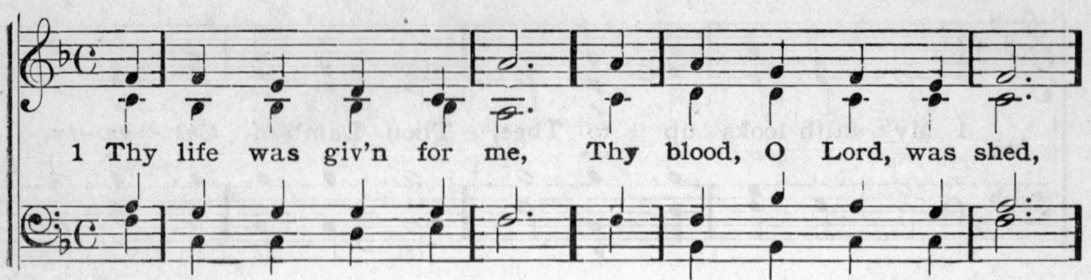
1 Thy life was giv'n for me, Thy blood, O Lord, was shed,

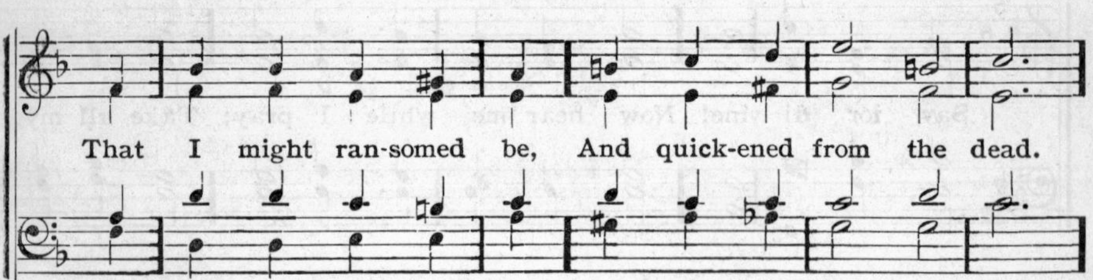
That I might ran-somed be, And quick-ened from the dead.

Thy life was giv'n for me: What have I giv'n for Thee?

2 Thy Father's home of light,
Thy rainbow-circled throne,
Were left for earthly night,
For wanderings sad and lone.
Yea, all was left for me:
Have I left aught for Thee?

3 And Thou hast brought to me,
Down from Thy home above,
Salvation full and free,
Thy pardon and Thy love.
Great gifts Thou broughtest me:
What have I brought to Thee?

4 Oh, let my life be given,
My years for Thee be spent,
World's fetters all be riven,
And pain with joy be blent!
Thou gavest Thyself for me;
I give myself to Thee.

F. R. Havergal, 1858 ab. and a

353 Winterton 6,4,6,4,6,6,6,4

J. BARNBY, 1892 (P)

1 Sav - ior, Thy dy - ing love Thou gav - est me, Nor should I

aught with-hold, Dear Lord, from Thee, In love my soul would bow,

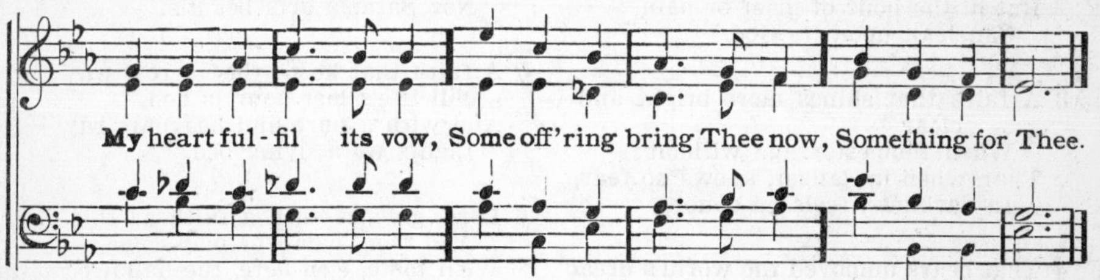
My heart ful - fil its vow, Some off'ring bring Thee now, Something for Thee.

2 O'er the blest mercy-seat,
Pleading for me,
My feeble faith looks up,
Jesus, to Thee:
Help me the cross to bear,
Thy wondrous love declare,
Some song to raise, or pray'r,
Something for Thee.

3 Give me a faithful heart—
Likeness to Thee—
That each departing day
Henceforth may see
Some work of love begun,
Some deed of kindness done,
Some wand'rer sought and won,
Something for Thee.

4 All that I am and have—
Thy gifts so free—
In joy, in grief, through life,
Dear Lord, for Thee!
And when Thy face I see,
My ransomed soul shall be,
Through all eternity,
Something for Thee.

S. D. Phelps, 1867

354 Mear C. M. AMERICAN TUNE, 1726

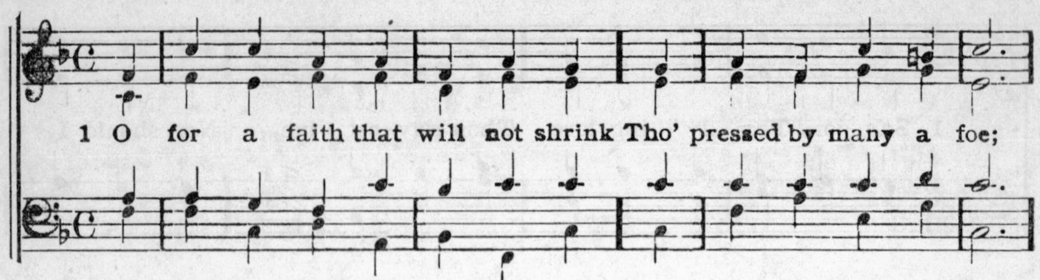
1 O for a faith that will not shrink Tho' pressed by many a foe;

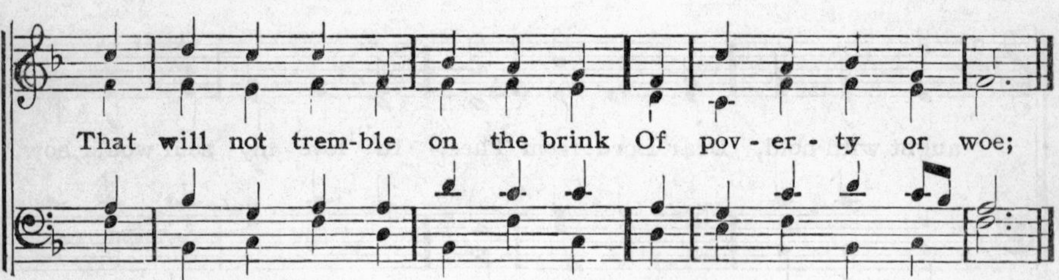
That will not trem-ble on the brink Of pov - er - ty or woe;

(*Or to St. Agnes Or to Beatitudo*)

2 That will not murmur nor complain
Beneath the chastening rod,
But in the hour of grief or pain
Can lean upon its God.

3 A faith that shines more bright and clear
When tempests rage without;
That, when in danger, knows no fear,
In darkness, feels no doubt.

4 That bears unmoved the world's dread frown,
Nor heeds its scornful smile;
That sin's wild ocean cannot drown,
Nor Satan's arts beguile.

5 A faith that keeps the narrow way
Till life's last hour is fled,
And with a pure and heavenly ray
Lights up a dying bed.

6 Lord, give us such a faith as this,
And then, whate'er may come,
We'll taste, e'en here, the hallowed bliss
Of an eternal home.

W. H. Bathurst, 1830 a

355 Patmos 7s W. H. HAVERGAL, 1869

1 Take my life, and let it be Con - se - cra - ted, Lord, to Thee.

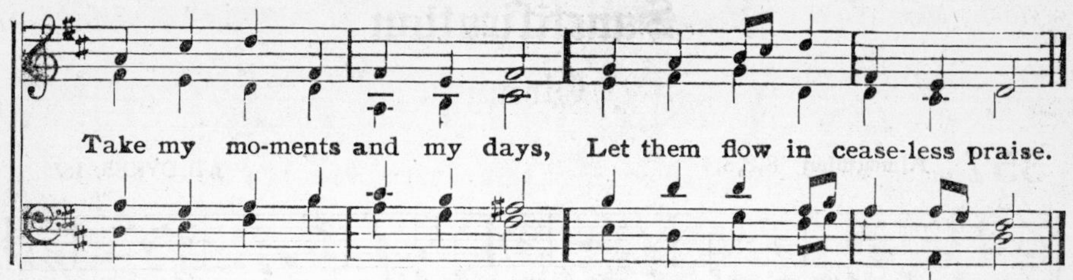
Take my mo-ments and my days, Let them flow in cease-less praise.

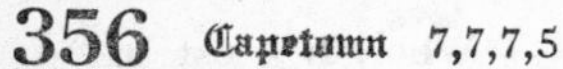
(Or to Holley)

2 Take my hands, and let them move
At the impulse of Thy love;
Take my feet, and let them be
Swift and beautiful for Thee.

3 Take my voice, and let me sing
Always, only, for my King;
Take my lips, and let them be
Filled with messages from Thee.

4 Take my silver and my gold,
Not a mite would I withhold;
Take my intellect, and use
Every power as Thou should choose.

5 Take my will and make it Thine,
It shall be no longer mine;
Take my heart, it is Thine own,
It shall be Thy royal throne.

6 Take my love, my Lord, I pour
At Thy feet its treasure-store;
Take myself, and I will be
Ever, only, all for Thee.

F. R. Havergal, 1874

356 Capetown 7,7,7,5

F. FILITZ

1 Je-sus, Shep-herd of the sheep, Who Thy Fa-ther's flock dost keep,
Safe we wake and safe we sleep, Guard-ed still by Thee.

2 In Thy promise firm we stand,
None can pluck us from Thy hand,
Speak—we hear—at Thy command,
We will follow Thee.

3 By Thy blood our souls were bought,
By Thy life salvation wrought,
By Thy light our feet are taught,
Lord, to follow Thee.

4 Father, draw us to Thy Son;
We with joy will follow on,
Till the work of grace is done,
And from sin set free—

5 We in robes of glory dressed,
Join the assembly of the blest,
Gathered to eternal rest,
In the fold with Thee.

Rev. Henry Cook, 1868

Sanctification

Giving

357 Almsgiving 8,8,8,4 J. B. DYKES, 1875

1 O Lord of heav'n, and earth, and sea, To Thee all praise and glo - ry be;
How shall we show our love to Thee, Who giv - est all?

2 Thou didst not spare Thine only Son,
But gav'st Him for a world undone,
And freely with that Blessed One
Thou givest all.

3 Thou giv'st the Spirit's holy dower,
Spirit of life, and love, and power,
And dost His sevenfold graces shower
Upon us all.

4 For souls redeemed, for sins forgiven,
For means of grace and hopes of heaven,
What can to Thee, O Lord, be given,
Who givest all?

5 We lose what on ourselves we spend,
We have, as treasure without end,
Whatever, Lord, to Thee we lend,
Who givest all.

6 Whatever, Lord, we lend to Thee,
Repaid a thousand-fold will be;
Then gladly will we give to Thee
Who givest all.

C. Wordsworth, ab.

358 Deerhurst 8,7 8 1 J. LANGRAN,

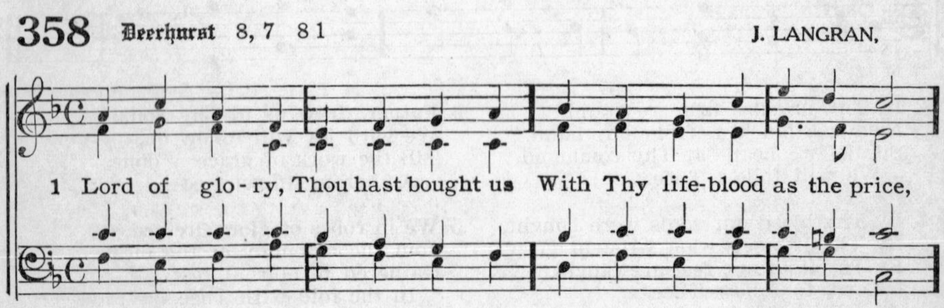

1 Lord of glo - ry, Thou hast bought us With Thy life-blood as the price,

Nev - er grudg-ing for the lost ones That tre - men-dous sac-ri - fice,

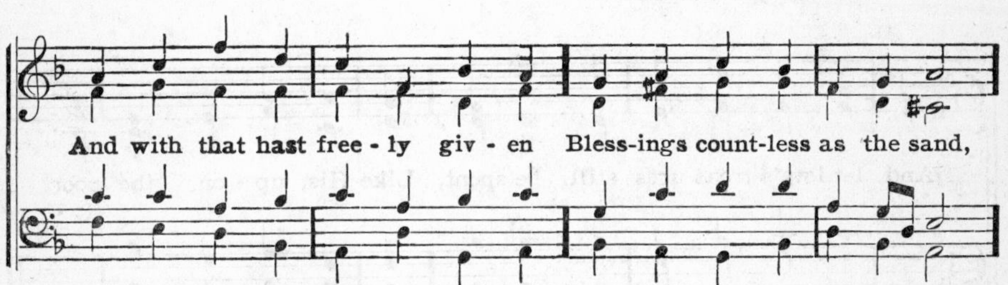
And with that hast free - ly giv - en Bless-ings count-less as the sand,

To th' un-thankful and the e - vil With Thine own un- spar-ing hand.

2 Grant us hearts, dear Lord, to yield
Thee,
Gladly, freely of Thine own;
With the sunshine of Thy goodness
Melt our thankless hearts of stone;
Till our cold and selfish natures,
Warmed by Thee, at length believe
That more happy and more blessed
'Tis to give than to receive.

3 Wondrous honor hast Thou given
To our humblest charity,
In Thine own mysterious sentence,
"Ye have done it unto Me."
Can it be, O gracious Master,
Thou dost deign for alms to sue,
Saying, by Thy poor and needy,
"Give as I have given to you?"

4 Lord of glory, who hast bought us
With Thy life-blood as the price,
Never grudging for the lost ones
That tremendous sacrifice,
Give us faith, to trust Thee boldly,
Hope, to stay our souls on Thee:
But oh! best of all Thy graces,
Give us Thine own charity.

E. S. Alderson. 1868 ab

359 Dalehurst C. M.

A. COTTMAN, 1872

1 Lord, lead the way my Sav - ior went, By lane and cell ob-scure,

And let love's treas-ures still be spent, Like His, up - on the poor.

2 Like Him thro' scenes of deep distress,
Who bore the world's sad weight,
We, in their crowded loneliness,
Would seek the desolate.

3 For Thou hast placed us side by side,
In this wide world of ill,
And, that Thy followers may be tried,
The poor are with us still.

4 Mean are all offerings we can make,
But Thou hast taught us, Lord,
If given for the Savior's sake,
They lose not their reward.

W. Crosswell, 1831

360 Keble L. M.

J. B. DYKES, 1875

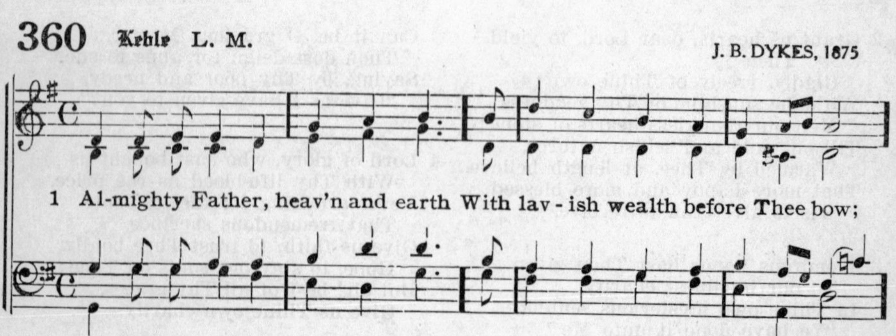
1 Al-mighty Father, heav'n and earth With lav - ish wealth before Thee bow;

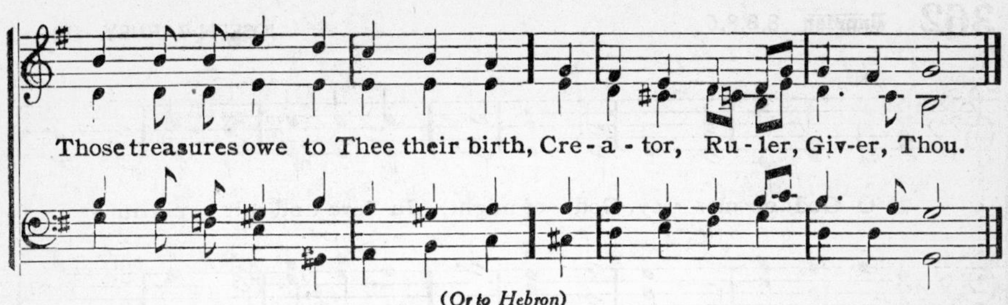
Those treasures owe to Thee their birth, Cre - a - tor, Ru - ler, Giv-er, Thou.

(Or to Hebron)

2 The wealth of earth, of sky, of sea,
The gold, the silver, sparkling gem,
The waving corn, the bending tree,
Are Thine; to us Thou lendest them.

3 To Thee, as early morning's dew,
Our praises, alms, and prayer shall rise;
As rose, when joyous earth was new,
Faith's patriarchal sacrifice.

4 We, Lord, would lay, at Thy behest,
The costliest offerings on Thy shrine;
But when we give, and give our best,
We only give Thee that is Thine.

5 O Father, whence all blessings come,
O Son, dispenser of God's store,
O Spirit, bear our offerings home,
Lord, make them Thine for evermore.

E. A. Dayman, 1868

361 Energy (St. Ethelwald) S. M. W. H. MONK

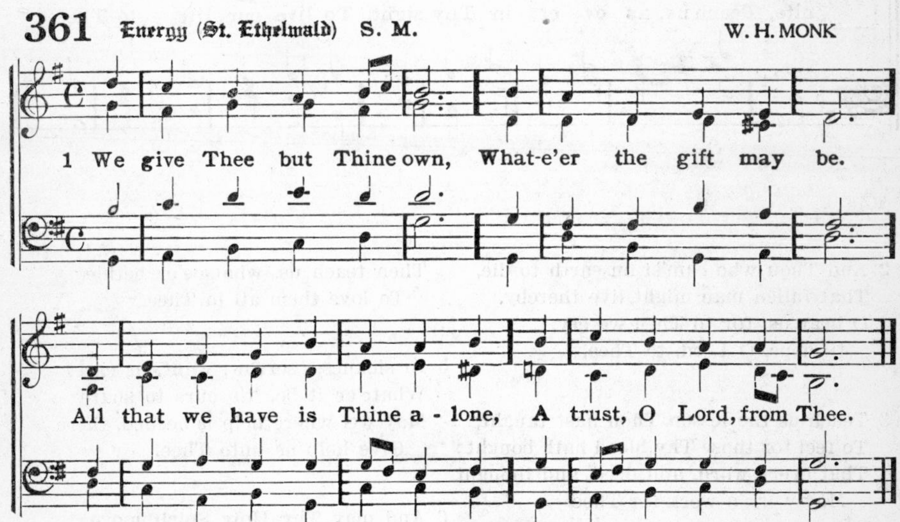
1 We give Thee but Thine own, What-e'er the gift may be.
All that we have is Thine a - lone, A trust, O Lord, from Thee.

2 May we Thy bounties thus
As stewards true receive,
And gladly, as thou blessest us,
To Thee our first-fruits give.

3 To comfort and to bless,
To find a balm for woe,
To tend the lone and fatherless—
Is angel's work below.

4 The captive to release,
To God the lost to bring,
To teach the way of life and peace—
It is a Christ-like thing.

5 And we believe thy Word,
Though dim our faith may be;
Whate'er for Thine we do, O Lord,
We do it unto Thee.

William W. How, ab

362 Dunstan 8,8,8,6

JOSEPH BARNBY, (P)

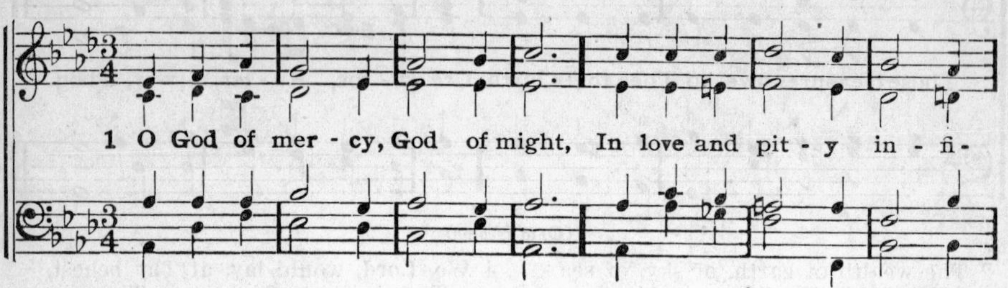
1 O God of mer - cy, God of might, In love and pit - y in - fi -

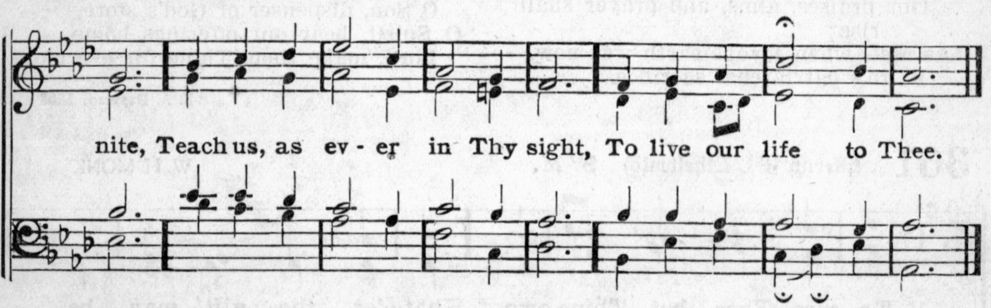
nite, Teach us, as ev - er in Thy sight, To live our life to Thee.

2 And Thou who cam'st on earth to die,
That fallen man might live thereby,
O hear us, for to Thee we cry,
In hope, O Lord, to Thee,

3 Teach us the lesson Thou hast taught,
To feel for those Thy blood hath bought;
That every word, and deed, and thought
May work a work for Thee.

4 For all are brethren, far and wide
Since Thou, O Lord, for all hast died:
Then teach us, whatsoe'er betide,
To love them all in Thee.

5 In sickness, sorrow, want, or care,
Whate'er it be, 'tis ours to share;
May we, where help is needed, there
Give help as unto Thee.

6 And may Thy Holy Spirit move
All those who live, to live in love,
Till Thou shalt greet in heaven above
All those who give to Thee.

G. Thring, 1879

Sanctification

Trust

363 Alles ist an Gottes Segen 8,8,7,8,8,7 KOENIG 1738

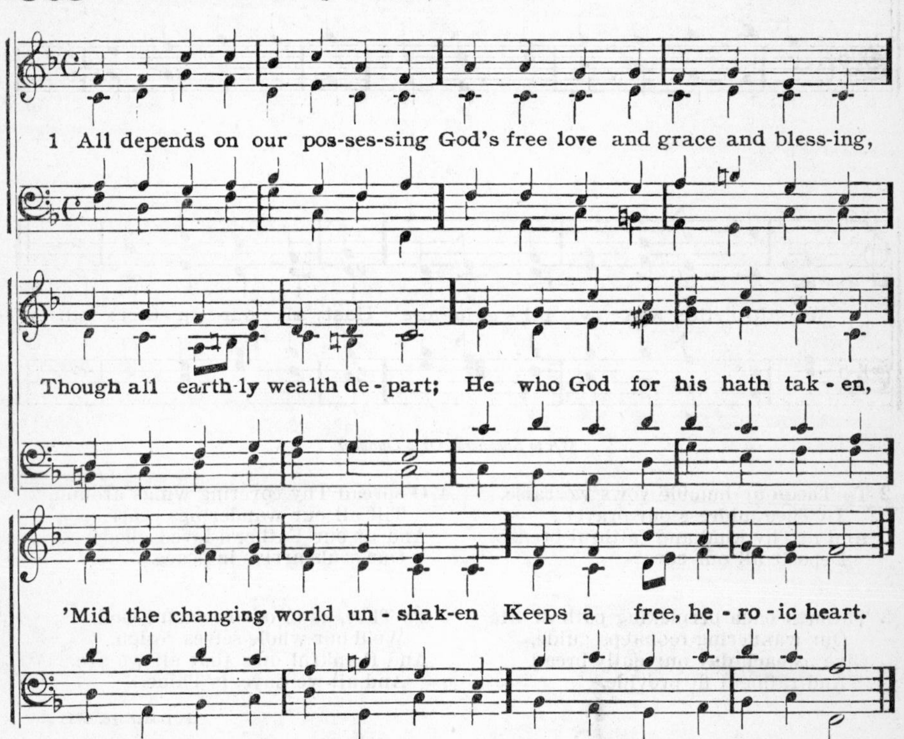

1 All depends on our pos-ses-sing God's free love and grace and bless-ing,
Though all earth-ly wealth de-part; He who God for his hath tak-en,
'Mid the changing world un-shak-en Keeps a free, he-ro-ic heart.

2 He who hitherto hath fed me,
And to many a joy hath led me,
Is and shall be ever mine;
He who did so gently school me,
He who still doth guide and rule me,
Will not leave me now to pine.

3 Shall I weary me with fretting
O'er vain trifles, and regretting
Things that never can remain?
I will strive but that to win me
Which can shed true rest within me,—
Rest the world must seek in vain.

4 When my heart with longing sickens,
Hope again my courage quickens,
For my wish shall be fulfilled,
If it please His will most tender,
Soul and body I surrender
Unto Him on whom I build.

5 Well He knows how best to grant me
All the longing hopes that haunt me;
All things have their proper day;
I would dictate to Him never,
As God wills, so be it ever,
When He wills I will obey.

6 If on earth He bids me linger,
He will guide me with His finger
Through the years that now look dim;
All that earth has fleets and changes,
As a river onward ranges,
But I rest in peace on Him.

Nuernberg H. B., 1676 C. Winkworth, Tr. a

364 St. Savior C. M.

T. G. BAKER, 1872

1 O God of Ja - cob, by whose hand Thy peo - ple still are fed;

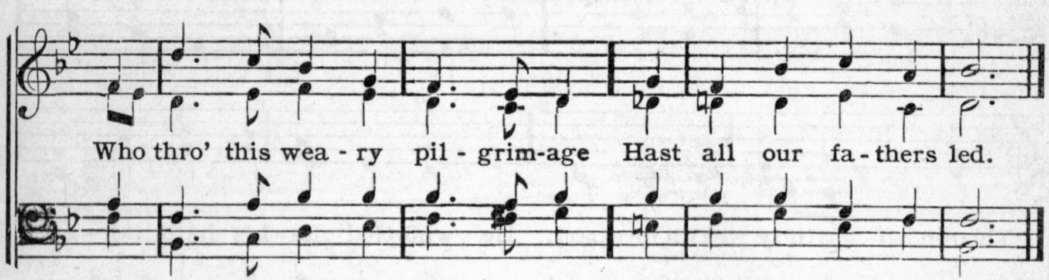
Who thro' this wea - ry pil - grim-age Hast all our fa - thers led.

(Or to Shepherd Or to Dundee)

2 To Thee our humble vows we raise,
To Thee address our prayer;
And in Thy kind and faithful breast
Deposit all our care.

3 Through each perplexing path of life
Our wandering footsteps guide,
Give us each day our daily bread
And raiment fit provide.

4 O spread Thy covering wings around,
Till all our wanderings cease,
And at our Father's loved abode
Our souls arrive in peace.

5 To Thee, as to our covenant God,
We'll our whole selves resign,
And thankful own that all we are,
And all we have, is Thine.

P. Doddridge, 1755 a

365 Ich ruf zu dir, Herr Jesu Christ 8,7,8,7,8,7,4,6,8

J. KLUGE, 1535

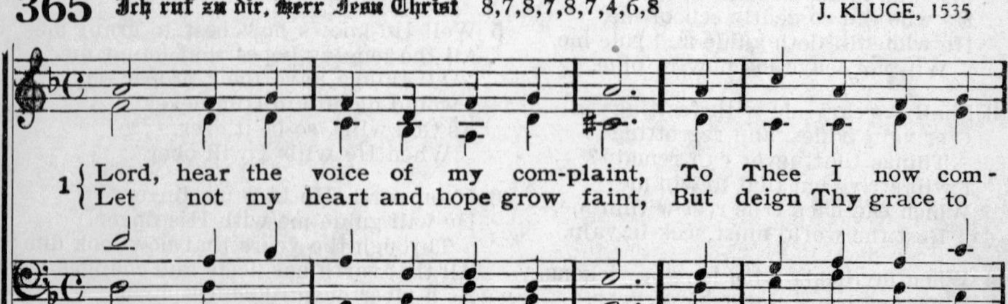
1 { Lord, hear the voice of my com-plaint, To Thee I now com-
Let not my heart and hope grow faint, But deign Thy grace to

mend me,
send me.
True faith from Thee, my God, I seek,
The faith that loves Thee sole - ly, Keeps me low - ly,
And prompt to aid the weak, And mark each word that Thou dost speak.

2 Yet more from Thee I dare to claim,
Whose goodness is unbounded;
O let me ne'er be put to shame,
My hope be ne'er confounded;
But e'en in death still find Thee true,
And in that hour else lonely,
Trust Thee only,
Not aught that I can do,
For such false trust I sore should rue.

3 O grant that from my very heart
My foes be all forgiven,
Forgive my sins and heal their smart,
And grant new life from heaven;
Thy Word, that blessed food, bestow,
Which best the soul can nourish;
Make it flourish
Through all the storms of woe
That else my faith might overthrow.

4 Then be the world my foe or friend,
Keep me to her a stranger,
Thy steadfast follower to the end,
Through pleasure and through danger;
From Thee alone comes such high grace,
No works of ours obtain it
Or can gain it;
Our pride hath here no place—
This Thy free promise we embrace.

5 Help me, for I am weak; I fight,
Yet scarce can battle longer;
I cling but to Thy grace and might,
'Tis Thou canst make me stronger;
When sore temptations are my lot,
And tempests round me lower,
Break the power:
So, through deliverance wrought,
I know that Thou forsak'st me not.

Paul Speratus, 1535 C. Winkworth, Tr. a

366 Herzlich lieb hab ich dich, o Herr MATTHIAS GASTRITZ, 1571

1 { O Lord, I love Thee from my heart; I pray Thee, ne'er from me de-part,
I scorn the rich-est earth-ly lot, E'en heav'n and earth at-tract me not,
With ten-der mer-cy cheer me;
If on-ly Thou be near (Omit.) me.
1 2
Yea, tho' my heart be like to break, Thou shalt my Trust that naught can shake, My Portion and my Comfort be, Who by Thy blood hast purchased me, Lord, Je-sus Christ! My God and

Lord! my God and Lord! For-sake me not who trust Thy Word.

2 Yea, Lord, 'twas Thy free bounty gave
My body, soul, and what I have
In this poor life of labor;
O grant that I may through Thy grace
Use all my powers to show Thy praise,
And serve and help my neighbor.
From all false doctrine keep me, Lord,
From Satan's lies and malice ward,
In every cross uphold Thou me,
That I may bear it patiently,
Lord Jesus Christ!
My God and Lord! my God and Lord!
In death Thy comfort still afford.

3 Ah! Lord, let Thy dear angels come
At my last end to bear me home,
That I may die unfearing;
And in its narrow chamber keep
My body safe in painless sleep
Until Thy reappearing;
And then from death awaken me,
That these mine eyes with joy may see,
O Son of God, Thy glorious face,
My Savior and my Fount of grace!
Lord Jesus Christ!
My prayer attend, my prayer attend,
And I will praise Thee without end.

Martin Schalling, 1571

367 Belmont (Vigils) C. M.

W. GARDINER, 1812

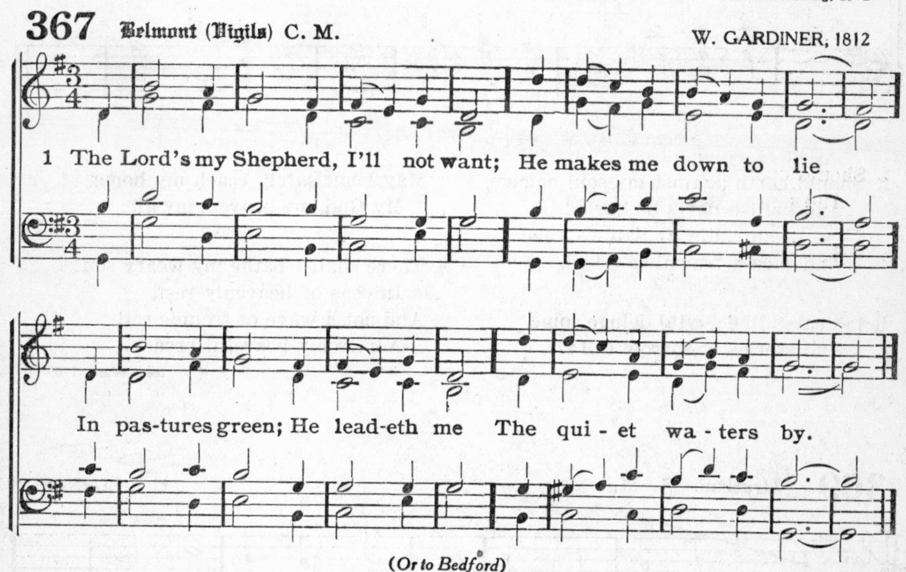
1 The Lord's my Shepherd, I'll not want; He makes me down to lie
In pas-tures green; He lead-eth me The qui - et wa - ters by.

(*Or to Bedford*)

2 My soul He doth restore again;
And me to walk doth make
Within the paths of righteousness,
E'en for His own name's sake.

3 Yea, though I walk in death's dark vale
Yet will I fear no ill;
For Thou art with me, and Thy rod
And staff me comfort still.

4 My table Thou hast furnished
In presence of my foes,
My head Thou dost with oil anoint
And my cup overflows .

5 Goodness and mercy, all my life,
Shall surely follow me;
And in God's house for evermore
My dwelling-place shall be.

F. Rouse, 1643

368 Marlow C. M.

J. CHETHAM, 1718

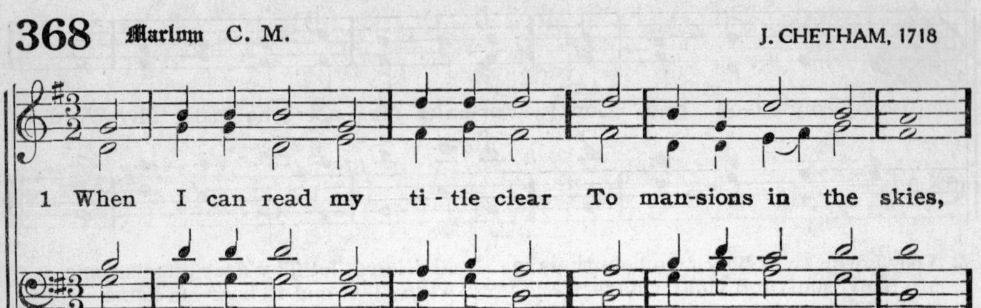
1 When I can read my ti-tle clear To man-sions in the skies,

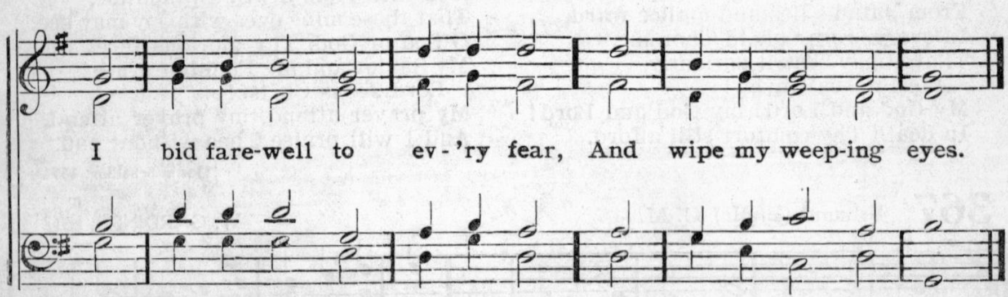
I bid fare-well to ev-'ry fear, And wipe my weep-ing eyes.

2 Should earth against my soul engage,
And hellish darts be hurled,
Then I can smile at Satan's rage,
And face a frowning world.

3 Let cares like a wild deluge come,
And storms of sorrow fall;
May I but safely reach my home,
My God, my heaven, my all:

4 There shall I bathe my weary soul
In seas of heavenly rest,
And not a wave of trouble roll
Across my peaceful breast.

Isaac Watts, 1709

369 Cleveland S. M.

U. C. BURNAP

1 My spir-it on Thy care, Blest Sav-ior, I re-cline;

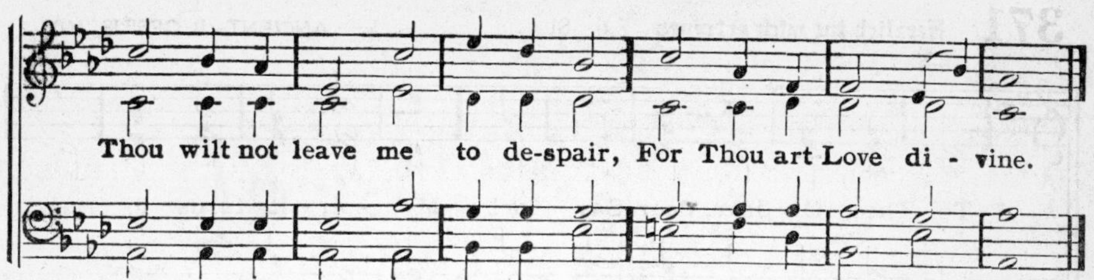
Thou wilt not leave me to de-spair, For Thou art Love di - vine.

2 In Thee I place my trust,
On Thee I calmly rest:
I know Thee good, I know Thee just,
And count Thy choice the best.

3 Whate'er events betide,
Thy will they all perform;
Safe in Thy breast my head I hide,
Nor fear the coming storm.

4 Let good or ill befall,
It must be good for me;
Secure of having Thee in all,
Of having all in Thee.

Henry Francis Lyte. 1834

370 Stephanos 8,5,8,3

H. W. BAKER 1861, (P)

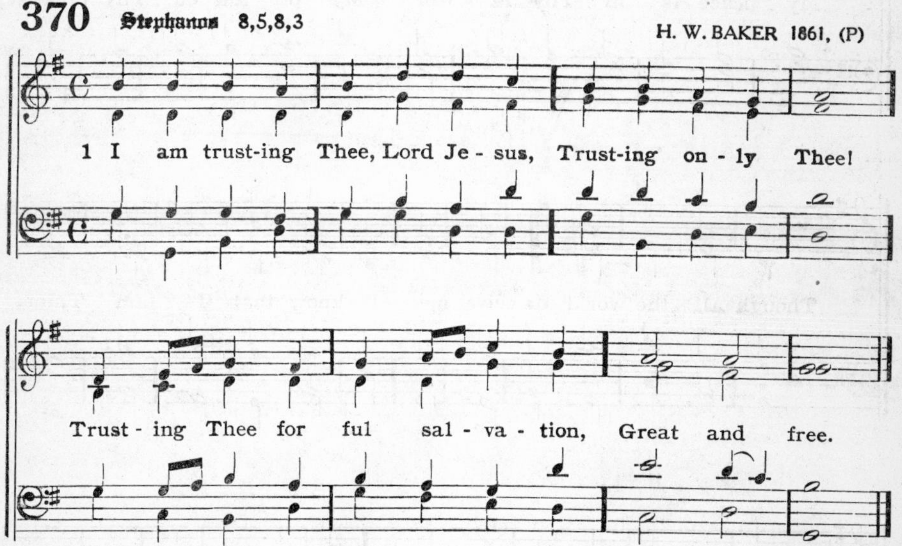
1 I am trust-ing Thee, Lord Je - sus, Trust-ing on - ly Thee!
Trust - ing Thee for ful sal - va - tion, Great and free.

2 I am trusting Thee for pardon,
At Thy feet I bow;
For Thy grace and tender mercy,
Trusting now.

3 I am trusting Thee for cleansing
In the crimson flood;
Trusting Thee to make me holy
By Thy blood.

4 I am trusting Thee to guide me;
Thou alone shalt lead,
Every day and hour supplying
All my need.

5 I am trusting Thee for power,
Thine can never fail;
Words which Thou Thyself shalt give me
Must prevail;

6 I am trusting Thee, Lord Jesus,
Never let me fall;
I am trusting Thee for ever,
And for all.

F. R. Havergal, 1874

371 Herzlich tut mich erfreuen 7,6 81 ANCIENT—B. GESIUS, 1605

1 To Thee, O dear, dear Sav - ior! My spir - it turns to rest,
My peace is in Thy fa - vor, My pil - low on Thy breast;
Though all the world de-ceive me, I know that I am Thine,
And Thou wilt nev - er leave me, O bless - ed Sav - ior mine.

2 In Thee my trust abideth,
On Thee my hope relies,
O Thou whose love provideth
For all beneath the skies;
O Thou whose mercy found me
From bondage set me free,
And then for ever bound me
With threefold cords to Thee.

3 My grief is in the dullness
With which this sluggish heart
Doth open to the fullness
Of all Thou wouldst impart;
My joy is in Thy beauty
Of holiness Divine,
My comfort in the duty
That binds my life in Thine.

4 Alas, that I should ever
Have failed in love to Thee,
The only One who never
Forgot or slighted me!
Oh, for a heart to love Thee
More truly as I ought,
And nothing place above Thee
In deed, or word, or thought.

5 Oh, for that choicest blessing
Of living in Thy love,
And thus on earth possessing
The peace of heaven above;
Oh, for the bliss that by it
The soul securely knows
The holy calm and quiet
Of faith's serene repose!

J. S. B. Monsell, 1863

372 Meribah 8,8,6,8,8,6 (C. P. M.)

1 Where'er I go, whate'er my task,
The counsel of my God I ask,
Who ruleth all things right;
Unless He give both thought and deed,
The utmost pains can ne'er succeed,
And vain must be man's might.

2 For what can all my toil avail?
My care, my watching,—all must fail,
Unless my God is there;
Then let Him order all for me
As in His will He shall decree,
On God I cast my care.

3 For naught can come, as naught has been,
But what my Father has foreseen,
And what shall work my good;
Whate'er He gives me I will take,
Whate'er He chooses I will make
My choice with thankful mood.

4 I lean upon His mighty arm,
Which shieldeth me from every harm
And all calamity;
If in His precepts I shall live,
Whate'er is useful He will give;
Nothing can injure me.

5 But only may He of His grace
The record of my guilt efface,
And wipe out all my debt;
Though I have sinned He will not straight
Pronounce His judgment, He will wait,
Have patience with me yet.

6 I travel to a distant land
To serve the post wherein I stand,
Which He hath bid me fill;
And He will bless me with His light,
That I may serve His world aright,
And make me know His will.

7 And though through desert wilds I fare,
Yet Jesus Christ is with me there,
The Lord Himself is near;
In all my dangers He will come,
And He who kept me safe at home,
Can keep me safely here.

8 Yes, He will speed me on my way,
And point me where to go and stay,
And help me still and lead;
Let me in health and safety live,
And time and wind and weather give,
And whatsoe'er I need.

9 His holy angel being near,
My enemies I need not fear,
For He protects me well;
I owe it to my faithful Guide,
Who never yet hath left my side,
That I in peace may dwell.

10 When late at night my rest I take,
When early in the morn I wake,
Halting, or on my way,
In hours of weakness or in bonds,
When vexed with fears my heart desponds,
God's Word is e'er my stay.

11 Since then my course is traced by Him,
I will not fear that future dim,
But go to meet my doom,
Well knowing, naught awaits me there
Too hard for me through Him to bear;
All evil I o'ercome.

12 To Him myself I wholly give,
At His command I die or live,
I trust His love and power;
Whether to-morrow or to-day
His summons come, I will obey,
He knows the proper hour.

13 But if it please that love most kind,
And if this voice within my mind
Be whispering not in vain,
I yet shall praise my God ere long
In many a sweet and joyful song,
When in my home again.

14 To those I love will He be near,
With his consoling light appear,
Who is my Shield and theirs;
And He will grant beyond our thought
What they and I alike have sought
With tears and fervent prayers.

Paul Flemming, 1633 C. Winkworth, Tr. a

(Or to Kommt her zu mir)

373 Swabia S. M.

OLD GERMAN CHORAL Arr. by REV. W. H. HAVERGAL, 1849

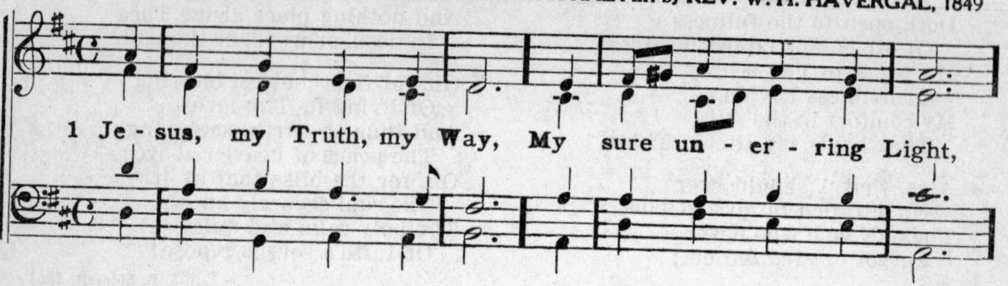
1 Je - sus, my Truth, my Way, My sure un - er - ring Light,

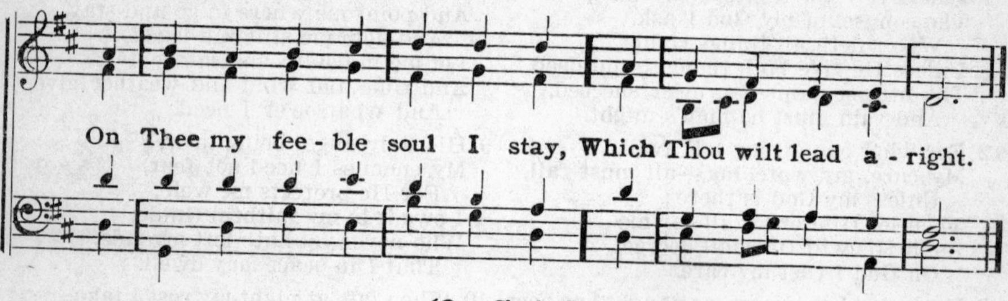
On Thee my fee - ble soul I stay, Which Thou wilt lead a - right.

(*Or to Cleveland*)

2 My Wisdom and my Guide,
My Counsellor Thou art:
O let me never leave Thy side,
Nor from Thy paths depart.

3 Thou seest my feebleness;
Jesus, be Thou my Power,
My Help and Refuge in distress,
My Fortress and my Tower.

4 Give me to trust in Thee;
Be Thou my sure Abode:
My Horn, and Rock, and Buckler be,
My Savior and my God.

5 Myself I cannot save,
Myself I cannot keep;
But strength in Thee I surely have,
Whose eyelids never sleep.

6 My soul to Thee alone
Now, therefore, I commend:
Thou, Jesus, having loved Thine own,
Wilt love me to the end!

Charles Wesley, 1749

374 Swabia S. M.

1 The Lord my shepherd is,
I shall be well supplied:
Since He is mine, and I am His,
What can I want beside.

2 He leads me to the place
Where heavenly pasture grows,
Where living waters gently pass,
And full salvation flows.

3 If e'er I go astray,
He doth my soul reclaim,
And guides me in His own right way,
For His most holy Name.

4 While He affords His aid,
I can not yield to fear:
Though I should walk through death's dark shade,
My Shepherd's with me there.

5 The bounties of Thy love
Shall crown my following days;
Nor from Thy house will I remove,
Nor cease to speak Thy praise.

Isaac Watts, 1719

375 Portuguese Hymn 11s 41

1 How firm a foundation, ye saints of the Lord,
Is laid for your faith in His excellent Word;
What more can He say, than to you He hath said,
Who unto the Savior for refuge have fled?

2 In every condition,—in sickness, in health,
In poverty's vale, or abounding in wealth,
At home and abroad, on the land, on the sea,
As thy days may demand shall thy strength ever be.

3 Fear not, I am with thee, oh be not dismayed;
For I am thy God, and will still give thee aid;
I'll strengthen thee, help thee, and cause thee to stand,
Upheld by my righteous, omnipotent hand.

4 When through the deep waters I call thee to go,
The rivers of sorrow shall not overflow;
For I will be with thee, thy troubles to bless,
And sanctify to thee thy deepest distress.

5 When through fiery trials thy pathway shall lie,
My grace, all-sufficient, shall be thy supply;
The flames shall not hurt thee; I only design
Thy dross to consume and thy gold to refine.

6 E'en down to old age my people shall prove
My sovereign, eternal, unchangeable love;
And when hoary hairs shall their temples adorn,
Like lambs they shall still in my bosom be borne.

7 The soul that on Jesus hath leaned for repose
I will not, I will not desert to His foes;
That soul, though all Hell should endeavor to shake,
I'll never, no never, no never forsake!

G. Keith (?). publ., 1787

Sanctification

Warfare

376 Sampson L. M. HANDEL

1 Fight the good fight with all thy might; Christ is thy strength, and Christ thy right:

Lay hold on life, and it shall be Thy joy and crown e - ter-nal - ly.

2 Run the straight race
Through God's good grace,
Lift up thine eyes, and seek His face;
Life with its way before us lies,
Christ is the path, and Christ the prize.

3 Cast care aside;
Upon thy guide
Lean, and His mercy will provide;
Lean, and the trusting soul shall prove,
Christ is its life, and Christ its love.

4 Faint not, nor fear,
His arms are near;
He changeth not, and thou art dear;
Only believe, and thou shalt see
That Christ is all in all to thee.

J. S. B. Monsell, 1863

377 Jeg vil mig Herren love 7,6 81

ZINCK'S KORALBOG, 1801

1 { Stand up!—stand up for Jesus! Ye soldiers of the cross;
Lift high His roy - al ban - ner, It must not suf - fer loss;

From vic - t'ry un - to vic - t'ry His arm - y shall He lead,

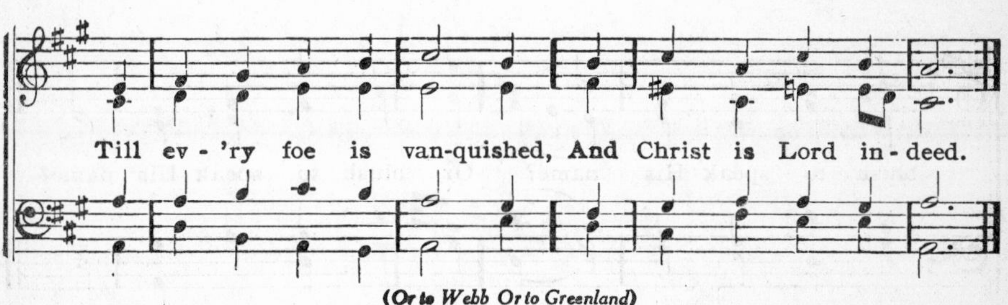
Till ev - 'ry foe is van-quished, And Christ is Lord in - deed.

(Or to Webb Or to Greenland)

2 Stand up!—stand up for Jesus!
The trumpet call obey;
Forth to the mighty conflict,
In this His glorious day.
Ye that are men, now serve Him
Against unnumbered foes;
Let courage rise with danger,
And strength to strength oppose.

3 Stand up!—stand up for Jesus!
Stand in His strength alone;
The arm of flesh will fail you,
Ye dare not trust your own:
Put on the gospel armor,
Each piece put on with prayer;
Where duty calls, or danger,
Be never wanting there.

4 Stand up!—stand up for Jesus!
The strife will not be long;
This day the noise of battle,
The next, the victor's song.
To him that overcometh,
A crown of life shall be;
He with the King of Glory
Shall reign eternally!

G. Duffield, 1858

378 Christmas C. M.

HAENDEL, 1728

1 Am I a sol-dier of the cross, A fol-l'wer of the

Lamb? And shall I fear to own His cause, Or

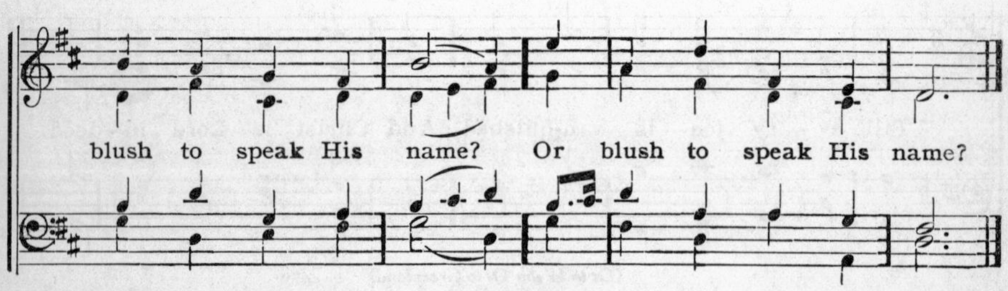
blush to speak His name? Or blush to speak His name?

(Or to Marlow)

2 Must I be carried to the skies
On flowery beds of ease,
While others fought to win the prize,
And sailed through bloody seas?

3 Are there no foes for me to face?
Must I not stem the flood?
Is this vile world a friend to grace,
To help me on to God?

4 Sure I must fight, if I would reign:
Increase my courage, Lord;
I'll bear the toil, endure the pain,
Supported by Thy Word.

5 Thy saints, in all this glorious war,
Shall conquer, though they die;
They see the triumph from afar,
With faith's discerning eye.

6 When that illustrious day shall rise,
And all Thine armies shine
In robes of victory through the skies,
The glory shall be Thine.

Isaac Watts, 1709 a

379 Laban S. M.

LOWELL MASON

1 My soul, be on thy guard, Ten thous-and foes a - rise; And

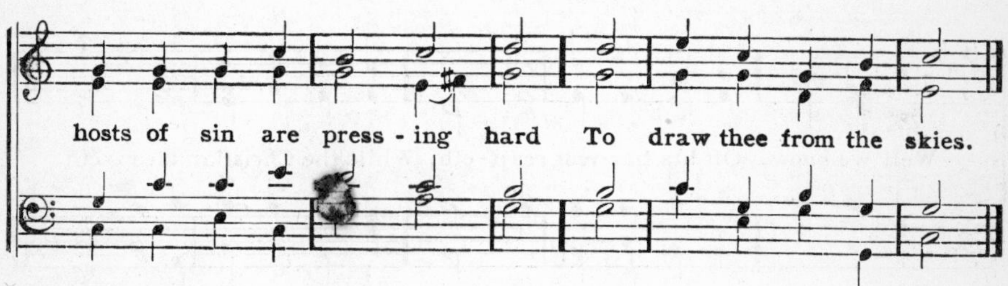
hosts of sin are press - ing hard To draw thee from the skies.

(Or to Schumann)

2 O watch, and fight, and pray,
The battle ne'er give o'er;
Renew it boldly every day,
And help divine implore.

3 Ne'er think the victory won,
Nor lay thine armor down;
Thine arduous work will not be done,
Till thou receive thy crown.

4 Fight on, my soul, till death
Shall bring thee to thy God;
He'll take thee at thy parting breath,
To His divine abode.

George Heath, 1781

380 Laban S. M.

1 Soldiers of Christ, arise,
And put your armor on;
Strong in the strength which God supplies,
Through His eternal Son.

2 Strong in the Lord of hosts,
And in His mighty power;
Who in the strength of Jesus trusts
Is more than conqueror.

3 Stand then in His great might,
With all His strength endued;
But take, to arm you for the fight,
The panoply of God:

4 That having all things done,
And all your conflicts past,
Ye may o'ercome through Christ alone,
And stand entire at last.

5 From strength to strength go on,
Wrestle, and fight, and pray;
Tread all the powers of darkness down,
And win the well-fought day.

6 Still let the Spirit cry,
In all His soldiers, "Come,"
Till Christ the Lord descends from high,
And takes the conquerors home.

Charles Wesley, 1749

(Or to Silver St. Or to St. Thomas)

381 Straf mich nicht in deinem Zorn 7,6,7,6,6,6,6,6 J. ROSENMUELLER (?), 1694

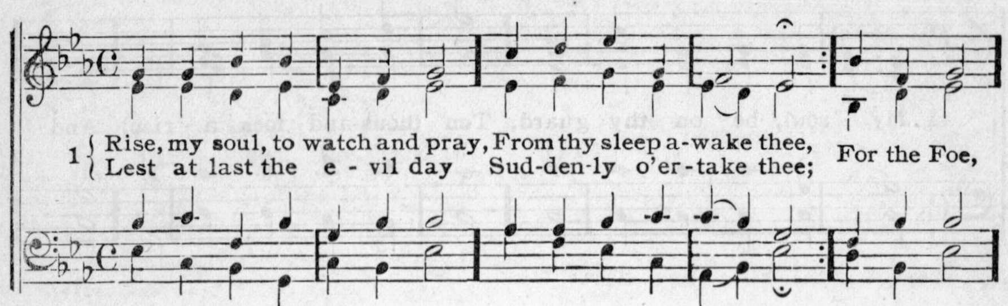
1 { Rise, my soul, to watch and pray, From thy sleep a-wake thee,
Lest at last the e - vil day Sud-den-ly o'er-take thee; For the Foe,

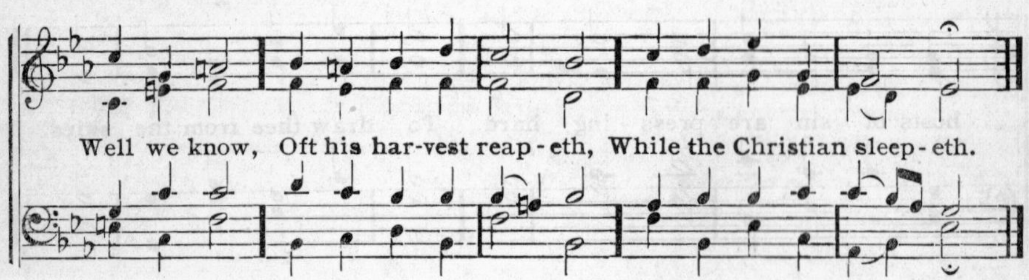
Well we know, Oft his har-vest reap - eth, While the Christian sleep - eth.

2 But first rouse thee, and awake
From secure indiff'rence;
Else will follow in its wake
Woe without deliv'rance.
O beware! Soul, take care!
Death in sins might find thee,
Ere thou look behind thee.

3 Wake and watch, or else thy night
Christ can ne'er enlighten;
Far off still will seem the light
That thy path should brighten;
God demands Eyes and hands
Open for the offers
He so richly proffers.

4 Watch against the Devil's snares,
Lest asleep he find thee;
For, indeed, no pains he spares
To deceive and blind thee;
Satan's prey Oft are they,
Who are soundly sleeping,
And no good watch keeping.

5 Watch against the world that frowns
Darkly to dismay thee;
Watch, when she thy wishes crowns,
Smiling to betray thee;
Watch and see Thou art free
From false friends that charm thee,
While they seek to harm thee.

6 Watch against thyself, my soul,
See thou do not stifle
Grace that should thy thoughts control,
Nor with mercy trifle;
Pride and sin Lurk within,
All thy hopes to scatter;
List not, when they flatter.

7 But while watching, also see
That thou pray unceasing,
For the Lord must make thee free,
Strength and faith increasing,
So to do Service true;
Let not sloth enslave thee;
Pray, and He will save thee.

8 Yea, indeed, He bids us pray,
Promising to hear us,
E'er to be our Staff and Stay,
Ever to be near us.
Ere we plead Will He heed,
Strengthen, keep, defend us,
And deliv'rance send us.

9 Courage then, for all things must
Work for good, and bless us,
If we but in prayerful trust
To His Son address us;
For He will Richly fill,
And His Spirit send us,
Who to Him commend us.

10 Therefore let us watch and pray
Ever without ceasing,
For we know, with every day
Dangers are increasing,
And the end Doth impend;
When the trumpet calleth,
Earth in ruins falleth.

J. Burkhard Freystein, 1704

382 Olney S. M.

LOWELL MASON (P)

1 Ye ser-vants of the Lord, Each in his of - fice wait,

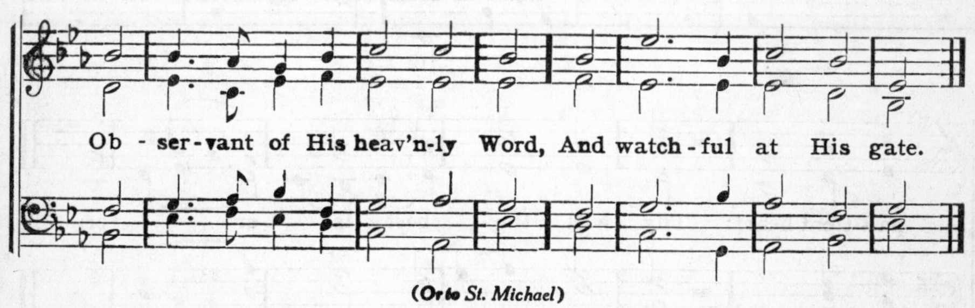
Ob - ser-vant of His heav'n-ly Word, And watch - ful at His gate.

(Or to St. Michael)

2 Let all your lamps be bright,
And trim the golden flame;
Gird up your loins, as in His sight,
For awful is His name.

3 Watch! 'tis your Lord's command;
And while we speak, He's near:
Mark the first signal of His hand,
And ready all appear.

4 O happy servant he,
In such a posture found!
He shall his Lord with rapture see,
And be with honor crowned.

P. Doddridge, 1755

Sanctification

Resignation

383 Herr, wie du willt, so schicks mit mir 8,7,8,7,7,8,8,7 GREITER, 1524

1 { Lord, as Thou wilt, deal Thou with me, No oth - er wish I cher - ish;
In life and death I cling to Thee, O Lord, let me not per - ish!
Let but Thy grace ne'er from me part, Else as Thou wilt; grant
pa - tient heart: Thy will the best is ev - - - er.

2 Grant honor, truth, prosperity,
 And love thy Word to ponder;
False doctrines, Lord, keep far from me,
 And grant both here and yonder
What serves my everlasting bliss;
Preserve me from unrighteousness
 In all my life and doings.

3 When, at Thy summons, I must leave
 This world of sin and sadness,
Grant me Thy grace, Lord, not to grieve,
 But to depart with gladness;
My spirit I commend to Thee,
O Lord, a blessed end give me
 Through Jesus Christ;—Yea, Amen.

Caspar Melissander, 1574

384 Mein Schœpfer steh mir bei 6s 81

F. H. MEYER, 1740, ad. by I

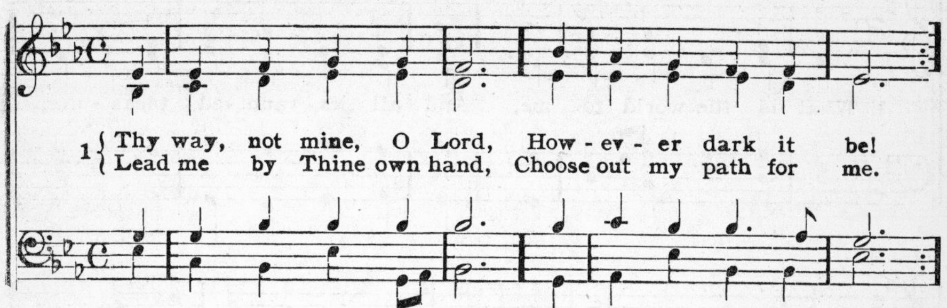
1 { Thy way, not mine, O Lord, How - ev - er dark it be!
Lead me by Thine own hand, Choose out my path for me.

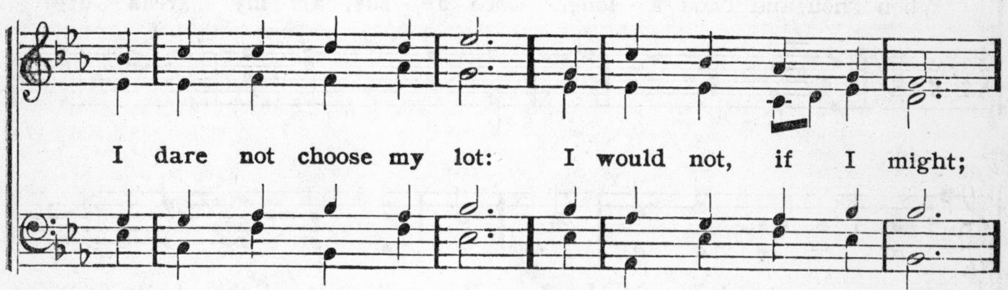
I dare not choose my lot: I would not, if I might;

Choose Thou for me, my God, So shall I walk a - right.

(Or to Weber)

2 The kingdom that I seek
Is Thine; so let the way
That leads to it be Thine,
Else I must surely stray,
Take Thou my cup and it
With joy or sorrow fill,
As best to Thee may seem;
Choose Thou my good and ill.

3 Choose Thou for me my friends,
My sickness or my health;
Choose Thou my cares for me,
My poverty or wealth.
Not mine, not mine the choice,
In things or great or small;
Be Thou my Guide, my Strength,
My Wisdom and my All.

Horatius Bonar, 1857

385 Was frag ich nach der Welt 6,7,6,7,6,6,6,6 A. FRITZSCH, 1675

1 What is the world to me, And all its vaunt-ed pleas-ure,
When Thou, and Thou a-lone, Lord Je-sus, art my treas-ure!
Thou on-ly, dear-est Lord, My soul's de-light shalt be,
Thou art my peace, my rest— What is the world to me!

(*Or to O Gott du frommer*)

2 The world is like the smoke,
A fleeting exhalation,
A shadow faint and dim
Of very short duration;
My Jesus doth abide,
Though all things fade and flee;
My everlasting Rock—
What is the world to me!

3 The world strives to be praised
And honored by the mighty,
Nor will at all reflect
How frail they are and flighty;
But what I glory in
Above all things, is He,
My Jesus, He alone—
What is the world to me!

4 The world seeks after wealth,
And unto Mammon offers
Its all, content if gold
Is hoarded in its coffers;
I know a higher good,
Which e'er my joy shall be;
My Jesus is my Wealth—
What is the world to me!

5 The world is sorely grieved,
If ever it is slighted,
As though an enemy
Its honor would have blighted;
Christ, I bear Thy reproach,
While thus it pleaseth Thee!
I'm honored by my Lord—
What is the world to me!

6 The world cannot extol
Too highly sinful pleasures,
And foolishly resigns
For them the heavenly treasures.
Let others love the world,
To please their vanity:
I love the Lord, my God—
What is the world to me!

7 What is the world to me,
It rapidly must vanish;
With all its gorgeous pomp
Pale death it cannot banish;
Its riches pass away,
And all its joys must flee,
But Jesus doth abide—
What is the world to me!

8 What is the world to me!
My Jesus is my Treasure,
My Life, my Wealth, my All,
My Friend, my Love, my Pleasure,
My heavenly Happiness
And Bliss eternally;
Once more, then, I would say,
What is the world to me!

G. Michael Pfefferkorn, 1667 A. Crull, Tr.

386 Southport 8,8,8,4

G. LOMAS

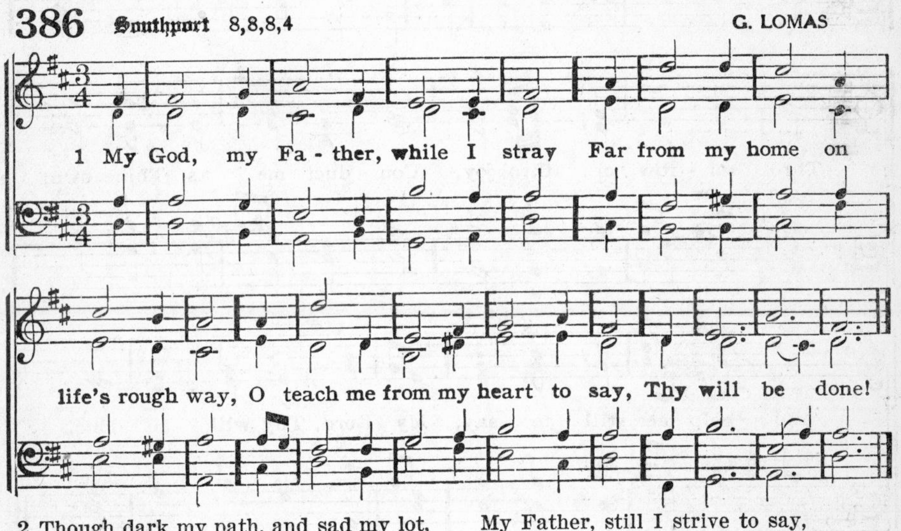
1 My God, my Fa - ther, while I stray Far from my home on
life's rough way, O teach me from my heart to say, Thy will be done!

2 Though dark my path, and sad my lot,
Let me be still and murmur not,
Or breathe the prayer divinely taught,
Thy will be done!

3 What though in lonely grief I sigh
For friends beloved, no longer nigh;
Submissive still would I reply,
Thy will be done!

4 Though Thou hast called me to resign
What most I prized, it ne'er was mine;
I have but yielded what was Thine:
Thy will be done!

5 Should grief or sickness waste away
My life in premature decay,
My Father, still I strive to say,
Thy will be done!

6 Let but my fainting heart be blest
With Thy sweet Spirit for its guest,
My God, to Thee I leave the rest:
Thy will be done!

7 Renew my will from day to day;
Blend it with Thine, and take away
All that now makes it hard to say,
Thy will be done!

8 Then, when on earth I breathe no more,
The prayer oft mixed with tears before,
I'll sing upon a happier shore,
Thy will be done!

Charlotte Elliott, 1834

387 Weber (Jewett) 6s 8l C. M. von WEBER, 1821

1 My Je - sus, as Thou wilt! O may Thy will be mine;
In - to Thy hand of love I would my all re - sign.
Thro' sor - row, or thro' joy, Con - duct me as Thine own;
And help me still to say, My Lord, Thy will be done.

2 My Jesus, as Thou wilt!
If needy here and poor,
Give me Thy people's bread,
Their portion rich and sure.
The manna of Thy word
Let my soul feed upon;
And if all else should fail,
My Lord, Thy will be done.

2 My Jesus, as Thou wilt!
Though seen through many a tear,
Let not my star of hope
Grow dim or disappear,
Since Thou on earth hast wept
And sorrowed oft alone,
If I must weep with Thee,
My Lord, Thy will be done.

4 My Jesus, as Thou wilt!
All shall be well for me;
Each changing future scene
I gladly trust with Thee.
Straight to my home above
I travel calmly on,
And sing, in life or death,
My Lord, Thy will be done.

Benjamin Schmolck, c. 1704 Jane Borthwick, Tr. 1854

388 Moravia S. M.

L. R. WEST

1 Blest be Thy love, dear Lord, That taught us this sweet way,
To love Thee on - ly for Thy - self, And for that love o - bey.

(Or to Monsell)

2 O Thou, our soul's chief hope,
We to Thy mercy fly;
Where'er we are Thou canst protect,
Whate'er we need, supply,

3 Whether we sleep or wake,
To Thee we both resign;
The darkest night is as the day,
If Thy light on us shine.

4 Whether we live or die,
Both we submit to Thee;
In death we live, as well as life,
If Thine in death we be.

John Austin 1868

389 Elvet C. M.

DYKES

1 O Lord, my best de - sire ful - fil, And help me to re - sign
Life, health, and com - fort to Thy will, And make Thy pleas - ure mine.

2 Why should I shrink at Thy command,
Whose love forbids my fears?
Or tremble at the gracious hand
That wipes away my tears?

3 No, rather let me freely yield
What most I prize to Thee,
Who never hast a good withheld,
Nor wilt withhold, from me.

4 Thy favor, all my journey through,
Thou art engaged to grant:
What else I want, or think I do,
'Tis better still to want.

William Cowper, 1779

Catechism

Law

390 Herr Jesu Christ, meins L. M.

1 Lord, grant that we e'er pure retain
The catechismal doctrine plain,
As Luther taught the heavenly truth
In simple words to tender youth.

2 That we Thy holy Law may know
And mourn our sin and all its woe,
And yet believe in Father, Son,
And Holy Spirit, Three in One.

3 That we on Thee, our Father, call
Who canst and wilt give help to all;
That as Thy children we may live,
Whom Thou in Baptism didst receive.

4 That, if we fall, we rise again,
Repentingly confess our sin,
And take the Sacrament in faith;—
Amen. God grant a happy death!

Ludwig Helmbold, 1577 M. Loy, Tr. a

(Or to *Erhalt uns Herr*)

391 Dies sind die heil'gen zehn Gebot 8,8,8,7,4 13th CENTURY, J. WALTHER, 1524

1 That man a god - ly life might live, God did these
ten com - mand-ments give By His true ser - vant Mos - es, high
Up - on the mount Si - na - i. Have mer - cy, Lord!

2 I am Thy God and Lord alone,
No other God beside me own;
Put Thy whole confidence in me,
And love me e'er cordially.
Have mercy, Lord!

3 By idle word and speech profane
Take not my holy name in vain,
And praise but that as good and true
Which I myself say and do.
Have mercy, Lord!

4 Hallow the day which God hath blest,
That thou and all thy house may rest;
Keep hand and heart from labor free,
That God may so work in thee.
Have mercy, Lord!

5 Give to thy parents honor due,
Be dutiful, and loving too,
And help them when their strength decays,
So shalt thou have length of days.
Have mercy, Lord!

6 In sinful wrath thou shalt not kill,
Nor hate, nor render ill for ill;
Be patient and of gentle mood,
And to thy foe do thou good.
Have mercy, Lord!

7 Be faithful to thy marriage vows,
Thy heart give only to thy spouse;
Thy life keep pure, and lest thou sin,
Use temp'rance and discipline.
Have mercy, Lord!

8 Steal not; all usury abhor,
Nor wring their life-blood from the poor;
But open wide thy loving hand
To all the poor in the land.
Have mercy, Lord!

9 Bear not false witness, nor belie
Thy neighbor by foul calumny;
Defend his innocence from blame,
With charity hide his shame.
Have mercy, Lord!

10 Thy neighbor's house desire thou not,
His wife, nor aught that he hath got,
But wish that his such good may be,
As thy heart doth wish for thee.
Have mercy, Lord!

11 God these commandments gave, therein
To show thee, child of man, thy sin,
And make thee also well perceive,
How man unto God should live.
Have mercy, Lord!

12 Help us, Lord Jesus Christ, for we
A Mediator have in Thee;
Our works cannot salvation gain.
They merit but endless pain.
Have mercy, Lord!

Dr. Martin Luther, 1524 R. Massie, Tr. a

392 Mensch, willt du leben seliglich 8,8,8,7,4 J. WALTHER, 1524

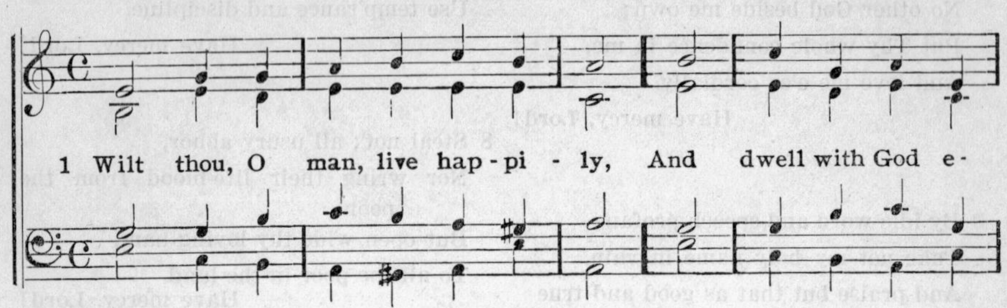
1 Wilt thou, O man, live hap-pi-ly, And dwell with God e-

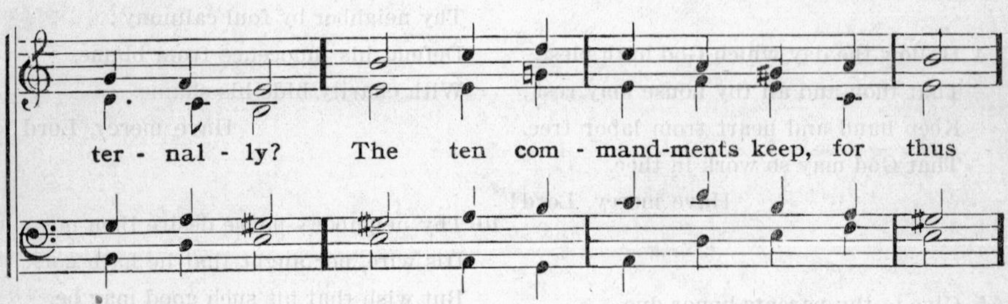
ter-nal-ly? The ten com-mand-ments keep, for thus

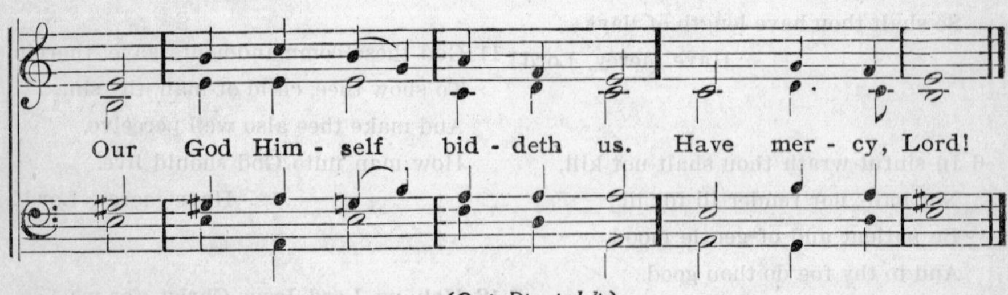
Our God Him-self bid-deth us. Have mer-cy, Lord!

(Or to Dies sind die)

2 I am thy Lord and God! take heed
Lest other gods do thee mislead;
Thy heart shall trust alone in me,
Thou shalt my own kingdom be.
Have mercy, Lord!

3 Honor my name in word and deed,
And call on me in time of need;
Hallow the Sabbath, that I may
Work in thy heart on that day.
Have mercy, Lord!

4 Obedient always, next to me,
To father and to mother be;
Kill no man, but to wrath be slow;
Be true to thy marriage vow.
Have mercy, Lord!

5 Steal not, nor do thy neighbor wrong
By bearing witness with false tongue;
Thy neighbor's wife desire thou not,
Nor grudge him aught he hath got.
Have mercy, Lord!

Dr. Martin Luther, 1525 Richard Massie, Tr. a

Catechism

Creed

393 **Wir glauben all an einen Gott,** 8,7,7,7,7,7 DARMST. H. B. 1699

1 We all be-lieve in One true God, Fa-ther, Son, and Ho-ly Ghost,
Pres - ent Help - er in all need, Praised by all the heav'n-ly host,
By whose might-y power a - lone All is made, and wrought, and done.

2 And we believe in Jesus Christ,
Son of God, and Mary's Son,
Who from heaven above came down,
And leads us to heaven's throne;
By whose blood and death are we
Rescued from all misery.

3 And we confess the Holy Ghost,
Who from both fore'er proceeds;
Who upholds and comforts us
In the midst of fears and needs.
Blest and holy Trinity,
Praise forever be to Thee!

Tobias Clausnitzer, 1671

394 Wir glauben all an einen Gott 8s 10 1 MARTIN LUTHER, 1524

1 We all be - lieve in one true God, Mak - er
of the earth and heav - en, The Fa - ther, who to us in love
Hath the claim of child - ren giv - en: He in soul and bod - y feeds us,
All we want His hand pro - vides us, Thro' all snares and per - ils

leads us, Watch - es that no harm be - tides us; He

cares for us by day and night, ...

3rd verse.
. . . . All things are gov-erned by His might. A - men.

2 And we believe in Jesus Christ,
His own Son, our Lord, possessing
An equal Godhead, throne and might,
Through whom comes the Father's blessing;
Conceived of the Holy Spirit,
Born of Mary, virgin-mother,
That lost man might life inherit,
Made true man, our Elder Brother,
Was crucified for sinful men,
And raised by God to life again.

3 We in the Holy Ghost believe,
Who sweet grace and comfort giveth,
And with the Father and the Son
In eternal glory liveth;
Who the Christian Church doth even
Keep in unity of spirit;
Sins are truly here forgiven
Through the blest Redeemer's merit;
All flesh shall rise again, and we
Shall live with God eternally; Amen.

Dr. Martin Luther, 1525

394b Pomerania 8s 101 J. C. KITTEL, 1790

1
2
1 { We all be-lieve in one true God, Mak-er of the earth and heav-
The Fa-ther, who to us in love Hath the claim of child-ren giv-
en,
- - - - en. He in soul and bod-y feeds us, All we want His hand provides us,
Thro' all snares and per-ils leads us, Watches that no harm be-tides us;
3rd verse
He cares for us by day and night, All things are governed by His might. A-men.

Prayer

395 Friend 8,7 81 CHARLES C. CONVERSE

1 What a Friend we have in Je - sus, All our sins and griefs to bear;
What a priv-i-lege to car - ry Ev-'ry thing to God in prayer.
Oh, what peace we oft - en for - feit, Oh, what needless pain we bear—
All because we do not car - ry Ev-'ry thing to God in prayer.

2 Have we trials and temptations?
Is there trouble anywhere?
We should never be discouraged,
Take it to the Lord in prayer.
Can we find a Friend so faithful,
Who will all our sorrows share?
Jesus knows our every weakness,
Take it to the Lord in prayer.

3 Are we weak and heavy laden,
Cumbered with a load of care?
Precious Savior, still our refuge,—
Take it to the Lord in prayer.
Do thy friends despise, forsake thee?
Take it to the Lord in prayer;
In His arms He'll take and shield thee,
Thou wilt find a solace there.

Joseph Scriven, 1855

396 Vater unser im Himmelreich L. M. 61

KOEPHL, 1538

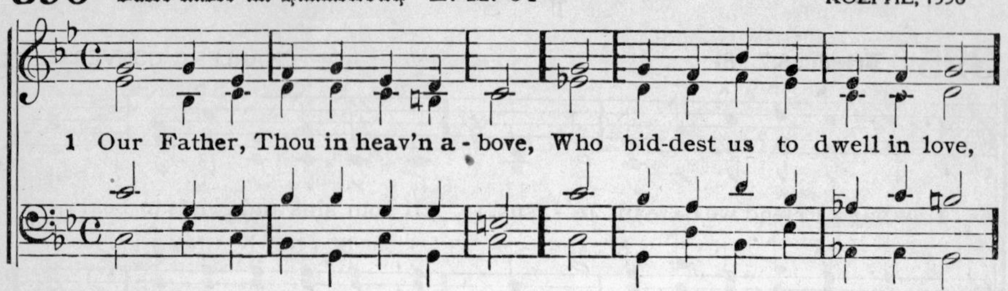
1 Our Father, Thou in heav'n a - bove, Who bid-dest us to dwell in love,

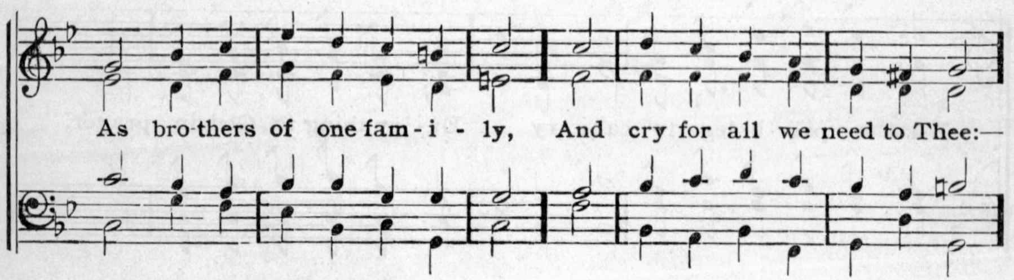
As bro-thers of one fam - i - ly, And cry for all we need to Thee:—

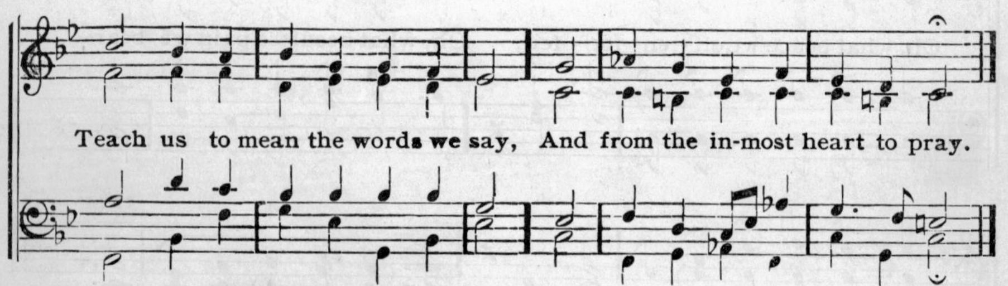
Teach us to mean the words we say, And from the in-most heart to pray.

2 Thy name be hallowed! help us Lord,
To keep in purity Thy Word,
And lead according to Thy name,
A holy life, untouched by blame;
Let no false teachings do us hurt,
All poor deluded souls convert.

3 Thy kingdom come! Thine let it be
In time, and through eternity!
O let Thy Holy Spirit dwell
With us, to rule and guide us well;
From Satan's mighty power and rage
Preserve Thy Church from age to age.

4 Thy will be done on earth, O Lord,
As where in heaven Thou art adored!
Patience in time of grief bestow,
Obedience in weal and woe;
Our sinful flesh and blood control
That thwart Thy will within the soul.

5 Give us this day our daily bread
And all that for this life we need;
From war and strife be our Defence,
From famine and from pestilence,
That we may live in godly peace,
Unvexed by cares and avarice.

6 Lord, all our trespasses forgive,
That they our hearts no more may grieve,
As we forgive their trespasses
Who unto us have done amiss;
Thus let us dwell in charity,
And serve each other willingly.

7 Into temptation lead us not;
And when the Foe doth war and plot
Against our souls on every hand,
Then armed with faith, O may we stand
Against him as a valiant host,
Through comfort of the Holy Ghost.

8 From evil, Lord, deliver us!
The times and days are perilous;
Redeem us from eternal death;
And when we yield our dying breath,
Console us, grant us calm release,
And take our souls to Thee in peace.

9 Amen! that is, So let it be!
Confirm our faith continually,
That we may doubt not, but believe
That what we ask we shall receive;
Thus in Thy name and at Thy word;
We say: Amen; O hear us, Lord!

Dr. Martin Luther, 1539

397 Boylston S. M.

1 Our heavenly Father, hear
The prayer we offer now;
Thy name be hallowed far and near,
To Thee all nations bow.

2 Thy kingdom come; Thy will
On earth be done in love,
As saints and seraphim fulfill
Thy holy will above.

3 Our daily bread supply
While by Thy word we live;
The guilt of our iniquity
Forgive as we forgive.

4 From dark temptation's power,
From Satan's wiles defend;
Deliver in the evil hour,
And guide us to the end.

5 Thine shall forever be
Glory and power divine;
The sceptre, throne, and majesty,
Of heaven and earth are Thine.

James Montgomery, 1825

(Or to Cleveland)

398 Spohr C. M.

1 Prayer is the soul's sincere desire,
Uttered or unexpressed;
The motion of a hidden fire
That trembles in the breast.

2 Prayer is the burden of a sigh,
The falling of a tear,
The upward glancing of an eye,
When none but God is near.

3 Prayer is the simplest form of speech
That infant lips can try;
Prayer the sublimest strains that reach
The Majesty on high.

4 Prayer is the contrite sinner's voice,
Returning from his ways,
While angels in their songs rejoice,
And cry, "Behold he prays!"

5 Prayer is the Christian's vital breath,
The Christian's native air;
His watchword at the gate of death—
He enters heaven with prayer.

6 The saints in prayer appear as one
In word, and deed, and mind,
While with the Father and the Son
Sweet fellowship they find.

7 Nor prayer is made by man alone,—
The Holy Spirit pleads,
And Jesus on the eternal throne
For sinners intercedes.

8 O Thou, by whom we come to God,
The Life, the Truth, the Way,
The path of prayer Thyself hast trod—
Lord, teach us how to pray!

James Montgomery, 1818

(Or to St. Agnes)

399 Spohr C. M.

L. SPOHR, (1784—1859)

1 Ap-proach, my soul the mer - cy - seat, Where Je - sus an-swers prayer;

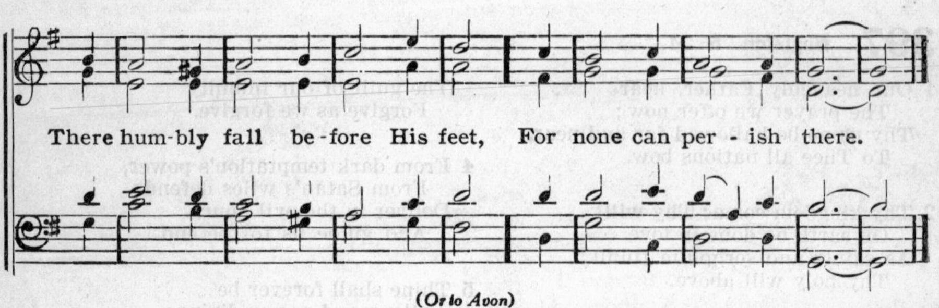
There hum-bly fall be-fore His feet, For none can per - ish there.

(Or to Avon)

2 Thy promise is my only plea,
With this I venture nigh;
Thou callest burdened souls to Thee,
And such, O Lord, am I.

3 Bowed down beneath a load of sin,
By Satan sorely pressed,
By wars without and fears within,
I come to Thee for rest.

4 Be Thou my shield and hiding-place,
That, sheltered near Thy side,
I may my fierce Accuser face
And tell him, Thou hast died.

5 O wondrous Love, to bleed and die,
To bear the cross and shame,
That guilty sinners such as I
Might plead Thy gracious name!

John Newton, 1779

Catechism

Baptism

400 Doles 9,8,9,8,8,8 DOLES, 1785

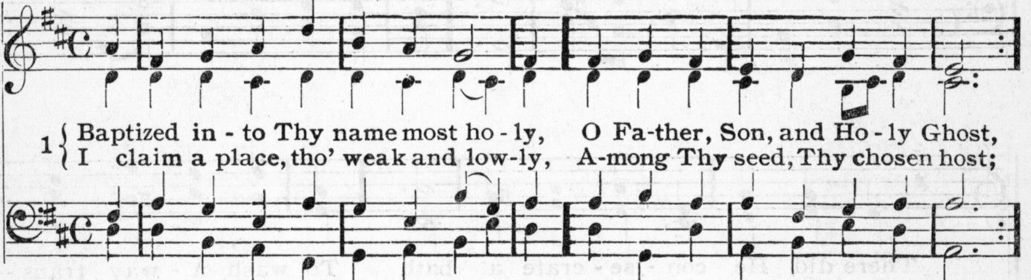
1 { Baptized in - to Thy name most ho - ly, O Fa-ther, Son, and Ho - ly Ghost,
I claim a place, tho' weak and low-ly, A-mong Thy seed, Thy chosen host;

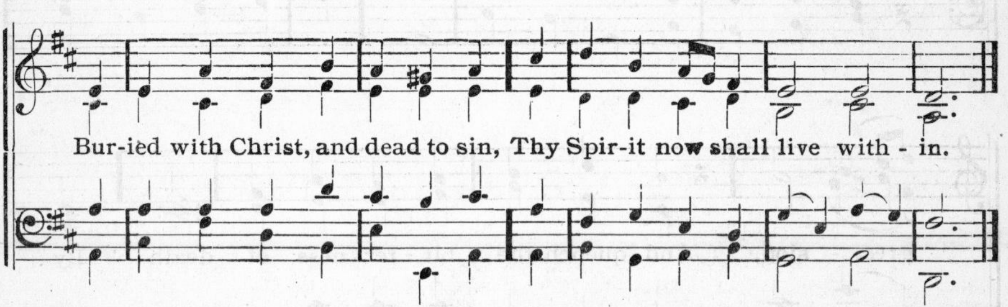
Bur-ied with Christ, and dead to sin, Thy Spir-it now shall live with - in.

(Or to O dass ich tausend zungen, by Koenig)

2 My loving Father, Thou dost take me
To be henceforth Thy child and heir;
My faithful Savior, Thou dost make me
The fruit of all Thy sorrows share,
Thou, Holy Ghost, wilt comfort me,
When darkest clouds around I see.

3 And I have vowed to fear and love Thee,
And to obey Thee, Lord, alone;
I felt Thy Holy Spirit move me,
And freely pledged myself Thine own,
Renouncing sin to keep the faith,
And war with evil unto death.

4 My faithful God, Thou failest never,
Thy covenant surely will abide;
O cast me not away forever,
Should I trangress it on my side;
If I have sore my soul defiled,
Yet still forgive, restore Thy child.

5 Yea, all I am, and love most dearly,—
To Thee I offer new the whole;
O let me make my vows sincerely,
Take full possession of my soul,
Let naught within me, naught I own,
Serve any will but Thine alone.

6 Depart, depart! Thou Prince of darkness!
No more by thee I'll be enticed.
Mine is indeed a tarnished conscience,
But sprinkled with the blood of Christ.
Away, vain world! O sin, away!
Lo! I renounce you all this day.

7 And never let my purpose falter,
O Father, Son, and Holy Ghost,
But keep me faithful to Thine altar,
Till Thou shalt call me from my post;
So unto Thee I live and die,
And praise Thee evermore on high.

J. J. Rambach, 1735, C. Winkworth, Tr. a

401 Christ unser Herr zum Jordan kam 8,7,8,7,8,7,8,7,7 J. WALTHER, 1524

1 { To Jordan came our Lord, the Christ, To do God's pleasure will-ing,
And there was by Saint John baptized, All righteousness ful-fill-ing;
There did He con-se-crate a bath To wash a-way trans-
gres-sion, And quench the bit-ter-ness of death By
His own blood and pas-sion; He would a new life give us.
(Or to Es wollt uns Gott)

2 So hear ye all, and well perceive
What God doth call a Baptism,
And what a Christian should believe
Who error shuns and schism:
That we should water use, the Lord
Declareth in His pleasure,
Not simple water, but the Word
And Spirit without measure;—
He is the true Baptizer.

3 To show us this, He hath His word
With signs and symbols given;
On Jordan's banks was plainly heard
The Father's voice from heaven:
"This is my well-beloved Son,
In whom my soul delighteth;
Hear him!" Yea, hear Him every one,
Whom He Himself inviteth;
Hear and obey His teaching!

4 In tender manhood God the Son
In Jordan's water standeth;
The Holy Ghost from heaven's throne
In dove-like form descendeth;
That thus the truth be not denied,
Nor should our faith e'er waver,
That the Three Persons all preside
At Baptism's holy laver,
And dwell with the believer.

5 Thus Jesus His disciples sent
Go, teach ye every nation,
That, lost in sin, they must repent,
And flee from condemnation;
He that believes and is baptized
Shall thereby have salvation,
A new-born man he is in Christ,
From death free and damnation,
He shall inherit heaven.

6 Who in this mercy hath not faith
Nor aught therein discerneth,
Is yet in sin, condemned to death
And fire that ever burneth;
His holiness avails him not,
Nor aught which he is doing;
His inborn sin brings all to naught,
And maketh sure his ruin;
Himself he cannot succor.

7 The eye of sense alone is dim,
And nothing sees but water;
Faith sees Christ Jesus, and in Him
The Lamb ordained for slaughter;
It sees the cleansing fountain, red
With the dear blood of Jesus,
Which from the sins, inherited
From fallen Adam, frees us,
And from our own misdoings.

Dr. Martin Luther, 1543 Richard Massie, Tr. a

402 Liebster Jesu, wir sind hier 7,8,7,8,8,8

1 Blessed Jesus, here we stand,
Met to do as Thou hast spoken;
And this child, at Thy command,
Now we bring to Thee, in token
That to Christ it here is given;
For of such shall be Thy heaven.

2 Yes, Thy warning voice is plain,
And we would obey it duly:
"He who is not born again,
Heart and life renewing truly,
Born of water and the Spirit,
Will My kingdom ne'er inherit."

3 Therefore hasten we to Thee;
Take the pledge we bring, O take it!
Let us here Thy glory see,
And in tender pity make it
Now Thy child, and leave it never,
Thine on earth, and Thine forever.

4 Wash it, Jesus, in Thy blood,
From the sin-stain of its nature;
Let it rise from out this flood
Clothed in Thee, a new born creature;
May it, washed as Thou hast bidden,
In thine innocence be hidden.

5 Turn its darkness into light,
To Thy grace receive and save it;
Heal the Serpent's venomed bite,
In the font where now we lave it;
Here let flow a Jordan river,
And from leprosy deliver.

6 Make it, Head, Thy member now;
Shepherd, take Thy lamb and feed it;
Prince of peace, its peace be Thou;
Way of life, to heaven lead it;
Vine, this branch may nothing sever,
Graft by faith in Thee forever.

7 Now into Thy heart we pour
Prayers, that from our hearts proceeded;
Let our sighing heavenward soar,
Let our warm desires be heeded;
Write the name we now have given,
Write it in the book of heaven.

Benj. Schmolck. 1794

403 Uxbridge L. M.

LOWELL MASON

1 Now Christ, the ver-y Son of God, On sinners sends an-oth - er flood;

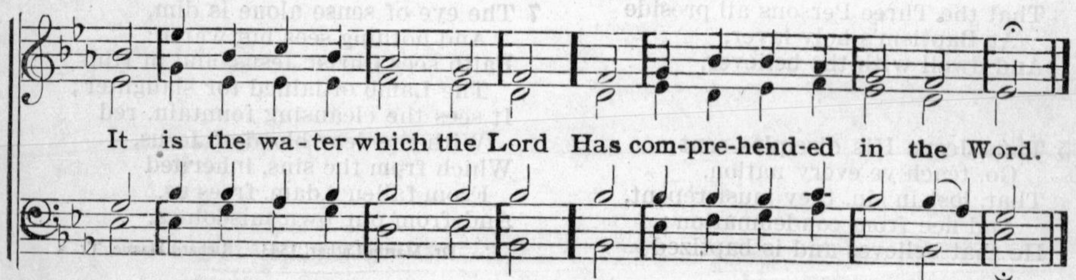
It is the wa-ter which the Lord Has com-pre-hend-ed in the Word.

2 This flood, to cleanse sin's leprosy.
Mere earthly water cannot be;
But water and God's gracious Word
Conjoined, this saving bath afford.

3 "Go ye," says Christ, "my Word proclaim,
Baptize the nations in God's name;
All who are baptized and believe
My full salvation shall receive."

4 God, Father, Son, and Holy Ghost,
To be baptized invites the host;
He will be present, though unseen,
From all their sins to wash them clean.

5 So, too, by our repentance, must
The old man, with his sins and lust,
Be daily drowned, and then arise
A new man, righteous, pure, and wise.

6 That by the water and the Word
We're born again, we thank Thee, Lord!
In life and death Thine let us be,
And Thine in all eternity.

17th Century, C. H. L. Schuette, Tr.

404 Uxbridge L. M.

1 This child we dedicate to Thee,
O God of grace and purity!
Shield it from sin and threatening wrong,
And let Thy love its life prolong.

2 Oh, may Thy Spirit gently draw
Its willing soul to keep Thy Law,
May virtue, piety, and truth,
Dawn even with its dawning youth.

3 We too, before Thy gracious sight,
Once shared the blest baptismal rite,
And would renew its solemn vow
With love, and thanks, and praises, now.

4 Grant that, with true and faithful heart,
We still may act the Christian's part,
Cheered by each promise Thou hast given,
And laboring for the prize in heaven.

S. Gilman Tr.

(Otto Hursley)

405

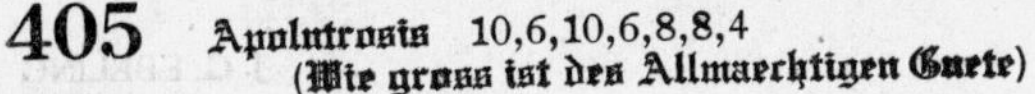
Apolutrosis 10,6,10,6,8,8,4
(Wie gross ist des Allmaechtigen Guete)

K. P. E. BACH, d. 1783—arr.

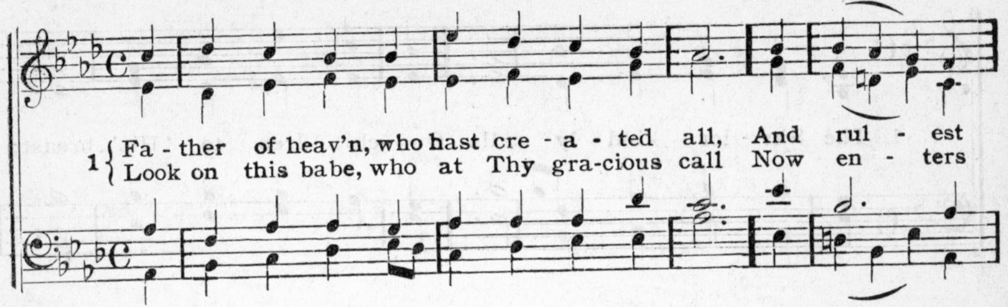
1 { Fa - ther of heav'n, who hast cre - a - ted all, And rul - est
Look on this babe, who at Thy gra-cious call Now en - ters

all, we pray,
on life's way: Oh, make it Thine; Thy bless-ing give,

That to Thy glo - ry it may live, Fa - ther of heav'n.

2 O Son of God, atoning Lord, behold,
We bring the babe to Thee:
Take it, O loving Shepherd, to Thy fold,
Forever Thine to be;
Defend it through this early strife,
And lead it on the path of life,
O Son of God.

3 O Holy Ghost, who broodest o'er the wave,
Descend upon this child;
Give it undying life, its spirit lave
With waters undefiled:
And make it evermore to be
An heir of bliss, a shrine for Thee,
O Holy Ghost.

4 O Triune God, what Thou hast willed is done;
We speak, but Thine the might:
This babe hath hardly seen our earthly sun.
Yet on it pour Thy light
Of faith and hope and joyful love,
Thou Sun of all below, above,
O Triune God.

Albert Knapp, 1850 C. Winkworth, Tr.

406 Franconia S. M.

J. G. EBELING

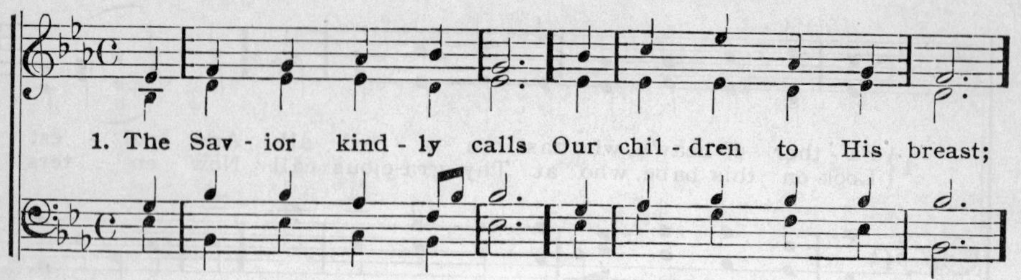
1. The Sav - ior kind - ly calls Our chil - dren to His breast;

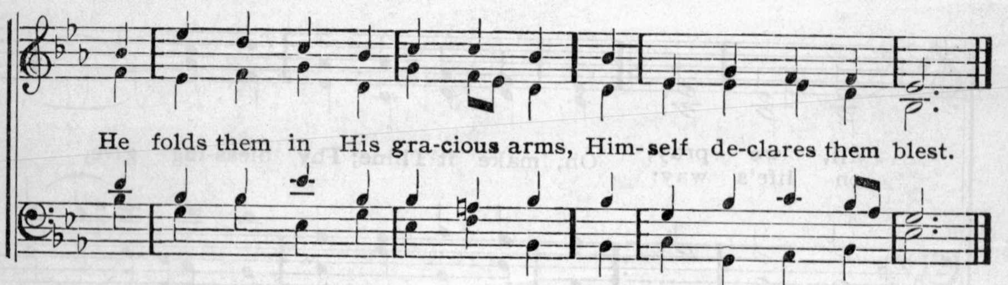
He folds them in His gra-cious arms, Him-self de-clares them blest.

2 "Let them approach," He cries,
"Nor scorn their humble claim,
The heirs of heaven are such as these,
For such as these I came."

3 With joy we bring them, Lord,
Devoting them to Thee,
Imploring, that, as we are Thine,
Thine may our offspring be.

H. U. Onderdonk

407 Franconia S. M.

1 Stand, soldier of the cross,
Thy high allegiance claim,
And vow to hold the world but loss
For Thy Redeemer's name.

2 Arise, and be baptized,
And wash thy sins away;
Thy league with God be solemnized,
Thy faith confessed to-day.

3 No more thine own, but Christ's;
With all the saints of old,
Apostles, seers, evangelists,
And martyr-throngs enrolled:

4 In God's whole armor strong,
Front hell's embattled powers:
The warfare may be sharp and long,
The victory must be ours.

5 O bright the conqueror's crown,
The song of triumph sweet.
When faith casts every trophy down
At our great Captain's feet!

E. H. Bickersteth. 1870 a

(Or to Silver St.)

Catechism

Confirmation

408 Ich dank Dir, lieber Herre 7,6 81 1536

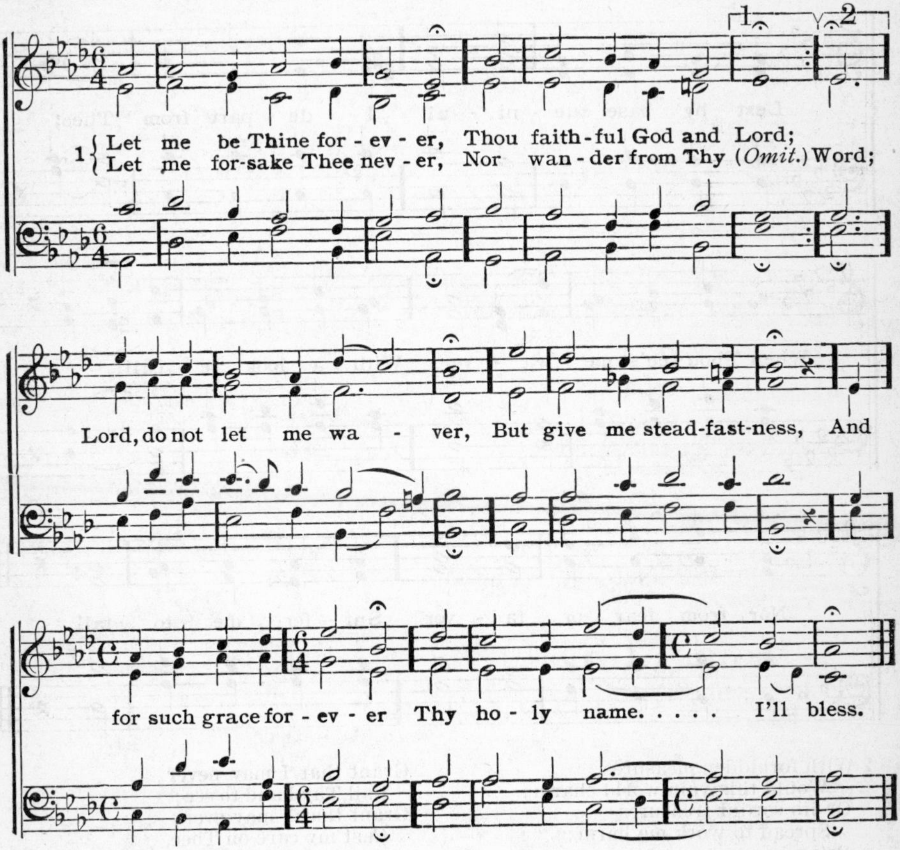

1 { Let me be Thine for - ev - er, Thou faith - ful God and Lord;
Let me for - sake Thee nev - er, Nor wan - der from Thy (*Omit.*) Word;

Lord, do not let me wa - ver, But give me stead - fast - ness, And

for such grace for - ev - er Thy ho - ly name. . . . I'll bless.

2 Lord Jesus, my Salvation,
My Light, my Life divine,
My only Consolation,
O make me wholly Thine!
For Thou hast dearly bought me
With blood and bitter pain;
Let me, since Thou hast sought me,
Eternal life obtain.

3 And Thou, O Holy Spirit,
My Comforter and Guide,
Grant that in Jesus' merit
I always may confide,
Him to the end confessing,
Whom I have known by faith.
Give me Thy constant blessing,
And grant a Christian death.

Nikolaus Selnecker, 1587 v. 2 & 3 Anon

409 Penitence 6,5 81 S. LANE, 1878

1 In the hour of tri - al, Je - sus, plead for me;
Lest by base de - ni - al I de - part from Thee;
When Thou see'st me wa - ver, With a look re - call;
Nor from fear or fa - vor Suf - fer me to fall.

2 With forbidden pleasures
Would this vain world charm;
Or its sordid treasures
Spread to work me harm;
Bring to my remembrance
Sad Gethsemane,
Or, in darker semblance,
Cross-crowned Calvary.

3 Should Thy mercy send me
Sorrow, toil, and woe;
Or should pain attend me
On my path below;
Grant that I may never
Fail Thy hand to see;
Grant that I may ever
Cast my care on Thee.

4 When my last hour cometh,
Fraught with strife and pain,
When my dust returneth
To the dust again;
On Thy truth relying,
Through that mortal strife,
Jesus, take me, dying,
To eternal life.

410 Valete L. M. 81

ARTHUR SULLIVAN, 1842—1900

1 { Arm these Thy sol-diers, might-y Lord, With shield of faith and Spir-it's sword; With ban-ner of the cross un-furled, And by it o-ver-come the world; And so at last re-ceive from Thee The palm and crown of vic-to-ry.
Forth to the bat-tle may they go And bold-ly fight a-gainst the foe,

2 Come, ever-blessed Spirit, come,
And make Thy servants' hearts Thy home;
May each a living temple be
Hallowed forever, Lord, to Thee;
Enrich that temple's holy shrine
With sevenfold gifts of grace Divine;
With wisdom, light, and knowledge bless
Strength, counsel, fear, and godliness.

3 O Trinity in Unity
One only God, and Persons Three;
In whom, thro' whom, by whom we live,
To Thee we praise and glory give;
O grant us so to use Thy grace,
That we may see Thy glorious face,
And ever with the heavenly host,
Praise Father, Son, and Holy Ghost.

C. Wordsworth, 1862

411 Holley 7s

G. HEWS, 1835

1 Thine for - ev - er! God of love, Hear us

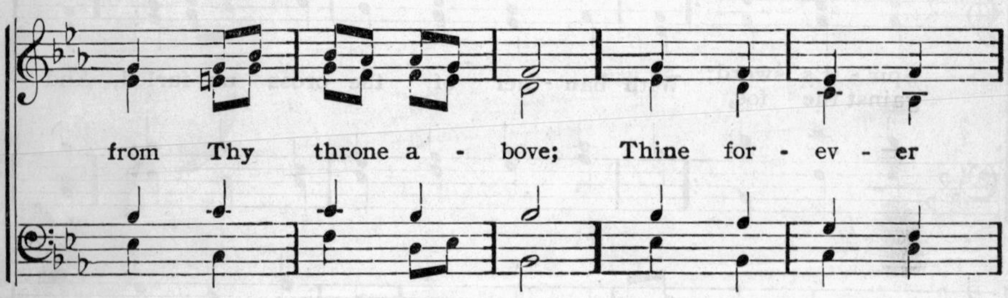
from Thy throne a - bove; Thine for - ev - er

may we be, Here and in e - ter - ni - ty.

(Or to Seymour)

2 Thine forever! Lord of life,
Shield us through our earthly strife;
Thou, the Life, the Truth, the Way,
Guide us to the realms of day.

3 Thine forever! O how blest
They who find in Thee their rest!
Savior, Guardian, heavenly Friend,
O defend us to the end.

4 Thine forever! Savior, keep
These Thy frail and trembling sheep!
Safe alone beneath Thy care,
Let us all Thy goodness share.

5 Thine forever! Thou our Guide,
All our wants by Thee supplied,
All our sins by Thee forgiven,
Lead us, Lord, from earth to heaven.

Mary F. Maude, 1848

412 Remembrance C. M. R. H. McCARTNEY

1 My God, ac - cept my heart this day, And make it al - ways Thine,

That I from Thee no more may stray, No more from Thee de - cline.

(Or to Beatitudo)

2 Before the cross of Him who died,
Behold, I prostrate fall;
Let every sin be crucified,
Let Christ be all in all!

3 Anoint me with Thy heavenly grace,
Adopt me for Thine own;
That I may see Thy glorious face,
And worship at Thy throne!

4 May the dear blood, once shed for me,
My blest atonement prove,
That I from first to last may be
The purchase of Thy love!

5 Let every thought, and work, and word,
To Thee be ever given:
Then life shall be Thy service, Lord,
And death the gate of heaven!

Matthew Bridges, 1848

Catechism

Confession

413 Allein zu dir 8,8,8,8,8,8,8,4,8 SCHNEESING, 1541

1 { Lord Je - sus Christ, in Thee a - lone My on - ly hope on earth I place,
For oth - er com - fort - er is none, No help have I but in . . . Thy grace.
There is no man nor crea - ture here,
No an-gel in the heav'n-ly sphere, Who in my need can suc-cor me
I cry to Thee, For Thee I trust im - plic - it - ly.

2 My sin is very sore and great,
I mourn beneath its dreadful load;
O free me from this heavy weight,
My Savior, through Thy precious blood;
And with Thy Father for me plead
That Thou hast suffered in my stead;
From me the burden then is rolled.
Lord, I lay hold
On Thy dear promises of old.

3 And in Thy mercy now bestow
True Christian faith on me, O Lord!
That all the sweetness I may know
Which in Thy holy cross is stored,
Love Thee o'er earthly pride or pelf,
And love my neighbor as myself;
And when, at last, is come my end,
Be Thou my Friend,
From Satan's wiles my soul defend.

4 Glory to God in highest heaven,
The Father of eternal love;
To His dear Son, for sinners given,
Whose watchful grace we daily prove;
To God the Holy Ghost on high;
O ever be His comfort nigh,
And teach us, in His love and fear
To please Him here,
And serve Him in the heavenly sphere!

Dr. John Schneesing, 1541 C. Winkworth, Tr. a

414 Meinen Jesum lass ich nicht 7,8,7.8,7,7

C. F. WITT, 1715

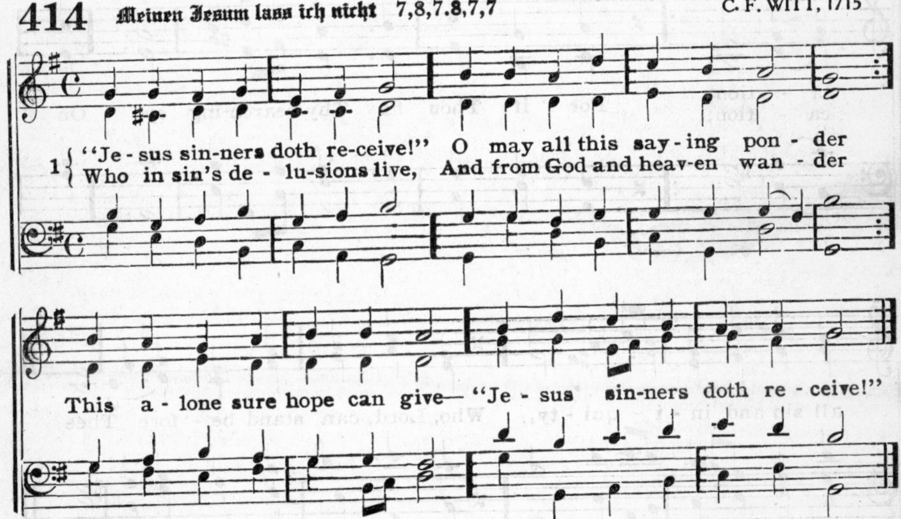
1 "Je - sus sin-ners doth re-ceive!" O may all this say - ing pon - der
Who in sin's de - lu-sions live, And from God and heav-en wan - der
This a - lone sure hope can give— "Je - sus sin-ners doth re - ceive!"

2 We deserve but grief and shame,
Yet His words, rich grace revealing,
Pardon, peace, and life proclaim;
Here their ills have perfect healing
Who with humble hearts believe—
"Jesus sinners doth receive!"

3 Sheep that from the fold did stray,
Every faithful shepherd seeketh;
Weary souls that lost their way,
Christ the Shepherd seeks and taketh
In His arms, that they may live—
"Jesus sinners doth receive!"

4 Come, ye sinners, one and all,
Come, ye all have invitation;
Come, obey His gracious call,
Come and take His free salvation!
Firmly in these words believe:
"Jesus sinners doth receive!"

5 I, a sinner, come to Thee,
And acknowledge my trangression;
Tender mercy show to me,
Grant me graciously remission;
Let these words my soul relieve:
"Jesus sinners doth receive!"

6 Henceforth I need fear no foe;
Were as scarlet my transgression,
It shall be as white as snow
By the virtue of Thy passion;
For in these words I believe:
"Jesus sinners doth receive!"

7 Now my conscience is at ease,
Now I fear no condemnation.
He who grants me full release
Hath atoned for my transgression;
In true faith to Him I cleave—
"Jesus sinners doth receive!"

Erdmann Neumeister, 1719

415 Aus tiefer not schrei ich zu dir

LUTHER (?), 1524

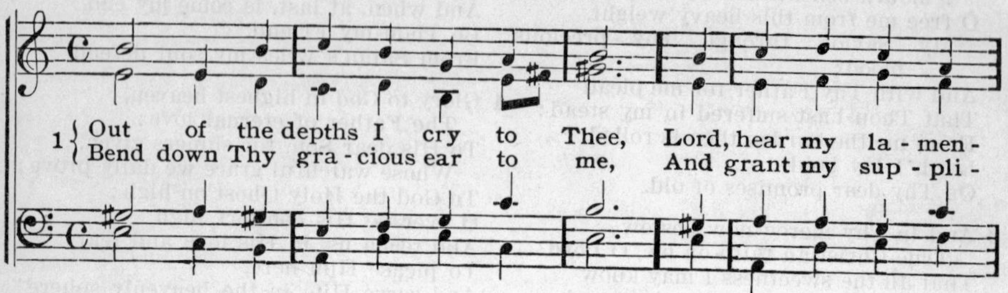
1 { Out of the depths I cry to Thee, Lord, hear my la - men -
Bend down Thy gra - cious ear to me, And grant my sup - pli -

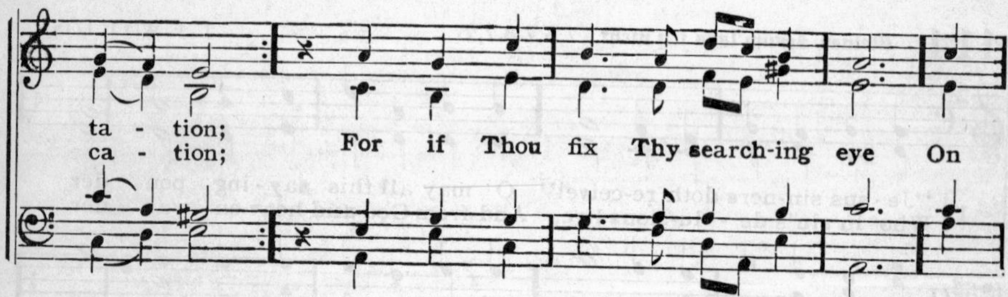
ta - tion;
ca - tion; For if Thou fix Thy search-ing eye On

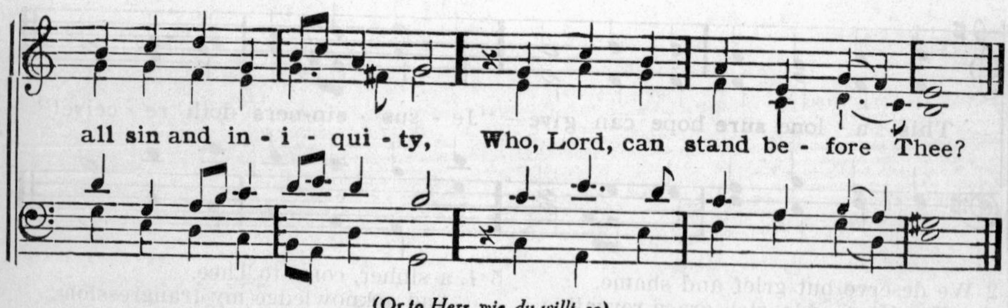
all sin and in - i - qui - ty, Who, Lord, can stand be - fore Thee?

(Or to Herr, wie du willt, so)

2 But love and grace with Thee prevail,
O God, our sins forgiving;
The best and holiest deeds must fail
Of all before Thee living;
Before Thee none can boasting stand,
But all must fear Thy strict demand,
And live alone by mercy.

3 My hope I rest then on the Lord,
And build not on my merit;
My heart shall trust His gracious Word,
His goodness stays my spirit.
His precious word assureth me,
He will my Joy and Comfort be;
This is my firm reliance.

4 And though it tarry till the night
And till the morn appeareth,
My heart still trusteth in His might,
It doubteth not, nor feareth.
Do thus, O ye of Israel's seed,
Ye of the Spirit born indeed,
Wait for your God's appearing.

5 Though great our sins and sore our woes,
His grace much more aboundeth;
His helping love no limit knows,
Our utmost need it soundeth,
Our Shepherd is the Lord, and He
At last shall set his Israel free
From all their sin and sorrow.

Dr. Martin Luther, 1524

416 Herr, ich habe missgehandelt 8,7,8,7,8,8

J. CRUEGER, 1649

1 { Lord, to Thee I make con - fes - sion, I have
I have mul - ti - plied trans - gres - sion, Cho - sen

1 2
sinned and gone a - stray,
for my - self my (Omit.) way. Led at last to see my

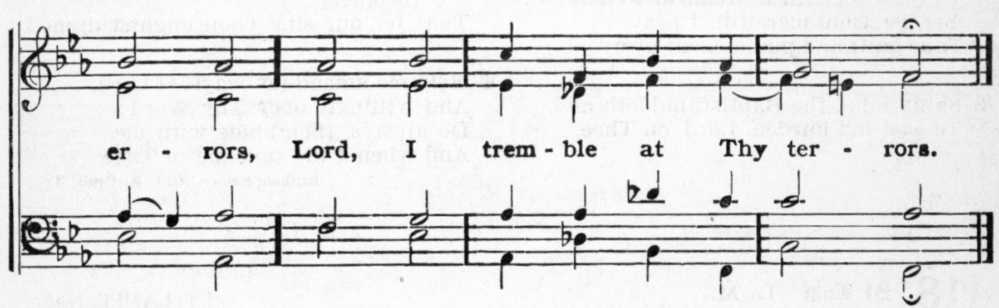
er - rors, Lord, I trem - ble at Thy ter - rors.

2 Yet, though conscience' voice appall me,
Father, I will seek Thy face;
Though Thy child I dare not call me,
Yet receive me to Thy grace;
Do not for my sins forsake me,
Let not yet Thy wrath o'ertake me.

3 For Thy Son hath suffered for me,
And the blood He shed for sin,
That can heal me and restore me,
Quench this burning fire within;
'Tis alone His cross can vanquish
These dark fears, and soothe this anguish.

4 Then on Him I cast my burden,
Sink it in the depths below!
Let me feel Thy gracious pardon,
Wash me, make me white as snow.
Let Thy Spirit leave me never,
Make me only Thine for ever!

John Franck, 1649 C. Winkworth, Tr. 1862

417 Weimar L. M.

C. P. E. BACH, 1784 (I)

1 O Je-sus, Lamb of God, who art The life and com-fort of my heart,

I, wretch-ed sin-ner, come to Thee And bring so man - y sins with me.

(*Or to Wenn wir in hoechsten*)

2 O God, my sinfulness is great,
I groan beneath a dreadful weight;
Yet, be Thou merciful, I pray,
Take guilt and punishment away.

3 Saint John, the Baptist, biddeth me
To cast my burden, Lord, on Thee,
Since Thou hast left Thy heavenly throne,
That for our sins Thou mightst atone.

4 Help me amend my ways, O Lord,
And willingly obey Thy Word;
Do always, then abide with me,
And when I die take me to Thee.

Barthold Helder. 1620 A. Crull, Tr

418 St. Luke L. M.

J. F. LAMPE, 1746

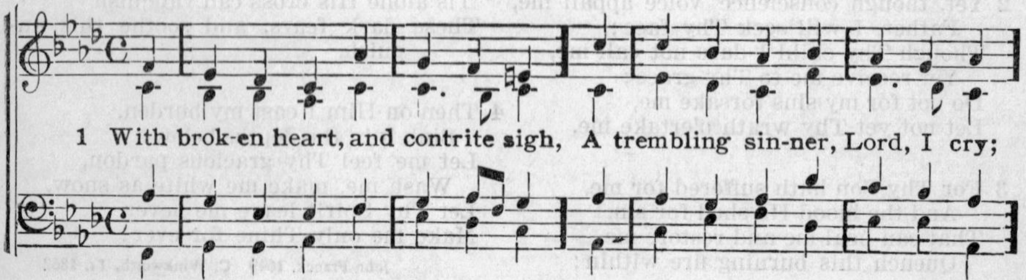
1 With brok-en heart, and contrite sigh, A trembling sin-ner, Lord, I cry;

Thy pard'ning grace is rich and free; O God, be mer-ci-ful to me!

2 I smite upon my troubled breast,
With deep and conscious guilt oppressed;
Christ and His Cross my only plea;
O God, be merciful to me!

3 Far off I stand with tearful eyes
Nor dare uplift them to the skies;
But Thou dost all my anguish see;
O God, be merciful to me!

4 Nor alms, nor deeds that I have done
Can for a single sin atone;
To Calvary alone I flee;
O God, me merciful to me!

5 And when, redeemed from sin and hell,
With all the ransomed throng I dwell,
My raptured song shall ever be,
God has been merciful to me!

C. Elven, 1852

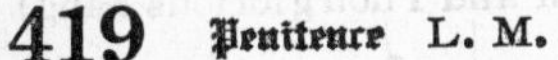

419 Penitence L. M.

ST. ALBAN'S TUNE BOOK

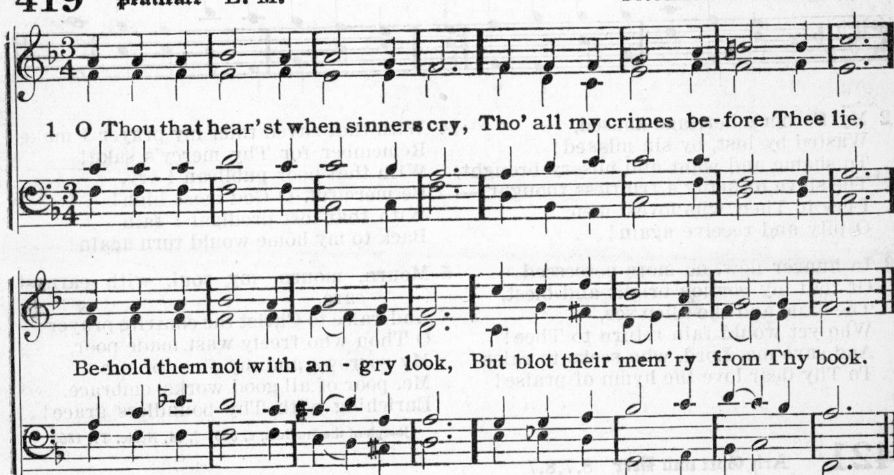
1 O Thou that hear'st when sinners cry, Tho' all my crimes be-fore Thee lie,
Be-hold them not with an-gry look, But blot their mem'ry from Thy book.

2 Create my nature pure within,
And form my soul averse to sin;
Let Thy good Spirit ne'er depart,
Nor hide Thy presence from my heart.

3 I cannot live without Thy light,
Cast out and banished from Thy sight;
Thy holy joys, my God, restore,
And guard me that I fall no more.

4 Though I have grieved Thy Spirit, Lord,
His help and comfort still afford;
And let me now come near Thy throne,
To plead the merits of Thy Son.

5 A broken heart, my God, my King,
Is all the sacrifice I bring;
Look down, O Lord, with pitying eye
And save the soul condemned to die.

6 O may Thy love inspire my tongue!
Salvation shall be all my song;
And all my powers shall join to bless
The Lord, my Strength and Righteousness.

Isaac Watts, 1719 a

420 O dass ich tausend L. M. 61

GNADAUER CHORALB., 1784

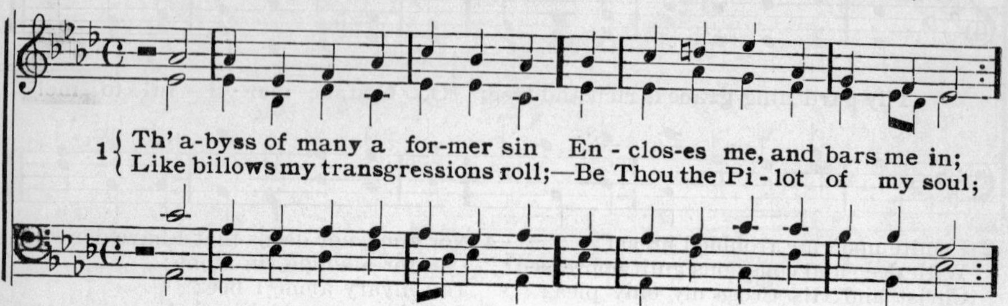
1 { Th' a-byss of many a for-mer sin En - clos-es me, and bars me in;
Like billows my transgressions roll;—Be Thou the Pi - lot of my soul;

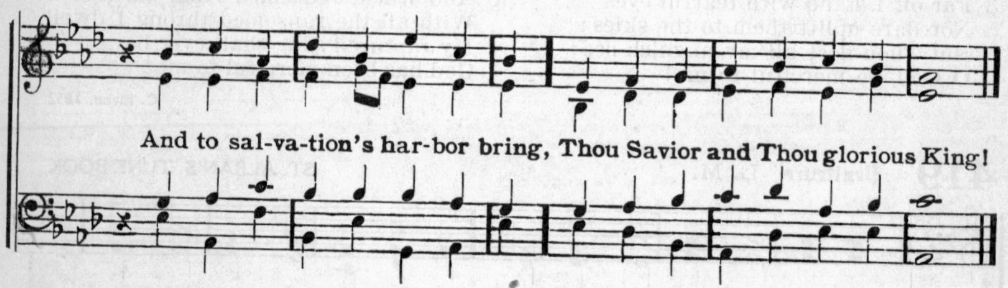
And to sal-va-tion's har-bor bring, Thou Savior and Thou glorious King!

2 My Father's heritage abused,
Wasted by lust, by sin missed;
To shame and want and misery brought,
The slave to many a fruitless thought:—
I cry to Thee, who lovest men,
O pity and receive again!

3 In hunger now, no more possessed
Of that my portion bright and blest,
The exile and the alien see,
Who yet would fain return to Thee!
And save me, Lord, who seeks to raise
To Thy dear love the hymn of praise!

4 With that saved thief my prayer I make,
Remember for Thy mercy's sake!
With that poor publican I cry,
Be merciful, O God most high!
With that lost prodigal I fain
Back to my home would turn again!

5 Mourn, mourn, my soul, with earnest care,
And raise to Christ the contrite prayer:—
O Thou who freely wast made poor,
My sorrows and my sins to cure,
Me, poor of all good works, embrace,
Enriching with Thy boundless grace!

Joseph of the Studium, c. 860 J. M. Neale. Tr. 1862

421 Ach Gott und Herr 8,7,8,7

1 Alas, my God! my sins are great,
My conscience doth upbraid me;
And now I find that in my strait
No man hath power to aid me.

2 And fled I hence, in my despair,
In some lone spot to hide me,
My griefs would still be with me there,
And peace still be denied me.

3 Lord, Thee I seek;—I merit naught,
Yet pity and restore me;
Be not Thy wrath, just God, my lot,
Thy Son hath suffered for me.

4 If pain and woe must follow sin,
Then be my path still rougher,
Here spare me not; if heaven I win,
On earth I gladly suffer.

5 But curb my heart, forgive my guilt,
Make Thou my patience firmer,
For they must miss the good Thou wilt,
Who at Thy chastenings murmur.

6 Then deal with me as seems Thee best,
Thy grace will help me bear it,
If but at last I see Thy rest,
And with my Savior share it.

Martin Rutilius, 1604 C. Winkworth, Tr. a

422 St. Bride S. M.

SAMUEL HOWARD, † 1782

1 And wilt Thou par - don, Lord, A sin - ner such as I?

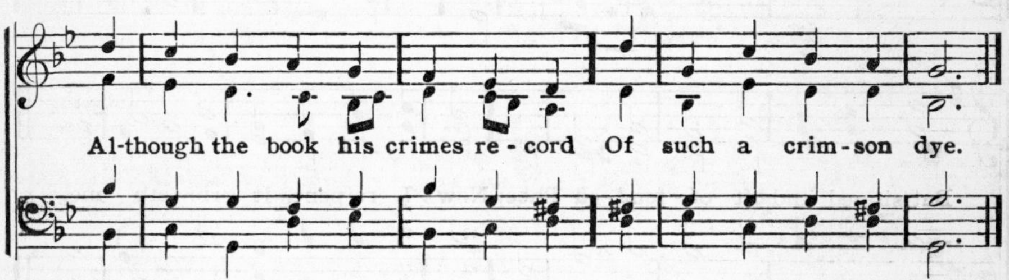
Al-though the book his crimes re - cord Of such a crim - son dye.

2 So deep are they engraved,
So terrible their fear:
The righteous scarcely shall be saved,
And where shall I appear?

3 O Thou Physician blest,
Make clean my guilty soul!
And me, by many a sin oppressed,
Restore, and keep me whole.

4 I know not how to praise
Thy mercy and Thy love;
But deign Thy servant to upraise,
And I shall learn above.

Joseph of the Studium c. 860 J. M. Neale, Tr. 1862

423 St. Bride S. M.

1 Out of the deep I call
To Thee, O Lord, to Thee;
Before Thy throne of grace I fall,
Be merciful to me.

2 Out of the deep I cry,
The woeful deep of sin,
Of evil done in days gone by,
Of evil now within.

3 Out of the deep of fear,
And dread of coming shame.
From morning watch till night is near
I plead the precious name.

4 Lord, there is mercy now,
As ever was, with Thee;
Before Thy throne of grace I bow;
Be merciful to me.

H. W. Baker, 1868

(Or to Aberystwyth)

Catechism

Absolution

424 Wenn wir in hœchsten Nœthen sein L. M. J. GERARD, 1555

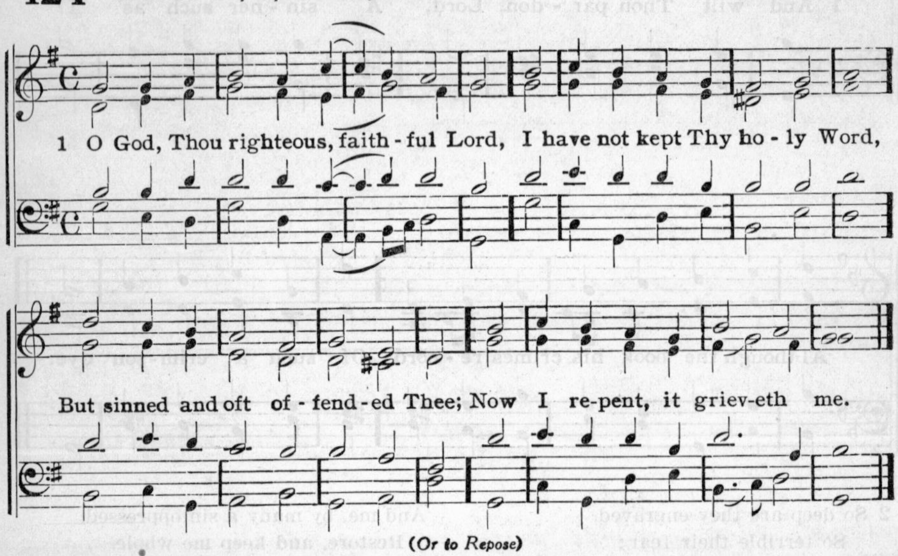
1 O God, Thou righteous, faith - ful Lord, I have not kept Thy ho - ly Word,
But sinned and oft of - fend - ed Thee; Now I re - pent, it griev - eth me.

(Or to Repose)

2 Thou, Father, merciful and kind,
No pleasure in my death dost find,
But strong desire doth in Thee burn,
That I should unto Thee return.

3 Since Thou, dear Father, callest me,
I, poor lost sinner, come to Thee,
Relying on Christ's precious blood
Which from His holy five wounds flowed.

4 I pray through Christ, Thine only Son,
Who for my good here flesh put on;
Thy love to me let never fail;
O'er justice let Thy grace prevail.

5 In mercy, Father, let Thy grace
Through Jesus' blood my sins efface;
Then I, the poor lost child, will be
From all my sins forever free.

6 Grant that, according to Thy Word,
I lead a godly life, O Lord,
And let me, after time is o'er,
Inherit life forevermore.

B. Ringwald, 1598 A. Crull, Tr.

425 Wenn wir in hœchsten Nœthen sein L. M.

1 O faithful God, we worship Thee!
Thou pardon'st our iniquity,
Thou grantest help in sin's distress,
And soul and body Thou dost bless.

2 Thou, through Thy servant, say'st to me:
"Thy sins are all forgiven thee,
Depart in peace; but sin no more,
And e'er my pardoning grace adore."

3 O Lord, we bless Thy gracious heart,
For Thou Thyself dost heal our smart,
Through Christ our Savior's precious blood,
Which for the sake of sinners flowed.

4 Give us Thy Spirit, peace afford
Now and forever, gracious Lord!
Thy Word and holy Sacrament
Preserve to us, till life is spent.

Nik. Selnecker, 1587

(Or to O Jesu Christ meins)

426 So wahr ich leb, spricht Gott der Herr L. M. J. G. SCHOTT, 1603

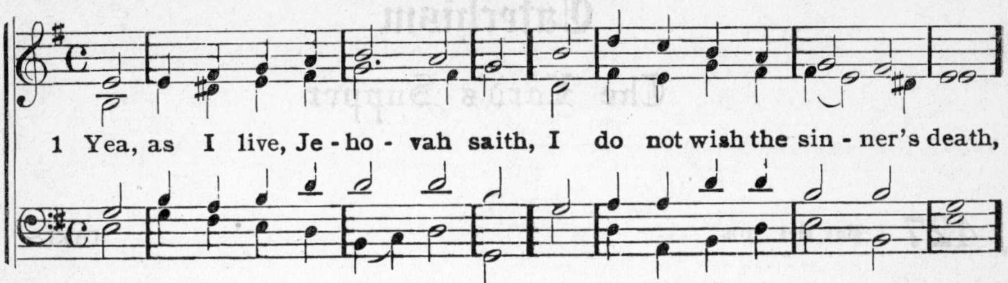
1 Yea, as I live, Je - ho - vah saith, I do not wish the sin - ner's death,

But that he turn from error's ways, Re-pent and live thro' end - less days.

(Or to Wenn wir in hoechsten)

2 Hence Christ, His foll'wers gave command:
Go forth and preach in every land;
Pardon to every soul extend
That mourns, believes, and will amend.

3 Whose sins soever ye remit,
I truly pardon and acquit;
Whose sins soever ye retain,
Condemned and guilty shall remain.

4 What ye shall bind, that bound shall be;
What ye shall loose, that shall be free;
To all alike the keys are given
To ope and close the gates of heaven.

5 They who believe, when ye proclaim
The joyful tidings in my name,
That I for them my blood have shed,
Are free from guilt and judgment dread.

6 The words which absolution give
Are His who died that we might live;
The minister whom Christ has sent
Is but His humble instrument.

7 However great our sin may be,
The absolution sets us free,
Appointed by God's own dear Son
To bring the pardon He has won.

8 When ministers lay on their hands,
Absolved by Christ the sinner stands;
He who by grace the Word believes,
The purchase of His blood receives.

9 This is the power of holy keys,
It binds and doth again release;
The Church retains them at her side,
Our mother and Christ's holy bride.

10 Let those who stings of conscience bear,
Whom sin would drive to dark despair,
To Jesus come with trustful mind
And peace in absolution find.

11 All praise, Eternal Son, to Thee
For absolution full and free,
In which Thou showest forth Thy grace;
From false indulgence guard our race.

12 Praise God, the Father and the Son
And Holy Spirit, Three in One,
As 'twas, is now, and so shall be,
World without end, eternally!

N. Hermann, 1560 M. Loy, Tr.

Catechism

The Lord's Supper

427 Pax Dei 10s DYKES

1 Draw nigh and take the bod - y of your Lord, And drink the
ho - ly blood for you out-poured. Of - ferred was He for
great-est and the least, Him - self the vic - tim and Him-self the priest.

(Or to Eventide)

2 He that in this world rules His saints, and shields,
To all believers life eternal yields;
With heavenly bread makes them that hunger whole,
Gives living waters to the thirsting soul.

3 Approach ye then with faithful hearts sincere,
And take the pledges of salvation here.
O Judge of all, our only Savior Thou,
In this Thy feast of love be with us now.

428 Truro L. M.

C. BURNEY, 1789

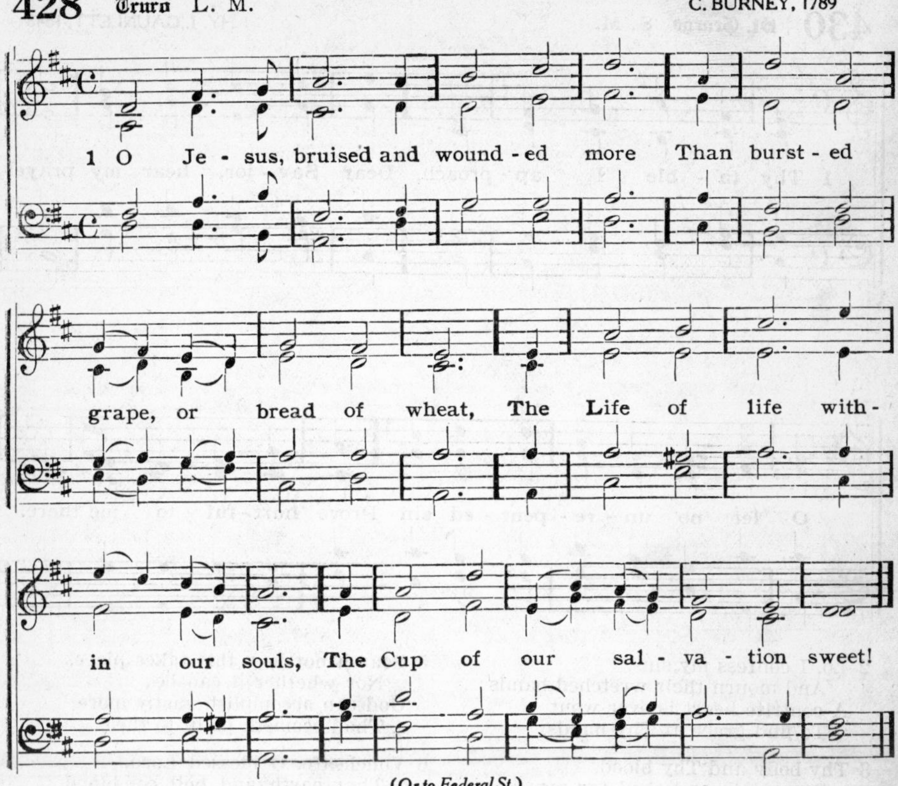
1 O Je - sus, bruised and wound - ed more Than burst - ed
grape, or bread of wheat, The Life of life with -
in our souls, The Cup of our sal - va - tion sweet!

(Or to Federal St.)

2 We come to show Thy dying hour,
Thy streaming vein, Thy broken flesh;
And still the blood is warm to save,
And still the fragrant wounds are fresh.

3 O Heart! that with a double tide
Of blood and water maketh pure,
O Flesh! once offered on the cross,
The gift that makes our pardon sure;

4 Let never more our sinful souls
The anguish of Thy cross renew;
Nor forge again the cruel nails
That pierced Thy victim body through.

5 Come, Bread of heaven, to feed our souls.
And with Thee, Jesus enter in!
Come, Wine of God! and as we drink,
His precious blood wash out our sin!

Mrs. C. F. Alexander

429 Truro L. M.

1 My God, and is Thy table spread?
And does Thy cup with love o'erflow?
Thither be all Thy children led,
And let them all its sweetness know.

2 Hail, sacred feast, which Jesus makes,
Rich banquet of His flesh and blood!
Thrice happy he who here partakes
That sacred stream, that heavenly food!

3 Why are its blessings all in vain
Before unwilling hearts displayed?
Was not for us the Victim slain?
Are we forbid the children's bread?

4 O let Thy table honored be,
And furnished well with joyful guests;
And may each soul salvation see,
That here its sacred pledges tastes.

P. Doddridge, 1755 ab.

(Or to Rockingham)

430 St. George S. M.

HY. J. GAUNLETT, 1848

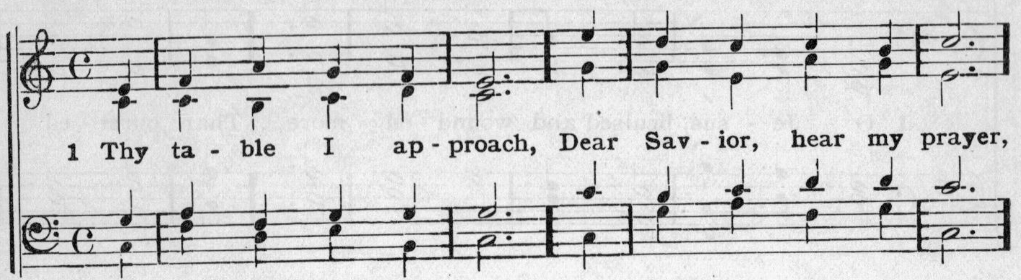
1 Thy ta - ble I ap - proach, Dear Sav - ior, hear my prayer,

O let no un - re - pent - ed sin Prove hurt - ful to me there.

2 Lo, I confess my sins,
And mourn their wretched bands;
A contrite heart is ever wont
To find grace at Thy hands.

3 Thy body and Thy blood,
Once slain and shed for me,
Are taken at Thy table here—
A wondrous mystery!

4 Here I with mouth and soul,
Incomprehensibly,
Shall eat the precious flesh of Christ
In blest reality.

5 Search not how this takes place,
Nor whether it can be;
God can accomplish vastly more
Than seemeth plain to thee.

6 Vouchsafe, O blessed Lord,
That earth and hell combined,
May ne'er about this Sacrament
A doubt raise in my mind.

7 And may I never fail
To thank Thee day and night
For Thy true body and true blood,
O God, my Peace and Light!

431 Gott sei gelobet und gebenedeiet 11,8,11,8,5,9,9,6,7,5

ANCIENT J. WALTHER, 1524

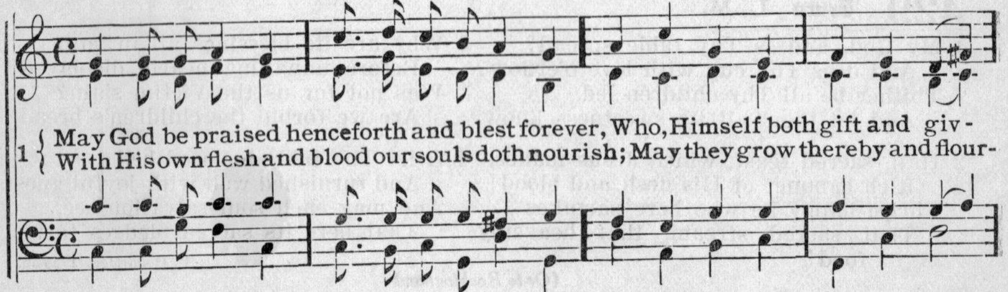
1 { May God be praised henceforth and blest forever, Who, Himself both gift and giv-
With His own flesh and blood our souls doth nourish; May they grow thereby and flour-

er,
ish!
O Lord, have mer - cy! By Thy ho - ly bod - y, the self-same

Which from Thine own moth-er Ma - ry came, By the drops Thou didst bleed,

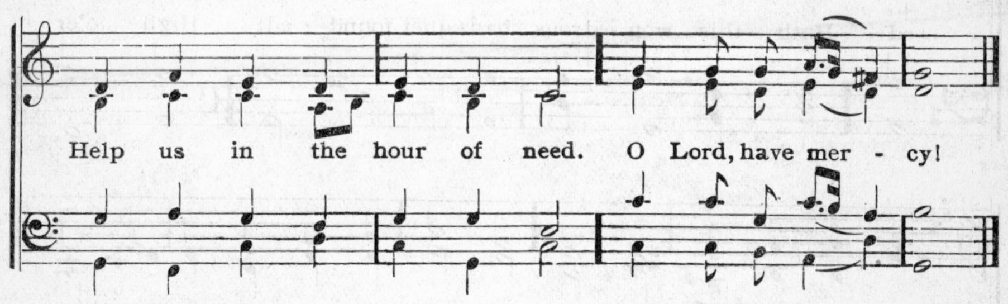
Help us in the hour of need. O Lord, have mer - cy!

2 Thou hast to death Thy holy body given,
Life to win for us in heaven;
By stronger love, dear Lord, Thou couldst not bind us,
Whereof this should well remind us.
O Lord, have mercy!
Lord, Thy love constrained Thee for our good
Mighty things to do by Thy dear blood;
Thou hast paid all we owed,
Thou hast made our peace with God.
O Lord, have mercy!

3 May God bestow on us His grace and blessing,
That, His holy footsteps tracing,
We walk as brethren dear in love and union,
Nor repent this sweet communion.
O Lord, have mercy!
Let not Thy good Spirit forsake us,
Grant that heavenly minded He make us,
That Thy poor Church may see
Days of peace and unity.
O Lord, have mercy!

Dr. Martin Luther, 1524 Richard Massie, Tr. a

432 Schmuecke dich, o liebe Seele L. M. 81 J. CRUEGER, 1649

1 { Deck Thy - self, my soul, with glad - ness, Leave the
Come un - to the day - light's splen - dor, There with
gloom-y haunts of sad - ness,
joy thy prais-es ren - der
Un - to Him whose grace un - bound - ed
Hath this won - drous ban-quet found - ed;
High o'er all the heav'ns He reign-eth,
Yet to dwell with thee He deign-eth.

2 Hasten as a bride to meet Him,
And with loving reverence greet Him,
For with words of life immortal
Now He knocketh at thy portal;
Haste to ope the gates before Him,
Saying, while thou dost adore Him,
"Suffer, Lord, that I receive Thee,
And I never more will leave Thee."

3 He who costly goods desireth
To obtain, much gold requireth;
But to freely give the treasure
Of Thy love is Thy good pleasure,
For on earth there is no coffer
Which as payment we might offer
For this cup Thy blood containing,
And this manna, on us raining.

4 Ah, how hungers all my spirit
For the love I do not merit!
Oft have I, with sighs fast thronging,
Thought upon this food with longing,
In the battle well-nigh worsted,
For this cup of life have thirsted,
For the Friend, who here invites us,
And to God Himself unites us.

5 Now I sink before Thee lowly,
Filled with joy most deep and holy,
As with trembling awe and wonder
On Thy mighty works I ponder,
How, by mystery surrounded,
Depths no man hath ever sounded,
None may dare to pierce unbidden,
Secrets that with Thee are hidden.

6 Nay, though reason here doth ponder,
It can never reach this wonder,
That this bread is never lessened,
Though it nourish thousands present,
And that Christ His blood is giving
With the wine we are receiving.
O, these mysteries unsounded
Are by God alone expounded!

7 Sun, who all my life doth brighten,
Light, who dost my soul enlighten,
Joy, the sweetest man e'er knoweth,
Fount, whence all my being floweth,—
At Thy feet I cry, my Maker,
Let me be a fit partaker
Of this blessed food from heaven,
For our good, Thy glory, given.

8 Lord, Thy fervent love hath driven
Thee to leave Thy throne in heaven,
For us on the cross to languish,
And to die in bitter anguish,
To forego all joy and gladness,
And to shed Thy blood in sadness,
Which we drink now; grant that never
We forget Thy love, dear Savior!

9 Jesus, Bread of life, I pray Thee,
Let me gladly here obey Thee,
Never to my hurt invited,
Be Thy love with love requited;
From this banquet let me measure,
Lord, how vast and deep love's treasure;
Through the gifts Thou here dost give me
As Thy guest in heaven receive me.

Joh. Franck, 1649

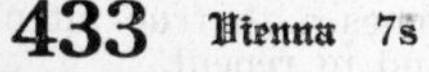
433 Vienna 7s

J. H. KNECHT, 1797

1 Lo, up - on the al - tar lies Bread of heav - en from the skies:

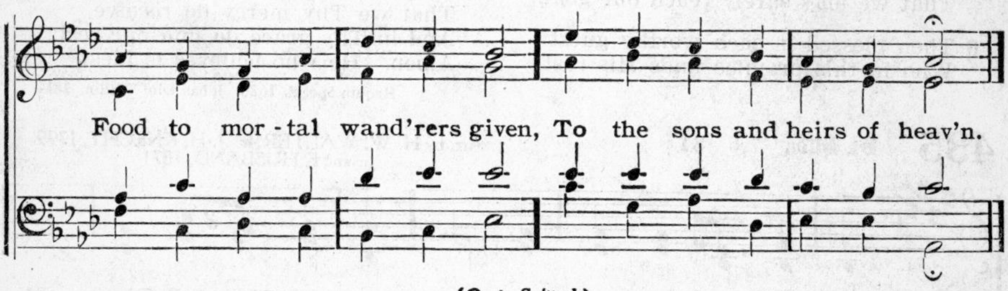
Food to mor - tal wand'rers given, To the sons and heirs of heav'n.

(Or to Solitude)

2 Jesus, Shepherd of the sheep!
Thou Thy flock in safety keep.
Living Bread! Thy life supply,
Strengthen us, or else we die.

3 Thou, who feedest us below!
Source of all we have or know!
Grant that with Thy saints above
We may reach Thy feast of love!

Thomas Aquinas, † 1274 Edward Caswall, Tr. 1848

434 Mein Seel, o Gott, muss loben dich L. M. (1569) B. GESIUS, 1603

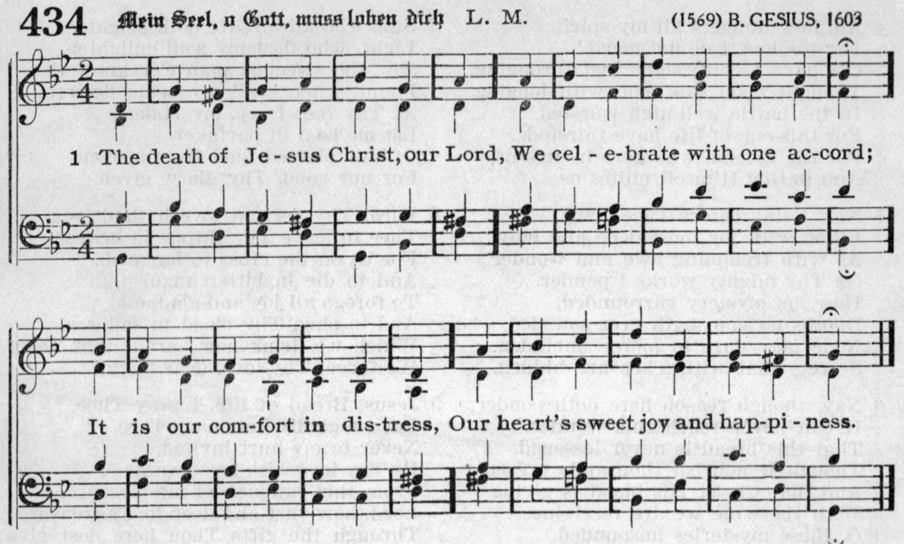
1 The death of Je - sus Christ, our Lord, We cel - e-brate with one ac-cord;
It is our com-fort in dis-tress, Our heart's sweet joy and hap-pi - ness.

2 He blotted out with His own blood
The judgment that against us stood;
He full atonement for us made,
And all our debt He fully paid.

3 That this is so and ever true
He gives an earnest ever new,
In this His holy Supper, here
We taste His love so sweet, so near.

4 For His true body, as He said,
And His true blood, for sinners shed,
In this communion we receive,
His sacred Word we do believe.

5 A precious food this is indeed,
It never faileth, such we need,
A heavenly manna for our soul,
That we may safely reach our goal.

6 Then blessed is each worthy guest
Who in this promise finds His rest,
For Jesus will in love abide
With those who do in Him confide:

7 The guest that comes with true intent
To turn to God and to repent,
To live for Christ, to die to sin,
And thus a holy life begin.

8 Who does unworthy here appear,
Does not believe, nor is sincere,
Salvation here he can not find.
May we this warning bear in mind.

9 O Jesus Christ, our Brother dear,
Unto Thy cross we now draw near;
Thy sacred wounds indeed make whole
A wounded and afflicted soul.

10 Help us sincerely to believe
That we Thy mercy do receive,
And in Thy grace do find our rest,
Amen. He who believes is blest.

Haquin Spegel, 1686 Johan Olof Wallin, 1814

435 St. Hilda 7,6 81 Arr. by H. W. WALTER, fr. J. H. KNECHT, 1799 and E. HUSBAND, 1871

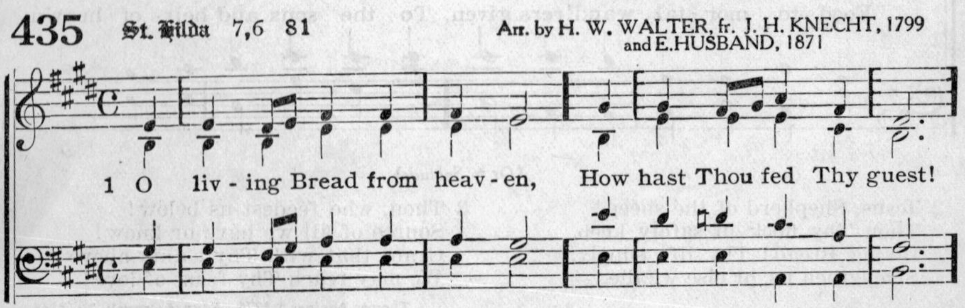
1 O liv - ing Bread from heav - en, How hast Thou fed Thy guest!

The gifts Thou now hast giv - en Have filled my heart with rest.

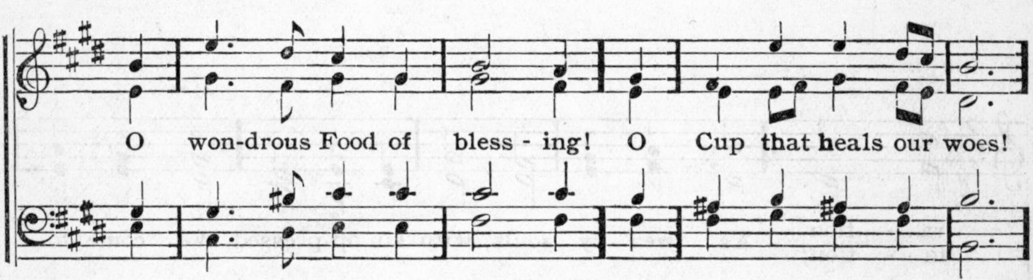
O won-drous Food of bless - ing! O Cup that heals our woes!

My heart, this gift pos - sess - ing, In thank-ful song o'er-flows.

(*Or to Herzlich thut   Or to Aurelia*)

2 My Lord, Thou here hast led me
Within Thy holiest place,
And there Thyself hast fed me
With treasures of Thy grace:
And Thou hast freely granted
What earth could never buy,
The Bread of life from heaven,
That now I shall not die!

3 Thou givest all I wanted
The food can death destroy;
And Thou hast freely granted
The cup of endless joy,
Ah, Lord, I do not merit
The favor Thou hast shown,
And all my soul and spirit
Bow down before Thy Throne!

4 Lord, grant me that, thus strengthened
With heavenly food, while here
My course on earth is lengthened,
I serve with holy fear;
And when Thou call'st my spirit
To leave this world below,
I enter, through Thy merit,
Where joys unmingled flow.

John Rist, 1651 a C. Winkworth, Tr.

436 Herr Jesu Christ, du hast bereit 8,7,8,7,8,8,7 P. SOHREN, 1668

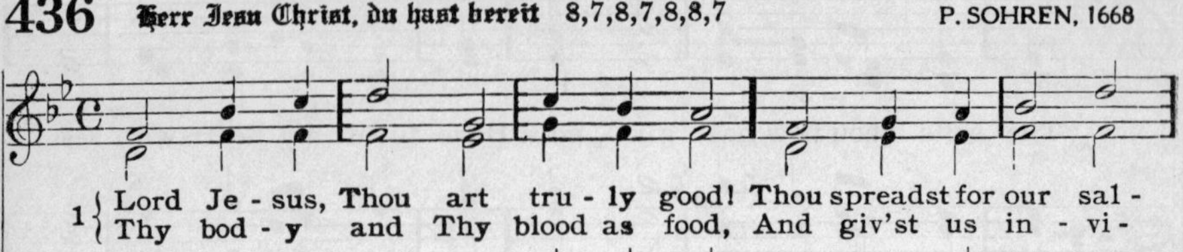
1 { Lord Je - sus, Thou art tru - ly good! Thou spreadst for our sal -
Thy bod - y and Thy blood as food, And giv'st us in - vi-

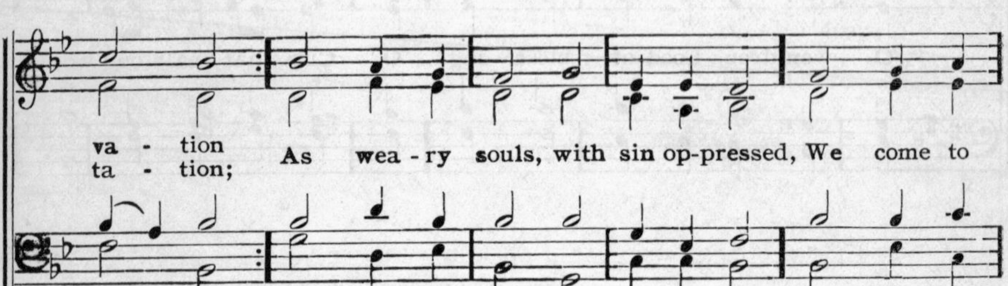
va - tion
ta - tion; As wea - ry souls, with sin op-pressed, We come to

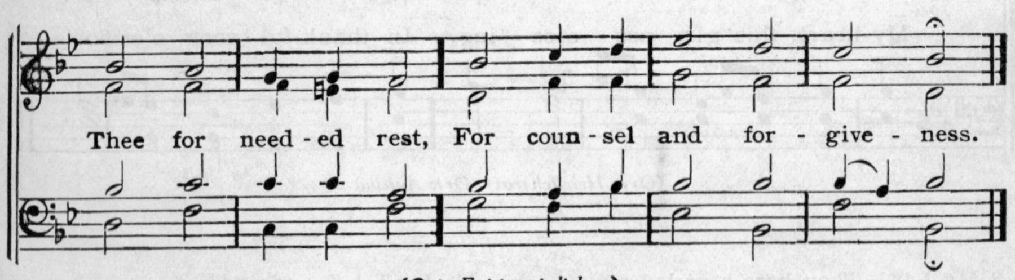
Thee for need - ed rest, For coun - sel and for - give - ness.

(Or to *Es ist gewisslich an*)

2 Although Thou didst ascend to heaven,
Where angels bow before Thee,
And now to mortals 'tis not given
By sight here to adore Thee,
Until begins Thy judgment grand,
When we before Thy throne shall stand,
And cheerfully behold Thee;

3 Yet art Thou ever with us, Lord,
And with Thy congregation,
And not confined—so says Thy Word—
To any habitation.
Firm as a rock Thy Word still stands,
Unshaken by the en'mies' hands,
Though they be e'er so cunning.

4 Thou say'st: "This is my body; eat,
And orally receive me!
This is my blood; drink all of it,
And henceforth never leave me!"
What Thou hast spoken, true must be:
Thou art almighty, and with Thee
Impossible is nothing.

5 Although my reason cannot see
How in so many places
Thy body at one time may be,
Yet faith Thy Word embraces.
How it can be, I leave to Thee,
Thy Word alone sufficeth me,
For Thou wilt that we trust it.

6 Lord, I believe in simple trust,
Strength in my weakness give me,
For I am naught but sinful dust,
Nor of Thy Word bereave me!
Thy Baptism, Supper, and Thy Word,
My consolation are, O Lord,
For they contain my treasure.

7 Grant that we worthily receive
Thy Supper, Lord our Savior,
That for our sins we truly grieve,
And prove by our behavior
That we obtained Thy saving grace,
And trust in it throughout our days;
Then will our life be godly.

8 For Thy consoling Supper, Lord,
Be praised throughout all ages!
Preserve it, for with one accord
The world against it rages.
Grant that Thy body and Thy blood
May be my comfort and sweet food
In my last moments. Amen!

Samuel Kinner, 1638

437 Repose L. M. F. R. STATHAM

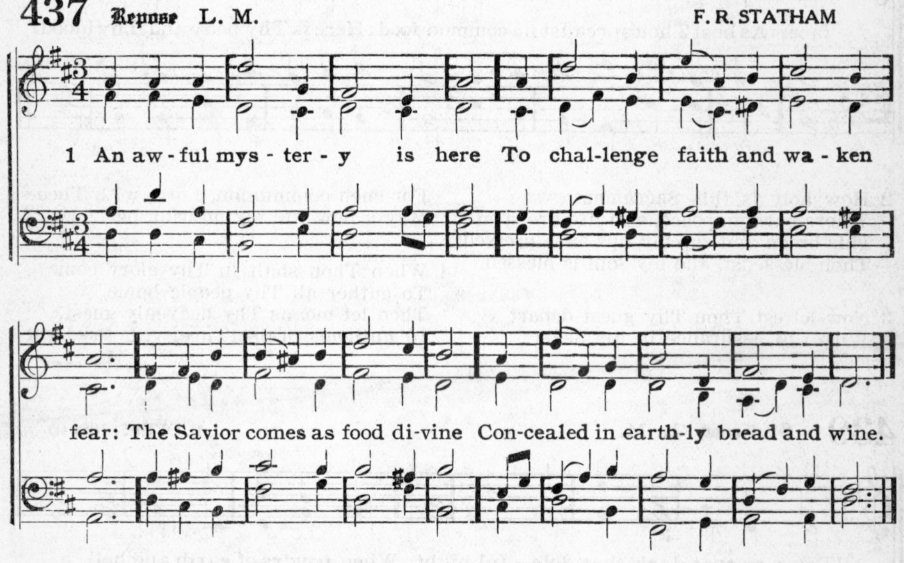
1 An aw-ful mys-ter-y is here To chal-lenge faith and wa-ken
fear: The Savior comes as food di-vine Con-cealed in earth-ly bread and wine.

(*Or to St. Crispen Or to Rest*)

2 This world is loveless—but above,
What wondrous boundlessness of love!
The King of glory stoops to me,
My spirit's life and strength to be.

3 In consecrated wine and bread
No eye perceives the mystery dread,
But Jesus' words are strong and clear:
"My body and my blood are here."

4 How dull are all the powers of sense,
Employed on proofs of love immense!
The richest food remains unseen,
And highest gifts appear how mean!

5 But here we have no boon on earth,
And faith alone discerns its worth;
The Word, not sense, must be our guide,
And faith assure, since sight's denied.

6 Lord show us still that Thou art good,
And grant us evermore this food,
Give faith to ev'ry wav'ring soul,
And make each wounded spirit whole.

M. Loy

438 Vetters L. M.

Pub. 1713 by VETTERS

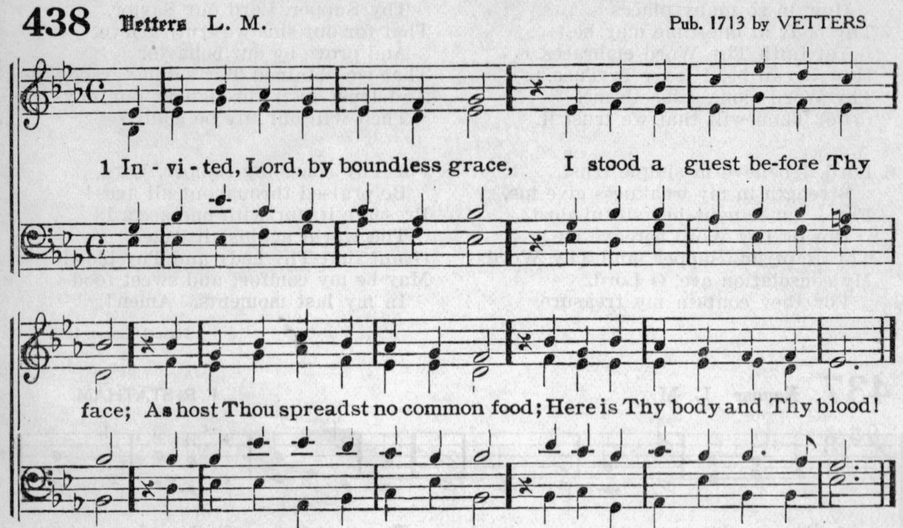
1 In - vi - ted, Lord, by boundless grace, I stood a guest be-fore Thy
face; As host Thou spreadst no common food; Here is Thy body and Thy blood!

2 How holy is this Sacrament,
Where pardon, peace, and life are spent!
This bread and cup my lips have pressed,
Thou blessedst, and my soul is blessed.

3 Now lettest Thou Thy guest depart
With full assurance in his heart;
For such communion, Lord, with Thee
May a new life my offering be.

4 When Thou shalt in Thy glory come
To gather all Thy people home,
Then let me, as Thy heavenly guest,
In anthems praise Thee with the blest!

E. Cronenwett

439 St. Cross L. M.

J. B. DYKES, 1861 (I)

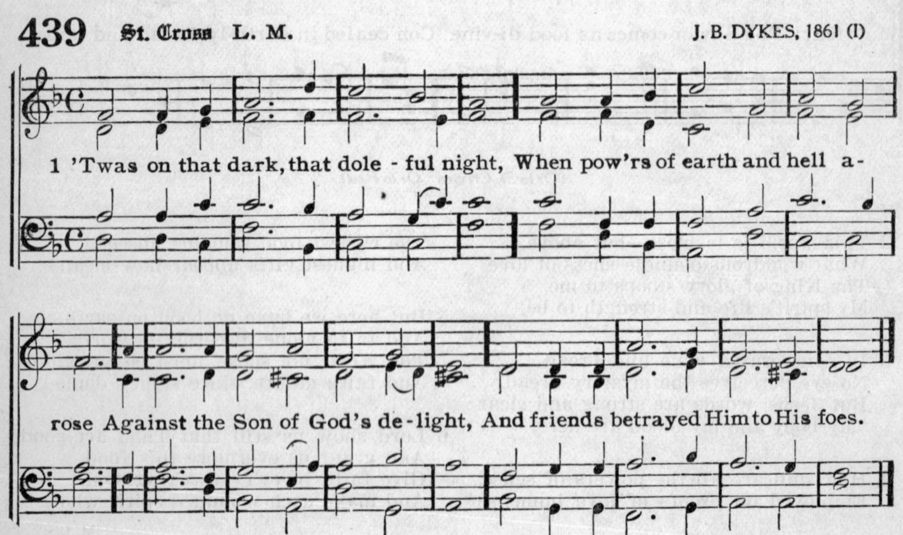
1 'Twas on that dark, that dole - ful night, When pow'rs of earth and hell a-
rose Against the Son of God's de-light, And friends betrayed Him to His foes.

2 Before the mournful scene began,
He took the bread, and blessed, and brake;
What love through all His actions ran!
What wondrous words of grace He spake!

3 "This is my body, broke for sin;
Receive and eat the living food:"
Then took the cup and blessed the wine;
"'Tis the new covenant in my blood."

4 "Do this," He said, "till time shall end,
In memory of your dying Friend
Meet at my table and record
The love of your departed Lord."

5 Jesus, Thy feast we celebrate;
We show Thy death, we sing Thy name,
Till Thou return, and we shall eat
The marriage supper of the Lamb.

Isaac Watts, a

440 St. Cross L. M.

1 At Thy command, our dearest Lord,
Here we attend Thy dying feast;
Thy blood, like wine, adorns the board,
And Thine own flesh feeds every guest.

2 Our faith adores Thy bleeding love,
And trusts for life in one that died;
We hope for heavenly crowns above
From a Redeemer crucified.

3 Let the vain world pronounce it shame,
And fling their scandals on the cause;
We come to boast our Savior's name,
And make our triumphs in His cross.

4 With joy we tell the scoffing age,
He that was dead has left His tomb;
He lives above their utmost rage,
And we are waiting till He come.

Isaac Watts.

441 Jesus Christus, unser Heiland, der 8,8,7,8 KLUGE, 1535

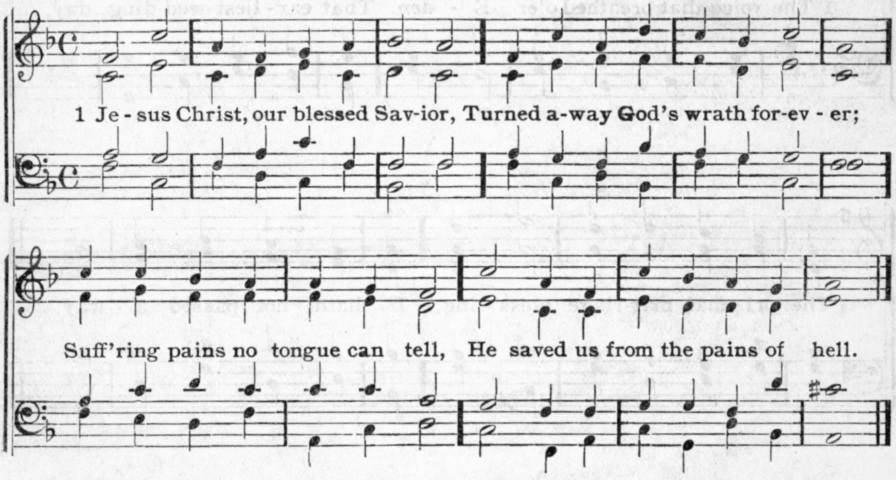

1 Je - sus Christ, our blessed Sav-ior, Turned a-way God's wrath for-ev - er;
Suff'ring pains no tongue can tell, He saved us from the pains of hell.

2 To remind us that, to save us,
He hath died, His flesh He gave us,
With this bread, a quick'ning food,
And with this wine, His precious blood.

3 Whoso to this board repaireth,
Take good heed how He prepareth;
Death instead of life shall he
Receive who comes unworthily.

4 Thou shalt hold with faith unshaken,
That this food is to be taken
By the sick who are distressed,
By those whose heart is sin-oppressed.

5 Christ says: Come, ye heavy-laden,
I your weary hearts will gladden;
They that are yet strong and well,
Despise the best physician's skill.

6 Couldst thou earn thine own salvation,
Useless were my death and passion;
This feast is not spread for thee,
If thine own helper thou wilt be.

7 If thou this believest truly,
And confession makest duly,
Thou a welcome guest art here,
This heavenly food thy soul shall cheer.

8 But the fruits must not be missing,
Love thy neighbor without ceasing,
That true love let him receive,
Which here to thee thy God doth give.

John Hus Dr. Martin Luther, Tr.

Catechism

Home, Marriage, Family, Children

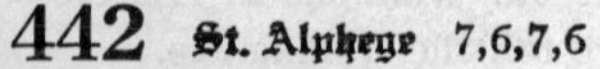

442 St. Alphege 7,6,7,6 — Dr. GAUNTLETT, 1852

1 The voice that breathed o'er E - den, That ear - liest wed-ding day,

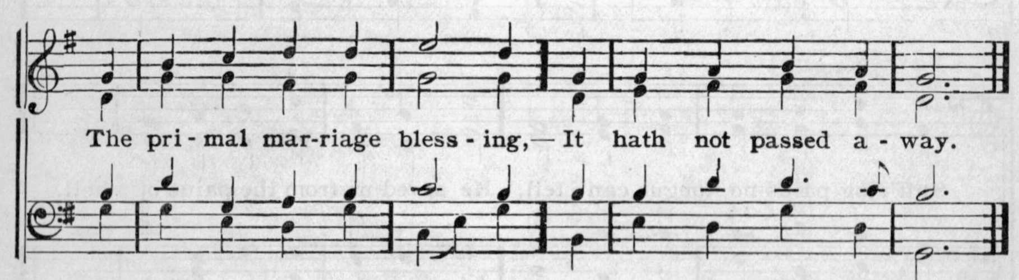
The pri - mal mar-riage bless - ing,— It hath not passed a - way.

2 Still in the pure espousal
Of Christian man and maid,
The Holy Three are with us,
The threefold grace is said.

3 Be present, loving Father,
To give away this bride,
As Eve Thou gav'st to Adam
Out of His own pierced side.

4 Be present, Son of Mary,
To join their loving hands,
As Thou didst bind two natures
In Thine eternal bands.

5 Be present, Holiest Spirit,
To bless them as they kneel,
As Thou for Christ, the Bridegroom,
The heavenly spouse dost seal.

6 O spread Thy pure wings o'er them,
Let no ill power find place,
When onward to Thine altar
Their hallowed path they trace.

7 To cast their crowns before Thee
In perfect sacrifice,
Till to the home of gladness
With Christ's own Bride they rise.

John Keble 1857 a

443 Stuyvesant C. M. 81 W. B. GILBERT

1 Lord, who at Ca-na's wed-ding feast Didst as a guest ap-pear,
Thou dear-er far than earth-ly guest Vouch-safe Thy pres-ence here,
For ho-ly Thou in-deed dost prove The mar-riage vow to be;
ritard.
Pro-claim-ing it a type of love Be-tween the Church and Thee.

2 The holiest vow that man can make,
  The golden thread in life,
The bond that none may dare to break,
  That bindeth man and wife;
Which, blest by Thee, whate'er betides,
  No evil shall destroy,
Thro' care-worn days each care divides,
  And doubles every joy.

3 On those who now before Thee kneel,
  O Lord, Thy blessing pour,
That each may wake the other's zeal
  To love Thee more and more:
Oh, grant them here in peace to live,
  In purity and love,
And this world leaving, to receive
  A crown of life above.

A. Thrupp, 1853 a

444 O Perfect Love 11,10,11,10

Arr. fr. J. BARNBY, 1889

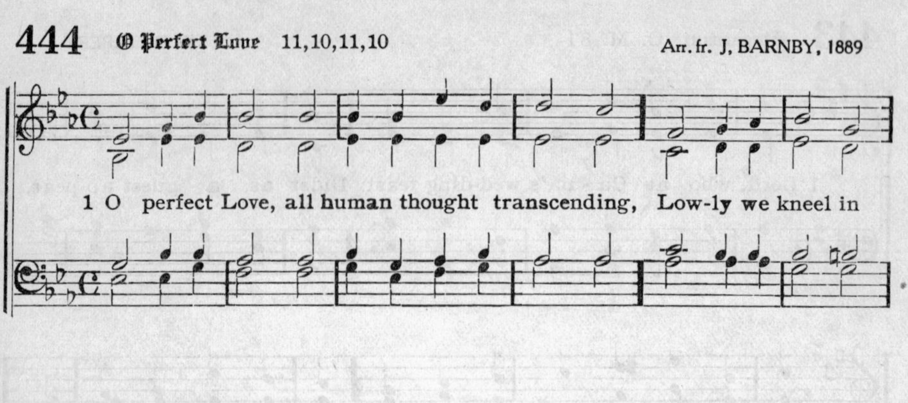
1 O perfect Love, all human thought transcending, Low-ly we kneel in

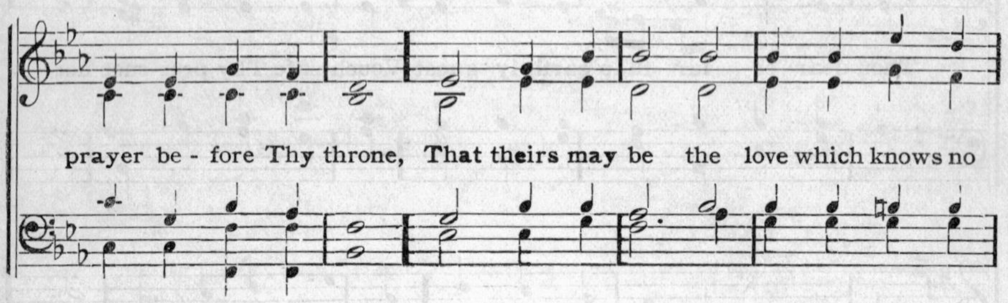
prayer be - fore Thy throne, That theirs may be the love which knows no

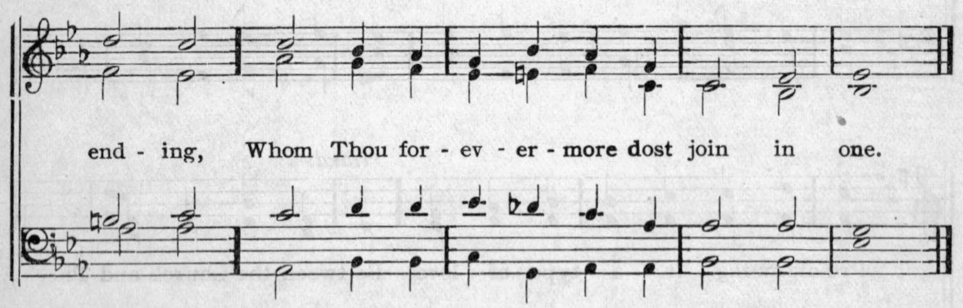
end - ing, Whom Thou for - ev - er - more dost join in one.

2 O perfect Life, be Thou their full assurance,
Of tender charity and steadfast faith,
Of patient hope, and quiet, brave endurance
With childlike trust that fears nor pain nor death.

3 Grant them the joy which brightens earthly sorrow;
Grant them the peace which calms all earthly strife,
And to life's day the glorious unknown morrow
That dawns upon eternal love and life.

Dorothy F. Bloomfield, 1883

445 Wo Gott zum Haus nicht gibt L. M. KLUGE, 1535

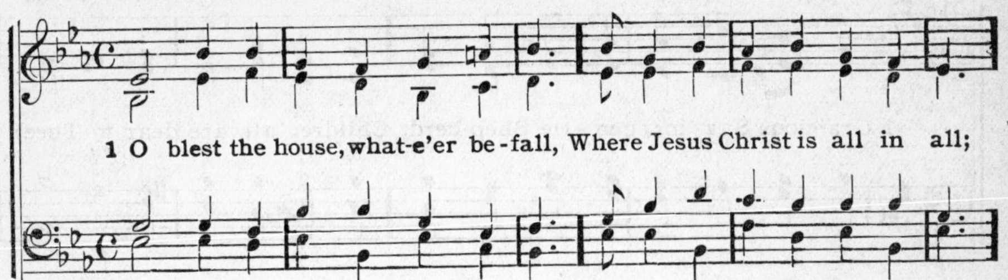
1 O blest the house, what-e'er be-fall, Where Jesus Christ is all in all;

Yea, if He were not dwell-ing there, How poor, and dark, and void it were!

2 O blest that house where faith ye find,
And all within have set their mind
To trust their God and serve Him still,
And do in all His holy will.

3 O blest the parents who give heed
Unto their children's foremost need,
And weary not of care or cost:
To them and heaven shall none be lost.

4 Blest such a house, it prospers well,
In peace and joy the parents dwell,
And in their children's lot is shown
How richly God can bless His own.

5 Then here will I, and mine to-day
A solemn cov'nant make and say:
Though all the world forsake Thy Word,
I and my house will serve the Lord.

C. H. von Pfeil

446 Wo Gott zum Haus nicht gibt L. M.

1 Happy the man who feareth God,
Whose feet His holy ways have trod;
Thine own good hand shall nourish thee,
And well and happy shalt thou be.

2 Lo! to the man these blessings cleave
Who in God's holy fear doth live;
From him the ancient curse hath fled
By Adam's race inherited.

3 Out of Mount Zion God shall send,
And crown with joy thy latter end,
That thou Jerusalem mayst see
In favor and prosperity.

4 He shall be with thee in thy ways,
And give thee health and strength of days;
Yea, thou shalt children's children see,
And peace on Israel shall be.

5 Praise God the Father, God the Son,
And God the Spirit, Three in One;
As 't was through ages heretofore,
Is now, and shall be evermore.

Dr. Martin Luther, 1524 Richard Massie, Tr ab.

447 Spes Unica 8,7 61 COOPER PERRY, 1889

1 Gra-cious Sav-ior, gen-tle Shep-herd, Children all are dear to Thee;

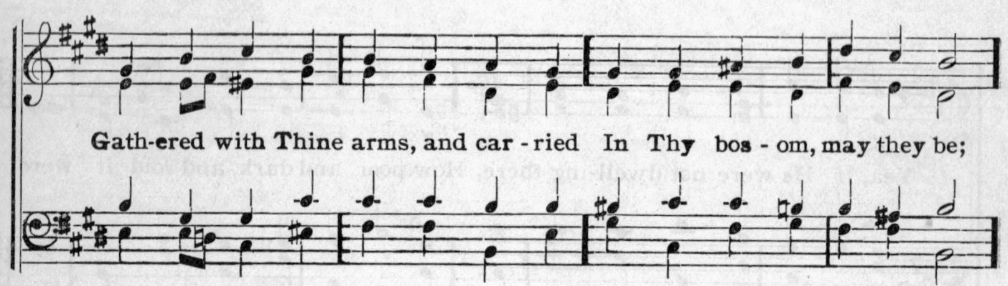
Gath-ered with Thine arms, and car-ried In Thy bos-om, may they be;

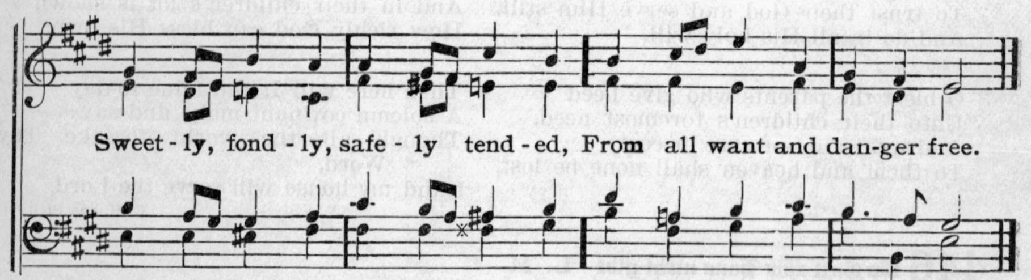
Sweet-ly, fond-ly, safe-ly tend-ed, From all want and dan-ger free.

2 Tender Shepherd, never leave them
From Thy fold to go astray;
By Thy warning love directed,
May they walk the narrow way;
Thus direct them, thus defend them,
Lest they fall an easy prey.

3 Cleanse their hearts from sinful folly
In the stream Thy love supplied,
Mingled stream of blood and water
Flowing from Thy wounded side;
And to heavenly pastures lead them,
Where Thine own still waters glide.

4 Let Thy holy Word instruct them;
Fill their minds with heavenly light;
Let Thy powerful grace constrain them
To approve whate'er is right;
Let them feel Thy yoke is easy,
Let them prove Thy burden light.

5 Taught to lisp Thy holy praises
Which on earth Thy children sing,
Both with lips and hearts, unfeigned,
Glad thank-offerings may they bring;
Then with all the saints in glory,
Join to praise their Lord and King.

Jane E. Leeson 1857

448 St. Ambrose 6,6,4,6,6,6,4

W. H. MONK (P)

1 Shep-herd of ten-der youth, Guid-ing in love and truth

Through de-vious ways; Christ our tri-um-phant King, We

come Thy name to sing, And here our children bring, To join Thy praise.

(Or to Italian Hymn)

2 Thou art our holy Lord,
O all-subduing Word,
Healer of strife:
Thou didst Thyself abase,
That from sin's deep disgrace
Thou mightest save our race,
And give us life.

3 Thou art the great High Priest;
Thou hast prepared the feast
Of holy love:
And in our mortal pain
None calls on Thee in vain;
Help Thou dost not disdain,
Help from above.

4 Ever be near our side,
Our Shepherd and our Guide,
Our Staff and Song;
Jesus, Thou Christ of God,
By Thine enduring Word,
Lead us where Thou hast trod,
Make our faith strong.

5 So now, and till we die,
Sound we Thy praises high,
And joyful sing;
Let all the holy throng
Who to Thy Church belong,
Unite and swell the song
To Christ our King!

Clement of Alexandria, 211 Henry M. Dexter, Tr. 1846

449 Batty (Ringe recht) 8,7,8,7 THOMMEN, 1745

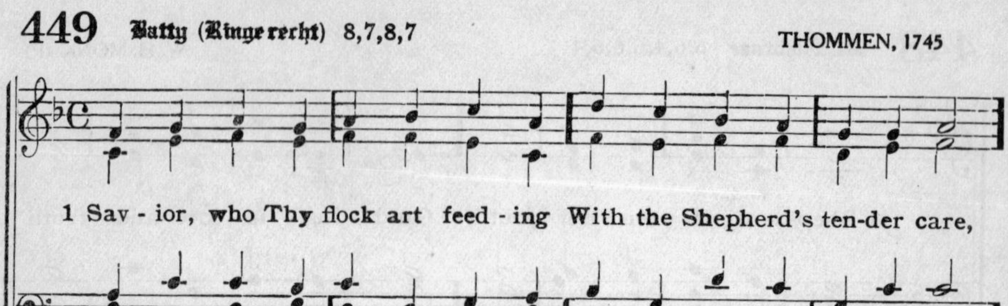
1 Sav - ior, who Thy flock art feed - ing With the Shepherd's ten-der care,

All the fee - ble gen - tly lead - ing, While the lambs Thy bos-om share.

2 Now, these little ones receiving,
Fold them in Thy gracious arm;
There, we know, Thy Word believing,
Only there secure from harm.

3 Never, from Thy pasture roving,
Let them be the Lion's prey;
Let Thy tenderness, so loving,
Keep them through life's dangerous way.

4 Then within Thy fold eternal
Let them find a resting-place:
Feed in pastures ever vernal,
Drink the rivers of Thy grace.

W. A. Muehlenberg, 1826

Church

Laying of the Corner-Stone

450 Bowen (Otterbourne) L. M. HAYDN, 1732—1809

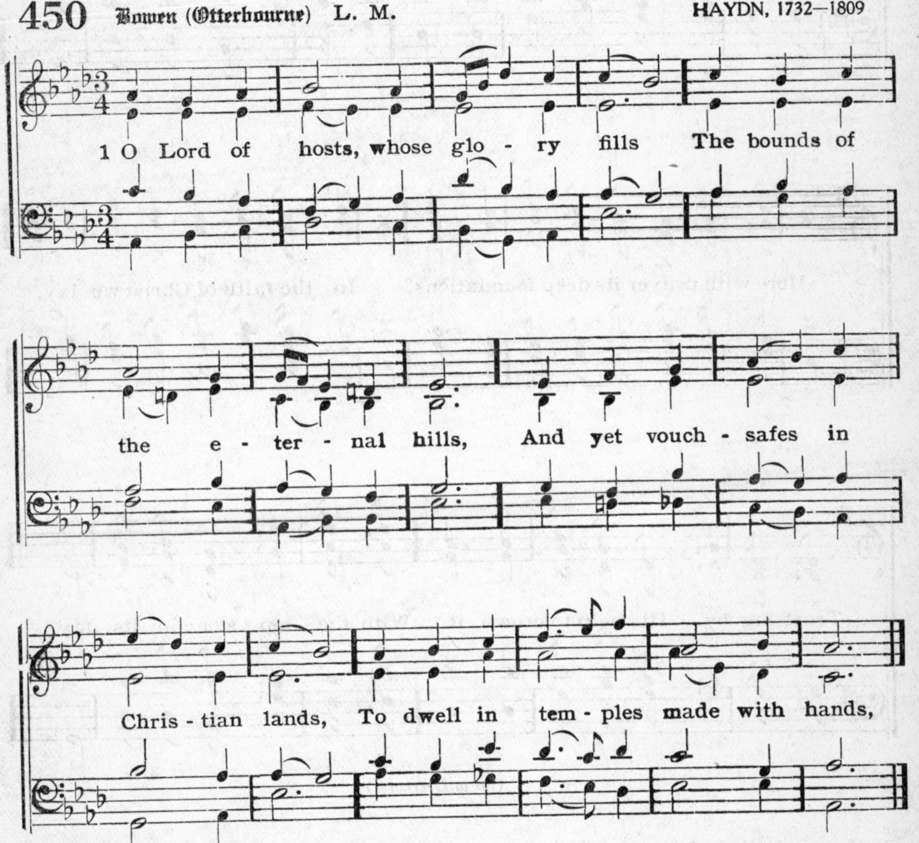

1 O Lord of hosts, whose glo - ry fills The bounds of
the e - ter - nal hills, And yet vouch - safes in
Chris - tian lands, To dwell in tem - ples made with hands,

2 Grant that all we, who here to-day
Rejoicing this foundation lay,
May be in very deed Thine own,
Built on the precious corner-stone.

3 The heads that guide endue with skill,
The hands that work preserve from ill,
That we, who these foundations lay,
May raise the topstone in its day.

4 But now and ever, Lord, protect
The temple of Thine own elect;
Be Thou in them, and they in Thee,
O ever-blessed Trinity!

J. M. Neale, 1844 ab.

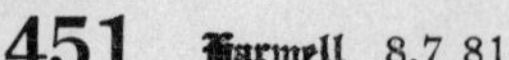

451 Harwell 8,7 8l

LOWELL MASON

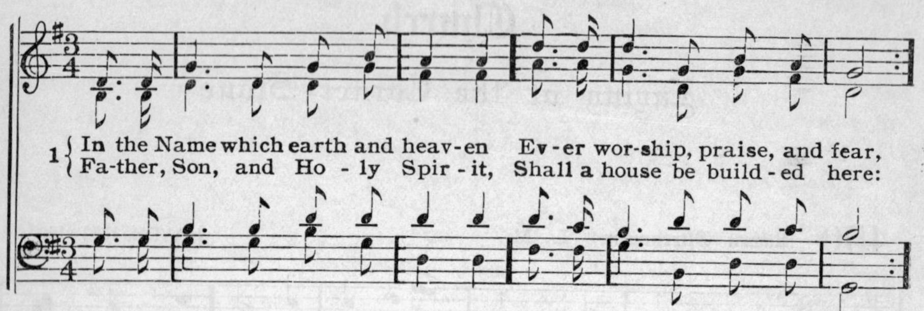
1 { In the Name which earth and heav-en Ev-er wor-ship, praise, and fear,
Fa-ther, Son, and Ho - ly Spir - it, Shall a house be build - ed here:

Here with prayer its deep foundations, In the faith of Christ we lay,

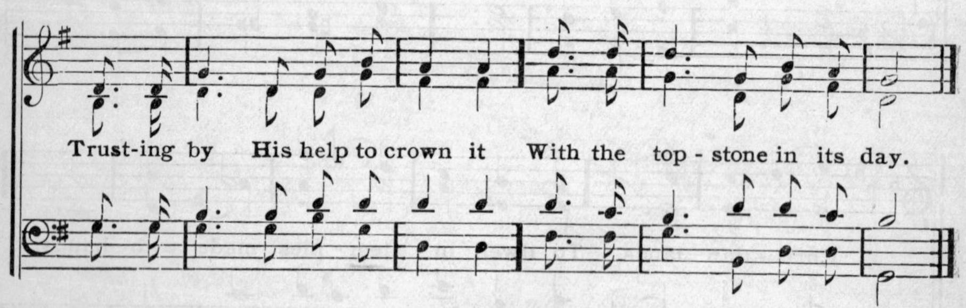
Trust-ing by His help to crown it With the top - stone in its day.

(*Or to Deerhurst*)

2 Here as in their due succession
  Stone on stone the workmen place,
Thus, we pray, unseen but surely,
  Jesu, build us up in grace;
Till, within these walls completed,
  We complete in Thee are found;
And to Thee, the one Foundation,
  Strong and living stones, are bound.

3 Fair shall be Thine earthly temple:
  Here the careless passer-by
Shall bethink him, in its beauty,
  Of the holier House on high;
Weary hearts and troubled spirits
  Here shall find a still retreat;
Sinful souls shall bring their burden
  Here to the Absolver's feet.

4 Yet with truer, nobler beauty,
Lord, we pray, this house adorn,
Where Thy Bride, Thy Church redeemed,
Robes her for her marriage morn;
Clothed in garments of salvation,
Rich with gems of heavenly grace,
Spouse of Christ, arrayed and waiting
Till she may behold His face.

5 Here in due and solemn order
May her ceaseless prayer arise;
Here may strains of holy gladness
Lift her heart above the skies;
Here the word of life be spoken;
Here the child of God be sealed;
Here the Bread of Heaven be broken,
"Till He come," Himself revealed.

6 Praise to Thee, O Master-Builder,
Maker of the earth and skies;
Praise to Thee, in Whom Thy temple
Fitly framed together lies;
Praise to Thee, eternal Spirit,
Binding all that lives in one:
Till our earthly praise be ended,
And the eternal song begun!

J. Ellerton, a

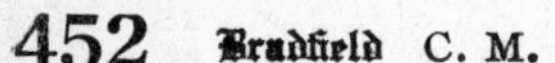

452 Bradfield C. M. J. B. CALKIN, 1872.

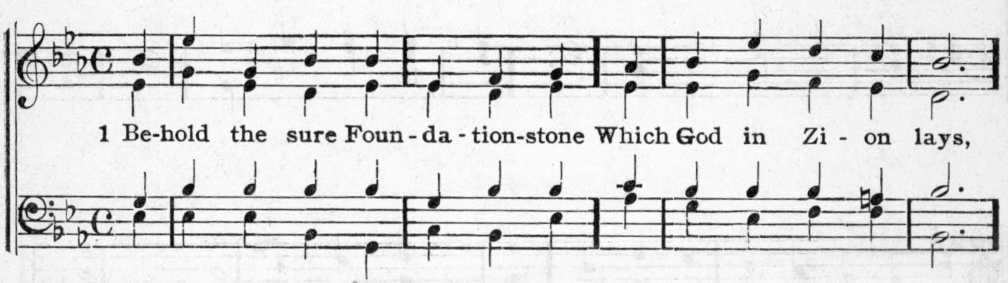
1 Be-hold the sure Foun-da-tion-stone Which God in Zi-on lays,

To build our heav'n-ly hopes up-on, And His e-ter-nal praise.

2 Chosen of God, to sinners dear,
Let saints adore the name;
They trust their whole salvation here,
Nor shall they suffer shame.

3 The foolish builders, scribe and priest,
Reject it with disdain;
Yet on this Rock the Church shall rest
And envy rage in vain.

4 What though the gates of hell withstood,
Yet must this building rise:
'Tis Thine own work, Almighty God,
And wondrous in our eyes.

Isaac Watts, 1719

453 Harewood 6,6,6,6,8,8 (H. M.) S. S. WESLEY, 1868.

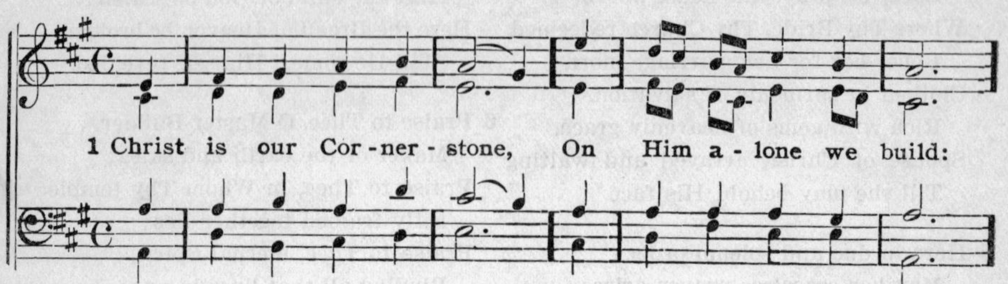
1 Christ is our Cor - ner - stone, On Him a - lone we build:

With His true saints a - lone The courts of heav'n are filled; On

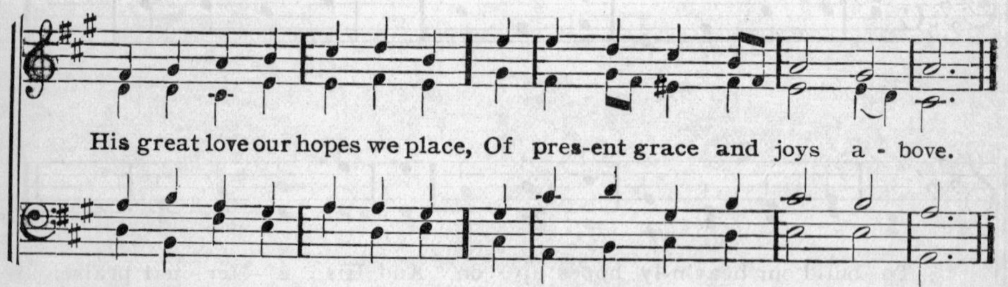
His great love our hopes we place, Of pres-ent grace and joys a - bove.

(Or to St. Godric)

2 Oh, then with hymns of praise
These hallowed courts shall ring;
Our voices we will raise,
The Three in One to sing;
And thus proclaim in joyful song
Both loud and long, that glorious name.

3 Here, gracious God, do Thou
For evermore draw nigh;
Accept each faithful vow,
And mark each suppliant sigh;
In copious shower, on all who pray,
Each holy day, Thy blessing pour.

4 Here may we gain from heaven
The grace which we implore,
And may that grace, once given,
Be with us evermore,
Until that day when all the blest
To endless rest are called away.

Anon, (Latin, 6th or 7th Century) J. Chandler, Tr. 1837

Church

Dedication

454 Regent Square 8,7 61 H. SMART, (P)

1 Christ, Thou art the sure Foun-da-tion, Thou the Head and Cor - ner-stone;
Cho - sen of the Lord, and pre-cious, Bind-ing all the Church in one;
Thou Thy Zi - on's help for - ev - er, And her Con - fi - dence a - lone.

2 To this temple, where we call Thee,
Come, O Lord of hosts, to-day!
With Thy wonted loving-kindness
Hear Thy servants as they pray;
And Thy fullest benediction
Shed within these walls alway.

3 Here vouchsafe to all Thy servants
What they ask of Thee to gain,
What they gain from Thee forever
With the blessed to retain,
And hereafter in Thy glory
Evermore with Thee to reign.

4 Praise and honor to the Father,
Praise and honor to the Son,
Praise and honor to the Spirit,
Ever Three and ever One;
One in might, and one in glory,
While eternal ages run.

From the Latin, John Mason Neale, 1851, a

455 Leigh L. M.

A. R. REINAGLE, (1799—1877)

1 Come, Je-sus, from the sapphire throne, Where Thy redeemed behold Thy face,

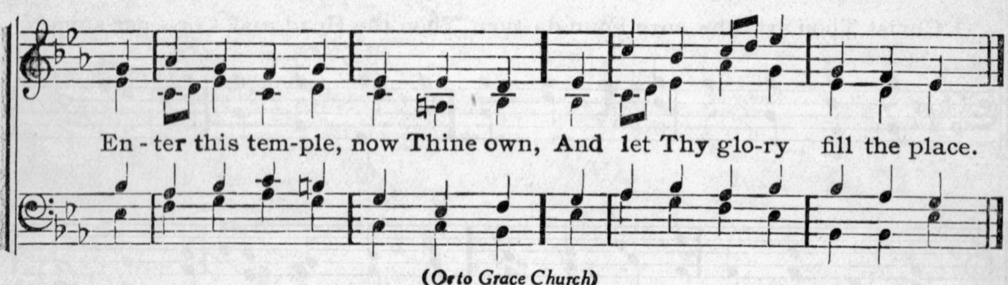
En-ter this tem-ple, now Thine own, And let Thy glo-ry fill the place.

(*Or to Grace Church*)

2 We praise Thee that to-day we see
Its sacred walls before Thee stand;
'Tis Thine for us: 'tis ours for Thee;
Reared by Thy kind assisting hand.

3 Oft as returns the day of rest,
Let heartfelt worship here ascend;
With Thine own joy fill every breast,
With Thine own power Thy word attend.

4 Here in the dark and sorrowing day,
Bid Thou the throbbing heart be still;
Oh, wipe the mourner's tears away,
And give new strength to meet Thy will.

5 When at Thine Altar we shall meet,
And keep the feast of dying love,
Be our communion ever sweet
With Thee, and with Thy Church above.

6 Come, faithful Shepherd, feed Thy sheep;
In Thine own arms the lambs infold;
Give help to climb the heavenward steep,
Till Thy full glory we behold.

R. Palmer, a and ab.

456 Hursley L. M.

1 Eternal Son of God, O Thou,
Before whom earth and heaven bow,
Regard Thy people as they raise
To Thee their songs of prayer and praise.

2 This house they dedicate to Thee,
That here Thy glory they may see,
Thy body and Thy blood they here
Receive, their fainting souls to cheer.

3 Here in baptismal water pure
They find for sin a gracious cure;
Their children here to Thee they bring,
O Thou our death-subduing King.

4 Here sin's diseases healing find.
The weak grow strong, light cheers the blind;
The troubled heart with peace is blest,
And weariness finds heavenly rest.

5 When tempests shake the world around,
The rock-built Church secure is found;
The gates of hell may here assail
Whom Christ defends, but not prevail.

6 To God the Father, God the Son,
And God the Spirit, Three in One,
Be praise: do Thou, whom we adore,
Teach us to praise Thee evermore.

3rd Century

457 Darwall 6,6,6,6,8,8 (H. M.)

J. DARWALL, 1770

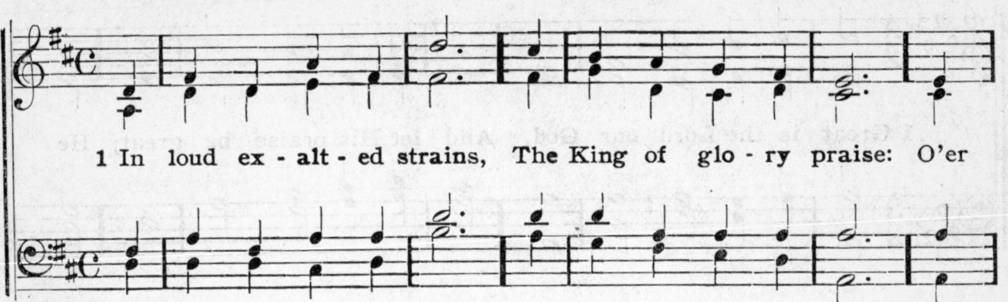
1 In loud ex - alt - ed strains, The King of glo - ry praise: O'er

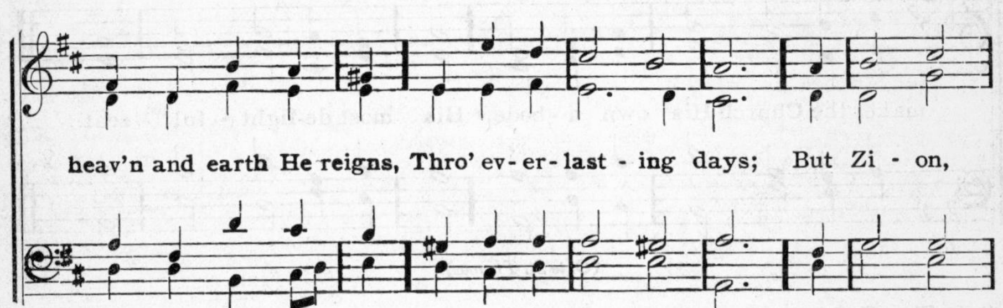
heav'n and earth He reigns, Thro' ev - er - last - ing days; But Zi - on,

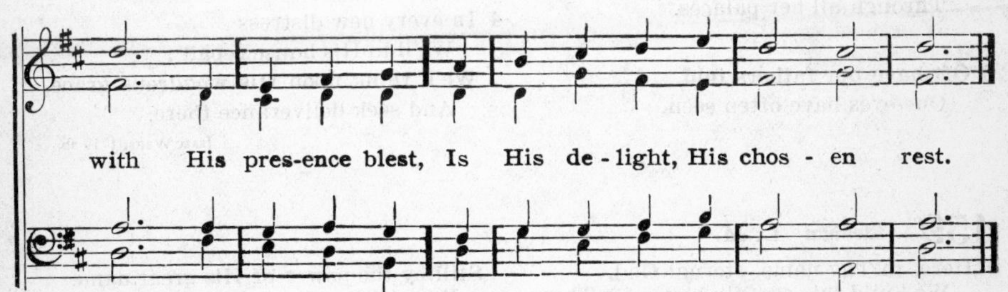
with His pres-ence blest, Is His de - light, His chos - en rest.

2 O King of glory, come
And with Thy favor crown
This temple as Thy home,
This people as Thy own;
Beneath this roof vouchsafe to show
How God can dwell with men below.

3 Now let Thine ear attend
Our supplicating cries;
Now let our praise ascend,
Accepted, to the skies;
Now let Thy Gospel's joyful sound
Spread its celestial influence round.

4 Here may the listening throng
Imbibe Thy truth and love;
Here Christians join the song
Of seraphim above:
Till all who humbly seek Thy face
Rejoice in Thy abounding grace.

B. Francis, 1774

458 State Street S. M.

J. C. WOODMAN, 1844

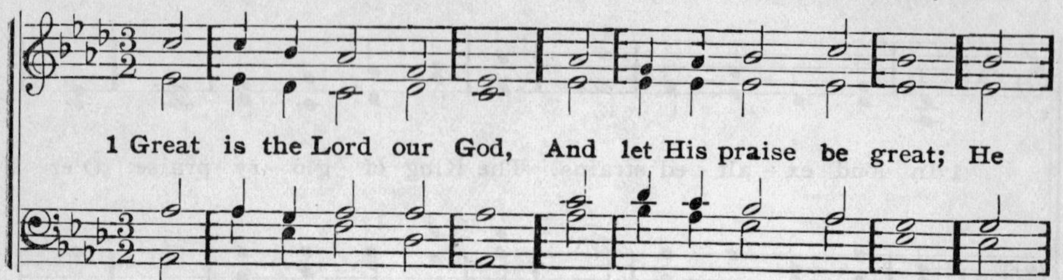
1 Great is the Lord our God, And let His praise be great; He

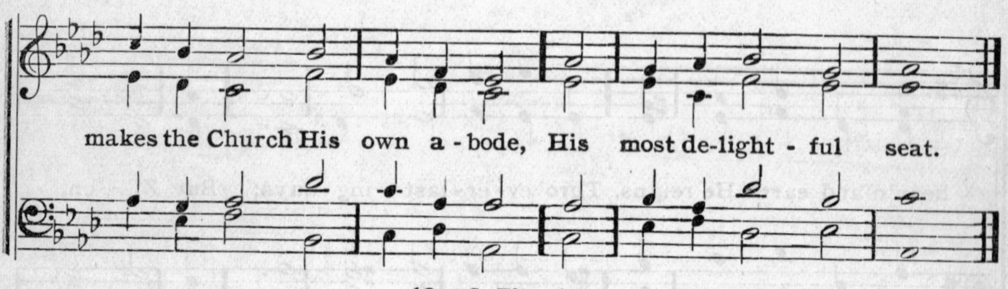
makes the Church His own a - bode, His most de-light - ful seat.

(*Or to St. Thomas*)

2 In Zion God is known,
A refuge in distress;
How bright has His salvation shone
Through all her palaces.

3 Oft have our fathers told,
Our eyes have often seen,
How well our God secures the fold,
Where His own sheep have been.

4 In every new distress
We'll to His house repair;
We'll think upon His wondrous grace,
And seek deliverance there.

Isaac Watts, 1719 ab.

459 Mendon L. M.

1 Here, in Thy name, eternal God,
We build this earthly house for Thee;
O choose it for Thy fixed abode,
And keep it from all error free.

2 Here, when Thy people seek Thy face,
And dying sinners pray to live,
Hear Thou in heaven, Thy dwelling place,
And when Thou hearest, Lord, forgive.

3 Here, when Thy messengers proclaim
The blessed Gospel of Thy Son,
Still by the power of His great name
Be mighty signs and wonders done.

4 When children's voices raise the song,
Hosanna to the heavenly King!
Let heaven, with earth, the strain prolong,
Hosanna! let the angels sing.

5 Thy glory never hence depart;
Yet choose not, Lord, this house alone:
Thy kingdom come to every heart,
In every bosom fix Thy throne.

James Montgomery, 1822

(*Or to Federal St. Or to Duke St.*)

Church

The Communion of Saints

460 Desire L. M. J. B. WOODBURY, (P)

1 There is with - in this heart of mine A lit - tle
church, with sa - cred shrine, And stained for - ev - er
with the blood Of Je - sus Christ, the Lamb of God.

(Or to Wo Gott zum Haus)

2 Here dwelleth God the Father, Son,
And Holy Spirit, Three in One;
He is my soul's beloved Guest,
And grants my heart true peace and rest.

3 This little church looks poor and odd;
But being the abode of God
It has a glorious, peerless grace:
It is God's royal dwelling-place.

4 This little church, Lord, I commend
Unto Thy care, and pray: Defend
And shield it from calamity,
Dwell there now and eternally.

From the Latin of B. Walther, B. Derschau, † 1639 A. Crull, Tr.

461

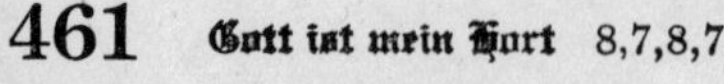

Gott ist mein Hort 8,7,8,7 — H. EGLI (?), 1787

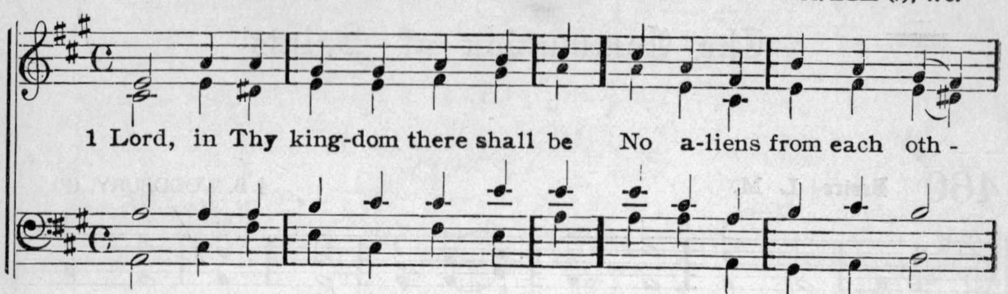
1 Lord, in Thy king-dom there shall be No a-liens from each oth -

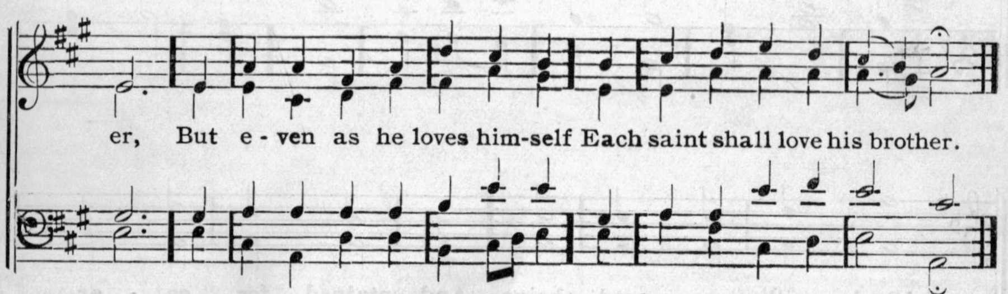
er, But e - ven as he loves him-self Each saint shall love his brother.

2 When in Thy courts below we meet
To mourn our sinful living,
And with united hearts repeat
Confession, creed, thanksgiving:

3 Make us to hear in each sweet word
Thy Holy Spirit calling
To oneness with Thy Church and Thee,
That heavenly bond forestalling.

4 One Baptism and one faith have we,
One Spirit sent to win us,
One Lord, one Father, and one God,
Above, and through, and in us.

5 Never, by schism, or by sin,
May we that union sever,
Till all, to perfect stature grown,
Are one with Thee forever.

J. Anstice

462

Boylston (Mixolydian) S. M. — L. MASON, 1832 (P)

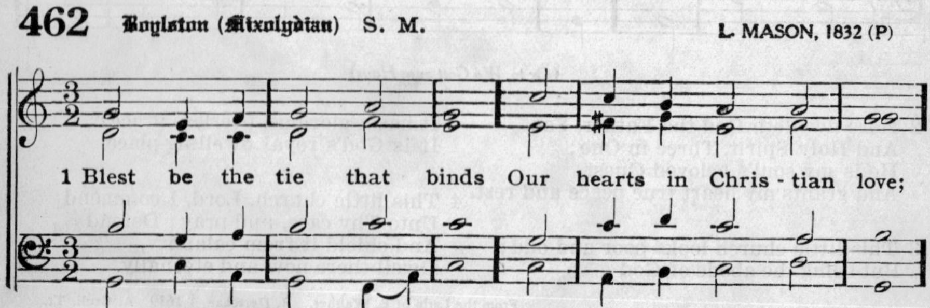
1 Blest be the tie that binds Our hearts in Chris - tian love;

The fel - low - ship of kin-dred minds Is like to that a - bove.

2 Before our Father's throne
We pour our ardent prayers;
Our fears, our hopes, our aims are one,
Our comforts and our cares.

3 We share our mutual woes;
Our mutual burdens bear;
And often for each other flows
The sympathizing tear.

4 When we asunder part,
It gives us inward pain;
But we shall still be joined in heart,
And hope to meet again.

5 This glorious hope revives
Our courage by the way;
While each in expectation lives,
And longs to see the day.

6 From sorrow, toil, and pain,
And sin we shall be free;
And perfect love and friendship reign
Through all eternity.

J. Fawcett,. 1772

463 St. Flavian C. M.

DAYE'S PSALTER, 1562 (P)

1 The saints on earth and those a - bove But one com-mun - ion make;

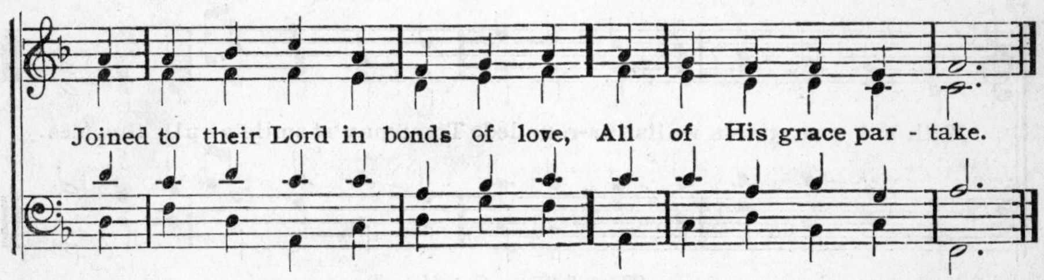
Joined to their Lord in bonds of love, All of His grace par - take.

2 One family we dwell in Him,
One Church above, beneath;
Though now divided by the stream,—
The narrow stream of death.

3 One army of the living God,
To His commands we bow:
Part of the host have passed the flood,
And part are crossing now.

4 Lo! thousands to their endless home
Are swiftly borne away;
And we are to the margin come,
And soon must launch as they.

5 Lord Jesus, be our constant guide,
Then, when the word is given,
Bid death's cold flood its waves divide,
And land us safe in heaven.

C. Wesley, a

Church

Glory of the Church

464 Silcher 8,7 81 — Ad. fr. FR. SILCHER, 1825

1 { Glor - ious things of Thee are spok - en, Zi - on, cit - y of our God;
He, whose word can not be brok - en, Formed Thee for His own a - bode;
On the Rock of a - ges found - ed, What can shake thy sure re-pose?
With sal - va - tion's walls sur-rounded, Thou may'st smile at all thy foes.

(*Or to Autumn* *Or to Harwell*)

2 See, the streams of living waters
Springing from eternal love,
Well supply thy sons and daughters,
And all fear of want remove.
Who can faint while such a river
Ever flows their thirst to assuage?
Grace, which, like the Lord, the Giver,
Never fails from age to age.

3 Savior, since of Zion's city
I, through grace, a member am,
Let the world deride or pity,
I will glory in Thy name.
Fading is the worldling's pleasure,
All his boasted pomp and show;
Solid joys and lasting treasure
None but Zion's children know.

John Newton, 1779

465 Zion (Holborn) 8,7,8,7,4,7

T. MORLEY

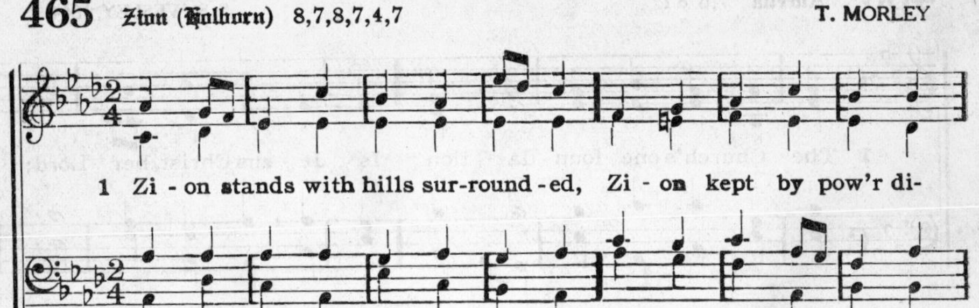
1 Zi - on stands with hills sur-round - ed, Zi - on kept by pow'r di-

vine; All her foes shall be con - found-ed, Though the world in

arms com - bine, Hap - py Zi - on, What a hap - py lot is thine!

(Or to Her vil ties)

2 Every human tie may perish;
Friend to friend unfaithful prove;
Brothers cease their own to cherish;
Heaven and earth at last remove:
But no changes
Can attend Jehovah's love.

3 In the furnace God may prove thee,
Thence to bring thee forth more bright,
But can never cease to love thee;
Thou art precious in His sight;
God is with thee,
God, thine everlasting Light.

Thomas Kelly, 1806

466 Aurelia 7,6 8l

S. S. WESLEY, 1864

1 The Church's one foun-da-tion Is Je-sus Christ, her Lord;
She is His new cre-a-tion By wa-ter and the word;
From heav'n He came and sought her, To be His ho-ly bride;
With His own blood He bought her, And for her life He died.

2 Elect from every nation,
  Yet one o'er all the earth,
Her charter of salvation
  One Lord, one faith, one birth;
One holy name she blesses,
  Partakes one holy food,
And to one hope she presses,
  With every grace endued.

3 Though with a scornful wonder,
  Men see her sore oppressed,
By schisms rent asunder,
  By heresies distressed;
Yet saints their watch are keeping,
  Their cry goes up, "How long?"
And soon the night of weeping
  Shall be the morn of song.

4 'Mid toil and tribulation,
And tumult of her war,
She waits the consummation
Of peace for evermore;
Till with the vision glorious
Her longing eyes are blest,
And the great church victorious
Shall be the church at rest.

5 Yet she on earth hath union
With God the Three in One,
And mystic sweet communion
With those whose rest is won;
O happy ones and holy!
Lord, give us grace, that we,
Like them, the meek and lowly,
On high may dwell with Thee.

S. J. Stone, 1866

467 Mabyn 8,7,8,7

A. H. BROWN (1830–)

1 Hark! the Church proclaims her hon-or, And her strength is on - ly this:
God hath laid her choice up - on her, And the work she doth is His.

(Or to Rathbun)

2 He His Church has firmly founded,
He will guard what He began;
We by sin and foes surrounded,
Build her bulwarks as we can.

3 Frail and fleeting are our powers,
Short our days, our foresight dim,
And we own the choice not ours,
We were chosen first by Him.

4 Onward, then! for nought despairing,
Calm we follow at His Word,
Thus through joy and sorrow bearing
Faithful witness to our Lord.

5 Though we here must strive in weakness,
Though in tears we often bend,
What His might began in meekness
Shall achieve a glorious end.

Paul Flemming C. Winkworth, Tr.

468 St. Thomas S. M.

1 I love Thy Zion, Lord,
The house of Thine abode,
The Church our blest Redeemer saved
With His own precious blood.

2 I love Thy Church, O God!
Her walls before Thee stand,
Dear as the apple of Thine eye,
And graven on Thy hand.

3 Should I with scoffers join
Her altars to abuse?
No! better far my tongue were dumb,
My hand its skill should lose.

4 For her my tears shall fall;
For her my prayers ascend;
To her my cares and toils be given,
Till toils and cares shall end.

5 Beyond my highest joy
I prize her heavenly ways,
Her sweet communion, solemn vows,
Her hymns of love and praise.

6 Jesus, Thou Friend divine,
Our Savior and our King,
Thy hand from every snare and foe
Shall great deliverance bring.

7 Sure as Thy truth shall last,
To Zion shall be given
The brightest glories earth can yield,
And brighter bliss of heaven.

T. Dwight, 1800 a

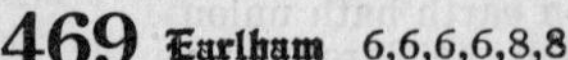

469 Earlham 6,6,6,6,8,8

J. BOOTH, 1852

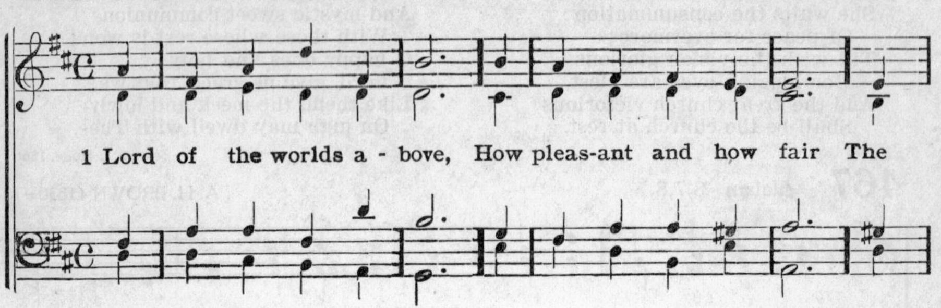
1 Lord of the worlds a - bove, How pleas-ant and how fair The

dwel - lings of Thy love, Thine earth-ly tem - ples are! To Thine a-

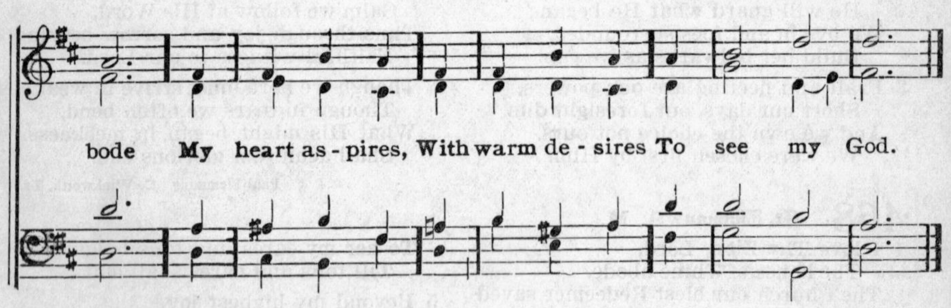
bode My heart as - pires, With warm de - sires To see my God.

(Or to Darwall)

2 Oh, happy souls who pray
Where God appoints to hear!
Oh, happy men who pay
Their constant service there!
They praise Thee still;
And happy they
Who love the way
To Zion's hill.

3 They go from strength to strength
Through this dark vale of tears,
Till each arrives at length,
Till each in heaven appears.
Oh, glorious seat,
When God our King
Shall thither bring
Our willing feet!

Isaac Watts, 1719

Church

Mission

470 Her vil ties, her vil bies 8,7 6 1 L. M. LINDEMAN, (1812–87)

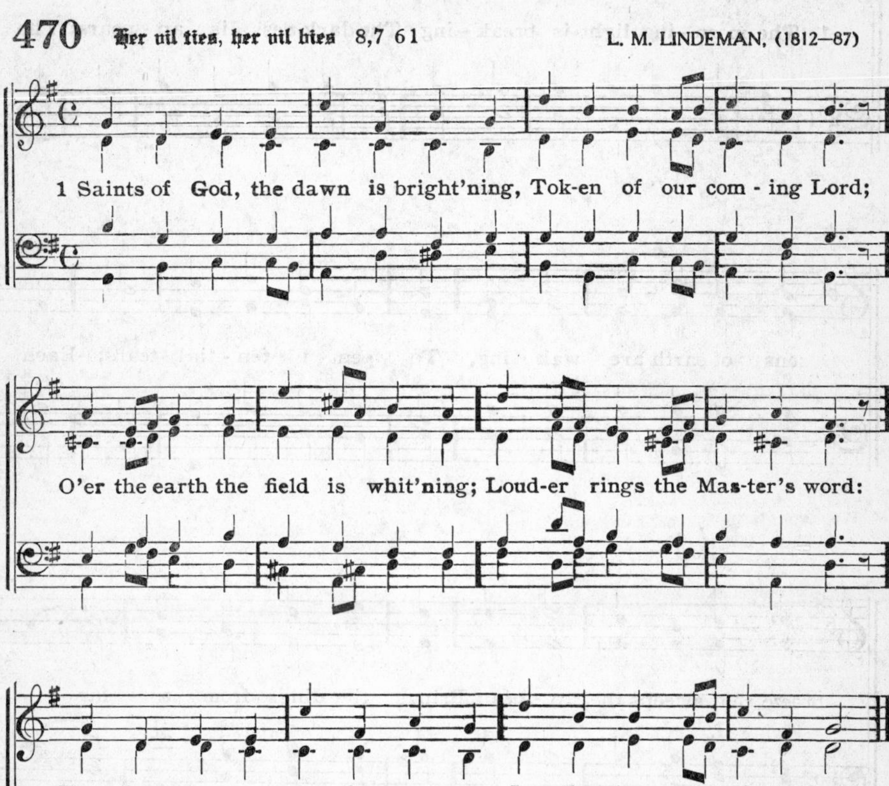

1 Saints of God, the dawn is bright'ning, Tok-en of our com - ing Lord;
O'er the earth the field is whit'ning; Loud-er rings the Mas-ter's word:
Pray for reap-ers, pray for reap - ers, In the har - vest of the Lord!

(Or to Regent Square)

2 Now, O Lord, fulfil Thy pleasure,
Breathe upon Thy chosen band,
And, with Pentecostal measure,
Send forth reapers o'er our land;
Faithful reapers
Gathering sheaves for Thy right hand.

3 Broad the shadow of our nation,
Eager millions hither roam;
Lo! they wait for Thy salvation;
Come, Lord Jesus, quickly come;
By Thy Spirit
Bring Thy ransomed people home.

4 Soon shall end the time of weeping,
Soon the reaping time will come;
Heaven and earth together keeping
God's eternal Harvest-Home.
Saints and angels
Shout the world's great Harvest-Home.

M. Maxwell, 1849

471 Webb 7,6 8 l

G. J. WEBB, 1830

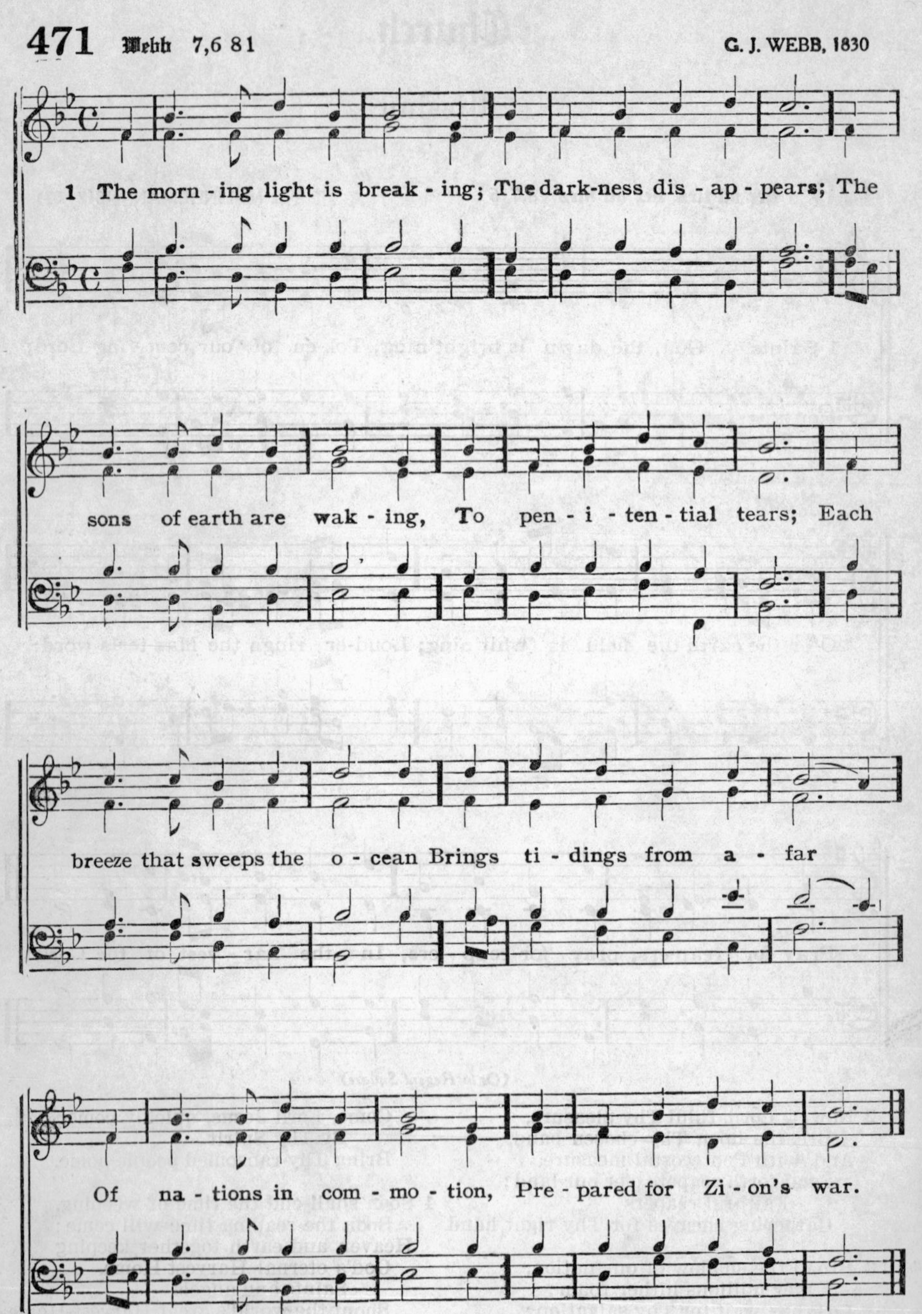
1 The morn - ing light is break - ing; The dark-ness dis - ap - pears; The
sons of earth are wak - ing, To pen - i - ten - tial tears; Each
breeze that sweeps the o - cean Brings ti - dings from a - far
Of na - tions in com - mo - tion, Pre - pared for Zi - on's war.

2 See heathen nations bending
Before the God we love,
And thousand hearts ascending
In gratitude above;
While sinners, now confessing,
The Gospel call obey,
And seek the Savior's blessing,
A nation in a day.

3 Blest river of salvation,
Pursue thy onward way;
Flow thou to every nation,
Nor in thy richness stay;
Stay not till all the lowly
Triumphant reach their home;
Stay not till all the holy
Proclaim "The Lord is come!"

S. F. Smith, 1832

472 Webb 7,6, 81

1 Our country's voice is pleading,
Ye men of God, arise!
His providence is leading,
The land before you lies;
Day-gleams are o'er it brightening,
And promise clothes the soil;
Wide fields, for harvest whitening,
Invite the reaper's toil.

2 Go, where the waves are breaking
On California's shore,
Christ's precious Gospel taking,
More rich than golden ore;
On Alleghany's mountains,
Through all the western vale,
Beside Missouri's fountains,
Rehearse the wondrous tale.

3 The love of Christ unfolding,
Speed on from east to west,
Till all, His cross beholding,
In Him are fully blessed.
Great author of salvation,
Haste, haste the glorious day,
When we, a ransomed nation,
Thy scepter shall obey.

Maria F. Anderson, 1848

(Or to Jeg vil mig Herren love)

473 Welcombe L. M.

1 O Spirit of the living God,
In all Thy plenitude of grace,
Where'er the foot of man hath trod,
Descend on our apostate race.

2 Give tongues of fire and hearts of love,
To preach the reconciling Word;
Give power and unction from above,
Where'er the joyful sound is heard.

3 Be darkness, at Thy coming, light;
Confusion—order, in Thy path;
Souls without strength inspire with might;
Bid mercy triumph over wrath.

4 O Spirit of the Lord, prepare
A sinful world their God to meet;
Breathe Thou abroad like morning air,
Till hearts of stone begin to beat.

5 Baptize the nations; far and nigh
The triumphs of the cross record;
The name of Jesus glorify,
Till every kindred call Him Lord.

6 God from eternity hath willed,
All flesh shall His salvation see:
So be the Father's love fulfilled,
The Savior's sufferings crowned through Thee.

James Montgomery, 1825

474 Missionary Hymn 7,6 8 1

L. MASON, 1823

1 From Greenland's i - cy mount-ains, From In - dia's co - ral strand,
Where Af - ric's sun - ny fount - ains Roll down their gold - en sand;
From many an an - cient riv - er, From many a palm-y plain,
They call us to de - liv - er Their land from er - ror's chain.

2 What though the spicy breezes
Blow soft o'er Ceylon's isle;
Though every prospect pleases,
And only man is vile;
In vain with lavish kindness
The gifts of God are strown;
The heathen in his blindness,
Bows down to wood and stone.

3 Shall we, whose souls are lighted
With wisdom from on high,—
Shall we to men benighted
The lamp of life deny?
Salvation, O salvation!
The joyful sound proclaim,
Till earth's remotest nation
Has learned Messiah's name.

4 Waft, waft, ye winds, His story,
And you, ye waters, roll,
Till, like a sea of glory,
It spreads from pole to pole;
Till o'er our ransomed nature
The Lamb for sinners slain,
Redeemer, King, Creator,
In bliss returns to reign.

R. Heber, 1819

475 O Jesu Christ, meins Lebens Licht L. M.

NUERNBERG H. B. 1676

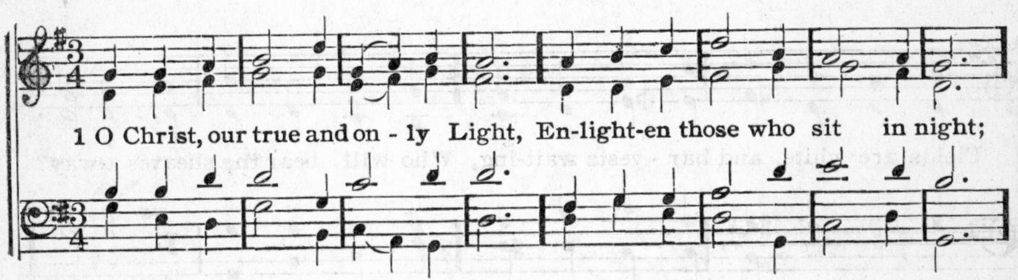
1 O Christ, our true and on - ly Light, En-light-en those who sit in night;

Let those a - far now hear Thy voice, And in Thy fold with us re-joice.

2 Fill with the radiance of Thy grace
The souls now lost in error's maze,
And all whom in their secret minds
Some dark delusion haunts and blinds.

3 And all who else have strayed from Thee,
O gently seek! Thy healing be
To every wounded conscience given,
And let them also share Thy heaven.

4 O make the deaf to hear Thy Word,
And teach the dumb to speak, dear Lord,
Who dare not yet the faith avow,
Though secretly they hold it now.

5 Shine on the darkened and the cold,
Recall the wanderers from Thy fold,
Unite all those who walk apart,
Confirm the weak and doubting heart.

6 So they with us may evermore
Such grace with wondering thanks adore,
And endless praise to Thee be given
By all Thy Church in earth and heaven.

Martin Behm, 1608 C. Winkworth, Tr. a

476 Galilean 8,7 8 l J. BARNBY, 1883 (P)

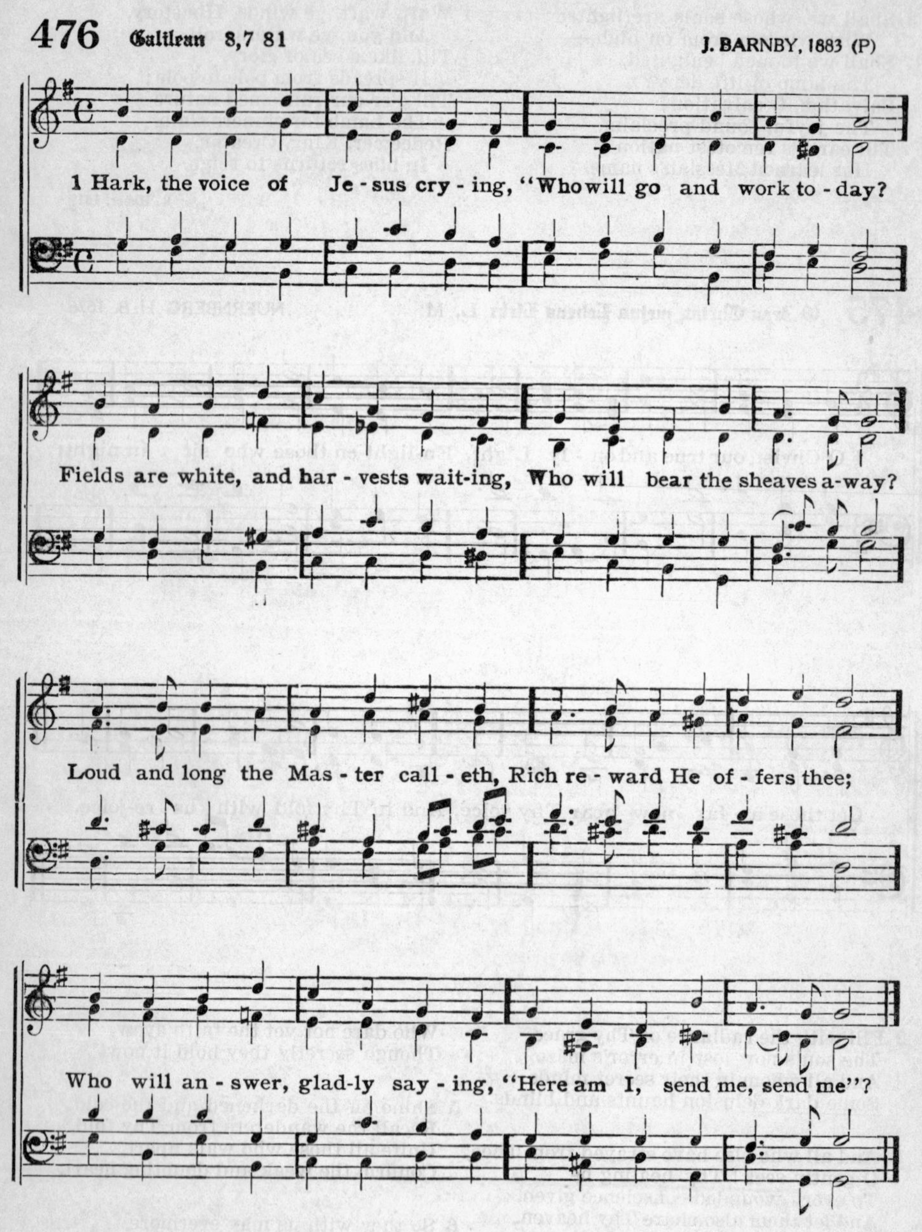
1 Hark, the voice of Je - sus cry - ing, "Who will go and work to - day?
Fields are white, and har - vests wait-ing, Who will bear the sheaves a-way?
Loud and long the Mas - ter call - eth, Rich re - ward He of - fers thee;
Who will an - swer, glad-ly say - ing, "Here am I, send me, send me"?

2 If you cannot cross the ocean,
And the heathen lands explore,
You can find the heathen nearer,
You can help them at your door;

If you cannot give your thousands,
You can give the widow's mite,
And the least you give for Jesus
Will be precious in His sight.

3 If you cannot speak like angels,
If you cannot preach like Paul,
You can tell the love of Jesus,
You can say He died for all.
If you cannot rouse the wicked,
With the judgment's dread alarms,
You can lead the little children
To the Savior's waiting arms.

4 Let none hear you idly saying,
"There is nothing I can do,"
While the souls of men are dying,
And the Master calls for you.
Take the task He gives you gladly,
Let His work your pleasure be;
Answer quickly when He calleth—
"Here am I, send me, send me."

D. March 1808

477 Galilean 8,7 81

1 Savior, sprinkle many nations;
Fruitful let Thy sorrows be;
By Thy pains and consolations
Draw the Gentiles unto Thee!
Of Thy cross the wondrous story,
Be it to the nations told;
Let them see Thee in Thy glory
And Thy mercy manifold.

2 Far and wide, though all unknowing,
Pants for Thee each mortal breast,
Human tears for Thee are flowing,
Human hearts in Thee would rest.
Thirsting as for dews of even,
As the new-mown grass for rain,
Thee they seek as God of heaven,
Thee as Man for sinners slain.

3 Savior, lo! the isles are waiting!
Stretched the hand and strained the sight,
For Thy Spirit, new creating,
Love's pure flame, and wisdom's light.
Give the word, and of the preacher
Speed the foot and touch the tongue,
Till on earth by every creature
Glory to the Lamb be sung!

Bishop Coxe 1851

(Or to Autumn   Or to O mein Jesu)

478 Ellers 10s

1 Rise, crowned with light, imperial Salem, rise!
Exalt thy towering head, and lift thine eyes;
See heaven its sparkling portals wide display,
And break upon thee in a flood of day.

2 See a long race thy spacious court adorn;
See future sons and daughters yet unborn
In crowding ranks on every side arise,
Demanding life, impatient for the skies.

3 See barbarous nations at thy gates attend,
Walk in the light and in thy temple bend;
See thy bright altars thronged with prostrate kings,
While every land its joyful tribute brings.

4 The seas shall waste, the skies to smoke decay,
Rocks fall to dust, and mountains melt away;
But fixed this Word, this saving power remains;
Thy realms shall last, thy own Messiah reigns!

Alexander Pope, 1720

479 Quebec (Hesperus) L. M. H. BAKER, 1866

1 Look from Thy sphere of endless day, O God of mer - cy and of night;

In pit - y look on those who stray Be-night-ed, in this land of light.

2 In peopled vale, in lonely glen,
In crowded mart, by stream or sea,
How many of the sons of men
Hear not the message sent from Thee!

3 Send forth Thy heralds, Lord, to call
The thoughtless young, the hardened old,
A scattered, homeless flock, till all
Be gathered to Thy peaceful fold.

4 Send them Thy mighty Word to speak,
Till faith shall dawn, and doubt depart,
To awe the bold, to stay the weak,
And bind and heal the broken heart.

5 Then all these wastes, a dreary scene,
That makes us sadden as we gaze,
Shall grow with living waters green,
And lift to heaven the voice of praise.

W. C. Bryant, 1859

480 Es wollt uns Gott genädig 8,7,8,7,8,7,8,7,7 M. GREUTER, 1524

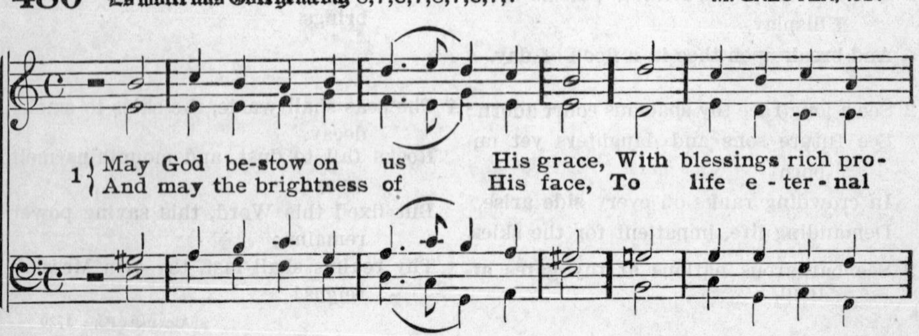
1 May God be-stow on us His grace, With blessings rich pro-
And may the brightness of His face, To life e - ter - nal

vide . . . . us,
guide . . . . us; That we His gracious work may know, And

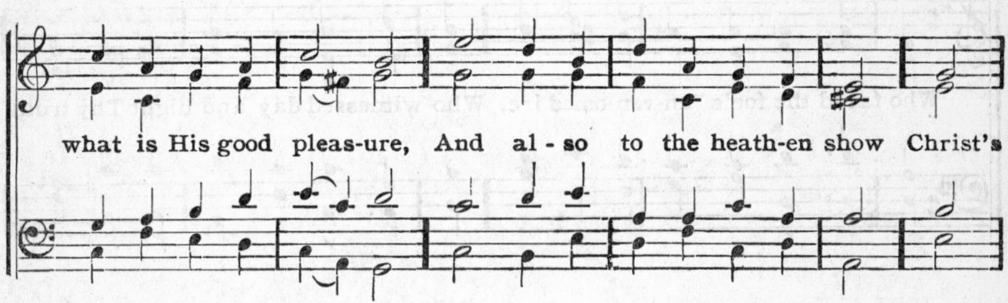
what is His good pleas-ure, And al - so to the heath-en show Christ's

rich-es with-out meas - ure, And un - to God con - vert them.

2 Thine over all shall be the praise
And thanks of every nation,
And all the world with joy shall raise
The voice of exultation;
For Thou shalt judge the earth, O Lord,
Nor suffer sin to flourish;
Thy people's pasture is Thy Word
Their souls to feed and nourish,
In righteous paths to keep them.

3 O let the people praise Thy worth,
In all good works increasing;
The land shall plenteous fruit bring forth,
Thy word is rich in blessing.
May God the Father, God the Son,
And God the Spirit bless us!
Let all the world praise Him alone,
Let solemn awe possess us.
Now let our hearts say, Amen.

Dr. Martin Luther, 1524

481 Saints of God L. M. 61 A. S. SULLIVAN (P and I)

1 Awake, Thou Spir-it, who didst fire The watchmen of the Church's youth,
Who faced the foe's en-ven-omed ire, Who witnessed day and night Thy truth,
Whose voi - ces loud are ring-ing still, And bringing hosts to know Thy will.

2 Lord, let our earnest prayer be heard,
The prayer Thy Son hath bid us pray,
For lo, Thy children's hearts are stirred
In every land in this our day,
To cry with fervent soul to Thee,
O help us, Lord! so let it be!

3 O haste to help, ere we are lost!
Send preachers forth, in spirit strong,
Armed with Thy Word, a dauntless host,
Bold to attack the rule of wrong;
Let them the earth for Thee reclaim,
Thy heritage, to know Thy name.

4 Would there were help within our walls!
O let Thy Spirit come again,
Before whom every barrier falls,
And now once more shine forth as then!
O rend the heavens and make us free!
Come, Lord, and bring us back to Thee!

5 And let Thy Word have speedy course,
Through every land be glorified,
Till all the heathen know its force,
And fill Thy churches far and wide;
Wake Israel from his sleep, O Lord,
And spread the conquest of Thy Word!

6 The Church's desert paths restore;
Let stumbling-blocks that in them lie
Hinder Thy Word henceforth no more:
Error destroy, and heresy,
And let Thy Church, from hirelings free,
Bloom as a garden fair to Thee!

Charles Henry Bogatsky 1750 C. Winkworth, Tr. 1855

482 Torgau 7s

Ad. fr. J. GROBE, 1840

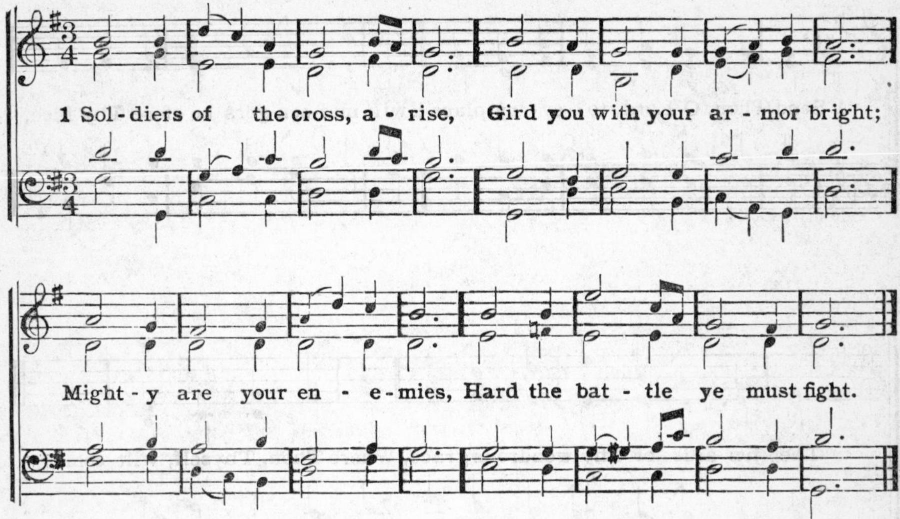
1 Sol - diers of the cross, a - rise, Gird you with your ar - mor bright;
Might - y are your en - e - mies, Hard the bat - tle ye must fight.

(Or to Redhead Or to Innocents)

2 O'er a faithless fallen world
Raise your banner in the sky;
Let it float there wide unfurled;
Bear it onward; lift it high.

3 'Mid the homes of want and woe,
Strangers to the living word,
Let the Savior's herald go,
Let the voice of hope be heard.

4 Where the shadows deepest lie,
Carry truth's unsullied ray;
Where are crimes of blackest dye,
There the saving sign display.

5 To the weary and the worn
Tell of realms where sorrows cease;
To the outcast and forlorn
Speak of mercy and of peace.

6 Guard the helpless; seek the strayed;
Comfort troubles; banish grief;
In the might of God arrayed,
Scatter sin and unbelief.

7 Be the banner still unfurled,
Still unsheathed the Spirit's sword,
Till the kingdoms of the world
Are the kingdom of the Lord.

W. W. How, 1854

483 Duke Street L. M.

1 Jesus shall reign where'er the sun
Does his successive journeys run;
His kingdom stretch from shore to shore,
Till moons shall wax and wane no more.

2 For Him shall endless prayer be made,
And endless praises crown His head;
His name, like sweet perfume, shall rise
With every morning sacrifice.

3 People and realms of every tongue
Dwell on His love with sweetest song;
And infant voices shall proclaim
Their early blessings on His name.

4 Blessings abound where'er He reigns;
The prisoner leaps to loose his chains;
The weary find eternal rest,
And all the sons of want are blest.

5 Where He displays His healing power,
Death and the curse are known no more;
In Him the tribes of Adam boast
More blessings than their father lost.

6 Let every creature rise and bring
Peculiar honors to our King;
Angels descend with songs again,
And earth repeat the loud Amen.

Isaac Watts, 1719

484 Elmhurst 8,8,8,6 E. D. DREWETT, 1887 (P)

1 Send Thou, O Lord, to ev-'ry place Swift mes-sen-gers be-fore Thy face,

The her-alds of Thy wondrous grace, Where Thou, Thyself, wilt come.

(Or to Dunstan)

2 Send men whose eyes have seen the King,
Men in whose ears His sweet words ring;
Send such Thy lost ones home to bring;
Send them where Thou wilt come.

3 To bring good news to souls in sin;
The bruised and broken hearts to win;
In every place to bring them in;
Where Thou, Thyself, wilt come.

4 Thou who hast died, Thy victory claim;
Assert, O Christ, Thy glory's name,
And far to lands of pagan shame,
Send men where Thou wilt come.

5 Gird each one with the Spirit's sword,
The sword of Thine own deathless word;
And make them conquerors, conquering Lord,
Where Thou, Thyself, wilt come.

6 Raise up, O Lord the Holy Ghost,
From this broad land a mighty host,
Their war-cry, "We will seek the lost,
Where Thou, O Christ, wilt come!"

Mrs. Merrill E. Gates, 1889

Church

The Ministry

485 Purleigh 8,8,6,8,8,6 (C. P. M.) ARTH. H. BROWN

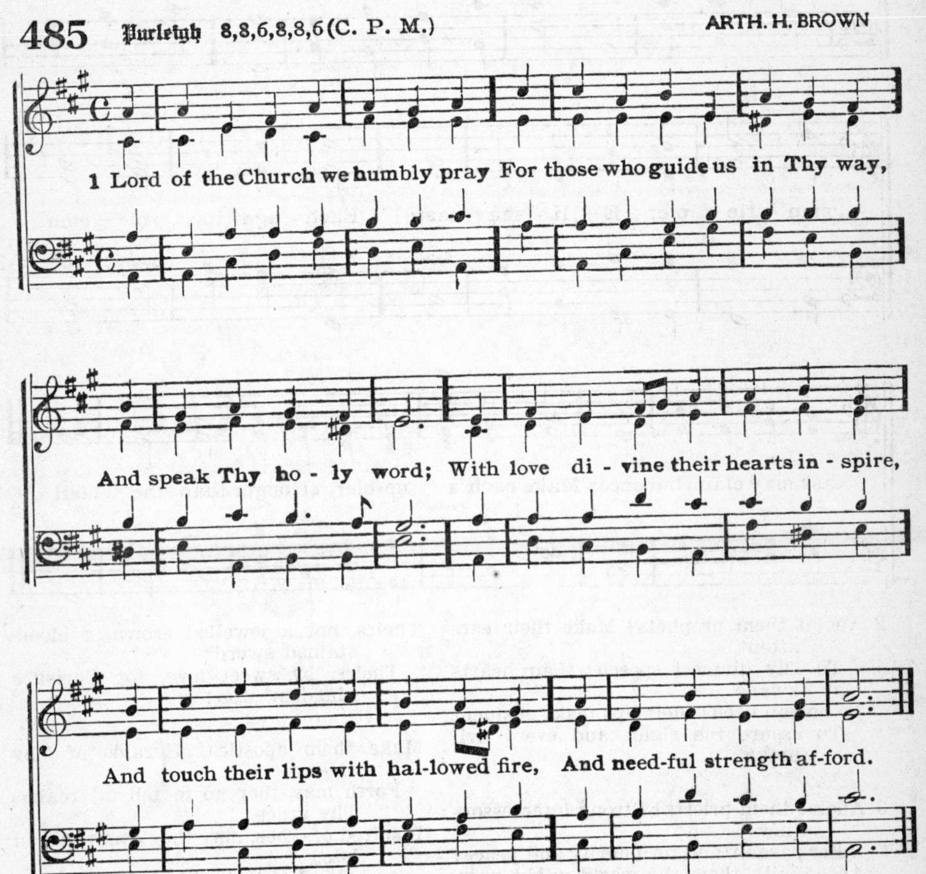

1 Lord of the Church we humbly pray For those who guide us in Thy way,
And speak Thy ho - ly word; With love di - vine their hearts in - spire,
And touch their lips with hal-lowed fire, And need-ful strength af-ford.

2 Help them to preach the truth of God,
Redemption through the Savior's blood;
Nor let the Spirit cease
On all the Church His gifts to shower;
To them a messenger of power,
To us, of life and peace.

3 So may they live to Thee alone;
Then hear the welcome word, "Well done!"
And take their crown above;
Enter into their Master's joy,
And all eternity employ
In praise, and bliss, and love.

E. Osler, 1836

486 Toulon (Old 124th) 10,10,10,10 L. BOURGEOIS, GENEVA PSALTER, 1543

1 God of the proph - ets! bless the proph-ets' sons; E - li - jah's
man - tle o'er E - li - sha cast; Each age its sol - emn
task may claim but once; Make each a no-bler, stronger than the last!

2 Anoint them prophets! Make their ears attent
To Thy divinest speech; their hearts awake
To human need; their lips make eloquent
To assure the right, and every evil break.

3 Anoint them priests! Strong intercessors they
For pardon, and for charity and peace!
Ah, if with them the world might pass, astray,
Into the dear Christ's life of sacrifice!

4 Anoint them kings! aye kingly kings, O Lord!
Anoint them with the spirit of Thy Son!
Theirs, not a jewelled crown, a blood-stained sword;
Theirs, by sweet love, for Christ a kingdom won!

5 Make them apostles! Heralds of Thy cross;
Forth may they go to tell all realms Thy grace;
Inspired of Thee, may they count all but loss,
And stand at last with joy before Thy face.

6 O mighty age of prophet-kings, return!
O truth, O faith, enrich our urgent time!
Lord Jesus Christ, again with us sojourn;
A weary world awaits Thy reign sublime!

D. Wortman, 1884

487 Leominster S. M. 81

GEO. WILLIAM MARTIN, 1862
Har. by SIR ARTHUR SULLIVAN, 1874

Slowly.
1 Lord, when at Thy com - mand, The word of life we sow,
Wa-tered by Thy al-might-y hand, The seed shall sure - ly grow:
The vir - tue of Thy grace A large in-crease shall give,
And mul - ti - ply the faith-ful race Who to Thy glo - ry live.

(Or to *Dulce Domum*)

2 Now then the ceaseless shower
Of gospel blessings send,
And let the soul-converting power
Thy ministers attend.

On multitudes confer
The heart-renewing love,
And by the joy of grace prepare
For fuller joys above.

C. Wesley.

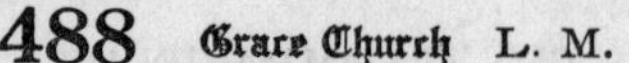

488 Grace Church L. M.

Fr. I. J. PLEYEL, 1800

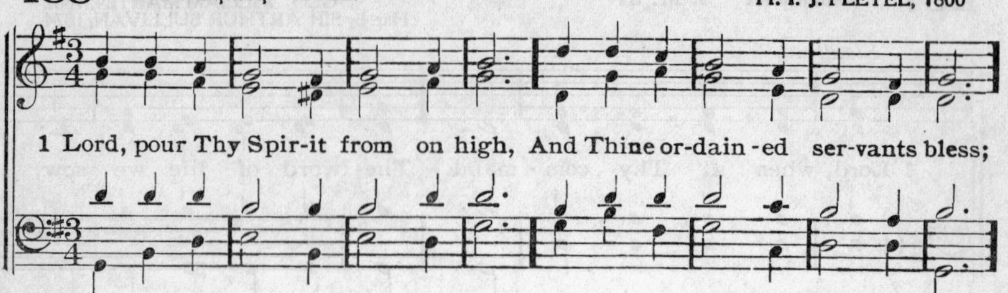
1 Lord, pour Thy Spir-it from on high, And Thine or-dain -ed ser-vants bless;

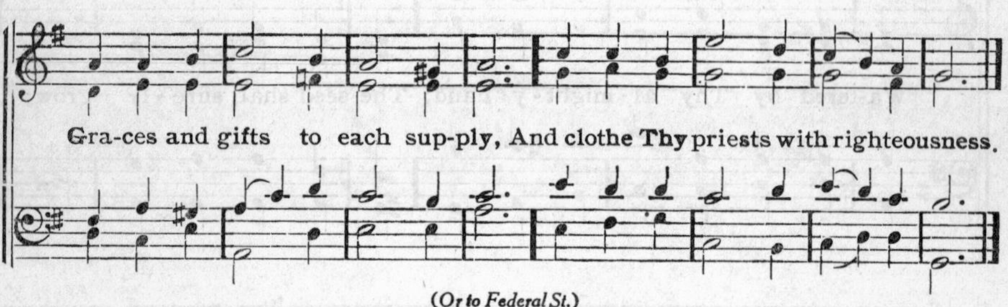
Gra-ces and gifts to each sup-ply, And clothe Thy priests with righteousness.

(*Or to Federal St.*)

2 Within Thy temple when they stand,
To teach the truth as taught by Thee,
Savior, like stars in Thy right hand,
Let all Thy Church's pastors be.

3 Wisdom, and zeal, and faith impart,
Firmness and meekness from above,
To bear Thy people in their heart,
And love the souls whom Thou dost love;

4 To watch and pray, and never faint,
By day and night strict guard to keep,
To warn the sinner, cheer the saint,
To feed Thy lambs, and fold Thy sheep.

5 So, when their work is finished here,
They may in hope their charge resign;
So, when their Master shall appear,
They may with crowns of glory shine.

James Montgomery, 1833

489 Grace Church L. M.

1 We bid thee welcome, in the name
Of Jesus, our exalted Head:
Come as a servant, so He came,
And we receive thee in His stead.

2 Come as a shepherd; guard and keep
This fold from hell, and earth, and sin,
Nourish the lambs, and feed the sheep
The wounded heal, the lost bring in.

3 Come as a teacher, sent from God,
Charged His whole counsel to declare;
Lift o'er our ranks the prophet's rod,
While we uphold thy hands with prayer.

4 Come as a messenger of peace,
Filled with the spirit, fired with love;
Live to behold our large increase,
And die to meet us all above.

James Montgomery ab.

490 St. Michael S. M.

L. BOURGEOIS, GENEVA PSALTER, 1543

1 How beau-teous are their feet, Who stand on Zi - on's hill;

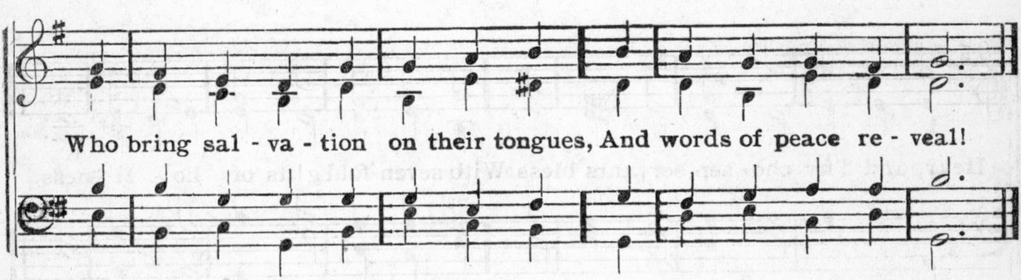
Who bring sal - va - tion on their tongues, And words of peace re - veal!

(*Or to Thatcher Or to St. Thomas*)

2 How charming is their voice;
How sweet their tidings are!
"Zion, behold thy Savior-King;
He reigns and triumphs here."

3 How happy are our ears
That hear this joyful sound,
Which kings and prophets waited for,
And sought, but never found.

4 How blessed are our eyes
That see this heavenly light;
Prophets and kings desired it long,
But died without the sight.

5 The watchmen join their voice,
And tuneful notes employ;
Jerusalem breaks forth in songs,
And deserts learn the joy.

6 The Lord makes bare His arm
Through all the earth abroad:
Let every nation now behold
Their Savior and their God.

Isaac Watts, 1707

491 St. Michael S. M.

1 Lord of the harvest, hear
Thy needy servants' cry;
Answer our faith's effectual prayer,
And all our wants supply.

2 On Thee we humbly wait,
Our wants are in Thy view:
The harvest, truly, Lord, is great,
The laborers are few.

3 Convert and send forth more
Into Thy Church abroad,
And let them speak Thy Word of power,
As workers with their God.

4 Oh, let them spread Thy name,
Their mission fully prove:
Thy universal grace proclaim,
Thine all-redeeming love.

Charles Wesley, 1742

(*Or to Mornington*)

492 Wavertree L. M. 61

W. SHORE (P)

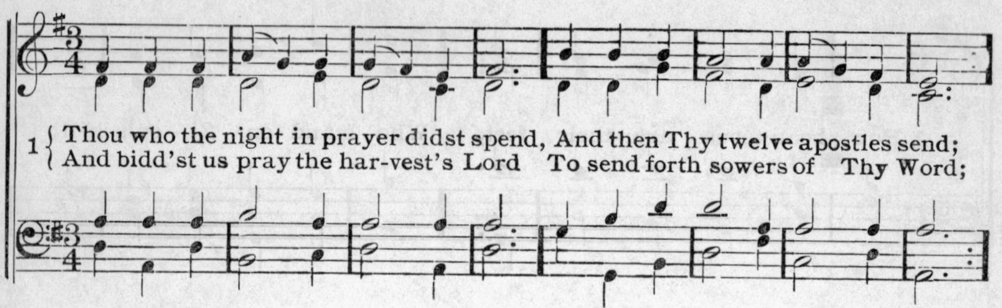
1 { Thou who the night in prayer didst spend, And then Thy twelve apostles send;
And bidd'st us pray the har-vest's Lord To send forth sowers of Thy Word;

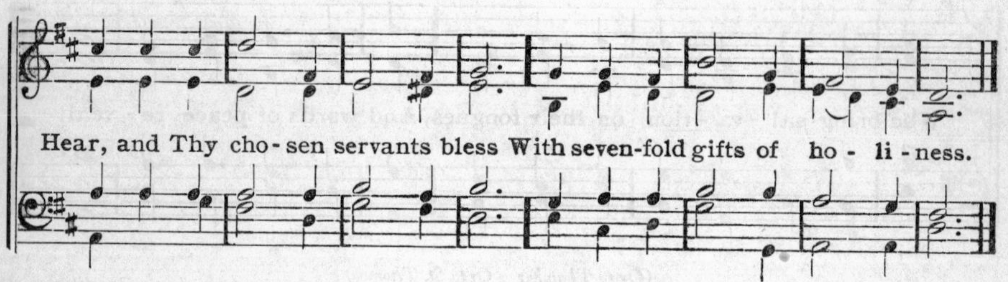
Hear, and Thy cho-sen servants bless With seven-fold gifts of ho - li - ness.

2 Oh, may Thy pastors faithful be,
Not laboring for themselves, but Thee;
Give grace to feed with wholesome food;
The sheep and lambs bought by Thy blood;
To tend Thy flock, and thus to prove
How dearly they the Shepherd love!

3 Oh, may Thy people faithful be,
And in Thy pastors honor Thee,
And with them work, and for them pray,
And gladly Thee in them obey;
Receive the prophet of the Lord,
And gain the prophet's own reward!

4 So may we, when our work is done,
Together stand before the throne;
And joyful hearts and voices raise
In one united song of praise,
With all the bright celestial host,
To Father, Son, and Holy Ghost.

C. Wordsworth

493 Quebec L. M.

1 Bow down Thine ear, almighty Lord,
And hear Thy Church's suppliant cry
For all who preach Thy saving Word,
And wait upon Thy ministry.

2 In mercy, Father, now give heed,
And pour Thy quickening Spirit's breath
On those whom Thou dost call to feed
Thy flock redeemed by Jesus' death.

3 O Savior, from Thy pierced hand
Shed o'er them all Thy gifts divine:
That those who in Thy presence stand
May do Thy will with love like Thine.

4 Blest Spirit, in their hearts abide,
And give them grace to watch and pray;
That as they seek Thy flock to guide,
Themselves may keep the narrow way.

5 O God, Thy strength and mercy send
To shield them in their strife with sin;
Grant them, enduring to the end,
The crown of life at last to win.

Thos. Edw. Powell, 1864

Cross and Comfort

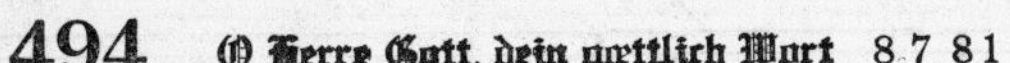
494 O Herre Gott, dein göttlich Wort

8,7 8 1 ERFURT ENCHIRIDION, 1527

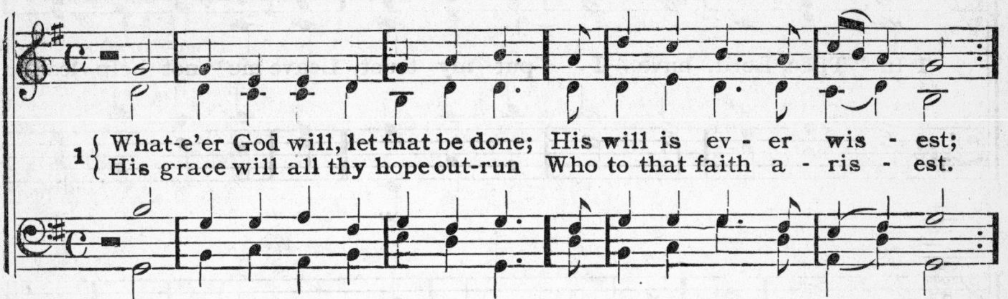
1 { What-e'er God will, let that be done; His will is ev - er wis - est;
His grace will all thy hope out-run Who to that faith a - ris - est.

The gracious Lord Will help af-ford, He chas-tens with for - bear - ing;

Who God believes, And to Him cleaves, Shall not be left de - spair - ing.

2 My God is my sure Confidence,
My Hope and my Existence;
His counsel is beyond my sense,
Yet I'll not make resistance.
His Word declares The very hairs
Upon my head are numbered;
His mercy large Holds me in charge,
With care that never slumbered.

3 The time has come when, at His will,
My life in this world ceases;
I think upon it, and am still,
Let come whate'er He pleases.
To Him I trust My soul, my dust,
When flesh and spirit sever,
The Christ we sing Has plucked the sting
Away from death forever.

4 Yet one thing, Lord, I ask of Thee,
O grant my supplication:
When Satan sorely tempteth me,
Save me from desperation.
O God my Lord, True to Thy Word,
Do Thou my soul deliver!
Who doth believe, He shall receive.
Thy name be praised forever!

Anon. N. L. Frothingham, Tr. a

495 In dich hab ich gehoffet 8,8,7,8,7

S. CALVISIUS, 1594
MELCH. VULPIUS, 1604

1 In Thee, Lord, have I put my trust, Leave me not help-less
in the dust, Let me not be con-found-ed; Let
in Thy Word My faith, O Lord, Be al-ways firm-ly ground-ed.

2 Bow down Thy gracious ear to me,
And hear my prayers, Lord, speedily
O grant me Thy protection;
For woes and fear Surround me here
Help me in my affliction.

3 My God and shield, now let Thy power
Be unto me a mighty tower,
Whence bravely I defend me
Against the foes That round me close;
O Lord, assistance lend me!

4 Thy Word hath said, Thou art my rock,
The fortress than can fear no shock,
My help, my life, my treasure;
Howe'er distress And dangers press,
All must perform Thy pleasure.

5 The world for me has falsely set
Full many a secret snare and net,
Dark lies and sore temptations;
Lord hear my prayers, And break these snares
And hellish machinations.

6 With Thee, Lord, would I cast my lot;
My God, my God, forsake me not,
For, Lord, I am commending
My soul to thee; Deliver me
Now and when life is ending.

7 All honor, praise, and majesty
To Father, Son, and Spirit be,
Our God forever glorious,
In whose rich grace We'll run our race,
Till we depart victorious.

Adam Reussner, 1533 C. Winkworth, Tr. a

496 St. Bernard C. M.

J. RICHARDSON

1 Lord, it be - longs not to my care, Wheth-er I die or live;

To love and serve Thee is my share, And this Thy grace must give.

(Or to St. Agnes)

2 If life be long, I will be glad
That I may long obey;
If short, yet why should I be sad
To soar to endless day?

3 Christ leads me through no darker rooms
Than He went through before;
He that into God's kingdom comes
Must enter by this door.

4 Come, Lord, when grace has made me meet
Thy blessed face to see;
For if Thy work on earth is sweet,
What will Thy glory be?

5 Then shall I end my sad complaints,
And weary sinful days,
And join with the triumphant saints,
That sing Jehovah's praise.

6 My knowledge of that life is small,
The eye of faith is dim;
But 'tis enough that Christ knows all,
And I shall be with Him.

Richard Baxter, 1681 a

497 St. Bernard C. M.

1 O Thou, from whom all goodness flows,
I lift my heart to Thee;
In all my sorrows, conflicts, woes,
Dear Lord, remember me!

2 When on my aching, burdened heart
My sins lie heavily,
My pardon speak, new peace impart;
In love remember me.

3 Temptations sore obstruct my way,
And ills I cannot flee;
O give me strength, Lord, as my day;
For good remember me.

4 Distrest with pain, disease, and grief,
This feeble body see;
Grant patience, rest, and kind relief;
Hear, and remember me!

5 When in the solemn hour of death
I wait Thy just decree,
Be this the prayer of my last breath,
Good Lord, remember me!

6 And when before Thy throne I stand
And lift my soul to Thee;
Then with the saints at Thy right hand,
Good Lord, remember me!

T. Haweis and T. Cotterill, 1792, a

(Or to Winchester Old)

498 Wer nur den lieben Gott laesst 9,8,9,8,8,8

G. NEUMARK, 1640

1 { If Thou but suf - fer God to guide thee; And hope in
He'll give thee strength, what-e'er be - tide thee, And bear thee
Him through all thy ways,
through the e - vil ways, Who trusts in God's un -
chang - ing love Builds on the Rock that naught can move.

2 What can these anxious cares avail thee,
These never-ceasing moans and sighs?
What can it help, if thou bewail thee
O'er each dark moment as it flies?
Our cross and trials do but press
Thee heavier for our bitterness.

3 Only be still and wait His leisure
In cheerful hope with heart content,
To take whate'er thy Father's pleasure
And His discerning love hath sent;
Nor doubt our inmost wants are known
To Him who chose us for His own.

4 He knows the time for joy, and truly,
Will send it when He sees it meet;
When He has tried and purged thee duly
And finds thee free from all deceit,
He comes to thee all unaware,
And makes thee own His loving care.

5 Nor think amid the heat of trial
That God hath cast thee off unheard;
That he whose hopes meet no denial
Must surely be of God preferred;
Time passes and much change doth bring,
And sets a bound to everything.

6 All are alike before the Highest;
'Tis easy to our God, we know,
To raise thee up, though low thou liest,
To make the rich man poor and low;
True wonders still by Him are wrought,
Who setteth up and brings to naught.

7 Sing, pray, and keep His ways unswerving;
So do thine own part faithfully,
And trust His word, though undeserving,
Thou yet shalt find it true for thee;
God never will forsake in need
The soul that trusts in Him indeed.

Georg Neumark, 1657 C. Winkworth, Tr. a

499 Wer nur den lieben Gott laesst walten 9,8,9,8,8,8

1 I leave all things to God's direction,
He loveth me in weal and woe;
His will is good, true His affection,
With tender love his heart doth glow.
My fortress and my rock is He:
What pleaseth God, that pleaseth me.

2 My God hath all things in His keeping,
He is the ever faithful Friend,
He grants me laughter after weeping,
And all His ways in blessings end.
His love endures eternally:
What pleaseth God, that pleaseth me.

3 The will of God shall be my pleasure,
While here on earth is mine abode;
My will is wrong beyond all measure,
It doth not will what pleaseth God.
The Christian's maxim e'er must be:
What pleaseth God, that pleaseth me.

4 God knows what must be done to save me,
His love for me will never cease,
For He upon His palms did grave me
With purest gold of loving grace.
Avaunt, my own will, off with thee!
What pleaseth God, that pleaseth me.

5 My God desires the soul's salvation,
Me also He desires to save;
Therefore, with Christian resignation,
All earthly troubles I will brave.
His will be done eternally:
What pleaseth God, that pleaseth me

Anon. Before 1697 A. Crull, Tr.

500 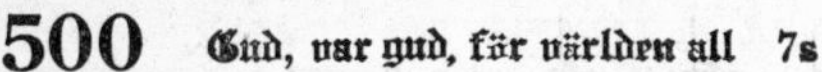
Gud, var gud, för världen all 7s

J. F. LAGERGREN

1 Oft in sor - row, oft in woe, On-ward, Christians, on-ward go;

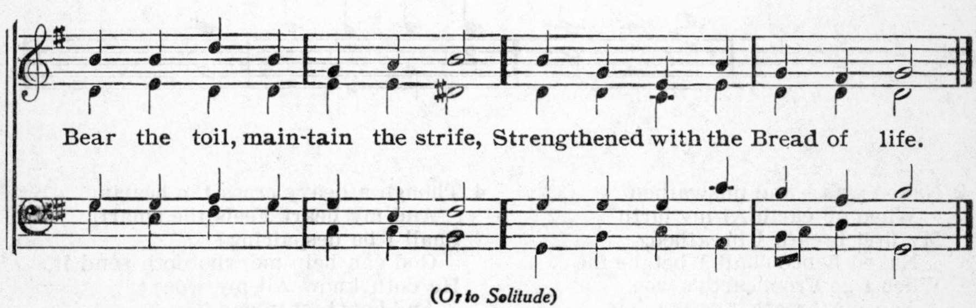
Bear the toil, main-tain the strife, Strengthened with the Bread of life.

(Or to Solitude)

2 Let not sorrow dim your eye,
Soon shall every tear be dry;
Let not woe your course impede,
Great your help, if great your need.

3 Let your drooping hearts be glad;
March, in heavenly armor clad;
Fight, nor think the battle long;
Victory soon shall tune your song.

4 Onward then to battle move,
More than conquerors you shall prove;
Though begirt with many a foe,
Onward, Christians, onward go!

H. K. White, 1806 a

501 Warum sollt ich mich denn grämen 8,6,6,8,6,6

J. G. EBELING, 1666

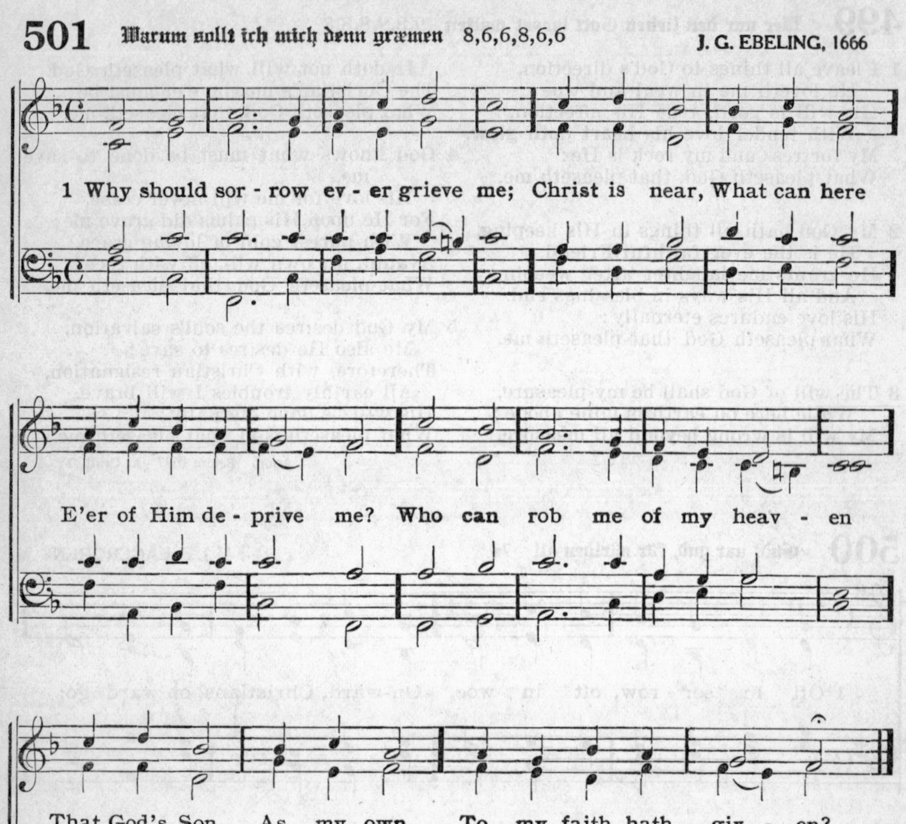
1 Why should sor - row ev - er grieve me; Christ is near, What can here
E'er of Him de - prive me? Who can rob me of my heav - en
That God's Son As my own To my faith hath giv - en?

2 Naked was I and unswathed
When on earth At my birth
My first breath I breathed.
Naked hence shall I betake me
When I go From earth's woe,
And my breath forsakes me.

3 Naught—not e'en the life I'm living,
Is my own, God alone
All to me is giving.
Must I then His own restore Him?
Though bereft Of each gift
Still shall I adore Him.

4 Though a heavy cross I'm bearing,
And my heart Feels the smart,
Shall I be despairing?
God can help me who doth send it,
He doth know All my woe
And how best to end it.

5 God oft gives me days of gladness,
Shall I grieve If He give
Seasons, too, of sadness?
God is good, and tempers ever
Every hurt; Me desert
Wholly can He never.

6 Though united world and Devil,
All their power Can no more
Do than mock and cavil.
Let derision now employ them,
Christ e'en here Will appear
And 'fore all destroy them.

7 True believers, shrinking never,
Where they dwell, Should reveal
Their true colors ever.
When approaching death would scare them,
Still should they Patient stay
And with courage bear them.

8 Death can never kill us even
But relief From all grief
To us then is given.
It doth close life's mournful story,
Makes a way That we may
Pass to heavenly glory.

9 There I'll reap enduring pleasure,
After woe Here below
Suffered in large measure.
Lasting good we find here never,
All the earth Deemeth worth
Vanisheth forever.

10 What is all this life possesseth?
But a hand Full of sand
That the heart distresseth.
Noble gifts that pall me never,
Christ so free There gives me
To enjoy forever.

11 Lord, Thou fount of joy forever,
Thou art mine, I am Thine,
No one can us sever.
I am Thine, because Thou gavest
Life and blood For my good,
By Thy death me savest.

12 Thou art mine, I love and own Thee,
Ne'er shall I, Light of joy,
From my heart dethrone Thee.
Let me, let me soon behold Thee
Face to face, Thy embrace—
May it soon enfold me!

Paul Gerhardt, 1653 J. Kelly, Tr. a

502 Windsor C. M.

G. KIRBYE, 1592 (P)

1 Dear Ref - uge of my wear - y soul, On Thee, when sor-rows rise,

On Thee, when waves of trou - ble roll, My faint - ing hope re - lies.

(Or to Avon)

2 To Thee I tell each rising grief,
For Thou alone canst heal;
Thy Word can bring a sweet relief
For every pain I feel.

3 Hast Thou not bid me seek Thy face?
And shall I seek in vain?
And can the ear of sovereign grace
Be deaf when I complain?

4 No, still the ear of sovereign grace
Attends the mourner's prayer;
O may I ever find access,
To breathe my sorrows there!

Anne Steele, 1760

503 Gibbons L. M.

O. GIBBONS (P)

1 O God, my days are dark in-deed, How oft this

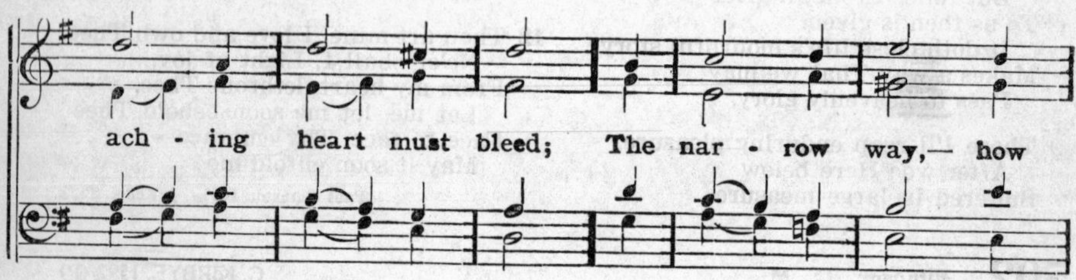
ach-ing heart must bleed; The nar-row way,— how

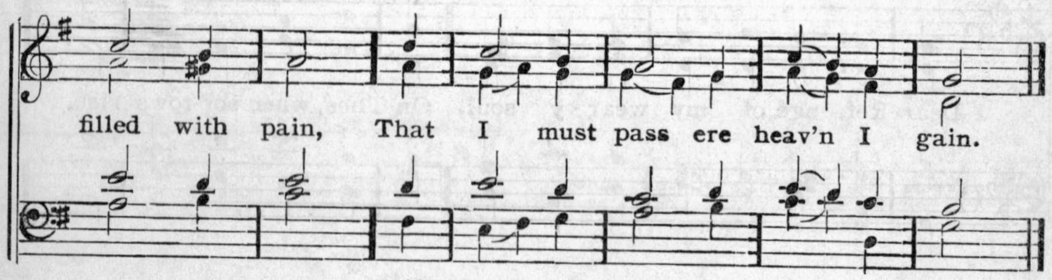
filled with pain, That I must pass ere heav'n I gain.

(Or to Herr Jesu Christ, meins)

2 How hard to teach this flesh and blood
To seek alone th' eternal God!
Ah! whither now for comfort turn?
For Thee, my Jesus, do I yearn.

3 In Thee have I, howe'er distressed,
Found ever counsel, aid, and rest!
I can not all forsaken be,
While still my heart can trust in Thee.

4 Thine office and Thy person show
That Thou great miracles canst do;
Miraculous was, Lord, Thy birth
When Thou wert born a child on earth.

5 And by Thy death Thou mak'st me free
So strangely from all misery.
Jesus, my only God and Lord,
What sweetness in Thy name is stored!

6 No grief can ever be so sore,
But Thy sweet name can cheer me more;
So keen no sorrow's rankling dart,
But thy sweet name can heal my heart.

7 Although my flesh and heart may fail,
I'll heed it not, I shall not quail;
My Savior, if I have but Thee,
I shall be blest eternally.

8 With heart and soul I'm Thine fore'er;
Sin, death, and health I need not fear.
The world can show no truth like Thine,
And therefore will I not repine.

9 I know Thou wilt forsake me not,
Thy truth is fixed, though dark my lot,
Thou art my Shepherd, and Thy sheep
From harm forever Thou wilt keep.

10 Jesus, my Boast, my Light, my Joy,
The Treasure naught can e'er destroy,
No words, no song that I can frame
Speak half the sweetness of Thy name.

11 They only all its power shall prove
Whose hearts have learnt Thy faith and love;
How many a time I've sadly said,
Far better were it I were dead;

12 Far better ne'er the light to see
If I had not this joy in Thee;
For he who hath not Thee in faith,
His very life is merely death.

13 Jesus, my Bridegroom and my Crown,
If Thou but smile, the world may frown,
In Thee lie depths of joy untold,
Far richer than the richest gold.

14 Whene'er I do but think of Thee,
Thy dews drop down and solace me;
Whene'er I hope in Thee, my Friend,
Thy comfort and Thy peace descend.

15 Where'er in grief I pray and sing,
I feel new courage in me spring;
Thy Spirit witnesses that this
Is foretaste of th' eternal bliss.

16 Therefore, while life remains in me,
I'll bear Thy cross and follow Thee,
Grant me a patient, willing mood;
I know that it shall work my good.

17 Help me to do my task aright,
That it may stand before Thy sight;
Let me this flesh and blood control,
From sin and shame preserve my soul.

18 O keep me steadfast in the faith,
Then I am Thine in life and death;
Jesus, my Comfort, bend to me,
Ah, would I were e'en now with Thee!

Conrad Hojer, 1597

504 Bethlehem S. M.

SAMUEL WESLEY, 1798 (P)

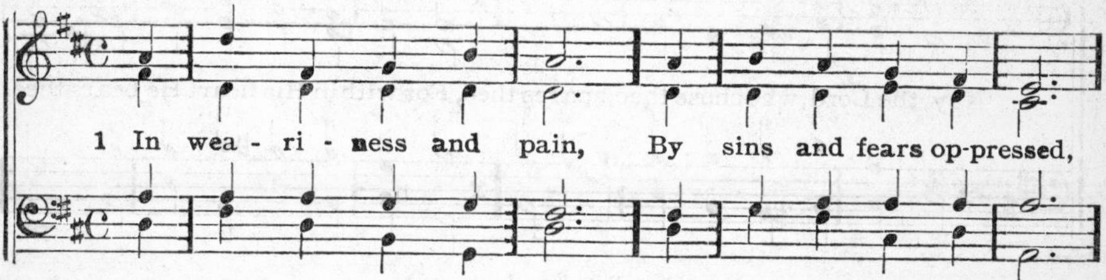
1 In wea-ri-ness and pain, By sins and fears op-pressed,

I turn me to my Rest a-gain, My soul's e-ter-nal Rest.

(*Or to Franconia* *Or to Greenwood*)

2 The Lamb that died for me,
And still my load doth bear;
To Jesus' streaming wounds I flee,
And find my quiet there.

3 Jesus, was ever grief,
Was ever love like Thine?
Thy sorrow, Lord, is my relief,
Thy life hath ransomed mine.

4 O may I rise with Thee,
And soar to things above,
And spend a blest eternity
In praise of dying love.

Charles Wesley 1749 a

505 Zion klagt mit Angst und Schmerzen 8,7,8,7,7,7,8,8 J. CRUEGER, 1640

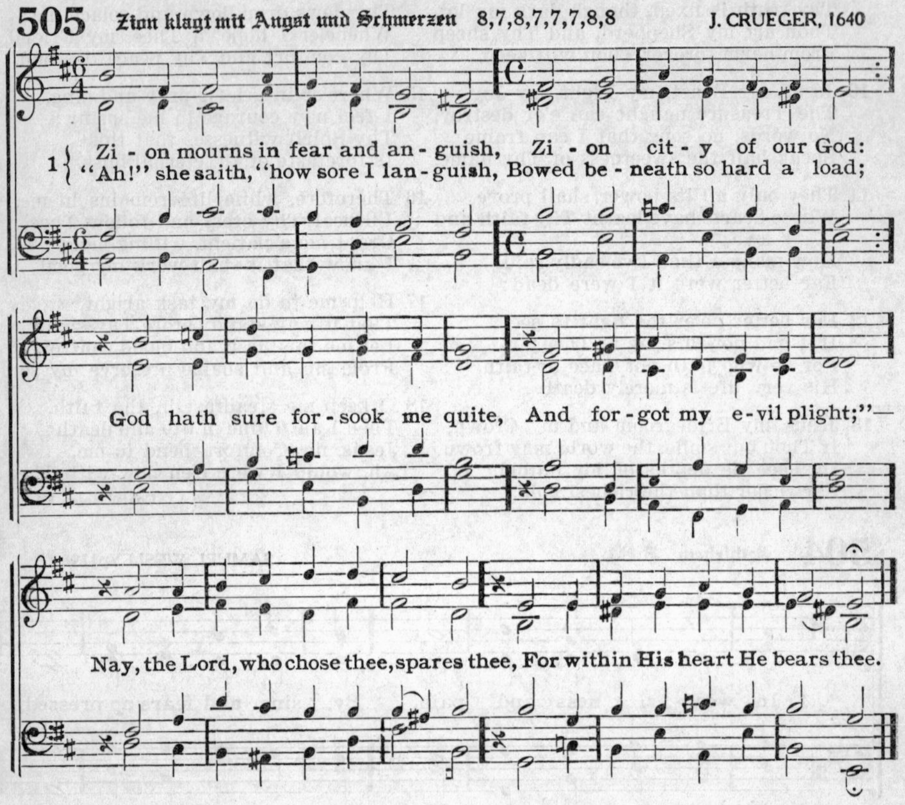
1 Zi - on mourns in fear and an - guish, Zi - on cit - y of our God:
"Ah!" she saith, "how sore I lan - guish, Bowed be - neath so hard a load;
God hath sure for - sook me quite, And for - got my e - vil plight;"—
Nay, the Lord, who chose thee, spares thee, For within His heart He bears thee.

(Or to Freu dich sehr, o meine)

2 "Once," she mourns, "He promised plainly
That His help should aye be near,
Yet I now must seek Him vainly
In my days of woe and fear.
Will He then forevermore
Keep His anger, and no more
Help His chosen generation
In their present tribulation?"

3 "Zion, surely I have loved thee!"
Thus to her the Highest saith,
"Although many woes have proved thee,
And thy soul is sad to death,
Yet now cast thy griefs behind;
Where wilt thou a mother find,
For her own child not providing,
Or in hatred with it chiding?"

4 "And if thou couldst find a mother
Who forgot her infant's claim,
Or whose wrath her love could smother,
Yet would I be still the same;
For my truth is pledged to thee,
Zion, thou art dear to me,
I within my heart have set thee,
And I never can forget thee."

5 "Let not Satan make thee craven,
He can fight but cannot harm;
On my hands thy name is graven,
And thy shield is still my arm.
How, then, could it ever be
That I failed to think of thee,
Build the wall of my own city,
And look down on thee with pity?"

6 "Thou before my eyes art ever,
In my bosom thou art laid
As a nursing child, and never
Shalt thou lack my timely aid.
Me and thee no time, nor stress,
War, nor danger, nor distress,
No, nor Satan's self shall sever,—
Only be thou faithful ever."

Joh. Heermann, 1630 C. Winkworth, Tr. a

506 Zion klagt mit Angst und Schmerzen 8,7,8,7,7,7,8,8

1 Let not such a thought e'er pain thee
As that thou art cast away,
But within God's Word restrain thee,
That far otherwise doth say.
E'en though thou unrighteous art,
True and faithful is God's heart.
Hast thou death deserved forever?
God's appeased, despond thou never!

2 Thou art, as is every other,
Tainted by the poison sin,
That the Serpent, and our father
Adam, by the fall, brought in.
But if thou God's voice dost hear,
"Turn to me, do good," ne'er fear,
Be of good cheer, He thy yearning
Will regard, thy prayer ne'er spurning.

3 He is not a bear or lion
Thirsting only for thy blood,
Faithful is thy God in Zion,
Gentle ever is His mood.
God aye as a Father feels,
He's afflicted by our ills,
Our misfortune sorrow gives Him,
And our dying ever grieves Him.

4 "Truly," saith He, "as I'm living,
I the death of none desire,
But that men themselves upgiving,
May be rescued from sin's mire."
When a prodigal returns,
God's heart then with rapture burns,
Wills that not the least one even
Ever from his flock be driven.

5 Shepherd was so faithful never,
Seeking sheep that go astray;
Couldest thou God's heart see ever
How He cares for them alway,
How it thirsts and sighs and burns,
After him who from Him turns,
From His people's midst doth wander,
Love would make thee weep and ponder.

6 God the good not only loveth
Who in His house ever dwell,
But His heart compassion moveth
Tow'rds those whom the Prince of hell
Hath enslaved, the cruel foe,
Who men's hearts with hate to glow
Makes 'gainst Him, who when he ever
Moves His foot, can make earth quiver.

7 Deep His love is and enduring,
His desire is ever great,
He is calling and alluring
Us to enter heaven's wide gate.
When they come, whoe'er they be,
Seeking now that liberty
From the Devil's fangs be given,
Glad are all the hosts of heaven.

8 God and all on high who're dwelling
'Fore whom heaven must hush its voice,
When their Maker's praise forth telling,
O'er our penitence rejoice;
But what has been done amiss
Covered now and buried is,
All offence to Him we've given,
All, yea all, is now forgiven.

9 From no lake so much is gushing,
No depth is so deep at all,
With such force no stream is rushing,
All compared with God is small;
Naught is like His grace so great,
That remits our mighty debt,
That He ever throweth over
All our lives e'en as a cover.

10 Soul, why art thou sad and dreary?
Rest now and contented be!
Why wilt thou thyself so weary
When there is no need for thee?
Though thy sins appear to thee
Like a vast and shoreless sea,
If thou with God's heart compare them,
'Twill a trifle seem to bear them.

11 Could we myriad worlds discover
All sunk in apostacy,
Had the sins there o'er and over
Every one been done by thee,
Oh! still they were less by far
Than the light of grace so clear
Could on earth extinguish ever,
God from greater could deliver.

12 Of such wondrous love and favor
Open wide the door to me;
Everywhere and aye, my Savior,
Tasted be thy grace by me
Love me, Lord! and let me be
Nearer ever drawn to Thee,
That I may embrace and love Thee,
Never more to anger move Thee.

Paul Gerhardt, 1653 J. Kelly, Tr.

507 Was Gott tut, das ist wohlgetan 8,7,8,7,8,7,7 G. GASTORIUS, 1670

1 What-ev-er God or-dains is good! Ho-ly His will a-bi-deth; He is my God; Though dark my road, He know-eth how to shield me, Where-fore to Him I yield me.
I will be still what-e'er He doth, And fol-low where He guid-eth,

2 Whatever God ordains is good!
He never will deceive me;
He leads me by the proper path,
I know He will not leave me,
And take content What He hath sent;
His hand that sends my sadness
Will turn my tears to gladness.

3 Whatever God ordains is good!
His loving thought attends me;
No poisoned draught the cup can be
That my Physician sends me,
But medicine due; For God is true,
Of doubt, then, I'll divest me,
And on His goodness rest me.

4 Whatever God ordains is good!
My Life, my Light can never
Intend me harm; then, to His care
I give myself forever
In weal or woe; For well I know,
Some day I shall see clearly,
That God did love me dearly.

5 Whatever God ordains is good!
Though now this cup in drinking
May bitter to my taste appear,
I take it all unshrinking;
For to my heart God will impart
A timely balm of healing,
And end each painful feeling.

6 Whatever God ordains is good!
Here shall my stand be taken;
Though sorrow, need, or death be mine,
Yet am I not forsaken;
My Father's care Is round me there,
His arms embrace and shield me;
Then to my God I yield me.

Samuel Rodigast, 1675

508 Auf meinen lieben Gott 6,6,7,7,7,7 1574

1 In God, my faith - ful God, I trust when dark my road;

Though man - y woe's o'er - take me, Yet He will not for - sake

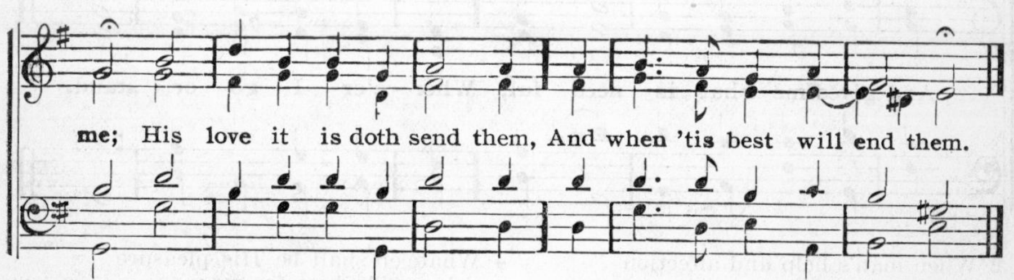
me; His love it is doth send them, And when 'tis best will end them.

2 My sins assail me sore,
But I despair no more;
I build on Christ who loves me,
From this rock nothing moves me;
To Him I all surrender
To Him, my soul's Defender.

3 If death my portion be,
Then death is gain to me,
And Christ my life forever,
From whom death cannot sever;
Come when it may, He'll shield me,
To Him I wholly yield me.

4 O Jesus Christ, my Lord,
So meek in deed and word,
Thou once didst die to save us,
Because Thou fain wouldst have us
After this life of sadness
Heirs of Thy heavenly gladness.

5 "So be it," then I say,
With all my heart each day;
We too, dear Lord, adore Thee,
Guide us while here we wander,
Till safely landed yonder,
We sing for joy before Thee.

Sigismund Weingaertner, c. 1609 C. Winkworth, Tr. a

Cross and Comfort

509 Von Gott will ich nicht lassen 7,6,7,6,6.7,7,6 J. MAGEDEBURG, 1571

1 { From God shall naught di - vide me, For He is true for aye,
{ And on my path will guide me, Who else should oft - en stray;

His ev - er - boun-teous hand By night and day is heed - ful,

And gives me what is need - ful, Wher - e'er I go or stand.

2 When man's help and affection
Shall unavailing prove,
God grants me His protection,
And proves His power and love;
He helps me in my need,
Delivers me from evil,
From sin, and death, and Devil,
He is my Friend indeed.

3 If sorrow comes, He sent it,
In Him I put my trust;
I never shall repent it,
For He is true and just,
And endeth every ill;
My life and soul I render,
To God, my strong Defender,
Let Him do as He will.

4 Whate'er shall be His pleasure
Is surely best for me;
He gave His dearest Treasure,
That our weak hearts may see
How good His will is toward us;
And in His Son He gave us
Whate'er could bless and save us;
Praise Him who loveth thus!

5 O praise Him, for He never
Forgets our daily need;
O blest the hour whenever
Our thoughts to Him can speed;
Yea, all the time we spend
Without Him is but wasted,
Till we His joy have tasted,
The joy that hath no end.

6 The world away is passing
With all its pomp and pride,
All we have been amassing
No longer may abide:
But in our earthly bed,
When safely we are sleeping,
God hath us in His keeping,
To wake us from the dead.

7 Our soul shall never perish,
But in yon paradise
The joys of heaven shall cherish;
Our body shall arise
Pure holy, new-born, free
From every sin and evil;
The tempting of the Devil
We then no more shall see.

8 Then, though on earth I suffer
Much trial, well I know
I merit ways still rougher,
And 'tis to heaven I go;
For Christ I know and love,
To Him I now am hasting,
And gladness everlasting
With Him my heart shall prove.

9 Such is His will that made us,
The Father seeks our good;
The Son of sin doth rid us,
And saves us by His blood;
His Spirit rules our ways,
Through faith in us abiding,
To heaven our footsteps guiding;
To Him be thanks and praise!

Ludwig Helmbold, 1563

510 Keston (Oxford) 8,7,8,7 J. STAINER, (1890—) (P)

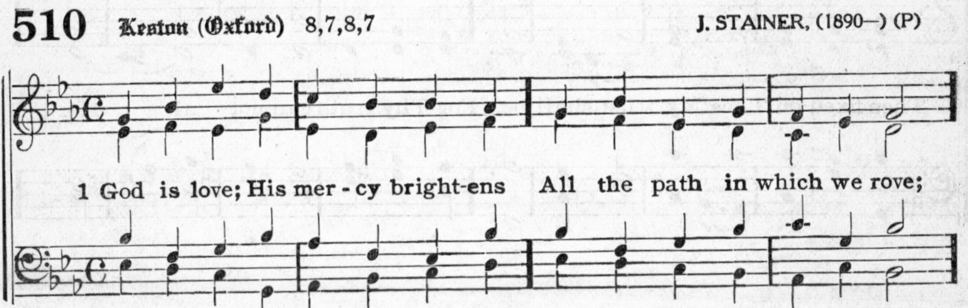
1 God is love; His mer - cy bright-ens All the path in which we rove;

Bliss He wakes, and woe He light-ens: God is wis-dom, God is love.

(*Or to Rathbun*)

2 Chance and change are busy ever,
Man decays, and ages move:
But His mercy waneth never:
God is wisdom, God is love.

3 E'en the hour that darkest seemeth
Will His changeless goodness prove;
From the gloom His brightness streameth:
God is wisdom, God is love.

4 He with earthly cares entwineth
Hope and comfort from above;
Everywhere His glory shineth:
God is wisdom, God is love.

J. Bowring, 1825

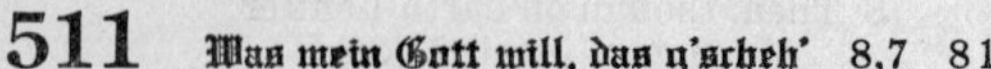
511 Was mein Gott will, das g'scheh' 8,7 81

FRENCH FOLKSONG, 1529
ANTWERP, 1540 (P)

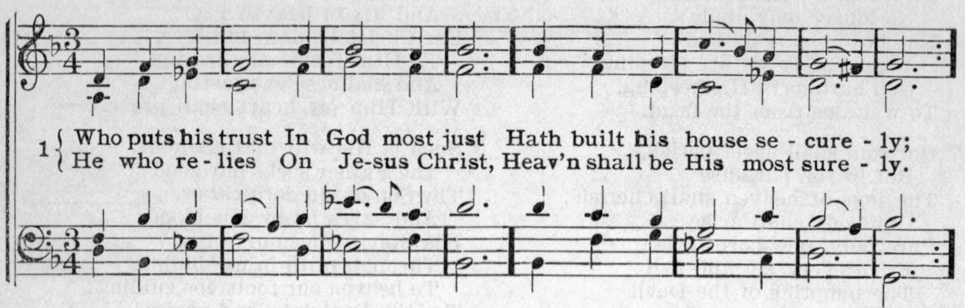
1 { Who puts his trust In God most just Hath built his house se - cure - ly;
He who re - lies On Je-sus Christ, Heav'n shall be His most sure - ly.

Then fixed on Thee My trust shall be, For Thy truth can-not al - ter;

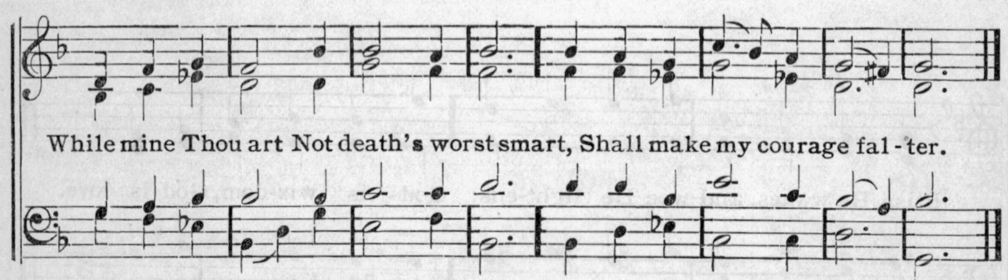
While mine Thou art Not death's worst smart, Shall make my courage fal - ter.

(*Or to Herre Gott*)

2 Though fiercest foes My course oppose,
A dauntless front I'll show them:
My Champion Thou, Lord Christ art now,
Who soon shalt overthrow them;
And if but Thee I have in me
With Thy good gifts and Spirit,
Nor death nor hell, I know full well,
Shall hurt me, through Thy merit.

3 I rest me here Without a fear;
By Thee shall all be given
That I can need, O Friend indeed;
For this life or for heaven.
O make me true, My heart renew,
My soul and flesh deliver!
Lord hear my prayer, And in Thy care
Keep me in peace forever.

J. Muehlmann, 1598 C. Winkworth, Tr.

512 Consolator 11,10,11,10 S. WEBBE, 1792

1 Come, ye dis - con - so - late, wher - e'er ye lan - guish, Come to the

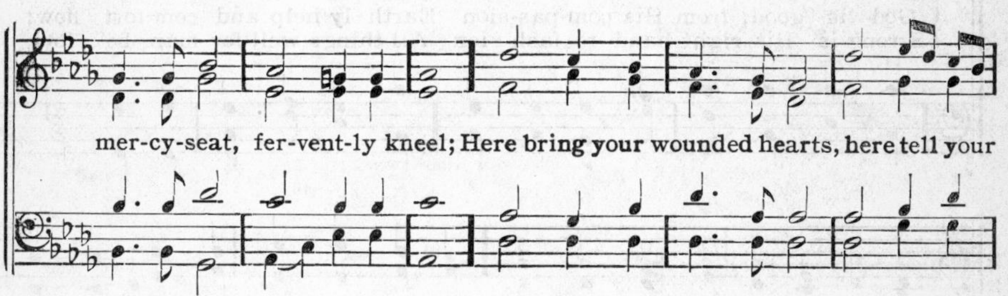
mer-cy-seat, fer-vent-ly kneel; Here bring your wounded hearts, here tell your

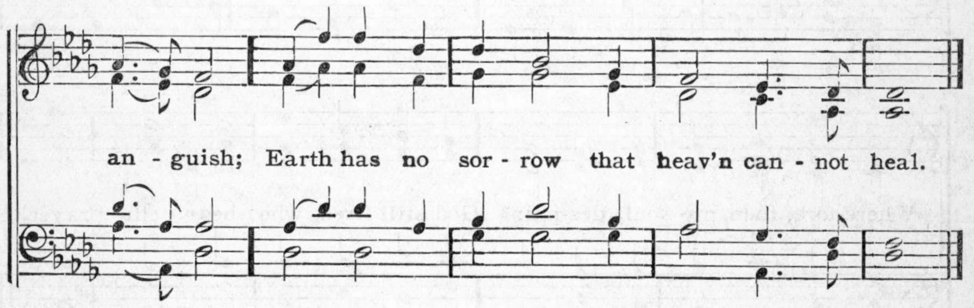
an - guish; Earth has no sor - row that heav'n can - not heal.

2 Joy of the desolate, light of the straying,
Hope of the penitent, fadeless and pure,
Here speaks the Comforter, tenderly saying,
Earth has no sorrow that heaven cannot cure.

3 Here see the Bread of life, see water flowing
Forth from the throne of God, pure from above;
Come to the feast of love, come, ever knowing
Earth has no sorrow but heaven can remove.

T. Moore, 1816 a V. 3 Hastings, 1832

513 Gott lebet noch 4,7,8,7,8,7,8,8,7,7

F. LAYRIZ

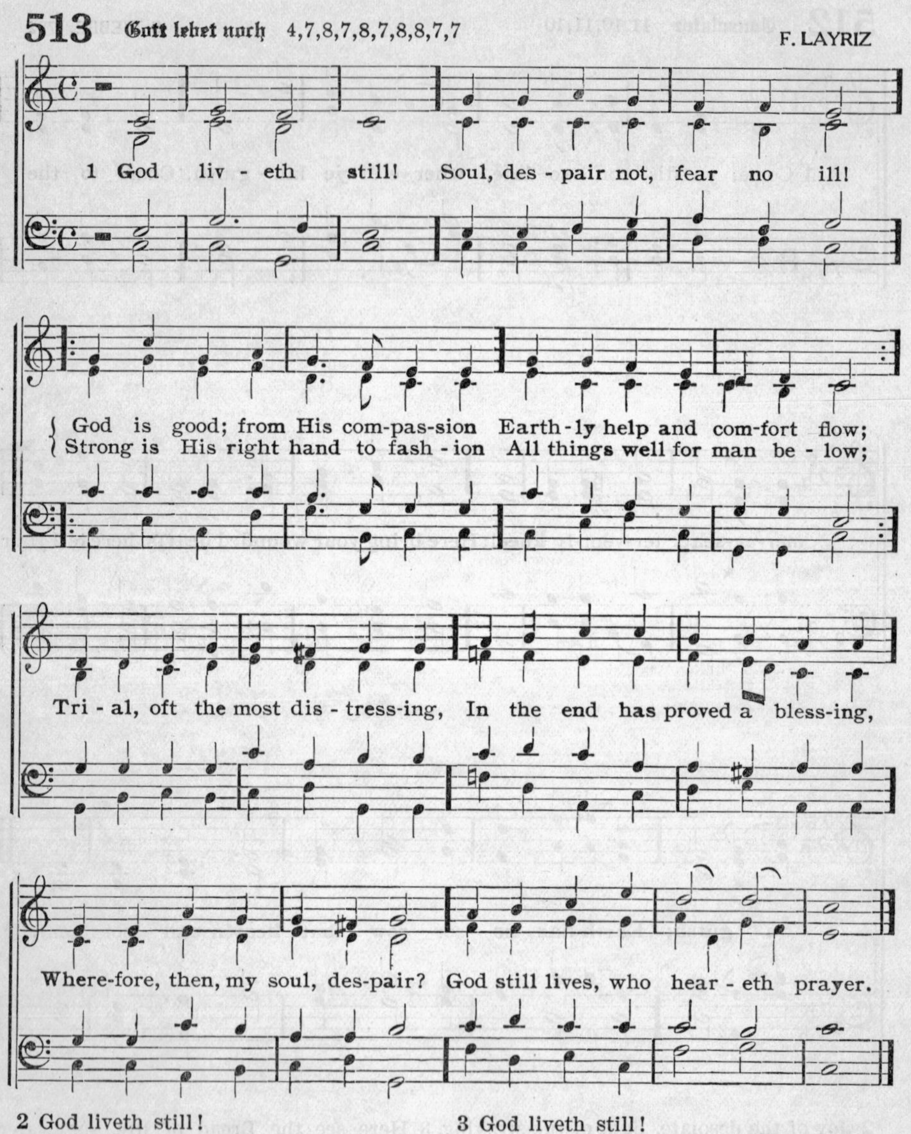

1 God liv - eth still! Soul, des - pair not, fear no ill!
God is good; from His com-pas-sion Earth-ly help and com-fort flow;
Strong is His right hand to fash - ion All things well for man be - low;
Tri - al, oft the most dis - tress-ing, In the end has proved a bless-ing,
Where-fore, then, my soul, des-pair? God still lives, who hear - eth prayer.

2 God liveth still!
Soul, despair not, fear no ill!
He who gave the eye its vision,
Shall He slumber once or sleep?
He who gave the ear its mission,
Hears He not His children weep?
God is God; His ear attendeth
When the sigh our bosom rendeth.
Wherefore, then, my soul, despair?
God still lives, who heareth prayer.

3 God liveth still!
Soul, despair not, fear no ill!
He who gives the clouds their measure,
Stretching out the heavens alone;
He who stores the earth with treasure,
Is not far from every one.
God in the hour of need defendeth
Him whose heart in love ascendeth.
Wherefore, then, my soul, despair?
God still lives, who heareth prayer.

4 God liveth still!
Soul, despair not, fear no ill!
Is thy cross too great and pond'rous,
Cast on Him thy grievous load;
God is great, His love is wondrous,
He will speed thee on the road.
For His truth endureth ever,
And His mercy ceaseth never.
Wherefore, then, my soul, despair?
God still lives, who heareth prayer.

5 God liveth still!
Soul, despair not, fear no ill!
Is the yoke of sin too galling?
Christ Himself has set thee free,
Borne for thee their weight appalling,
Cast them in oblivion's sea!
In thy deepest grief and sadness
He can grant thee joy and gladness.
Wherefore, then, my soul, despair?
God still lives, who heareth prayer.

6 God liveth still!
Soul, despair not, fear no ill!
When the world would let thee perish,
Pathless all thy tangled way,
God the nearer draws, to cherish
Him who makes the Lord his stay.
Children oft that most He loveth
Thus with strictest rod He proveth.
Wherefore, then, my soul, despair?
God still lives, who heareth prayer.

7 God liveth still!
Soul, despair not, fear no ill!
Heaven's huge vault may cleave asunder,
Earth's round globe in ruins burst,
Satan's fellest rage may thunder,
Death and hell may spend their worst;
Yet will God keep safe and surely
Those who trust in Him securely.
Wherefore, then, my soul, despair?
God still lives, who heareth prayer.

8 God liveth still!
Soul, despair not, fear no ill!
Be thy life, until its ending,
Full of thorns, of grief or need,
God, in love the trial sending,
Thus His child would heavenwards lead.
For this life's long night of sadness
He will give thee peace and gladness.
Wherefore, then, my soul, despair?
God still lives, who heareth prayer.

Johann Friedr. Zihn, 1682 F. E. Cox, Tr. a

514 Saxby L. M. T. R. MATTHEWS, 1826

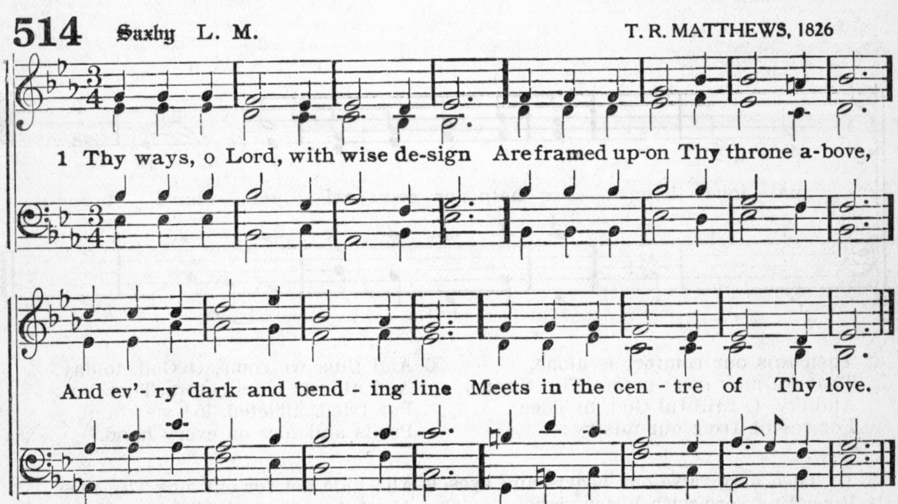
1 Thy ways, o Lord, with wise de-sign Are framed up-on Thy throne a-bove,
And ev'- ry dark and bend - ing line Meets in the cen - tre of Thy love.

2 With feeble light and half obscure,
Poor mortals Thine arrangements view;
Not knowing that the least are sure,
And the mysterious just and true.

3 Thy flock, Thine own peculiar care,
Though now they seem to roam uneyed;
Are led or driven only where
They best and safest may abide

4 They neither know nor trace the way;
But whilst they trust Thy guardian eye,
Their feet shall ne'er to ruin stray,
Nor shall the weakest fail or die.

5 My favored soul shall meekly learn
To lay her reason at Thy throne;
Too weak Thy secrets to discern,
I'll trust Thee for my guide alone.

Ambrose Serle, 1786

Cross and Comfort

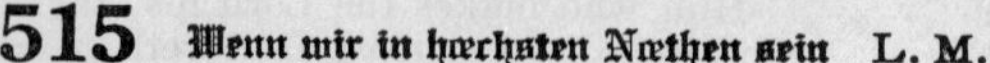

515 Wenn wir in hœchsten Nœthen sein L. M. J. GERARD, 1555

1 When in the hour of ut - most need We

know not where to look for aid; When days and nights of

anx - ious thought Nor help nor coun - sel yet have brought:

2 Then this our comfort is alone,
That we may meet before Thy throne,
And cry, O faithful God, to Thee
For rescue from our misery;

3 To Thee may raise our hearts and eyes,
Repenting sore with bitter sighs,
And seek Thy pardon for our sin,
And respite from our griefs within.

4 For Thou hast promised graciously
To hear all those who cry to Thee,
Through Him whose name alone is great,
Our Savior and our Advocate.

5 And thus we come, O God, to-day,
And all our woes before Thee lay;
For tried, afflicted, lo! we stand,
Perils and foes on every hand.

6 Ah! hide not for our sins Thy face,
Absolve us through Thy boundless grace,
Be with us in our anguish still,
Free us at last from every ill.

7 That so with all our hearts we may
Once more our glad thanksgivings pay,
And walk obedient to Thy Word,
And now and ever praise Thee, Lord.

Paul Eber, 1547 C. Winkworth, Tr.

516 Sollt es gleich bisweilen scheinen 7s

A. FRITSCH, 1675 (P)

1 Seems it in my an-guish lone, As if God for-sook His own,

Yet I hold the knowl-edge fast, God will sure-ly help at last.

2 Though awhile it be delayed,
He denieth not His aid;
Though it come not oft with speed,
It will surely come at need.

3 As a father not too soon
Grants his child the longed-for boon,
So our God gives when He will;
Wait His pleasure and be still.

4 I can rest in thoughts of Him,
When all courage else grows dim,
For I know my soul shall prove
His is more than father's love.

5 Would the powers of ill affright,
I can smile at all their might;
Or the cross be pressing sore,
God, my God, lives evermore!

6 Man may hate me causelessly,
Man may plot to ruin me,
Foes my heart may pierce and rend;
God in heaven is still my Friend.

7 Earth against me may declare,
For her love I do not care,
Though the world bear me a grudge,
God my Father is my Judge.

8 Earth may all her gifts deny,
Safe my treasure is on high;
And if heaven at last be mine,
All things else I can resign

9 I renounce thee willingly,
World, I hate what pleases thee;
Baneful every gift of thine,
Only be my God still mine.

10 Ah! Lord, if but Thee I have,
Naught of other good I crave,
Bright is even death's dark road,
If but Thou art there, my God!

Christoph Titius, c. 1663 C. Winkworth, Tr. a

517 Erhalt uns Herr bei L. M.

1 Lord God, who art my Father dear,
I pray in Jesus' name: O hear
What, trusting in His promised word,
I humbly ask of Thee, good Lord.

2 Grant us Thy Word, Thy Spirit give,
That by His grace we godly live,
Give shelter, peace, good friends, and food,
Protect our native land, O God.

3 Save us from sin and Satan's fraud,
Deliver us from evil, God,
Be with us in our dying hour;
Thine is the kingdom, glory, power.

4 Lord, at Thy word, Amen, I say;
Increase my feeble faith, I pray.
Thou lead'st me with a father's care,
O let me be Thy child and heir!

Johann Mathesius, 1564 A. Crull, Tr.

518 Cambridge S. M. R. HARRISON, 1784

1 Be - lov - ed, "It is well!" God's ways are al - ways right;

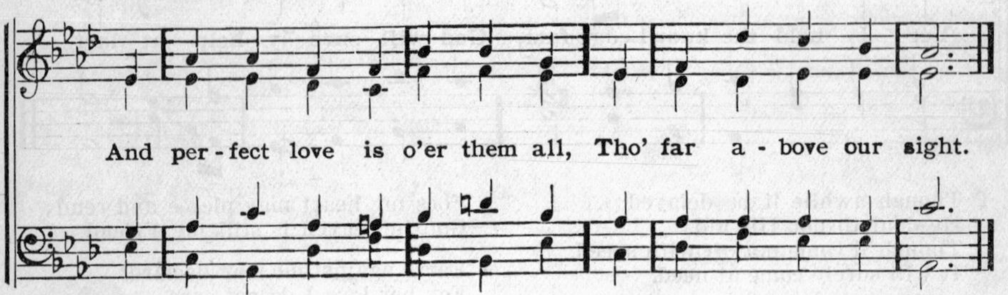
And per - fect love is o'er them all, Tho' far a - bove our sight.

2 Beloved, "It is well!"
Though deep and sore the smart,
The hand that wounds knows how to bind
And heal the broken heart.

3 Beloved, "It is well!"
Though sorrow clouds our way,
'T will only make the joy more dear
That ushers in the day.

4 Beloved, "It is well!"
The path that Jesus trod,
Though rough and straight and dark it be,
Leads home to heaven and God.

George W. Doane, 1833

519 Cambridge S. M.

1 My Father! cheering name!
O may I call Thee mine!
Give me with humble hope to claim
A portion so divine.

2 Whate'er Thy will denies,
I calmy would resign;
For Thou art just, and good, and wise,
O bend my will to Thine!

3 Whate'er Thy will ordains,
O give me strength to bear;
Still let me know a Father reigns,
And trust a Father's care.

4 Thy ways are little known
To my weak, erring sight;
Yet shall my soul, believing, own
That all Thy ways are right.

Anon

520 Bethany 6,4,6,4,6,6,6,4

L. MASON, 1856

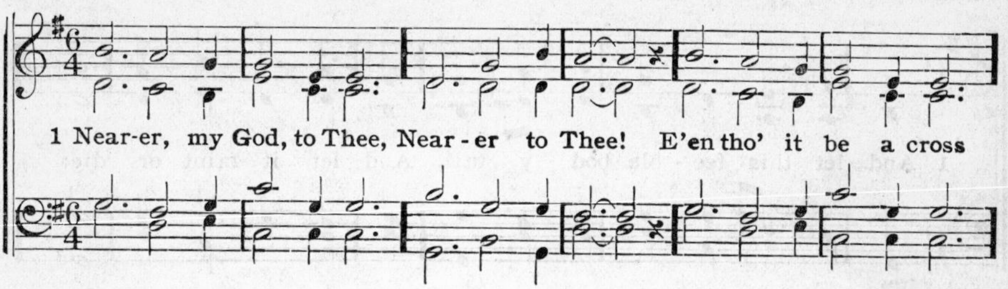
1 Near-er, my God, to Thee, Near-er to Thee! E'en tho' it be a cross

That rais-eth me; Still all my song shall be, Near-er my

God, to Thee, Near-er, my God, to Thee, Near-er to Thee!

2 Nearer, my Lord, to Thee,
 Nearer to Thee!
Who to Thy cross didst come
 Dying for me!
Strengthen my willing feet!
Hold me in service sweet
 Nearer, O Christ, to Thee,
 Nearer to Thee!

3 Nearer, O Comforter,
 Nearer to Thee!
Who with my loving Lord
 Dwellest with me!
Grant me Thy fellowship!
Help me each day to keep
 Nearer, my guide, to Thee,
 Nearer to Thee!

4 But to be nearer still,
 Bring me, O God!
Not by the visioned steeps
 Angels have trod.
Here where Thy cross I see
Jesus, I wait for Thee,
 Then evermore to be
 Nearer to Thee!

H. D. Ganse

521 Old 137th C. M. 81 — J. DAYE, 1562

1 And let this fee - ble bod - y fail, And let it faint or die;
My soul shall quit the mourn-ful vale And soar to worlds on high;
Shall join the dis - em - bod - ied saints And find its long sought rest.
That on - ly bliss for which it pants, In my Re - deem - er's breast.

2 In hope of that immortal crown
I now the cross sustain,
And gladly wander up and down,
And smile at toil and pain:

I suffer on my threescore years
Till my Deliverer come,
And wipe away His servant's tears,
And take His exile home.

3 O what hath Jesus bought for me!
Before my ravished eyes
Rivers of life divine I see,
And trees of paradise!
I see a world of spirits bright
Who reap the pleasures there;
They all are robed in spotless white,
And conquering palms they bear.

4 O what are all my sufferings here,
If, Lord, Thou count me meet,
With that enraptured host t' appear,
And worship at Thy feet!
Give joy or grief, give ease or pain,
Take life or friends away;
But let me find them all again
In that eternal day.

C. Wesley a

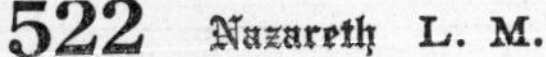

522 Nazareth L. M.

SAM. WEBBE

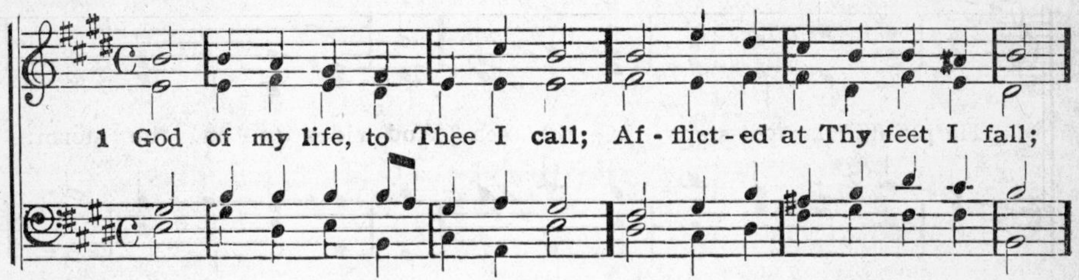
1 God of my life, to Thee I call; Af - flict - ed at Thy feet I fall;

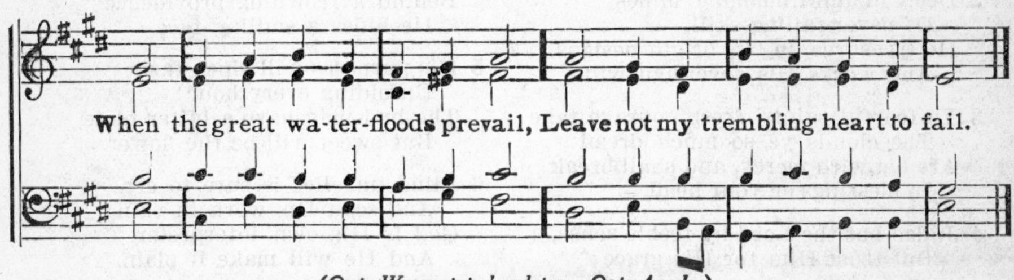
When the great wa-ter-floods prevail, Leave not my trembling heart to fail.

(Or to Wenn wir in hoechsten Or to Angelus)

2 Friend of the friendless and the faint,
Where should I lodge my deep complaint?
Where but with Thee, whose open door
Invites the helpless and the poor?

3 Did ever mourner plead with Thee,
And Thou refuse that mourner's plea?
Does not the word still fixed remain,
That none shall seek Thy face in vain?

4 That were a grief I could not bear,
Didst Thou not hear and answer prayer;
But a prayer-hearing, answering God,
Supports me under every load.

5 Fair is the lot that's cast for me;
I have an Advocate with Thee;
They whom the world caresses most
Have no such privilege to boast.

6 Poor though I be, despised, forgot,
Yet God, my God, forgets me not;
And he is safe, and must succeed,
For whom the Lord Himself does plead.

W. Cowper, 1779 a

523 Nazareth L. M.

1 Help, Helper, help in fear and need,
Have mercy, to my prayer give heed!
I know Thou lov'st me still as Thine,
Though 'gainst me world and hell combine.

2 My God and Lord, I trust in Thee;
What need I, if Thou art with me?
And Thou, Lord Jesus Christ, art mine;
My God and Savior, I am Thine.

3 Therefore my happiness is great,
I am content, for Thee I wait,
Trust wholly in Thy name, and then
I pray: Help, Helper, help! Amen.

Martin Moller, 1593

(Or to Erhalt uns Herr)

524 Farrant C. M. R. FARRANT, 1585

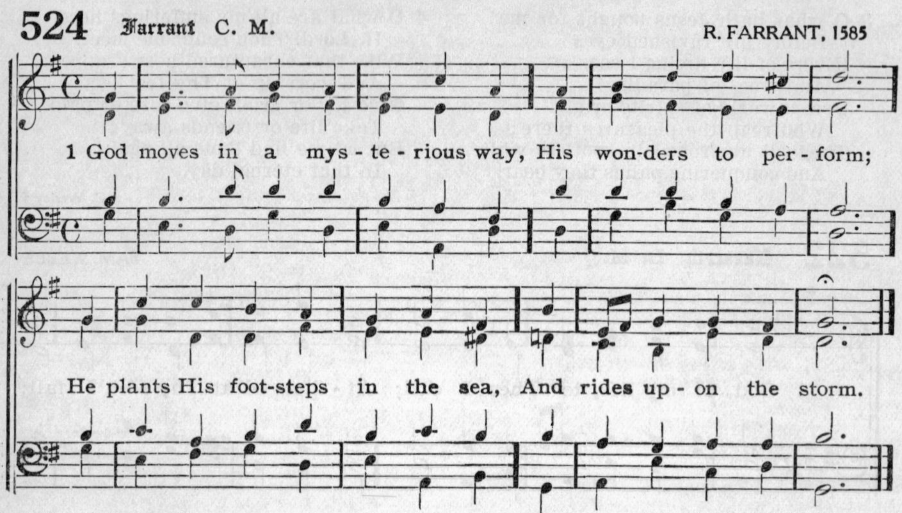
1 God moves in a mys - te - rious way, His won-ders to per - form;
He plants His foot-steps in the sea, And rides up - on the storm.

2 Deep in unfathomable mines
Of never-failing skill,
He treasures up His bright designs,
And works His sovereign will.

3 Ye fearful saints, fresh courage take;
The clouds ye so much dread
Are big with mercy, and shall break
In blessings on your head.

4 Judge not the Lord by feeble sense,
But trust Him for His grace;
Behind a frowning providence
He hides a smiling face.

5 His purposes will ripen fast,
Unfolding every hour;
The bud may have a bitter taste,
But sweet will be the flower.

6 Blind unbelief is sure to err,
And scan His work in vain:
God is His own interpreter,
And He will make it plain.

W. Cowper, 1772

525 Herzlich tut mich verlangen (Befiehl du) 7,6 8 1 H. SCHEIN, 1627

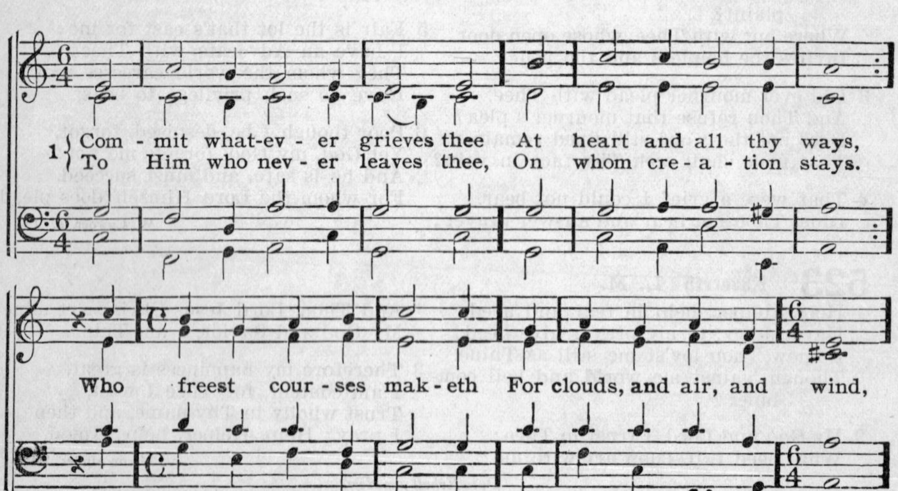
1 { Com - mit what-ev - er grieves thee At heart and all thy ways,
To Him who nev - er leaves thee, On whom cre - a - tion stays.
Who freest cour - ses mak - eth For clouds, and air, and wind,

And who care ev - er tak - eth A path for thee to find.

2 The Lord thou must repose on
If thou wouldst prosper sure,
His work must ever gaze on
If thine is to endure.
By anxious care and grieving.
By self-consuming pain,
God is not moved to giving;
By prayer must thou obtain.

3 Thy grace that ever floweth,
O Father! what is good,
Or evil, ever knoweth,
To mortal flesh and blood.
What to Thine eye all-seeing,
And to Thy counsel wise
Seems good must into being,
O mighty Prince arise!

4 For means it fails Thee never,
Thou always findst a way,
Thy deeds are blessing ever,
Thy path like brightest day.
Thy work can no one hinder,
Thy labor cannot rest,
If Thou design'st Thy tender
Children should all be blessed.

5 Though all the power of evil
Should rise up to resist,
Without a doubt or cavil
God never will desist;
His undertakings ever
At length He carries through;
What He designs He never
Can fail at all to do.

6 Hope on, thou heart, grief-riven,
Hope, and courageous be,
Where anguish thee had driven
Thou shalt deliverance see.
God from Thy pit of sadness
Shall raise thee graciously;
Wait and the sun of gladness
Thine eyes shall early see.

7 Arise! to pain and anguish
A long good night now say;
Drive all that makes thee languish
In grief and woe away.
Not thine 'tis to endeavor
The ruler's part to play,
God sits as ruler ever,
Guides all things well each day.

8 Let Him alone, and tarry,
He is a Prince all-wise,
He shall Himself so carry
'Twill strange seem in thine eyes.
When He, as Him beseemeth,
In wonderful decree,
Shall as Himself good deemeth,
O'errule what grieveth thee.

9 He may, awhile still staying,
His comforts keep from thee,
And, on His part delaying,
Seem to have utterly
Forgotten and forsaken
And put thee out of mind,
Though thou'rt by grief o'ertaken,
No time for thee to find.

10 But if thou never shrinkest,
And true dost still remain,
He'll come when least thou thinkest,
And set thee free again,
Thee from the load deliver,
That burdeneth thy heart,
That thou hast carried never
For any evil part.

11 Hail! child of faith, who gainest
The victory alway,
Who honor's crown obtainest,
That never fades away.
God in thy hand will give thee
One day the glorious palm;
Who ne'er in grief did leave thee,
To Him thou'llt sing thy psalm.

12 O Lord, no longer lengthen
Our time of misery;
Our hands and feet do strengthen;
And until death may we
By Thee be watched and cared for,
In faithfulness and love:
So come we where prepared for
Us is our blessed abode.

Paul Gerhardt, 1656 J. Kelly, Tr. a

526 Herzlich tut mich verlangen 7,6 81

1 If God Himself be for me,
I may a host defy,
For when I pray, before me
My foes confounded fly.
If Christ, my head and master,
Befriend me from above,
What foe or what disaster
Can drive me from His love?

2 This I believe—yea, rather,
Of this I make my boast,
That God is my dear Father,
The Friend who loves me most;
And that, whate'er betide me,
My Savior is at hand,
Through stormy seas to guide me,
And bring me safe to land.

3 I build on this foundation,
That Jesus and His blood
Alone are my salvation,
The true, eternal good;
Without Him, all that pleases
Is valueless on earth;
The gifts I owe to Jesus
Alone my love are worth.

4 My Jesus is my Splendor,
My soul's bright-beaming Sun;
Were He not my Defender
Before God's awful throne,
I never should find favor
And mercy in His sight,
But be destroyed forever,
As darkness by the light.

5 He canceled my offences,
And saved my soul from death;
'Tis He who ever cleanses
Me from my sins through faith.
In Him I can be cheerful,
Bold, and undaunted aye:
In Him I am not fearful,
Of God's great judgment-day.

6 Naught, naught can e'er condemn me,
Nor set my hope aside;
Now hell no more can claim me,
Its fury I deride.
No sentence e'er reproves me,
No ill destroys my peace,
For Christ, my Savior, loves me
And screens me with His grace.

7 His Spirit in me dwelleth
And o'er my mind He reigns.
All sorrow He dispelleth
And soothes away all pains.
He crowns His work with blessing,
And helpeth me to cry
"My Father!" without ceasing,
To Him who dwells on high.

8 To mine His Spirit speaketh
Sweet words of holy cheer,
How God, to Him that seeketh
For rest, is always near,
And how He hath erected
A city fair and new,
Where what our faith expected
We evermore shall view.

9 In yonder home doth flourish
My heritage, my lot,
Though here I die and perish,
My heaven shall fail me not.
Though care my life oft saddens
And causeth tears to flow,
The light of Jesus gladdens
And sweetens every woe.

10 Who clings with resolution
To Him whom Satan hates,
Must look for persecution;
For him the burden waits
Of mockery, shame, and losses,
Heaped on his guiltless head;
A thousand plagues and crosses
Shall be his daily bread.

11 All this I am prepared for,
Yet am I not afraid;
By Thee shall all be cared for,
To whom my vows were paid.
Though life and limb it cost me
And everything I have,
Unshaken shall I trust Thee,
Thee never shall I leave.

12 Though earth be rent asunder,
Thou'rt mine eternally;
Not fire, nor sword, nor thunder,
Shall sever me from Thee;
Not hunger, thirst, nor danger,
Not pain nor poverty,
Nor mighty princes' anger,
Shall ever hinder me.

13 No angel, and no gladness,
No throne, no pomp, no show,
No love, no hate, no sadness,
No pain, no depth of woe,
No scheme of man's contrivance,
However small or great,
Shall draw me from Thy guidance,
Nor from Thee separate.

14 My heart for joy is springing,
And can no more be sad,
'Tis full of mirth and singing,
Sees naught but sunshine glad:
The Sun that cheers my spirit
Is Jesus Christ my King,
That which I shall inherit
Hereafter, makes me sing.

Paul Gerhardt, 1664

(*Or to Valet will*)

Death and Burial

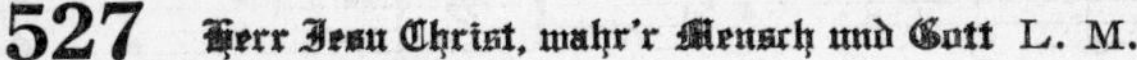
527 Herr Jesu Christ, wahr'r Mensch und Gott L. M.

J. ECCARD, 1597

1 Lord Je-sus Christ, true man and God, Who bor-est an-guish, scorn, the rod,

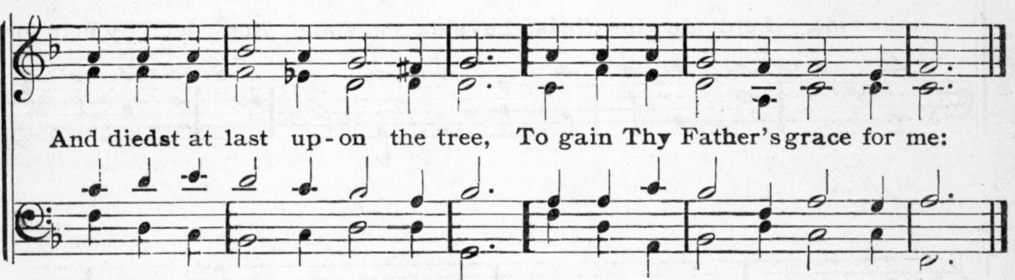
And diedst at last up-on the tree, To gain Thy Father's grace for me:

(Or to Wenn wir in hoechsten Noeten)

2 I pray Thee, through that bitter woe,
Let me, a sinner, mercy know,
When comes the hour of failing breath,
And I must wrestle, Lord, with death,

3 When from my sight all fades away,
And when my tongue no more can say,
And when mine ears no more can hear,
And when my heart is racked with fear,

4 When all my mind is darkened o'er,
And human help can do no more;
Then come, Lord Jesus, come with speed,
And help me in the hour of need.

5 Lead me from this dark vale beneath,
And shorten then the pangs of death;
All evil spirits drive away,
But let Thy Spirit with me stay,

6 Until my soul the body leave;
Then in Thy hands my soul receive,
And let the earth the body keep,
Till the last day shall break its sleep.

7 Joyful my resurrection be,
Thou in the Judgment plead for me,
And hide my sins, Lord, from Thy face,
And give me life, of Thy dear grace!

8 Implicitly I trust Thee, Lord,
For Thou hast promised in Thy Word:
"In truth I tell you, who receives
My Word, and keeps it, and believes,

9 Shall never fall God's wrath beneath,
Shall never taste eternal death;
Though here he must return to dust,
He still is noways therefore lost;

10 For I will with a mighty hand
Deliver him from death's strong band,
And lift him hence that he shall be
Forever in my realm with me,

11 Forever living there in bliss."
O let us not that glory miss!
Dear Lord, forgive us all our guilt,
Help us to wait until Thou wilt

12 That we depart; and let our faith
Be brave, and conquer even in death,
Firm resting in Thy sacred Word,
Until we sleep in Thee, our Lord.

Paul Eber, 1557 C. Winkworth, Tr. a

528 Wenn mein Stuendlein 8,7,8,7,7,8,8,7 WOLFF, 1509

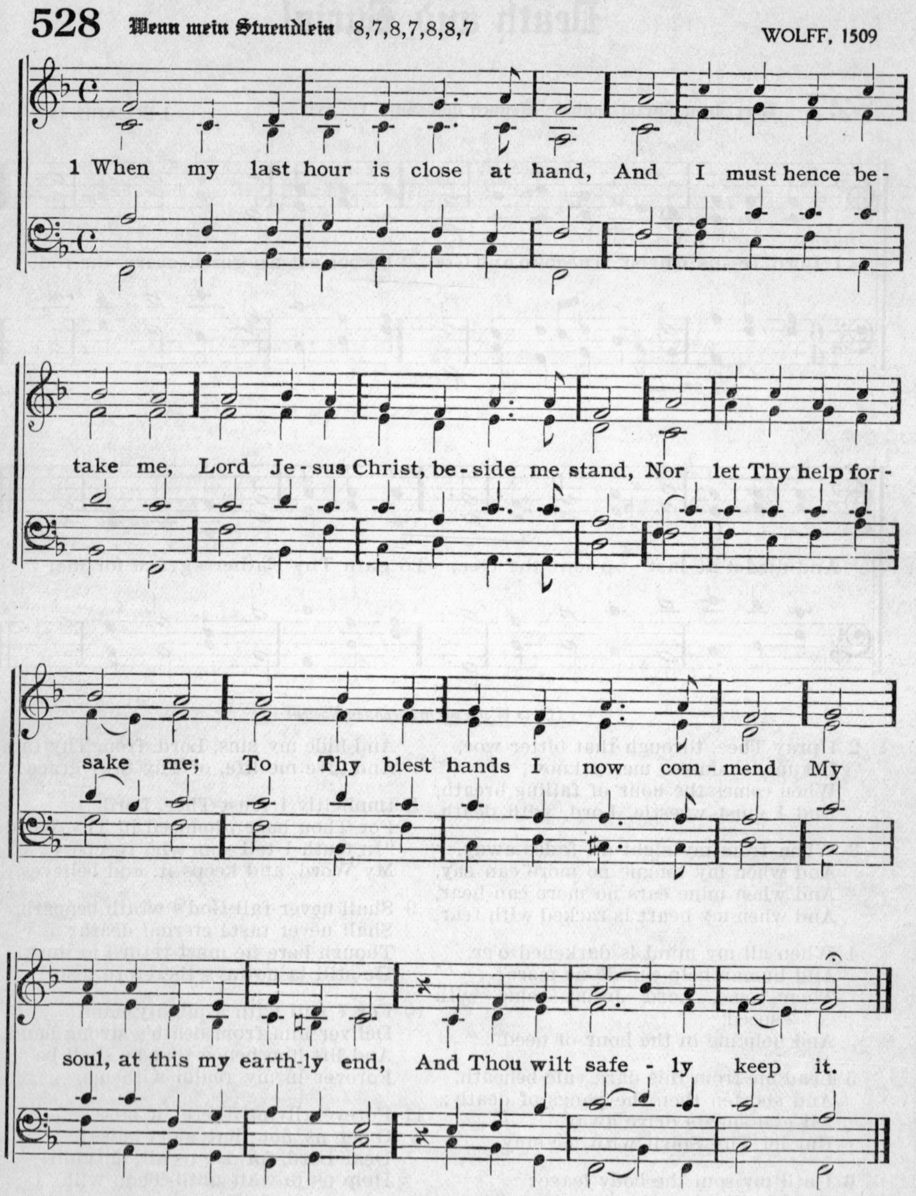
1 When my last hour is close at hand, And I must hence be-
take me, Lord Je-sus Christ, be-side me stand, Nor let Thy help forsake me; To Thy blest hands I now com-mend My
soul, at this my earth-ly end, And Thou wilt safe - ly keep it.

(*Or to Herr wie du willt*)

2 My sins, dear Lord, disturb me sore,
My conscience cannot slumber;
But though as sands upon the shore,
My sins may be in number,
I will not quail, but think of Thee;
Thy death, Thy sorrow, borne for me,
Thy sufferings shall uphold me.

3 I have been grafted in the Vine,
And hence my comfort borrow,
For Thou wilt surely keep me Thine
Through fear, and pain, and sorrow;
Yea, though I die, I die to Thee,
Who through Thy death hast won for me
The right to life eternal.

4 Since Thou from death didst rise again,
In death Thou wilt not leave me;
Lord, Thy ascension soothes my pain,
No fear of death shall grieve me;
For Thou wilt have me where Thou art,
And so with joy I can depart
To be with Thee forever.

5 And so I stretch mine arms to Thee,
And gladly hence betake me:
Peaceful and calm my sleep shall be,
No human voice can wake me.
But Christ is with me through the strife,
And He will bear me into life,
And open heaven before me.

Nikolaus Hermann, 1560 V. 5 Anon C. Winkworth, Tr. a

529 Christus der ist mein Leben 7,6,7,6

VULPIUS. 1609

1 For me to live is Je - sus, To die is gain for me,

To Him I glad - ly yield me, And die right cheer - ful - ly.

2 From hence I go with gladness
To Christ my Brother's side,
That I may soon be with Him,
And e'er with Him abide.

3 I have o'ercome life's crosses;
Grief, pain, and sorrow cease;
Through His five wounds most holy
With God I am at peace.

4 When all my powers are breaking,
My breath comes heavily,
Nor word more I can utter,
Lord, hear my sighs to Thee!

5 When reason, sense, and thinking,
Fail like a flickering light,
That to and fro doth waver,
Ere 'tis extinguished quite:

6 Then let me softly, gently,
Lord, fall asleep in Thee,
When by Thy will and counsel
My last hour comes to me.

7 As to the oak the ivy,
So let me cleave to Thee,
And live in heavenly glory
With Thee eternally.

8 Amen! This wilt Thou, Jesus,
Grant graciously to me:
Endow me with Thy Spirit,
That I die happily.

Anna, Countess von Stolberg, 1600

530 Alle Menschen muessen sterben 8,7,8,7,8,8,7,7 J. HINTZE, 1678

1 { Hark! a voice saith, All are mor - tal. Yea, all flesh must fade as grass,
On - ly thro' death's gloom-y por - tal To a bet - ter land we pass;
This frail bod - y here must per - ish, Ere the heav'n-ly joys it cher-ish,
Ere it gain the free re - ward For the ran-somed of the Lord.

(*Or to Jesu meines Lebens*)

2 Therefore, when my God doth choose it,
Willingly I'll yield my life,
Nor will grieve that I should lose it,
For with sorrows it was rife;
In my dear Redeemer's merit
Peace hath found my troubled spirit,
And in death my comfort is
Jesus' death—sweet comfort this!

3 For my sake He went before me,
And His death is now my gain;
Peace and hope He conquered for me;
So without regret or pain,
Yea, with joy I'll quit earth's sadness
For the beauteous heaven of gladness,
Where I shall eternally
See the holy Trinity.

4 There is joy beyond our telling,
Where so many saints have gone;
Thousands, thousands there are dwelling,
Worshipping before the throne,
There the Seraphim are shining,
Evermore in chorus joining:
"Holy, holy, holy, Lord!
Triune God, for aye adored!"

5 There great men, of sacred story,
Prophets, Patriarchs, are met;
There Apostles too in glory
Fill twelve thrones by Jesus set;
All the saints that have ascended
Age on age, through time extended,
There in blissful concert, sing
Hallelujahs to their King.

6 O Jerusalem, how glorious
Dost thou shine, thou city fair!
Lo! I hear the tones victorious
Ever sweetly sounding there!
O the bliss that there surprises!
Lo! the sun of morn now rises,
And the breaking day I see
That shall never end for me!

7 Yea, I see what here was told me,
See that wondrous glory shine;
Feel the spotless robes enfold me,
Know a golden crown is mine,
Thus before the throne so glorious
Now I stand, a soul victorious,
Gazing on that joy for aye
That shall never pass away

Joh. Georg Albinus, 1652

531 Dulce Domum S. M. R. S. AMBROSE

1 One sweet-ly sol - emn thought Comes to me o'er and o'er,—

Near - er my home, to - day, am I Than e'er I've been be - fore.

(Or to Leominster)

2 Nearer my Father's house,
Where many mansions be;
Nearer to-day the great white throne,
Nearer the crystal sea.

3 Nearer the bound of life
Where burdens are laid down;
Nearer to leave the heavy cross;
Nearer to gain the crown.

4 But, lying dark between,
Winding down through the night,
There rolls the silent, unknown stream
That leads at last to light.

5 E'en now, perchance, my feet
Are slipping on the brink,
And I, to-day, am nearer home,—
Nearer than now I think.

6 Father, perfect my trust;
Strengthen my spirit's faith;
Nor let me stand, at last alone
Upon the shore of death.

Phebe Cary, 1852

532 Valet will ich dir geben 7,6 81

M. TESCHNER, 1613

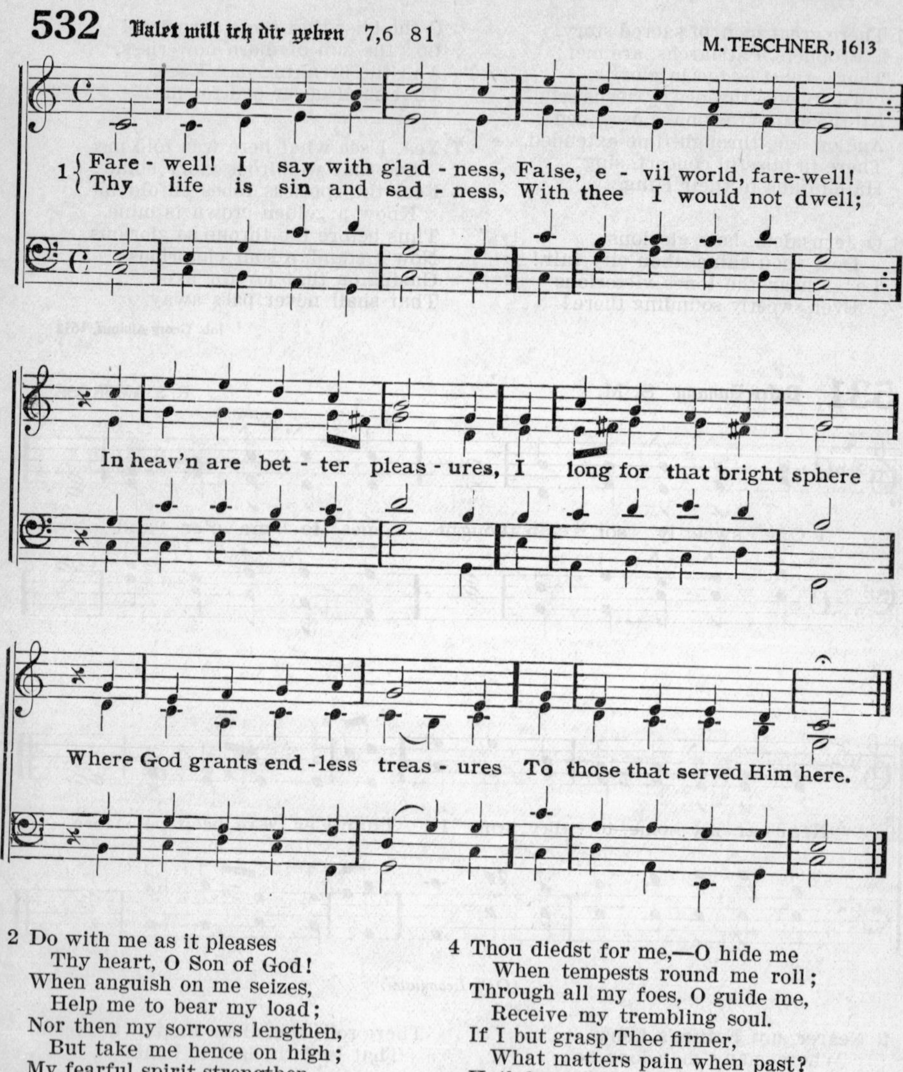
1 { Fare - well! I say with glad - ness, False, e - vil world, fare-well!
Thy life is sin and sad - ness, With thee I would not dwell;
In heav'n are bet - ter pleas - ures, I long for that bright sphere
Where God grants end - less treas - ures To those that served Him here.

2 Do with me as it pleases
Thy heart, O Son of God!
When anguish on me seizes,
Help me to bear my load;
Nor then my sorrows lengthen,
But take me hence on high;
My fearful spirit strengthen,
And let me calmly die.

3 When all around is darkling,
Thy name and cross, still bright,
Deep in my heart are sparkling,
Like stars in blackest night.
Appear Thou in Thy sorrow,
For Thine was woe indeed,
And from Thy cross I borrow
All comfort heart can need.

4 Thou diedst for me,—O hide me
When tempests round me roll;
Through all my foes, O guide me,
Receive my trembling soul.
If I but grasp Thee firmer,
What matters pain when past?
Hath he a cause to murmur
Who reaches heaven at last?

5 O write my name, I pray Thee,
Now in the book of life;
So let me here obey Thee,
And there, where joys are rife,
Forever bloom before Thee,
Thy perfect freedom prove,
And tell, as I adore Thee,
How faithful was Thy love.

Valerius Herberger, 1613 C. Winkworth, Tr. a

533 Aberystwyth S. M.

F. A. G. OUSELEY, 1861

1 It is not death to die; To leave this wea - ry road,

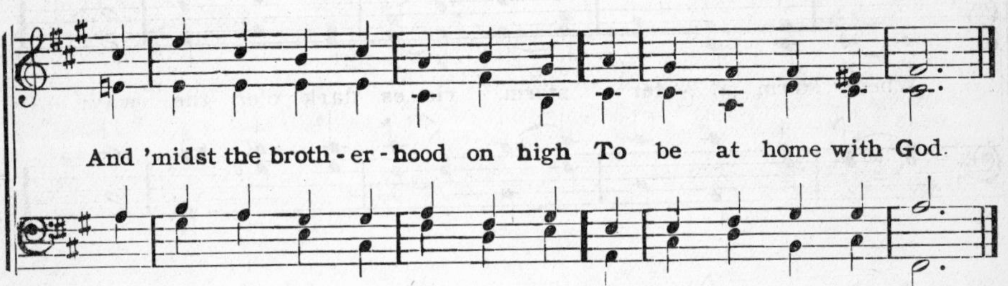
And 'midst the broth - er - hood on high To be at home with God.

2 It is not death to close
The eye long dimmed by tears,
And wake, in glorious repose
To spend eternal years.

3 It is not death to bear
The wrench that sets us free
From dungeon chain, to breathe the air
Of boundless liberty.

4 It is not death to fling
Aside this sinful dust,
And rise, on strong exulting wing,
To live among the just.

5 Jesus, Thou Prince of life!
Thy chosen cannot die;
Like Thee, they conquer in the strife,
To reign with Thee on high.

H. A. C. Malan, 1832 Tr. G. W. Bethune, 1847

534 Aberystwyth S. M.

1 And must this body die,
This mortal frame decay?
And must these active limbs of mine
Lie mouldering in the clay?

2 God my Redeemer lives,
And ever from the skies
Looks down and watches all my dust,
Till He shall bid it rise.

3 Arrayed in glorious grace
Shall these vile bodies shine,
And every shape, and every face,
Look heavenly and divine.

4 These lively hopes we owe
To Jesus' dying love:
We would adore His grace below
And sing His power above.

5 Dear Lord, accept the praise
Of these our humble songs,
Till tunes of nobler sound we raise
With our immortal tongues.

Isaac Watts, 1709

535 Frederick 11s G. KINGSLEY, 1833

1 I would not live al - way; I ask not to stay
Where storm af - ter storm ris - es dark o'er the way:
The few lu - rid morn - ings that dawn on us here
Are e - nough for life's woes, full e - nough for its cheer.

2 I would not live alway; thus fettered by sin,
Temptation without and corruption within:
E'en the rapture of pardon is mingled with fears,
And the cup of thanksgiving with penitent tears.

3 I would not live alway; no, welcome the tomb;
Since Jesus hath lain there, I dread not its gloom:
There sweet be my rest till He bid me arise
To hail Him in triumph descending the skies.

4 Who, who would live alway, away from his God?
Away from yon heaven, that blissful abode,
Where the rivers of pleasure flow o'er the bright plains,
And the noontide of glory eternally reigns:

5 Where the saints of all ages in harmony meet,
Their Savior and brethren transported to greet,
While the anthems of rapture unceasingly roll,
And the smile of the Lord is the feast of the soul.

W. A. Muehlenberg, 1826

536 Culbach

7s — GEORGE W. DOANE, 1826

1 Hark! a voice di - vides the sky: Hap - py are the faith - ful dead,

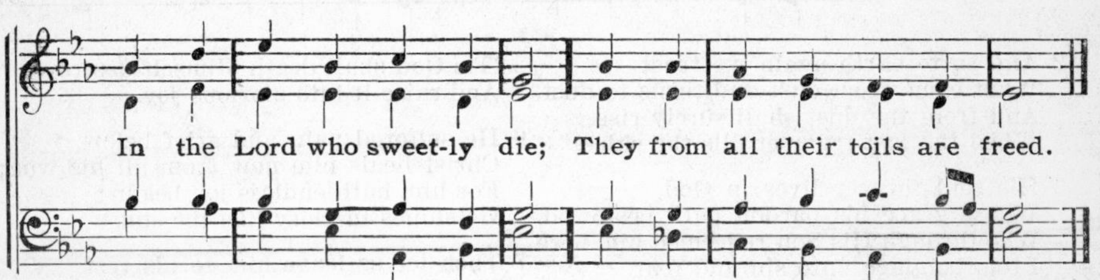
In the Lord who sweet-ly die; They from all their toils are freed.

2 Them the Spirit hath declared
Blest, unutterably blest;
Jesus is their great Reward,
Jesus is their endless Rest.

3 Followed by their works, they go
Where their Head had gone before;
Reconciled by grace below,
Grace hath opened mercy's door.

4 Justified through faith alone,
Here they knew their sins forgiven;
Here they laid their burden down,
Hallowed and made meet for heaven.

5 When from flesh the spirit freed
Hastens homeward to return,
Mortals cry: "A man is dead!"
Angels sing: "A child is born!"

Charles Wesley, 1742

537 Meinen Jesum 7,8,7,8,7,7

1 Gentle Shepherd, Thou hast stilled
Now Thy little lamb's brief weeping;
Ah, how peaceful, pale, and mild,
In its narrow bed 'tis sleeping,
And no sigh of anguish sore
Heaves that little bosom more.

2 In this world of care and pain,
Lord, Thou wouldst no longer leave it;
To the sunny, heavenly plain
Dost Thou now with joy receive it;
Clothed in robes of spotless white,
Now it dwells with Thee in light.

3 Ah, Lord Jesus, grant that we
Where it lives may soon be living,
And the lovely pastures see
That its heavenly food are giving:
Then the gain of death we prove
Though Thou take what most we love.

J. W. Meinhold, 1835 C. Winkworth, Tr. 1858

538 Nun lasst uns den Leib L. M.

Pub. by RHAU, 1544

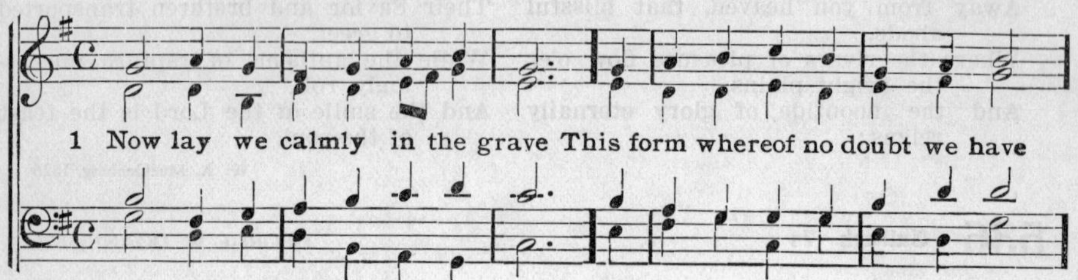
1 Now lay we calmly in the grave This form whereof no doubt we have

That it shall rise a - gain that day, In glor-ious triumph o'er de-cay.

2 And so to earth again we trust
What came from dust and turns to dust,
And from the dust shall surely rise,
When the last trumpet fills the skies.

3 His soul forever lives in God,
Whose grace his pardon hath bestowed,
Who through His Son redeemed him here
From bondage unto sin and fear.

4 His trials and his griefs are past;
A blessed end is his at last;
He bore Christ's yoke and did His will,
And though he died he liveth still.

5 He lives where none do mourn and weep,
And calmly shall his body sleep,
'Tis God shall death Himself destroy,
And raise it into glorious joy.

6 He suffered pain and grief below,
Christ heals him now from all his woe;
For him hath endless joy begun;
He shines in glory like the sun.

7 Then let us leave him to his rest,
And homeward turn, for he is blest:
And we must well our souls prepare,
For death may seize us everywhere.

8 So help us, Christ, our Hope in loss;
Thou hast redeemed us by Thy cross
From endless death and misery;
We praise, we bless, we worship Thee.

M. Weiss, 1531 V.8 Dr. Martin Luther C. Winkworth, Tr. a

539 Nun lasst uns den Leib L. M.

1 Now hush your cries and shed no tear,
On such death none should look with fear;
He died a faithful Christian man,
And with his death true life began.

2 Coffin and grave we deck with care,
His body reverently bear,
It is not dead, but rests in God,
And softly sleeps beneath the sod.

3 It seems as all were over now,—
The heavy limbs, the soulless brow,—
Yet through these rigid limbs once more
A noble life, ere long, shall pour.

4 These bones, now dead, again shall feel
New warmth and vigor through them steal,
And reunited they shall soar
On high to live for evermore.

5 This body, lying stiff and stark,
Shall soon rise upward from the dark,
And swiftly mount up to the skies,
Even as the spirit heavenward flies.

6 The buried grain of wheat must die,
Withered and worthless long must lie,
Yet springs to light all sweet and fair,
And proper fruits shall rightly bear.

7 Even so this body, made of dust,
To earth we once again entrust,
Where it shall slumber free from pain,
Till from the dead it rise again.

8 God breathed into this house of clay
The spirit that hath passed away;
The righteous mind, the noble heart,
The living faith did Christ impart.

9 Now earth has hid it from our eyes,
Till God shall bid it wake and rise,
Who ne'er the creature will forget,
On whom his image He hath set.

10 Ah! would that promised day were here,
When Christ will once again appear,
And bring them to their heavenly home
Who have been buried in the tomb.

Nikolaus Hermann, † 1561 C. Winkworth, Tr. a

540 Rest L. M.

W. B. BRADBURY. 1843

1 A - sleep in Je - sus! bless - ed sheep, From which none
ev - er wakes to weep, A calm and un - dis - turbed repose, Un - brok - en by the last of foes.

(Or to St. Crispin Or to Repose)

2 Asleep in Jesus! Oh, how sweet
To be for such a slumber meet;
With holy confidence to sing
That death has lost his venomed sting.

3 Asleep in Jesus! peaceful rest,
Whose waking is supremely blest;
No fear, no woe, shall dim that hour
That manifests the Savior's power.

4 Asleep in Jesus! Oh, for me
May such a blissful refuge be;
Securely shall my ashes lie,
And wait the summons from on high.

Mrs. Margaret Mackay, 1832 ab.

Death and Burial

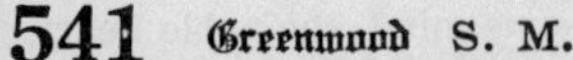

541 Greenwood S. M. — J. E. SWEETSER (P)

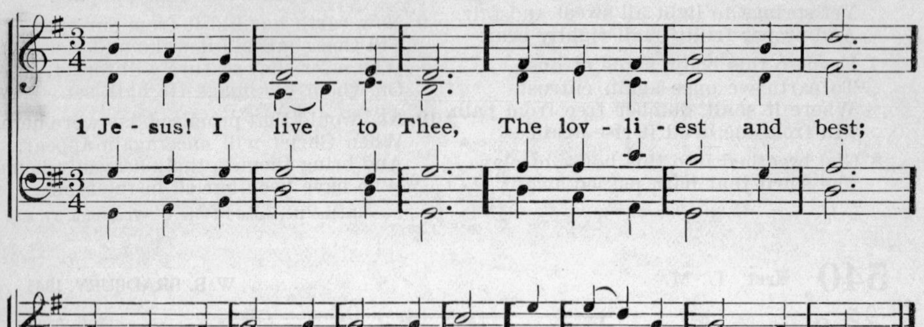
1 Je - sus! I live to Thee, The lov - li - est and best;

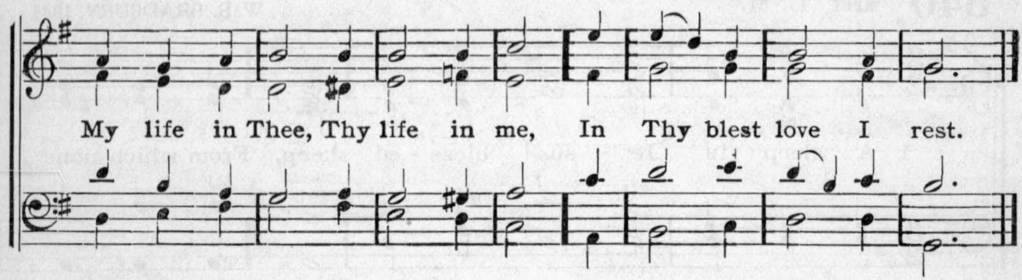
My life in Thee, Thy life in me, In Thy blest love I rest.

2 Jesus! I die to Thee,
Whenever death shall come;
To die in Thee is life to me
In my eternal home.

3 Whether to live or die,
I know not which is best;
To live in Thee is bliss to me,
To die is endless rest.

4 Living or dying, Lord,
I ask but to be Thine;
My life in Thee, Thy life in me,
Make heaven forever mine.

H. Harbaugh, 1850

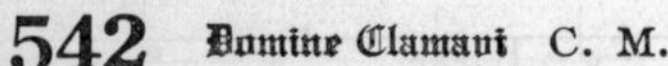

542 Domine Clamavi C. M. — J. H. KNECHT, 1797

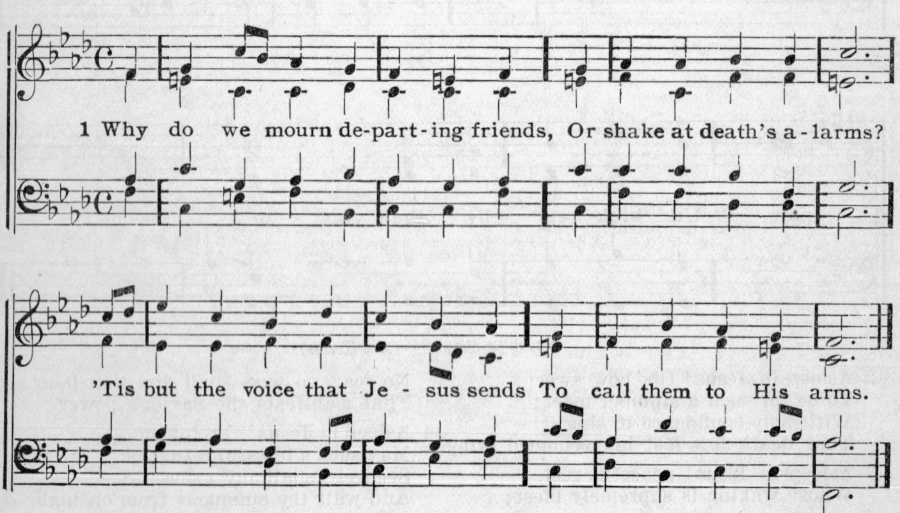
1 Why do we mourn de-part-ing friends, Or shake at death's a-larms?
'Tis but the voice that Je - sus sends To call them to His arms.

2 Are we not tending upward, too,
As fast as time can move?
Nor would we wish the hours more slow,
To keep us from our love.

3 Why should we tremble to convey
Their bodies to the tomb?
There the dear flesh of Jesus lay,
And scattered all the gloom.

4 The graves of all the saints He blessed,
And softened every bed;
Where should the dying members rest,
But with their dying Head?

5 Thence He arose, ascending high,
And showed our feet the way;
Up to the Lord we, too, shall fly
At the great rising-day.

6 Then let the last loud trumpet sound,
And bid our kindred rise;
Awake! ye nations under ground,
Ye saints, ascend the skies!

Isaac Watts, 1709

543

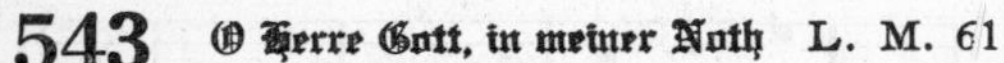
O Herre Gott, in meiner Noth L. M. 61

REIMANN, 1747

1 { O Lord my God, I cry to Thee, In my dis-tress Thou help-est me.
My soul and bod-y I com-mend In - to Thy hands; Thine an-gel send

To guide me home, and cheer my heart, Since Thou dost call me to de - part.

2 O Jesus Christ, Thou Lamb of God,
Once slain to take away our load,
Now let Thy cross, Thine agony,
Avail to save and solace me;
Thy death to open heaven, and there
Bid me the joy of angels share.

3 O Holy Spirit, at the end,
Sweet Comforter, be Thou my Friend.
When death and hell assail me sore,
Leave me, O leave me nevermore,
But bear me safely through the strife,
As Thou hast promised, into life.

N. Selnecker, 1587 C. Winkworth, Tr. a

544 Wer weiss wie nahe mir mein Ende 8s 61 CHR. MOECK, † 1818 (Ad. by P)

1 { Who knows how near my end may be? Time speeds away, and death comes on;
How swift-ly, ah! how sud - den-ly, May death be here and life be gone!

My God, for Je - sus' sake I pray Thy peace may bless my dy - ing day.

2 The world that smiled when morn was come
May change for me ere close of eve;
So long as earth is still my home
In peril of my death I live;
My God, for Jesus' sake I pray
Thy peace may bless my dying day.

3 Teach me to ponder oft my end,
And ere the hour of death appears,
To cast my soul on Christ, her Friend,
Nor spare repentant cries and tears;
My God, for Jesus' sake I pray
Thy peace may bless my dying day.

4 And let me now so order all,
That ever ready I may be
To say with joy, Whate'er befall,
Lord, do Thou as Thou wilt with me;
My God, for Jesus' sake I pray
Thy peace may bless my dying day.

5 Let heaven to me be ever sweet,
And this world bitter let me find,
That I, mid all its toil and heat,
May keep eternity in mind;
My God, for Jesus' sake I pray
Thy peace may bless my dying day.

6 O Father, cover all my sins
With Jesus' merits, who alone
The pardon that I covet wins
And makes His long sought rest my own;
My God, for Jesus' sake I pray
Thy peace may bless my dying day.

7 His sorrows and His cross I know
Make death-beds soft, and light the grave,
They comfort in the hour of woe,
They give me all I fain would have;
My God, for Jesus' sake I pray
Thy peace may bless my dying day.

8 From Him can naught my soul divide,
Nor life nor death can part us now;
I thrust my hand into His side,
And say, My Lord and God art Thou!
My God, for Jesus' sake I pray
Thy peace may bless my dying day.

9 In holy Baptism long ago
I joined me to the living Vine;
Thou lovest me in Him I know,
In Him Thou dost accept me Thine;
My God, for Jesus' sake I pray
Thy peace may bless my dying day.

10 And I have eaten His own flesh
And drunk His blood,—nor can I be
Forsaken now, nor doubt afresh,
I am in Him, and He in me.
My God, for Jesus' sake I pray
Thy peace may bless my dying day.

11 Then death may come, or tarry yet,
I know in Christ I perish not,
He never will His own forget,
He gives me robes without a spot.
My God, for Jesus' sake I pray
Thy peace may bless my dying day.

12 And thus I live in God at peace,
And die without a thought of fear,
Content to take what God decrees,
For through His Son my faith is clear,
His grace shall be in death my stay,
And peace shall bless my dying day.

Emilie Juliane, Countess of Schwarzburg-Rudolstadt, 1686 C. Winkworth, Tr. 1858 a

545 Wer weiss wie nahe mir mein Ende L. M. 61

1 I fall asleep in Jesus' wounds,
There pardon for my sins abounds;
Yea, Jesus' blood and righteousness
My jewels are, my glorious dress,
Wherein before my God I stand,
When I shall reach the heavenly land.

2 With peace and joy I now depart,
God's child I am with all my heart;
I thank thee, death, thou leadest me
To that true life where I would be.
So cleansed by Christ I fear not death.
Lord Jesus, strengthen Thou my faith!

Paul Eber, † 1569 C. Winkworth, Tr. a

(Or to Vater unser im)

546 Vesperi Lux 7,7,7,5

J. B. DYKES, 1823—1876

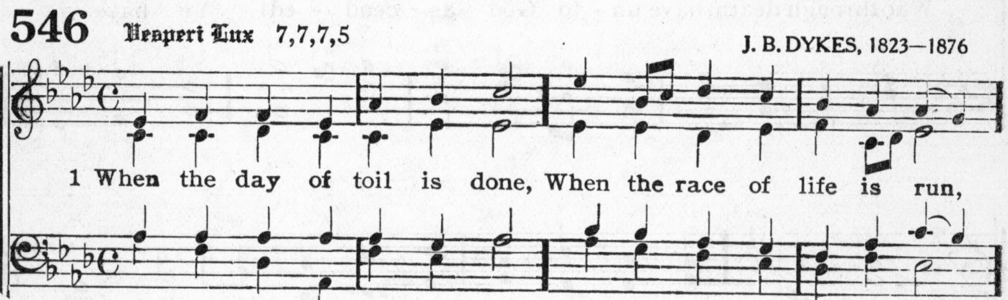
1 When the day of toil is done, When the race of life is run,

Fa - ther, grant Thy wea - ried one Rest for ev - er - more.

2 When the strife of sin is stilled,
When the foe within is killed,
Be Thy gracious word fulfilled,—
"Peace for evermore."

3 When the darkness melts away
At the breaking of the day,
Bid us hail the cheering ray,—
Light for evermore.

4 When the heart by sorrow tried
Feels at length its throbs subside,
Bring us, where all tears are dried,
Joy for evermore.

5 When for vanished days we yearn,
Days that never can return,
Teach us in Thy love to learn
Love for evermore.

6 When the breath of life is flown,
When the grave must claim its own,
Lord of life, be ours Thy crown,—
Life for evermore.

J. Ellerton, 1871

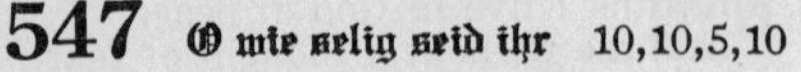

547 O wie selig seid ihr 10,10,5,10 STOEZEL, 1744

1 O how blest are ye, whose toils are end - ed!

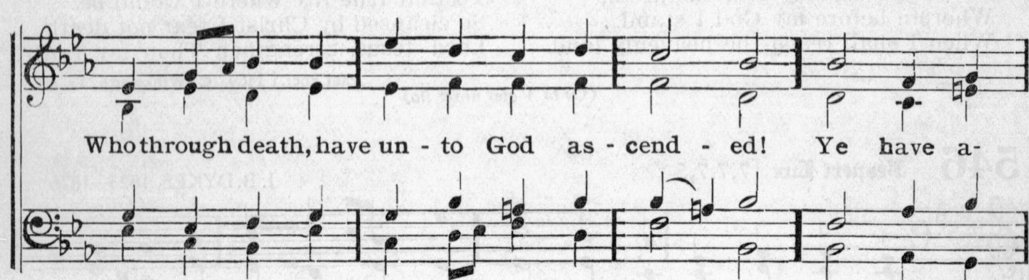
Who through death, have un - to God as - cend - ed! Ye have a-

ris - en From the cares which keep us still in pris - on.

2 We are still as in a dungeon living,
Still oppressed with sorrow and misgiving;
Our undertakings
Are but toils and troubles and heartbreakings.

3 Ye, meanwhile, are in your chambers sleeping,
Quiet, and set free from all our weeping;
No cross or sadness
There can hinder your untroubled gladness.

4 Christ has wiped away your tears forever;
Ye have that for which we still endeavor;
To you are chanted
Songs that ne'er to mortal ears were granted.

5 Ah! who would then not depart with gladness,
To inherit heaven for earthly sadness?
Who here would languish
Longer in bewailing and in anguish?

6 Come, O Christ, and loose the chains that bind us!
Lead us forth, and cast this world behind us!
With Thee, th' Anointed,
Finds the soul its joy and rest appointed.

Simon Dach, 1635 H. W. Longfellow, Tr. a

548 Storl (O Jerusalem, du schöne) 8,7 61
J. G. C. STOERL
1 O'er the dis-tant mountains breaking Comes the redd'ning dawn of day;
Rise, my soul, from sleep a-wak-ing, Rise, and sing, and watch, and pray,
'Tis thy Sav-ior, 'Tis thy Sav-ior, On His bright re-turn-ing way.

2 O Thou long-expected, weary
Waits my anxious soul for Thee,
Life is dark, and earth is dreary,
Where Thy light I do not see;
|: O my Savior, :|
When wilt Thou return to me?

3 Nearer is my soul's salvation,
Spent the night, the day at hand;
Keep me in my lowly station,
Watching for Thee, till I stand,
|: O my Savior, :|
In Thy bright, Thy promised land.

4 With my lamp well trimm'd and burning,
Swift to hear and loath to roam,
Watching for Thy glad returning
To restore me to my home.
|: Come, my Savior, :|
Thou hast promised: quickly come.

J. S. B. Monsell, 1863 a

549
Wachet auf, ruft uns die Stimme
8,9,8,6,6,4,8,8
P. NICOLAI, 1599
1 { Wake, a - wake, for night is fly - ing, The watch-men on the heights are cry - ing, A-wake, Je - ru - sa - lem, a - rise! The
Mid - night hears the wel-come voi - ces, And at the thrill-ing cry re - joi - ces; O where are ye, ye vir - gins (Omit.) wise?
1
2
Bride - groom comes, a - wake! Your lamps with glad - ness take!
Hal - le - lu - jah! With bri - dal care Your-selves pre -

pare To meet the Bride - groom, who is near!

2 Zion hears the watchmen singing,
And all her heart with joy is springing,
She wakes, she rises from her gloom;
For her Lord comes down all glorious,
The strong in grace, in truth victorious,
Her Star is risen, her Light is come!
Now come Thou Blessed One,
Lord Jesus, God's own Son,
Hail! Hosanna!
The joyful call We answer all,
And follow to the nuptial hall.

3 Glory unto Thee be given,
By men and by the host of heaven,
With harp and cymbal's clearest tone;
Of one pearl each shining portal,
Where we are with the choir immortal
Of angels round Thy dazzling throne,
Nor eye hath seen, nor ear
Hath yet attained to hear
Such great glory;
Therefore will we Eternally
Sing hymns of joy and praise to Thee.

Dr. Ph. Nicolai, 1599

550 St. Ambrose L. M.

ANCIENT MEL. HAR. W. H. MONK

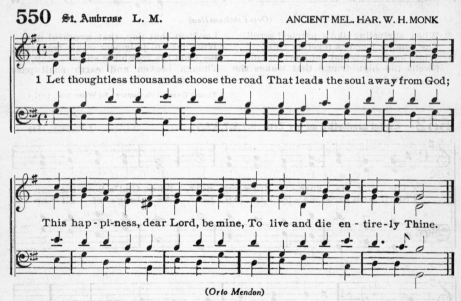

1 Let thoughtless thousands choose the road That leads the soul away from God;
This hap - pi-ness, dear Lord, be mine, To live and die en - tire-ly Thine.

(Orto Mendon)

2 On Christ, by faith, I fain would live,
From Him, my life, my all receive;
To Him devote my fleeting hours,
Serve Him alone with all my powers.

3 Christ is my everlasting All;
To Him I look, on Him I call;
He will my every want supply,
In time, and through eternity.

4 Soon will the Lord, my Life, appear;
Soon shall I end my trials here;
Leave sin and sorrow, death and pain,
To live is Christ, to die is gain.

5 Soon will the saints in glory meet,
Soon walk through every golden street,
And sing on every blissful plain,—
To live is Christ, to die is gain.

Hoskins

Judgment

551 Windham L. M. D. READ, 1785

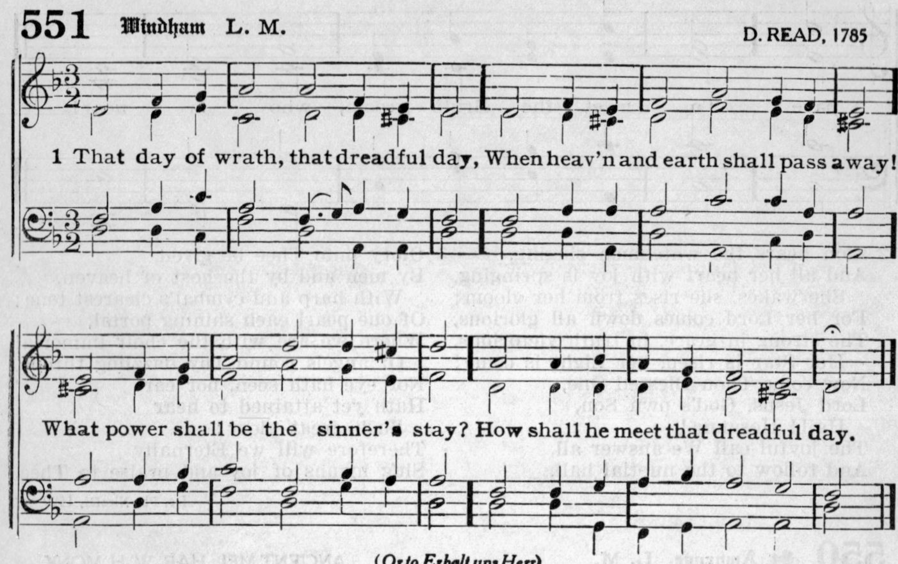
1 That day of wrath, that dreadful day, When heav'n and earth shall pass away!
What power shall be the sinner's stay? How shall he meet that dreadful day.

(Or to Erhalt uns Herr)

2 When, shriveling like a parched scroll,
The flaming heavens together roll;
When louder yet, and yet more dread,
Swells the high trump that wakes the dead:

3 Lord, on that day, that wrathful day,
When man to judgment wakes from clay,
Be Thou the trembling sinner's stay,
Though heaven and earth shall pass away.

Thomas Celano, 13th Century Sir Walter Scott, 1805 a

552 Es ist gewisslich an der Zeit 8,7,8.7,8,8,7 J. KLUGE, 1535

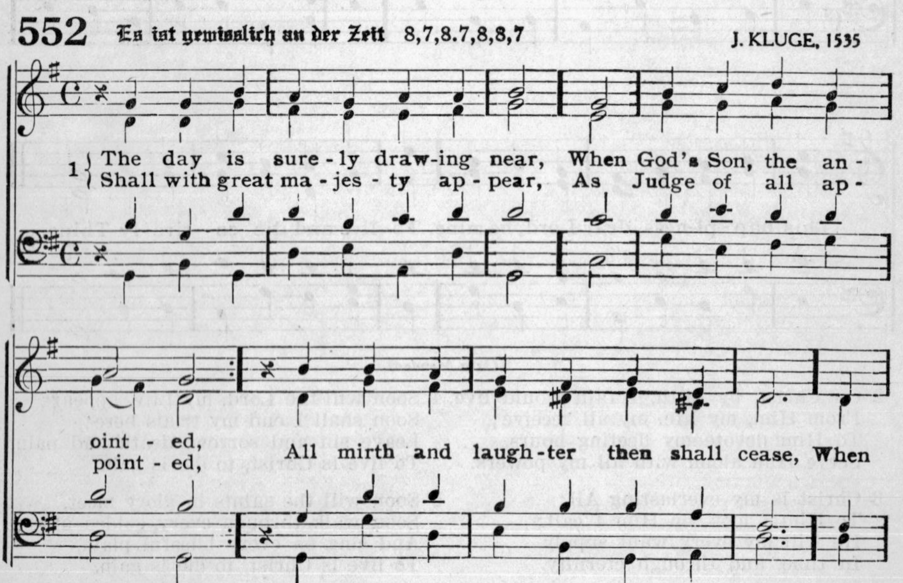
1 { The day is sure-ly draw-ing near, When God's Son, the an-oint-ed,
Shall with great ma-jes-ty ap-pear, As Judge of all ap-point-ed,
All mirth and laugh-ter then shall cease, When

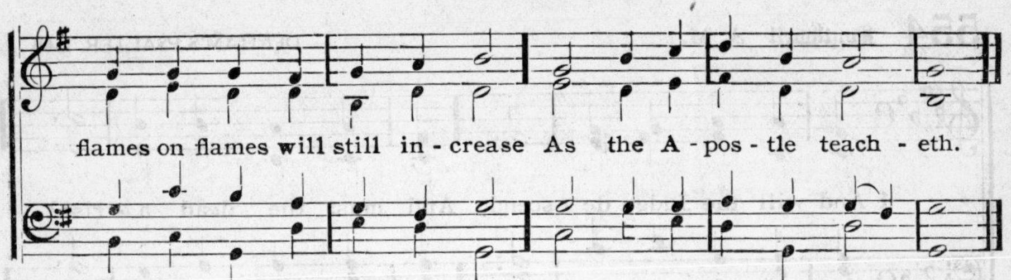
flames on flames will still in - crease As the A - pos - tle teach - eth.

2 A trumpet loud shall then resound,
And all the earth be shaken;
Then all who in their graves are found
Shall from their sleep awaken;
But all that live shall in that hour,
By the Almighty's boundless power,
Be changed at His commanding.

3 A book is opened then to all
A record truly telling
What each hath done both great and small,
When he on earth was dwelling;
And every heart be clearly seen,
And all be known as they have been,
In thoughts and words and actions.

4 Then woe to those who scorned the Lord,
And sought but carnal pleasures,
Who here despised His precious Word,
And loved their earthly treasures!
With shame and trembling they will stand,
And at the Judge's stern command
To Satan be delivered.

5 O Jesus, who my debt didst pay,
And for my sin wast smitten,
Within the book of life, O may
My name be also written!
I will not doubt; I trust in Thee,
From Satan Thou hast made me free,
And from all condemnation.

6 Therefore my Intercessor be,
And for Thy bloody merit
Declare my name from judgment free,
With all who life inherit;
That I may see Thee face to face,
With all Thy saints in that blest place,
Which Thou for us hast purchased.

7 O Jesus Christ, do not delay,
But hasten our salvation!
We often tremble on our way
In fear and tribulation.
Then hear us when we cry to Thee;
Come, mighty Judge, and make us free
From every evil. Amen!

Bartholomaeus Ringwald, 1581   A. Peter, Tr. a.

553 Es ist gewisslich an der Zeit 8,7,8,7,8,8,7

1 Great God, what do I see and hear?
The end of things created;
The Judge of mankind doth appear
On clouds of glory seated;
The trumpet sounds; the graves restore
The dead which they contained before:
Prepare, my soul, to meet Him.

2 The dead in Christ shall first arise,
At the last trumpet's sounding,
Caught up to meet Him in the skies;
With joy their Lord surrounding;
No gloomy fears their souls dismay;
His presence sheds eternal day
On those prepared to meet Him.

3 But sinners, filled with guilty fears,
Behold His wrath prevailing,
For they shall rise, and find their tears
And sighs are unavailing;
The day of grace is past and gone;
Trembling they stand before the throne,
All unprepared to meet Him.

4 O Christ, who diedst and yet dost live,
To me impart Thy merit;
My pardon seal, my sins forgive,
And cleanse me by Thy Spirit.
Beneath Thy cross I view the day
When heaven and earth shall pass away,
And thus prepare to meet Thee.

V. 1 Anon. 1802   Vs. 2, 3 William Bengo Collyer, 1812

554 Southwell S. M. DENHAM'S PSALTER. 1588

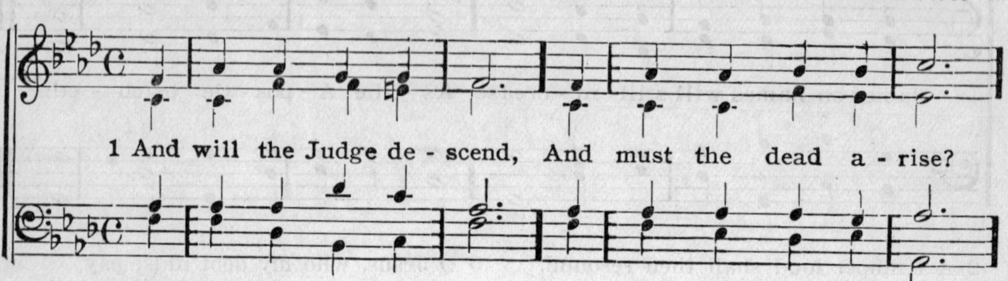
1 And will the Judge de - scend, And must the dead a - rise?

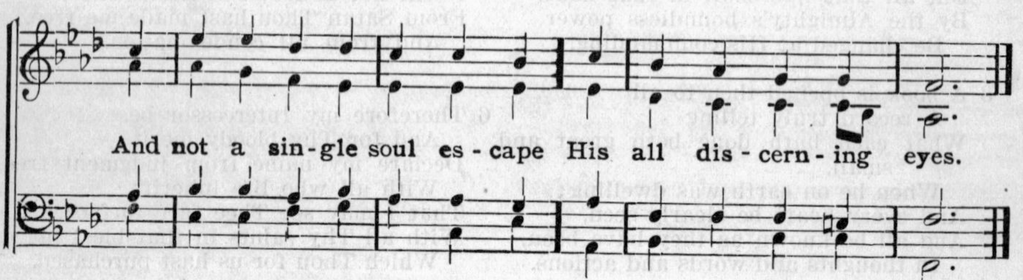
And not a sin-gle soul es - cape His all dis - cern - ing eyes.

2 And from His righteous lips
Shall this dread sentence sound;
And, through the numerous guilty throng,
Spread black despair around?

3 "Depart from me accursed,
To everlasting flame,
For rebel angels first prepared,
Where mercy never came."

4 How will my heart endure
The terrors of that day,
When earth and heaven before His face,
Astonished shrink away?

5 But ere that trumpet shakes
The mansions of the dead,
Hark, from the Gospel's cheering sound
What joyful tidings spread!

6 Ye sinners, seek His grace
Whose wrath ye cannot bear;
Fly to the shelter of His cross,
And find salvation there.

Philip Doddridge

555 Dies Irae 8s 31 OLD LATIN

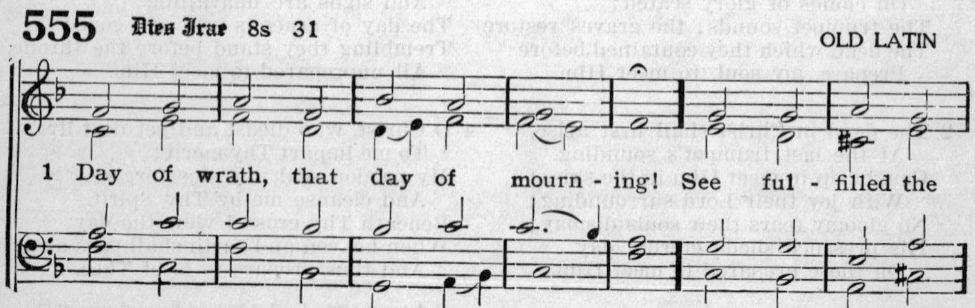
1 Day of wrath, that day of mourn - ing! See ful - filled the

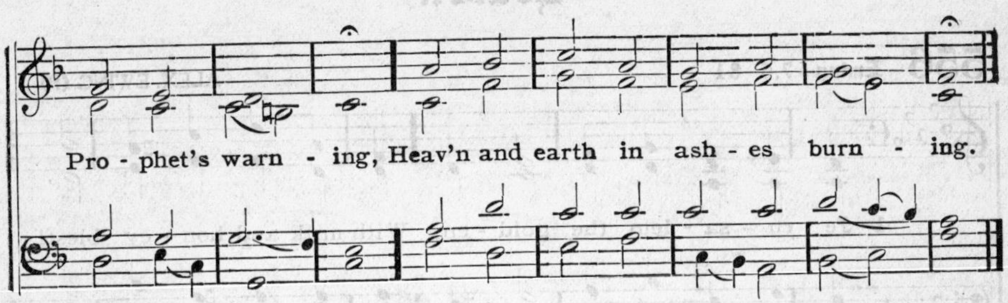
Pro - phet's warn - ing, Heav'n and earth in ash - es burn - ing.

2 O what fear man's bosom rendeth
When from heaven the Judge descendeth
On whose sentence all dependeth!

3 Wondrous sound the trumpet flingeth,
Through earth's sepulchers it ringeth,
All before the throne it bringeth.

4 Death is struck, and nature quaking;
All creation is awaking,
To its Judge an answer making.

5 Lo, the book, exactly worded,
Wherein all hath been recorded;
Thence shall judgment be awarded.

6 When the Judge His seat attaineth,
And each hidden deed arraigneth,
Nothing unavenged remaineth.

7 What shall I, frail man, be pleading?
Who for me be interceding,
When the just are mercy needing?

8 King of majesty tremendous,
Who dost free salvation send us,
Fount of pity, then befriend us!

9 Think, kind Jesus! my salvation
Caused Thy wondrous incarnation;
Leave me not to reprobation!

10 Faint and weary Thou hast sought me;
On the cross of suffering bought me;
Shall such grace in vain be brought me?

11 Righteous Judge of retribution,
Grant Thy gift of absolution,
Ere that day's dread execution.

12 Guilty, now I pour my moaning,
All my shame with anguish owning:
Spare, O God, Thy suppliant groaning!

13 Thou the women gav'st remission,
Heard'st the dying thief's petition;
Hopeless else were my condition.

14 Worthless are my prayers and sighing,
Yet, good Lord, in grace complying,
Rescue me from fires undying!

15 With Thy favored sheep, O place me!
Nor amid the goats abase me:
But to Thy right hand upraise me.

16 While the wicked are confounded,
Doomed to flames of woe unbounded,
Call me, with Thy saints surrounded.

17 Bows my heart in meek submission,
Strewn with ashes of contrition;
Succor Thou my lost condition!

18 Day of sorrow, day of weeping,
When in dust no longer sleeping,
Man awakes in Thy dread keeping!

19 To the rest Thou didst prepare me,
On Thy cross, O Christ, upbear me!
Spare, O God, in mercy spare me!

Thomas de Celano, 1520 ab. William Joseph Irons, Tr. 1848 a

556 Ewing 7,6 8l
ALEX. EWING (P)
1 Je - ru - sa - lem the gold - en, With milk and hon - ey blest!
Be - neath thy con - tem - pla - tion Sink heart and voice op - pressed,
I know not, O I know not What joys a - wait us there,
What ra - dian - cy of glo - ry, What bliss be - yond com - pare!

2 There is the throne of David;
And there, from care released,
The songs of them that triumph,
The shout of them that feast;
And they who, with their Leader,
Have conquered in the fight,
Forever, and forever,
Are clad in robes of white!

3 Exult, O dust and ashes!
The Lord shall be thy Part:
His only, His forever,
Thou shalt be and thou art!
Jesus, in mercy bring us
Soon to that land of rest:
Who art, with God the Father
And Spirit ever blest!

Bernard of Cluny, 12th Cent. J. M. Neale, Tr. 1851

557 Ewing 7,6 8 1

1 Brief life is here our portion;
Brief sorrow, shortlived care;
The life that knows no ending,
The tearless life, is there.
O happy retribution!
Short toil, eternal rest;
For mortals and for sinners
A mansion with the blest!

2 And now we fight the battle,
But then shall wear the crown
Of full and everlasting
And passionless renown;
And now we watch and struggle,
And now we live in hope,
And Zion in her anguish,
With Babylon must cope;

3 But He, whom now we trust in,
Shall then be seen and known;
And they that know and see Him
Shall have Him for their own.
And there is David's fountain,
And life in fullest glow;
And there the light is golden,
And milk and honey flow.

4 The morning shall awaken,
And shadows shall decay,
And each true-hearted servant
Shall shine as doth the day;
Yes! God my King and portion,
In fullness of His grace,
We then shall see for ever,
And worship face to face.

5 O sweet and blessed country,
The home of God's elect!
O sweet and blessed country
That eager hearts expect!
Jesus, in mercy bring us
To that dear land of rest;
Who art, with God the Father.
And Spirit, ever blest.

Bernard of Cluny, 12th Cent. J. M. Neale, Tr. 1851

558 Southwell C. M. H. S. IRONS (P)

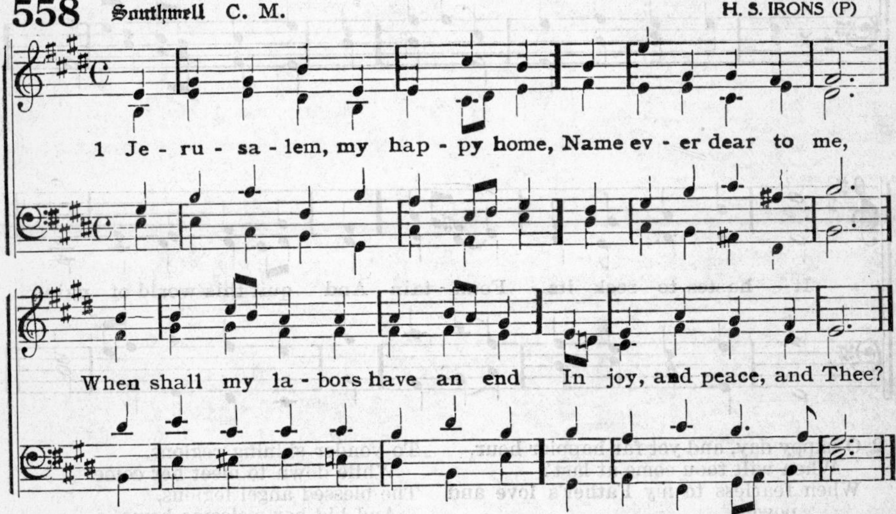
1 Je - ru - sa - lem, my hap - py home, Name ev - er dear to me,
When shall my la - bors have an end In joy, and peace, and Thee?

2 When shall these eyes thy heaven-built walls
And pearly gates behold;
Thy bulwarks with salvation strong,
And streets of shining gold?

3 O when, thou city of my God,
Shall I thy courts ascend,
Where evermore the angels sing,
Where sabbaths have no end?

4 There happier bowers than Eden's bloom,
Nor sin nor sorrow know;
Blest seats! through rude and stormy scenes
I onward press to you.

5 Why should I shrink from pain and woe,
Or feel at death dismay?
I've Canaan's goodly land in view,
And realms of endless day.

6 Apostles, martyrs, prophets, there
Around my Savior stand;
And soon my friends in Christ below
Will join the glorious band.

F. B. P. Re-written by James Montgomery, c. 1796

559 Jerusalem, du hochgebaute Stadt

H. FRANK, † 1639

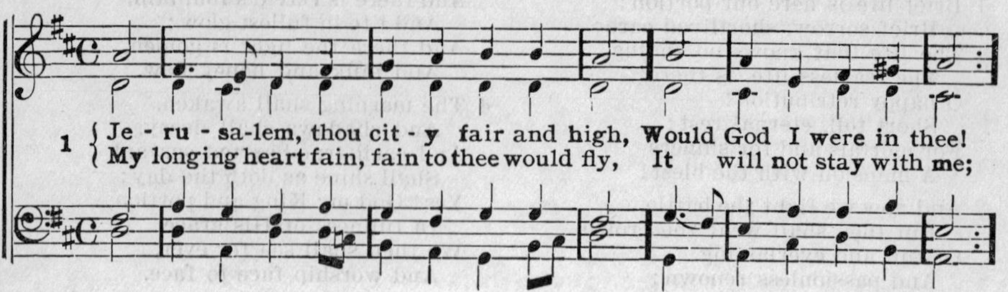
1 { Je - ru - sa-lem, thou cit - y fair and high, Would God I were in thee!
My longing heart fain, fain to thee would fly, It will not stay with me;

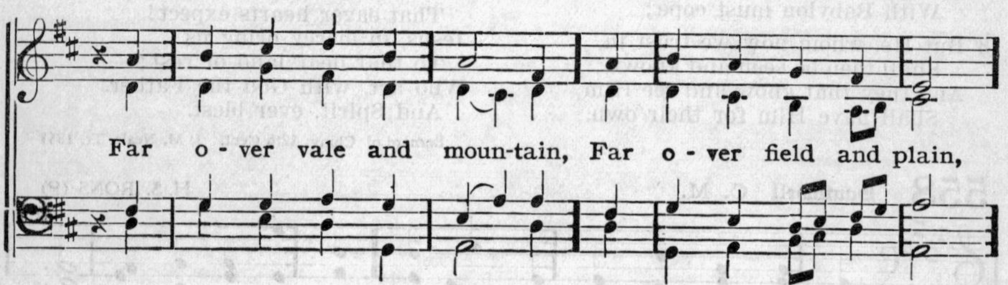
Far o - ver vale and moun-tain, Far o - ver field and plain,

It hastes to seek its Foun - tain And quit this world of pain.

2 O happy day, and yet far happier hour,
When wilt thou come at last?
When fearless to my Father's love and power,
Whose promise standeth fast,
My soul I gladly render,
For surely will His hand
Lead her, with guidance tender,
To heaven, her fatherland.

3 A moment's space, and gently, wondrously,
Released from earthly ties,
Elijah's chariot bears her up to thee,
Through all these lower skies,
To yonder shining regions,
While down to meet her come
The blessed angel legions,
And bid her welcome home.

4 O Zion, hail! Bright city, now unfold
The gates of grace to me!
How many a time I longed for thee of old,
Ere yet I was set free
From yon dark life of sadness,
Yon world of shadowy naught,
And God had given the gladness,
The heritage I sought.

5 O what the tribe, or what the glorious host,
Comes sweeping swiftly down?
The chosen ones on earth who wrought the most,
The Church's brightest crown,
Our Lord hath sent to meet me,
As in the far-off years
Their words oft came to greet me
In yonder land of tears.

6 The Patriarchs' and Prophets' noble train,
With all Christ's followers true,
Who bore the cross, and could the worst disdain
That tyrants dared to do,
I see them shine forever,
All glorious as the sun,
'Mid light that fadeth never,
Their perfect freedom won.

7 And when within that lovely paradise
At last I safely dwell,
From out my soul what songs of bliss shall rise,
What joy my lips shall tell,
While holy saints are singing
Hosannas o'er and o'er,
Pure Hallelujahs ringing
Around me evermore!

8 Innumerous choirs before the shining throne
Their joyful anthems raise,
Till heaven's glad halls are echoing with the tone
Of that great hymn of praise,
And all its host rejoices,
And all its blessed throng
Unite their myriad voices
In one eternal song.

Joh. Matthaeus Meyfart, 1648 C. Winkworth, Tr. a

560 Shepherd C. M.

ARTHUR SULLIVAN, (1842—1900)

1 There is a land of pure de-light, Were saints im - mor - tal reign;

E - ter - nal day ex - cludes the night, And pleas-ures ban - ish pain.

2 There everlasting spring abides,
And never-withering flowers;
Death, like a narrow sea, divides
This heavenly land from ours.

3 Sweet fields, beyond the swelling flood,
Stand dressed in living green;
So to the Jews old Canaan stood,
While Jordan rolled between.

4 But timorous mortals start and shrink
To cross this narrow sea,
And linger, shivering, on the brink,
And fear to launch away.

5 O could we make our doubts remove,
Those gloomy doubts that rise,
And view the Canaan that we love,
With unbeclouded eyes:

6 Could we but climb where Moses stood,
And view the landscape o'er,
Not Jordan's stream, nor death's cold flood,
Should fright us from the shore.

Isaac Watts, 1707

(Or to Heber)

561 Paradise 8,6,8,6,6,6,6,6 J. BARNBY, 1866 (P)

1 O Par-a-dise, O Par-a-dise, Who doth not crave for rest?
Who would not seek the hap-py land Where they that loved are blest;
Where loy-al hearts and true
Where loy - - al hearts and true Stand ev-er in the light,
All rap-ture through and through, In God's most ho - ly sight?

2 O Paradise, O Paradise,
The world is growing old;
Who would not be at rest and free
Where love is never cold;
Where loyal hearts, etc.

3 O Paradise, O Paradise,
I greatly long to see
The special place my dearest Lord
In love prepares for me;
Where loyal hearts, etc.

4 Lord Jesus, King of Paradise,
Oh, keep me in Thy love,
And guide me to that happy land
Of perfect rest above,
Where loyal hearts, etc.

F. W. Faber, 1862

562 Homeland 7,6 8 l

ARTHUR SULLIVAN, 1872

1 The Home-land! O the Home-land! The land of souls free born!
No gloom - y night is known there, But aye the fade - less morn:
I'm sigh - ing for that Coun - try, My heart is ach - ing here;
There is no pain in the Homeland, To which I'm draw-ing near.

2 My Lord is in the Homeland,
With angels bright and fair;
No sinful thing nor evil,
Can ever enter there;
The music of the ransomed
Is ringing in my ears,
And when I think of the Homeland,
My eyes are wet with tears.

3 For loved ones in the Homeland
Are waiting me to come
Where neither death nor sorrow
Invade their holy home:
O dear, dear native Country!
O rest and peace above!
Christ bring us all to the Homeland
Of His eternal love.

H. R. Haweis, 1872

463 **St. Edmund** 6,4,6,4,6,6,6,4 A. S. SULLIVAN

1 I'm but a stran-ger here, Heav'n is my home; Earth is a

des-ert drear, Heav'n is my home; Danger and sorrow stand Round me on

ev-ery hand; Heav'n is my fa-ther-land, Heav'n is my home.

2 What though the tempest rage,
Heav'n is my home;
Short is my pilgrimage,
Heav'n is my home;
And time's wild wintry blast
Soon shall be over-past;
I shall reach home at last,
Heav'n is my home.

3 There at my Savior's side,
Heav'n is my home;
I shall be glorified,
Heav'n is my home;
There are the good and blest,
Those I love most and best;
And there I, too, shall rest,
Heav'n is my home.

4 Therefore I murmur not,
Heav'n is my home;
Whate'er my earthly lot,
Heav'n is my home,
And I shall surely stand
There at my Lord's right hand;
Heav'n is my fatherland,
Heav'n is my home.

Thomas R. Taylor, 1836 a

564 Elton 8,6,8,8,6 F. C. MAKER, 1844

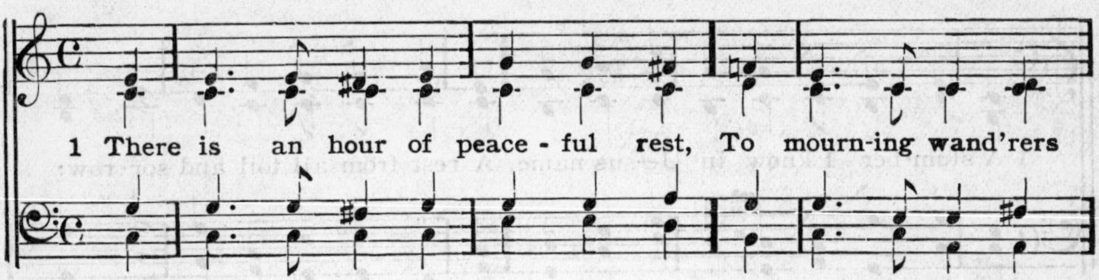
1 There is an hour of peace - ful rest, To mourn-ing wand'rers

given; There is a joy for souls dis-tressed, A

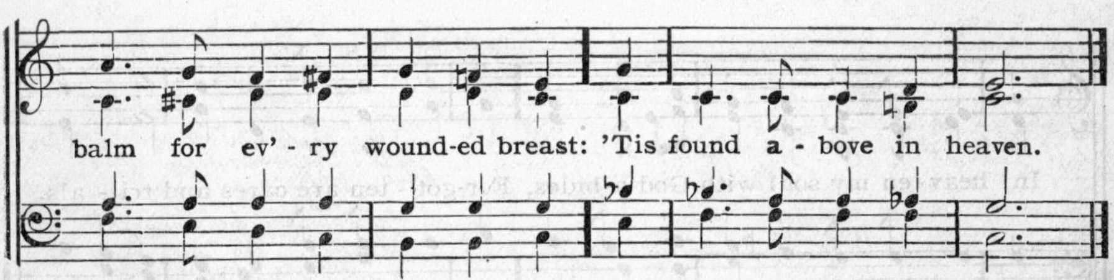
balm for ev' - ry wound-ed breast: 'Tis found a - bove in heaven.

2 There is a soft, a downy bed,
'Tis fair as breath of even;
A couch for weary mortals spread
Where they may rest the aching head,
And find repose—in heaven.

3 There is a home for weary souls,
By sin and sorrow driven,—
When tossed on life's tempestuous shoals,
Where storms arise and ocean rolls,
And all is drear—but heaven.

4 There faith lifts up her cheerful eye,
To brighter prospects given;
And views the tempest passing by,
The evening shadows quickly fly,
And all serene—in heaven.

5 There fragrant flowers immortal bloom,
And joys supreme are given;
There rays divine disperse the gloom;
Beyond the confines of the tomb
Appears the dawn of heaven!

N. B. Tappan, 1818

565 Den signede Dag, som vi nu ser 9,8 6 1 C. E. F. WEYSE, 1826

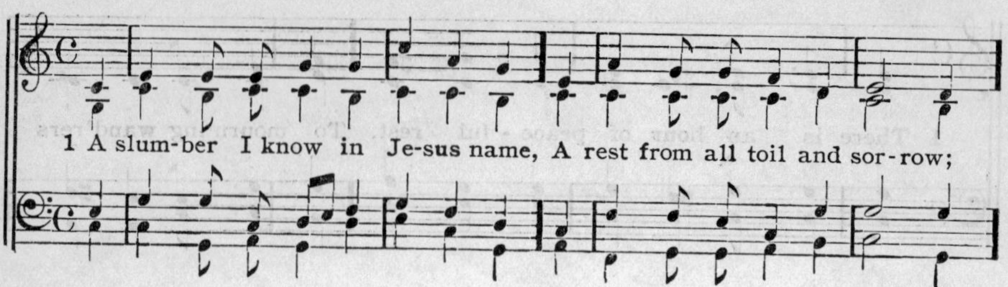
1 A slum-ber I know in Je-sus name, A rest from all toil and sor-row;

Earth ten-der-ly takes My wear-y frame, To sleep till the blissful mor-row;

In heav-en my soul with God a-bides, For-got-ten are cares and tri-als.

2 An even I know, serene and blest,
And oft is my spirit longing,
When, weary and worn, it finds no rest,
While woes on the way are thronging,—
Oft longing to see the journey's end,
And rest in a blissful slumber.

3 A morning I know, so bright and fair,
When tidings of joy shall wake us,
When anthems from high shall fill the air,
And God to His glory take us,
When Jesus shall bid us rise from sleep—
How joyous that hour of awaking!

4 Oh, dear is that morning fair to me!
And oft, o'er the mountains beaming,
In spirit its heavenly light I see,
As golden the peaks are gleaming—
For joy I must sing, as birds at dawn
Their carols in lofty lindens.

5 The Savior then comes unto our graves;
His mighty command is given:
Then break from the deep the ocean waves,
Each tomb and restraint is riven.
All earth hears the cry: Ye dead, come forth!
In glory we go to meet Him.

M. B. Landstad, † 1880

566 Wie wohl ist mir, o Freund der Seelen

1 Yes, there remaineth still a rest!
Arise, sad heart, that darkly pines,
By heavy care and pain opprest,
On whom no sun of gladness shines;
Look to the Lamb! in yon bright fields
Thou'lt know the joy His presence yields;
Cast off thy load and thither haste;
Soon shalt thou fight and bleed no more,
Soon, soon thy weary course be o'er,
And deep the rest thou then shalt taste.

2 The rest appointed thee of God,
The rest that naught shall break or move,
That ere this earth by man was trod
Was set apart for thee by love.
Our Savior gave His life to win
This rest for thee; O enter in!
Hear how His voice sounds far and wide,
Ye weary souls no more delay,
Loiter not faithless by the way,
Here in my peace and rest abide.

3 Ye heavy laden, come to Him!
Ye who are bent with many a load,
Come from your prisons drear and dim,
Toil thus not sadly on your road!
Ye've borne the burden of the day,
And hear ye not the Savior say:
"I am your refuge and your rest"?
His children ye, of heavenly birth,
Howe'er may rage sin, hell, or earth,
Here ye are safe, here calmly blest.

4 O what contentment fills the breast
Of wanderers through the desert plains,
If they have found a place to rest,
To quench their thirst and cure their pains!
How welcome is an humble bed,
Where they may rest their weary head,
To persons that are sick and sore!
Such hours of sweet repose soon fly,
But there remains a rest on high
Where we shall rest forevermore.

5 Yonder in joy the sheaves we bring,
Whose seed was sown on earth in tears;
There in our Father's house we sing
The song too sweet for mortal ears.
Sorrow and sighing all are past,
And pain and death are fled at last;
There with the Lamb of God we dwell,
He leads us to the crystal river,
He wipes away all tears forever;
What there is ours no tongue can tell.

6 Nor thirst nor hunger pains us there,
The time of recompense is come,
Nor cold nor scorching heat we bear,
We're sheltered in our Savior's home.
The Lamb is in the midst; and those
Who followed Him through shame and woes,
Are crowned with honor, joy, and peace.
The dry bones gather life again,
One Sabbath over all shall reign,
Wherein all toil and labor cease.

7 There is untroubled calm and light,
No gnawing care shall mar our rest;
Ye weary, heed this word aright
Come, lean upon your Savior's breast.
Fain would I linger here no more,
Fain to yon happier world upsoar,
And join that bright expectant band.
O raise, my soul, the joyful song
That rings through yon triumphant throng;
Thy perfect rest is nigh at hand.

J. S. Knudt, 1337 C. Winkworth, Tr. a

567 Schumann

1 "Forever with the Lord!"
Amen! so let it be;
Life from the dead is in that word,
'Tis immortality.

2 Here in the body pent,
Absent from Him I roam,
Yet nightly pitch my moving tent
A day's march nearer home.

3 My Father's house on high,
Home of my soul! how near
At times to faith's fore-seeing eye
The golden gates appear!

4 Ah! then my spirit faints
To reach the land I love,
The bright inheritance of saints
Jerusalem above!

5 "Forever with the Lord!"
Father, if 'tis Thy will,
The promise of that faithful word
E'en here to me fulfill.

6 Be Thou at my right hand,
Then I can never fail;
Uphold Thou me, and I shall stand,
Fight, and I must prevail.

7 So when my latest breath
Shall rend the veil in twain,
By death I shall escape from death,
And life eternal gain.

8 Knowing as I am known,
How shall I love that word,
And oft repeat before the throne,
"Forever with the Lord!"

J. Montgomery, 1835

Chants

568 Gloria in Excelsis

From SPANGENBERG, 1545

Congregation
Glo-ry be to God on high, and on earth peace, good will toward men.
Choir or Congregation
We praise Thee, we bless Thee, we wor-ship Thee, we glo-ri-fy
Thee, we give thanks to Thee for Thy great glo-ry. O

Lord God, Heavenly King, God the Fa - ther, Al - might - y.

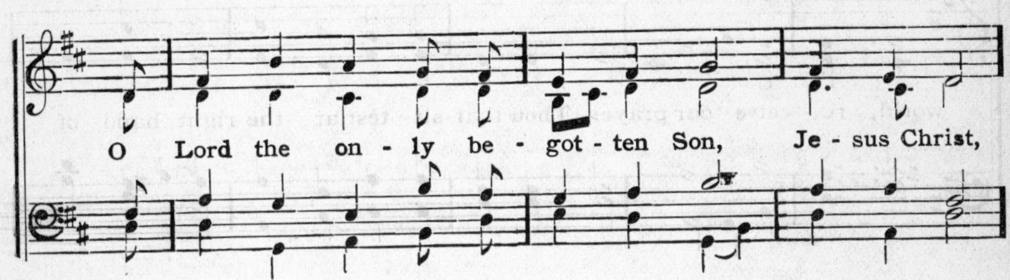

O Lord the on - ly be - got - ten Son, Je - sus Christ,

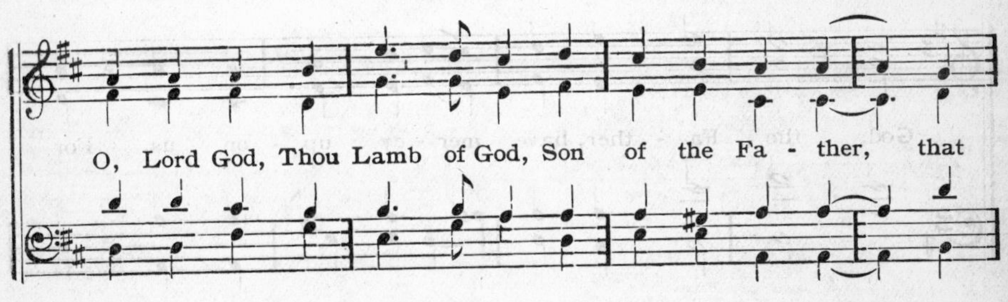

O, Lord God, Thou Lamb of God, Son of the Fa - ther, that

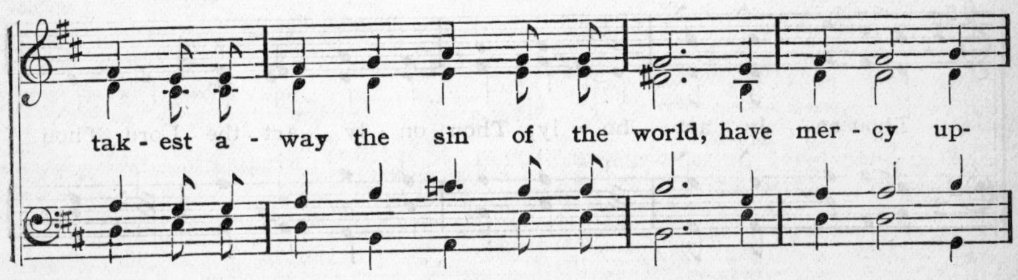

tak - est a - way the sin of the world, have mer - cy up-

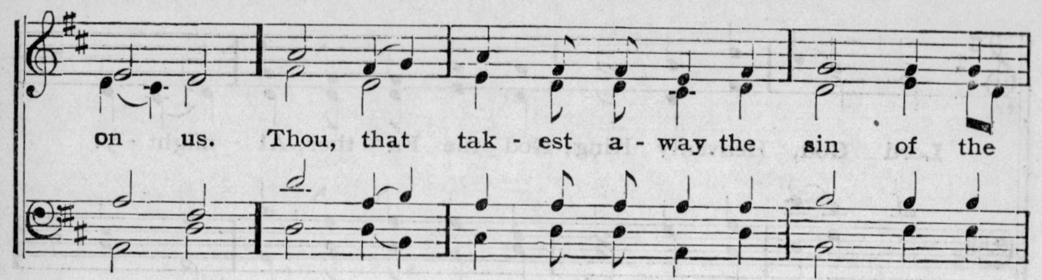
on us. Thou, that tak - est a - way the sin of the

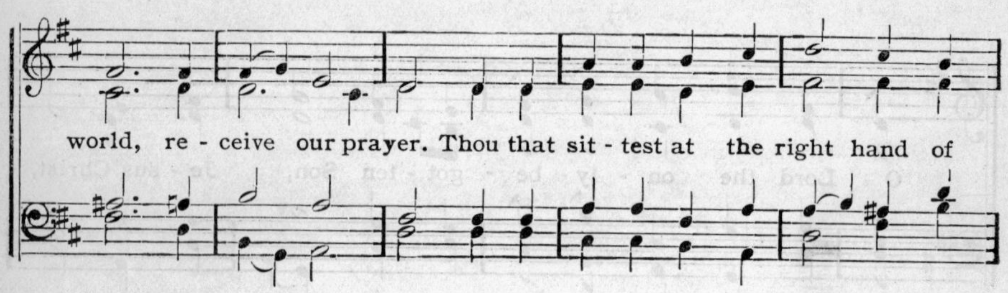
world, re - ceive our prayer. Thou that sit - test at the right hand of

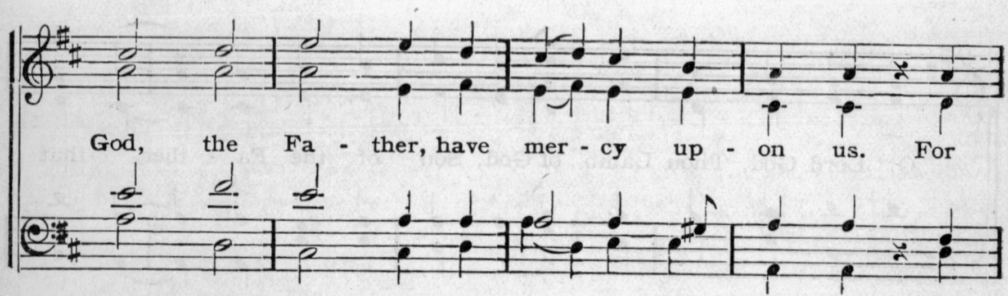
God, the Fa - ther, have mer - cy up - on us. For

Thou on - ly art ho - ly, Thou on - ly art the Lord, Thou

on - ly, O Christ, with the Ho - ly Ghost, art most

high in the glo - ry of God the Fa - ther, A - - men.

569 Levavi Oculos

No. 1 JOHN F. BURROWES, 1787—1852 No. 2 EDWARD J. HOPKINS, 1818

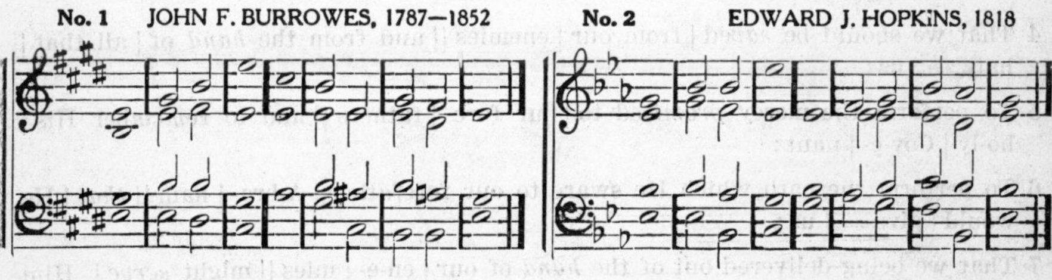

1 I WILL lift up mine *eyes* un- | to the | hills || From *whence* | com-eth | my — | help.
2 My help *come*th | from the | Lord || *Who* hath | made — | heaven · and | earth.
3 He will not *suf*fer thy | foot · to be | moved || *He* that | keepeth · thee | will not | slumber.
4 Behold, *He* that | keep-eth | Israel || *Shall* | nei-ther | slumber · nor | sleep.
5 The *Lord* Him- | self · is thy | keeper: || The *Lord* is thy de- | fence up- · on | thy right | hand;
6 So that the sun shall not *burn* | thee by | day || *Nor* the | moon — | by — | night.
7 The Lord shall pre*serve* thee | from all | evil || *He* | shall pre- | serve thy | soul.
8 The Lord shall preserve thy going *out* and thy | coming | in || From *this* time | forth for- | ev-er- | more.

Glory be to the *Fa*ther | and · to the | Son || *And* | to the | Ho-ly | Ghost;
As it was in the beginning, is *now* and | ev-er | shall be || *World* without | end. — | *A-* — | *men.*

570 Benedictus

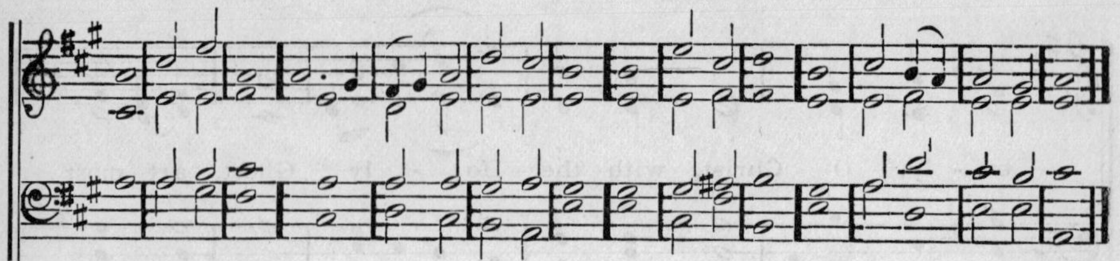

TRENT

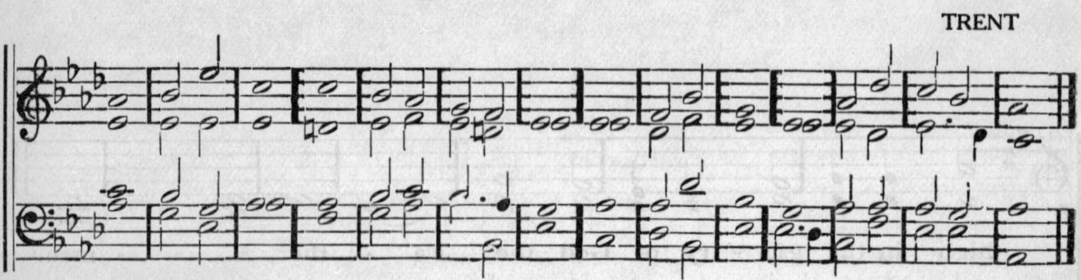

1 Blessed be the Lord *God* of | Is-ra- | el || for He hath *visit*ed | and re- | deem-ed His | people:

2 And hath raised up a *mighty* sal- | va-tion | for us || in the *house* | of His | servant | David;

3 As He spake by the *mouth* of His | ho-ly | Prophets || which have *been* | since the | world be- | gan;

4 That we should be *sav*ed | from our | enemies || and from the *hand* of | all that | hate — | us;

5 To perform the mercy *promis*ed to | our fore- | fathers || and to re*mem*ber His | ho-ly | Cov-e- | nant;

6 To perform the oath which He sware to our fore*fa*ther | A-bra- | ham || *that* | He would | give — | us;

7 That we being delivered out of the *hand* of our | en-e- | mies || might *serve* | Him with- | out — | fear;

8 In holiness and *right*eous- | ness be- | fore Him || *all* the | days of | our — | life.

9 And thou Child, shalt be called the *Proph*et | of the | Highest || for thou shalt go before the face of the *Lord* | to pre- | pare His | ways;

10 To give knowledge of sal*va*tion | unto · His | people || *for* the re- | mis-sion | of their | sins,

11 Through the tender *mer*cy | of our | God || whereby the day-spring *from* on | high hath | visit- · ed | us;

12 To give light to them that sit in darkness, and *in* the | shadow · of | death || and to guide our *feet* | into · the | way of | peace.

Glory be to the *Fa*ther | and · to the | Son || *and* | to the | Ho-ly | Ghost;
As it was in the beginning, is *now* and | ev-er | shall be || *world* without | end.— | *A-* — | *men.*

571 Te Deum Laudamus H. LAWES (1596–1662)

1 WE *praise* | Thee O | God || we ac*know*ledge | Thee to | be the | Lord.
2 All the *earth* doth | wor-ship | Thee || *the* | Fa-ther | ev-er- | lasting.
3 To Thee all *An*gels | cry a- | loud || the *Heavens* and | all the | Powers there- | in.
4 To Thee Cheru*bim* and | Ser-a- | phim || *con-* | tin-ual- | ly do | cry,
5 *H*oly | Ho-ly | Ho-ly || *Lord* | God of | Sab-a- | oth;
6 Heaven and earth are *full* of the | Maj-es- | ty || *of* | Thy — | Glo- — | ry.
7 The glorious *com*pany | of · the A- | postles || *praise* | — — | — — | Thee.
8 The goodly *fel*lowship | of the | Prophets || *praise* | — — | — — | Thee.
9 The *no*ble | army · of | Martyrs || *praise* | — — | — — | Thee.
10 The holy *Church* throughout | all the | world || *doth* | — ac- | knowl-edge | Thee;
11 *The* | Fa- — | ther || *of* an | in- · finite | Maj-es- | ty;
12 *Thine* a- | dor- · able, | true || *and* | on- — | — ly | Son;
13 *Al*so* the | Holy | Ghost || *the* | Com- — | fort- — | er.
14 *Thou* art the | King of | Glory || O | — — | — — | Christ.
15 Thou art the *ever-* | last-ing | Son || *of* | — the | Fa- — | ther.

* Last half of chant.

R. COOKE (1768–1814)

16 When Thou tookest upon *Thee* to de- | liv-er | man || Thou didst humble Thy*self* to be | born — | of a | Virgin.
17 When Thou hadst over*come* the | sharpness · of | death || Thou didst open the *King*dom of | Heaven · to | all be- | lievers.
18 Thou sittest at the *right* | hand of | God || *in* the | Glo-ry | of the | Father.
19 We be*lieve* that | Thou shalt | come || *to* | be — | our — | Judge.
20 We therefore *pray* Thee | help Thy | servants || whom Thou hast *redeem*ed | with Thy | pre-cious | blood.
21 Make them to be *num*bered | with Thy | Saints || *in* | glo-ry | ev-er- | lasting.
22 O *Lord* | save Thy | people || *and* | bless Thine | her-it- | age.
23 *Gov-* | — ern | them || *and* | lift them | up for- | ever.

Return to chant in B♭ at the top of page.

24 *Day* | by — | day || *we* | mag-ni- | fy — | Thee;
25 *And* we | worship · Thy | Name || *ever* | world with- | out — | end.
26 *Vouch-* | safe O | Lord || to keep *us* this | day with- | out — | sin.
27 O *Lord* · have | mercy · up- | on us || *have* | mercy · up- | on — | us.
28 O Lord, let Thy *mercy* | be up- | on us || *as* our | trust — | is in | Thee.
29 O Lord, in *Thee* | have I | trusted || *let* me | nev-er | be con- | founded.

572 Magnificat (Luke i 45–55)

G. A. MACFARREN (1813–1887) J. BARNBY, (1838–1896)

H. SMART (1813–1879)

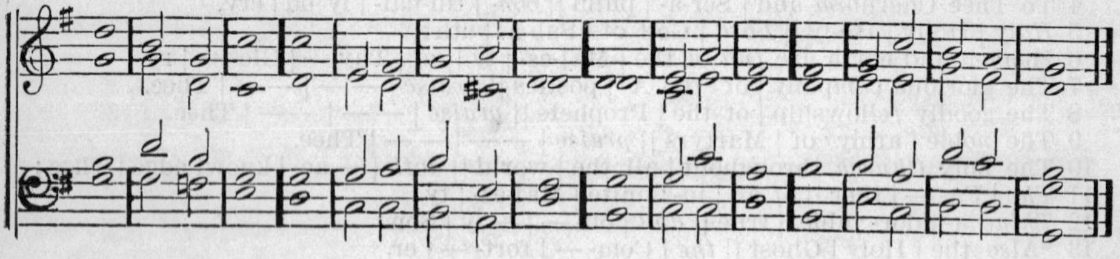

1 My soul doth *magni-* | fy the | Lord || and my spirit *hath* re- | joiced · in | God my | Saviour.

2 *For* He | hath re- | garded || the *low*li- | ness of | His hand- | maiden.

3 *For* be- | hold from | henceforth || all *gen*er- | ations · shall | call me | blessed.

4 For He that is *migh*ty hath | magni- · fied | me || *and* | ho-ly | is His | name.

5 And His mer*cy* is on | them that | fear Him || *through-* | out all | gen-er- | ations.

6 He hath showed *strength* | with His | arm || He hath scattered the proud in the ima*gin*- | a-tion | of their | hearts.

7 He hath put down the *migh*ty | from their | seat || and *hath* ex- | alted · the | humble · and | meek.

8 He hath filled the *hun*gry | with good | things || and the *rich* He hath | sent — | empty · a- | way.

9 *He remembering His mercy, hath holpen His *ser*vant | Is-ra- | el || as He promised to our forefathers, Abra*ham* | and his | seed for- | ever.

Glory be to the *Fa*ther | and · to the | Son || *and* | to the | Ho-ly | Ghost;

As it was in the beginning, is *now* and | ev-er | shall be || *world* without | end.— | *A*- — | *men.*

* Last half of Double Chant.

573 Dominus regit me (Ps. xxiii) ANON

1 The *Lord* | is my | shepherd || *I* | shall — | not — | want.

2 He maketh me to lie *down* in | green — | pastures || He leadeth *me* be- | side the | still — | waters.

3 *He* re- | storeth · my | soul || He leadeth me in the paths of righteous*ness* | for His | name's — | sake.

4 Yea though I walk through the valley of the shadow of *death* I will | fear no | evil || for Thou art with me; Thy *rod* and Thy | staff they | com-fort | me.

5 Thou preparest a table before me in the *pres*ence | of mine | enemies || Thou anointest my head with *oil* my | cup — | run-neth | over.

6 Surely goodness and mercy shall follow me all the *days* | of my | life || and I will dwell in the *house* | of the | Lord for- | ever.

Glory be to the *Fa*ther | and · to the | Son || *and* | to the | Ho-ly | Ghost;

As it was in the beginning, is *now* and | ev-er | shall be || *world* without | end.— | A- — | *men.*

574

De Profundis (Ps. cxxx)

1 Out of the deep have I called unto *Thee* O | Lord || *Lord* hear my | voice.

2 O let Thine ears con*sid*er | well || the voice of *my* com- | plaint.

3 If Thou, Lord, wilt be extreme to mark what is *done* a- | miss || O Lord, who *may* a- | bide it.

4 For there is mer*cy* with | Thee || therefore shalt *Thou* be | feared.

5 I look for the Lord, my soul doth *wait* for | Him || in His *word* is my | trust.

6 My soul *fleeth* unto the | Lord || before the morning watch, I say before the *morn*ing | watch.

7 O Israel, trust in the Lord, for with the *Lord* there is | mercy || and with Him is plent*eous* re- | demption.

8 And He shall re*deem* Isra- | el || from *all* his sins.

Glory be to the *Fa*ther, and to the | Son || and to the *Ho*ly | Ghost;

As it was in the beginning, is now, and *ev*er shall be || world without *end.* A- | *men.*

575 Venite Exultemus (Ps. 95)

From HANDEL

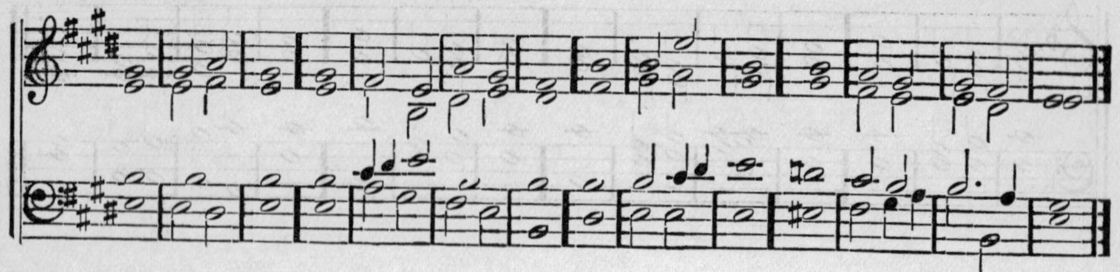

1 O Come, let us sing | unto...the | Lord || let us make a joyful noise to the | Rock of | our Sal- | vation.

2 Let us come before His presence | with thanks- | giving || and make a joyful | noise..unto | Him with | psalms.

3 For the Lord is a | great | God || and a great | King a- | bove all | gods.

4 In His hand are the deep places | of the | earth || the strength of the | hills is | His | also.

5 The sea is His, and | He | made it || and His hands | form-ed | the | dry | land.

6 O come, let us worship | and bow | down || let us kneel be- | fore the | Lord our | Maker.

7 For He | is our | God || and we are the people of His pasture, | and the | sheep of..His | Hand.

8 Glory be to the Father, and to the Son: and to the Holy Ghost.

9 As it was in the beginning, is now, and ever shall be: world without end. *Amen.*

576 The Lord's Prayer

J. BLOW (1648–1708)

1 Our Fa*ther* which | art in | heaven! || *Hal*lowed | be — | Thy — | name.

2 *Thy* | kingdom | come || Thy will be done in *earth* | as it | is in | heaven.

3 Give us this *day* our | daily | bread || and forgive us our *debts* as | we for- | give our | debtors.

4 And lead us *not* | into · temp- | tation || *but* de- | liv-er | us from | evil:

5 For Thine is the king*dom* and the | power · and the | glory || *for* | ever. | *A-* — | *men.*

577 The Beatitudes (Matthew v. 3--12) J. TURLE (1802—1882)

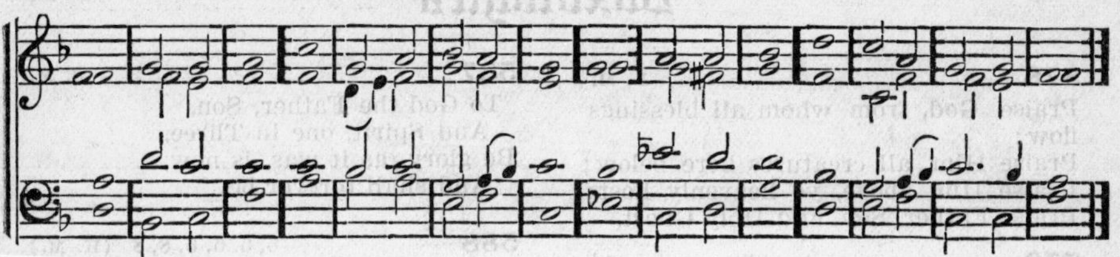

S. P. WARREN, 1872

1 BLESS*ed* are the | poor in | spirit || *for* | theirs · is the | kingdom · of | heaven.

2 Bless*ed* are | they that | mourn || *for* | they — | shall be | comforted.

3 Bless*ed* | are the | meek || *for* | they · shall in- | herit · the | earth.

4 Blessed are they which do hunger and *thirst* after | right-eous- | ness || *for* | they — | shall be | filled.

5 Bless*ed* are the | mer-ci- | ful || *for* | they · shall ob- | tain — | mercy.

6 Bless*ed* are the | pure in | heart || *for* | they shall | see — | God.

7 Bless*ed* are the | peace- — | makers || for they shall be *call*ed the | children | of — | God.

8 Blessed are they which are persecut*ed* for | righteous- · ness' | sake || *for* | theirs · is the | kingdom · of | heaven.

9 Blessed are ye, when men shall revile *you* and | perse- · cute | you || and shall say all manner of evil a*gainst* you | false-ly | for my | sake.

10 Rejoice and be exceeding glad, for great is *your* re- | ward in | heaven || for so persecuted *they* the | prophets · which | were be- | fore you.

Glory be to the *Fa*ther | and · to the | Son || *and* | to the | Ho-ly | Ghost;

As it was in the beginning, is *now* and | ev-er | shall be || *world* without | end.— | *A*- — | *men.*

Doxologies

578 L. M.

Praise God, from whom all blessings flow;
Praise Him, all creatures here below;
Praise Him above, ye heavenly host;
Praise Father, Son, and Holy Ghost.

579 L. M. 6 l

To God the Father, God the Son,
And God the Spirit, Three in One,
Be glory in the highest given,
By all on earth, and all in heaven;
As was through ages heretofore,
Is now, and shall be evermore.

580 C. M.

To Father, Son, and Holy Ghost,
The God whom we adore,
Be glory, as it was, is now,
And shall be ever more.

581 6, 5, 6, 5

Father, Son, and Spirit
Endless one in Three,
Now, henceforth, forever,
Glory be to Thee.

582 7, 6, 7, 6

To Father, Son, and Spirit,
Eternal One and Three,
As was and is forever,
All praise and glory be.

583 TROCHAIC 7, 6, 7. 6

Glory be to God most high,
Glory to the Saviour,
Glory to the Holy Ghost,
Now, henceforth, forever.

584 7,6 8 l

O Mighty God and Holy,
Fount of unchanging grace,
Whose mercy ever shineth—
The brightness of Thy face;
To Thee, all praise and glory,
Thou God of love and might!
The Father, Son, and Spirit—
Thou uncreated Light!

585 7 s

Thee, Eternal God, Most High,
Thee we laud and magnify;
Glorious o'er the heavenly host—
Father, Son, and Holy Ghost.

586 TROCHAIC 7 s

Holy Father, holy Son,
Holy Spirit, Three in One!
Glory, as of old, to Thee
Now and evermore shall be.

587 S. M.

To God the Father, Son,
And Spirit, one in Three,
Be glory, as it was, is now,
And shall forever be.

588 6, 6, 6, 6, 8, 8 (H. M.)

O Blessed, Holy One!
All worship, praise, and love,
To Thee—the Father, Son,
And Spirit—God above!
Let earth and heaven with one accord
Sing Thine eternal glory, Lord.

589 S. M.

Eternal, Holy Lord!
Thy Name we glorify—
The Father, Son, and Holy Ghost—
Jehovah, God Most High.

590 8, 7, 8, 7

Praise the Father, earth and heaven,
Praise the Son, the Spirit praise,
As it was, and is, be given
Glory through eternal days.

591 8, 7 6 l

Praise and honor to the Father,
Praise and honor to the Son,
Praise and honor to the Spirit,
Ever Three and ever One;
One in might and one in glory
While eternal ages run.

592 8, 7, 8, 7, 4, 7

Glory be to God the Father,
Glory be to God the Son,
Glory be to God the Spirit,
Great Jehovah, Three in One:
Glory, Glory,
While eternal ages run.

593 8, 7, 8, 7, 4, 7

Great Jehovah we adore Thee,
God the Father, God the Son,
God the Spirit, joined in glory
On the same eternal throne;
Endless praises
To Jehovah, Three in One.

594 8, 7, 8, 7, 7, 7

Glory be to God the Father,
Glory be to God the Son,
Glory be to God the Spirit,
Everlasting Three in One:
Thee let heaven and earth adore,
Now, henceforth, and evermore.

Festivals of the Church

I.

Immovable Festivals

CHIEF FESTIVALS.

Christmas, or the Nativity of our Lord..............................December 25
The Circumcision of Christ, and New Year's Day..............................January 1
The Epiphany, or the Manifestation of Christ to the Gentiles..............................January 6
The Festival of the Reformation..............................October 31

MINOR FESTIVALS,

OBSERVED IN SOME PARTS OF THE LUTHERAN CHURCH.

St. Andrew the Apostle's Day..............................November 30
St. Thomas the Apostle's Day..............................December 21
St. Stephen the Martyr's Day..............................December 26
St. John the Apostle's Day..............................December 27
The Conversion of St. Paul..............................January 25
The Presentation of Christ..............................February 2
St. Matthias the Apostle's Day..............................February 24
The Annunciation ....March 25
St. Philip and St. James the Apostles' Day..............................May 1
The Birthday of St. John the Baptist..............................June 24
St. Peter and St. Paul the Apostles' Day..............................June 29
The Visitation ....July 2
St. James the elder, the Apostle's Day..............................July 25
St. Bartholomew the Apostle's Day..............................August 24
St. Matthew the Apostle's Day..............................September 21
St. Michael the Archangel's Day..............................September 29
St. Simon and St. Jude the Apostles' Day..............................October 28
All Saints Day..............................November 1

II.

Movable Festivals

RULES

TO FIND THE MOVABLE FESTIVALS.

The *Movable Festivals* all depend upon *Easter* except *Advent.*

Advent Sunday is always the nearest *Sunday* to the thirtieth day of *November,* whether before or after.

Easter is always the first *Sunday* after the Full Moon, which happens upon, or next after the twenty-first day of *March;* and if the Full Moon happen upon a *Sunday, Easter* is the *Sunday* after.

The time of *Easter* being found, the other *Festivals* occur as follows:

Septuagesima Sunday is nine weeks before *Easter.*

Ash-Wednesday, or the beginning of *Lent,* is forty-six days before *Easter.*

Palm Sunday, or the beginning of *Holy Week,* is eight days before *Easter.*

Holy Thursday is the *Thursday* before *Easter.*

Good-Friday is the *Friday* before *Easter.*

Ascension-Day is forty days after *Easter.*

Whitsunday is seven weeks after *Easter.*

Trinity Sunday is eight weeks after *Easter.*

Table of the Days on which Easter will Fall from 1913—2000.

Year	Easter	Year	Easter	Year	Easter	Year	Easter	Year	Easter
1913.	March 23	1931.	April 5	1949.	April 17	1967.	March 26	1985.	April 7
1914.	April 12	1932.	March 27	1950.	“ 9	1968.	April 14	1986.	March 30
1915.	“ 4	1933.	April 16	1951.	March 25	1969.	“ 6	1987.	April 19
1916.	“ 23	1934.	“ 1	1952.	April 13	1970.	March 29	1988.	“ 3
1917.	“ 8	1935.	“ 21	1953.	“ 5	1971.	April 11	1989.	March 26
1918.	March 31	1936.	“ 12	1954.	“ 18	1972.	“ 2	1990.	April 15
1919.	April 20	1937.	March 28	1955.	“ 10	1973.	“ 22	1991.	March 31
1920.	“ 4	1938.	April 17	1956.	“ 1	1974.	“ 14	1992.	April 19
1921.	March 27	1939.	“ 9	1957.	“ 21	1975.	March 30	1993.	“ 11
1922.	April 16	1940.	March 24	1958.	“ 6	1976.	April 18	1994.	“ 3
1923.	“ 1	1941.	April 13	1959.	March 29	1977.	“ 10	1995.	“ 16
1924.	“ 20	1942.	“ 5	1960.	April 17	1978.	March 26	1996.	“ 7
1925.	“ 12	1943.	“ 25	1961.	“ 2	1979.	April 15	1997.	March 30
1926.	“ 4	1944.	“ 9	1962.	“ 22	1980.	“ 6	1998.	April 12
1927.	“ 17	1945.	“ 1	1963.	“ 14	1981.	“ 19	1999.	“ 4
1928.	“ 8	1946.	“ 21	1964.	March 29	1982.	“ 11	2000.	“ 23
1929.	March 31	1947.	“ 6	1965.	April 18	1983.	“ 3		
1930.	April 20	1948.	March 28	1966.	“ 10	1984.	“ 22		

A Table of the Movable Festivals.
According to the several days that Easter can possibly fall upon.

Easter.	Sundays after Epiphany.*	Septuagesima Sunday.	Ash Wednesday.	Ascension-Day.	Whitsunday.	Sundays after Trinity.	First Advent Sunday.
March 22	1	Jan. 18	Feb. 4	April 30	May 10	27	Nov. 29
—— 23	1	—— 19	—— 5	May 1	—— 11	27	—— 30
—— 24	1	—— 20	—— 6	—— 2	—— 12	27	Dec. 1
—— 25	2	—— 21	—— 7	—— 3	—— 13	27	—— 2
—— 26	2	—— 22	—— 8	—— 4	—— 14	27	—— 3
—— 27	2	—— 23	—— 9	—— 5	—— 15	26	Nov. 27
—— 28	2	—— 24	—— 10	—— 6	—— 16	26	—— 28
—— 29	2	—— 25	—— 11	—— 7	—— 17	26	—— 29
—— 30	2	—— 26	—— 12	—— 8	—— 18	26	—— 30
—— 31	2	—— 27	—— 13	—— 9	—— 19	26	Dec. 1
April 1	3	—— 28	—— 14	—— 10	—— 20	26	—— 2
—— 2	3	—— 29	—— 15	—— 11	—— 21	26	—— 3
—— 3	3	—— 30	—— 16	—— 12	—— 22	25	Nov. 27
—— 4	3	—— 31	—— 17	—— 13	—— 23	25	—— 28
—— 5	3	Feb. 1	—— 18	—— 14	—— 24	25	—— 29
—— 6	3	—— 2	—— 19	—— 15	—— 25	25	—— 30
—— 7	3	—— 3	—— 20	—— 16	—— 26	25	Dec. 1
—— 8	4	—— 4	—— 21	—— 17	—— 27	25	—— 2
—— 9	4	—— 5	—— 22	—— 18	—— 28	25	—— 3
—— 10	4	—— 6	—— 23	—— 19	—— 29	24	Nov. 27
—— 11	4	—— 7	—— 24	—— 20	—— 30	24	—— 28
—— 12	4	—— 8	—— 25	—— 21	—— 31	24	—— 29
—— 13	4	—— 9	—— 26	—— 22	June 1	24	—— 30
—— 14	4	—— 10	—— 27	—— 23	—— 2	24	Dec. 1
—— 15	5	—— 11	—— 28	—— 24	—— 3	24	—— 2
—— 16	5	—— 12	Mar. 1	—— 25	—— 4	24	—— 3
—— 17	5	—— 13	—— 2	—— 26	—— 5	23	Nov. 27
—— 18	5	—— 14	—— 3	—— 27	—— 6	23	—— 28
—— 19	5	—— 15	—— 4	—— 28	—— 7	23	—— 29
—— 20	5	—— 16	—— 5	—— 29	—— 8	23	—— 30
—— 21	5	—— 17	—— 6	—— 30	—— 9	23	Dec. 1
—— 22	6	—— 18	—— 7	—— 31	—— 10	23	—— 2
—— 23	6	—— 19	—— 8	June 1	—— 11	23	—— 3
—— 24	6	—— 20	—— 9	—— 2	—— 12	22	Nov. 27
—— 25	6	—— 21	—— 10	—— 3	—— 13	22	—— 28

*In a Leap Year, the number of Sundays after Epiphany is the same as if Easter had fallen one day later than it really does; and Septuagesima Sunday and Ash-Wednesday fall one day later than that given in the Table, unless the Table gives some day in March for Ash-Wednesday; for in that case the day in the Table is right.

SCRIPTURE LESSONS FOR THE SUNDAYS AND FESTIVALS OF THE CHURCH YEAR.			EPISTLES AND GOSPELS FOR THE SUNDAYS AND FESTIVALS OF THE CHURCH YEAR.			PSALMS FOR SUNDAYS AND FESTIVALS.	
OLD TESTAMENT.	EPISTLES.	GOSPELS.	SUNDAYS AND CHIEF FESTIVALS.	EPISTLES.	GOSPELS.	MATINS.	VESPERS.
Jer. xxxiii. 14-18	Colossians i. 12-23	Luke i. 1-25	*1 Sunday in Advent,*	Romans xiii. 11-14	Matthew xxi. 1-9	Ps. 1	Ps. 143
Micah iv. 1-7	Romans ii. 1-16	Luke i. 26-35	*2 Sunday in Advent,*	Romans xv. 4-13	Luke xxi. 25-36	Ps. 42	Ps. 91
Malachi iii. 1-6	Romans i. 16-25	Luke i. 39-56	*3 Sunday in Advent,*	1 Cor. iv. 1-5	Matthew xi. 2-10	Ps. 4	Ps. 98
Isaiah xl. 1-8	Hebrews xii. 15-29	Luke i. 67-80	*4 Sunday in Advent,*	Philippians iv. 4-7	John i. 19-28	Ps. 5	Ps. 145
Isaiah vii. 10-14	Hebrews i. 1-12	John i. 1-14	*Christmas Day,*	Tit.ii.11-14; Is.ix.2-7	Luke ii. 1-14	Ps. 19, 45, 85	Ps. 89, 110, 132
Micah v. 2-4	1 John iv. 7-16	John i. 15-18	*2 Christmas Day,*	Tit. iii. 4-7	Luke ii. 15-20		
Isaiah xi. 1-5	Hebrews ii. 9-16	Luke ii. 22-32	*Sunday after Christmas,*	Galatians iv. 1-7	Luke ii. 33-40	Ps. 121	Ps. 111
Isaiah lxiii. 7-18	1 Peter i. 22-25	Luke xiii. 6-10	*New Year's Eve,*	....	....	....	....
Isaiah iv. 1-13	James iv. 13-17	Luke iv. 16-21	*Circumcision New Year,*	Galatians iii. 23-29	Luke ii. 21	Ps. 122, 72	Ps. 90, 115
Isaiah xlii. 1-9	Romans iii. 19-22	Matthew iii. 1-12	*Sunday after New Year,*	1 Peter iv. 12-19	Matthew ii. 13-23	....	....
Isaiah xlix. 1-7	Romans iii. 23-31	Matthew iii. 13-17	*Epiphany,*	Isaiah lx. 1-6	Matthew ii. 1-12	Ps. 96	Ps. 72
Isaiah lxi. 1-3	Ephesians vi. 1-4	Mark x. 13-16	*1 Sun. after Epiphany,*	Romans xii. 1-5	Luke ii. 41-52	Ps. 13.	Ps. 86
Deut. xviii. 15-19	Ephesians v. 21-33	Luke xix. 1-10	*2 Sun. after Epiphany,*	Romans xii. 6-16 *a*	John ii. 1-11	Ps. 14	Ps. 16
Jer. xxxiii. 6-9	Hebrews xi.1-16	Luke xvii. 5-10	*3 Sun. after Epiphany,*	Romans xii. 16-21 *b*	Matthew viii. 1-13	Ps. 15	Ps. 33
Isaiah xliii. 1-3	Romans iv. 16-25	Matt xiv. 22-33	*4 Sun. after Epiphany,*	Romans xiii. 8-10	Matthew viii. 23-27	Ps. 2	Ps. 97
Jer. xvii. 5-10	1 Cor. iii. 3-23	Matt. xiii. 44-52	*5 Sun. after Epiphany,*	Colossians iii. 12-17	Matthew xiii. 24-30	Ps. 20	Ps. 86
Isaiah lxi. 10, 11	2 Cor. iv. 5-6	Matt. xi. 25-27	*6 Sun. after Epiphany,*	2 Peter i. 16-21	Matthew xvii. 1-9	Ps. 87	Ps. 8
Jeremiah i. 4-10	Acts xvii. 22-34	Matt. xxv. 14-30	*Septuagesima Sunday,*	1 Cor. ix. 24—x. 5	Matthew xx. 1-16	Ps. 23	Ps. 114
Isaiah lv. 10-13	2 Tim. iii. 10; iv. 5	Mark iv. 26-32	*Sexagesima Sunday,*	2 Cor. xi. 19—xii. 9	Luke viii. 4-15	Ps. 24	Ps. 25
Isaiah xxxv. 3-7	1 Peter iii. 18-22	John xii. 23-36	*Quinquagesima Sunday,*	1 Cor. xiii. 1-13	Luke xviii. 31-43	Ps. 26	Ps. 27
Jonah iii. 1-10; or	1 John i. 5-10	Luke vi. 20-49	*Ash Wednesday,*	Joel ii. 12-19	Matthew vi. 16-21	Ps. 6	Ps. 51
Isaiah lix. 12-21							
Genesis iii. 1-24	James i. 2-15	Luke xxii. 24-32	*1 S. in Lent, Invocavit,*	2 Cor. vi. 1-10	Matthew iv. 1-11	Ps. 32	Ps. 16
Isaiah xlv. 20-25	James v. 13-20	Mark ix. 17-29	*2 S. in Lent, Reminiscere,*	1 Thess. iv. 1-7	Matthew xv. 21-28	Ps. 130	Ps. 25
2 Samuel xxii. 1-7	Revelation ii. 1-7	John viii. 42-51	*3 S. in Lent, Oculi,*	Ephesians v. 1-9	Luke xi. 14-28	Ps. 43	Ps. 86
Isaiah xlix. 8-13	2 Peter i. 2-11	John vi. 36-51	*4 S. in Lent, Laetare,*	Galatians iv. 21-31	John vi. 1-15	Ps. 46	Ps. 139
Genesis xii. 1-3	1 Cor. i. 21-31	Matthew x. 32-42	*5 S. in Lent, Judica,*	Hebrews ix. 11-15	John viii. 46-59	Ps. 54	Ps. 27
Zechariah ix. 9, 10	Hebrews xii. 1-11	Mark xiv. 3-9	*6 S. in Lent, Palmarum,*	Philippians ii. 5-11	Matthew xxi. 1-9	Ps. 61	Ps. 67
....	....	....	*Monday in Holy Week,*	Isaiah l. 5-10	John xii. 1-23	....	....
....	....	....	*Tuesday,*	Jeremiah xi. 18-20	John xii. 24-43	....	....
....	....	....	*Wednesday,*	Is. lxii. 11; lxiii. 1-7	Lk. xxii. 1—xxiii. 42	....	....
Exodus xii. 1-14	1 Cor. x. 16, 17	Luke xxii. 14-20	*Holy Thursday,*	1 Cor. xi. 23-32	John xiii. 1-15	Ps. 116	Ps. 70
Isaiah l. 6-9	Revelation v. 6-10	Matt. xxvii. 33-54	*Good Friday,*	Is. lii. 13—liii. 12	John xviii.1—xix.42	Ps. 22, 40, 54	Ps. 69, 88
Isaiah lii. 13-15	1 Peter i. 3-12	Matt. xxviii. 1-8	*Easter Sunday,*	1 Cor. v. 6-8	Mark xvi. 1-8	Ps. 2, 57, 111	Ps. 113, 114, 118
Hosea xiii. 14	1 Cor. xv. 12-20	John xx. 1-18	*Easter Monday,*	Acts x. 34-41	Luke xxiv. 13-35	Ps. 62	Ps. 30
			Sundays after Easter,				
Job xix. 25-27	1 Peter i. 17—ii: 3	John xxi. 15-19	*1 Quasimodogeniti,*	1 John v. 4-12	John xx. 19-31	Ps. 111	Ps. 4
Eze. xxxiv. 11-16	Heb. xiii. 20-21	John v. 22-30	*2 Misericordias,*	1 Peter ii. 21-25	John x. 11-16	Ps. 70	Ps. 23
Lam. iii. 18-26	Hebrews iv. 14-16	John xiv, 1-11	*3 Jubilate,*	1 Peter ii. 11-20	John xvi. 16-23 *c*	Ps. 75	Ps. 146
Isaiah xii. 1-6	2 Cor. v. 14-21	John viii. 21-36	*4 Cantate,*	James i. 16-21	John xvi. 5-15	Ps. 82	Ps. 126
Jer. xxix. 11-14	Romans viii. 24-28	John xvii. 1-19	*5 Rogate,*	James i. 22-27	John xvi. 23-30 *d*	Ps. 84	Ps. 124
Isaiah lvii. 15	Ephesians i. 3-14	Luke xxiv. 46-53	*Ascension Day,*	Acts i. 1-11	Mark xvi. 14-20	Ps. 8, 15, 21, 47	Ps. 24, 68, 148
Eze. xxxvi. 25-27	Romans viii. 29-39	John xvii. 20-26	*Sunday after Ascension,*	1 Peter iv. 7-11 *e*	John xv. 26—xvi. 4	Ps. 93.	Ps. 97
Joel ii. 28-32	Ephesians iv. 7-16	John xiv. 15-21	*Whitsunday,*	Acts ii. 1-13	John xiv. 23-31	Ps. 48, 68, 45	Ps. 104, 145
Isaiah xxxii. 14-20	Acts ii. 42-47	John iv. 5-26	*Whit-Monday,*	Acts x. 42-48 *f*	John iii. 16-21	Ps. 90	Ps. 19
Eze. xviii. 30-32	2 Cor. xiii. 14	Matt. xxviii. 18-20	*Trinity Sunday,*	Romans xi. 33-36	John iii. 1-15	Ps. 67, 8, 148	Ps. 115, 143
Jer. ix. 23, 24	1 Timothy vi. 6-19	Luke xii. 13-21	*1 Sunday after Trinity,*	1 John iv. 16-21 *g*	Luke xvi. 19-31	Ps. 119—1st part	Ps. 34

a End: "Men of low estate."
b Begin: "Be not wise in your own conceits."
c End: "ye shall ask me nothing."
d Begin: "Verily, verily, I say."
e Begin: "Be ye therefore sober."
f End: "In the name of the Lord."
g Begin: "God is love."

TABLE OF SCRIPTURE LESSONS—*Continued.*			TABLE OF EPISTLES AND GOSPELS—*Continued.*			TABLE OF PSALMS—*Cont.*	
OLD TESTAMENT	EPISTLES.	GOSPELS.	SUNDAYS AND CHIEF FESTIVALS.	EPISTLES.	GOSPELS.	MATINS.	VESPERS.
Isaiah xxv. 6-9	Rev. iii. 14-22	Luke xiv. 25-35	*2 Sunday after Trinity,*……	1 John iii. 13-18	Luke xiv. 16-24	Ps. 119—2d part	Ps. 28
Micah vii. 18-20	Acts ix. 1-18	Luke xv. 11-32	*3 Sunday after Trinity,*……	1 Peter v. 6-11	Luke xv. 1-10	Ps. 119—3d "	Ps. 25
Isaiah lviii. 6-12	Romans xiv. 7-17	Matthew v. 43-48	*4 Sunday after Trinity,*……	Romans viii. 18-23	Luke vi. 36-42	Ps. 119—4th "	Ps. 92
Jer. xvi. 14-21	1 Peter ii. 4-10	Matt. xvi. 13-26	*5 Sunday after Trinity,*……	1 Peter iii. 8-15 *h*	Luke v. 1-11	Ps. 119—5th "	Ps. 113
Exodus xx. 1-17	Ephesians ii. 4-10	Matt. xix. 16-30	*6 Sunday after Trinity,*……	Romans vi. 3-11	Matthew v. 20-26	Ps. 119—6th "	Ps. 114
Jer. xxxi.23-25	Acts xiv. 8-23	Matthew x. 24-31	*7 Sunday after Trinity,*……	Romans vi. 19-23	Mark viii. 1-9	Ps. 119—7th "	Ps. 125
Jer. xv. 19-21	Acts xx. 17-38	Matt. vii. 22-29	*8 Sunday after Trinity,*……	Romans viii. 12-17	Matthew vii. 15-23	Ps. 119—8th "	Ps. 126
1 Chr. xxix. 10-13	2 Timothy i. 3-14	Luke xii. 32-48	*9 Sunday after Trinity,*……	1 Cor. x. 6-13	Luke xvi. 1-9	Ps. 119—9th "	Ps. 139
Jeremiah vii. 1-7	Hebrews iii. 7-15	Matthew xi. 16-24	*10 Sunday after Trinity,*……	1 Cor. xii. 1-11	Luke xix. 41-48	Ps. 119—10th "	Ps. 143
2 Sam. xxii. 21-29	Romans x. 4-18	Luke vii. 36-50	*11 Sunday after Trinity,*……	1 Cor. xv. 1-10	Luke xviii. 9-14	Ps. 119—11th "	Ps. 147
Isaiah xxix. 18, 19	James iii. 1-12	Matt xii. 31-42	*12 Sunday after Trinity,*……	2 Cor. iii. 4-11	Mark vii. 31-37	Ps. 119—12th "	Ps. 104
Lev. xviii. 1-5	1 Timothy i. 5-17	Matt. xx. 20-28	*13 Sunday after Trinity,*……	Galatians iii. 15-22	Luke x. 23-37	Ps. 119—13th "	Ps. 84
Jer. xvii. 13, 14	Acts iii. 1-10	John v. 1-15	*14 Sunday after Trinity,*……	Galatians v. 16-24	Luke xvii. 11-19	Ps. 119—14th "	Ps. 66
Deut. vi. 4-7	Acts viii. 26-39	Luke x. 38-42	*15 Sunday after Trinity,*……	Gal. v. 25—vi. 10	Matthew vi. 24-34	Ps. 119—15th "	Ps. 34
Deut. xxxii. 39, 40	1 Cor. xv. 21-28	John xi. 19-45	*16 Sunday after Trinity,*……	Ephesians iii. 13-21	Luke vii. 11-17	Ps. 119—16th "	Ps. 36
1 Samuel ii. 1-10	Jude 20-25	Mark ii. 18-28	*17 Sunday after Trinity,*……	Ephesians iv. 1-6	Luke xiv. 1-11	Ps. 119—17th "	Ps. 56
Deut. x. 12-21	1 John iii. 1-8	John xv. 1-17	*18 Sunday after Trinity,*……	1 Cor. i. 4-9	Matt. xxii. 34-46	Ps. 119—18th "	Ps. 54
Isaiah xliv. 21-23	1 Cor. xii. 12-27	John i. 35-51	*19 Sunday after Trinity,*……	Ephesians iv. 22-28	Matthew ix. 1-8	Ps. 119—19th "	Ps. 61
Isaiah lxv. 1, 2	Romans xi. 25-32	Matt. xxi. 28-44	*20 Sunday after Trinity,*……	Ephesians v. 15-21	Matthew xxii. 1-14	Ps. 119—20th "	Ps. 57
Hosea xiii. 14	Rev. iii. 7-13	John iv. 31-42	*21 Sunday after Trinity,*……	Ephesians vi. 10-17	John iv. 46-54 *i*	Ps. 119—21st "	Ps. 31—1st part
Deut. vii. 9-11	Ephes iv. 30-32	Matt. xviii. 1-20	*22 Sunday after Trinity,*……	Philippians i. 3-11	Matt. xviii. 23-35	Ps. 119—22d "	Ps. 31—2d "
Isaiah xxxii. 1-8	Romans xiii. 1-7	Mark xii. 41-44	*23 Sunday after Trinity,*……	Phil. iii. 17-21	Matt. xxii. 15-22	Ps. 124	Ps. 31—3d "
Isaiah li. 9-16	2 Cor. v. 1-10	John v. 17-29	*24 Sunday after Trinity,*……	Colossians i. 9-14	Matt. ix. 18-26	Ps. 125	Ps. 18—1st "
Isaiah xlix. 12-17	2 Peter iii. 3-15	Luke xvii. 20-33	*25 Sunday after Trinity,*……	1 Thess. iv. 13-18	Matt. xxiv. 15-28	Ps. 116	Ps. 18—2d "
Isaiah xl. 9-11	Hebrews iv. 9-13	Matthew xi. 25-30	*26 Sunday after Trinity,*……	2 Peter iii. 3-14, or 2 Thess. i. 3-10	Matt xxv. 31-46	Ps. 111	Ps. 18—3d "
Isaiah lxv. 17-19	Rev. xxi. 1-7	Matthew v. 13-16	*27 Sunday after Trinity,*……	1 Thess. v. 1-11	Matt. xxv. 1-13	Ps. 103	Ps. 27, 97
Deut. xxvi.1-11, or Malachi iii. 10-12	Acts xiv. 15, 16, or James i. 17-18	Matt. vi. 24-34 or Luke xii. 13-21	*Harvest,*……	……	……	Ps. 65, 100	Ps. 67
2 Chr. xxix. 12-19	Galatians ii. 16-21	John ii. 13-17	*Reformation,*……	Galatians ii. 16-21 Revelation xiv. 6-7	John ii. 13-17	Ps. 126, 48	Ps. 138, 87
Lam. iii. 22-25	Galatians vi. 7-10	Luke xvii. 11-19	*Thanksgiving,*……	……	……	Ps. 136, 104	Ps. 92
Daniel ix. 3-19	Hebrews x. 1-31	Matthew iii. 1-12	*Humiliation,*……	……	……	Ps. 6	Ps. 32
……	……	……	*Apostles', Evangelists' and Martyrs' Days,*…	……	……	Ps. 70, 138, 143, 148	Ps. 113, 115, 117, 145
……	……	……	*St. Michael's Day,*……	……	……	Ps. 8, 19	Ps. 24, 34

h End: "sanctify the Lord God in your hearts."   *i* Begin: "And there was a certain nobleman."

APOSTLES' DAYS AND OTHER MINOR FESTIVALS.

MINOR FESTIVAL DAYS.	EPISTLES.	GOSPELS.	MINOR FESTIVAL DAYS.	EPISTLES.	GOSPELS.
St. Andrew the Apostle,……	Romans x. 10-18	Matthew iv. 18-22	*St. John the Baptist,*……	Isaiah xl. 1-5	Luke i. 57-80
St. Thomas the Apostle,……	Ephesians i. 3-6	John xx. 24-31	*St. Peter and St. Paul, Apostles,*…	Acts xii. 1-11	Matthew xvi. 13-20
St. Stephen the Martyr,……	Acts vi. 8—vii. 60	Matt. xxiii. 34-39	*The Visitation,*……	Isaiah xi. 1-5	Luke i. 39-56
St. John the Apostle,……	1 John i, 1-10	John xxi. 19-24	*St. James the Elder, Apostle,*……	Romans viii. 28-39	Matthew xx. 20-33
The Conversion of St. Paul,……	Acts ix. 1-22	Matt. xix. 27-30	*St. Bartholomew the Apostle,*……	2 Cor. iv. 7-10	Luke xxii. 24-30
The Presentation of Christ,……	Malachi iii. 1-4	Luke ii. 22-32	*St. Matthew the Apostle,*……	Ephesians iv. 7-14	Matthew ix. 9-13
St. Matthias the Apostle,……	Acts i. 15-26	Matthew xi. 25-30	*St. Michael the Archangel,*……	Revelation xii. 7-12	Matthew xviii. 1-11
The Annunciation,……	Isaiah vii. 10-16	Luke i. 26-38	*St. Simon and St. Jude, Apostles,*…	1 Peter i. 3-9	John xv. 17-21
St. Philip and St. James, Apostles,.	Ephesians ii. 19-22	John xiv. 1-14	*All Saints Day,*……	Revelation vii. 2-17	Matthew v. 1-12

Lessons for Morning and Evening throughout the Year.

These Lessons may be used at Matins and Vespers, or at Morning and Evening Prayer of the household, on the days of the week.

The Lessons appointed for days between the *Fourth Sunday in Advent* and the *First Sunday after Epiphany* are to be omitted when the days for which they are appointed do not occur.

When there are not six *Sundays after Epiphany*, the Lessons for the week after the *First Sunday* may be omitted one year; and those which follow another *Sunday*, the second year; and so on: in order that in the course of several years all the Lessons provided may be read.

The Lessons appointed for the days from the *Twentieth Sunday after Trinity* to the end of the year are to be read in every year, and those appointed for the weeks before the *Twentieth Sunday after Trinity* are to be omitted so far as necessary to this end.

[In this Table the first Lesson is for the Morning, and the second for the Evening of each day.]

1st Sunday in Advent.

Mon.	Matt. 11: 25-30.	Gen. 3: 1-24
Tues.	Acts 3: 22-26.	Gen. 9: 1-19
Wed.	Col. 1: 15-29.	Gen. 22: 1-19
Th.	Heb. 1: 1-4.	Gen. 49: 1-28
Fri.	Heb. 2: 1-4.	Num. 24: 14-25
Sat.	Eph. 3: 1-12.	Deut. 18: 15-19

2d Sunday in Advent.

Mon.	Acts 17:16-34.	1 Chr. 17:1-27
Tues.	1 John 4:9-16.	2 Chr. 7:11-22
Wed.	Col. 1: 1-8.	Is. 11: 1-10
Th.	Phil. 2: 12-18.	Jer. 23: 2-8
Fri.	Phil. 3: 12-16.	Jer. 30: 1-22
Sat.	Col. 3: 1-11.	Jer. 33: 14-26

3d Sunday in Advent.

Mon.	Heb. 10: 35-39.	Is. 2: 1-5
Tues.	Lk. 21:5-24.	Is. 24:21—25:5
Wed.	Luke 12: 35-59.	Is. 25: 6-10
Th.	James 5: 7-11.	Is. 26: 1-21
Fri.	Luke 1: 1-25.	Is. 51: 1-16
Sat.	Luke 1: 26-38.	Is. 52: 1-12

4th Sunday in Advent.

Mon.	Matt. 1: 18-25.	Is. 40: 1-11
Tues.	Luke 1: 39-45.	Mal. 3: 1-7
Wed.	Luke 1: 46-56.	Mal. 4: 1-6
Th.	Luke 1: 57-66.	Is. 28: 14-19
Fri.	Luke 1: 67-80.	Is. 7: 1-17
Sat.	Matt. 1: 1-17.	Mic. 5: 1-5

Christmas.

Dec. 27.	John 1: 15-18.	Mic. 4: 1-8
Dec. 28.	Luke 2: 15-20.	Is. 32: 1-8
Dec. 29.	Luke 2: 22-24.	Is. 46: 3-13
Dec. 30.	Luke 2: 25-32.	Is. 49: 1-13
Dec. 31.	Matt. 2: 13-15.	Is. 55: 1-13
Jan. 2.	Matt. 2: 16-18.	Is. 42: 1-9
Jan. 3.	Matt. 2: 19-23.	Is. 61: 1-11
Jan. 4.	Matt. 3: 1-12.	Is. 56: 1-8
Jan. 5.	Luke 3: 1-9.	Is. 12: 1-6

Epiphany.

Mon.	Luke 3: 10-14.	Gen. 1: 1-31
Tues.	Luke 3: 15-20.	Gen. 2: 1-25
Wed.	Mark 1: 1-8.	Gen. 4: 1-26
Th.	Mark 1: 9-11.	Gen. 5: 1-32
Fri.	Luke 3: 21, 22.	Gen. 6: 9-22
Sat.	Luke 3: 23-38.	Gen. 7: 1-24

1st Sunday after Epiphany.

Mon.	John 1: 29-34.	Gen. 8: 1-22
Tues.	John 1: 35-42.	Gen. 11: 1-9
Wed.	John 1: 43-51.	Gen. 12: 1-20
Th.	Luke 4: 1-13.	Gen. 13: 1-18
Fri.	Mark 1: 12-15.	Gen. 14: 8-24
Sat.	Matt. 4: 12-17.	Gen. 15: 1-21

2d Sunday after Epiphany.

Mon.	Matt. 4: 18-25.	Gen. 17: 1-22
Tues.	Matt. 5: 1-9.	Gen. 18: 1-33
Wed.	Matt. 5: 27-48.	Gen. 19: 1-29
Th.	Matt. 6: 1-23.	Gen. 21: 1-8
Fri.	Matt. 7: 1-14.	Gen. 24: 1-28
Sat.	Matt. 7: 24-29.	Gen. 24: 29-67

3d Sunday after Epiphany.

Mon.	Matt. 8: 14-22.	Gen. 25: 19-34
Tues.	Matt. 8: 28-34.	Gen. 27: 1-45
Wed.	Mat. 9:9-17.	Gen. 27:46—28:22
Th.	Matt. 9: 27-38.	Gen. 29: 1-20
Fri.	Matt. 10: 1-16.	Gen. 31: 1-18
Sat.	Mat. 10:17—11:1.	Gen. 32:3-32

4th Sunday after Epiphany.

Mon.	Mat. 11: 11-24.	Gen. 33: 1-20
Tues.	Matt. 12: 1-21.	Gen. 35: 1-21
Wed.	Mat. 12: 22-50.	Gen. 37: 1-36
Th.	Matt. 13: 1-23.	Gen. 39: 1-23
Fri.	Matt. 14: 1-36.	Gen. 40: 1-23
Sat.	Matt. 15: 1-20.	Gen. 41: 1-37

5th Sunday after Epiphany.

Mon.	Mat. 15: 29-39.	Gen. 41: 38-57
Tues.	Matt. 16: 1-12.	Gen. 42: 1-38
Wed.	Mat. 16: 21-28.	Gen. 43: 1-34
Th.	Matt. 17: 9-27.	Gen. 44: 1-34
Fri.	Matt. 19: 1-15.	Gen. 45: 1-28
Sat.	Matt. 20: 17-34.	Gen. 46: 1-34

6th Sunday after Epiphany.

Mon.	Matt. 21: 10-46.	Gen. 47: 1-31
Tues.	Matt. 23: 1-39.	Gen. 48: 1-22
Wed.	Mark 1: 16-45.	Ex. 1: 1-22
Th.	Mark 2: 1-28.	Ex. 2: 1-25
Fri.	Mark 3: 1-35.	Ex. 3: 1-22
Sat.	Mark 5: 1-20.	Ex. 4: 1-31

Septuagesima Sunday.

Mon.	Mark 5: 21-43.	Ex. 5: 1-23
Tues.	Mark 6: 1-29.	Ex. 6: 1-13
Wed.	Mark 6: 30-56.	Ex. 11: 1-10
Th.	Mark 7: 1-30.	Ex. 12: 1-28
Fri.	Mk. 8: 10—9: 1.	Ex. 12: 29-42
Sat.	Mark 9: 2-32.	Ex. 13: 1-22

Sexagesima Sunday.

Mon.	Mark 10: 1-31.	Ex. 14: 1-31
Tues.	Mark 10: 32-52.	Ex. 15: 1-21
Wed.	Mk. 11:1-33.	Ex. 15:22—16:36
Th.	Mark 12: 13-44.	Ex. 17: 1-16
Fri.	Luke 4: 14-44.	Ex. 19: 1-25
Sat.	Luke 5: 12-39.	Ex. 20: 1-23

Quinquagesima Sunday.

Mon.	Luke 6:1-35.	Ex. 24:1—25:9
Tues.	Lk. 6:33-49.	Ex. 31:18—32:35
Wed.	Luke 7: 1-10.	Ex. 33: 1-23
Th.	Luke 7: 18—8: 3	Ex. 34: 1-10
Fri.	Luke 8: 16-56.	Ex. 34: 27-35
Sat.	Luke 9: 1-27.	Ex. 40: 1-38

1st Sunday in Lent.

Mon.	Luke 9: 28-62.	Num. 3: 5-13
Tues.	Luke 10:1-22.	Num. 10:11-36
Wed.	Lk. 10:38—11:13.	Nu. 11:1-35
Th.	Luke 11:29-36.	Num. 12:1-15
Fri.	Lk. 11: 37-54.	Num. 13: 1-25
Sat.	Lk. 12:1-34.	Num. 13: 26-33

2d Sunday in Lent.

Mon.	Luke 13: 1-17.	Num. 14: 1-45
Tues.	Lk. 14: 25-35.	Num. 16: 1-22
Wed.	Lk. 15:11-32.	Num. 16:23-50
Th.	Lk. 16: 10-18.	Num. 17: 1-13
Fri.	Lk. 17: 1-10.	Num. 20: 1-29
Sat.	Lk. 18:1-8.	Num. 21:1—22:1

3d Sunday in Lent.

Mon.	Lk. 18: 15-30.	Num. 22: 2-41
Tues.	Lk. 19: 1-40.	Num. 23: 1-30
Wed.	Lk. 20:1—21:4.	Num. 24:1-13
Th.	Lk. 21:37—22:38.	Nu. 27:12-23
Fri.	Lk. 22: 39-71.	Deut. 5: 1-33
Sat.	Luke 23: 1-25.	Deut. 8: 1-20

4th Sunday in Lent.

Mon.	Lk. 23: 26-56.	Deut. 9: 1-29
Tues.	Matt. 26: 1-35.	Deu. 10: 1-22
Wed.	Matt. 26:36-75.	Deut. 11:1-32
Th.	Matt. 27: 1-38.	Deut. 28: 1-14
Fri.	Matt. 27:39-66.	Deut. 28:15-68
Sat.	Mark 14: 1-31.	Deut. 34: 1-12

5th Sunday in Lent.

Mon.	Mark 14: 32-72.	Jer. 2: 1-19
Tues.	Mk. 15: 1-19.	Hosea 13: 9-14
Wed.	Mark 15: 20-47.	Zeph. 3: 1-8
Th.	John 12: 1-19.	Micah 3: 9-12
Fri.	John 12: 20-50.	Is. 66: 1-9
Sat.	John 13: 16-38.	Zech. 9: 1-17

Palm Sunday.

Mon.	John 18: 1-18.	Jer. 7: 1-15
Tues.	John 18: 19-40.	Is. 50: 4-11
Wed.	John 19: 1-12.	Jer. 11: 18-23
Th.	John 19: 13-24.	Zech. 3: 1-10
Fri.	John 19: 25-37.	Lam. 2: 8-15
Sat.	John 19: 38-42.	Is. 52: 13-15

LESSONS FOR MORNING AND EVENING THROUGHOUT THE YEAR.—*Continued.*

Easter.		
EASTER MONDAY.		
Tues.	Matt. 28: 1-15.	Eze. 21: 25-27
Wed.	John 20:1-18.	Haggai 2:20-23
Th.	Luke 24: 1-12.	Zech. 6: 9-15
Fri.	Luke 24:36-49.	Eze. 17:22-24
Sat.	Mark 16: 9-14.	Is. 44: 21-28

1st Sunday after Easter.		
Mon.	John 21: 1-25.	Jonah 1: 1-16
Tues.	Jno.2:12-25.	Jonah 1:17—2:10
Wed.	John 3: 22-36.	Jonah 3: 1-10
Th.	John 4: 1-27.	Jonah 4: 1-11
Fri.	John 4: 28-38.	Is. 33: 2-6
Sat.	John 4: 39-45.	Is. 42:10-17

2d Sunday after Easter.		
Mon.	John 5: 1-17.	Micah 2: 12-13
Tues.	John 5: 18.30.	Is. 30: 19-26
Wed.	John 5: 31-47.	Jer. 3: 11-19
Th.	John 6: 16-29.	Eze. 34:1-11
Fri.	John 6: 30-40.	Eze. 34: 12-22
Sat.	John 6: 41-59.	Eze. 34: 23-31

3d Sunday after Easter.		
Mon.	John 6: 60-71.	Eze. 36: 1-15
Tues.	John 7: 1-13.	Eze. 36: 16-32
Wed.	John 7: 14-24.	Eze. 36: 33-38
Th.	John 7: 25-36.	Haggai 2: 2-9
Fri.	John 7: 37-53.	Zech. 2: 1-13
Sat.	John 8: 1-11.	Zech. 11: 1-17

4th Sunday after Easter.		
Mon.	John 8: 12-20.	Zech. 12: 1-14
Tues.	John 8: 21-29.	Is. 65: 1-7.
Wed.	John 8: 30-45.	Is. 65: 8-16
Th.	John 9: 1-13.	Jer. 8: 4-13
Fri.	John 9: 14-34.	Zech. 8: 18-23
Sat.	John 9: 35-41.	Is. 49: 22-26

5th Sunday after Easter.		
Mon.	John 10: 1-5.	Amos 9: 8-15
Tues.	John 10: 6-10.	Is. 4: 2-6
Wed.	Matt. 28: 16-20.	Is. 29: 18-24
ASCENSION DAY.		
Fri.	Lk. 24: 50-53.	Micah 7: 7-13
Sat.	Acts 1: 12-26.	Micah 7: 14-20

Sunday after Ascension.		
Mon.	John 10: 17-21.	Zech. 13: 7-9
Tues.	John 10: 22-31.	Zech. 14:1-21
Wed	John 10: 32-42.	Is. 66: 10-24
Th.	John 11: 1-27.	Jer. 46: 27, 28
Fri.	John 11: 28-44.	Is. 32: 9-20
Sat.	John 11: 45-57.	Is. 57: 15-21

Whitsunday.		
MONDAY.		
Tues.	Acts 2: 14-36.	Eze. 47: 1-12
Wed.	Acts 2: 37-47.	Is. 45: 18-21
Th.	John 14: 1-22.	Is. 45: 22-25
Fri.	John 15: 1-25.	Jer. 9: 23-26
Sat.	John 16:31—17:26.	Is.44:6-8

Trinity Sunday.		
Mon.	Acts 3: 1-21.	Josh. 1: 1-18
Tues.	Acts 4: 1-37.	Josh. 3: 1-17
Wed.	Acts 5: 1-42.	Josh. 4: 1-24
Th.	Acts 6: 1-15.	Josh. 6: 1-27
Fri.	Acts 7: 1-60.	Josh. 8: 1-35
Sat.	Acts 8: 1-40.	Josh. 9: 1-27

1st Sunday after Trinity.		
Mon.	Acts 9: 1-43.	Josh. 10: 1-15
Tues.	Acts. 10: 1-33.	Josh. 11: 1-23
Wed.	Acts 11: 1-30.	Josh. 23: 1-16
Th.	Acts 12: 1-25.	Josh. 24: 1-31
Fri.	Acts 13: 1-52.	Judges 2: 1-23
Sat.	Acts 14: 1-28.	Judges 6: 1-40

2d Sunday after Trinity.		
Mon.	Acts 15: 1-41.	Judges 7: 1-25
Tues.	Acts 16: 1-40.	Jud. 13: 1-25
Wed.	Acts 17: 1-15.	Jud. 14: 1-20
Th.	Acts 18: 1-28.	Jud. 15: 1-20
Fri.	Acts 19: 1-41.	Jud. 16: 4-31
Sat.	Acts 20: 1-38.	1 Sam. 1: 1-28

3d Sunday after Trinity.		
Mon.	Acts 21: 1-39.	1 Sam. 2: 1-21
Tues.	Acts 21:40-22:29.	1Sam.3:1-21
Wed.	Acts 22:30-23-35.	1Sam.4:1-22
Th.	Acts 24: 1-27.	1 Sam. 5: 1-12
Fri.	Acts 25: 1-27.	1 Sam. 7: 1-17
Sat.	Acts 26: 1-32.	1 Sam. 8: 1-22

4th Sunday after Trinity.		
Mon.	Acts 27: 1-44.	1 Sam. 9: 1-27
Tues.	Acts 28: 1-31.	1 Sam. 10: 1-27
Wed.	Rom. 1: 1-15.	1 Sam. 12: 1-25
Th.	Rom. 1:16-32.	1 Sam. 13:1-14
Fri.	Rom. 2: 1-29.	1 Sam. 15: 1-35
Sat.	Rom. 3: 1-31.	1 Sam. 16: 1-23

5th Sunday after Trinity.		
Mon.	Rom. 4: 1-25.	1 Sam. 17: 1-58
Tues.	Rom. 5:1—6:2.	1Sam.18:1-21
Wed.	Rom. 6:12-18.	1 Sam. 19:1-24
Th.	Rom. 7: 1-25.	1 Sam. 20: 1-42
Fri.	Rom. 8: 1-11.	1 Sam. 22: 1-23
Sat.	Rom. 13: 1-7.	1 Sam. 24: 1-22

6th Sunday after Trinity.		
Mon.	Rom.14:1-15:3.	1Sam.26:1-25
Tues.	Rom.14:14-33.	1 Sam.28:3-25
Wed.	Rom. 16:1-27.	1 Sam. 31:1-13
Th.	1 Cor. 1: 10-31.	2 Sam. 1:1-27
Fri.	1 Cor. 2: 1-16.	2 Sam. 5: 1-25
Sat.	1 Cor.4:6—5:5.	2 Sam.6:1-23

7th Sunday after Trinity.		
Mon.	1Cor.5:9—6:20.	1Chr.16:1-43
Tues.	1 Cor. 7: 1-40.	2 Sam. 7: 1-29
Wed.	1 Cor. 8:1-13.	2 Sam. 12:1-23
Th.	1 Cor. 9:1-23.	2 Sam. 15:1-15
Fri.	1 Cor.10:14-33.	2Sam.16:5-35
Sat.	1 Cor. 11:1-22.	2 Sam.18:1-13

8th Sunday after Trinity.		
Mon.	1 Cor.12:12-31.	2Sam.19:1-23
Tues.	1 Cor. 14:1-40.	1 Chr.21:1-30
Wed.	1Cr.15:58-16:24.	1Ch.22:1-19
Th.	2 Cor. 1:1-24.	1 Chr. 28:1-21
Fri.	2 Cor.2:1—3:3.	2 Chr.29:1-23
Sat.	2Cor.6:11—7:16.	2Chr.1:1-13

9th Sunday after Trinity.		
Mon.	2 Cor. 8: 1-24.	1 Ks. 3: 16-28
Tues.	2 Cor. 9: 1-15.	1 Ks. 4: 22-34
Wed.	2 Cor. 10: 1-18.	1 Ks. 5: 1-18
Th.	2 Cor. 11:1-18.	2 Chr. 3: 1-17
Fri.	2Cor.12:19-13:13.	1Ks.8:1-66
Sat.	Gal. 1: 1-24.	1 Ks. 7: 1-12

10th Sunday after Trinity.		
Mon.	Gal. 2: 1-21.	1 Ks. 9: 1-28
Tues.	Gal. 3: 1-14.	I Ks. 10: 1-29
Wed.	Gal. 4: 8-20.	1 Ks. 11: 1-43
Th.	Gal. 5: 1-15.	1 Ks. 12: 1-33
Fri.	Gal. 6:11-18.	1 Ks. 13: 1-34
Sat.	Eph. 6: 1-9.	1 Ks. 14: 1-31

11th Sunday after Trinity.		
Mon.	Eph.6:18-24.	1Ks.16:29-17:24
Tues.	Phil. 1:12—2:4.	1 Ks.18:1-46
Wed.	Phil. 2: 19-30.	1 Ks. 19: 1-21
Th.	Phil. 3: 1-11.	1 Ks. 21: 1-29
Fri.	Phil.4:1-3.	1K.22:52. 2K.1:17
Sat.	Phil. 4: 8-23.	2 Ks. 2: 1-25

12th Sunday after Trinity.		
Mon.	Col. 2: 1-23.	2 Ks. 4: 1-44
Tues.	Col. 3:18—4:18.	2 Ks. 5:1-27
Wed.	1 Thess. 1: 1-10.	2 Ks. 6:1-23
Th.	1 Thess.2:1-20.	2Ks.6:24-7:20
Fri.	1 Thess. 3: 1-13.	2 Ks. 8: 1-15
Sat.	1 Thess. 4: 8-12.	2 Ks.9: 1-37

13th Sunday after Trinity.		
Mon.	1 Thess.5:12-28.	2 Ks.10:1-36
Tues.	1 Tim. 1:1-20.	2 Chr. 22:1-12
Wed.	1 Tim. 2:1-15.	2 Chr. 23:1-21
Th.	1 Tim. 3:1-16.	2 Chr. 24:1-27
Fri.	1 Tim. 4: 1-16.	2 Ks. 14: 1-29
Sat.	1 Tim. 5: 1-25.	2 Ks. 15: 1-38

14th Sunday after Trinity.		
Mon.	1 Tim. 6: 1-21.	Is. 6: 1-13.
Tues.	2 Tim. 1: 1-18.	Amos 7: 7-17
Wed.	2 Tim. 2:1-26.	2 Ks. 16:1-20
Th.	Titus 1: 1-16.	2 Ks. 17: 1-23
Fri.	Titus 2: 1-10.	2 Ks. 18: 1-37
Sat.	Titus 2:15—3:3.	2Ks.19:1-37

15th Sunday after Trinity.		
Mon.	Titus 3: 8-15.	2 Ks. 20: 1-21
Tues.	Philemon 1:25.	2 Ks. 21:1-26
Wed.	Heb. 1: 1-14.	2 Chr. 34: 1-33
Th.	Heb.2:5-3:6.	2Ch.35:20-36:10
Fri.	Heb. 4:14—5:14.	Jer.22:1-30
Sat.	Heb. 6: 1-20.	Jer. 25: 1-14

16th Sunday after Trinity.		
Mon.	Heb. 7: 1-28.	Jer. 37: 1-21
Tues.	Heb. 8: 1-13.	Jer. 38: 1-28
Wed.	Heb. 9: 1-10.	Jer. 32: 1-44
Th.	Heb. 9: 16-28.	Jer. 39: 1-18
Fri.	Heb. 10: 1-34.	Jer. 29: 1-23
Sat.	Heb. 11: 1-7.	Daniel 1: 1-21

17th Sunday after Trinity.		
Mon.	Heb. 11: 17-40.	Dan. 3: 1-30
Tues.	Heb. 12: 1-17.	Dan. 4: 1-37
Wed.	Heb. 13: 1-25.	Dan. 5: 1-30
Th.	James 1:1-15.	Dan. 5:31-6:28
Fri.	James 2: 1-13.	Ezra 1: 1-11
Sat.	James 2: 14-26.	Ezra 3: 1-13

18th Sunday after Trinity.		
Mon.	James 3: 1-18.	Ezra 4: 1-24
Tues.	James 4:1-5:6.	Haggai 1:1-15
Wed.	James 5: 12-20.	Ezra 5: 1-17
Th.	1 Peter 3: 1-7.	Ezra 6: 1-22
Fri.	1 Peter 3: 15-22.	Ezra 7: 1-28
Sat.	1 Peter 5:1-5.	Ezra 8:31-9:15

Lessons for Morning and Evening throughout the Year.—*Concluded.*

19th Sunday after Trinity.

Day	Morning	Evening
Mon.	1 John 1: 1-10.	Neh. 1: 1-11
Tues.	1 John 2: 1-17.	Neh. 2: 1-20
Wed.	1 John 5: 1-3.	Neh. 4:1-23
Th.	1 John 5: 10-21.	Neh. 8: 1-18
Fri.	2 John 1:13.	Neh. 9: 1-38
Sat.	3 John 1:14.	Zech. 8: 1-23

20th Sunday after Trinity.

Day	Morning	Evening
Mon.	Mark 4: 1-41.	Is. 43: 1-13
Tues.	Luke 13: 18-35.	Is. 41: 1-20
Wed.	Matt. 13: 31-58.	Hab. 2: 1-4
Th.	Matt. 16: 13-20.	Is. 63: 7-19
Fri.	2 Cor. 3:10—4:18.	Is. 64:1-12
Sat.	2 Cor. 5: 1-21.	Is. 5: 1-7

21st Sunday after Trinity.

Day	Morning	Evening
Mon.	Eph. 1: 1-23.	Micah 6: 1-9
Tues.	Eph. 2: 1-22.	Is. 58: 1-14
Wed.	Eph. 4: 7-21.	Is. 59: 1-21
Th.	Eph. 4: 29-32.	Jer. 31: 1-22
Fri.	Eph. 5: 10-14.	Jer. 31: 23-40
Sat.	Eph. 5: 22-23.	Is. 48: 1-22

22d Sunday after Trinity.

Day	Morning	Evening
Mon.	Matt. 18:1-22.	Micah 4:9-5:1
Tues.	Mark 9: 33-50.	Is. 49: 14-21
Wed.	Luke 17: 20-37.	Is. 2:10-21
Th.	Rom. 8: 24-39.	Is. 63: 1-6
Fri.	Mark 12: 1-12.	Joel 2: 1-11
Sat.	Matt. 25: 14-30.	Joel 2: 12-27

23d Sunday after Trinity.

Day	Morning	Evening
Mon.	1 Cor. 3: 1-23.	Joel 3: 1-13
Tues.	Matt. 19: 16-30.	Joel 3:14-21
Wed.	Luke 14: 12-15.	Obad. 1:21
Th.	Mark 13: 1-37.	Nah. 1: 1-14
Fri.	Rom. 9:1-33.	Nah. 1:15-3:19
Sat.	Rom. 10: 1-21.	Is. 10: 5-27

24th Sunday after Trinity.

Day	Morning	Evening
Mon.	Rom. 11: 1-33.	Is. 13: 1-22
Tues.	2 Thess. 1:11-2:17.	Is.14:1-27
Wed.	2 Thess. 3: 1-18.	Is. 47: 1-15
Th.	2 Tim. 3: 1-17.	Dan. 2: 27-45
Fri.	2 Tim. 4: 1-22.	Dan. 7: 1-28
Sat.	Matt. 24: 1-14.	Dan. 9: 1-27

25th Sunday after Trinity.

Day	Morning	Evening
Mon.	Mat. 24:29-51.	Dn.11:36-12:13
Tues.	Matt. 22: 23-33.	Eze. 38: 1-23
Wed.	1 Cor. 15:11-50.	Eze. 39:1-29
Th.	Heb. 3:7—4:13.	Is. 43:14-25
Fri.	Heb. 11: 8-16.	Is. 33: 17-24
Sat.	Heb. 12: 18-29.	Eze. 37: 1-14

26th Sunday after Trinity.

Day	Morning	Evening
Mon.	1 Peter 1: 1-12.	Zep. 3: 9-20
Tues.	1 Peter 1:13-2:10.	Is. 34:1-17
Wed.	1 Peter 4: 1-7.	Is. 35: 1-10
Th.	1 Peter 4: 12-19.	Is. 54: 1-17
Fri.	2 Peter 1: 1-15.	Is. 60: 7-22
Sat.	2 Peter 2: 1-22.	Is. 62: 1-12

27th Sunday after Trinity.

Day	Morning	Evening
Mon.	2 Peter 3: 1-18.	Is. 65: 17-25
Tues.	Jude 1:25.	Eze. 37: 15-28
Wed.	1 John 2: 18-29.	Hab. 3: 1-19
Th.	1 John 3: 1-12.	Is. 40: 27-31
Fri.	1 John 3: 19-24.	Jer. 14: 7-9
Sat.	1 John 4: 1-8.	Mal. 3: 7-18

THE PSALMS

With reference to the Sundays and Festivals of the Church Year.

SUNDAYS AND HOLYDAYS.	PSALMS.
1. Advent	2, 8, 24, 102, 118.
2. "	29, 50, 70, 93, 98.
3. "	24, 98 132.
4. "	24, 93, 45, 110.
1. Christmas	45, 92, 148.
2. "	42, 98, 121.
Sunday after Christmas	117, 135.
New Year	30, 34, 40, 65, 148.
After New Year	62.
Epiphany (Jan. 6th)	5, 8, 72.
1. Sunday after Epiphany	121, 122, 127.
2. " "	104, 127, 128.
3. " "	13, 33, 127.
4. " "	46, 65, 87.
5. " "	17, 91, 129.
6. " "	15.
Septuagesima	38.
Sexagesima	1.
Estomihi	31.
Invocavit	91.
Reminiscere	25.
Oculi	25.
Lætare	84.
Judica	7, 43.
Palmarum	92.
Maundy-Thursday	23, 111, 114.
Good-Friday	22, 40, 69.
Easter-Festival	16, 41, 110.
Easter-Monday	1, 62, 19.
Quasimodogeniti	22, 29, 116, 133.
Misericordias Domini	23, 100.
Jubilate	12, 45, 56, 66, 126.
Cantate	29, 41, 98, 140.
Rogate	1, 50, 54, 104, 141.
Ascension-Day	33, 47, 68.
Exaudi	27, 36, 44, 83, 110.
Pentecost	27, 33, 46, 78, 143.
Pentecost-Monday	30, 103.
Trinity-Festival	2, 27, 33, 110.

Sundays and Holydays	Psalms
1. Sunday after Trinity	4, 49, 53, 62.
2. " "	19, 22, 72, 78, 144.
3. " "	25, 32, 51, 95.
4. " "	15, 112.
5. " "	8, 117, 127, 128, 130.
6. " "	15, 32, 133.
7. " "	107, 145.
8. " "	5, 12, 81.
9. " "	14, 50, 112.
10. " "	3, 21, 59, 95, 137.
11. " "	32, 51, 130.
12. " "	34, 90, 115, 117.
13. " "	70, 143.
14. " "	50, 117, 136.
15. " "	23, 49, 65.
16. " "	90, 116.
17. " "	50, 113.
18. " "	34, 110.
19. " "	7, 32, 39, 103.
20. " "	1, 45, 99.
21. " "	27, 39, 42, 48, 86.
22. " "	6, 32, 133.
23. " "	7, 64, 82, 85.
24. " "	25, 28, 38, 90.
25. " "	10, 70, 74.
26. " "	41, 112, 126.
27. " "	41, 91.
The presentation of Jesus in the temple	12, 66.
Annunciation-Day	91, 125, 135.
John the Baptist-Day	33, 45, 50.
Presentation of the Augsburg Confession	103, 134, 150.
Visitation of Mary	12.
Michaels-Day	91.
Harvest-Festival	65, 95, 104.
Reformation-Festival	46, 126.
All Saints Day (Nov. 1st)	116.
Church Dedication Festival	23, 27, 84.
Mission-Festival	19, 72, 96.
Times of War	91, 121.
Jubilee-Festival	46.
Close of the Church-Year	27.
Close of the Year	90, 121.

THE PSALMS

With reference to their import.

I. OF PRAYERS:

For the Church: 3, 5, 28, 59, 64, 71, 74, 77, 79, 80, 83, 94, 112, 125.
Against the Enemies of the Church: 7, 19, 26, 27, 42, 54, 56, 57, 62, 141.
Against the Pope and the Papists: 10, 12, 36, 44, 55, 69, 70, 94, 109, 120.
For Peace in the Church: 60, 86, 137, 140.
For the divine Word: 67, 69, 119.
For Forgiveness of sin and spiritual direction: 38, 59, 86, 90, 130, 141, 142.
For the State: 20, 62.
Against an evil Conscience: 6, 38, 88.

II. OF REPENTANCE:

6, 32, 38, 51, 102, 130, 143.

III. OF THANKSGIVING:

For the divine Word and other spiritual gifts: 34, 42, 66, 103, 109, 122, 138, 145, 147.
For bodily Blessings: 33, 105, 107, 108, 114, 116, 139, 144, 146.
For the Preservation of the Church: 76, 86, 108, 111, 116, 135, 136.
For Deliverance from Tyranny and other distresses: 9, 18, 30, 66, 113.

IV. OF DOCTRINE:

Concerning the Forgiveness of sin: 51, 139.
Concerning Trust in God alone: 4, 33, 91, 112, 115, 131, 146, 148.
Concerning God's Word and the Fear of God: 1, 15, 41, 78, 81, 92, 95, 96, 100, 112, 149.
Concerning the Prosperity of the wicked and the misfortunes of the godly: 37, 39, 49, 52, 63, 73, 92, 129.
For the Teachers of the Church: 134, 150.
For Rulers and for the Household: 2, 82, 101, 125, 127, 128, 133, 144.

V. OF CONSOLATION:

God preserves the Church and destroys her Enemies: 3, 11, 23, 33, 36, 46, 47, 76, 124, 125, 126.

VI. OF PROPHESIES:

Concerning Christ's Person and Office: 2, 110, 118, 138.
Concerning Christ's Sufferings and Exaltation: 2, 8, 16, 21, 22, 41, 68, 69, 109.
Concerning the Spread of the Gospel: 19, 40, 45, 47, 50, 72, 78, 93, 97, 98.

VII. OF PARTICULAR SEASONS:

Morning: 63, 103, 130.
Midday: 4, 7, 19, 104, 121.
Evening: 3, 4, 8, 91, 104, 127, 134, 139.

Index of First Lines

Index of First Lines

Index of First Lines

Index of First Lines

Index of First Lines

Index of First Lines

Index of First Lines

Index of First Lines

Index of First Lines

Index of First Lines

INDEX OF SELECTIONS FOR CHANTING.

INDEX OF DOXOLOGIES.

INDEX TUNES ALPHABETICAL.

Index Tunes Alphabetical

Index Tunes Alphabetical

Index Tunes Alphabetical

Index Tunes Alphabetical

Index Tunes Alphabetical

Index Tunes Alphabetical

Index Tunes Alphabetical

Index Tunes Alphabetical

Index Tunes Metrical

S. M.

S. M. 8 LINES.

C. M.

Index Tunes Metrical

C. M. 8 LINES.

Index Tunes Metrical

L. M.

6. 7. 6. 7. 6. 6. 6. 6.

7 s.

7 s. 6 LINES.

7 s. 8 LINES.

7. 4. 7. 4. 7. 4. 6.

7. 5. 8 LINES.

7. 6. 7. 6.

7. 6. 8 LINES.

7. 6. 7. 6. 6. 6. 6.

7. 6. 7. 6. 6. 6. 6. 6.

7. 6. 7. 6. 6. 7. 7. 6.

7. 6. 7. 6. 8. 7. 6.

7. 6. 8. 6. 8 LINES.

7. 7. 6. 7. 7. 8.

7. 7. 7. 5.

Index Tunes Metrical

8. 7. 8. 7. 8. 7. 4. 6. 8.

8. 7. 8. 7. 8. 7. 7.

8. 7. 8. 7. 8. 7. 7. 8. 7. 7.

8. 7. 8 LINES.

8. 7. 8. 7. 8. 7. 8. 7. 7.

8. 7. 8. 7. 8. 8.

8. 7. 8. 7. 8. 8. 7.

8. 7. 8. 7. 8. 8. 7. 7.

8. 7. 8. 7. 8. 8. 7. 8. 8. 7.

8. 7. 8. 8. 4.

Index Tunes Metrical

Index Tunes Metrical

9. 8. 6 LINES.

Translated Hymns

Translated Hymns

Translated Hymns

Translated Hymns

A Short Form for Holy Baptism in Cases of Necessity

In urgent cases, in the absence of the Pastor, any Christian may administer Holy Baptism.

Take water, call the child by its name, pour or sprinkle the water on the child, saying:

I baptize thee in the name of God the Father, and of the Son, and of the Holy Ghost. Amen.

If there is time, the baptism may be preceded by the following prayer:

Eternal, merciful God! We pray Thee extend Thy goodness and mercy unto this child, who now asks, open the door to it who knocks! That it may enjoy the everlasting blessing of Thy heavenly washing, and may come to the eternal kingdom which Thou hast prepared through Christ our Lord! Amen.

Our Father who art in heaven, hallowed be Thy name. Thy kingdom come. Thy will be done on earth, as it is in heaven. Give us this day our daily bread. And forgive us our trespasses, as we forgive those who trespass against us. And lead us not into temptation, but deliver us from evil: For Thine is the kingdom, and the power, and the glory, forever and ever. Amen.